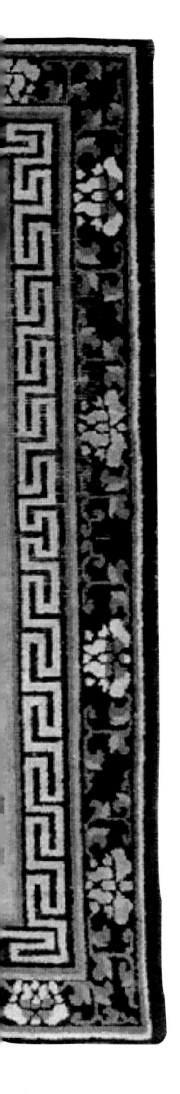

oriental rugs

An Illustrated Lexicon of Motifs, Materials, and Origins

Peter F. Stone

TUTTLE Publishing

Tokyo | Rutland, Vermont | Singapore

contents

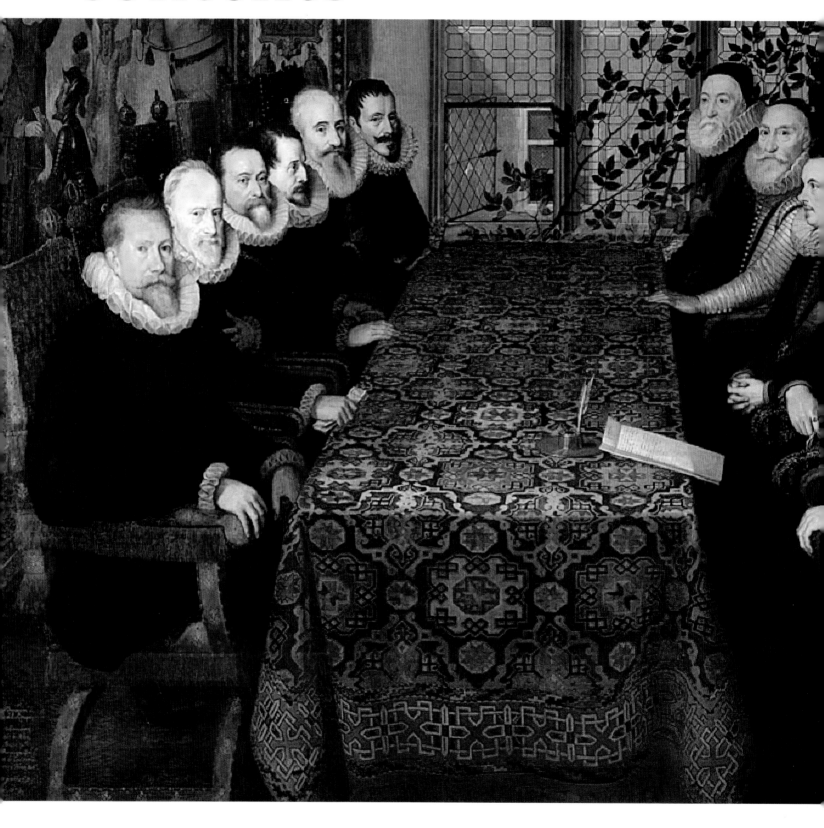

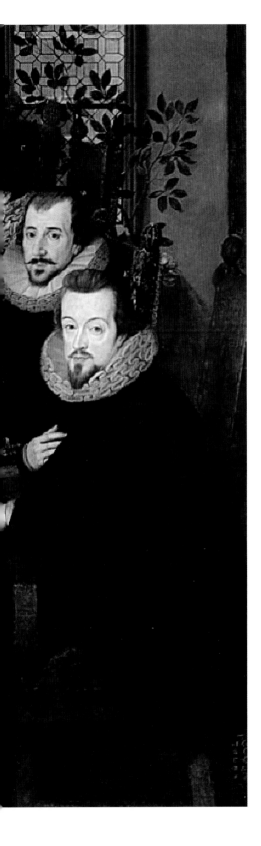

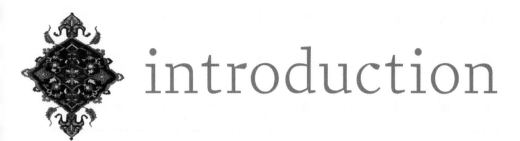

introduction

Rugs terms are confusing. The same rug may have a baffling variety of names. Some names refer to geographic or ethnic origin. Others refer to structure, design, or function. The names themselves may offer no clue as to the type of reference. Variant spellings of these names compound the problem. This confusion of terms discourages those seeking a beginning understanding of oriental rugs. It also frustrates those researching the subject. Even a Linnaeus could not bring order out of this chaos of names. However, a single source for commonly accepted definitions of oriental rug terms can dispel much of the confusion.

There is a growing wealth of research in rug attribution, technical structures, ethnography, and history. This research is published in monographs, periodicals, and survey texts. By organizing this research under alphabetical entries, we can increase its usefulness for those seeking specific information about oriental rugs.

SCOPE.

This lexicon includes definitions and explanations for names and terms referring to:

- **pile rugs and flatweaves of the Near East, North Africa, continental Asia, Europe, and the United States**

- **geographic locations and ethnic groups noted for their rugs and weavings**

- **functional weavings of tribal and nomadic origin**

- **the rug trade and the rug-weaving craft and industry**

- **designs, motifs, and symbols of pile rugs and flatweaves**

- **rug and textile structures**

- **specific rugs of historical significance.**

RUG RESEARCH.

Rugs have received greater recognition as art in recent years. During the same period, rug research has developed in scope and quality. Researchers in oriental rug studies have adopted the scientific methods of art historians. These include detailed technical structural analysis, chemical and chromatographic dye analysis, and microscopic identification of fibers.

Tribal weavings have received greater research attention. Recently, our understanding of southwest Persian tribal weavings, Baluchi weavings, and Kurdish weavings has grown tremendously.

These are very positive trends. At the same time, there are problems in rug research. Because oriental rugs are relatively fragile artifacts, the historical record is incomplete.

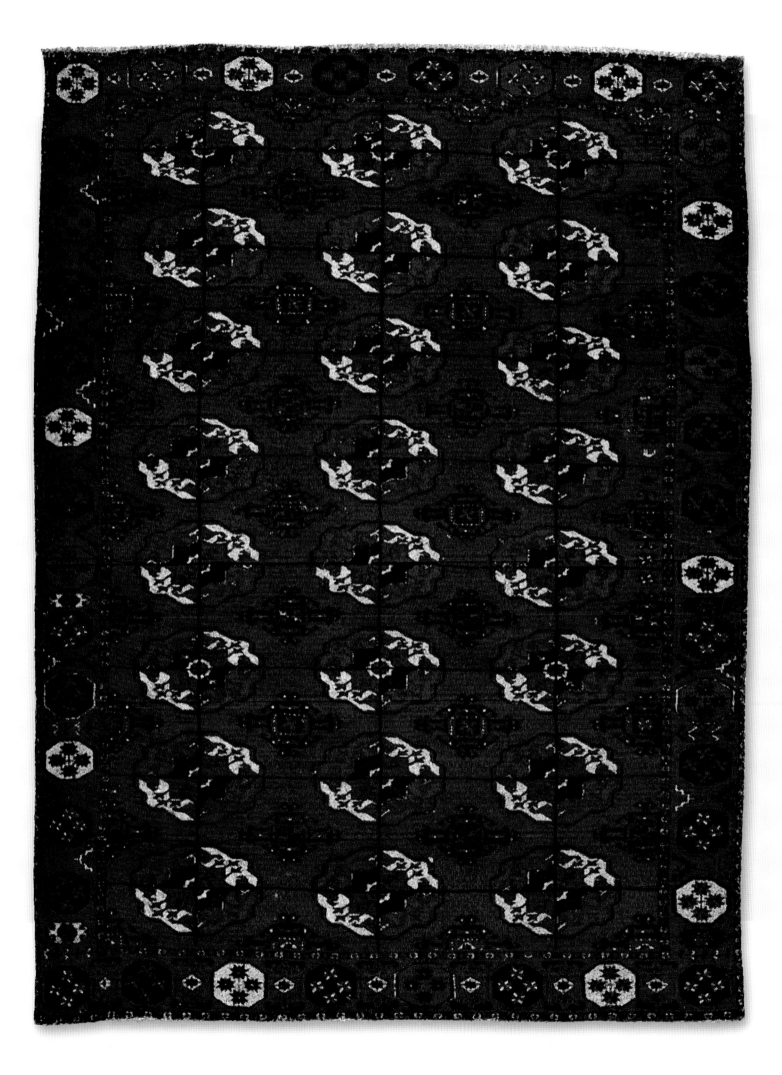

There is no direct and continuous chain of evidence linking some types of rugs and their origins or documenting the evolution of rug designs.

Tribal peoples do not usually leave written records. The history, migrations, cultures, and crafts of many rug-weaving tribal peoples are poorly documented or not documented at all.

Recent wars and revolutions in the Near East have radically altered historic patterns of rug production and distribution. Current rug production conditions have not been thoroughly studied or documented.

Due to these and other research problems, there are gaps in our knowledge. In some cases, the gaps are occupied by partial research and reasoned speculation. In other cases, unverified knowledge and trade lore fills the void. Where information in the lexicon is speculative, we have tried to indicate this. There are controversies in rug attribution and design origin. Generally, where there are opposing views, the concepts and information are described in the lexicon as questioned. To present current and generally accepted views, information has been cross-checked against recently published research.

FORM OF ENTRIES.

A primary entry consists of a term or name followed by less common equivalent terms or names, cross-referenced. The language of origin, other than English, is enclosed in parentheses following the primary term. If there are additional foreign terms, their languages of origin also appear in parentheses. The same parentheses may enclose the original form of the foreign term or place name in italics. A literal translation of foreign terms and place names may be included in quotes. The definition or explanation follows. Then, cross-references are provided to related topics and terms. Strict letter-by-letter alphabetical order, regardless of spaces or hyphens, is used in sequencing primary entries. The format of entries is shown here:

primary entry (language of origin, *original foreign term*, "literal translation"),

secondary entry. Definition or explanation. See "cross-reference."

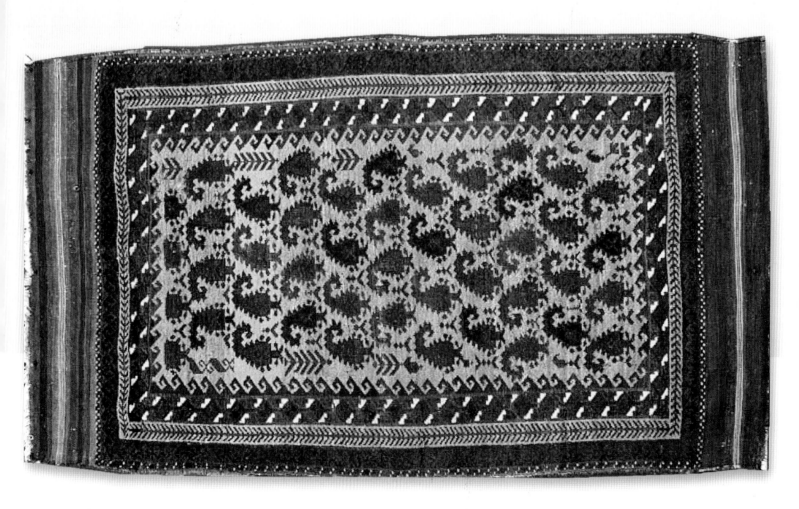

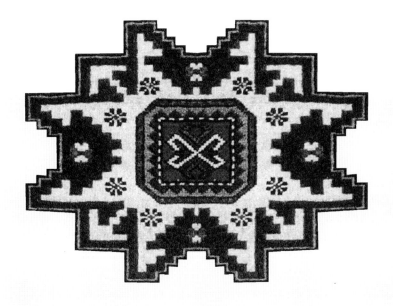

DEFINITIONS.

The first definition of a term is usually the technical definition within the field of oriental rug and textile studies. This is followed by more specific definitions or definitions of the term in general usage. For place names, the location is given first followed by a description of weavings of that area. For names of ethnic groups, the geographical location of the group or other identifying information is given first followed by a description of their weavings.

TYPOGRAPHIC USAGE.

Boldface is used for primary and secondary terms or cross-referenced terms defined or explained within an entry. Parentheses enclose the language of origin of the entries. Capitalized initial letters are used for proper nouns and terms that are usually capitalized. Quotation marks or parentheses enclose references to other entries and translations of foreign words. Italics present foreign words in the context of an entry, scientific Latin names, subheadings, and publication titles.

TERMS FOR TEXTILE STRUCTURES.

In defining terms for textile structures, the common meaning of the term is presented first. This is usually followed by a definition using the system of classifying and describing rug structures in *The Primary Structure of Fabrics* by Irene Emery or *Woven Structures* by Marla Mallet. The terms "asymmetric knot" and "symmetric knot" are used in describing structure of pile fabrics. These are not technically correct terms, but they are used because they are generally understood in rug studies. The terms "soumak" and "weft wrapping" are used in the absence of more specific information. There are many types of weft wrapping, but published descriptions rarely differentiate these types for flatweaves.

Where structure or design information is given for rugs from a specific source, the structure or design is "average" or "typical," unless otherwise noted. For a specific source, structural or design variation may be very great. For hand-knotted pile rugs, the pile is assumed to be wool unless otherwise noted.

For any specific source of rug production, structural and technical details may change over time according to commercial demand. Generally, there is an historical trend from higher to lower knot densities, from wool to cotton foundation, and from vegetable to synthetic dyes.

BIOGRAPHICAL DATA.

Brief biographical sketches are included of deceased individuals who achieved international prominence in rug studies or through their association with oriental rugs. A lexicon is about language. This lexicon is about the language of oriental rugs. It is analytical in that it presents very specific terms for rug origins, structures, and designs. Examining the parts rather than the whole makes this book useful. However, the attraction, charm, and beauty of oriental rugs is not in the parts, but in the whole. Many oriental rugs and other weavings are works of art, from the narrowest to the grandest meaning of the word "art." An analytical understanding of oriental rugs is ultimately justified by the experience of oriental rugs as art.

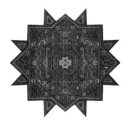

Foreign Terms And Place Names by John R. Perry

A good part of the confusion surrounding rug terminology stems from the variety of languages used by the weavers, sellers, buyers, and connoisseurs of this most cosmopolitan of products. Very few of the names for relevant peoples, places, techniques, and types are to be found consistently spelled in the literature. Much of this inconsistency reflects dialect differences or a clash of sound, writing, and transcription systems in the languages subsequently involved. Thus "alcatif," "qtifa," and "kadife" all go back to the same Arabic term for a pile or nap rug, independently processed through Portuguese, Moroccan/French, and Turkish.

Some variants result simply from slips of the pen or typewriter. Many a sensible word has been turned into nonsense by the miswriting of *u* for *n* or *b* for *h,* or vice versa. Thus *Murdschekar, Murchehkbur* and *Murcheh Khvort* are all the same place to a Persian; it was a German (with a poor ear or a poor informant), a Frenchman (with poor eyesight or working from scribbled notes), and an Englishman (working from literary Persian) who carved "Murcheh Khurt" into such varied shapes.

There are no universal systems of transcription (written representation of the sounds of words) or transliteration

(representation of the written form of words in a different writing system). In a work of reference, pedantry must give way to conciseness and accuracy, which involves compromises. Wherever possible, first place has been given to a widely accepted form, whether rigorously transcribed or not. A few general observations must suffice here on the relations between the language systems that are encountered in this field, with a note where these systems typically break down. This will help the reader identify analogous spellings, read and pronounce an unfamiliar term with confidence, and recognize a variant of a familiar term, however outlandishly disguised.

ARABIC-SCRIPT LANGUAGES AND THE WEST.

From the eighth century, throughout most of the Near East, Central Asia, and north India, Arabic script was widely used for literary languages (including Arabic, Persian, western and eastern Turkish, and Urdu). The Arabic "alphabet" is deficient, in that it does not have characters for most vowels. It is particularly unsuited to representing the eight-vowel system of Turkic languages.

Literacy was not—and still is not—widespread in rural and nomadic areas. Thus the early Western rug-collectors had little more than their ears to work with; and since these were attuned to English, French, German, or Russian sounds, the resulting transcriptions of native terms left much to be desired. All the more since the orthography of their own languages (particularly English and French) was—and still is —a chaos of historically conditioned letter-combinations. The final stage of confusion is reached when we try to interpret another's transliterations in ignorance of the conventions of the original or an intermediate language.

For example, the sound represented in English by *j*, as in *judge* (or by *dge*, of course!) also occurs commonly in Arabic, Persian, and Turkish. It does not occur natively in French, German, or Russian, where it has to be represented by unfamiliar letter-combinations. Thus an Iranian of Central Asia, properly known in English as a "Tajik," is in German *Tadschik,* in French *tadjik,* and in Russian appears with the same *dj* combination written in Cyrillic characters. Since it

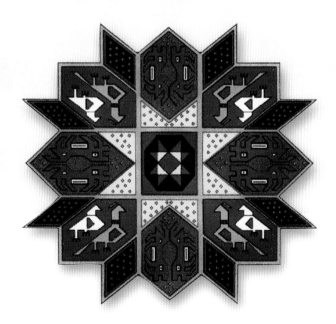

| ORIGINAL SOUND, as in | AS TRANSCRIBED VIA: | | | EXAMPLES |
	FRENCH	GERMAN	RUSSIAN	
Bach	c, k, kh	ch	kh	chalat, khalat
ship	ch	sch	sh	frach, alloucha
chop	tch	tsch	ch	Tchetchen, tschoval
job	dj	dsch	dzh	dzhidzhim
very	v, w	w	v	Zejwa, Zeyva
war, how	ou	w, u	u	Chichaoua
yes, say	i, y	j, i	i, y	Zeyva, Zejwa
q (see Persian)	k, g, gh	k, g	k, g	germez, ghermez

was through the Russians that the Western world was introduced to the peoples of Central Asia and the Caucasus, the Russian form was transliterated into English; and since there was no "French *j*" sound in English, the Russian letter following *d* was represented as *zh*—hence the "English" form *Tadzhik*, with three letters for the value of one. The same cycle of analysis and resynthesis of one sound produces the forms *Azerbaidschan, Azerbaidjan,* and *Azerbaidzhan* for "Azerbaijan."

Similarly, our perception of a Berber term from North Africa may have been filtered first through a local spoken form of Arabic and/or literary Arabic, then through written French (e.g. "Ouaouzguite," to be pronounced approximately *wa-ooz-keet*). English itself is notorious for its spelling traps, as the tourist visiting Cirencester (*sisister*) or Godmanchester (*gumster*) can attest. Thus a short "a" vowel common in north Indian languages sounds like the English vowel of such words as *sung, luck, but, hurry.* English speakers therefore represented this Indian vowel as "u" in writing *Lucknow, suttee, curry,* etc. *Lucknow,* luckily, preserves the context of the substitution; the unfamiliar

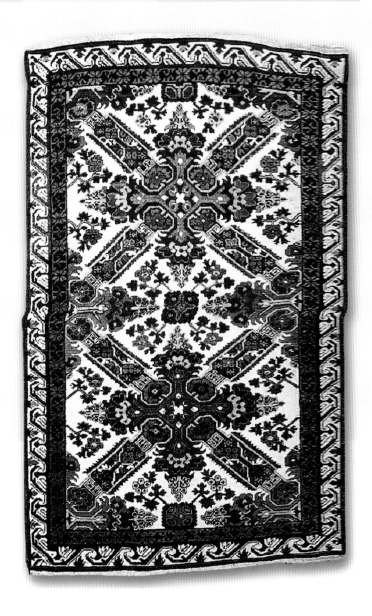

"dhurrie" (pronounced *darry*) is likely to be mispronounced as *doory*.

To pronounce a term with confidence, it helps to know the word's linguistic lineage. This is not always possible, but the table of systematic correspondences of sounds and spellings on the previous page will guide the reader in making an educated guess.

It can be seen from several of the examples how, once the language context has been established from one orthographic feature, other conventions become clear. Since in "Chichaoua" (a town in Morocco) *ch* must be French for *sh*, the *ou* lurking between two other vowels must represent *w*, to yield a pronunciation *shishawa*. German-processed "Zejwa" and "chalat" will respond to similar reasoning. Occasional words imported into Italian or Spanish will, of course, follow the conventions established for, say, *e* and *g* in those languages.

TURKISH.

Since 1928 Turkish (in the narrower sense of the term, i.e. the language of the Republic of Turkey) has used the Latin alphabet with a completely regular orthography. Those few letters that do not approximate English usage are as follows.

c: *j* as in *jog,* **e.g. cicim.**

ç: *ch* as in *chip,* **e.g. Çanakkale.**

ı: *e* as in *the* or *i* in *sir,* **e.g. Topkapı.**

ş: *sh* as in *ship,* **e.g. Uşak.**

ğ: **silent; lengthens the preceding vowel, e.g. Niğde (nee-deh).**

ö: **approx. as in** *nurse,* **with lips rounded; German** *böse,* **French** *peu,* **e.g. Gördes (=Ghiordes).**

ü: **approx. as in** *few,* **with lips rounded; German** *für,* **French** *lune,* **e.g. Yörük.**

In Turkish words, each syllable is pronounced separately: Tekke is *tek-keh*. The vowels *a, e, i, o, u* are pronounced approximately as in Spanish.

The designation "Turk." for the language of origin generally means modern Turkish or its ancestor, Ottoman Turkish. However, it may also stand for "Turkic," an adjective embracing the closely related language family of the Azerbaijani Turks, Turkmens, Uzbeks, Kazakhs, Kirghiz and Qashqa'i. A term designated as "Turk." may be common to two or more of these varieties of Turkish, and particularly in its transcribed form it may not be possible to assign it a definitive origin. Most of these languages are spoken in the Russian Caucasus and Central Asia, and were originally transcribed with the Cyrillic alphabet: see the "Russian" column in the preceding table.

Some of the Turkic languages have consonants which may be written as *q*, *kh*, and *gh* (see under Persian). These are usually equivalent to the modern Turkish *k*, *h*, and *ğ* respectively (e.g. qanât, kanat). The vowel *y* in Turkic words transliterated through Russian is equivalent to the undotted i (e.g. "asmalyk").

PERSIAN AND ARABIC.

Persian was for many centuries both the principal literary language and the spoken lingua franca of the eastern Islamic world, supplementing Turkic, Kurdish, Pashto, Baluch, and other vernaculars. It is still widely used in Central Asia, Afghanistan, and Pakistan as well as Iran. As such it has borrowed freely from other local languages and in turn provided them with vocabulary of its own and many terms taken from Arabic.

Most terms of Arabic origin that appear in this lexicon have been "processed" through Persian. Persian still uses a modified form of Arabic script, and systems of transliteration are almost identical for the two languages. It is thus convenient to treat them together from the viewpoint of unfamiliar sounds and spellings.

dh: (Arabic only) like th as in *the, wither*, e.g. *dhar'* (see "zar").

gh: like French uvular r, but produced even farther back in the throat (Arabic, Turkic langs, e.g. Ghormaj). In Persian of Iran it is pronounced the same as *q*, e.g. ghermez.

kh: like ch as in German *Bach*, Scottish *loch*. E.g. Khila, Bakhtiari.

q: like k, but farther back in the throat, e.g. Qajar.

â: In Persian, long "a" as in *raw* or *war;* to be distinguished from *a*, as in *bat*, e.g. Râvar, kenâreh. In Arabic and Turkish, generally the long equivalent of *a*, e.g. salât, lâle.

The apostrophe is used to represent one of two letters sounded differently in Arabic, but pronounced identically in Persian, as a slight hiatus between vowels (Sa'idâbâd) or between vowel and consonant (Za'farânlu). The vowels *a, e, i, o, u* are pronounced approximately as in Spanish. The other letters and combinations used are roughly equivalent to English usage or otherwise self-evident.

Adjacent letters found in transliterations of Turkish, Persian, etc., may sometimes stand for separate letters (hence distinct sounds) and not the combinations listed above: thus Akhisar is Ak-hisar, Mashhad is Mash-had.

FORMATIVES.

There are several suffixes in Persian and Turkish used to form adjectives or otherwise expand the meaning of a base word in predictable ways. The most common of these, and their typical uses in rug terminology, are as follows.

-âbâd (Persian): forms names of inhabited places, settlements, cities, e.g. Meshkâbâd (from *meshk*, "musk").

-dân (Persian): "container," e.g. qâshoq-dân, "spoonbag."

-i (Persian and Arabic): forms an attributive adjective and related nouns, "from/belonging to a place, tribe, etc.; characterized by," e.g. Baluchi, "of the Baluch people," aksi, "pictorial," from *aks* "picture."

-li, -lu (Turk.): similar in function to -i, e.g. parmakli, "fingerlike, finger-shaped" (parmak, "finger"); Qaragözlü, tribal name (qara göz, "black eye").

-lik, -luk, -lyk (Turk.): something made for, appropriate to, or containing the base referent, e.g. eyerlik, "saddle cloth" (eyer, "saddle").

CHINESE PLACE NAMES.

Since about 1975 the so-called Pinyin system of romanization has been universally accepted for Chinese geographical names. Thus the older form "Peking" is written "Beijing," which more closely approximates the sound of the Chinese word in the Mandarin dialect. This standard is adopted for Chinese place names in this lexicon, with cross-references to variant spellings. The only relevant conventions of Pinyin that do not approximate English usage are as follows.

x: like *sh* as in *ship*, e.g. Xinjiang (shin-jang).

zh: like *j* as in *job*, e.g. Guizhou (gway-joe).

The traditional spellings are retained for place names in East Turkestan, such as "Khotan," since these are familiar in rug literature.

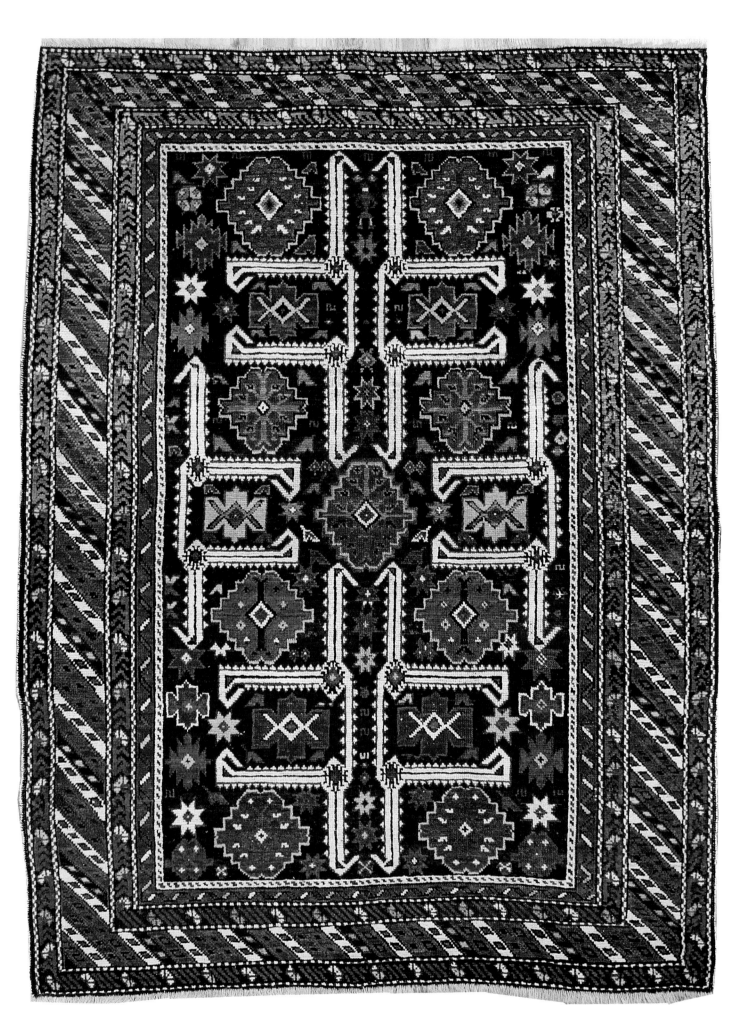

aba (Arabic). A striped fabric or a sleeveless, loose outer garment. Also, a heavy wool cloth.

Abadah. See "Abâdeh."

Abâdeh, Abadah. A town in southwestern Iran on the highway between Isfahan and Shiraz. Some rugs woven in this town have designs similar to Persian city rugs. Others copy local tribal rugs. Knot density is about 80 to 160 symmetric knots per square inch on a cotton foundation. Wefts are sometimes dyed blue. See "Iran."

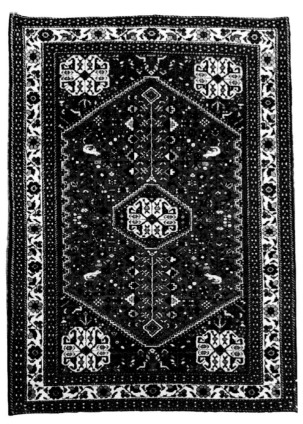

Abâdeh carpet *Dilmaghani & Co.*

Abbas I, Shah. Abbas I, called "the Great," shah of Persia, reigned from 1587 to 1629. In wars with the Uzbeks, Ottoman Turks, and Portuguese, he consolidated the dominion of Persia from the Tigris to the Indus. His reign was distinguished by a magnificent court, the construction of mosques and public buildings, and a great expansion of commerce. He established workshops which produced carpets for his palaces and for state gifts. Approximately 300 silk carpets woven during or shortly after his reign have survived. Most of these silk carpets have been attributed to Isfahan and Kashan. See "Iran," "Polonaise carpets," and "Vase carpets."

Abbasid caliphate. Caliphs ruling at Baghdad from 750 to 1258 C.E. who claimed descent from Abbas, uncle of Muhammad.

Abkhazia. An area of the northwestern Caucasus inhabited by the Abkhaz, a sub-group of the Circassians. They are Sunni Muslims and may have been a very minor source of nineteenth-century Caucasian pile rugs. See "Caucasus."

abr (Persian). Sky-blue, cloud. Also, Persian for ikat fabrics. See "ikat."

abrash (Arabic, "dappled, piebald"). A change in color in the field and border of pile rugs due to differences in wool or dye batches. Abrash may develop as different dye batches in a rug fade at different rates. The color change extends across the rug, weft-wise. Abrash is more likely to occur at the top of a rug than at the bottom, as beginning yarn batches are used up. Abrash is sometimes imitated in new commercial production of hand-knotted and power-loomed rugs.

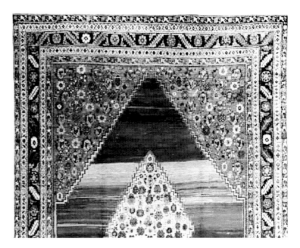

Abrash in a Bakshaish rug (detail) *Alberto Levi*

abrisham, abrishom (Persian). Silk.

Abruzzi. A district of central Italy. From the seventeenth century, Abruzzi has been the source of flatwoven furniture covers and hand-knotted rugs. These are woven on narrow looms. Designs are usually geometricized floral, animal, or heraldic motifs. See "Italy."

acanthus. A plant of the Mediterranean area having toothed leaves, Acanthus spinosus, Acanthus mollis. Stylized representations of the acanthus leaf are familiar as architectural ornamentation and have been recognized in some oriental rug designs. Acanthus leaves are a common motif in Savonnerie rugs.

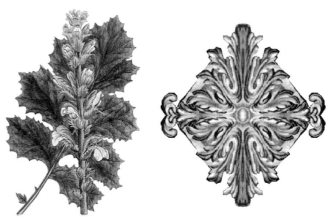

Acanthus leaves *Savonnerie rug (detail)*

accessory fabric. A fabric superimposed (appliqué or quilted), inlaid, or seamed to a ground fabric.

accessory objects. Non-fabric objects attached to a fabric. In tribal weavings, such accessory objects as beads, sea shells, bells, bones, feathers, buttons, or coins are sometimes attached to the fabric as non-functional decorative or shamanistic additions.

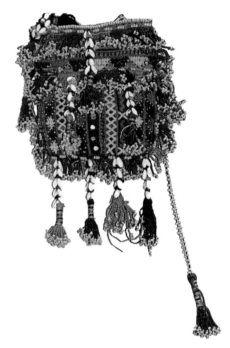

Uzbek bag with accessory objects
R. John Howe

accessory stitches. Functional or decorative stitches in a fabric that include flat stitches, looped stitches, and knot stitches.

acrylic. A synthetic fiber of acrylonitrile. Acrylic may be dyed before extrusion as filaments to be spun. When dyed in this manner, acrylic is very color-fast. It is static-free and stain resistant. Acrylic is used as a substitute for wool, but is not resistant to crushing.

Achaemenian dynasty. Rulers of ancient Persia from about 550 B.C.E. to 331 B.C.E. Certain designs in the Pazyryk carpet are very similar to decorative motifs used in Achaemenian architecture. See "Pazyryk carpet."

acid dyes. Dyes derived from coal tar through the action of nitric acid. They produce bright colors in animal fibers. They are soluble in water and must be used in an acid solution. The first such dye was Bismarck brown developed in 1862. See "basic dyes" and "dye, synthetic."

A.C.O.R., American Conference on Oriental Rugs. An association of approximately 25 local rug societies. Its goal has been to present a national oriental rug conference every two years. These conferences have included seminars, exhibitions, and sales of rugs of interest to collectors.

A.D. (Latin *Anno Domini*, "In the year of our Lord"). The year counted from the time of Christ, a system of date designation generally used by western countries. See "A.H.," "C.E.," "Islamic dates," and "Gregorian date."

Ada-Milas. The peninsula south of Milas in southwestern Anatolia. The area is a source of prayer rugs and rugs with a narrow, vertical, central panel containing a highly abstract tree-of-life design. The field is filled with repeated geometric figures in brownish red.

Adam. A style of architectural and interior decoration in vogue from about 1765 through 1790. The Adam brothers were architects in England whose decorative style consisted of motifs drawn from Roman, Pompiian, and Etruscan work. Ovals, octagons, fans, wreaths, garlands, and medallion shapes were common features of their decoration. Rugs were made to the designs of the Adam brothers in Moorfields, England. Often these rug designs reflected the paneled relief ceilings of the rooms in which the rugs were to be used. Colors were gray, light blue, and jasper. See "Moorfields."

Adana. A town of south central Anatolia, and a source of multi-panel kilims. Adana is a trading center for rugs. See "Turkey."

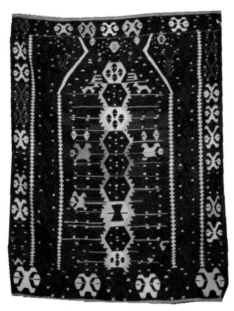

Adana kilim *Simon Knight*

Adıyaman. A city of eastern Anatolia and a source of tülüs and Kurdish rugs. See "Turkey."

Adler Kazak. See "Chelaberd."

Admiral carpets. Carpets of fifteenth-century Spain with armorial bearings of the hereditary admiral of Castile. Many of these carpets bear the arms of the Enriquez family. The field is a lattice of octagons containing geometricized blossoms, with a few containing geometricized birds or animals. Heraldic shields are arranged on this field. These rugs are all wool with the Spanish knot. See "Spain" and "Williams Admiral Carpet."

Adraskand. A town of western Afghanistan, south of Herat, in a district that is a source for kilims and pile rugs woven by Pashtun and Baluchi peoples. See "Afghanistan."

Afghan. A trade term for certain Turkmen carpets of the Ersari tribe. These are main carpets, coarsely woven, with the gulli gul design and are about 8 feet by 10 feet. Also, a woven or knitted coverlet (general usage). A native of Afghanistan. See "Ersari."

Afghanistan. A country of Central Asia bordered by Iran, Turkmenistan, Uzbekistan, Tajikistan, China, and Pakistan. About 75 percent of the population is Sunni Muslim. Rugs are woven by native Afghans (Pashtun) and by Turkmen tribes, most of whom migrated to Afghanistan in the 1920s. These tribes include Ersari, Tekke, Yomud, and Sariq. There is some rug production from Baluchi and Uzbek peoples in Afghanistan. Pile rug production consists largely of pieces with traditional Turkmen guls and geometric designs in shades of red. A wide variety of flatweaves is produced along with bags, animal trappings, and other special-function tribal weavings.

Rug export from Afghanistan increased in the 1970s with the large-scale production of lower-quality rugs. Afghanistan carpets that are single-wefted and without offset warps may be termed *yaktâr* and those that are double-wefted with offset warps may be termed *dotâr*. Soviet Russian troops occupied Afghanistan in December of 1979 in support of a communist régime. Armed resistance to the occupying forces and to the civil government involved much of the rural population. Soviet troops withdrew in February of 1989 and the communist régime was defeated in May of 1992. Warfare resumed in 2002 with the United States incursion into Afghanistan. Rug production, marketing, and distribution were disrupted by warfare. Most descriptions of rug production and marketing centers refer to conditions in prewar Aghanistan. See "Afghanistan war rugs."

There are entries under the following Afghanistan geographic names:

Adraskand	Kabul
Alti Bolaq	Khairabad
Andkhoy	Kunduz
Aq Chah	Labijar
Babaseqal	Laghari
Balkh	Lokari
Barmazid	Maimana
Behsud	Maurchaq
Chakhansur	Qaisar
Charshango	Qala-i Nau
Chichaktu	Qala-i Zal
Daulatabad	Qarqin
Ghorian	Samangân
Ghormaj	Sar-e Pol
Herat	Sharkh
Jengal Arjuk	Shebergân

Afghanistan war rugs. Beginning with Baluchi weavers in Herat, rugs were woven with weapons and war imagery shortly after the Soviet invasion of Afghanistan in 1979. The earliest of these rugs showed a few weapons within traditional fields and borders. In later rugs, war imagery displaced most traditional motifs in the field. Finally, in the latest rugs, both traditional field and border motifs were displaced completely by war imagery. See "Baluchi."

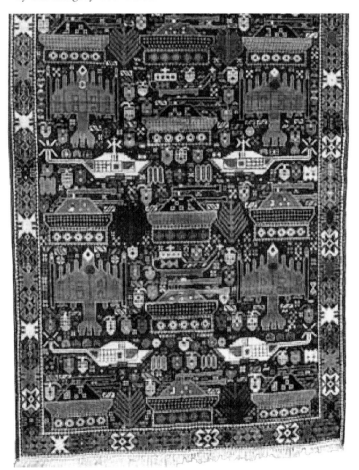

Afghanistan war rug (detail) *Smithsonian*

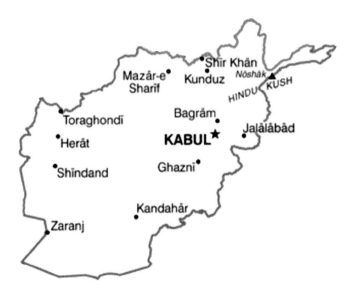

Afghanistan

afshan, avshan (Persian *afshân*, "scattered"). An all-over design found in Caucasian, Indian, Persian, and Turkish rugs. It consists of stylized, right-angle blossom cups or calyxes on a stem surrounded by florets.

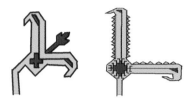

Afshan motifs

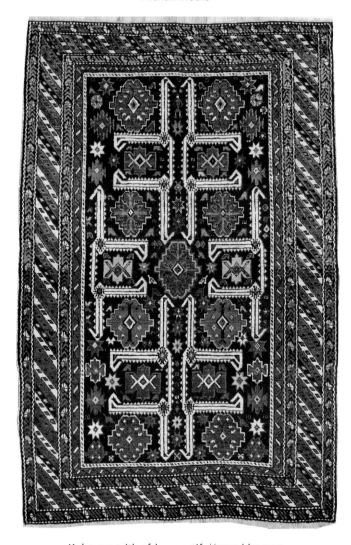

Kuba rug with afshan motif *Hagop Manoyan*

Afshar, Avşar. A Turkic tribe (called "Turkmen" in earlier histories) with scattered groups in Turkey, the Caucasus, and Iran. The largest group is located in Iran south of Kerman. There are both nomadic and village pieces produced by the tribe. Structural characteristics of their pile weaves include primarily wool foundation with pink or orange wefts and warp offset. Twentieth-century Afshar rugs may have a cotton foundation. Rugs of the Afshars are squarish with increasingly geometricized designs in later rugs. There is great variation in rug design, but one of the most common is a floral central medallion with floral spandrels and an opposing vase of

flowers at the top and bottom of the rug. Afshars produce flatweaves in slit tapestry, soumak, weft substitution, and double interlocking weft structures. See "DaHaj," "rakhat," and "Sirjân."

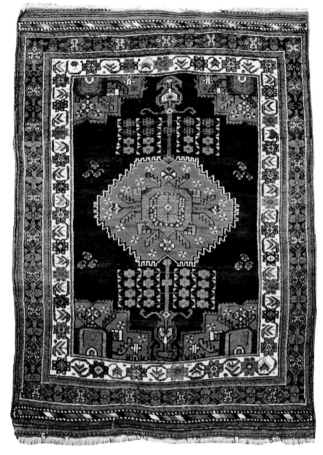

Afshar rug *John Collins*

aft rang. See "haft rang."

Afyon (Turk., "opium"). A town of central Anatolia now referred to as Karahisar. It is a source of rugs similar to those of Konya. See "Karahisar."

age in rugs. See "dating rugs."

agedyna (Swedish). A Flemish type weaving. A flatwoven, long cushion used in carriages and sleighs and on short benches. See "rölaken."

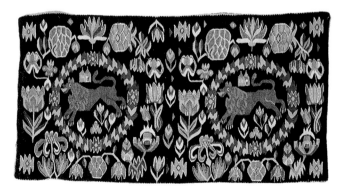

Agedyna *Peter Willborg*

Agra. An ancient city of north central India and former capital of the Mughal Empire. Carpet workshops were in production in Agra in 1619. After the partition of India in 1947, many Muslim weavers immigrated to Pakistan. The industry has recovered, and presently there is an active carpet-weaving industry in Agra. Some rugs are woven by prisoners of the Agra Central Jail. See "India."

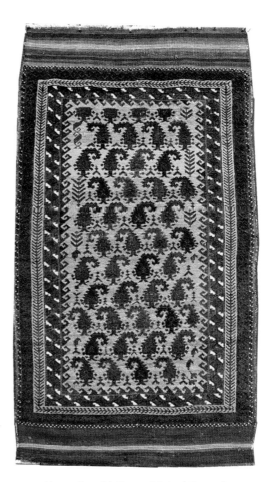

Aimaq (Jamshidi) rug *Michael Craycraft*

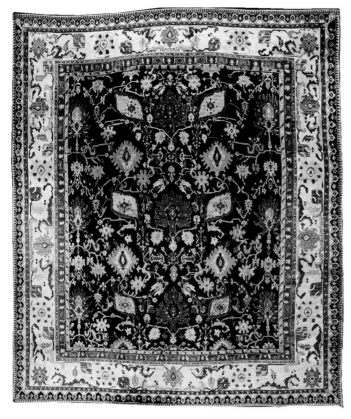

Agra rug *Doris Leslie Blau*

A.H. See "Anno Hegirae."

Ahar, Ahjar. A town in the Heriz region of northwest Iran. A designation of fine weave or curvilinear design in Heriz rugs. Contemporary rugs of Ahar have medallions and spandrels. The symmetric knot is used at a density of about 65 per square inch on a cotton foundation. The wefts may be blue. Single-wefted rugs of the Heriz area may be termed "Ahar." See "Iran."

Ahmedabad. Formerly a rug-weaving center in west central India. There is no significant current production. See "India."

Ahura Mazda. See "Zoroastrianism."

Aibak. See "Samangân."

Aimaq, Chahar Aimaq (Turk. or Mongol, "four tribes"). Four semi-nomadic tribes of partly Turko-Mongol origin inhabiting Afghanistan and Iran: the Hazara, Firozkohi, Jamshidi, and Taimani. See entries under these names. Some of these tribes are noted for their rug production. Their weavings are sometimes confused with those of the Baluch. See "Afghanistan" and "Timuri."

aina gul, mirror gul (Persian *âyena*, "mirror"). A Turkmen gul consisting of a quartered diamond in a rectangle or a stepped diamond within a regular diamond within a rectangle. These are termed "compartment guls."

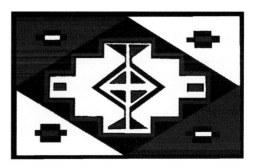

Aina gul *After Moshkova*

Ainabad. See "Bibikabad."

aina-kotchak. See "kochak."

aina khalata. Small mirror bag.

Ainalu. A tribe of the Khamseh Confederacy of southwest Iran. See "Khamseh Confederacy."

Aintab, Aintap. See "Gaziantep."

ajdaha, ejderha, (Persian *azhdahâ*, "dragon"). A dragon motif in Persian rugs, usually reduced to an "S" shape or "Z" shape. It is common in borders as overlapping or sequential "S" or "Z" shapes. See "dragon and phoenix" and "S-borders."

ak, aq (Turk.) White.

ak chuval. A joval with a white ground pile skirt and white flatwoven stripes. See "joval."

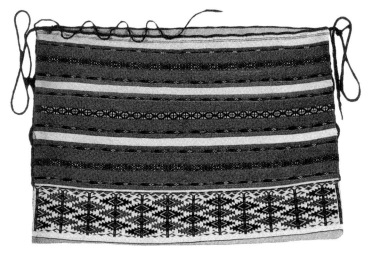

Ak Chuval *Collection of Mr. and Mrs. Steven Price*

Akhisar (Turk. *ak hisar,* "white castle"). A town of northwest Anatolia. The town is a minor source of prayer rugs in red and orange. Small pompons may be attached to the selvedge. Kilim ends may be ornamented with pile buttons. See "Turkey."

Ak Karaman. A breed of fat-tailed sheep of central and east Anatolia.

Aksaray. A town of central Anatolia and a center of Turkmen carpet weaving during the Seljuk period. Aksaray is a source of kilims. Often, there is a design offset between the two halves of these kilims. See "Turkey."

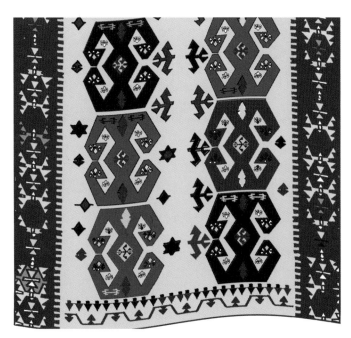

Aksaray kilim (detail)

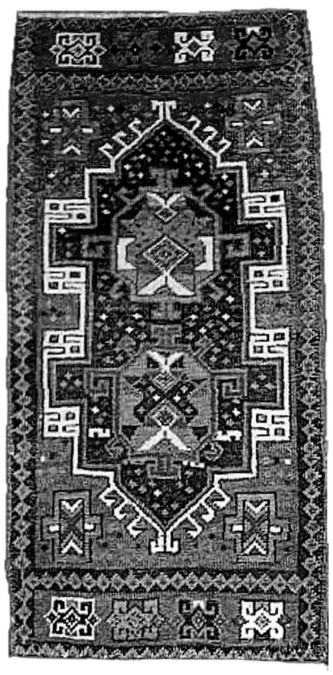

Aksaray yastik *R. John Howe*

Akşehir (Turk., white town). A town of western Anatolia and a rug weaving center in the sixteenth and seventeenth centuries.

aksi (Persian, "pictorial"). Used to describe rugs with a pictorial emphasis rather than a design emphasis. See "pictorial rug" and "war rugs."

Akstafa, Akstafa peacock. The town of Akstafa and the river Akstafa are located in the Transcaucasus. The Akstafa peacock motif is a geometricized bird with an elaborate tail. As a design element, it is found on rugs of Shirvân in the Caucasus and in Turkish rugs. Akstafa design rugs of nineteenth-century Shirvân are woven with the symmetric knot at a density of about 107 knots per square inch. Average size is about 34 square feet. Warps are wool and wefts may be cotton or wool. See "Shirv-ân."

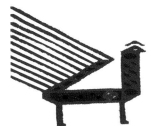

Akstafa peacock

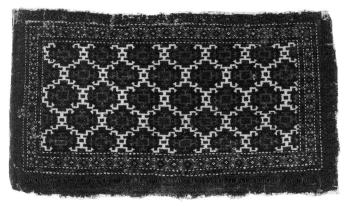

Torba with ak-su motif *Sothebys*

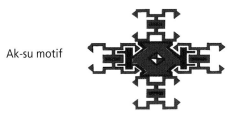

Ak-su motif

ak yup (Turk.). White tent band.

alachiq. A domed felt tent of the Moghân Shahsavan.

ala chuval. Anatolian flatwoven storage bags. These bags are made in pairs. Designs are woven in horizontal or vertical panels. Sizes are about 2 feet to 4 feet high and about 20 inches to 30 inches wide. The bag is open on a short side. See "joval."

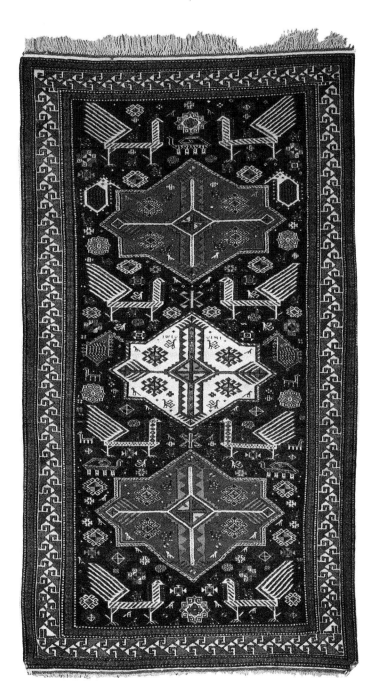

Akstafa rug *Sothebys*

ak-su (Turk. "white water"). A repeated design motif consisting of interlocking quadrilaterals with projections.

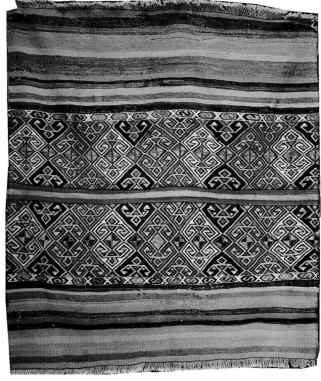

Anatolian brocaded ala chuval (opened up) *Hugh Rance*

alam. See "elem."

Alamdâr. A village of the Hamadan area in northwest Iran. The village is a source of rugs with a geometric Herati pattern on a blue field.

Alanya. A coastal town of south central Anatolia and a minor source of rugs and kilims. See "Turkey."

alasa, alasha. In Kazakhstan, a flatwoven rug consisting of woven bands sewn together. See "gadzhari" and "jijim."

Albania. Since World War II, a source of contemporary, very well-made pile rugs with Persian designs.

alcatif (Portuguese *alcatifa* from Arabic *al-qatif(a)*, "velvet, plush"). An archaic term for rugs of India.

Alcaraz. A textile and rug-weaving center in Spain from the fifteenth to the mid-seventeenth centuries. Spanish wreath design, armorial carpets, ogival lattice carpets, and copies of Holbein rugs are attributed to Alcaraz. See "Spain" and "wreath carpets."

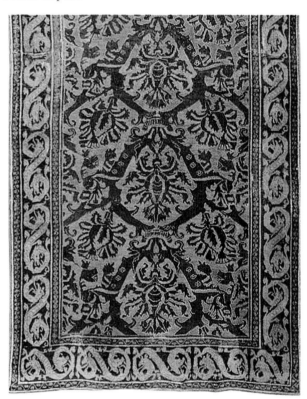

Alcaraz rug (detail) *Jason Nazmiyal*

alem. See "elem."

Aleppo, Halep. A city of northwest Syria, now called Haleb. It was formerly in southeast Anatolia and an administrative center during the Ottoman period. In the last half of the nineteenth century many kilims were woven in this area. They were used as curtains and wall hangings. These kilims were woven in two pieces. Cochineal was used in many of these kilims. Borders are usually white with a repeated winged or hourglass figure. Diamonds and octagons are the primary repeated field motif. Some of the kilims are woven with the sandıklı or compartment motif.

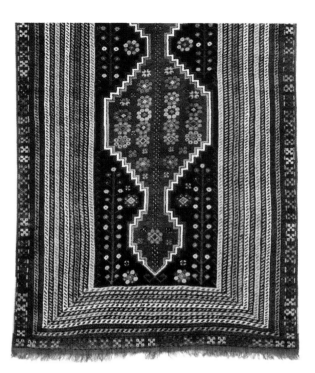

Aleppo rug (detail) *Peter Willborg*

Algeria. A country of North Africa. Algerian rugs are similar to those of Morocco and Tunisia. Sétif is a town southeast of Algiers that is noted for its rug production. Pile rugs are all-wool and woven with the symmetric knot. Traditionally, pile rugs are woven by men (*reggema*) with women as assistants. Currently, women are designing and weaving pile rugs. There are a few pile rug types unique to Algeria. These are the Algerian *qtif* and *tanchra* with uncut looped pile and the *frach* and Kalâa pile carpets with large flatwoven ends. See "frach," "Guergour carpets," "Kalâa," "Maadid tribe," "metrah," "qtif," "reggema," "tanchra," and "zerbiya."

The flatweaves of Algeria are similar to those of Tunisia. The *melgout, hamel, tag,* and *draga* are flatwoven tent dividers used in different ways. Blankets (*hambel*), flatwoven carpets, sacks, shawls (*ddil*), and saddle blankets (*dokkala*) are also woven.

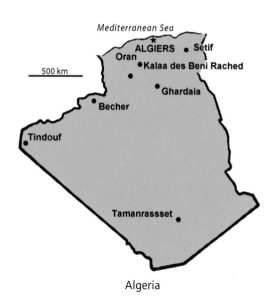

Algeria

Ali Eli. A subtribe of the Ersari in the area of the Amu Darya river.

alınık (Turk., "place where the forehead meets the ground during prayer"). In a prayer rug, a panel above a mihrab that may contain a Koranic inscription. See "elem."

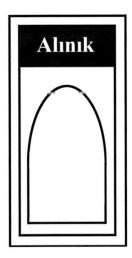
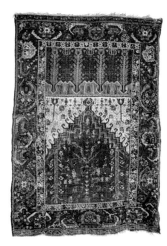

Alınık

alizarin (from Spanish *alizari*, "madder," from Arabic al-'asâra, "juice, extract"). A primary active agent in the dye derived from madder, an anthraquinone that produces shades of red in combination with metals. It provides a red component of the dye. Alizarin was produced synthetically in 1870. A variety of dyes of different colors were developed from compounds of alizarin. See "madder."

alloucha. A pile carpet of Tunisia in white, beige, brown, and gray. This rug was formerly woven of naturally colored wools. See "Tunisia."

all-over pattern field repeat. A design in the field of a rug consisting of vertically and horizontally repeated geometrical or floral elements. Usually, the pattern is interrupted or cut off by the borders. Sometimes borders awkwardly interrupt the pattern. Such rugs may suggest that the weaver has a mental image of an infinitely repeated pattern with an arbitrary segment framed by the border. See "boteh," "gul," "Herati pattern," "lattice," "minâ khâni," "mir-i boteh," and "Lotto."

alpaca. A domesticated South American ruminant related to the lama. It has long silky wool used in South American weaving.

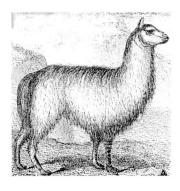

 alpaca

Alpan Kuba. A design of rugs from nineteenth-century Kuba in the Caucasus that may be a simplified version of either the Seishour Cross or the Kasim Ushag design. A medallion is surrounded by four elongated hexagons. See "Kuba."

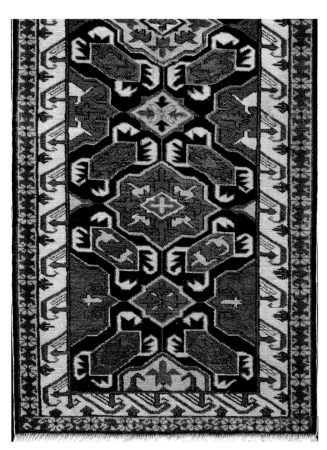

Alpan Kuba rug (detail) *Richard Rothstein & Co.*

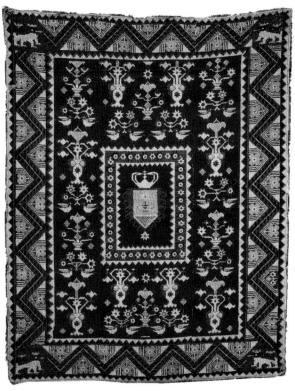

Alpujarra rug *Grogan & Company*

Alpujarra. Alpujarra means "grassland." The term refers to rugs first woven in Alpujarra in the province of Granada, Spain. These rugs were first woven in the fifteenth or sixteenth centuries during the Moorish period and continued to be woven into the nineteenth century. They have a coarsely-woven looped pile and are very heavy. Usually, a separately produced elaborate fringe was attached to all four sides of the rug. Often, the date and name of the person for whom the rug was woven was included in the design. Designs were simple floral and animal motifs. Often, only two colors were used. Later rugs of Alpujarra include Christian symbols. See "Spain."

Altai culture, Altay culture. Altai is an area of Inner Asia taking its name from the Altai mountains. From the second millennium B.C.E., the area has been inhabited by cattle-rearing nomads and agriculturists. Many objects employing distinctive stylized animal motifs of wood, bone, bronze, and gold have been found in burial sites. Felts, fabrics, and pile rugs have also been found at these sites. In the eastern Altai, a pile rug was discovered at Pazyryk that has been radiocarbon-dated to about 500 to 300 B.C.E. See "Pazyryk carpet."

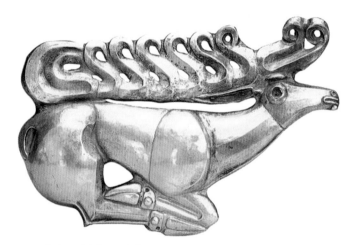

Altaic gold deer of the same period as the Pazyrik carpet

Alti Bolaq. A village of north central Afghanistan near the Turkmen border. The village is a source of rugs woven by Ersaris. The rugs are double-wefted and the asymmetric knot is used.

alum mordant. Aluminum sulfate (and sometimes potassium sulfate) are both called alum. These water-soluble salts are used in dyeing as a mordant. With many dyes, they produce lighter colors than tin or chrome mordants.

Alvand. See "Qazvin."

Amaleh. A subtribe of the Qashqa'i of southwest Iran, noted for its kilims. See "Qashqa'i."

American Conference on Oriental Rugs. See "A.C.O.R."

American Indian rugs. See "Navajo rugs," "Pueblo weaving," and "Rio Grande blankets."

Ames Pictorial Rug. This Mughal rug, a gift of Mrs. F. L. Ames, is in the Museum of Fine Arts, Boston. It shows scenes from the hunt, domestic scenes, and mythological beasts. The border includes grotesque faces. This rug is thought to be a copy of a painting. It was woven in the first half of the seventeenth century and is eight feet by five feet.

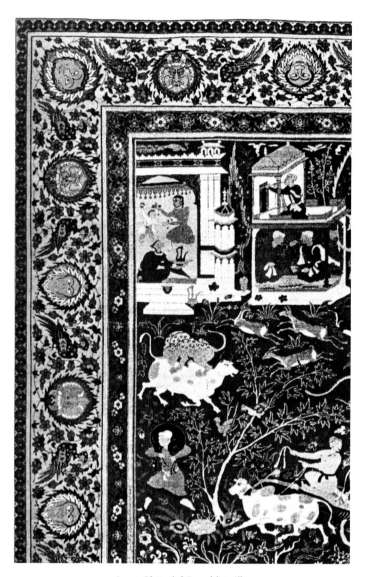

Ames Pictorial Rug (detail)

Amo Oghli, Amoghli, Emoghli. An early 20th-century rug workshop owner, rug weaver, and rug designer of Mashhad, Iran. "See Mashhad."

Amritsar (Sanskrit, "lake of immortality"). A city of the Punjab in northwest India, the major Sikh center. Rug manufacturing began in Amritsar in about 1860, using unemployed shawl weavers. Early production copied Turkmen designs. Production in Amritsar declined during the depression in the 1920s and during the partition of India, but has since recovered. Currently, floral designs are woven based on Persian models. The asymmetric knot is used. Contemporary rugs have a knot density of about 200 to 400 knots per square inch. See "India."

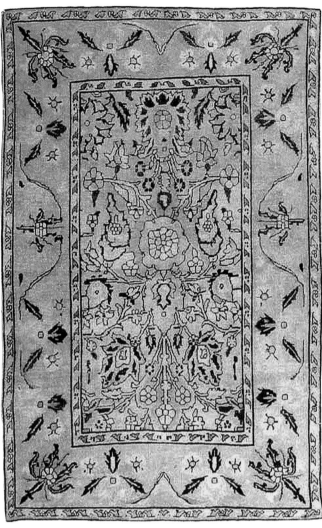

Amritsar rug *Jason Nazmiyal*

AMTORG. Acronym for American Trading Organization, an export-import company representing Soviet Russian interests in the United States. The company was active from about 1926 to 1937, exporting commodities to the United States and importing machinery to Russia. From 1926 to about 1930, AMTORG exported old Caucasian and Turkmen rugs to the U.S. After 1931, it exported five-year plan rugs to the U.S. See "five-year plan rugs."

Amu Darya. A river (the ancient Oxus) near the northern boundary of Afghanistan and the southern boundary of Turkmenistan. Several different Turkmen tribes live along this river. These include the Ersari, Salor, Saryk, and Tekke.

amulet. See "muska."

analysis. See "technical analysis" and "dye analysis."

Anatolia. A peninsula between the Black Sea and the Mediterranean Sea constituting Asiatic Turkey or Asia Minor. The rug-weaving population includes Turkmen, Yörük, and Kurdish peoples. Armenian and Greek peoples in Anatolia also wove rugs. Anatolian rugs are the products of workshops such as those of Ushak, Kayseri, and Bandirma, of nomadic Kurds and

Yörük, and of thousands of villages scattered through Anatolia. The foundation and pile are wool with very few exceptions. Warps are undyed and 2-ply "S" twist; wefts are unplied. The symmetric knot is used consistently. Except in a few rugs of central and east Anatolia, there is no warp offset. Pile rug weaving is an ancient craft of Anatolia. There are fragments of thirteenth-century rugs woven during the Seljuk period. See "Turkey."

andhani. A camel's head covering of Pakistan.

Andhra Pradesh. A province of southern India (capital, Hyderabad) and the location of several weaving centers. See "Ellore," "India," "Masulipatam," and "Warangal."

Andkhoy. A town of north central Afghanistan near the Turkmen border. The town is a collecting point and market for rugs made in the area, primarily woven by Ersaris. Most of these rugs are based on Turkmen designs in shades of red, indigo, and white. The asymmetric knot is used. Usually, these rugs are double-wefted. Typical rug sizes are about 5 feet by 6 feet and 9 feet by 12 feet.

angle of twist. A measure of the tightness to which yarn is twisted in spinning. The angle between the longitudinal axis of the yarn and the plane of the fibers in a single or the plane of the last ply in plied or cabled yarns. The direction of spin is taken into account when measuring this angle. A twist angle of about 5 degrees is a soft-spun yarn; 20 degrees is a medium-spun yarn; and 30 to 45 degrees is a hard-spun yarn. Crêpe spun yarns crinkle and have an angle of twist of 65 degrees or more. See "twist."

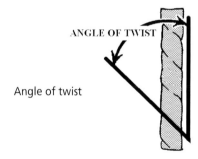

Angle of twist

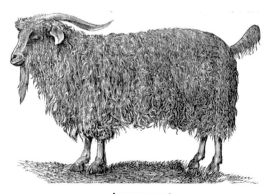

Angora goat

Angora goat. A goat of Turkish origin and the source of mohair, a long, coarse, and lustrous fiber. See "mohair."

Anhalt Medallion Carpet. A sixteenth-century carpet of northwest Persia. It formerly belonged to the Dukes of Anhalt of Dessau and is now in the collection of the Metropolitan Museum of Art, New York. This carpet is in excellent condition. It has a circular lobed medallion with pendants on a yellow field of arabesques with leaves, blossoms, and palmettes. Among the arabesques are peacocks with plumage displayed. It has a knot density of 400 asymmetric knots per square inch. The warp is cotton and the weft is silk. The size of this rug is 26 feet 6 inches by 13 feet 7 inches.

aniline dyes. Direct dyes derived from aniline, which is in turn a derivative of coal tar. The first such dye, mauve, was invented by Perkin in 1856. By 1870, aniline dyes were inexpensive and widely used. Some of the aniline dyes used in rugs were not colorfast. See "acid dyes," "basic dyes," and "synthetic dyes."

animal carpet. Any carpet design including animal motifs. More particularly, Persian and Indo-Persian rugs with representations of a variety of animals in the field of the rug. See "Animal Carpet of Leopold I," "animal motifs," "hunting carpets," "Sackville Mughal Animal and Tree Carpet," and "Widener Animal Carpet."

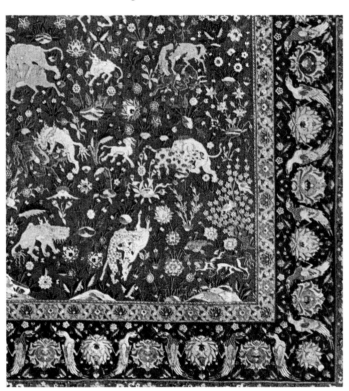

Animal carpet (detail)

Animal Carpets of Leopold I, Emperor. A pair of late sixteenth-century Persian carpets given to the Austrian Emperor Leopold I by Peter the Great of Russia. The field is red and filled with animals in combat, cloud bands, blossoms, and palmettes. The inner minor border contains lines from a poem. The knot density is 320 asymmetric knots per square inch. Warps are cotton and wefts are silk. The size of the rugs is 11 feet 6 inches by 24 feet 4 inches. One rug is in Vienna and the other is in the collection of the Metropolitan Museum of Art, New York.

animal head motif, animal head column. A motif also known as "latch hooks" consisting of a triangle offset on a column. The animal head sometimes possesses an eye. A short line may trail from the point of the triangle. This motif may be repeated in rows or columns and as a border or medallion outline. This motif is common in tribal and Turkic weavings.

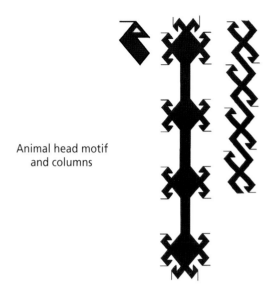

Animal head motif and columns

animal motifs. A very wide range of animals has been used in oriental rug designs. Animals have been represented naturalistically, as in the Persian hunting carpets. Through progressive stylization and abstraction, they have been represented as geometric symbols, as in Turkmen rugs. Even extinct animals may be represented. The aurochs, an extinct ox, is thought to be represented in certain ancient designs in Anatolian kilims. Domesticated animals are common in the weavings of nomadic peoples. These include goats, horses, camels, and roosters. The tiger is often represented in the rugs of Tibet and the lion in the rugs of southwest Iran. The bat is common in Chinese rugs.

For some cultures, the animals represented may symbolize a trait or condition as the crane in China symbolizes long life. The animal may symbolize a particular ethnic group or tribe, as in the tauk noska gul of the Chodor Turkmen.

A geometric design may suggest an animal form to those wishing to label and classify the design where the weavers had no intention of any animal representation. Such is the case with the "Eagle Kazak" and the "running dog" border. See "symbolism in rugs."

animal trapping. Weavings used primarily for ornament for horses, camels, and donkeys. These include blankets that cover the back and cross the chest of the animal, as well as head ornaments. See "andhani," "asmalyk," "at-joli," "cherlyk," "chul," "dzo ke-thil," "jol," "kapan," "khalyk," "knee caps," "sar," "shabrak," "takheb" and "ushter-i jol."

Anno Hegirae, A.H. Latinate designation of years in accordance with the Islamic calendar, beginning in 622 C.E., the year of Muhammad's emigration (Arabic hijra) from Mecca to Medina. See "Islamic dates."

Antalya. A town on the Gulf of Antalya in Anatolia, located just south of Döşmealtı. Carpets made in Döşmealtı are sometimes incorrectly termed Antalya. Antalya is a trading center for rugs. See "Turkey."

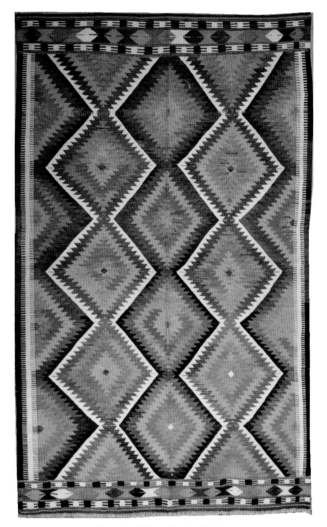

Antalya kilim *Kazim Yildiz*

Antheraea pernyi. A silk-producing moth that feeds on oak leaves. See "silk."

antique. This term is ambiguous and variously interpreted. An antique rug may be one thought to be at least 100 years old. See "dating rugs."

antique wash. The application of chemicals to a rug to soften colors and simulate the appearance of an older rug. See "luster" and "bleaching."

appliqué. Superimposed fabrics in which the pattern is created by an accessory fabric (or tape, ribbon, or cord) overlaid on a ground fabric or the pattern is created by cutouts in the ground fabric with the accessory fabric underlaid beneath the cutout.

appraisal. Determining the monetary value of a rug. In formal appraisal, the rug is identified and described. These properties are considered: attribution, age, condition, rug structure, design, and color.

Generally, auction prices are the best guide to the value of oriental rugs of interest to collectors. Easily identified types of rugs have a relatively narrow range of prices in the auction market. Rugs in exceptionally good or bad condition or having exceptional aesthetic merit fall outside this price range. Rugs of less popular or rare attribution have more variable auction prices. Prices are affected by changing interests of collectors and by changing tastes in interior decoration.

The valuation of contemporary decorative oriental rugs depends on current production and changing trends in interior decoration. Current retail prices are the comparative basis for valuing decorative rugs.

Monetary valuation is likely to be influenced by the motive of the person desiring the appraisal. Low appraisals may occur if the owner's motive for valuation is purchase or estate taxation. High appraisals may occur if the owner's motive is sale, an insurance claim, or gift deduction for tax purposes. Usually, replacement cost is the basis for declared value for insurance premium determination. Some consider it unethical for an appraiser to charge a fee based on the appraised value of the rug. See "attribution," "condition," "dating rugs," "decorative rug," "design classification," and "technical analysis."

apricot. A light yellowish red color, either the result of initial dye colors or the result of fading.

Aq Chah. A town and district of northern Afghanistan. The town is the chief market for rugs in Afghanistan. Rugs from the villages surrounding Aq Chah are woven by Turkmen. These rugs are in traditional designs and woven with the asymmetric knot. Colors used are red, indigo, and black, with some white, orange, and green

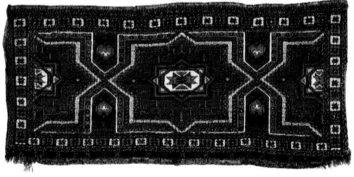

Arabatchi joval *Sothebys*

Arabatchi (from Turk. *arabacı* "(driver of) wheeled vehicle.") A Turkmen tribe of the Amu Darya (Oxus) region of central Turkestan. Older main carpets attributed to this tribe carry the tauk noska gul. The dominant field color in their weavings is purplish-brown. Outlines are formed in natural brown wool. There is some warp offset and the knot is asymmetric and open to the left. Wefts are spun of wool and white cotton. However, the attribution of specific rugs to this tribe is questioned. See "Turkmen."

arabesque. A design motif of intertwining or scrolling vines, tendrils, straps, or branches. These may be classified as geometric, floral, or vegetal, including the split-leaf type known as "*rumî.*" Arabesques usually include leaves, profile buds, and blossoms. They are a common device in oriental rug designs. Systems of arabesques may be superimposed in rug designs. See "islimi," "saz," "split leaf arabesque," "Vase carpet," and "Strapwork carpets."

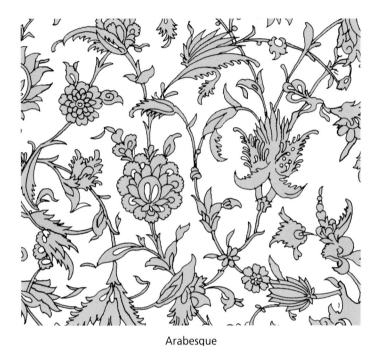

Arabesque

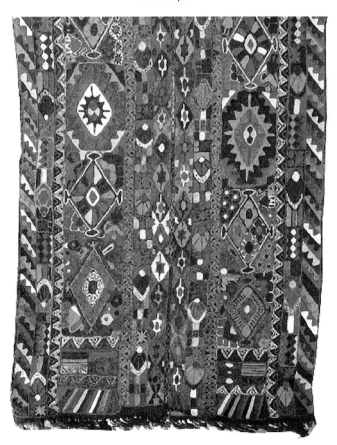

Iraqi Arabic embroidered rug (detail) *Tribal Collections*

Arabs. Arabic-speaking peoples inhabiting the countries of Arabia, Jordan, Lebanon, Syria, Iraq, Egypt, and much of North Africa. There are scattered groups throughout the Middle East, including Iran, and Turkestan. There is no significant rug production in Arabia. However, a so-called Arab tribe in southwest Iran, a member of the Khamseh Confederacy, produces pile rugs, and Arab enclaves in Turkestan (both northern Afghanistan and Uzbekistan) are the source of kilims. See "Khamseh" and "Bedouin."

Arabia. A peninsula of the Near East bounded on the west by the Red Sea, on the south by the Indian Ocean, on the east by the Persian Gulf, and on the north by Iraq and Jordan. It presently comprises the states of Saudi Arabia, Kuwait, Yemen, Oman, and the United Arab Emirates. Mecca, the Muslim holy city, is near the west coast.

Arabic calligraphy and script. Arabic script derives from Nabataean script, and is a member of the family of Semitic writing systems which, via Phoenician, gave rise to the Greek and hence the Latin alphabet. The development and wide usage of Arabic script was due to the need to copy and distribute the Koran, beginning in the seventh century. Ornamented script or calligraphy developed from early Jazm script. There were many succeeding variations. These included Kufic, Thuluth, Naskhi, Nasta'liq, Muhaqqaq, Rayhani, Riqa', and Tawqi'. Of these, only Kufic, Thuluth, Naskhi, and Nasta'liq have been found in inscriptions in oriental rugs. The inscriptions in the Ardabil carpet are in Nasta'liq. Kufesque is a group of design motifs derived from Kufic script, but not directly readable as script. The calligraphic styles were first used for textile and rug inscriptions in this approximate time sequence:

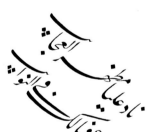

Kufic

Kufic:
seventh to tenth centuries

Kufesque:
eleventh to fifteenth centuries

Nasta'liq:
sixteenth to eighteenth centuries

Nasta'liq

Thuluth:
nineteenth to twentieth centuries

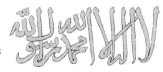

Thuluth

See "cartouche," "Kufesque," and "inscriptions."

Arabic numbers, Arabic numerals. See "Islamic dates."

Arâk, Sultanabad. A province and city of northwest Iran. The city of Arâk was formerly Sultanabad. The province was the source of much high-quality rug production, on a workshop basis, in the late nineteenth and early twentieth centuries. Notable rug-weaving centers in Arâk province include Sarouk, Mahal (Mahallât), Lillihan, and the districts of Farâhân and Serabend. See entries under these names.

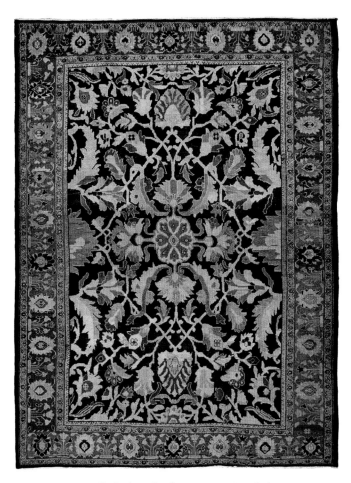

Arâk (Sultanabad) rug *Jason Nazmiyal*

ara-khachi (Turk.). Middle or main stripe in a rug border.

arbabash (cart cover or head). A felt carpet of Daghestan in which the design is produced by appliquéd felt. See "Daghestan," "istang," and "kiyiz."

archaeological sites. See "Altai culture," "At-Tar," "Çatal Hüyük," "Fustat," "Fustat carpet," "Kizil," "Lop Nor," "Lop Sanpra," "Lou lan," "Niya," "Pazyryk carpet," "Quseir al-Qadim," and "Shahr-i Qumis."

Ardabil, Ardebil. A town in Iranian Azerbaijan east of Tabriz. It is the site of the shrine of Shaikh Safi (ancestor of the Safavid dynasty), first begun in the fourteenth century. Contemporary rugs of this area employ designs similar to Caucasian designs. They have symmetric knots at a density up to 160 per square inch on a cotton foundation. See "Persia."

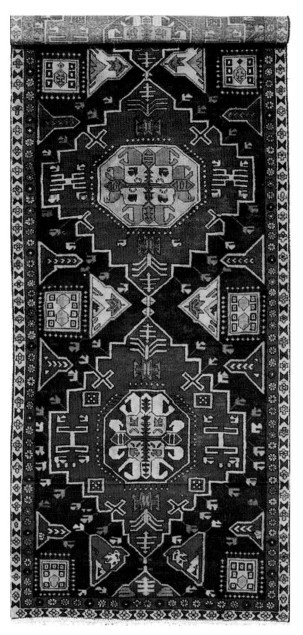

Ardabil rug (detail) *J. Barry O'Connell*

Ardabil Carpets. Two nearly identical Ardabil carpets were woven in 1535 or 1540, according to inscriptions on the carpets. One carpet, repaired with fragments from its twin, is in the Victoria and Albert Museum. A major central portion of the other is in the Los Angeles County Museum of Art. Both these magnificent carpets were woven in the reign of Shah Tahmâsp. Both carpets have the same original dimesions, about 34½ feet by 17½ feet. The carpets are woven on a silk foundation with an asymmetric knot at approximately 300 knots per square inch. The carpet in the Victoria and Albert museum has the higher knot count. The name of the designer, Maqsud of Kashan, is woven into the rugs. Their specific function and city of origin is conjectural. They were originally thought to have been woven for the shrine at Ardabil, but this use has been questioned due to the size of the rugs. The origin of the carpets has been assigned to Ardabil, Kashan, Mashhad, Tabriz, and other locations. See "Persia."

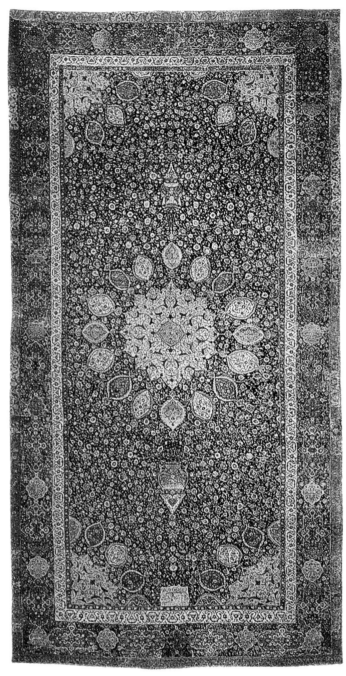

Ardabil Carpet *Victoria and Albert Museum*

Ardakān. A town southeast of Nain in Iran and a source of rugs with Kashan designs, though more coarsely woven.

area rug. In the rug trade, any rug that is not cut and installed to cover the floor from wall to wall. Also a rug of about 4½ feet by 7 feet.

Armenia. An ancient country of western Asia, professing Christianity since ca. 300 C.E., that once included parts of eastern Turkey, northern Persia, and the southern Caucasus. There are rugs from all of these areas that carry Armenian inscriptions. The Republic of Armenia occupies a southern portion of the Caucasus. See "Caucasus."

Often, dates in Armenian rugs appear in letter form. The date can be translated to the Gregorian calendar by

determining the sum of the numbers represented by each letter and adding 551 to this sum.

Ա	ա	1	Մ	ս	200
Բ	բ	2	Յ	յ	300
Գ	գ	3	Ն	ն	400
Դ	դ	4	Շ	շ	500
Ե	ե	5	Ո	ո	600
Զ	զ	6	Չ	չ	700
Է	է	7	Պ	պ	800
Ը	ը	8	Ջ	ջ	900
Թ	թ	9	Ռ	ռ	1000
Ժ	ժ	10	Ս	ս	2000
Ի	ի	20	Վ	վ	3000
Լ	լ	30	Տ	տ	4000
Խ	խ	40	Ր	ր	5000
Ծ	ծ	50	Ց	ց	6000
Կ	կ	60	Ւ	ւ	7000
Հ	հ	70	Փ	փ	8000
Ձ	ձ	80	Ք	ք	9000
Ղ	ղ	90	Օ	օ	10000
Ճ	ճ	100	Ֆ	ֆ	20000

Armenian alphabet with numerical equivalents

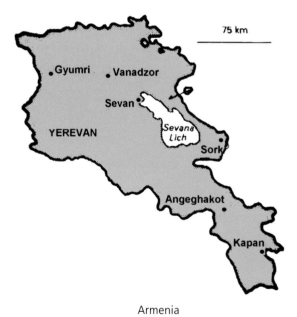

Armenia

Armenian rugs. There are rugs with Armenian inscriptions from Iran, Turkey, and the Caucasus. Most are from the Caucasus. Much of the rug production of Shusha in nineteenth-century Karabagh is thought to have been woven by Armenians. Caucasian rugs with western dates are probably Armenian in origin. Some scholars believe the early Caucasian Dragon Carpets are attributable to Armenians of the southern Caucasus. See "Caucasus," "Dragon carpets," "Echmiadzin," "Erivan," and "Gohar carpet."

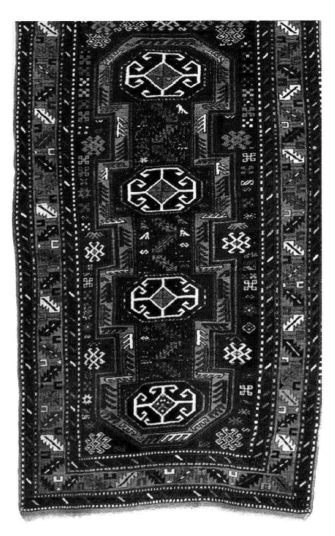

Armenian rug (detail) *Wikimedia Commons*

armorial carpet. Any carpet bearing a coat of arms or heraldic device. More particularly, carpets woven in Spain by the Moors which were commissioned by Spanish royalty and bore their coats of arms. These carpets are dated as early as 1405. See "Admiral carpets," "Alpujarra," "escutcheon," "Fremlin carpet," "Girdler's carpet," "Kerman armori," and "Polonaise"

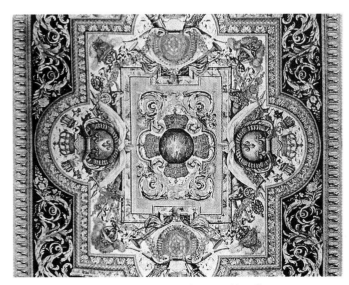

Savonnerie armorial carpet (detail)

Aroon. A lower grade of Kashan. See "Kashan."

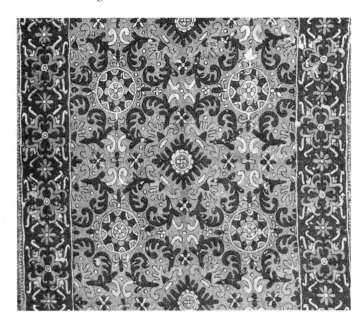

Arraiolos needlework carpet (detail)

Arraiolos. A town of Portugal and a source of needlework carpets beginning in the sixteenth century. Originally designs were based on models from Persia and Anatolia. Later designs include boldly drawn floral and animal motifs of a more European character. The field of these rugs was usually yellow.

Arras. A city of the Netherlands (presently in northern France) famed for tapestries woven from the 13th through the 15th centuries. The name has become synonymous with tapestries, wall hangings, and curtains.

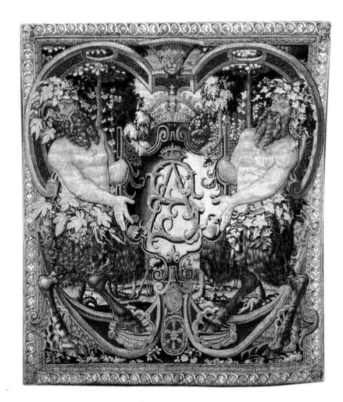

Arras tapestry

Ashkhabad. Ashkhabad (Ashgabat) is the capital of Turkmenistan, a center for commercial rug manufacture, and a trading center for other Turkmen rugs and weavings. See "Turkmenistan."

artel. An artisans' cooperative. Cooperatives of rug weavers were organized in the 1920s in Soviet Russia to weave rugs for export. See "five-year plan rugs."

artemisia leaf. One of the eight precious things of Confucianism. A Chinese symbol of dignity and happiness sometimes used in rug designs. In the Near East, artemisia stems are used as a yellow dye. In Europe, it is used as a flavoring herb and narcotic (wormwood).

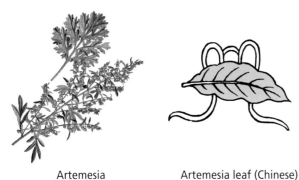

Artemesia   Artemesia leaf (Chinese)

Art Moderne, Art Décoratif, Art Deco, Modern Movement.
A style of interior decoration having its origin in the Bauhaus movement. It developed between World Wars One and Two and involved the design of furnishings compatible with modern machine production methods. Art Moderne rug designs were influenced by such artists as Braque, Léger, Mondrian, and Miró. Geometric shapes, blocks of color, straight lines, and curving lines were used to form non-objective designs. These carpets were designed and woven in England, China, Scotland, France, and the United States.

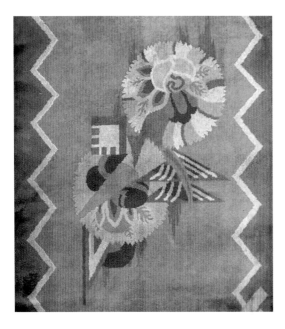

French Art Deco rug (detail) *Peter Pap Oriental Rugs Inc*

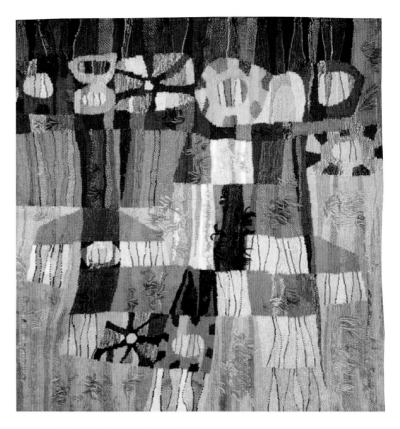

Scandanavian Modern Movement (detail) *Doris Leslie Blau*

Art Nouveau. The decorative style of Art Nouveau flourished in the last decade of the nineteenth century. It influenced the design of architecture, graphics, and domestic furnishings. A return to high standards of craftsmanship was a goal of this movement. The style is characterized by the exuberant use of plant forms (stems, vines, leaves, flowers) attenuated and integrated into the shape of the object. Outstanding examples of Art Nouveau carpets were designed with these highly stylized plant forms by Sir Frank Brangwyn, Gallén-Kallela of Finland, and Victor Horta of Belgium.

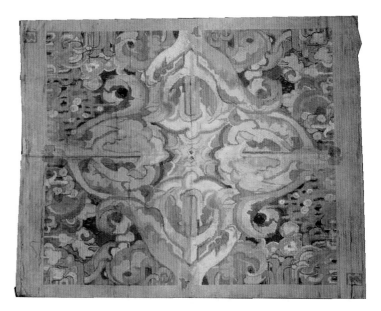

Art Nouveau rug by Frank Brangwyn (detail) *Doris Leslie Blau*

Arts and Crafts. A design movement of the last quarter of the nineteenth century and the early twentieth century originating in Great Britain. Supporters of the movement were committed to craftsmanship in the applied arts and the production of domestic furnishings. They rejected the elaborate decorative styles of manufactured goods then popular on the continent. A guiding concept was that of the designer artisan who executed his or her own designs. The Arts and Crafts movement fostered Art Nouveau. Arts and Crafts rugs were designed by William Morris and C.F.A. Voysey. Hand-knotted Arts and Crafts rugs were woven and many others were designed for production as power-loomed Axminsters. Large scale or out-sized floral motifs were dominant and some pictorial designs were used. See "Art Nouveau," "Voysey, Charles," and "Morris, William."

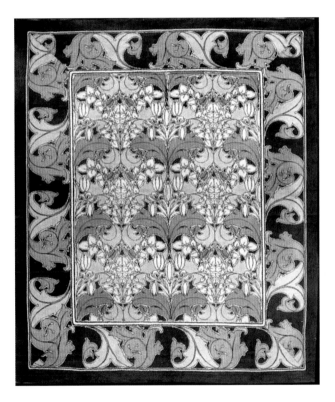

Arts and Crafts rug (C.F. A. Voysey) *Doris Leslie Blau*

art silk. A trade term for artificial silk or mercerized cotton. See "floss" and "mercerized."

art squares. Late nineteenth-century, power-loomed English carpets. These carpets were woven as whole, independent carpets, rather than as carpeting strips to be sewn together according to prior practice.

asab (Arabic). Ikat.

asachu. Moroccan long, narrow, mixed-technique fabric used as a tent divider.

Asadâbâd, Assadabad. A town of the Hamadan region in northwest Iran. The town is a source of red, coarsely woven rugs with an open variation of the Herati pattern.

asan (Sanskrit "seat, pose"). A small rug of India, usually in a square format, used for meditation or prayer.

ashik (Turk. *aşık*, "knuckle bone"). A stepped motif used in borders or stripes and, sometimes as a field design.

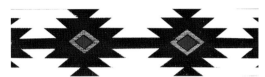

Ashik border *After Moshkova*

ashik gul. A gul of serrated or stepped diamonds. The diamonds may be concentric.

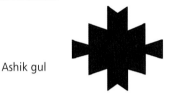

Ashik gul

Ashkali. An ambiguous term for a Qashqa'i medallion and border design. See "Qashqa'i."

asmalyk, osmulduk (Turk., "hanging"). A five-sided or seven-sided Turkmen camel trapping made in pairs and worn by the camel carrying the bride in wedding celebrations. See "bird asmalyk" and "jewelry asmalyk."

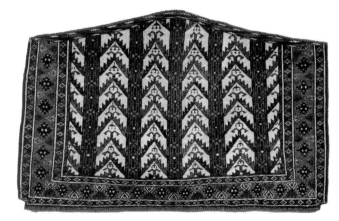

Asmalyk (Yomud) *Richard Golder, Jr.*

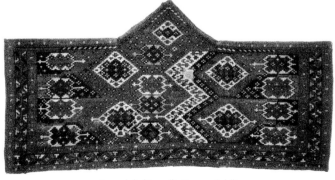

Asmalyk (Ersari) *Grover Schiltz*

Assadabad. See "Asadâbâd."

assyuti. An Egyptian kilim of traditional design, woven in bright colors. Attributed to Asyut, a city of central Egypt.

asymmetric knot. A pile knot. The Persian (Farsibaff) or (incorrectly described) Senneh knot. This knot may be open to the right or left.

Open to the left

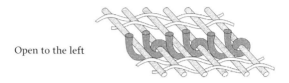

Open to the right

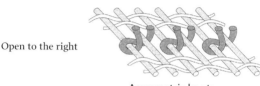

Asymmetric knots

Atabei. A sub-tribe of the Yomud. They are associated with the erre gul. See "erre gul" and "Yomud."

atelier (French). A workshop where artisans are employed or an artist's studio.

at-joli (Turk.). Horse blanket.

atkı (Turk.). Weft.

At-Tar. See "Iraq."

at-torba (Turk.) Horse feed bag.

attribution. Attribution is assigning a geographic and/or ethnic origin to a weaving, sometimes including dating. More formally, attribution is assigning a geographic, ethnic, or commercial origin to a weaving (with or without dating) by reference to detailed criteria and persuasive evidence. Persuasive evidence should show that the criteria are valid and that the rug in question satisfies the criteria. Criteria should be explicit, detailed, observable, and relate the properties of a weaving to the weavers.

Evidence for the validity of criteria may be classified as follows:

1. Certain knowledge. A reliable witness saw rugs woven in a specific place or by persons of a specific ethnic group and documented the shared properties of these rugs. This is the rarest and most persuasive form of evidence.

2. Inference from specific contemporary circumstances. Local inhabitants claim the rug as their product. Someone purchased the rug in a specific area or shipped it from a specific area. Dealers identify an area, ethnic group, or commercial entity as a source for certain rugs. The shared properties of these rugs were documented. This form of evidence is more common and less persuasive than certain knowledge.

3. Inference from historical and cultural circumstances. One deduces the origin of rugs with shared properties from historical and cultural circumstances. For example, comparison of rug motifs with decorative motifs from other sources can support the criteria for attribution. Generally, this form of evidence is more speculative and less persuasive than other classifications. A particular weaving should be shown to satisfy the criteria for attribution based on internal evidence (properties of the rug itself) or external evidence such as history of ownership, fitness of a weaving for its supposed purpose, or information about the site where the weaving was found. Also, attribution may be a socially acceptable fib about the origin of a rug. In rug literature, a question mark in parenthesis following an attribution indicates it is speculative. See "provenance" and "provocation."

aubergine. Eggplant; the color of this, a blackish purple. Bishop's purple.

Aubusson. Carpets woven at the factories first established in Aubusson, France, in about 1665. Initially, carpet designs copied Turkish models, but later designs were based on those of the Savonnerie workshops, although simpler.

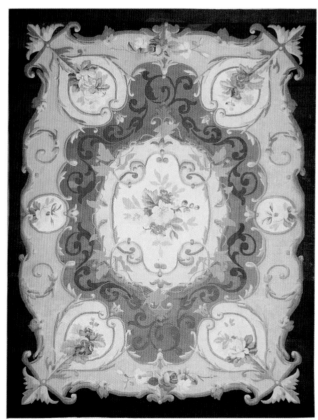

Aubusson rug *Jason Nazmiyal*

auction pool, auction ring, knockout. A group of individuals (usually dealers) attending an auction who agree not to bid against each other in order to lower the auction price. One individual bids for the group. The group holds another auction for group members only after the rugs are purchased. Individuals who do not bid successfully for the rugs in this second auction are compensated according to some predetermined rate depending on the spread between the first and second auction prices.

audience rug, triclinium. In certain Islamic countries, it was customary in important dwellings to arrange rugs in the main chamber as shown.

When a single rug is woven to represent this arrangement, it is known as an audience rug or triclinium rug (after the three couches surrounding the meal table in ancient Rome). These terms are not native to Islamic countries nor do they correctly suggest the function of the rug in a household.

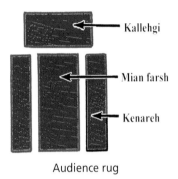

Audience rug

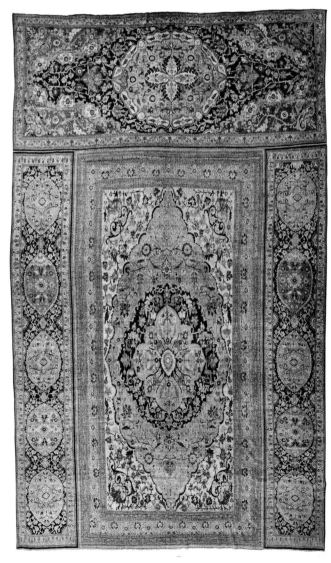

Tabriz audience rug *Sothebys*

Austria. A factory for hand-knotted carpets was set up in Vienna in 1810 and production continued through 1929.

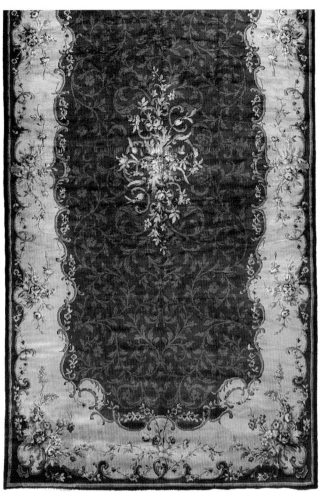

Austrian carpet (detail) *Peter Willborg*

Avanos. See "Cappadocia."

Avar. An ethnic group of Daghestan in the Caucasus. Their religion is Sunni Muslim. In the nineteenth century, they wove rugs and kilims (*davaghins*). Many have a distinctive design of angular branching structures or hooked diamonds (*rukhzal*) in light red on an indigo blue field. Some of these pieces include dates in the last half of the nineteenth century. See "Daghestan" and "davaghin."

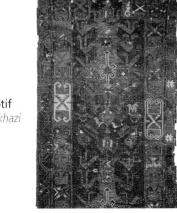

Avar motif (detail) *Rukhazi*

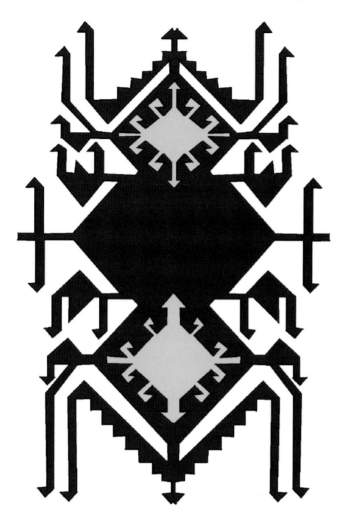

Avar kilim (detail)

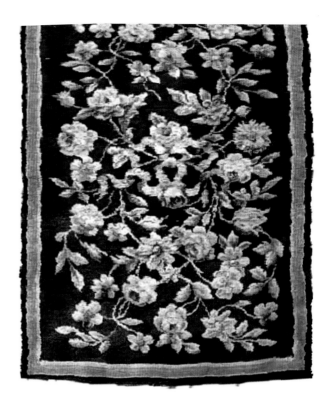

Axminster carpet (detail) *Haliden*

ayatalak (Turk.) A funerary rug. See "landscape carpet."

Aybak. See "Samangân."

Avşar. See "Afshar."

avshan. See "afshan."

Avunya. See "Ezine."

Axminster. From the mid-eighteenth century to 1835, hand-knotted rugs were woven in the town of Axminster, England, in a factory founded by Thomas Whitty. These were woven in designs compatible with Adams interiors and in imitation of Persian models. After 1835, so called "Axminster" carpets were hand-knotted in Wilton factories up to the beginning of the twentieth century.

Spool Axminster or Moquette rugs woven on power looms employ a system in which pile yarn is laid against a weft and inserted between warps by means of small tubes, through which the pile yarn passes. Wefts, locking the pile in place, are stitched by means of needles rather than interlaced by means of a shuttle. In another power loom system, termed seamless Axminster, a Jacquard system raises lengths of pile to mechanical fingers which grasp and insert pile lengths between warps and hold them in place until they are locked by wefts. See "Brussels," "Chenille," "England," "Moorfields," and "Wilton."

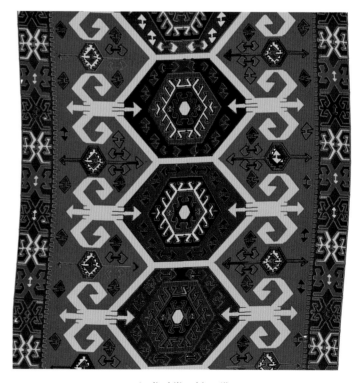

Aydin kilim (detail)

Aydın. A town in western Anatolia and a source of kilims and cicims. Most kilims from the area are woven in three parts, a central panel with two edge strips. A distinctive design feature is that main borders at the ends are followed by colored stripes and a single row of weft twining. See "Turkey."

ay gul. A generally circular medallion of Eastern Turkestan rugs, especially rugs of Khotan. There are many variations, but the most common ay gul medallions contain rosettes, pomegranates, or cloud bands.

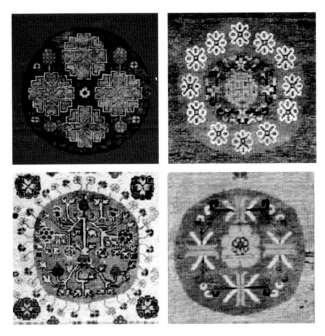

Ay guls *Doris Leslie Blau*

Ayvacık. A town south of Çanakkale in Anatolia, the headquarters of the DOBAG project and a source of DOBAG rugs. See "DOBAG" and "Turkey."

Azerbaijan. A large region south of the Caucasus mountains and west of the Caspian Sea, now divided by the River Aras (Araxes) into the Republic of Azerbaijan (north) and the Iranian province of Azerbaijan (south). Tabriz is a major city and rug production center of Iranian Azerbaijan. Rug production centers in the Republic of Azerbaijan include Kuba, Karabagh, Shirvân, and Baku. Azerbaijan is inhabited by Turks who are currently (or formerly) Shi'i Muslim in religion, but the population also includes Shi'i Persians, Sunni Kurds, and Christian Armenians and Assyrians.

Carpet production was primarily for domestic use until the mid-nineteenth century. In the last quarter of the nineteenth century and early twentieth century, carpet production was a major export industry. Turkey was the largest importer of Azerbaijanian carpets throughout this period. Pile rugs of Azerbaijan are primarily Turkish knotted.

There is a group of Azerbaijan embroidery dating back to the seventeenth century, primarily from northern Azerbaijan. The foundation fabric is cotton and the embroidery is usually in silk. Often, these embroideries have a squareish format. They were usually used as kerchiefs. Most designs are similar to those of early Caucasian floral carpets. Designs of compact roundels, stars, and cartouche shapes are also common. Many nineteenth-century rug designs appear to have been developed or adopted from such embroideries (Swastika Kazak, Star Kazak, Karagashli, etc.).

A wide variety of bags, animal trappings, and flatweaves are produced in Iranian Azerbaijan. The structures used are kilim, soumak, cicim, and embroidery. See "Bakhshaish," "Baku," "Caucasus," "Nakhchivan," and "Sâliâni."

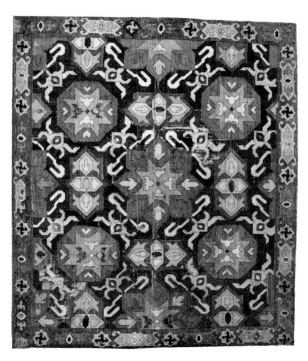

Azerbaijan silk embroidery *Sothebys*

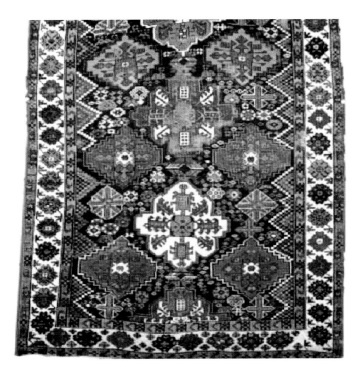

Azerbaijan rug (detail) *Haliden*

azo dyes. These are synthetic direct dyes introduced about 1880, including Ponceau 2R, Amaranth, and Roccelline. For the early azo dyes, particular acidity conditions were needed to fix the dye. These conditions were not always met in rug-producing areas with the result that these dyes bled and faded. See "dye, synthetic."

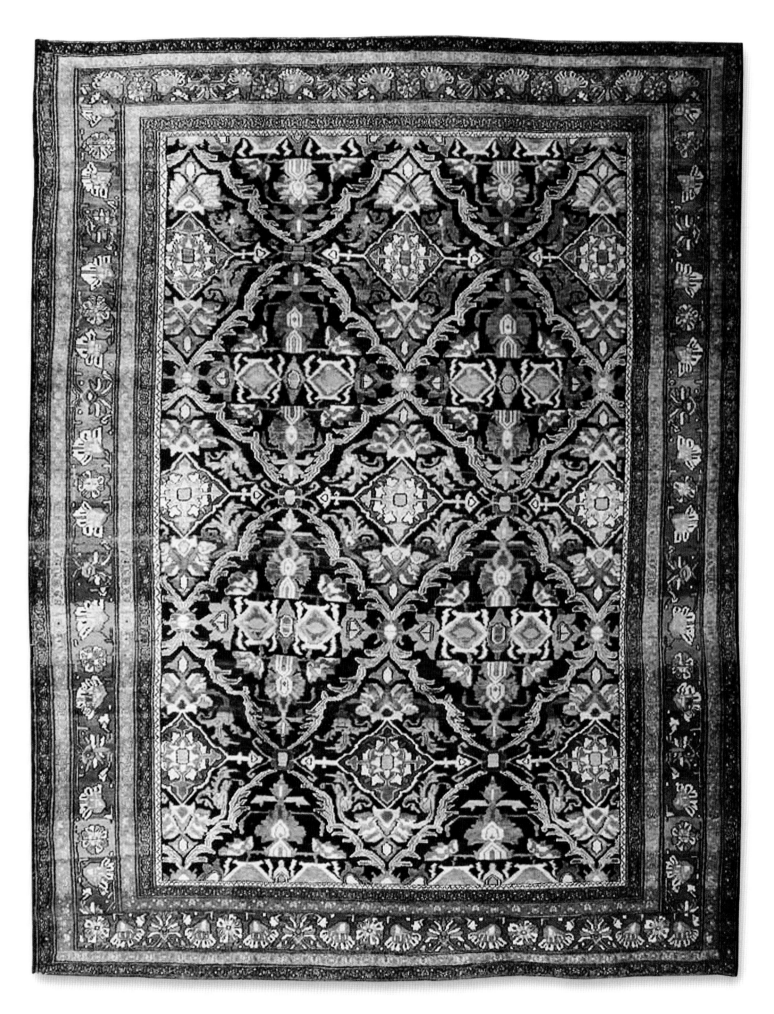

Baba Haidar. A village of western Persia, west of Isfahan. The village is a source of both single and double-wefted medallion rugs.

Babaseqal. A clan of Ersaris in Afghanistan between Andkhoy and Aq Chah.

baby. A trade term for an oriental rug about 4 feet by 2 feet.

back. That side of a rug normally placed against the floor. The side of a weaving not intended to be exposed.

backing. Cotton, jute, synthetics, or other flexible materials used to form the back of a machine-made rug.

backstrap loom. A narrow loom in which the weight of the weaver provides tension for the warps by means of a strap attached to the breast beam that passes around the weaver's back. The warp beam is tied to some stable object. The backstrap loom is used in Tibet, Nepal, and Central America.

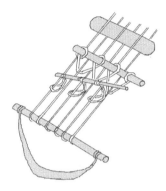

Backstrap loom (schematic)

Badahoi. See "Bhadohi."

badam border. See "gul-i badam."

badem. See "boteh."

badgashi (Persian). In Khurasan, "coarse wool."

badge of Tamerlane. See "chintamani."

badges, rank. See "rank badges."

bâfandeh (Persian). Weaver. See "nassâj."

baff (Persian, "weaving"). Knot or weave.

bag. See entries under these names.

ala chuval	galeh
at-torba	hurch
balisht	igsalik
bashtyk	jollar
beshek	joval
chanteh	kap
chavadan	karshin
chemche torba	kese
chupuqdân	khâbgâh

khorjin	rakhat
kif	saddlebags
kola-i chergh	scisssor bags
mafrash	schabadan
namakdan	spoon bag
napramach	tacheh
pul donneh	tarhalt
pushti	torba
qalyândân	torbak
qâshoqdân	tubreh

Bag closures. A very wide variety of closures is used for tribal and nomadic bags. These include ties, drawstrings, laceing, loop-through-loop, and the most common loop-through-slit closure.

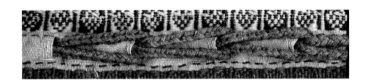

Loop-through-slit bag closure

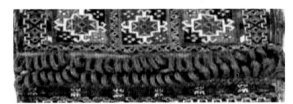

Loop-through-loop bag closure

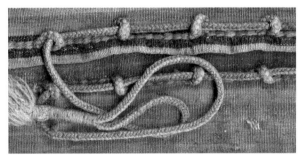

Drawstring bag closure

bag face. See "face."

bâgh (Persian). Garden.

baghmal (Tajik, variant of *makhmal*). An ikat of silk velvet.

Baharestan. See "Spring Carpet of Chosroes."

Baharlu. A Turkic tribe of the Khamseh Confederacy of southwest Iran. Their rugs usually have symmetric knots. See "Khamseh Confederacy."

Bahluli. A subtribe of the Baluchis inhabiting northern Iran.

baize. See "bayeta."

Bakhshaish. A village in Persian Azerbaijan, southwest of Heriz. Contemporary rugs of this village are of the Heriz design. Older rugs of Bakhshaish were woven with the Herati pattern. The symmetric knot is used.

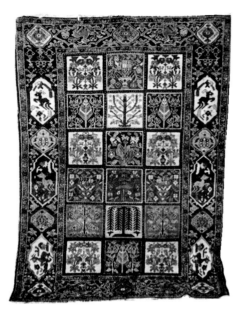

Bakhtiari rug (detal) *Grogan and Company*

baklava design. A design in Anatolian kilims and pile rugs of diamonds with saw-tooth or serrated edges. The diamonds may be medallions or small repeats. Baklava is a Turkish pastry traditionally cut in a diamond shape.

Baklava design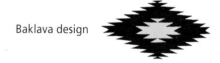

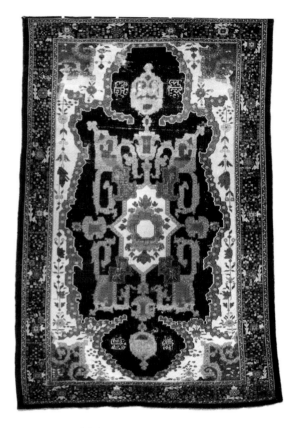

Bakhshaish rug *Grogan & Company*

Bakhtiari. A nomadic tribe (though two-thirds are now sedentary) inhabiting an area of west central Iran, southwest of Isfahan. The Bakhtiaris are a subtribe of the Lurs, speaking an Iranian language. Some researchers classify Bakhtiari pile rugs as nomadic or village based on structural distinctions. Symmetrically knotted double-wefted rugs on a wool foundation are regarded as nomadic or tribal. Symmetrically knotted single-wefted rugs on a cotton foundation are regarded as village production. Many of these have brown-black overcast edges. Designs are primarily rectangular or lozenge-shaped compartments filled with brightly-colored stylized floral or garden motifs and long rugs with vertical stripes containing small botehs. In the late nineteenth and early twentieth centuries, the Bakhtiari wove a number of fine rugs carrying inscriptions in an end strip or cartouche. These inscriptions were dates and dedications to Bakhtiari khans.

Bakhtiari flatweaves include kilims, saddlebags, salt bags, mafrash, and warp-faced tablet-woven bands. Many of the bags are woven in the soumak structure. The bags often have a pile strip at the bottom. Some kilims are woven in two strips. The interlocking weft structure is used in Bakhtiari kilims. End panels outside the kilim borders are a design feature of some Bakhtiari kilims. See "Chahâr Mahâl," "kheshti," "Lurs," and "Shushtar."

Baku. A city at the base of the Apsheron peninsula in the Caucasus, formerly in Persian Azerbaijan. Baku was a khanate until annexed by Russia in 1806. The term "Baku" is applied to nineteenth-century rugs of Baku, Chila, Surahani, and Sâliâni. Boteh are a common motif in Baku rugs. Colors are often turquoise blue and earth tones. These rugs have symmetric knots at an average density of 84 per square inch. The average area is 35 square feet. They are slightly more likely to be cotton-wefted (52%) than wool-wefted (45%). Wefts are usually white, but blue and red-wefted examples are found. See "Caucasus," "Chila," and "Surakhany."

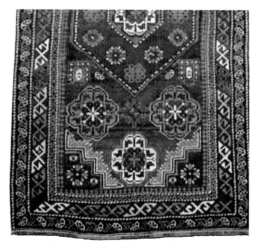

Baku rug (detail) *Azerbaijan Rug*

bala-khachi (Turk.). Narrow borders on either side of a main border.

balanced plain weave. A plain weave (the simplest interlacing of warp and weft) in which warp and weft are of the same size, equally spaced and have the same count. Both sides are structurally identical. See "plain weave."

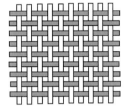

Balanced plain weave

balanced twill weave. A float weave in which continuous wefts systematically skip warps and/or warps systematically skip wefts in a diagonal alignment and warp and weft counts are equal. See "twill weave."

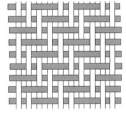

Balanced twill weave

bales. See "balisht"

Bahawalpur. A town and district of southeastern Pakistan. It is a source of commissioned workshop rugs.

Balıkesir. A town of northwest Anatolia. A market source of rugs woven on an all-wool foundation with knot densities of about 40 to 80 symmetric knots per square inch. Some rugs are produced in Kazak designs. There are small, one-piece, tapestry-woven kilims from the area. These are primarily red and blue with interlocking latch hook designs. See "Yüncü."

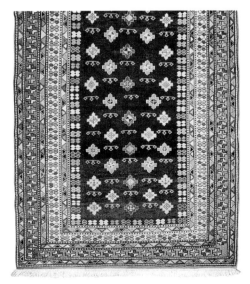

Balıkesir rug (detail) *Yuran*

balisht, bales, blesht, pushti (Persian, "cushion, bolster"). A bag woven by the Baluchis, Kurds, and Pashtuns. These bags are about 16 by 32 inches. They have one pile and one flatwoven face or they may be entirely flatwoven. They may be used as pillows.

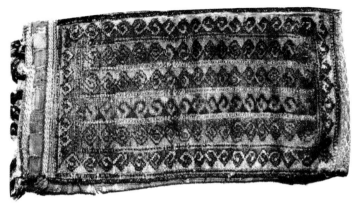

Baluchi balisht

Balkan carpets and kilims. Most of the weavings of Balkan countries have been strongly influenced by the occupation of the Ottoman Turks. Specific descriptions of the weavings of these countries are under these entries: Albania, Bessarabia, Bosnia, Bulgaria, Romania, Serbia, and Yugoslavia.

Balkh. A town of northern Afghanistan near Mazar-i Sharif, formerly a great city of the ancient world. The Balkh area is a major source of carpets based on Tekke designs. Colors are red, blue, and white. The asymmetric knot is tied on wool warps.

Ballard, James Franklin (1851-1931). Ballard was a pharmaceutical manufacturer who collected many eighteenth and nineteenth-century Turkish prayer rugs. At least six catalogs of his collections were published, one authored by Maurice S. Dimand. He gave valuable collections of oriental rugs to the Metropolitan Museum of Art, New York and to the St. Louis City Art Museum in 1929.

Baluchi, Baluch, Beloudge, Beluchi. The Baluch are a people inhabiting contiguous areas of Iran, Afghanistan, and Pakistan collectively called Baluchistan. There are also groups of Baluch in northern Iran and Afghanistan and in Central Asia. They speak a language of the Iranian family. Pile rugs are woven by the Baluch of Khurasan in Iran and Afghanistan. Their pile rugs are usually small and characteristically thin and floppy. Most have asymmetric knots and a very few have symmetric knots. Baluchi rugs are double-wefted. Traditional colors are dark browns, dark blues, orange-reds, dark reds, and black. White is used in border designs and for highlights in the field. Camel colored wool and camel hair are also used, often in a tree-of-life prayer rug design. Touches of orange, light blue, and green are sometimes used. Designs are usually all-over patterns of gul-like elements, botehs, or geometricized Mina Khani patterns. Usually, there is a flatwoven strip at top and bottom of the rug. It may be striped or woven in slit-weave tapestry and include designs of weft substitution patterning.

The Baluch weave sofrehs, ru-korsi, saddle bags, salt bags, balisht, and other bags. Weavings of the Aimaq, including Timuris, have often been confused with those of the Baluch. Rugs of the Quchân Kurds and the Ferdows Arabs have also been attributed to the Baluch. See "Bahluli," "black Baluchi," "Chakhansur," "Jan Mirzai," "Moreidari," "Yaqub Khani," and "Zâbol."

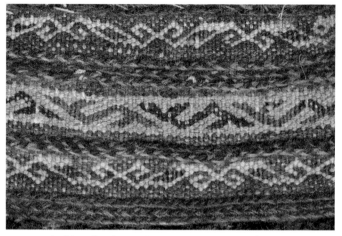

Baluchi weft substitution patterning and weft twining

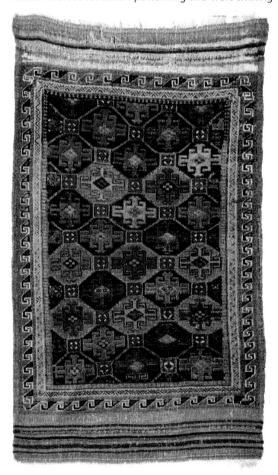

Baluchi rug *Moe Jamali*

Baluchistan. An area of southeastern Iran and western Pakistan. The inhabitants of this area produce flatwoven pieces, but very few pile rugs. Pile rugs generally attributed to the Baluch are woven in Khurasan and Afghanistan. Baluchistan is a harsh

and arid area. The native Baluch are primarily nomadic. They weave a wide variety of flatwoven articles on horizontal ground looms. Many of their weavings are intricate examples of weft float brocade structures. Shells, bones, beads, and buttons are often used as accessory ornaments. Functional articles consist of bedding covers (**shaffi**) and floor covers (**kont**). Animal trappings include camel collars (**gardan-band**), camel necklaces (**gutti**), and camel foreleg decorations (**shishajel**). The Baluch weave saddle bags, salt bags, flour bags (**gowalag**), and highly ornamented vanity bags (**istrajal**). See "Baluchi" and "Brahui."

Balvardi. See "Bulvardi."

bamboo. Bamboo is sometimes depicted in Chinese rugs. As a Taoist symbol, a bamboo tube is shown wrapped by a ribbon and containing several wands. It may be shown in full leaf as a motif in modern rugs. Generally, bamboo symbolizes endurance, the ability to bend without breaking.

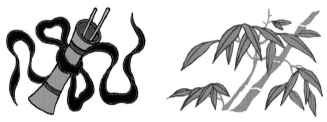

Bamboo

Banat. A province of Romania and a source of kilims, usually woven with the slit-weave tapestry structure. These kilims have stripes or geometrical medallion designs. Designs and structure suggest strong Turkish influence. See "Romania."

band. See "ghorband," "kanat," "mâlband," "navâr," "tablet weaving," "tang," and "tent band."

band-e kenâreh (Persian). Heavy selvage warps in a pile rug.

bandha (Oriya, "tied"). Ikat fabrics of Orissa, a province of central eastern India.

Bandırma, Panderma. Bandırma is a town in northwest Anatolia on the Sea of Marmara. Copies of Gördes prayer rugs and Ottoman court rugs were woven there until the end of the Second World War. These rugs are mostly wool on a cotton foundation. Some silk rugs were woven and some were all cotton. Many of these rugs were artificially aged and have been mistaken for genuine antique Gördes prayer rugs or Ottoman court rugs. Rugs based on Persian floral designs were also woven in Bandırma.

Bannu. A town of northwest Pakistan and a source of commissioned rugs.

Baotou, Paotou, Pao Tao. A town of Inner Mongolia in China northeast of Ningxia. Rugs of Baotou and surrounding villages are more densely knotted than those of Ningxia and use more blue in their designs. Early Baotou rugs have all-over repeating patterns while later rugs are more pictorial. See "China."

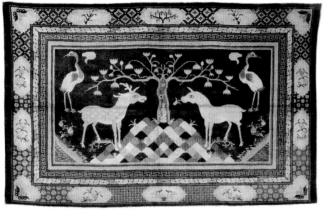

Baotou rug *Sothebys*

Barak. A town of southeast Anatolia and a source of kilims, often with a diamond or hexagon lattice design.

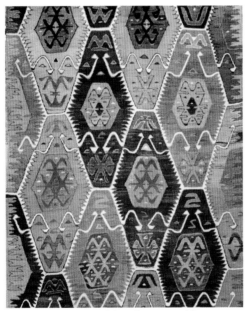

Barak kilim (detail) *Kazim Yildiz*

barberpole, barberpole border, gyak. Diagonal stripes. These are sometimes used in the field, but more often occur in borders and selvages of rugs. A selvedge overcast to produce diagonal stripes. A warp plied of yarn of two different colors.

Barberpole

Barmazid. A village of northern Afghanistan inhabited by Tekke Turkmen. They weave all-wool, double-wefted rugs in traditional Tekke designs.

Barjid. A town of Karadagh in Persian Azerbaijan and a source of rugs woven with Chelaberd or Eagle Kazak medallions. These rugs are woven on a cotton foundation and are single-wefted.

bar, yamany. In the Caucasus, a Kurdish kilim used as a cover.

Barujird. See "Borujerd."

Baseri, Basiri, Basseri. A Persian-speaking tribe of the Khamseh Confederacy of southwest Iran. Their rugs usually have asymmetric knots. See "Khamseh Confederacy."

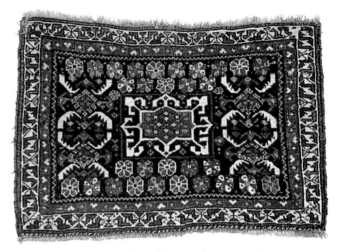

Baseri bag face *R. John Howe*

bashtyk. A Kirgiz rectangular storage bag with a flap and hung in the tent. The size is about 20 by 20 inches. The face may be ornamented with embroidery and the bottom hung with tassels.

basit elma (Turk. "simple apple"). A motif of an oval chain of small circles with a cross or diamond in the center, used in Makri and other rugs.

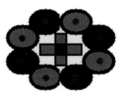

Basit elma motif

Basic dyes. Early coal tar derivative dyes developed by Perkin and Hoffman. These are salts of various organic bases. They produced bright colors on animal fibers, but were not colorfast. See "acid dyes" and "dye, synthetic."

basket weave. A plain weave in which there are multiple warps and multiple wefts (such as pairs or triplets) interlaced. In a basket weave, the number of warps woven as a group equals the number of wefts woven as a group.

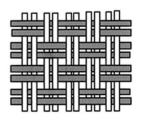

Basket weave

baskur. A tent band. See "tent band."

Basmakçı. A town of western Anatolia. It is the source of a large contemporary production of all-wool rugs in Caucasian designs. Knot densities are about 120 per square inch.

bast. Woody vegetable fibers used for weaving such as flax, hemp, jute, or straw.

bat. The bat is often represented singly or in groups in Chinese and Tibetan rugs. Five bats (*wufu*) are emblematic of blessings.

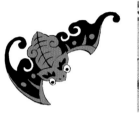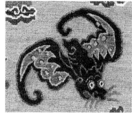

Bat

Bauhaus. A design movement in Germany founded by Hermann Muthesius and Walter Gropius in the early twentieth century. Rug weavers who participated in the movement produced pile and flatwoven rugs with designs of non-objective geometric shapes. See "Art Moderne."

Bavânât. See "Bowanat."

Bayburt. A town of northeast Anatolia. It is thought to be the source of kilims with stepped mihrabs and ornate multiple borders. Dominant colors are ochre and olive green. Many of these kilims are dated. Gilt metal threads and silk were used in some of these kilims.

bayeta. A fabric woven on treadle looms in New Mexico in the nineteenth century. The nap was raised on the fabric after it was taken from the loom. Also, wool yarn from blankets made in Spain and England that was unraveled by Navajos and rewoven into Navajo blankets. Dyes used in these yarns are critical in dating Navajo blankets of the 19th century. The English equivalent of bayeta is baize.

bayeta serapes. A type of Navajo blanket woven between 1830 and about 1850 and containing a high proportion of bayeta yarn. These blankets were of the highest weaving quality. A common design was diamonds superimposed on stripes.

beam. The horizontal member of the loom frame on which warps are wound or fastened. On a roller beam loom, warps are unwound from the top beam of the loom and the textile is rolled upon the lower beam of the loom as the textile is woven. Since the warps must be maintained in tension as the fabric is woven, there are various means of spreading the beams. Wedges or twisted ropes are used on primitive looms, screw and/or ratchet devices are used on commercial looms. See "breast beam," "loom," and "warp beam."

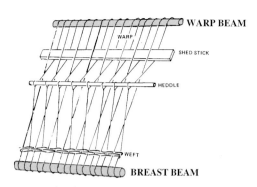

Beams on a loom

beater. A weighted wood or metal comb used to beat wefts down against each row of knots as a carpet is woven on the loom.

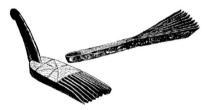

Beaters

Beattie, May H. (1908-1997). May Beattie was a British scholar of oriental rugs with a focus on rug structure as a key to rug origins. She began her rug studies in Iraq. Subsequently, she wrote extensively about Persian rugs. Her research is preserved in the Beattie Archive of the Ashmolean Museum.

beat up. The tufts per inch in Axminster and chenille carpeting.

bed covers. See "blankets."

Bedouin, Beduin. Nomadic Arabs inhabiting the deserts of North Africa and Arabia. They are sheep and camel herders. Bedouin weavings includes goat hair fabric for tents and wool dividing curtains, pillows, bags, animal trappings, and small articles. Designs consist mainly of stripes of geometric elements, diamonds, checks, and animal brands (*wasm*). Bright colors are characteristic. Ground looms are used to produce warp-faced plain weaves. Weft twining is used for decorative stripes and to strengthen edges. Some Bedouin men weave, but most weavers are women.

Behbehân. A town of southwestern Iran and a source of Luri rugs. Designs are hooked medallions in dark colors.

Behsud. A town west of Kabul in Afghanistan. The town is inhabited by Hazaras who weave coarse kilims, mainly with stripes. See "Hazara."

Beijing, Peking. The earliest rug weaving in Beijing is thought to have begun in 1860. Regular factory rug production began in 1880. The period of heaviest production was between 1880 and 1920, after which Tientsin became the major production center.

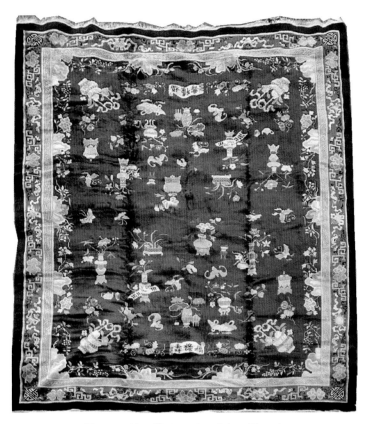

Beijing rug (detail) *Peter Pap Oriental Rugs Inc.*

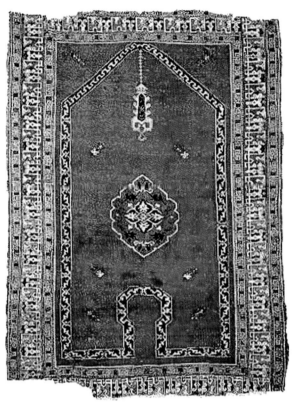

Bellini prayer rug

The best of the Beijing carpets imitated designs of older palace, court, and temple rugs. The more popular Beijing carpets had a blue field with designs and border in buff, white, or gold. Motifs included Buddhist and Taoist symbols, sometimes mixed in the same rug and used without regard for their meanings. Beijing rugs were usually woven with the asymmetric knot on warps without offset. There is contemporary rug production in Beijing. Current knot densities range from 34 knots per square inch to 100 knots per square inch. See "China."

Belgium. There is a large, contemporary production of power-loomed carpets in Belgium. Most of these are made in imitation of hand-knotted Near Eastern rug designs. From the thirteenth century, Flanders was famed for its tapestries and lace. See "Arras" and "Brussels."

Bellini rugs. Anatolian prayer rugs of the fifteenth and sixteenth centuries. These are rugs with a pointed mihrab and open field except for a distinctive indented or lobed quadrilateral medallion. The main border may be Kufesque. An inner border may have a reentrant octagon or "keyhole" at the bottom. This design is shown in rugs in paintings of northern Italy of the sixteenth and seventeenth centuries. The earliest representation of this prayer rug is in a painting in the National Gallery, London, by Gentile Bellini made in 1507. See "turret design."

bells. Small bells may be attached to animal trappings. See "accessory objects" and "knee caps."

Beloudge. See "Baluchi."

Beluchi. See "Baluchi."

Ben Adi. A town in Egypt producing naturally colored, tapestry-woven rugs in geometric designs.

Benares (modern Varanasi). An ancient city of north central India. The carpet center of this area is in the nearby city of Bhadohi. See "Bhadohi."

Bengal. A region of east India including the city of Calcutta. Rug weaving began in the region in the late seventeenth century, but rug production from the area was never great. See "Calcutta."

Benguiat, Vitall (1859-1937). A dealer and collector of rugs and textiles. Born in Izmir, Turkey, Vitall Benguiat moved from Europe to New York in 1898. Through his liaison with the American Art Association, Benguiat imported and auctioned some of the finest classical Turkish, Persian, Indian, and Mamluk oriental rugs.

Beni M'guild. A Berber tribe of the Middle Atlas region of Morocco. The weavers of this tribe generally use the symmetric knot, though they have sometimes used the asymmetric knot. Designs are repeated geometric elements. Rugs are often without side borders. The tribe produces flatwoven blankets, curtains, shawls, saddle bags, and cushion covers.

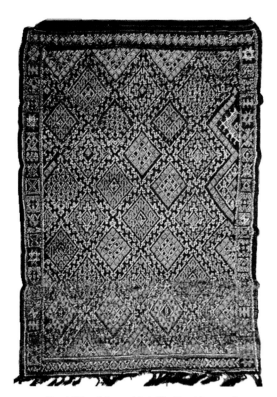

Beni M'guild rug (detail) *Lloyd Rowcroft*

Beni M'tir. A Berber tribe of the Middle Atlas region of Morocco. Their rugs are borderless and designs consist of repeated geometric elements. Weavers of this tribe use the asymmetric knot.

Berber knot. A rug knot used in Berber tribal weavings of the Middle Atlas region of Morocco. The Berber knot encircles two warps twice. On the front of the rug, tufts emerge in diagonal opposing directions from under a diagonal loop of the knot. The Berber knot may be offset one warp in either direction. It may also be used in combination with the symmetric knot tied on four warps. The amount of yarn used in the Berber knot is greater than that used in either the symmetric or asymmetric knots. The Berber knot is more durable than the asymmetric or symmetric knots.

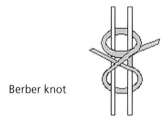

Berber knot

Berber rugs. See "Morocco."

berde (Greek). A flatwoven doorway hanging of northern Greece woven in three panels and stitched together.

berdelik. Textiles, including rugs, used as wall hangings. See "laicerul."

Bergama, Bergamo, Pergamum (Latin). A city of northwestern Anatolia (ancient Pergamum), near the Aegean Sea, with a long tradition of rug weaving. Fifteenth-century rugs have been attributed to Bergama. A wide variety of designs are identified as Bergama. The term is sometimes applied to western Anatolian rugs of indefinite origin. Some Transylvanian rugs of the seventeenth and eighteenth centuries are thought to derive from Bergama. Contemporary Bergama rugs have designs that suggest Caucasian types or are all-over geometricized floral patterns. Rugs of the Yağçibedir tribe are woven in the region and the nearby towns of Yuntdağ and Kozak are known for their rugs. Kilims from this area usually have geometric designs suggesting those of the Seljuk period.

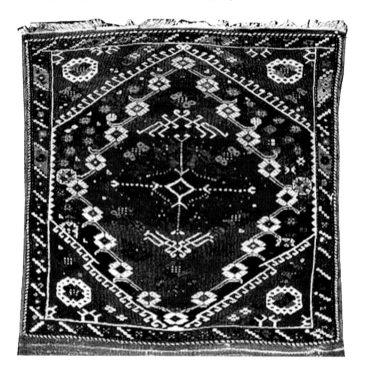

Bergama rug *James Allen*

beshek, beşik (Turk.). Bedding bag. See "mafrash."

Beshir, Beshire. A town on the Amu Darya river in west Turkestan. Rugs made in the area of Bokhara and along the Amu Darya into northern Afghanistan are often described as Beshir. Most of these rugs are thought to be woven by Ersari Turkmen. This general attribution is disputed by some scholars. Turkmen rugs labeled Beshir have designs derived from Ikat patterns, the Herati pattern, the Mina Khani pattern and 2-1-2 medallions. A large variety of geometric motifs and boteh patterns are also found in these rugs. A distinctive prayer rug with a large mihrab containing geometricized floral patterns is considered Beshiri. Beshiri rugs are woven with the asymmetric knot.

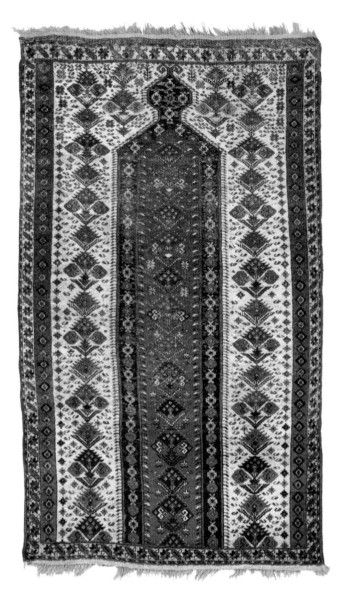

Beshir namazlyk *Sothebys*

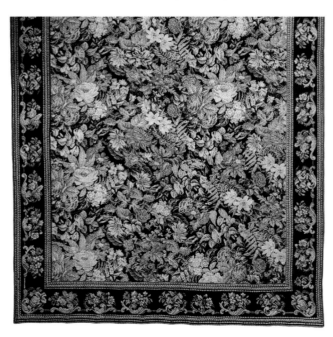

Bessarabian carpet (detail) *Sothebys*

Bessarabia. A region of southwest Russia bordering Romania on the south and the Black Sea on the east. "Bessarabian" is used loosely to describe Polish, Rumanian, and Bulgarian hand-knotted rugs. Bessarabia itself is the source of kilims similar to those of Moldavia. Inscriptions on Bessarabian kilims are in the Cyrillic alphabet. See "Moldavia."

Bezalel. Rugs made at the Bezalel School of Arts and Crafts in Jerusalem between 1906 and 1931. These rugs, produced by Jewish weavers, showed traditional Jewish ritual motifs, scenes from the Old Testament and conventional Persian designs. They were inscribed in Hebrew "Bezalel Yerushalem" or "Marvadia Yerushalem." These rugs were woven with the asymmetric knot. See "synagogue rug."

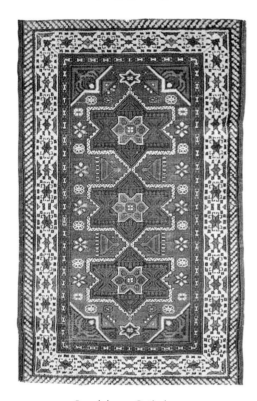

Bezalel rug *Sothebys*

Bhadohi, Badahoi. A city of northern India near Mirzapur and Benares. It is one of the major modern rug production centers of India. Bhadohi rugs are generally copies of Persian models with floral motifs. These rugs are woven on a cotton foundation using the asymmetric knot at densities between 30 and 225 knots per square inch.

The Bhadohi method of counting knots is uniquely complicated. A knot count is represented thus: 5/40. The first figure (5) is termed *bis*. It produces the horizontal or weft-wise knot count. Bis times 11% added to the bis is the horizontal or weft-wise knot count. Thus (5x.11)+5=5.55 knots per inch weft-wise. *Bhutan* is the term for the second figure (40). It produces the vertical or warp-wise knot count. Bhutan times 33.3% added to the bhutan and divided by 6 is the vertical or warp-wise knot count. Thus: ((40x.333)+40)/6=8.88 knots per inch warp-wise. The knot density represented by 5/40 is 5.55x8.88 or 48.8 knots per square inch. See "India."

Bhutan. A country located between Tibet to the north and India on the south. Bhutan is the source of rugs woven by Tibetan refugees who settled there after the Chinese occupation of Tibet in 1959.

bhutan. See "Bhadohi."

bibibaff (Persian, "grandmother's weave"). Particularly fine weaving of Chahâr Mahâl. See "Chahâr Mahâl."

Bibikabad, Ainabad. A village of the Hamadan region of Iran, northeast of Hamadan city. Rugs of this village often have boteh or Herati designs. They are single-wefted and woven with the symmetric knot. See "Hamadan."

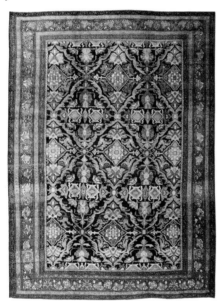

Bibikabad rug *Jason Nazmiyal*

Bidgeneh. A village of northwest Iran and a source of rugs similar to those of Bijâr. These are medallion rugs with pendants and spandrels.

Bidjar. See "Bijâr."

Bidjov. See "Bijov."

Bid Majnun. See "weeping willow design."

Bigelow, Erastus Brigham (1814-1879). The American inventor of power looms for Brussels, Wilton, tapestry, and velvet carpeting. He established weaving mills in Connecticut, Massachusetts, and New York. His looms and mills greatly increased rug production in the 1840s.

Bijâr, Bidjar. A town of northwest Iran surrounded by many rug-weaving villages whose output is also labeled "Bijâr." The area is inhabited by Kurds. Rugs of Bijâr and its immediate area are woven in a wide variety of patterns. Usually, in early rugs, three wefts are hammered down with heavy combs. One of these wefts is usually very heavy, so these rugs are very stiff due to great vertical knot packing. Later rugs have two wefts. Warps are completely offset and the knot is symmetric at densities of

about 100 to 160 per square inch. Formerly, wool foundation was used. Contemporary rugs have a cotton foundation.

Bijâr was the source of a group of fine arabesque (Garrus design) rugs woven in the late nineteenth century and early twentieth century. Rugs with a stylized willow and cypress design were woven in Bijâr in the early twentieth century. Bijâr samplers are relatively common compared to samplers from other areas of Persia. Bijâr kilims are woven with the slit weave tapestry structure. Designs of large Bijâr kilims are sometimes similar to those of Bijâr pile weaves. Smaller kilims are similar in design to those of Senneh. See "Garrus design," "Kurdish rugs," and "split leaf arabesque."

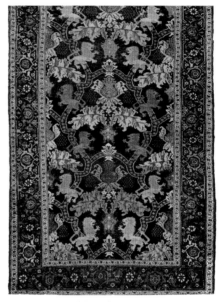

Bijâr rug (detail) *Jason Nazmiyal*

Bijov, Bidjov. A town located near Shemakha in the Caucasus. This is a design of nineteenth-century rugs of the Shirvân region which consists of a vertical arrangement of nested bracketing elements. Rugs of this design are the most coarsely woven (averaging 94 symmetric knots per square inch) of Shirvân rugs. Bijov design rugs are also the largest of Shirvân rugs. They are woven on an all-wool foundation. See "Shirvân."

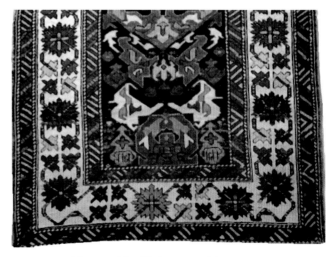

Bijov rug (detail) *Grogan and Company*

Bildrev (Norwegian). Early Norwegian tapestries, often portraying biblical scenes.

Bilverdi. A town of Persian Azerbaijan west of Heriz. Rugs of Bilverdi are woven in the Heriz design, with the symmetric knot and single wefts. See "Heriz."

binding. An edge or selvage treatment for rugs in which edge warps are wrapped with yarn to protect and strengthen them after the rug is woven. Less desirably, machine stitching may be used for this purpose. See "overcasting" and "serging."

Binding

Biographies. See entries under these names:

Ballard, James Franklin
Beattie, May H.
Benguiat, Vitall
Bigelow, Erastus B.
Bode, Wilhelm von
Dudin, Samul Martynovich
Edwards, A. Cecil
Ellis, Charles Grant
Erdmann, Kurt
Ettinghausen, Richard
Jenkins, Arthur D.
Jones, H. McCoy
Markarian, Richard B.

Martin, F.R.
McMullan, Joseph V.
Morris, William
Moshkova, V.G.
Myers, George Hewitt
Pinner, Robert H.
Pope, Arthur Upham
Schürmann, Ulrich
Tiffany, Louis Comfort
Tuduc, Theodore
Von Bode, Wilhelm
Voysey, Charles
Yerkes, Charles Tyson

bird asmalyks. Rare Tekke asmalyks with a repeated pattern of birds within a lattice of serrated leaves. The field is red and borders are white with a meandering vine motif. See "asmalyk."

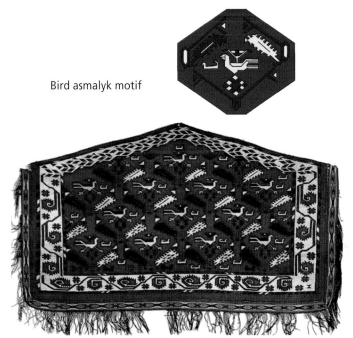

Bird asmalyk motif

Bird asmalyk (Tekke) *J. Barry O'Connell*

bird head border. A border design in Kurdish and Persian tribal rugs with many variations. This same border is occasionally used as a field repeat.

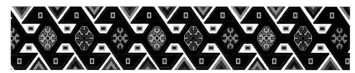

Bird head border

Bird Ushak. A group of sixteenth and seventeenth-century rugs woven in Ushak, Anatolia. Their common design feature is a repeated arrangement of four leaves or "birds" radiating from a blossom on a white field. The earliest known representation is in a rug in a painting by Hans Mielich done in 1557. These rugs usually have lines of reversing wefts or "lazy lines" on the back.

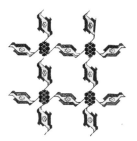

Bird Ushak motif

Birjand. A city of the Qainat region of eastern Iran. Rugs were woven on a factory basis in Birjand from the beginning of the twentieth century. Most of the rugs produced before World War II were Jufti knotted with poor wearing quality. The Jufti asymmetric knot is used at a density of about 100 knots per square inch on a wool foundation. Older pieces have higher knot densities. Later rugs have a cotton foundation. See "Qainat."

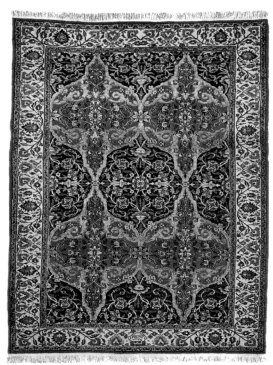

Birjand rug

birth symbol. A diamond with two in-curving arms at each end. This ancient motif is found in many weavings of Asia and the Near East. It is a common motif in Anatolian kilims.

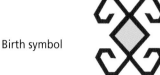

Birth symbol

bis. See "Bhadohi."

black. In Near Eastern weavings, this color may be produced by synthetic dyes, by vegetable dyes, or by the use of naturally black wool. As vegetable dyes, oak bark, oak galls, acorn cups, or walnut hulls were used with an iron mordant to produce black or brown. Wool so dyed is subject to etching. Naturally dark wool or dyed wool might be over-dyed with indigo to produce black. See "etching."

black Baluchi. Refers to Baluchi rugs with a very dark palette. The designs of such rugs are not easily visible except in very bright light.

black light. See "ultra-violet light."

black Marasalis. Marasali prayer rugs with a black or very dark field. See "Marasali."

blanket dress. Traditional Navajo dress for women made of two identical blankets sewn at the shoulders and sides. See "Navajo rugs."

blanket stitch, buttonhole stitch. A stitch using a single strand that loops through itself. This stitch may be used, very closely spaced, to strengthen edges or selvages or it may be used, more widely spaced, at the end of a weaving to prevent wefts from unraveling.

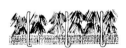 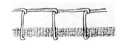

Front   Back

Blanket stitch

blankets, covers, sleeping rugs.
See the following entries:
bar
churga
colcha embroidery
farda
frach
frazada
hamel
huli
k'ang cover
karolya
khaden
kopan
moj
Navajo rugs
neyden
pardaghy
postaghi
pound blankets

blazon. An armorial bearing or heraldic device.

bleaching. Dyes in rugs may fade due to exposure to sunlight. Rugs may be deliberately bleached through a chemical wash. Chemical bleaching was used to produce the so-called "golden Afghans" and "golden Shirvans." Red Afghan rugs were bleached to a shade of yellow to satisfy market demand before yellow-dyed yarns were actually used in these rugs. Some Sarouks were bleached and then painted to satisfy color tastes of the American market. Bleaching is accomplished through a variety of chemical agents. These include oxidizing agents such as hydrogen peroxide, acids such as sulfuric acid, alkalis such as ammonia and lye, and chlorine and its compounds. See "burning," "chemical wash," "strip, "tip fading," "ultraviolet light," and "patina."

bleeding, running. Dyes that are improperly fixed or dyed yarn that has been inadequately washed after dyeing may bleed or run into other colors in a finished rug. Some red dyes are particularly susceptible to running. There are chemical washes that effectively remove some red dyes from areas into which they have run.

blocking. See "tentering."

bloom. To add ingredients to the dye bath which increase the brightness of colors.

Blossom carpet. See "floral carpet."

blue. A primary color. In Near Eastern weavings, this color may be produced by synthetic or vegetable dyes. By far the most common blue dye is indigo. See "indigo."

bobbin. A cylinder, spindle, or spool on which yarn, thread, or roving may be wound during the spinning or weaving process.

Bode, Wilhelm von. 1845-1929. German scholar, founder of the Museum for Islamic Art, Berlin, rug collector, and author of the first comprehensive treatise on the classic period of oriental rugs, *Vorderasiatische Knüpfteppiche aus alterer Zeit*, published in 1902.

body Brussels carpet. A loop pile rug in which different color warps are brought to the surface to form the pattern. Because colored warps are continuous beneath the pile, they provide "body" or thickness and weight to the rug.

bogu. A Chinese rug motif consisting of representations of bronze, jade, or porcelain vessels and other antique objects.

bohça. See "bokche"

bohça. See "bokche"

bokche, bohça, boqcheh (Turk.). A Turkmen envelope-like bag consisting of a square flatweave with pile woven triangles at each side of the rectangle. The triangular pieces are folded inwards to form a container. In general, any square piece of cloth used as a carrying bag for many different items.

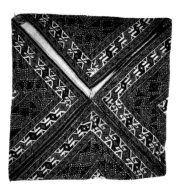

Dr. Herbert J. Exner
Turkmen bokche

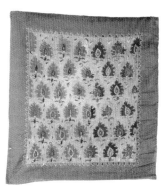

Ottoman embroidered bohça
Sothebys

Bokhara, Bukhara. An ancient city and emirate of West Turkestan, presently in Uzbekistan. The name is popularly used to describe any rug, Turkmen or otherwise, with designs consisting of or derived from Turkmen guls. Bokhara was an important rug trading and shipping center in the nineteenth century. A few scholars have attributed rugs to Bokhara, but such attributions are questioned.

Boldaji. A small town south of the Chahâr Mahâl region in western Iran. It is a source of Bakhtiari panel design rugs.

Bolvardi. See "Bulvardi."

Bombyx mori. The domesticated silkworm moth. See "silk."

Borchalu. A tribe of the Hamadan region of Iran. Contemporary rugs of this tribe have curvilinear, floral medallions. They are single-wefted and woven with the symmetric knot at a density of about 65 per square inch. The foundation is cotton and wefts may be blue. See "Borjalou" and "Hamadan."

border. A design around the edge of a rug and enclosing the field. The border usually includes a wide band of repeating design called the main border and subsidiary borders called guard stripes. See the following entries:

ashik	cloud band border
bala-khachi	çubuklu
barberpole border	curled leaf border
bird head border	dagdan
broken border	elibilinde
carnation border	flag border
cartouche border	fret
chamtos	Greek key
check border	gul-i badam
chichi border	Herati border
crab border	koca baş
crenellated border	kufesque

lab-i mazar	running dog border
leaf and calyx	sainak
Laleh Abbasi	sari gira border
medahil	sawtooth border
meander borders	"S" borders
Naldag border	shekeri border
palmette border	soldat border
pearl border	split leaf arabesque
Qashqa'i frieze	swastika border
rainbow border	T band
reciprocating border	turtle border
rosette border	

Bordjalou. See "Borjalou."

Borjalou, Bordjalou. A town located south of Tiflis (Tbilisi) in the Caucasus. Originally, this was a settlement for Borchalu tribespeople deported by Shah Abbas from the Hamadan district in the seventeenth century (cf. "Borchalu").

Nineteenth-century rugs attributed to Borjalou often have broad zig-zag borders with latch hooks projecting from both sides of the border. Rugs of Borjalou are classified as Kazak. Borjalou is the most coarsely knotted of the Kazak design types, with about 52 symmetric knots per square inch.

Average area is about 35 square feet. About half of Borjalou rugs have red wefts. Those with blue wefts are of later production. See "Borchalu" and "Kazak."

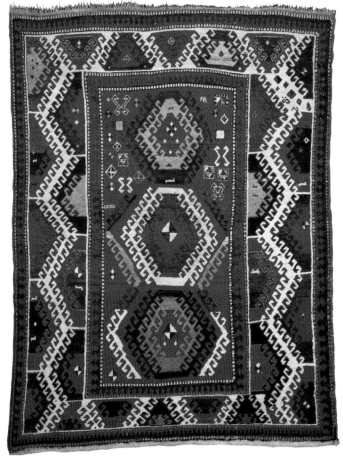

Borjalou Kazak (detail) *Sothebys*

Borodjert. See "Borujerd."

borpush (Uzbek, from Persian, meaning "load cover"). A Central Asian embroidery similar to a suzani, but smaller. It is often square.

Borujerd, Barujird, Borodjert, Borujird. A market center in northwest Iran for rugs of the area. These rugs are single-wefted with the symmetric knot. They have dark red designs on a dark blue field.

Bosnia and Herzegovina. Formerly, a large political subdivision of east central Yugoslavia. Now, an independent state. This region was a source of kilims very similar to those of Turkey. These kilims were used as carpets and bed covers.

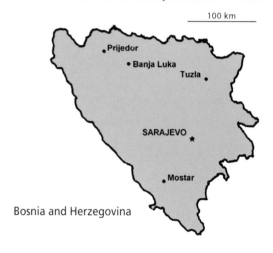

Bosnia and Herzegovina

Bosque Redondo. See "Navajo rugs."

boteh, buta, (Persian "bush"), **badem,** (Turk. "almond"). A pear-shaped figure common in oriental rug design. There are a great many variations, ranging from elaborate and highly detailed interpretations to simple, geometricized versions. Usually, this motif is used in the field as an all-over repeat pattern. It has been thought to represent a leaf, a bush, a flame, or a pine cone. It probably originated in Kashmir. The boteh is characteristic of the Paisley pattern. See "islimi," "Kashmir," "mir boteh," "mother and daughter boteh," and "Paisley."

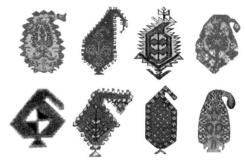

TOP ROW: Serabend, Karabagh, Marasali, Qashqa'i
BOTTOM ROW: Talish, Genje, Beshir, India *Botehs*

bottom. In knotted rugs, the end of the rug towards which the knot ends or pile were pulled when the rug was woven. The end of the rug woven first.

boucherouite, boucherwit, (Arabic *bu sherwit* "scrap"). Moroccan Berber rugs made from scraps of clothing and other fabrics.

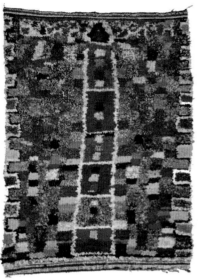

Boucherouite rug *Alberto Levi*

bouclé. A three-ply yarn, with one ply looser than the others, resulting in a rough fabric when woven.

bouharopodia (Greek, "chimney apron"). A flatwoven hanging of three panels stitched together and used above the fireplace in northern Greece.

Bou Sbaa. See "Oulad Bou Sbâa."

Bowanat, Bavânât. A market center of southwest Iran for rugs of Arab tribes in the area. These rugs have designs that are simplified versions of Qashqa'i designs.

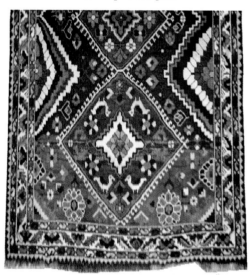

Bowanat rug (detail) *Manouchehr Haghighat*

boy (Turk., "family, class"). Ancient tribal grouping making up the Oghuz Turkmen confederation.

boya (Turk.). Dye.

Boyer Ahmadi. See "Lurs."

Brahui. The Brahuis are an ethnic group of Baluchistan often associated with the Baluchis. Their language is of the Dravidian family, akin to Tamil and other languages of south India, and unrelated to Baluchi, which is of the Iranian family. The Brahuis inhabit areas of Afghanistan. Pile rugs have been attributed to the Brahuis.

braid. A structure of oblique interlacing of a single set of elements, usually a narrow structure in one direction. No special tools are used in the process. Braids or braided structures are used in the end finish of rugs, in closures or fasteners for bags, and as ties for animal trappings. "Plaiting" is sometimes used interchangeably with "braiding." More strictly, plaiting is oblique interlacing of two or more sets of elements in two or more directions. See "oblique interlacing" and "plaiting."

 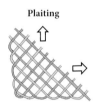

Braiding   **Plaiting**

braided rugs. Strips of cloth with edges folded inward are braided together and then the braids are wound to produce a circular or oval rug. The braids may be stitched together or otherwise linked. Usually, waste or used fabric was braided for the rug. This is an early American form of rug.

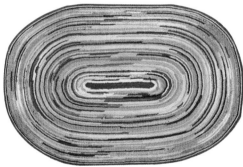

Braided rug *Jason Nazmial*

Braila. A city of Romania on the Danube and a major contemporary rug-weaving center. Also, a trade designation of quality for contemporary Romanian rugs with cotton foundation and a knot density of about 100 per square inch. See "Romania."

Bran. A trade designation of quality for contemporary Romanian pile rugs. These rugs are knotted on a wool foundation with knot densities of about 60 per square inch. See "Romania."

Brașov, (Hungarian Brassó), Kronstadt. A city of Romania and a contemporary trade designation of quality for Romanian rugs with woolen foundation and a knot density of about 100 per square inch. Inventory records show that hundreds of Turkish carpets were imported into the city during the early sixteenth century. The "Black Church" of Brașov held more than 100 of these "Transylvanian" carpets it received as gifts. See "Transylvania."

brazilwood dye. A dye made from any of a variety of leguminous trees of the genus *Caesalpinia*. The dye produces purple, red and black shades. The dye was a major export of colonial Brazil. This dye was used in early Chinese rugs.

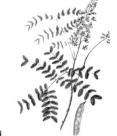

brazilwood

breast beam, cloth beam. The lower beam of a vertical loom. The beam nearest the weaver in any loom where the weaver has a fixed position. On a horizontal loom, the beam nearest the weaver's first weft. See "beam."

(British) East India Company. Strictly, "The Honorable East India Company." A company founded in England in 1600 to conduct trade with India. The trade included carpets woven in India. The Company's first carpet factory was established in Masulipatam in 1611. The British East India Company played a significant role in India carpet production and trade into the middle of the nineteenth century. See "India."

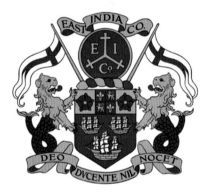

Arms of the East *India Company*

broadloom. A power-loomed rug. More specifically, a power-loomed rug in a solid color and/or more than 54 inches in width.

brocade. A patterning in a fabric achieved with interlaced supplementary wefts. Supplementary wefts may be continuous or discontinuous. The term is incorrectly applied to weft wrapping structures. Brocade and weft wrapping may occur in the same weaving. The term may be used to indicate patterning with metallic threads. See "embroidery," "extra weft patterning," "overlay brocading" and "overlay-underlay brocading."

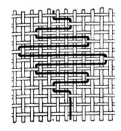 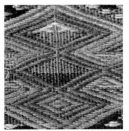

Brocade

broche carpet. A wool carpet of clipped and looped pile. Patterning is provided by the clipped areas. See "cut-and-loop."

broken border. A border which is not confined by a straight line around the field. The border design may occasionally penetrate the field or a field design may break into the border. Some Kerman rugs, some French rugs, and some Chinese rugs have such borders.

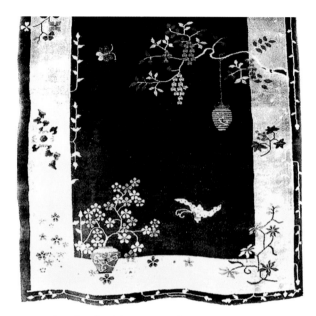

Broken border (Chinese rug detail) *Jason Nazmiyal*

Brousa. See "Bursa."

Brousse. See "Bursa"

brown. In Near Eastern weavings, this color may be produced by a variety of natural dyes or, more rarely, it may be the natural brown color of sheep's wool. Vegetable dyes for brown include oak bark and acorn cups, walnut husks and pomegranate rind. Cutch or catechu (the heartwood and pods of an Asiatic tree) is a brown dye used in Far Eastern weavings. Like black, brown dyes embrittle wool and produce etching when used with an iron mordant. See "etching."

Brusa, Brussa. See "Bursa."

Brussels. A power-loomed carpet in which extra warps are looped around wires in the weaving process. If the loops are left uncut, the rug is termed "Brussels." In some looms, the wire is grooved and a knife, running down the groove, cuts the loops to form cut pile. In this case, the rug is termed "Wilton." The Brussels carpet process was developed in Brussels in about 1710.

Bucharest. A trade designation of quality for contemporary Romanian rugs with cotton foundation and a knot count of about 70 knots per square inch.

buckles. Ridges or wrinkles in a carpet due to improper installation or weaving faults. See "cockle," "cornrowing," and "grinning."

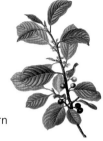

buckthorn. *Rhamnus petiolaris.* The unripe berries of this shrub produce a yellow dye with an alum mordant.

Buckthorn

Buddha's Hand, foshou. An Asiatic fruit, *citrus medica*, whose form suggests a hand. It is sometimes represented in Chinese and Tibetan rugs and symbolizes wealth and honor.

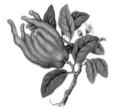 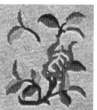

Buddha's Hand

Buddhist symbols. A collection of eight "precious things" or "treasures" symbolic of good fortune and emblematic of Buddhism. They are used singly or collectively as motifs in Chinese and Tibetan rugs. The symbols are the wheel, conch, umbrella, canopy, lotus, vase, fish and Ch'ang or endless knot. See entries under these names. See "Confucian symbols" and "Taoist symbols."

Bukhara, Bokhara. A city of Uzbekistan populated by Uzbeks and Tajiks. The city is a source of suzanis woven by Tajiks. Turkmen rugs are erroneously referred to as "Bokharas."

Bulgaria, Thrace. A country of southeast Europe. Bulgaria was a source of nineteenth-century rugs made in imitation of the Gördes prayer rug. Bulgaria is a minor source of contemporary pile rugs with floral designs based on Persian models. These rugs are woven in Kotel and Panagiurishte. Bulgarian kilims are sometimes referred to as "Thracian." The slit-weave tapestry structure is most common. Red is dominant and colors are stronger than those of Turkish kilims. Nineteenth-century sources of kilims include these towns: Berekovica, Chiprovtsy, Gabrovo, Kotel, Samokov, Şarköy, Sliven, Sumen, Teteven, and Zaribrod. There are some antique kilims with Bulgarian inscriptions. West Bulgarian kilims are finely woven and employ curvilinear wefts. East Bulgarian kilims are more coarsely woven, with darker colors than those from the west, and they are more like Anatolian kilims. Contemporary kilims are woven in Chiprovtsi. See "Cerga," "Kotel," and "Şarköy."

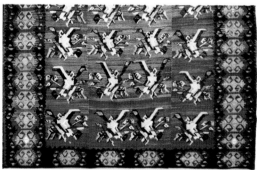

Bulgarian kilim *Kazim Yildiz*

buli. In Bangladesh, memorized verbal instructions for the creation of a specific pattern by a weaver. See "talim."

Bulvardi, Balvardi, Bolvardi. A subtribe of the Qashqa'i. They reside near Shiraz in southwest Iran. See "Qashqa'i."

Bünyan. See "Kayseri."

Burdur. A town of western Anatolia and a source of rugs in designs based on Persian models with modern colors. Knot densities are about 130 knots per square inch on a cotton foundation. The asymmetric knot is used.

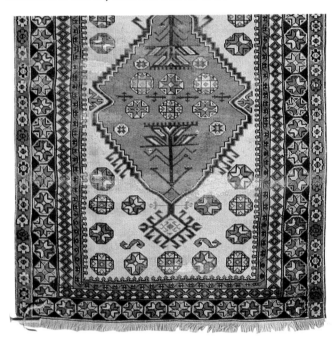

Burdur rug (detail) *Yurdan*

burling. Inspecting and repairing newly-woven factory-produced rugs. More specifically, hand-tufting void areas that occur in power-loomed rugs.

burning. When caustic solutions are used to fade a rug, an excessively strong solution may fuse some wool fibers in the pile. This condition is termed "burning."

burn test. Used to determine the type of fiber in rugs. A very small sample is exposed to flame. Bright burning, the smell of burning paper, and a fragile, fine ash indicate cotton. Barely sustains flame, strong odor of burning hair, and ash in an elongated ball indicate wool. Does not sustain flame, indistinct smell, and small ash ball indicate silk.

Burnt Water. See "Pine Springs."

Bursa, Brusa, Brousse, Prusa. A town of northwest Anatolia, south of Istanbul. Bursa was the first capital of the Ottoman Empire and Ottoman court rugs may have been woven there in the late sixteenth century. In the nineteenth century, Bursa was the source of rugs made in imitation of the Gördes prayer rug. Silk production from Bursa is used in contemporary Turkish rugs.

buta. See "boteh."

butterfly. In Chinese rugs, the butterfly symbolizes marital bliss.

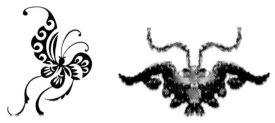

Chinese butterflies

butterfly saddle rugs. Tibetan saddle rugs woven in a trapezoidal shape. The corners of the shorter parallel edge may be rounded. The overall shape suggests a butterfly with spread wings.

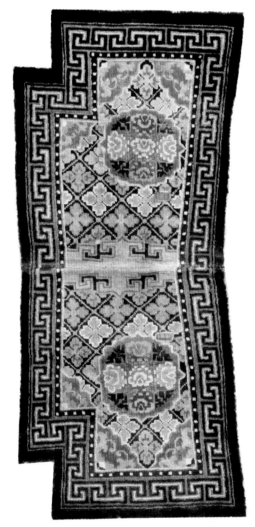

Butterfly saddle rug *Jason Nazmiyal*

button rugs. Rugs made by taking a fabric disk, folding it in quarters, and stitching the point to a backing material. This was an early American method for home-made rugs.

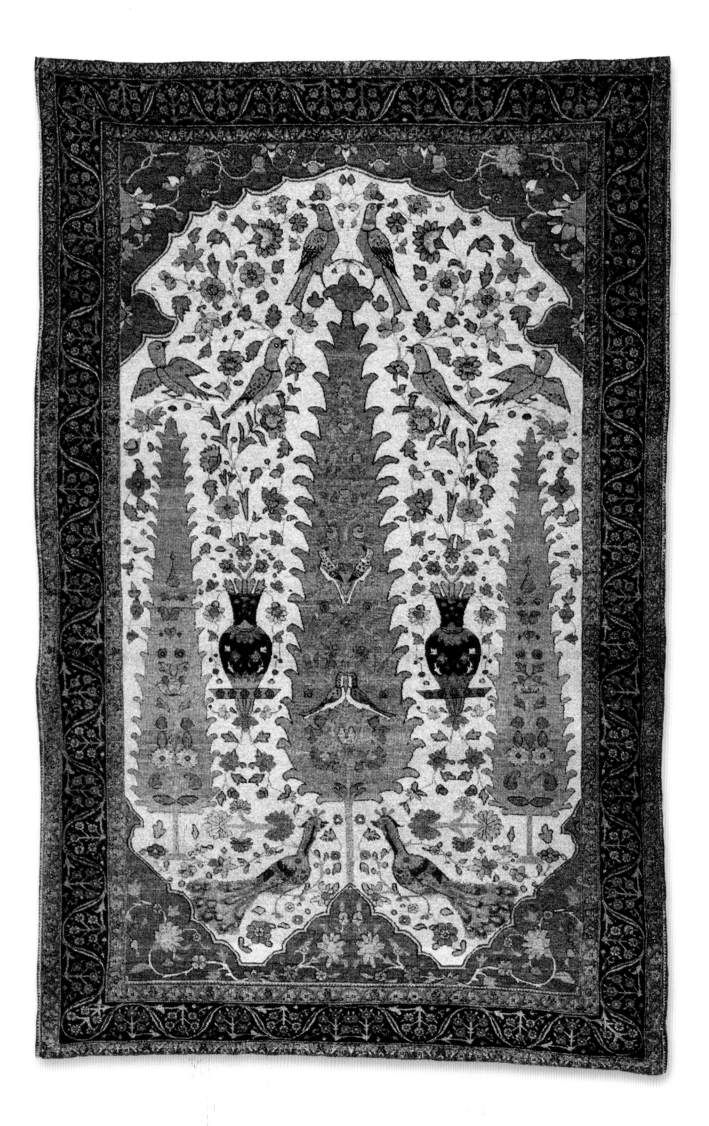

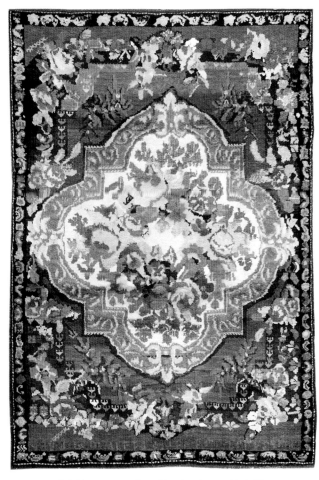

Cabbbage roses in a Karabagh rug (detail)
Jason Nazmiyal

cabbage rose. A rug motif based on European naturalistic rendition of a rose, usually a repeat of an overhead view of an outsized red rose in full bloom. The roses tend to dwarf any other elements in the design. Examples may be found in Savonnerie rugs, mid-nineteenth-century Turkish rugs (Mejidian style) and nineteenth-century rugs of Karabagh and Kuba. See "farangi gul" and "rose motif."

Cabistan, Kabistan. A term of controversial origin formerly used as an attribution for some Caucasian rugs. There is no such geographical location, and there are no certain structural or design features associated with rugs so attributed. This attribution is no longer used.

cabled, cable twist, cord. When plied yarns are plied again, the resulting yarn may be described as a "cable" or "cabled." Heavy cabled wefts every 3 to 8 inches are used in some Mashhad carpets and Dragon carpets. These wefts are clearly visible from the back of the rug and may appear as lines of wear on the front. Cabled yarns are often used in selvages. See "ply."

cable weft. When warps are offset or depressed, wefts are alternately straight or bending in their passage through the warps. The straight and tight weft is termed a "cable" weft and the bending weft is termed a "sinuous" weft. In some rugs, the cable weft is much thicker than the sinuous weft, thus forcing

the warps apart so that the thinner sinuous weft must bend. See "thari."

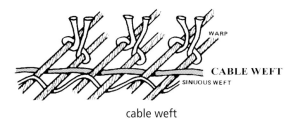

cable weft

Caesarea. See "Kayseri."

Cairene carpets. Floral and Mamluk carpets attributed to Cairo, Egypt of the fifteenth through seventeenth centuries. These carpets are constructed with the asymmetric knot and S-spun and Z-plied yarns. See "Egypt," "Mamluk," "Ottoman floral carpets," and "para-Mamluk."

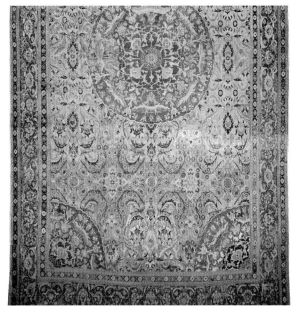

Cairene carpet (detail)

Çal. A town of southwest Anatolia where kilims and brightly colored, coarsely knotted rugs are woven.

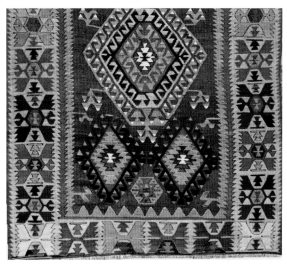

Çal kilim (detail) *Kazim Yildiz*

Calcutta (now Kolkata). A city of eastern India on the Bay of Bengal. In the nineteenth century, Calcutta jail served as a collection center for rugs and dhurries woven by prisoners of other jails in India.

calligraphy. See "Arabic calligraphy and script."

calyx. The outermost floral parts or sepals forming a cup shape. These may be shown in stylized cross section in oriental rug designs. See "Afshan" and "Rhodian lilly."

Çamardı, Maden. A town of south central Anatolia and the source of rugs sold as "Maden." These are prayer rugs with a red field.

camel hair. The wool or hair of the camel is used rarely in pile rug weaving and kilims. Camel hair is distinguished from wool by its fineness and pigmentation granules. The term may refer to the color of sheep wool. See "shotori."

Campeche wood. See "Logwood."

Çan. A town of northwestern Anatolia where rugs are woven. These rugs usually have a rust red field and green spandrels. See "Turkey."

Çanakkale. Turkish for "pottery castle." A town and district of northwest Anatolia, located on the Dardanelles. Rug weaving is an ancient craft in Çanakkale, some examples from the area having been woven in the fifteenth century. Rugs of the nineteenth and twentieth centuries are coarsely woven on a wool foundation with red wefts. Knot densities are about 40 to 80 symmetric knots per square inch. The number of wefts varies between rows of knots. Ends are usually a red plain weave. Within the rug trade, these rugs may be termed "Bergama." See "Turkey."

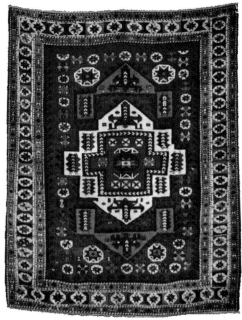

Çanakkale rug *Simon Knight*

cane pattern. A pattern of repeated stripes, each occupied by some repeated motif.

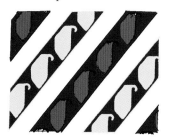 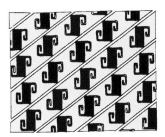

Cane patterns

canopy or standard motif. A Buddhist symbol of official authority sometimes used as a motif in Chinese rugs.

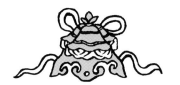 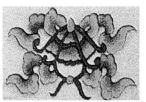

Canopy

Cappadocia. A province of central Anatolia. The town of Avanos in Cappadocia produces prayer rugs with a red field and an ornate suspended lamp. These rugs have many borders. Formerly there were Greek rug-weaving workshops in Avanos. See "Turkey."

carbon dating rugs. Naturally occurring radio carbon 14 decays at a fixed rate. Atmospheric carbon 14 is continuously created through cosmic ray bombardment. Accordingly, the relative quantity of radio carbon 14 in samples protected from the atmosphere or bound in organic matter for long periods differs from that in the present atmosphere. By comparing the relative amounts of carbon 14 in protected samples with atmospheric carbon 14, the age of organic matter, including animal fibers can be calculated. This method is useful in dating objects up to about 60,000 years old. The age of the Pazyryk carpet, the Shroud of Turin, and many other ancient textiles was determined through radiocarbon 14 dating. See "archeological sites," "dating rugs," and "Pazyryk carpet."

carding. To comb fibers prior to spinning with cards or brushes having wire bristles. Woolens are wool yarns that have been spun from carded wool. In the Near East, wool may be carded with a bow, its vibrations aligning the fibers. See "worsted."

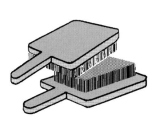 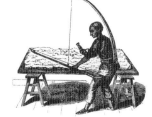

Carding brushes   Carding by bowing (India)

carminic acid. The essential red dye pigment of cochineal. See "cochineal."

carnation motif. The carnation is commonly used as a motif in oriental rugs, particularly in Turkey. It appears in naturalistic renderings in Mughal carpets and it is a geometricized motif in the field of certain rugs of Kuba, in Persian rugs and Kurdish meander borders.

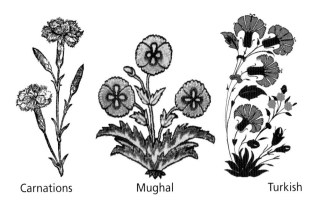

Carnations   Mughal   Turkish

carnation border. A meandering vine border of reversing fan-shaped carnation flowers, each separated by a diagonal leaf. This border may be more or less geometricized. It is a very common border found on rugs throughout the Middle East, including rugs of India.

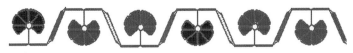

Carnation border

çarpana (Turk.). Tablet weave. See "tablet weaving."

carpet. Any fabric floor covering. Some make a distinction between carpets and rugs, the former being larger than 6 by 9 feet or 8 by 10 feet.

carpet beater. A paddle, usually made of wire or wicker, used to beat rugs to remove soil or dust. See "dusting."

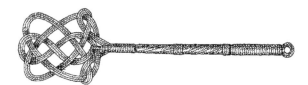

Carpet beater

carpet beetle. *Attegenus piceus.* A black beetle that feeds on the keratin in wool or hair when the beetle is in its larval state.

 Carpet beetle

carpet loom. Generally, carpet looms differ from other basic looms only in that the frame and beam structure is of stronger

members so as to tension the heavier yarns used for rug warps. The simplest form is a horizontal ground loom in which beams are attached to pegs driven into the ground. This is a primitive loom, formerly used by nomads. The horizontal frame loom consists of frame members and beams arranged parallel to the ground. The weaver sits on the completed portion of the rug as it is woven.

Vertical looms may have fixed or roller beams. With fixed beams, a scaffold arrangement is used to raise the seat of the weaver as the work area rises on the loom. With roller beams, warp is unwound from the upper roller beam and the finished portion is wound onto the lower roller beam as the work progresses. With all looms, some device is used to maintain the tension of the warps. These include wedges, twisted ropes and levers, ratchets and pawls, screw mechanisms, turnbuckles, and weights. See "loom" and "shed."

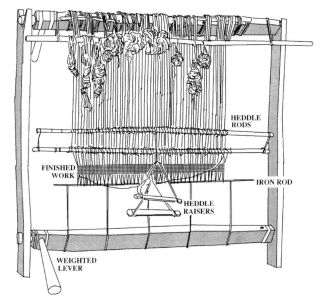

HEDDLE RODS

FINISHED WORK

IRON ROD

HEDDLE RAISERS

WEIGHTED LEVER

Carpet loom

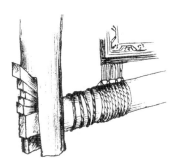

Warp tensioning by wedges

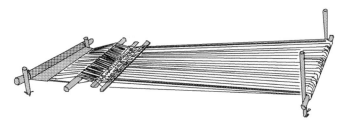

Horizontal ground loom

carpet moth, webbing moth. *Tineola bisseliella.* The larval form of the moth feeds on wool or hair. Wool rugs that are out of the light are subject to infestation and damage from this insect.

Carpet moth

carpet page. Pages of illuminated manuscript of the Hiberno-Saxon school of the eighth and nineth centuries. The pages are covered with intricate interlacing and scroll work, sometimes including ciphers. The designs suggest arabesques in carpets.

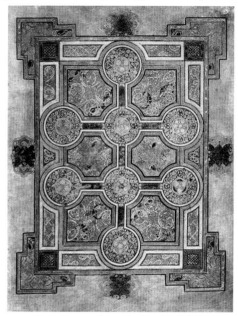

Carpet page from the Book of Kells

carpet slave. A decorative weight placed on a rug to keep it flat and prevent it from shifting. Used in India.

carpet tiles. Any power-loomed carpet cut in squares and finished so that the squares can be butted to cover larger areas.

carthamin. The essential yellow dye pigment derived from the safflower. See "safflower."

cartoon. A grid on paper with cells colored to guide rug weavers in selecting colored pile yarns when tying knots to execute a rug design. Usually, each cell represents a knot. See "buli," "design plate," "loom drawing," "naqsh," and "talim."

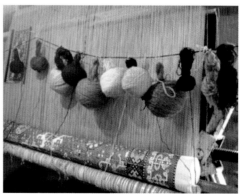

Carpet loom with cartoon *Azerbaijan Rugs*

cartouche. An enclosed area in the field or border of a rug, often containing an inscription, though other design elements may be so enclosed. The outline of the cartouche is usually a rectangle with rounded, cut, or scalloped corners. See "inscription."

Cartouche border. Any border containing repeated cartouches or cartouches alternating with other design elements.

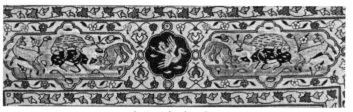

Cartouche border

cartouche carpet. See "compartment rug."

Casablanca. A city of Morocco, a source of contemporary factory rugs. See "Morocco."

casemaking moth. *Tinea pellionella.* The larvae of this moth feed on wool and hair. Wool rugs that are out of the light are subject to infestation and damage from this insect.

cashmere. See "Kashmir goat."

castellated border. See "crenellated border."

çatal (Turk.). A tool used to beat down weft.

Çatal Hüyük. The site of a neolithic settlement in central Anatolia. Archaeological excavation has uncovered painted walls and artifacts. Carbonized fabric from this site has been identified as linen. Images and designs suggest the worship of a mother goddess. James Mellaart, an archaeologist who worked at this site, theorized that some designs in contemporary Anatolian kilims are ultimately derived from these neolithic images of a mother goddess. This theory is disputed and the credibility of Mellaart's archaeological evidence has been challenged. See "elibelinde."

catechu dye, cutch. This brown dye is made from the heartwood of Acacia catechu, a tree. Catechu dye was used in rugs of India.

caterpillar rugs. A nineteenth-century American rug consisting of accordion-folded strips of fabric stitched to a fabric backing.

çatma, chatma. Orginally, an Ottoman fabric in which the motif was brocaded in silver-wrapped thread, rendered in raised velvet. Generally, a technically superior and dense form of velvet. Cushion covers were made from this fabric. Some yastik designs may derive from these cushion covers. See "kadife."

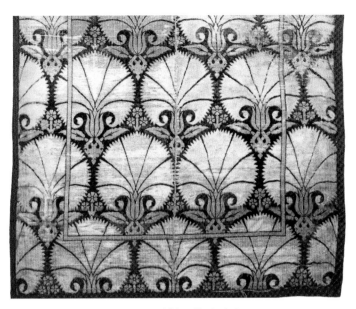

Çatma panel (detail) *Sothebys*

Caucasus. Formerly, southern Russia, an area bounded by the Caspian Sea on the east and the Black Sea on the west. The Caucasus mountain range, from the northwest to the southeast, diagonally divides the region. The area south of the mountain range is termed the Transcaucasus. This is the primary rug-producing area. The population is of varied ethnic origin. Rugs and carpets are woven by Azeri Turks, Kurds, and Armenians. Travelers refer to rug production in the Caucasus in the fifteenth century, and there are Dragon carpets from the seventeenth century attributed to the Caucasus. Rug production was a major cottage industry in the nineteenth century.

Rugs are brightly colored and generally have geometric designs. The symmetric knot is used with average knot densities ranging from 60 per square inch for Kazaks to 114 per square inch for Kuba rugs. Pile is wool. Warps are undyed. With few exceptions, these rugs have two or more wefts between each row of knots. Rugs with cotton foundations from the Caucasus have higher knot densities than those with wool foundations.

There is contemporary pile rug production in cooperative rug factories in Azerbaijan, Daghestan, and Armenia. The largest producer is Armenia. Designs are traditional or modern variations of traditional designs. Depending on commercial grade, knot densities vary from 78 knots per square inch to 162 knots per square inch. Export of these rugs was handled by a division of the Russian agency, Novoexport. After export, these rugs receive a chemical wash to improve their color tone and and color contrast.

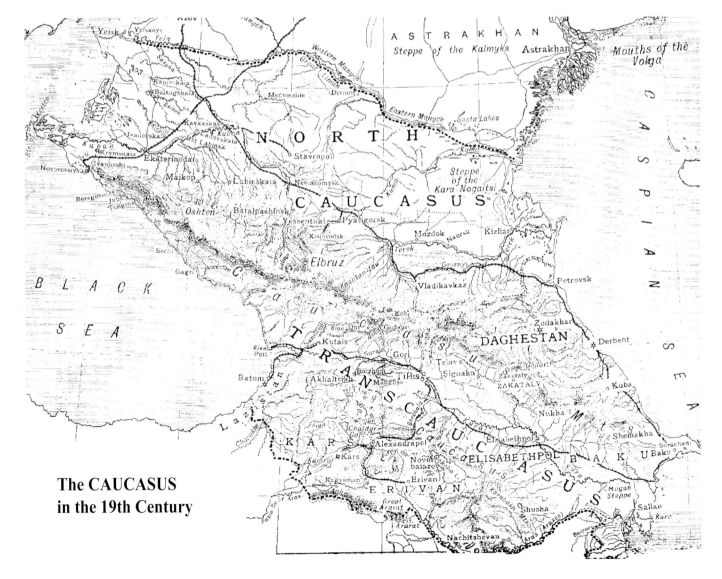

**The CAUCASUS
in the 19th Century**

See the following geographical entries:

Abkhazia	Goradis
Akstafa,	Karabagh
Armenia	Kazak
Azerbaijan	Konaghend
Baku	Kuba
Chelabi,	Lenkoran
Chondzoresk	Lori Pambak
Daghestan	Marasali
Dara Chichi	Moghân
Derbend	Shamshadnee
Dilijan	Shemakha
Echmiadzin	Surakhany
Elisavetpol	Shirvân
Erivan	Talish
Genje	Zakatala

Caucasian flatweaves. Caucasian kilims and palases are usually woven as a single piece. The slit weave tapestry structure is used. Warp ends are knotted to produce a web effect. Motifs consist of adjacent or compacted large geometric medallions suggesting palmettes or rows of smaller geometric motifs. A few kilims consist of all-over patterns of small, repeated geometric elements. Colors are bright and contrasting. Regional attribution of kilims within the Caucasus is problematic, despite trade designations such as "Kuba," "Shirvân," or "Talish."

Soumak bags and mafrash are attributed to Kurdish weavers in the Caucasus and similar pieces to the Shahsavan in Iran. Large soumaks were woven throughout the Caucasus, many of them from Kuba. Common designs in the nineteenth century were a vertically repeated diamond medallion alternating with two hexagons or circular motifs, and dragon soumaks based on the pile dragon rugs. A design of large "S" shapes thought to represent dragons was woven with the soumak structure. See "arbabash," "davaghin," "dragon soumaks," "dum," "istang," "kiyiz," "sileh," and "verneh."

C.E. Common era. Used as a religiously neutral replacement for A.D. in date designation.

çeki tülü. See "tülü."

cemetery carpet. See "landscape carpet."

centaury. *Centaurea acaulis*, a plant whose roots are used for a yellow dye.

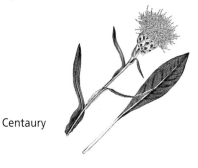

Centaury

centimeter. See "conversion factors."

Central Asia. See "Eastern Turkestan" and "Western Turkestan."

cerga, tsherga. A Bulgarian goat-hair flatweave of woven strips sewn together.

çeyrek (Turk., "quarter"). A Turkish term for village rugs of about 2.5 by 4.5 feet.

"C" gul. A Turkmen octagon gul in which C-shapes or crescents are arranged, with crescents facing both left and right. This gul is found in Yomud rugs.

"C" gul

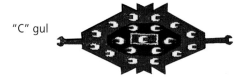

Chahal Shotur, Chehel Shotur (Persian, "forty camels"). A town of Iran west of Isfahan and a source of Bakhtiari rugs with a compartmented garden design.

Chahar aimaq. See "Aimaq."

chahar bagh (Persian, "quartered garden"). The design of compartmented carpets with the layout of a formal Persian garden. See "garden carpet."

Chahâr Mahâl (Persian, "four places"). A region of western Iran between Isfahan and the Zagros Mountains. The area is controlled by the Bakhtiaris. Rugs marketed as "Bakhtiari" are woven by natives of the area, who are not members of the Bakhtiari tribe. The "four places" are the towns and districts of Shahr-e Kord, Borujen, Farâhân, and Lordakân. See "Bakhtiari," "khod rang," and "Shahr-e Kord."

Chahâr-râ (Persian *chahâr-râh* "crossroads"). A district of Hamadan in Iran and the source of rugs with a black ground. Knots are symmetric on a cotton foundation with single wefts.

chain. A term for foundation warp in power-loomed pile carpets.

chain stitch. A stitch consisting of successive loops, the needle passing through each loop at the same relative position. The chain stitch is used for decorative purposes and sometimes to lock the final weft in place at the end of a rug. Rugs embroidered with chain-stitching are commercially produced in India.

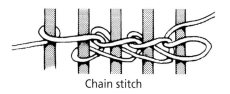

Chain stitch

chair covers, throne back. A Chinese or Tibetan special-purpose pile weaving consisting of two pieces, one for the back and the other for the bottom of the chair. The piece for the back is usually scalloped. See "thigyarbya."

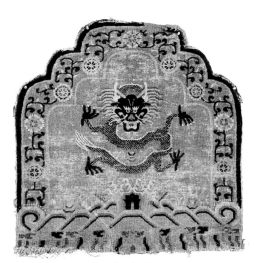

Chair back *Ningxia*

Chajli. A group of nineteenth-century rugs attributed to Shirvân in the Caucasus that display three or more large octagonal medallions. The medallions often resemble rectangles with clipped corners rather than true octagons. The medallions are in alternating light and dark colors. Knot density is about 100 symmetric knots per square inch. Their average area is about 40 square feet. Wefts may be cotton or wool. See "Caucasus" and "Shirvân."

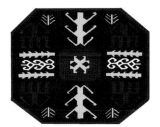

Chajli medallion

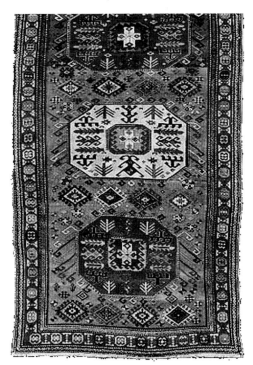

Chajli rug *James Allen*

Chakesh. A tribe of the Ersari located around Aq Chah in Afghanistan. The tribe weaves rugs in red and blue using traditional guls.

Chakhansur. A town in southwestern Afghanistan bordering Iran. Baluchi rugs of this area are finely knotted. Small, packed geometric elements are used in the field. Colors are dark brown, blue, and black with some red. See "Afghanistan."

chaklâ (Hindi). A cloth of silk and cotton.

chalat. See "khalat."

chalik. See "khalyk."

chamomile. *Anthemis tinctoria*, a flowering plant that may be used to produce a yellow dye.

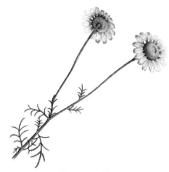

Chamomile

Chamtos border. A border used by the Salor Turkmen consisting of small rectangles arranged as diamonds with a mosaic effect.

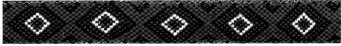

Chamtos border

Ch'ang. The Chinese endless knot and the Buddhist symbol for destiny, eternity, or longevity. This knot is used as a motif in some Chinese rugs.

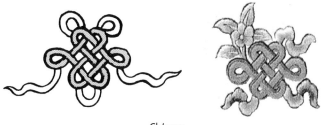

Ch'ang

Chan-Karabagh. A Caucasian rug type, identified by Schürmann, with a design consisting of large botehs. See "Karabagh."

chanteh (Persian). A small bag or satchel.

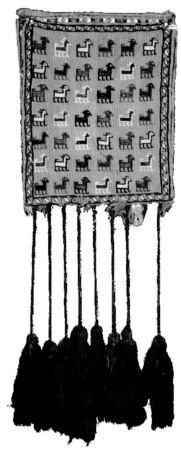

Qashga'i chanteh *Simon Knight*

chapan. A Turkmen or Uzbeki long-sleeved robe, often of silk and embroidered or of silk ikat. See "chirpy" and "khalat."

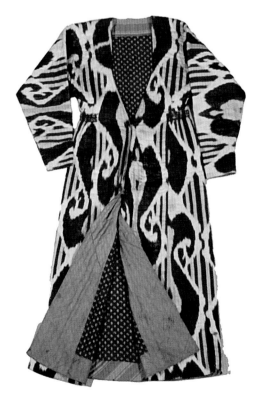

Chapan *Grogan and Company*

Chardjou (Persian *Châr-juy*, "four streams"). A town in Turkmenistan on the Amu Darya inhabited by Ersaris. Contemporary rugs from this area are woven with the Tekke gul and variations. Pile rugs are woven in two knot densities: one of about 55 knots per square inch and the other of about 120 knots per square inch.

Charshango, Charchangu, Charchangi. A town of northern Afghanistan. A term for rugs thought to be woven by a subtribe of the Salor or Ersari. The tribe inhabits an area on either side of the Amu Darya in Turkestan and Afghanistan.

chatma. See "çatma."

Chaudor, Chodor. A Turkmen tribe inhabiting the Khiva area of Turkestan. The ertman and tauk noska guls are used in their rugs, as well as a variety of other designs. The field color is often a distinctive purple-brown. These rugs have asymmetric knots, open to the right. Wefts are two-ply, sometimes wool and sometimes cotton. See "ertman gul" and "Turkmen."

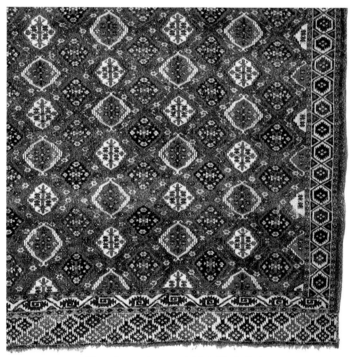

Chaudor main carpet (detail) *Sothebys*

chavadan, shabadan, shavadan. A Kirghiz long kit bag.

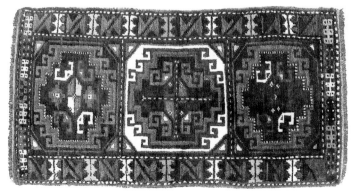

Chavadan face *Carpet Collection*

Chechens, Tchetchens, Krists. A people of northwest Daghestan (now the Chechniya Region) in the Caucasus. They are Sunni Muslims, fiercely independent and egalitarian. The term, "Chichi," applied to certain rug designs, is thought to derive from the name of this ethnic group. Whether rugs ascribed to this group were actually woven by them is problematic. See "Chichi."

check border. A very common minor border, especially in Kazak and Kurdish rugs

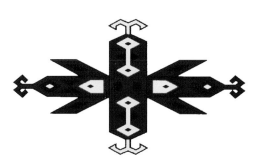

Check border

Chehel Shotur. See "Chahal Shotur."

Chelaberd, Eagle Kazak, Sunburst Kazak, Adler Kazak. Nineteenth-century rugs of Karabagh in the Caucasus with a medallion consisting of a lozenge with parallel radiating arms. Hooked brackets, facing outwards, are above and below the medallion. The design is thought to derive from Dragon carpets. Chelabi is a town of southern Karabagh. Chelaberd is a corruption of that name. There are seventeenth-century Caucasian carpets with this medallion. These rugs are published most frequently as representative of the Caucasus. Their average knot density is about 60 symmetric knots per square inch and the average rug area is about 35 square feet. They have an all-wool foundation. See "Caucasus," "Dragon carpet," and "Karabagh."

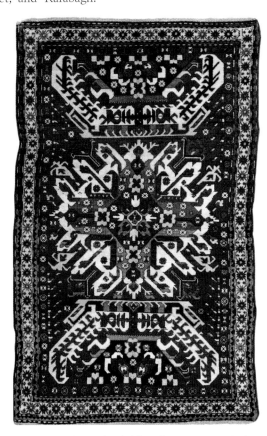

Chelaberd Karabagh (detail) *Jason Nazmiyal*

Chelsea Carpet. A sixteenth-century rug in the Victoria and Albert Museum, thought to have been woven in India or Herat. It has a cloud band border and multiple medallions. Birds and animals are represented in the field. It is 17 feet 9 inches by 10 feet 4 inches.

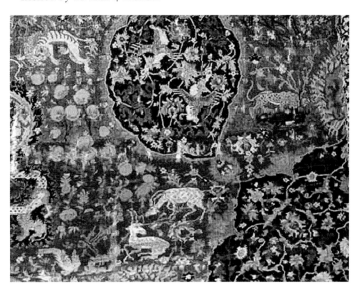

Chelsea carpet (detail)

Chemche gul. Chemche means "spoon" or "scoop." A common minor or secondary gul in Turkmen rugs. It consists of a quartered diamond and may have eight radiating arms, alternately terminating in the ram's horn motif.

Chemche gul

chemche torba (Turk). Spoon bag. See "spoon bag."

chemical wash. The application of chemicals (sometimes lime, chlorine compounds, or wood ash) to a rug to soften colors, soften the wool, and increase the sheen of the pile. Harsh chemical washes are cited as the cause of weakened or embrittled fibers in some old rugs. See "burning."

Chenâr, Çinar (Turk.). A town of Hamadan in Iran. It is a source of rugs and runners with vertically arranged, large diamond medallions. Also the name of the Asian plane tree (sycamore) and the name of a Turkmen design derived from the shape of the leaf, chenâr gul.

chenille rug. A fabric of warps holding cut wefts is slit, warpwise, into strips. These strips of warp with cut weft are then woven into the rug to form cut pile.

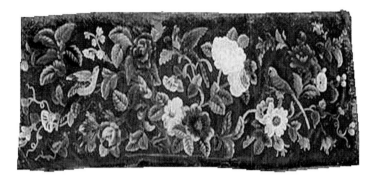

Chenille panel *Grogan and Company*

Cherkess, Circassian, Tcherkess. A Caucasian ethnic group including the Kabardians and Abkhazians. They inhabit the northwestern Caucasus. They are Sunni Muslims. These people may have been a minor source of rugs in the nineteenth century.

cherlyk (Turk.). Saddle cover. See "saddle cover."

chessboard. Any design of offset rows of adjacent rectangles, each rectangle alternating in color with vertical columns of rectangles, also alternating in color. This design is found in Chinese and Tibetan rugs. Usually, such Tibetan rugs are without borders. See "sadranji."

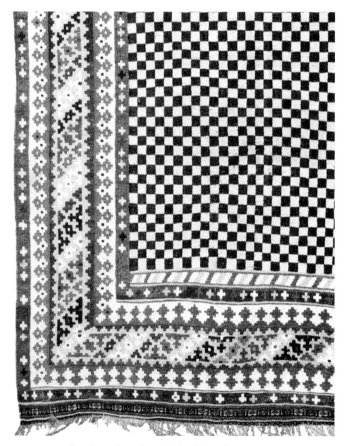

Chessboard Qashga'i kilim (detail) *Southebys*

Chessboard rugs, Damascus carpets. A group of 16th and 17th-century rugs. The field design is usually rows of hexagons, each containing small fish-like shapes radiating from a complex central star. The hexagons are in square compartments which are outlined by red bands. Chessboard rugs have asymmetric knots open to the left with Z-spun yarns. These rugs have been attributed to Cairo, Damascus, and Anatolia. They have been termed "Damascus rugs." See "Cairene rugs," "compartment rug," "Egypt," "Mamluk," and "para-Mamluk."

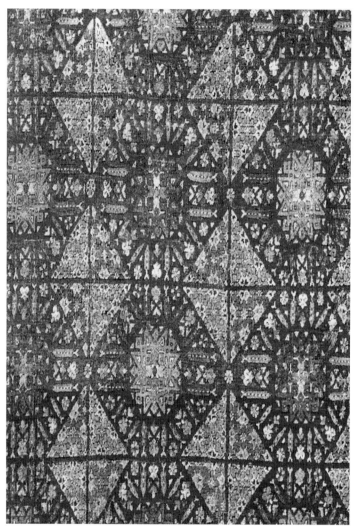

Chessboard rug (detail)

chi. A coiled cloud or a shell-like motif used in Chinese rugs. See "ruyi."

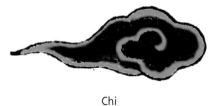

Chi

Chiadma. A tribe of southwest Morocco. Their rugs have a burgundy field with scattered diamonds or small geometric elements. Their flatweaves employ the slit tapestry structure.

chichak lameh. A design motif, flower and bud, used primarily by Turkish-speaking weavers. It consists of a single flower with leaves or buds on both sides springing from the same stem. There are many geometric versions of this motif.

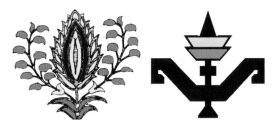

Chichak lameh

Chichaktu, Chichaksu, Tchitchaktu. A town of northern Afghanistan. Major rug production began in this town in the early 1970s. The designs used are prayer rugs and variations of ensi designs. Colors are dark, similar to Baluchi rugs. The asymmetric knot is used on a wool foundation.

Chichaoua. See "Oulad Bou Sbâa."

Chichi. A design attributed to Kuba in the Caucasus. The distinctive border consists of diagonal bars alternating with large blossoms. Kuba rugs with this border have a mean knot density of 105 symmetric knots per square inch. Their average area is 25 square feet. Wefts may be either cotton or wool. See "Chechens," "Dara-chichi," and "Kuba."

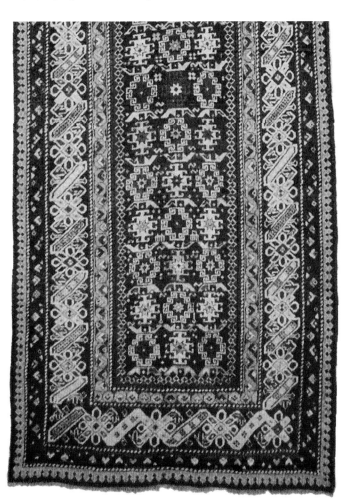

Chichi rug (detail) *Grogan & Company*

Chichi border. A distinctive border of Kuba rugs of the Caucasus attributed to the Chechens. It consists of a diagonal bar alternating with a large geometricized rosette.

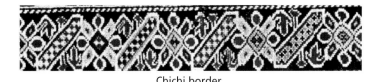

Chichi border

Chief's blanket. A flatweave blanket woven by Navajos with simple designs. This blanket is narrower warp-wise than it is weft-wise. Colors are some combination of red, black, blue, or brown on a white field. There were no chiefs among the Navajo, but these blankets did indicate some prestige because they were finely woven.

Chief's blankets are classified in three phases according to design evolution. First phase design consists of stripes only. Second phase design consists of stripes with blocks or groups of rectangles inserted within the stripes. Third phase design consists of diamonds or crosses superimposed over stripes. Third phase designs were created after the Navajo internment at Bosque Redondo. See "Navajo rugs" and "serape."

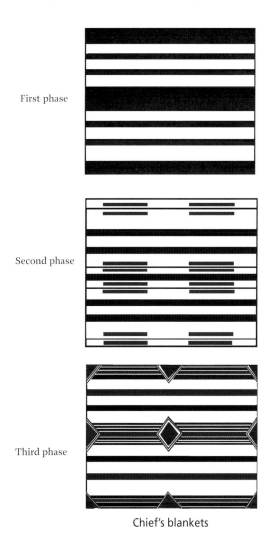

First phase

Second phase

Third phase

Chief's blankets

chikh. See "reed screens."

Chila, Khila. A town west of Baku in the Caucasus, to which are attributed nineteenth-century rugs with an all-over boteh field with stepped spandrels and containing a stepped central medallion. These are the largest of Baku rugs with an average rug area of 41 square feet. They have wool warps and either wool or cotton wefts. Their mean knot density is 88 symmetric knots per square inch. See "Baku."

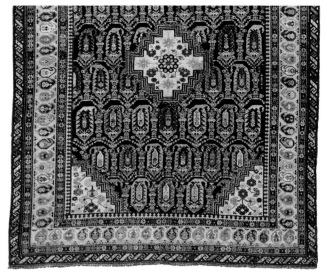

Chila rug (detail) *Sothebys*

Chila-boteh. See "Chila."

child's serape. A Navajo wearing blanket about 2½ feet by 4 feet. See "Navajo rugs."

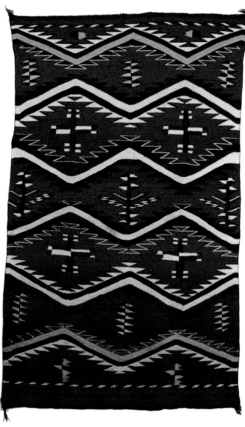

Child's serape *Grogan and Company*

chilin. See "ky'lin."

Chilkat. Indians of the Pacific Northwest. They weave fabrics on warp-weighted looms using a weft twining structure.

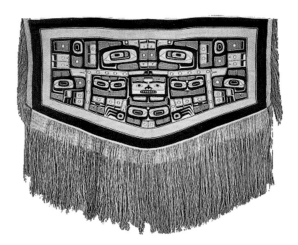

Chilkat apron *R. John Howe*

Chimayó. A town of New Mexico and a source of rugs and blankets of Navajo design. These are primarily stripes and diamonds.

China. Rugs of China are considered to include those of Manchuria, Mongolia, and Xinjiang. Rugs were primarily woven in northern China. A Chinese saddle blanket from Lop Sanpra was dated to about 100 B.C.E. A few pile rugs have been dated to the Ming dynasty. Domestic pile rug production in China was quite small until production for export began in about 1890. Rug-weaving centers predating rug production for export include Ningxia, Baotou, Suiyuan, and the towns of Gansu. See entries under these names.

Commercial rug production for export began late in the nineteenth century in Beijing and about the turn of the century in Tianjin. Tianjin became the center of large-scale commercial production from about 1910 to 1930 as foreign firms came to dominate the Chinese rug industry. American firms in China included Karagheusin, A. Beshar & Co., Donchian, Avanosian, Kent-Costikyan, Elbrook Inc., Nichols Super Yarn, and Fette-Li. Throughout the early twentieth century, the United States was the largest importer of Chinese rugs. The peak period of rug production and shipment to the United States was 1925. In the early 1930s, rug production was interrupted by the Japanese invasion. Large-scale commercial production was not resumed until the 1960s.

Chinese rugs use the asymmetric knot with occasional use of the symmetric knot in edges and ends of early examples. Chinese rugs are not finely knotted, varying between 30 and 120 knots per square inch. Some early Chinese rugs have asymmetric knots that are offset on warps or skip warps at curving borders of color changes. See "offset knots" and "packing knots." Early rugs have no warp offset, while later rugs have offset warps, some with closed backs.

Contemporary Chinese rugs are woven in cooperative factories. There is consistent quality in these rugs due to the use of steel looms, chrome dyes, and objective production standards. The "line" is the contemporary measure of knot density. See "line." Woolen carpets are woven in 70, 80, 90, and 120-line qualities. Silk rugs are woven in 120 to 300-line qualities. Pile heights for wool rugs are ⅜, ½, and ⅝ inch. The pile height for silk rugs is ½ inch. The Chinese rug trade designation "Super" means a 90-line rug with ⅝ inch pile height and a closed back.

See "Buddhist symbols," "chair covers," "Ch'ing dynasty," "closed back," "Confucian symbols," "Fette rugs," "fret rugs," "k'ang covers," "line," "Ming dynasty," "Nichols," "open back," "pillar rug," "Taoist symbols," "trigram," and "yin yang."

See the following geographic entries: Baotou, Beijing, Gansu, Guizhou, He-bei, Jehol, Lop Nor, Lop Sanpra, Mongolia, Ningxia, Niya, Shanghai, Shantung, Suiyuan, Tianjin, Xinjiang.

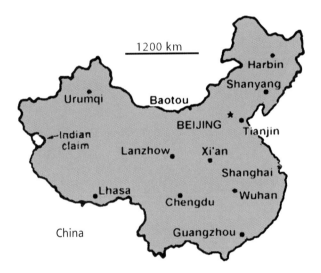

China

chinakap, chinikap. A Turkmen cup or bowl case. This may be a bag or a bowl-shaped container with a lid and a pendant strap. It has an overall length of about one foot. Chinakaps are made of pile, embroidered cloth, wood, or leather.

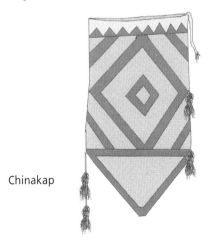

Chinakap

Chindi drugget. A drugget made of waste fabric. See "drugget."

chiné. A ply of yarns of different, but similar or closely related colors.

Chinese fret. A repeat pattern consisting of linked swastikas.

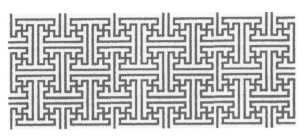

Chinese fret

Chinese tapestry weave. See "k'o-ssu."

Ch'ing dynasty. The Ch'ing or Manchu dynasty governed China from 1644 to 1912. Most of the older surviving pile Chinese carpets date from this period; large-scale rug production was introduced in about 1890. See "Ming dynasty."

chinikap. See "chinakap."

Chinle. A Navajo reservation area of east central Arizona. From the 1930s, Navajo weavers of the area wove rugs without borders and with horizontal bands in an effort to revive 19th century designs. Colors are earth tones from vegetable and synthetic dyes.

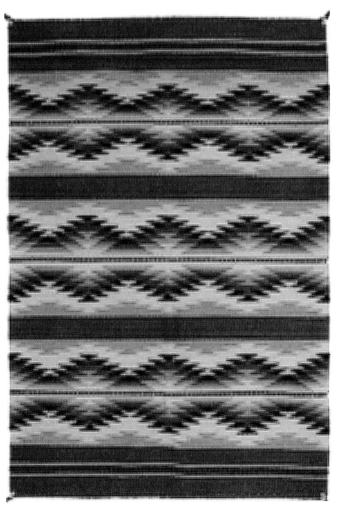

Chinle Navajo rug *Steve Getzwiller*

chintamani, badge of Tamerlane (Turk.). Ottoman court motif of a triangular arrangement of three balls above two cloudbands or waves. A repeat pattern of groups of three balls only may also be termed "chintamani." Also referred to as the "badge of Tamerlane." The motif was widely used in Ottoman ceramics and weavings from the fifteenth to the seventeenth century. This motif is probably of Buddhist or Chinese origin.

Chintamani

Chintamani Ushak. A rare group of sixteenth and seventeenth-century rugs from Ushak in Anatolia. These rugs have a white ground and an all-over pattern of the chintamani motif, a repeated figure of three balls in a pyramidal arrangement over two wavy lines or cloudbands. See "Ushak."

Chiprovtsi carpet. A handmade carpet of Bulgaria, the name is from the town of Chiprovtsi where their production started in the 17th century. The carpet is two-sided with both sides having an identical design.

chirpy. A Tekke Turkmen woman's cloak, often of embroidered silk. The chirpy has false sleeves sewed to the shoulder. The ground color is matched to the age of the wearer: *yashl chirpy* (green chirpy) for young women, *sary chirpy* (yellow chirpy) for middle-aged women, and *ak chirpy* (white chirpy) for old women. See "chapan" and "khalat."

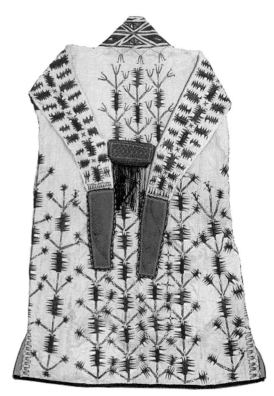

Chirpy *R. John Howe*

Chob Bash. See "Chub-bash."

chobi (Persian) "colored like wood." Describing Afghanistan and Pakistan rugs in shades of light brown or tan.

Chodor. See "Chaudor."

Chondzoresk, Cloudband Kazak. Chondzoresk or Khondzoresk is a village south of Shusha in southern Karabagh in the Caucasus. Khondzor is Armenian for "apple." Nineteenth century rugs of this design have one or more medallions containing motifs similar to cloudbands. The mean knot density of these rugs is 58 symmetric knots per square inch. These are the smallest rugs of Karabagh, with an average size of 33 square feet. See "Caucasus" and "Karabagh."

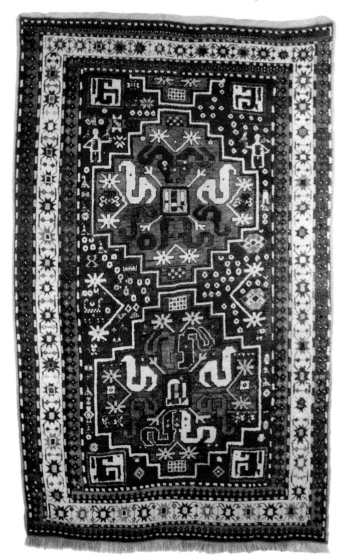

Chondzoresk Kazak *Grogan and Company*

Chosroes, Spring Carpet of. See "Spring Carpet of Chosroes."

chroma, saturation. The absence of an admixture of white, black, or gray in a color. See "Munsell's color theory."

chromatography. A chromatogram is the colored strip resulting from chromatographic analysis when constituents of a mixture are differentially absorbed by a strip of paper or column of some other material or a graph of color frequencies resulting from a chromatographic analysis. This form of chemical analysis is used to identify dye constituents in rugs.

chrome dyes. A group of modern synthetic dyes that are used with a mordant of potassium dichromate. These dyes are fast and non-fugitive.

chrome mordant. Potassium dichromate is used as a mordant and has a general tendency to darken colors.

chronogram. A date indicated by the sum of the numerical values of a sequence of letters. This form of date is sometimes found as an inscription in rugs. See "Armenia" and "dates."

Chronology of oriental rugs. The years are approximate. There is an entry for each listing.

300 B.C.E.	Pazyrik carpet
100 B.C.E.	Lop Sampra saddle blanket
600 C.E.	Shahr-i Qumis fragments
800	Fustat carpet
1200-1300	Seljuk carpets
1300-1924	Ottoman carpets
1350-1650	Ming dynasty rugs
1400-1500	Mamluk carpets
1400-1500	Star carpets
1400-1500	Admiral carpets
1400-1600	Para-Mamluk carpets
1400-1700	Cairene carpets
1450	Dragon and phoenix carpet - Berlin
1450	Marby rug
1500-1600	Salting group
1500-1650	Mughal carpets
1500-1700	"Portuguese" carpets
1500-1700	Chessboard rugs
1500-1720	Safavid carpets
1500-1800	Vase carpets
1500-1800	Transylvania carpets
1500-1900	Dragon carpets
1540	Ardabil carpets
1580-1630	Abassid carpets
1600-1700	"Polonaise" carpets
1600-1800	Lotto carpets
1600-1900	Dragon carpets
1630	Girdler's carpet
1650-	Savonnerie carpets
1660-1870	Aubusson carpets
1700	Gohar carpet
1840-1860	Medjid carpets
1880-1920	Arts and Crafts carpets
1880-1920	Ziegler and Co. carpets
1900-1930	Bezalel carpets
1917-1940	Art Deco carpets
1920-1935	Fette carpets
1979-	Afghanistan war rugs
1980-	DOBAG rugs

Missing from this chronology are tribal and village rugs which are usually of more recent origin. Note that a rug style or design can be copied long after the originating weaving culture has produced it. See "dating rugs" and "historical rugs and textiles."

chrysanthemum. This flower is used as a motif in Chinese carpets and symbolizes long life. It may be used in combination with the plum, bamboo, and orchid. In the rugs of India, the chrysanthemum is represented with naturalistic realism in Mughal carpets.

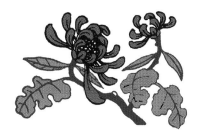

After Hackmack

Chub-bash, Chob Bash. A Turkmen tribe of northern Afghanistan, possibly a subtribe of the Ersaris. Weavings of the tribe display a variety of guls, including the ertman and the tauk noska. See "Ersari."

chul. See "horse cover."

chupuqdân. A shallow bag with a short flap in the center specifically intended to hold tobacco pipes and tobacco. With flap extended, the shape is similar to the top portion of a salt bag. Such bags are woven by the Afshars.

churga. A heavy, fulled blanket of northern Greece.

Churro. A hardy breed of Spanish sheep introduced by Coronado and the Conquistadors to North America in 1540. It was raised by the Pueblos and Navajos and was the early source of wool used in their blankets. These sheep produced a long and straight staple with a low grease content. See "Rambouillet-Merino Sheep."

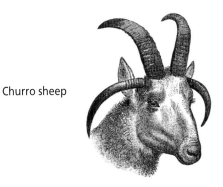

Churro sheep

chuval. See "joval."

çiçekli (Turk. "floral"). Any kilim or rug of Anatolia with a design primarily of flowers.

cicim (Turk.). This term has been used indiscriminately for flat-weaves. The term has referred to an Anatolian flatweave consisting of weft float or overlay-underlay brocade on a balanced or weft-faced plain weave. See "jijim."

Cihanbeyli. A town of central Anatolia inhabited by Kurds. They weave rugs of stepped designs, some of which have tufts of dyed mohair in rows on the back.

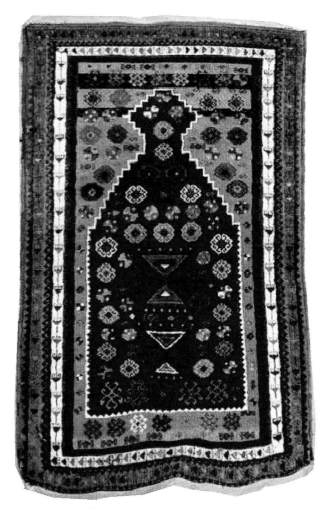

Cihanbeyli prayer rug *Mete Mutlu*

çıkrık (Turk.). Spinning wheel.

ciliated line. A line from which short parallel lines project. The lines may be either curved or straight. Ciliated lines are found in rug designs. See "pectinated line."

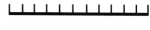

Ciliated line

Circassians. See "Cherkess."

circular carpets. The oldest circular carpet is a sixteenth-century Mamluk piece. There are later circular Cairene carpets. They were probably used to cover the tops of round tables. Chinese rugs with circular shapes or rounded ends were first woven in Tientsin and Beijing in the early

nineteenth century. Circular rugs are now a commercial product of many rug-weaving countries. See "table carpet."

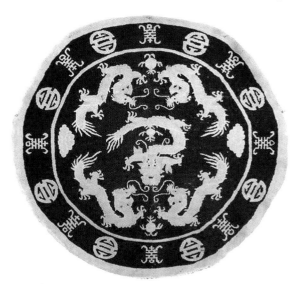

Chinese circular carpet *Grogan and Company*

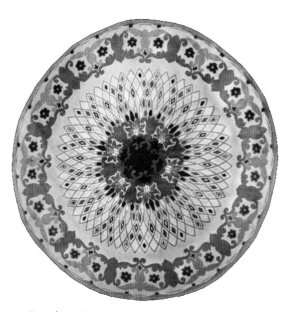

French Art Deco circular carpet *Doris Leslie Blau*

classification. See "design classification" and "rug classification."

closed back. When the asymmetric knot is tied on offset warps so the loop surrounds the warp closest to the back of the rug and wefts are not visible from the back of the rug, the structure is termed "closed back." In this case, the loop is not visible from the front of the rug when the pile is pulled to one side. This structure is used in rugs of Tianjin, China. See "open back."

cloth beam. See "breast beam."

cloud. Clouds are a common motif in Chinese rugs. One symmetrical stylized cloud form is known as "***ruyi.***" It is found in earlier Chinese rugs. Asymmetrical cloud shapes or "drifting clouds" are represented in later rugs. See "chi" and "ruyi."

cloud band. A re-curving, horseshoe-shaped motif originating in China and used in rugs throughout the Middle East.

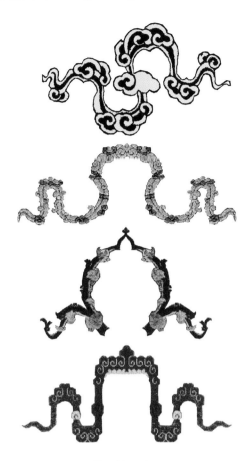

Cloud bands
FROM TOP TO BOTTOM: Chinese, Turkish, Persian, Caucasus

cloud band border. A border of repeated horseshoe-shaped cloud bands originating in sixteenth-century Persian rugs. The cloud bands alternate toward and away from the field.

Cloud band border

cloud collar, sky door, yün-chien. An outline and enclosing design of Chinese origin. It was originally used around the openings of vessels and the openings of garments. The design, or variations, is used around the smoke hole of eastern nomadic tents. It is used as a medallion outline in Near Eastern rugs and may have been the origin of outlines for some Turkmen guls.

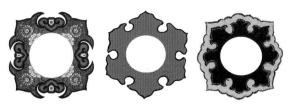

Cloud collars (various interpretations)

cloud lattice. A common all-over field design of Chinese and Eastern Turkestan rugs consisting of a four-sided figure, each side being a bar with in-curving ends. Where this design is used, the field is often yellow with the lattice in blue.

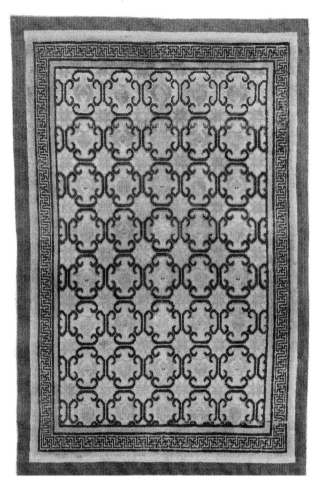

Ninghsia rug with cloud lattice *Sothebys*

Coal Mine Mesa. A Navajo weaving area south of Tuba City in Arizona. Beginning in about 1970, weavers of this area used eccentric weft to outline designs. They also produce twill weaves and saddle bags using eccentric weft for design outlining.

Coccus cacti. See "cochineal."

Coccus ilicis. See "kermes."

Coccus laccae. See "lac."

cochineal. A red dye derived from scale insects. The term "cochineal" usually describes dye made from the dried bodies of the female *coccus cacti*. This dye was imported from the New World as early as 1520 and produced in the Canary Islands in the 1820s. There are other cochineals that may have been used in rugs. These include Armenian Red or Ararat Cochineal from the insect *Porphyrophora hamelii* and Polish Cochineal from the insect *Margarodes polonicus*. The essential dye component of cochineal is carminic acid. Cochineal is far more effective by weight than madder or kermes. The effect of cochineal dye varies with the mordant. A chromium mordant produces purple, aluminum produces crimson, tin produces scarlet and iron mordant produces gray. See "carminic acid," "kermes," and "lac."

Coccus cacti

cockle. A wrinkle in a rug. See "buckle."

coir. Matting made from the spun fibers of coconut husks. It was commonly used for doormats. See "Mourzouck."

colcha embroidery. Colcha is Spanish for "bed covering." Floral motifs embroidered in wool using a self-couching stitch. The embroidery may be on wool or cotton. This style of embroidery was developed by Hispanic women of New Mexico, beginning in the early eighteenth century.

collecting. Oriental rugs and textiles are collected for their beauty, historical value, ethnographic significance, and as investments. Collectors acquire weavings from dealers, auctions (local, national, and on-line), and from local sales of household goods. Local and international societies foster these interests. See "ACOR," "ICOC," and "teppetophilia."

color. That portion of the visual electromagnetic spectrum reflected by objects. In rugs, color depends on the natural hue of the fibers used in combination with natural or synthetic dyes. See "chroma," "hue," "shade," "tint," "tone," "value, color" and "Munsell's color theory."

colorfast, fast. Any dye that retains its strength and vividness despite exposure to light and to washing. See "fading."

color poms. Small bundles of cut yarn to assist in color matching yarn for pile or selecting rug colors for interior decoration.

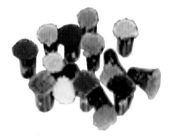

Color poms

colorways. The same design rendered in different color combinations. Used in describing commercial rugs and fabrics.

column rug. See "pillar rug."

comb. A weighted comb is used to beat down wefts over rows of knots in weaving pile rugs. An image of a comb is often used as a filler motif in tribal and nomadic rugs. See "beater," "hava," and "panja."

Commonwealth of Independent Nations (or States). See "Russia."

compartment gul. See "aina gul."

compartment rug, cartouche carpets, mosaic carpets. A term sometimes used as a synonym for chessboard rugs. Commonly applied to rugs of Persia and, perhaps, India that have a rug design consisting of repeated compartments in the field. Usually, the compartments are rectangular or interlocking ogival shapes and are occupied by some floral motif. These may also be called "cartouche" carpets. See "chahar bagh," "Chessboard rugs," "garden carpet," and "honeycomb design."

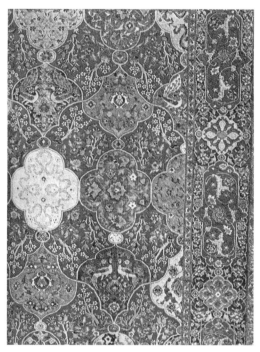

Compartment rug (detail)

complementary elements. Two or more sets of warps, wefts, or other elements of equal structural significance in a fabric.

compound weaves. In simple weaves, there are only two sets of weaving elements (warps and wefts). Compound weaves consist of more than two sets of elements. The additional elements may be supplementary wefts or supplementary warps, or they may be more complicated interconnected or integrated sets of elements.

conch shell. A Buddhist symbol signifying a call to prayer. This symbol is used in Chinese and Tibetan rug designs.

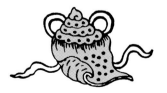
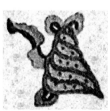

Conch shells

condition. Both beauty and monetary value of a rug are influenced by its condition. Usually, condition is described in technical analysis. These specific conditions are noted:

- Holes, tears, cuts, or alterations in size or shape.
- Extent of pile wear and etching.
- Insect damage in wool rugs
- Dry rot in cotton and wool
- Missing or replaced overcasting.
- Damaged, false, or replaced selvage warps.
- End damage and replaced or false fringe.
- Fading, fugitive colors, stains, bleeding, or discoloration.
- Repairs, darns, plugs, patches, or reknotting.

Confucian symbols. Symbols related to the Chinese philosopher Kong Fuzi (Confucius). The symbols suggest the scholarly life advocated by the philosopher; they are the harp, chessboard, books, and scrolls, each wrapped with ribbons. These symbols are sometimes used as motifs in Chinese rugs. See "Buddhist symbols" and "Taoist symbols."

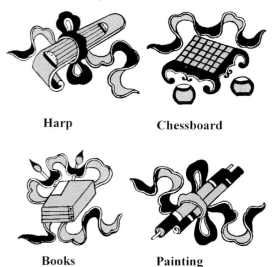

Harp   **Chessboard**

Books   **Painting**

Confucian symbols *After Hackmack*

conga. See "tilma."

Congo red. An azo dye that turns red in alkaline solutions and blue in acid solutions. It is used chiefly as an indicator and biological stain.

conservation. Preserving an object with as little change as possible. In conserving rugs and fabrics, the goal is to prevent further damage or deterioration. Mechanical methods of stabilization of damage, if sufficient, are generally preferable to chemical methods. Whatever method is used must be reversible. See "inherent vice" and "ultraviolet light."

Constantinople. See "Istanbul."

continuity line. A specific rug design for which the importer or distributor has committed to supply the rug dealer on a continuing basis. Often, the rug dealer sells such rugs from a catalog. See "program line."

continuous weft float. A fabric in which wefts systematically pass over two or more warps to form some pattern and the wefts are continuous from selvage to selvage.

contoured. See "sculpting."

conversion factors.
centimeter = 0.39 inch
decimeter = 3.94 inches
meter = 39.37 inches
square centimeter = 0.155 square inch
100,000 knots per square meter =
1,000 knots per square decimeter =
65 knots per square inch
See "knot density."

copper mordant. Copper sulfate is used as a mordant and adds a greenish tone to colors. See "mordant."

Coptic. Relating to Egyptian Christians (Copts). Coptic tapestry weaves and hand-knotted fabrics have survived from the fifth and sixth centuries in Egypt. Rugs, wall hangings, and funereal wrappings exhibit great weaving skill. See "Fustat."

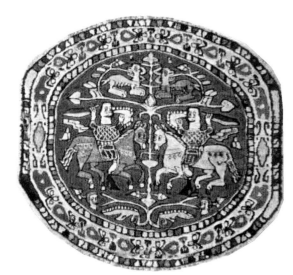

Warriors on Coptic fabric

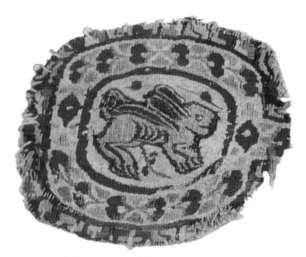

Rabbit on Coptic fabric *Grogan & Company*

Coptic knot. See "Senneh loop."

cord. Extra heavy edge warps in rugs. Also, any yarn that has been replied. See "cabled."

Corfu (Kerkira, Kerkyra). An island off the west coast of Greece, formerly a source of copies of Gördes prayer rugs.

corner. That portion of a rug where the border makes a right-angled turn, or designs in a portion of the field at a corner. See "spandrel" and "unresolved corners."

cornerpiece. See "spandrel."

corners, unresolved. See "unresolved corners."

cornhusk bags. Finger-woven, twined bags made by northwest native American women, particularly the Nez Percé. Carbon dating has shown such bags to be 9,000 years old. Bags were made of grasses, hemp, or cornhusks and designs were rendered in vegetable-dyed fibers.

cornrowing. A corrugated effect in a pile rug that occurs when the pile lies down in flat rows perpendicular to the flow of heavy traffic. See "grinning."

Coronation Carpet. A mid-seventeenth-century Safavid medallion carpet attributed to Isfahan. This rug is of the Polonaise type with gold and silver brocading. It has silk pile and is 17 feet 3 inches by 10 feet. This rug was displayed at the coronation of Frederik IV of Denmark in 1700. It is in the Danish Royal Collection.

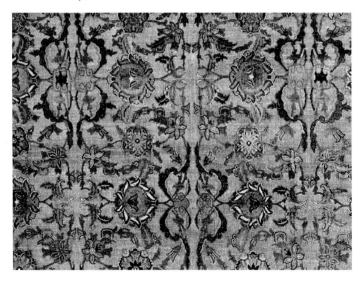

Danish Coronation Carpet (detail)

corridor carpet. A runner about 3½ feet to 4½ feet wide by 8 feet to 12 feet long.

corrosion. See "etching."

cottage industry. The production of goods within the home for sale. For rugs, this form of production is distinguished from workshop or factory production and nomadic weaving. Rugs produced through cottage industry may reflect local or tribal traditions in design and structure, or the dictates of foreign markets when rugs are commissioned by agents of distributors. A contract system has been used in Afghanistan and Iran in connection with cottage industry rug weaving. The contractor provides the weaver with a cartoon, dyed yarns, and rug specifications. The weaver is assured a market for her labor and is spared the investment in materials. She is paid for her labor when the rug is completed.

cotton. Fiber from the seed pod of the plant *Gossypium herbaceum*. The use of cotton in the foundation of pile rugs is a common and very old practice. Undyed cotton is used rarely for small areas of pile rugs where its hard white appearance provides contrast. Cotton is not generally used as an allover pile fiber because of its tendency to mat.

Cotton is grown throughout the Middle East and Asia. Egyptian cotton is known for its long staple, only exceeded in length by Georgia Sea Island cotton. Staple length varies from ⅜ to 2½ inches. Cotton fiber has the cross section of a flattened tube. It is naturally twisted, and this characteristic makes it easy to spin. See "mercerized cotton."

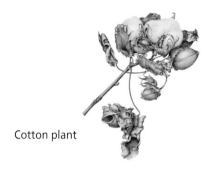

Cotton plant

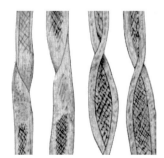

Microscopic view of cotton fiber

cotton count. A measure of size for cotton yarn. It is the number of 840-yard lengths of yarn in one pound. The higher the number, the smaller the yarn. See "yarn size."

countered soumak. See "soumak."

country of origin. The country producing a particular rug. Country of origin may be confused because a design originating in one country may be used in rugs produced by a different country, e.g., Indo-Persian rugs.

coupled-column prayer rugs. Prayer rugs from Ushak and other areas of Anatolia in which arches of the mihrab are supported by pairs of columns rather than by single columns. This design may have evolved into vertical-panel prayer rugs. Many of the coupled-column prayer rugs have lazy lines. Coupled-column prayer rugs are incorrectly attributed to Lâdik. See "Myers Coupled-Column Prayer Rug."

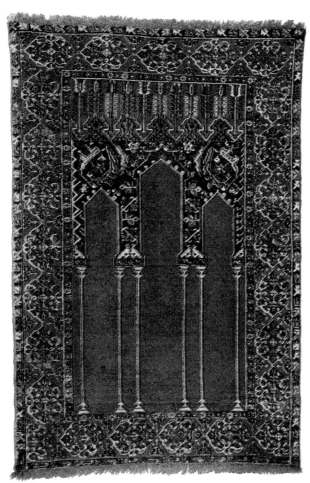

Coupled-column prayer rug

court rug. Chinese, Persian, Turkish, or Mughal rugs commissioned by the ruling court. Usually these were large rugs woven in workshops owned or sponsored by the ruler. These rugs are characterized by the highest standards of workmanship and great sophistication of design. Court rugs were used in royal residences and court buildings and presented as royal gifts, frequently for diplomatic purposes.

cover. See "blanket."

crab border. A border of repeated florets connected by radiating lines suggesting crab claws. This border is often found in rugs of Karabagh.

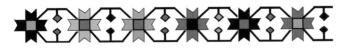

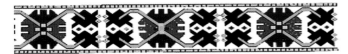

Crab borders

crab design. See "Harshang."

Crab Ushak. A small group of white-ground Anatolian rugs of the sixteenth or seventeenth centuries. These rugs have columns of palmettes vaguely resembling crabs.

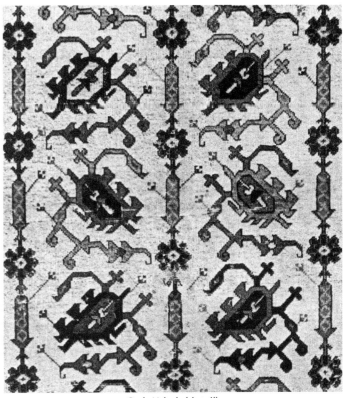

Crab Ushak (detail)

cradle. A bed for a baby. See "nanu" and "salıncak."

crane. The crane is a symbol of long life and is used in Chinese rug designs. It was also the emblem of first-degree officials in the Manchu court. The crane has been represented in Mughal carpets and in contemporary copies of those carpets.

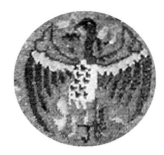 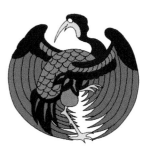

Cranes (Chinese)

crenellated border (French crenelle), castellated border. Suggesting the shape of the battlements of a castle. A reciprocal border design of regular, rectangular indentations and projections. See "reciprocal borders."

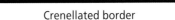

Crenellated border

crewel yarn. A trade designation for thin, lightweight, two-ply, medium-twist wool yarn used in embroidery.

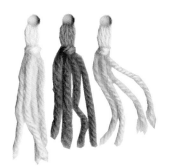

Crewel yarn

Crivelli rugs. Fifteenth and sixteenth-century rugs of Anatolia with large sixteen-pointed star medallions. These medallions are segmented, with segments containing stylized animal images. Rugs with this design were painted by the Venetian, Carlo Crivelli, in 1482 and 1486. An example is his painting "Annunciation" in the National Gallery, London. The sixteen-pointed star is a common motif in Caucasian soumaks and Kazakh pile weavings.

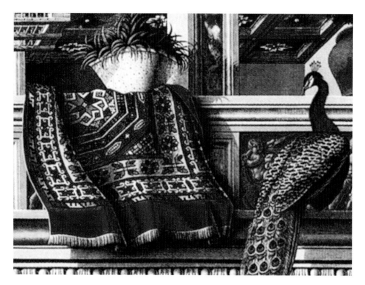

From a painting by Carlo Crivelli

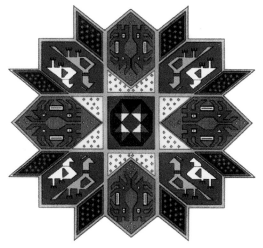

Crivelli star medallion

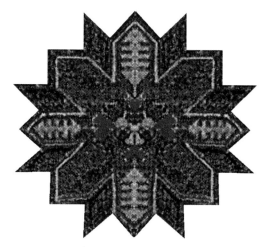

Soumak star medallion (Caucasian)

Pile rug star medallion (Kazakh)

crochet rug. An American rug crocheted of rag strips.

crocin. Yellow dye pigment of the saffron crocus. See "crocus."

crocking. A loss of dye color at points of friction or wear.

crocus. *Crocus sativa*, the saffron crocus, is the source of a yellow dye. Saffron or pollen from the stamens contains crocin, the essential yellow dye pigment of the crocus. Because of its value, saffron was very rarely used as a dye for rug yarns.

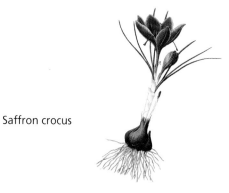

Saffron crocus

cross (Armenian *khach*, Turk. *haç*). Any device, symbol, or design element consisting of a primary vertical and a transverse member. Crosses are a fundamental design element in weavings of many cultures and do not necessarily possess Christian religious significance. The crosses found in weavings include the cross-crosslet, cross-quadrate, tau cross, cross-potent, cross-formée, Greek cross, and St. Andrew's cross. See "dorje" and "Seishour."

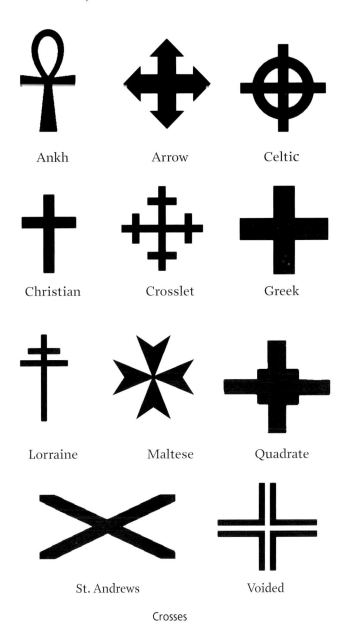

Ankh   Arrow   Celtic

Christian   Crosslet   Greek

Lorraine   Maltese   Quadrate

St. Andrews   Voided

Crosses

cross stitch. A stitch used in American embroidered rugs on a canvas foundation of the eighteenth and nineteenth century. A widely-used embroidery stitch. See "embroidered carpets."

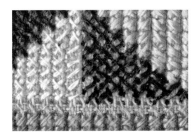

Cross stitch in Uzbek embroidery

cross-woven. A machine-made Wilton rug structure in which rugs are woven side-to-side rather than end-to-end, allowing for a greater variety of colors.

crumb carpet. A carpet cover used in the 18th and 19th centuries in dining areas.

Crystal. A trading post of New Mexico and a source of Navajo weaving. From 1897 through 1930, rugs of the area were woven using oriental rug motifs and diamond medallions with aniline-dyed yarn. During the 1930s and 1940s, some rugs of the area were woven with stripes, using earth-tone vegetable dyes. These rugs are without borders.

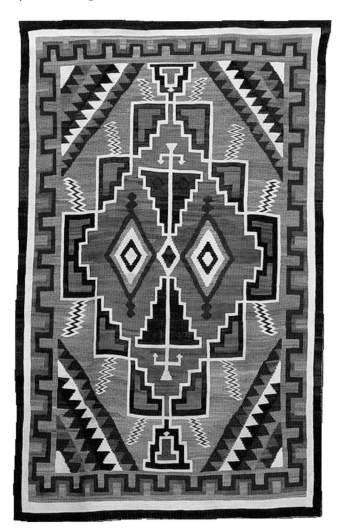

Crystal Navajo rug (detail) *Steve Getzwiller*

çubuklu, çubukli (Turk., "striped"). A border of five to seven parallel stripes in alternating colors, each stripe containing a column of small, stylized blossoms. This border is used in some Kula and Gördes prayer rugs.

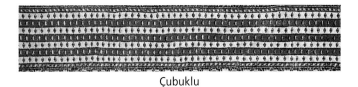

Çubuklu

Cuenca. A city of Spain noted for its wool rugs since the eleventh century. The symmetric knot first replaced the Spanish knot in Spain in seventeenth-century rugs of Cuenca.

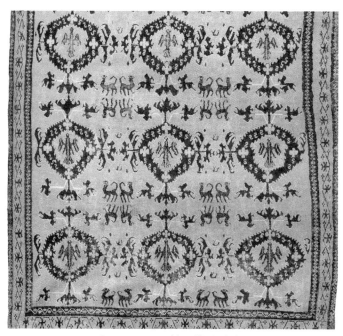

Cuenca carpet (detail) *Sothebys*

çul (Turk.) Fabric of coarse goat hair, loosely woven wool or camel hair. The term may also refer to pieces made of such fabric, to heavy brocading or to a finely woven horse blanket (in Azerbaijan).

cummerbund (Persian kamar-band, "waist band"). A sash worn around the waist by men. Some Shahsavan men wear warp-faced, hand-woven cummerbunds.

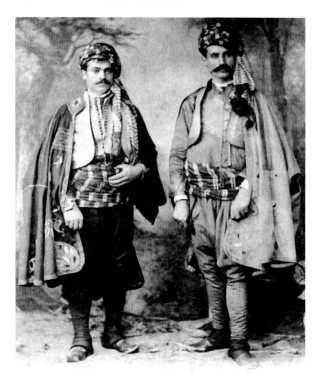

Kurdish men wearing cummerbunds
Foundation for Kurdish Library & Museum

curcuma. See "turmeric."

curled leaf border, ovadan. A main border design of a repeated geometricized curled leaf, one side of which is serrated. The leaves are connected by a vine. This border is used in Turkmen weavings.

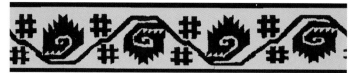

Curled leaf border

curved wefts. See "eccentric wefts."

curvilinear designs. Any design consisting primarily of curving lines. Generally, higher knot densities are associated with rugs of curvilinear design than with rugs of rectilinear or geometric design. See "Motif Variation Examples."

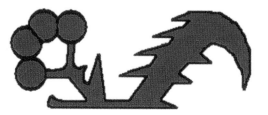

Curvilinear

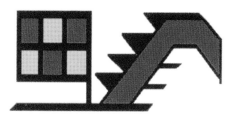

Rectilinear

Versions of a Makri rug border motif

cut-and-loop. A mixture of cut pile and looped pile in power-loomed rugs, originally found in early Italian velvets. Patterns may be created using the two pile structures in different areas and in different pile heights. See "broche carpet."

cut-and-shut. A trade term describing rugs that have been shortened by removing damaged areas and then re-joined.

cut-a-rug. A 1930s and 40s Swing era slang expression meaning to dance energetically or enthusiastically

cutch. See "catechu dye."

cut pile. Any form of weaving in which supplementary wefts or warps are cut at the surface of the fabric to produce tufts. See "loop pile" and "nap."

çuval (Turk.). See "joval."

cypress. An evergreen conifer that is common in countries around the Mediterranean. The cypress tree is a design motif in Near Eastern rugs. It may symbolize mourning. See "tree-of-life."

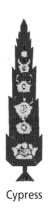

Cypress

Cyrillic alphabet. An alphabet based on the Greek and used in its modern form for Russian and other Slavic languages, as well as many non-Slavic languages of the U.S.S.R. Chronograms and, rarely, inscriptions in the Cyrillic alphabet have been used in Caucasian, Turkmen, and Slavic weavings.

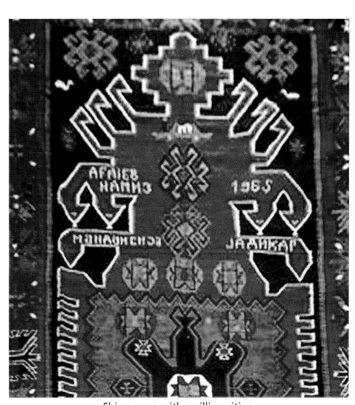

Shirvan rug with cyrillic writing
Azerbaijan Rugs

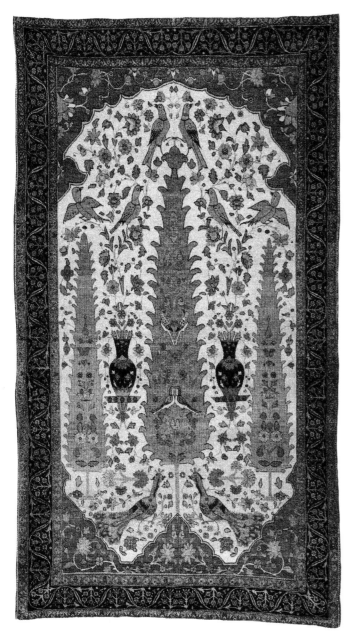

Kerman prayer rug with cypress *Sothebys*

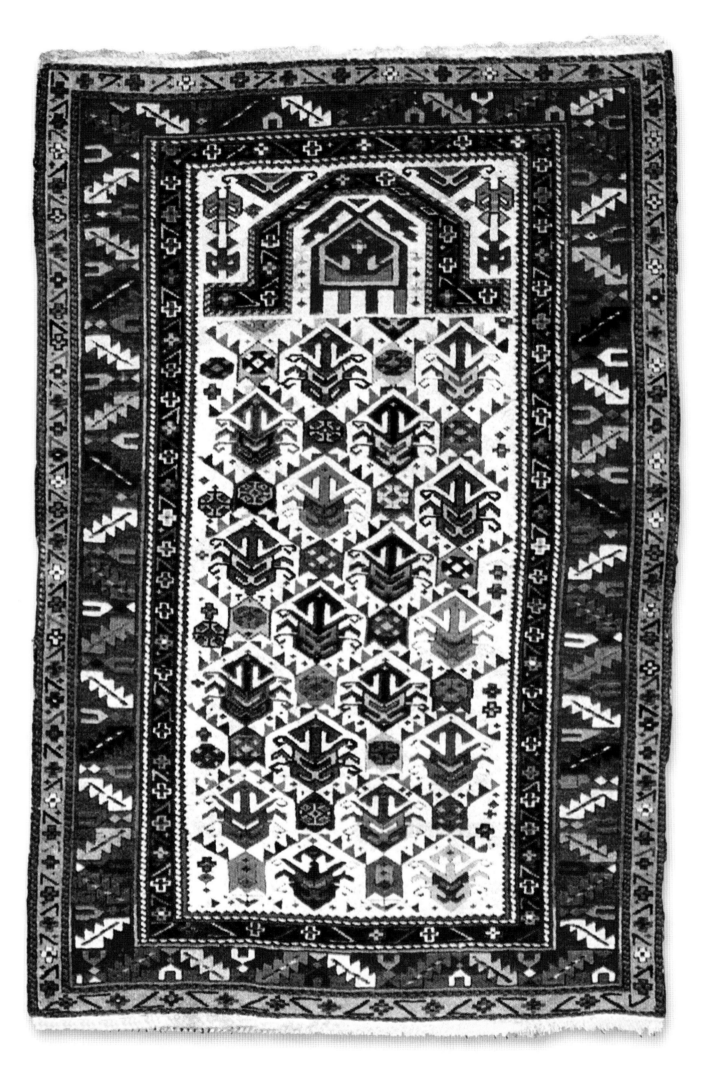

There are a variety of Daghestan flatweaves. Soumaks are woven by Kumyks and Lesghians. Lesghians also weave two-piece kilims or davaghins. Avars weave long mats called chibtas in a tapestry weave. Felt carpets are also produced in Daghestan. See "arbabash," "Avar," "Caucasus," "davaghin," "Derbend," "dum," "Lesghi," "Kumyk," "Kurin," "kiyiz," and "Tabassaran."

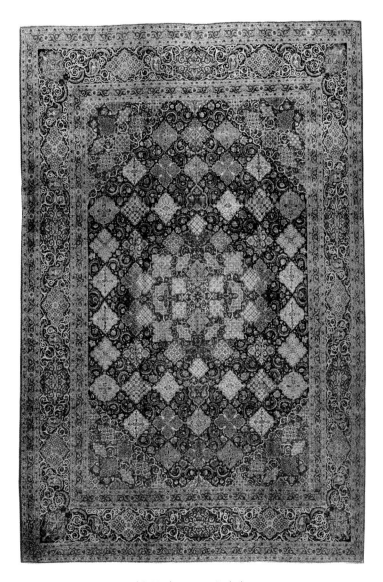

Dabir Kashan rug *Sothebys*

Dabir Kashan. A 20th century rug of Kashan, Iran, woven to the designs of Dabir Sanyen, a Kashan rug designer.

daeva. See "dev."

dagdan. A Turkmen amulet. A minor border design in Sariq weavings.

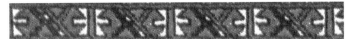

Dagdan border

Dâgh, dag (Turk.) Mountain.

Daghestan. Means "land of mountains." A mountainous region of the northeast Caucasus. Daghestan includes the city of Derbend (Darband) and the area formerly known as "Lesghistan." Nineteenth-century rugs from this region are small and usually have a lattice design, an all-over pattern or Lesghi star medallions. Many are prayer rugs in design, with a lattice or all-over pattern. Rugs of this area have symmetric knots on wool warps. Wefts may be wool or cotton.

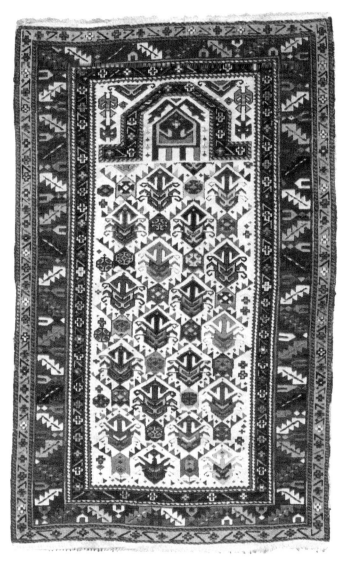

Daghestan prayer rug *Dr. Herbert Exner*

DaHaj. See "Dehaj."

daisy. The central yellow portion of the wild daisy may be used as a yellow vegetable dye in Near Eastern countries.

Dali. A subtribe of the Ersari Turkmen in Afghanistan. Their gul usually contains the trefoil or cloverleaf design element of the Ersari gul.

Damaq. A village of the Hamadan area producing single-wefted, cotton foundation rugs.

Damascus carpets. See "Chessboard rugs."

damga (Turk.). Insignia, totem, or brand. See "tamga."

Daoist symbols. See "Taoist symbols."

daphne. *Daphne gnidium,* a plant whose leaves are used for a yellow dye.

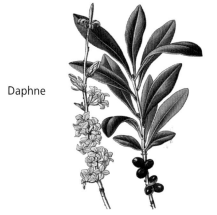

Daphne

Dara-chichi. A town of the eastern Caucasus cited as a source of rugs with the Chichi design. See "Chichi."

Darashuri. A subtribe of the Qashqa'i of southwest Iran whose weavings include rugs, kilims, and four-sided packing bags or mafrash. See "Qashqa'i."

Darband, Darbend. See "Derbend."

Dargazin, Dergazine, Derghezin. A district and village of the Hamadan region of Iran. In volume, this is the most productive of the rug-weaving districts of Hamadan. Many runners are woven here.

Darbar. See "dhurrie."

darn. To mend or patch a hole or other damage to a textile. The stitches used do not reproduce the original structure.

darvaza medallion. A medallion or gul used in Charshango Ersari, Salor, and Kizil Ayak Turkmen weavings. It is a complex symmetrical polygon including six to eight small hexagons.

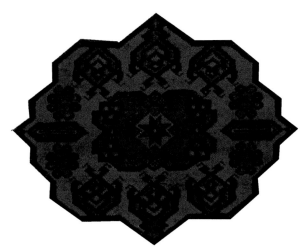

Darvaza medallion

dashgah, tezgâh (Turk., from Persian dastgâh). Loom.

dastarkhan. An Afghanistan embroidered eating cloth. See "sofreh."

dates. Dates may be woven into the design of rugs. Usually the date is presumed to be the year that the rug was woven or presented as a gift. There is some skepticism about the reliability of such dates because a weaver may use a much earlier date or may copy a date from an earlier rug. A little re-knotting may add decades or centuries to the date when a rug was woven. See "chronogram," "chronography of oriental rugs," "dating rugs," "Gregorian dates," "Islamic dates," and "post knotting."

dating rugs. A variety of methods are used to establish the age of oriental rugs. Purchase and inventory records may be used to determine the minimum age of rugs. Such data are useful where there is an unbroken trail of the history of ownership or provenance. Rugs have been dated by comparing their designs to those of rugs in old paintings. Since the age of most paintings can be reasonably determined, the painting sets the minimum age of the design type.

Rugs may have a date woven into the design and this is sometimes presumed to be the year the rug was woven. For some rugs, the evolution of the design is well established. A rug of that type may be dated according to the stage of design evolution of the rug. Within specific design types, a more curvilinear rendering of the motif or a comparatively narrow border may suggest an older rug.

Structural features may be useful in estimating age. For some types of rugs, a higher knot density or a wool foundation may suggest greater age. A simplified selvage or edge finish may suggest later production. A maximum age is set for rugs containing machine-spun yarn, depending on when such yarn was introduced into the area of attribution.

Dye analysis can be used to establish the approximate maximum age of rugs containing synthetic dyes when the dates and areas of initial distribution of those dyes are known. Archaeological techniques of carbon dating and stratigraphic dating are used for finds of ancient weavings. Silk may be dated by the ratios of amino acids it contains in a recently developed method. Since etching, fading, and pile wear increase with use and the passage of time, these conditions may be used to make a very rough estimate of the age of a rug. See "carbon dating rugs," "chronogram," "chronology of oriental rugs," "dates," "dye analysis," "Gregorian date," "Islamic dates," and "provenance."

datisca. *Datisca cannibina,* a hemp-like plant used as a yellow dye in the Caucasus.

Daulatabad. A town of northern Afghanistan. The town is a collection point for rugs woven in surrounding villages. Uzbeks and Turkmen of the area weave carpets. The term "Daulatabad" also refers to a design of large octagon guls surrounded by multiple borders. These are brownish-red carpets with designs in dark blue.

davaghin. A flatwoven rug of the Avars in Daghestan. The design consists of hooked diamond medallions called rukhzal ("house" or "cage"). The medallions are red on a blue field. See "Avar."

Dazkiri. Means "bare field." A village in central, western Anatolia. Rugs from the village have a design of a large lozenge with spandrels. The lozenge and field are filled with geometricized florets. Antique Dazkiri rugs often have an intense green.

dead wool. See "tabachi."

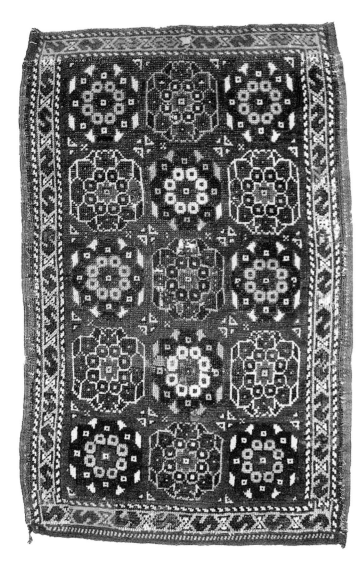

Dazkiri yastik *Wendel Swan*

Deccan. The lower or southern penninsula of India. Deccani embroideries are antique silk and metal thread embroideries from central India. Also, a breed of coarse-wooled Indian sheep. See "India."

decimeter. See "conversion factors."

decorative rugs. Contemporary hand-made, knotted pile or flat-woven rugs woven in factories from cartoons. Most of these rugs are designed for the Western market and produced for export. The term may also describe some older, large commercial carpets such as those known as Heriz, Serapi, Mahal, or Agra. See "workshop rugs."

decorative styles, interior decoration. See these entries: "Adam," "Art Moderne," "Art Nouveau," "Arts and Crafts," and "Bauhaus."

deer. Images of deer are used in rugs of India, Persia, and China. In Chinese rugs, the image of a deer may suggest longevity or money. See "ky'lin."

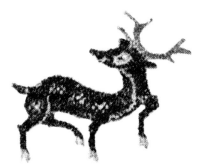

Deer (Chinese)

Dehaj, DaHaj. A town about half way between Yazd and Kerman and a source of Afshar rugs. See "Afshar."

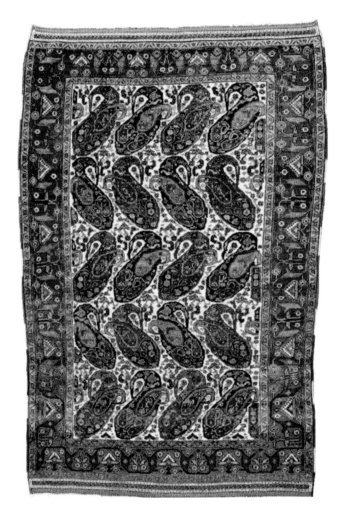

Dehaj rug *John Collins*

Dehbokri. A Kurdish tribe of western Azerbaijan in Iran. The tribe was a source of village rugs and kilims.

delphinium zalil. A source of yellow dye. It may be referred to as esparek. See *"esparek."*

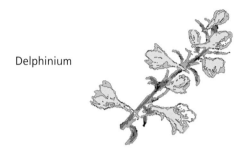

Delphinium

Demirci, Demirji (Turk.) "blacksmith," "ironmonger". A town of northwest Anatolia producing red-wefted rugs sometimes designated by the trade as ***Kömürcü Küla*** ("coalman's hat" or "charcoal burner's hat"). These rugs are single-wefted or alternately single and double-wefted within the same rug. They have dark colors and often have an arch at both ends.

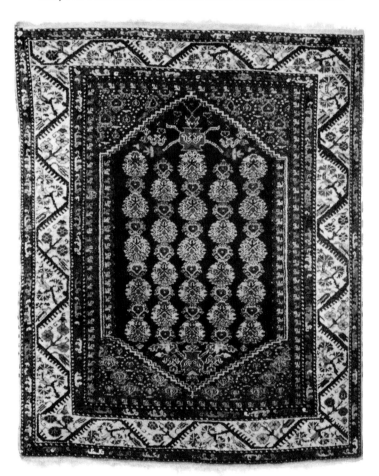

Demirci rug (detail) *Grogan & Company*

den (Tibetan). Pile rug.

denier. A measure of the fineness of single filaments or yarns, especially silk, rayon, and nylon. The denier equals the weight in grams of 9,000 meters of yarn or filament. The higher the denier, the larger the diameter of the yarn or filament.

Denizli. A town of southwest Anatolia and a source of kilims and jijims.

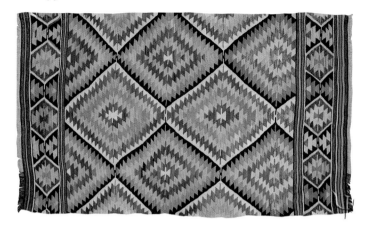

Denizli kilim (detail)

depressed warp. See "warp offset."

derakhti (Persian) "like a tree." A tree-of-life design in Persian rugs. See "tree-of-life."

Derbend, Darband, Darbend, Derbent (Persian, "defile, pass"). The major city of Daghestan, located on the coast between the Caspian Sea and the mountains. Nineteenth century rugs of Derbend have a lattice or all-over pattern of geometricized flowers. The term "Derbend" may suggest a Daghestan rug of lower knot density to those in the rug trade. See "Caucasus" and "Daghestan."

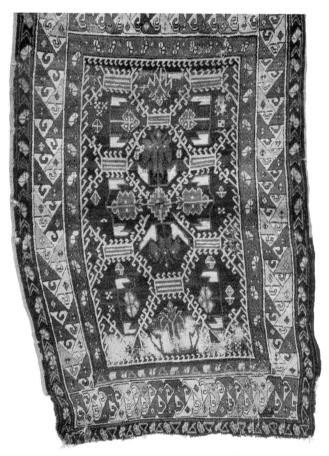

Derbend rug (detail) *Grover Schiltz*

Dereköy. A town of central Anatolia. This town is a minor source of small rugs with floral patterns.

Dergazine. See "Dargazin."

Derghezin. See "Dargazin."

design. The overall composition of decorative elements of a rug. The ornamental aspect of a rug or textile consisting of lines and/or colored areas. These make up images or patterns intended to be visually pleasing or symbolic. A design often consists of an arrangement of motifs. See "design classification," "drawing," "motif," and "pattern."

design classification and description. Generally, the overall character of a rug design can be described as geometric or curvilinear.

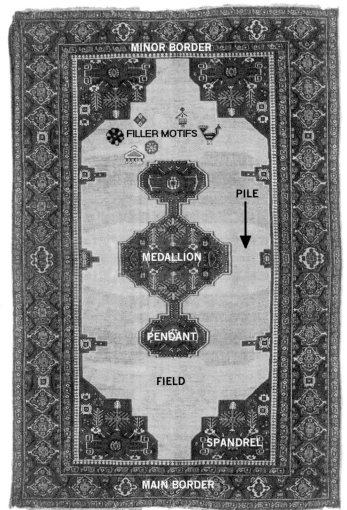

Typical parts of a rug design

Designs may be directional, in which case the rug is intended to be viewed from a specific vantage point (such as a prayer rug or pictorial rug) or non-directional (such as rugs with all-over repeated motifs). Within these broad categories, fields are classified as:

Single medallion
Multiple medallion
All-over repeat
Vase
Compartment or garden
Pictorial
Prayer
Empty field

The elements of the field may be described according to universal or specific motifs such as boteh, Herati, Memling gul, and so on. Other design elements may be cartouches, pendants, spandrels, panels, skirts, inscriptions, dates, and so on. Main borders may be classified as:

Meander
Reciprocating
Rosette
Palmette
Cartouche
See "border," "curvilinear," "field," "geometric," "medallion," and "rug classification."

design plate. A colored rug design drawn on graph paper. It usually shows one quarter of the rug. A row of color squares on the plate may show all the colors used in the rug. See "cartoon" and "loom drawing."

The design plate may be scaled up to actual size for a loom drawing from which weavers work. Color-matched yarn samples may be attached to the loom drawing. See "cartoon," "loom drawing," and "talim."

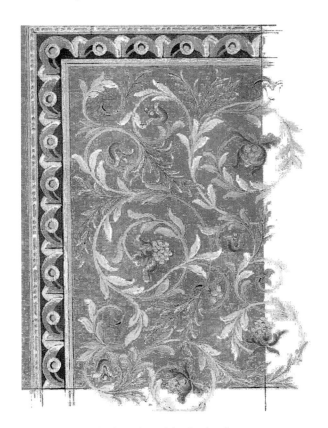

Design plate *John Stockwell*

dev (Turk.), **daeva, div.** In Zorastrianism and Near Eastern mythology, a demon or malevolent spririt, sometimes pictured in oriental rugs. See "Zoroastrianism."

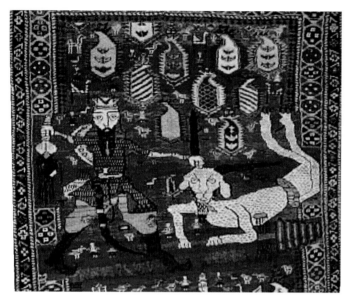

Caucasian rug showing Rustem fighting a dev
R. John Howe

dezlik (Turk.). See "dizlyk."

dhurrie, durrie, jamkhani, satrangi. A flatweave of India made of cotton. Dhurries are woven throughout India. Virtually all the kilim structures may be used in dhurries, including slit weave tapestry, interlocking wefts, dovetailed wefts, and eccentric wefts. Traditionally, dhurries are used as floor coverings and bed covers. Some dhurries have been woven with mihrabs for use as saffs and prayer rugs. Between 1880 and 1920, dhurries were woven in Indian prisons. Many of these dhurries meet the highest standards of design and structure. Dhurries may be referred to as satrangi (Persian, "checkerboard") and jamkhani. Darbar (Persian, "court") is a very large dhurrie woven for use as a floor covering in public buildings. See "Mourzouck."

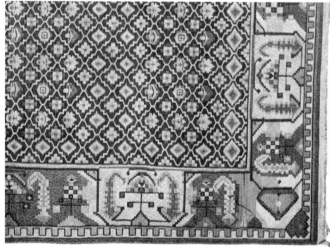

Dhurrie (detail) *Sothebys*

diagonal wefts. See "eccentric wefts."

diamond. A square or rhombus so oriented that a line connecting opposing corners is either horizontal or perpendicular to the horizon. See "lozenge."

diaper. An all-over pattern of small, repeated, and interconnected units of design, often geometric in character.

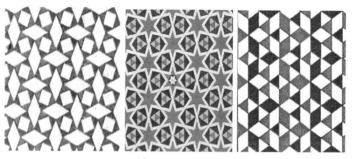

Diaper patterns

dihari. A unit of production for rug-weaving of 6,000 knots, used in India.

Dilijan. A town of the south central Caucasus thought to be a source of Kazak rugs. See "Kazak."

Dilley, Arthur Urbane. See "Hajji Baba Club."

dip khali. A mat or small rug placed at the entrance of a nomad's tent.

direct dye. A water-soluble dye that can be applied without a separate mordant process for the fiber. Congo red is such a dye.

directional field design. Any rug field design that is intended to be viewed from a particular vantage point. Prayer rugs and pictorial rugs have directional designs. See "non-directional design."

discontinuous wefts. Wefts that do not extend from selvage to selvage. They are either cut or reverse direction. See "lazy lines" and "tapestry weave."

distaff. A staff used to hold wool, flax, or cotton during spinning.

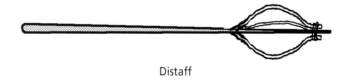

Distaff

distresssing. Treating rugs to make them appear older than they are. See "Tuduc, Theodore."

div. See "dev."

divan cover. Turkish, two-part pile pieces used as couch covers. These were made in mirror image strips with borders on the ends and outside edges and without borders where the two pieces meet at the back of the divan.

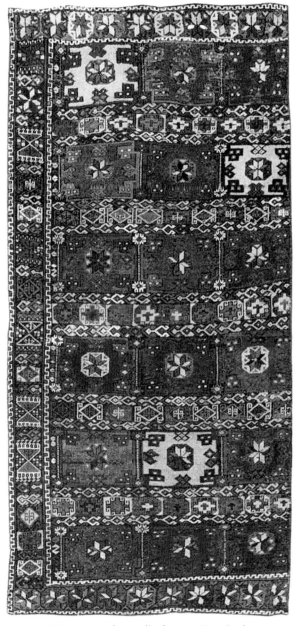

Divan cover (Anatolian) *Jason Nazmiytal*

divâri (Persian, "wall cover"). Vertical carpet loom.

Diyarbakır. A marketing center for Kurdish rugs in eastern Anatolia.

diyugi. Coarsely-woven all-purpose Navajo blankets. See "Navajo rugs."

Dizai. A Kurdish tribe of the Erbil plain in Iraq and a source of poorly dyed rugs. The more commercial variety is woven as runners. The tribe also weaves soumak and tapestry woven bags and banded kilims.

dizaine. Ten knots square, 100 knots. A measure of weaving production for Savonnerie rugs.

dizlik. See "dizlyk."

dizlyk, dezlik, dyslyk (Turk. *diz,* "knee"). A camel knee cover.

djidjim. See "jijim."

DOBAG. An acronym for *Dobğal Boya Araştırma ve Geliştirme Projesi,* a Turkish phrase meaning "Natural Dye Research and Development Project." The term describes contemporary natural-dyed, all-wool, symmetrically knotted rugs woven by cooperatives in Ayvacık and the Yuntdağ Anatolia. Production of these rugs began in 1981.

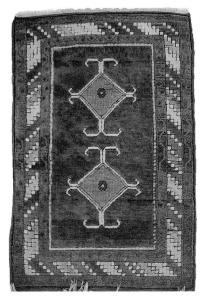

DOBAG rug (detail) *Lloyd Rowcroft*

Dobruja. A region of southeast Romania and northeast Bulgaria, along the Black Sea coast. It is a source of kilims with stripes or geometricized animal figures. See "Romania."

Dokhtar-e Gazi (*-qâzi*). Means "the judge's daughter." A sub-tribe of the Timuri inhabiting an area around Herat, Afghanistan. Many of their rugs have a prayer design with an all-over pattern of geometric elements and a six-sided mihrab. See "Timuri."

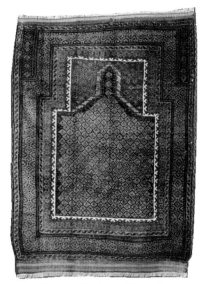

Dokhtar-e Gazi rug *Simon Knight*

dokumak (Turk.). To weave.

dollar rugs, penny rugs. Early American, home-made, small rugs consisting of fabric disks about the size of a silver dollar sewn to a fabric backing. A similar rug of penny-sized disks.

dome and squinch carpets. See "Holbein carpets."

DOMOTEX. An annual international carpet industry trade show.

Donegal. In 1858, a factory for weaving hand-knotted rugs was opened in the village of Killybegs in Donegal, Ireland. Hand-knotted rugs have continuously been woven at this factory. Contemporary rugs are woven at knot densities from 16 to 36 knots per square inch on linen warps. Designs tend to be neoclassical or reproductions for museums and estates. See "Ireland."

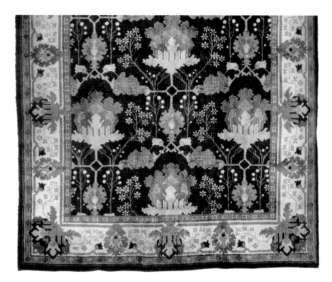

Donegal rug (detail) *Sothebys*

dorje, vajra. Dorje is Tibetan for "sacred stone." Ritual objects of the Lamaist Buddhist religion in Tibet. The dorje is shaped like a small bar bell and symbolizes coiled lightning. Crossed dorjes are sometimes shown in Tibetan rugs.

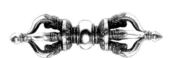

Dorje   Dorje motif

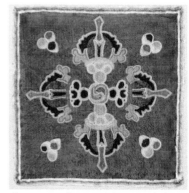

Tibetan small mat with crossed dorjes
Mae Festa & R. John Howe

Dorna. A trade designation for a grade of Romanian rug with 25 knots per square inch on a cotton foundation.

Dorokhsh, Doruksh, Dorukksh, Duruksh. A town of the Qainat region in northeast Iran noted for its rug production. Designs are floral motifs and medallions. Older rugs have wool foundations while newer rugs have cotton foundations. Knot densities are between 130 and 260 knots per square inch. The jufti knot is used. See "Qainat."

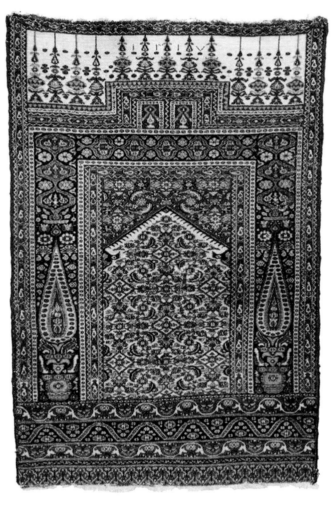

Dorokhsh Prayer Rug *Grogan and Company*

doruka. A double sided Kashmir shawl.

Doruksh, Dorukksh. See "Dorokhsh."

doshak. See "joval."

Döşemealtı, Dösmealti. A town of southwestern Anatolia, just north of Antalya. Only a few small rugs are woven in Döşemealtı. Rugs attributed to Döşemealtı may have been woven in Antalya. See "Antalya."

double ikat. Ikat for which both warp and weft are dyed before weaving. See "ikat."

double interlocking weft. In a tapestry weave, wefts that link or pass through two other wefts in reversing direction at the edge of differently colored adjacent areas. This structure is found in flatwaves of the Bakhtiari of Iran and the Kazakh or Uzbek weavers of Afghanistan. See "interlocking weft."

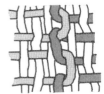

Double interlocking weft

double knotted, double faced, double sided. A very few Persian pile rugs have been woven with pile surfaces on both sides, each side presenting a different design. These rugs are reversible. They are noted as rare and novel demonstrations of the weaver's technical skill rather than as beautiful or artistic productions. Some early rya rugs were knotted on both sides. Double knotting may also refer to the Jufti ("double") knot. See "Jufti knot."

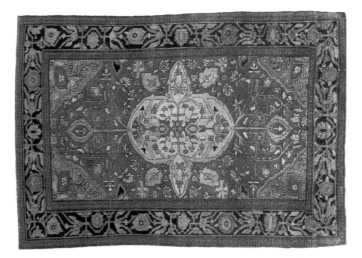

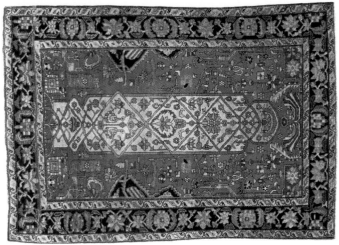

Double knotted Sarouk Farâhân rug *Grogan and Company*

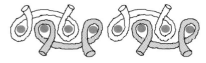

Double knotting (warp end view) *After Collingwood*

double outlining. Rugs in which two lines of contrasting color are used to outline and distinguish design elements from the ground or field. See "outlining."

double prayer rug. Rugs with opposing prayer niches or mihrabs. An apex of a mihrab is located at each end of the rug. See "opposed arch prayer rug."

doubling. Spinning plied yarn into cord.

Doukhobor rugs. The Doukhobors are a Russian religious sect that immigrated to Canada from the Caucasus in 1899. They wove knotted pile rugs (*kovri*) and kılıms (*polası*). Their pile rugs were woven with the symmetric knot on a wool foundation and sometimes with warps of hemp. The rugs are double wefted. Colors were bright and designs were usually composed of Caucasian motifs. Kilims were used as rugs, blankets, and wall hangings. They were woven in the slit weave tapestry structure with simple, bold designs.

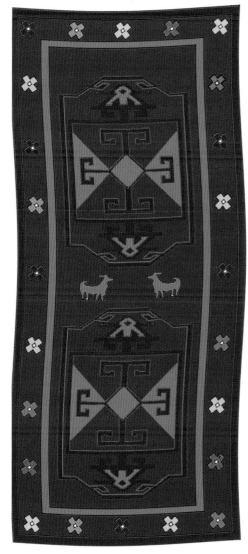

Doukhobor rug

doutakapi. In India, a jufti knot. See "jufti knot."

dovetailed. See "warp sharing."

dowry rugs. In many tribes of the Near East, it was customary for a woman of marriageable age and her female relatives to weave rugs and bags for her dowry. Since these pieces were for the weaver's own use, they were thought to be of higher quality and of more traditional design than other weavings. In the rug trade, dealers may refer to any high-quality tribal piece as a dowry rug.

dozar (Persian). A rug size, about 6 feet by 4 feet. The term is not correctly applied to a rug intended as a sleeping mat. "Dozar" means two zars. See "zar."

dragon. See "dragon and phoenix."

dragon and phoenix. The dragon (lung) is an important motif in Chinese rugs. It represents the Emperor and symbolizes the power of nature and the universe. Kuiluog refers to the stylized archaic dragon often seen in the medallions of Chinese rugs. Two opposing dragons are sometimes shown in combat over a flaming pearl, the symbol of perfection. These highly stylized opposing dragons may have been the source of the dragon designs in the Caucasian Dragon Carpets. "S" shapes in the fields and borders of Persian and Turkish rugs are thought to be versions of the dragon motif. An Anatolian dragon and phoenix carpet in the Islamische Museum, Berlin, is attributed to the fifteenth century, though this dating is questioned. See "ajdaha," "sileh," and "'S' motif."

The phoenix (feng huang), less frequently used in designs, represents the Empress in Chinese rugs, the colors of the phoenix symbolizing the five cardinal virtues. Sometimes the dragon is shown with the phoenix. Together, they symbolize happiness and good fortune. See "ajdaha," "kuilung," "phoenix," and "simurg."

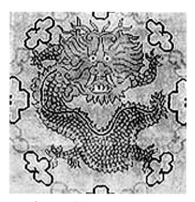

Dragon from a Chinese rug *Jason Nazmiyal*

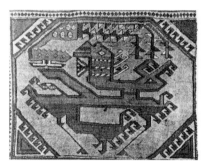

Panel from the Berlin dragon and phoenix carpet

Dragon carpets. The design of this carpet is a lattice of leaf shapes containing palmettes and stylized animals in combat, usually very highly geometricized dragons. Carpets of this design are among the oldest to be attributed to the Caucasus. There are sixteenth century examples. They were first thought to have originated in Kuba; now, it is believed they originated in Shusha. In these rugs, worn areas in the front reveal periodic heavy, cabled wefts in the foundation. The designs of dragon carpets were probably derived from earlier carpets of Kerman, themselves influenced by the vocabulary of Chinese art. See "kuilung."

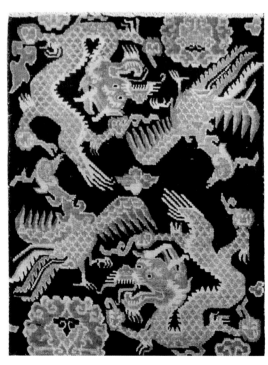

Tibetan rug with dragon and phoenix *Jason Nazmiyal*

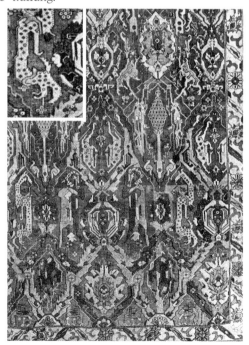

Dragon carpet (detail)

dragon soumaks. Nineteenth and twentieth-century Caucasian rugs in the soumak structure with designs derived from Caucasian Dragon carpets. Progressive abstraction has made the dragon unrecognizable in most of these soumaks. Recently, these flatweaves have been primarily attributed to the northeast Caucasus. See "soumak."

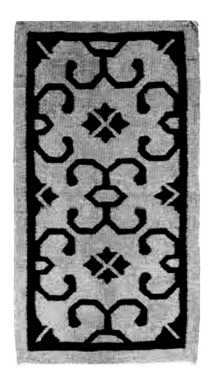

Drugget designed by Gustav Stickley *Treadway Galler*

drumze, dromze (Tibetan). Pile rug.

dry rot, mildew. Dry rot is the result of the growth of fungi. Damage to rug fiber occurs when the fungi produces hyphae which penetrate fibers and break them down. Fungi thrive especially on the cellulose in cotton, but they also grow on wool. Fungi grow in warm and humid or wet conditions. The ultra-violet rays of sunlight arrest growth. After a cotton foundation is exposed to fungi, it loses strength and becomes brittle. Cracking or creaking in a rug when it is bent indicates dry rot. A rug can be tested for dry rot by passing a fold down the length of the rug while listening for a cracking sound.

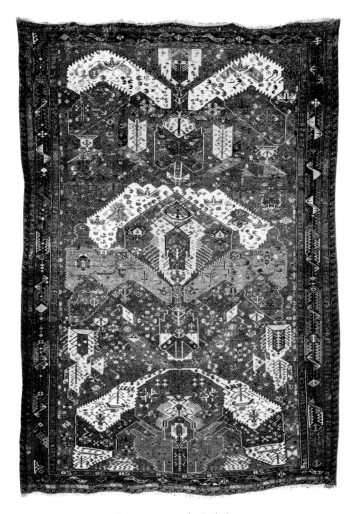

Dragon soumak *Sothebys*

drätt (Swedish). A flatwoven cover made for benches.

drawing. The fineness or degree of detail with which a rug design is executed.

draw-in rug. A hooked rug. See "hooked rug."

dromze. See "drumze."

drop match. A power-loomed carpet with a diagonal repeated pattern. Such patterns require more yardage when they must be matched at seams. See "set match."

drop repeat. An endless vertical repeat pattern.

drugget. A flatwoven rug of India with cotton warps and coarse wool wefts, wefts of rag strips or filling, made in solid colors, stripes, or checks. A heavy felted rug of wool or cotton. Any coarse woven fabric used as a rug. See "Chindi drugget."

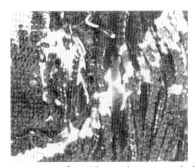

Dry rotted cotton wefts with wool warps and pile intact

dshudur. See "gul-i badam."

Dudin, Samul Martynovich (1863-1926). Curator of the Museum of Anthropology and Ethnography in Leningrad, scholar of Islamic and Buddhist art, and collector of Central Asian rugs and ethnic weavings. During expeditions to Central Asia for the Museum, Dudin collected more than 200 rugs and animal trappings. One hundred forty of these are of Turkmen origin. These constitute one of the largest, oldest, and most carefully documented collections of Turkmen weavings.

Dudley Carpet. Named for a Lady Dudley. A seventeenth-century Persian carpet with flowering trees, shrubs and plants in horizontal rows on a red field. This "Shrub" design is a possible precursor of the weeping willow design and the Joshegan design. The size of the rug is 11 feet 6 inches by 9 feet 5 inches. See "Shrub rugs."

düğüm (Turk.) Knot.

dulicha. A cotton pile rug of India.

dum. A kilim used as a cover of Kurds in the Caucasus and the Avar and Kumyk of Daghestan. The field includes three stepped diamond medallions or three Lesghi star medallions in red on a blue field. Borders are meandering floral vines. See "Avar" and "Kumyk."

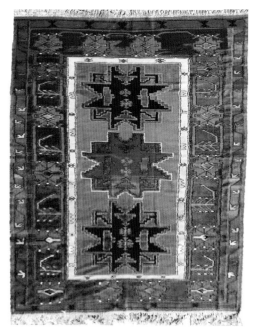

Avar dum *Michael Phillips*

dumba sheep. The fat-tailed sheep, *Ovis platura*, common throughout the Near East and Central Asia. See "Karaman" and "sheep."

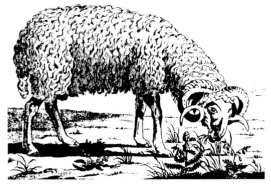

Dumba sheep

durbar carpet. A long Indian carpet, one that may be appropriate for state functions.

durrie. See "dhurrie."

Duruksh. See "Dorokhsh."

dusting. Removing dirt from a rug with a carpet beater. See "carpet beater."

Dutch East India Company (Vereenigde Oost-Indische Compagnie). The Dutch East India Company had trading settlements in Masulipatam and southern India from about 1600 to 1670. Indian rugs for import to Europe were a major commodity. In Holland, these were more often used as table coverings than on floors because of their costliness. Dutch paintings of the period show these rugs in use on tables. See "Holland."

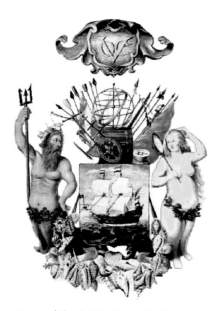

Arms of the Dutch East India Company

düz dokuma yaygi (Turk.). A flatwoven rug.

dye. A substance used to color fiber, yarn, or textiles with or without the use of a mordant. Originally, dyeing of rug wools was practiced by weavers. In countries with a long tradition of rug weaving, dyeing developed as an independent and skilled craft. The actual colors achieved in dyeing depend on many variables. These include dye quality, mordant, trace elements in water, acidity of the water, dye bath temperature and timing, fiber quality, and the amount of grease or soil in the fibers. See "acid dyes," "basic dyes," "direct dye," "dye analysis," "dye, natural," "dye, synthetic," "over-dyeing," "mordant," and "vat dye."

dye analysis. Determining the chemical composition of dyes used in oriental rugs and their natural or synthetic origins. This information is useful in establishing the age and attribution of oriental rugs. If one knows when a specific dye was first introduced to a region, then that date is the maximum age of any rug from the region containing that dye. If a rug contains dyes that are not characteristic for the region of attribution, then the rug's attribution to that region may be questioned. Chemical analysis is performed by treating sample fibers or extracts from fibers with reagents in a specified sequence. Analysis may also be conducted by means of chromatography or spectrophotometry. See entries under these names.

dye, natural. Dyes derived from botanical or animal sources. Natural dyes are prized in oriental rugs because such dyes generally produced a more harmonious color pallet than synthetic dyes. Natural dyes fade evenly and consistently. In addition, natural dyes suggest an older rug. Because natural dyes are prized, there is a movement to use them in contemporary rugs. See "DOBAG." Natural dyes are classified as vegetable or animal. The larger group is vegetable dyes. Here are some of the more common vegetable dyes used in rugs categorized by the colors they produce.

Blue: indigo.

Brown or black: catechu dye, oak bark, oak galls, acorn husks, tea, walnut husks

Green: indigo over-dyed with any of a variety of yellow dyes

Orange: henna

Red: madder, Brazilwood, logwood

Yellow: artemisia, buckthorn, centaury, chamomile, daphne, datisca, delphinium zalil, fustic, onion skin, pomegranate, safflower, saffron, sophora japonica, rhubarb, sumac, turmeric, weld

See entries under these names. The animal dyes are derived from scale insects, all producing shades of red. These are cochineal, kermes, and lac. See entries under these names.

dye, synthetic. Dyes prepared through chemical processing rather than the processing of botanical or animal sources. An early successful synthetic dye, mauve, was developed by Perkin in 1853. By 1870 synthetic dyes had begun to displace natural dyes in rug weaving areas.

Certain colors became available to weavers that had not been used previously and this changed the traditional color combinations in the rugs of some regions. Some early synthetic dyes changed color or faded rapidly. Others bled or washed out and some retained their original harsh intensity while different colors in the same rug faded gracefully.

Synthetic alizarin was introduced in about 1870 and devastated the agricultural production of madder. A wide variety of dyes for different colors were eventually developed from compounds of alizarin.

About 1880, azo dyes were generally available. Azo dyes produced red, yellowish orange, brown, and blue. Ponceau 2R and Roccelline are red azo dyes used in nineteenth-century oriental rugs. In 1910, synthetic indigo began to be used in rug yarns. In the fiber, this dye is chemically indistinguishable from vegetable indigo. It quickly supplanted vegetable indigo.

By 1920, analine dyes were widely used. They were, however, fugitive in color and prone to fading. Because these dyes were damaging to the Persian rug trade, Reza Shah prohibited their use and required only natural dyes for oriental rugs. His attempt to regulate dye use was unsuccessful.

Chrome dyes are modern synthetic dyes used with a mordant of potassium dichromate. These dyes produce an almost infinite variety of colors. They are fast and non-fugitive. See "acid dyes," "aniline dyes," "azo dyes," and "basic dyes."

Synthetic dye development chronology:

1774 Prussian blue

1853 mauve

1858 magenta

1861 methyl violet

1862 analine blue

1871 alizarin

1872 methyl green

1876 malachite green

1876 Orange II

1880 azo dyes (Ponceau 2R)

1884 Congo red

1885 benzopurpurine

1887 rhodamine B

1890 direct black BH

1891 diamine green

1891 sky blue FF

1897 indigo

1901 flantherene yellow

1908 hydron blue

1915 chrome dye

1956 Procion

dyers weed, dyers rocket. See "weld."

dyrnak gul (Turk. "claw"). A diamond gul, quartered, with external and internal hooks used in Yomud, Chaudor, Chubbash, and Ersari weavings. See "gul."

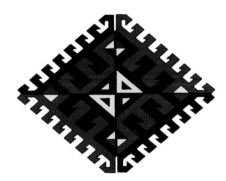

Dyrnak gul *After Moshkova*

dyzlyk. See "dizlyk."

dzheinamaz, jäynamäz (Persian, "place of prayer"). See "prayer rug."

dzhidzhim. See "jijim."

dzo ke-thil (Tibetan). A narrow, pile-woven band for decorating the neck of a yak or dzo (a cross between a yak and cow).

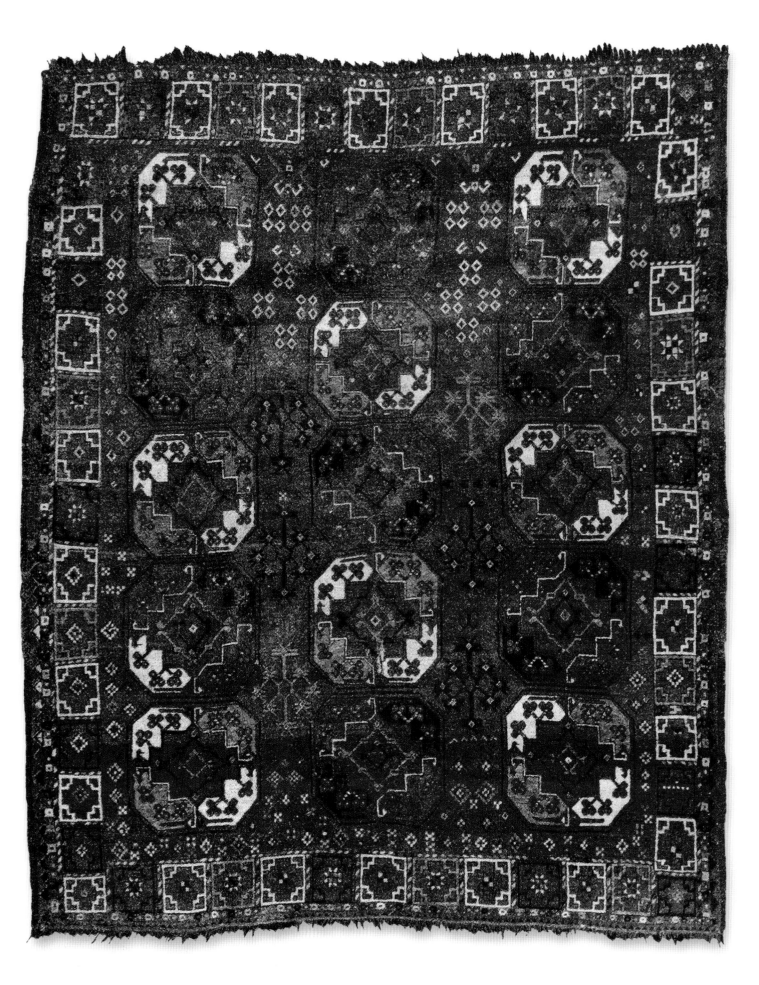

eagle group. Problematic subclassification of Yomud pile weavings based on structural properties.

eagle gul. A gul thought to be used by the Göklan Turkmen and, possibly, the Yomud. It is no longer associated with the Imreli. The gul is complex, consisting of a hexagon within a border of spikes and rams' horns. The gul is not quartered. The eagle gul is thought to be a stylized floral palmette. See "gul," and "Göklan Turkmen."

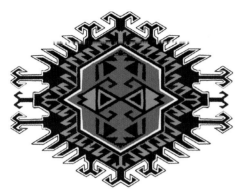

Eagle gul *After Moshkova*

Eagle Kazak. See "Chelaberd."

Eastern Turkestan, Chinese Turkestan. An area of southwestern Xinjiang province in western China. It is inhabited primarily by Turkic-speaking Muslims. Rugs of Eastern Turkestan may be termed "Samarkand" because Samarkand (in Western Turkestan) was once a trading center for Eastern Turkestan rugs. Wool rugs of this area usually have asymmetric knots with densities of about 40 to 100 knots per square inch. Silk rugs may have knot densities up to 300 knots per square inch. Designs are usually medallions or all-over geometric elements. A distinctive rug of eastern Turkestan is a long saff with different floral elements in each mihrab. See "Kâshgar," "Khotan," "Lop Nor," "Urumqi," "Xinjiang," and "Yarkand."

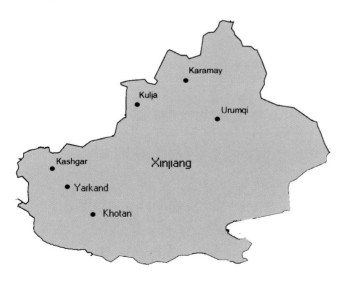

Eastern Turkestan

East India Company. See "British East India Company."

eccentric wefts, curvilinear wefts. Wefts that deviate from a perpendicular orientation to the warps. In kilims or tapestry weaves, diagonal or outlining supplementary wefts are sometimes used. These are eccentric wefts. See "kilim" and "tapestry weave."

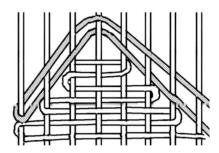

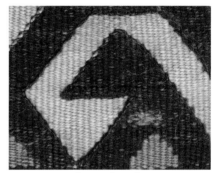

Eccentric weft

Echmiadzin. An ancient city located in southern Armenia. It is the seat of the primate of the Armenian church. Nineteenth-century rugs of this area are classified as Kazak rugs.

edge finish. An on-loom or off-loom treatment of edges of a fabric to protect, strengthen, or decorate them. The edge finish in rugs includes the outermost warps, ground wefts passing around those warps, selvage wefts or wefts that are not continuous with the foundation and overcasting, consisting of various accessory stitches to which accessory structures or objects may be attached. Edge finishes may be in colored segments, checkered, or barber pole stripes in nomadic or tribal rugs. Tassels, pompoms, cowries, or coins may be attached. The structure, fibers, and design of edge finishes are important features in rug attribution. See "overcasting" and "selvage."

Edwards, Arthur Cecil (1881-1951). Edwards was born in Turkey and entered the carpet trade at the age of 16. He was for many years the primary agent of OCM in Persia. In 1948 Edwards wrote *The Persian Carpet*, an authoritative description of rug production in Iran during the early twentieth century. See "OCM."

Egypt. A bed cover with symmetrically knotted linen pile was found in the tomb of Kha and dated to 1400 B.C.E. Cut pile rugs were woven in Egypt as early as the pre-Islamic period, in the sixth century. Heavy tapestry weaves were produced in Fustat in the ninth century. The greatest period of Egyptian carpet weaving was during the reign of the Mamluks, when brightly colored rugs with complex geometric designs were woven in Cairo beginning in the latter part of the fifteenth century. In the sixteenth century, after the Turkish conquest (1517), rugs were woven in Cairo in Ottoman designs. By the late seventeenth century knotted rug production had all but disappeared.

Due to limitations on imports, knotted rug production began again in the 1950s. There is no significant export of these rugs made in Persian, Turkish, and Caucasian designs. Knot counts in contemporary Egyptian rugs are expressed as 4 x 5, where the first number is knots per centimeter weft-wise and the second number is knots per centimeter warp-wise. Thus, 4 x 5 is 20 knots per square centimeter. See "assyuti," "Ben Adi," "Cairene carpets," "Coptic," "Fustat," "Harrânia tapestry," "Helwan," "Mamluk carpets," "para-Mamluk," "Quseir al-Qadin," and "Ramses Wissa Wassef."

ejderha. See "ajdaha."

Elaziğ. See "Rashwan."

elem, alam, alem (Turk., "banner, flag"). Skirt; the end panels outside the main border of Turkmen bags, ensis, and rugs. These end panels may be pile or flat-woven. In rugs, elems are at both ends, but only at the lower ends of ensis and bags. Also, a transverse panel above the mihrab in a prayer rug. See "alınık."

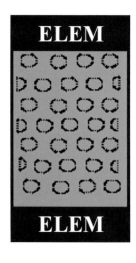 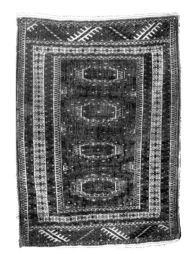

Rug with elems

elephant foot. A common reference to any octagonal Turkmen gul design in a rug.

elibelinde (Turk., "hands on hips"). This term describes a motif common in kilims consisting of a highly geometricized human figure with hands on hips. See "Çatal Hüyük."

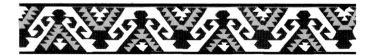

Elibelinde border

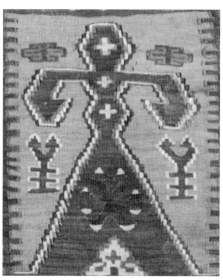

Elibelinde motif

ell. An old English and Flemish unit of linear measure equaling 27 inches. Until the development of broadloom carpeting, the ell was a standard measure of carpet width. See "gauge."

Ellis, Charles Grant (1908-1996). Charles Grant Ellis was a Research Associate of the Textile Museum in Washington and the leading scholar of classical oriental rugs. From 1940, he was devoted to rug research and by 1950, had translated the works of German rug scholars into English. He was noted for his phenomenal memory of specific rugs, their features, and locations. He authored many research publications.

Elisavetpol. See "Genje."

Ellora, Ellore, Eluru. A town of southeast India. It has been a rug weaving center since the seventeenth century and was formerly a source of finely woven rugs. Current rug production consists of small, coarsely knotted copies of Persian models. See "India."

embossing. See "sculpting."

embroidered carpets. Carpets of ornamental needlework, usually on a linen canvas base. A wide variety of embroidery stitches may be used. There are near eastern examples and large eighteenth and nineteenth-century English and European embroidered carpets with very sophisticated designs. There are many examples of small American embroidered rugs from the eighteenth and nineteenth centuries. These may be termed "yarn-sewn" rugs. They were often used as hearth rugs. Designs consisted of floral motifs, domestic animals, rural or domestic scenes, or nautical motifs. See "Arraiolos," "cross-stitch," "needlepoint," "Resht," and "suzani."

embroidery. Decorative needlework. More specifically, decorative accessory stitches made in a fabric. There is a great variety of such stitches. These are broadly classified as flat stitches, which may cross or overlap but do not interlock, looped stitches, where stitches are interlocked in various ways, and knot stitches, in which some type of knot is formed in the stitch. There is a very large production of contemporary machine-made needlepoint rugs. See "suzani."

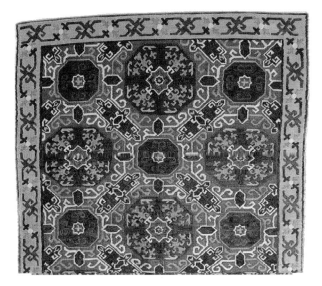

Caucasian embroidery (detail) *Peter Pap Oriental Rugs Inc.*

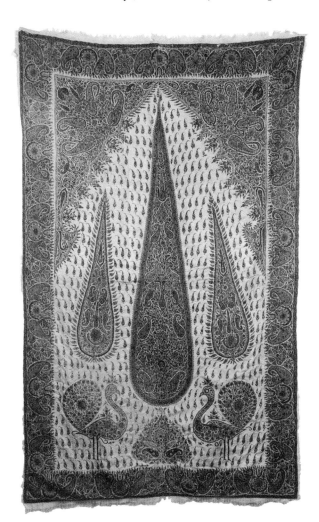

Persian embroidered shawl *Grogan and Company*

Emperor Carpets. See "Animal Carpets of Leopold I."

end. The top or bottom edges of a rug where the warps project from the foundation.

end dip. Warp ends that have been dyed after weaving to produce a colored fringe in the finished rug. A practice used in some Turkish rugs.

end finish. The end of a pile rug or flatweave, where the warps project from the foundation, must be finished in some way to prevent wefts or pile knots from unraveling. For a flatweave, the fabric may be folded and stitched to lock the ends. Warps may be braided, plaited, or knotted to hold wefts in place. A variety of macramé, systems may be used to lock the ends. Warps my be twisted in pairs or in groups. Weft twining, weft chaining, or soumak weave is sometimes used for the same purpose. See "fringe" and "saçak."

endless knot. A motif showing a symmetrically arranged strapwork or cable knot or loops with no ends or a design suggesting a knot. Design versions of an endless knot are used as a minor motif in Persian, Turkish, and Chinese rugs. See "ch'ang."

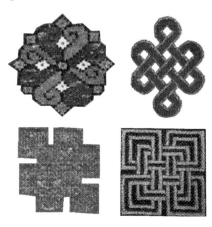

Endless knots
TOP: Qashqa'i, China. **BOTTOM:** China, Tibet

endless repeat. A motif or design repeated vertically and horizontally in the field of a rug and interrupted by the borders. See "all-over pattern" and "field repeat."

England. The earliest English hand-knotted rug dates from 1570. Most early hand-knotted and needlework rugs were copies of Turkish designs. Some early rugs were hand-knotted on a flax foundation. Early rugs were commissioned with armorial bearings. In the seventeenth century heavy, flatwoven carpets were produced in Kidderminster (Worcestershire) and Wilton (Wiltshire). Looms for weaving hand-knotted rugs, based on Brussels models, were set up in Wilton in 1720. In the late eighteenth century, Thomas Whitty began weaving hand-knotted rugs in Axminster. Designs incorporated Adam and Greco-Roman motifs. In the nineteenth century, production of hand-knotted carpets declined as power-loomed production of tufted carpets developed. See "Axminster," "Brussels," "ingrain," "Kidderminster," "Moorfields," "Morris, William," "Strathmore Carpet," "Voysey, Charles," and "Wilton."

enhancement. See "painting."

Enjelâs, Injilas, Enjilas. A town some ten miles southeast of Hamadan in Iran. Villagers in the area weave rugs with the symmetric knot on single-wefted, scatter-size rugs with a cotton foundation. The knot density is from 130 to 160 knots per square inch. The designs are Herati pattern or all-over botehs.

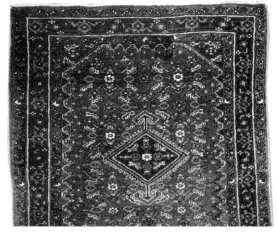

Enjelâs rug (detail) *Peter Pap Oriental Rugs Inc*

Enjilas. See "Enjelâs."

ensi, engsi (Turk.), **pardeh, purdah** (Persian, "curtain"), **goyo** (Tibetan). A felt or pile rug hung over the door of Turkmen tents. The pile ensi design usually includes four compartments with these divisions creating a cross or "khatch" in the center of the rug. See "berde," "eshik tysh," "germesh," "goyo," and "khatchli."

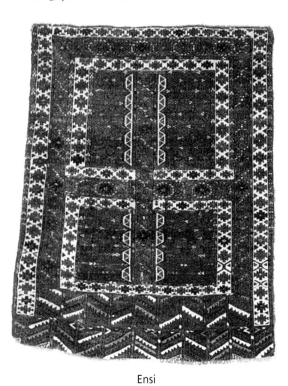

Ensi

Epirus. A Greek province and the source of silk embroideries dating back to the 17th century. It is also a source of contemporary flokati rugs.

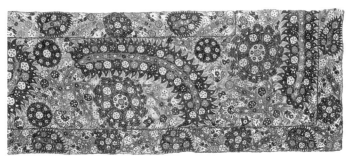

Epirus embroidered panel (detail) *Sothebys*

Erbil. A town of north central Iraq and a market for Kurdish rugs. These rugs are woven in the area by members of the Dizai, Girdi, and Mantik Kurdish tribes.

Erdmann, Kurt (1901-1964). A scholar of early oriental rugs and the author of many publications on oriental rugs. He was director of the Islamic Department, Berlin State Museums, and Professor of Islamic Art at the University of Istanbul.

Erivan, Erevan, Yerevan. A city and province in the south central Caucasus, now Armenia. Nineteenth-century rugs of this area are usually classified as Kazak rugs. There is contemporary production of rugs in Erivan. These have a cotton foundation. See "Armenia," "Echmiadzin," and "Kazak."

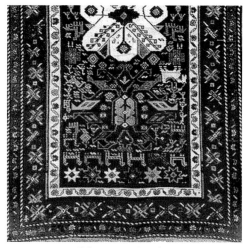

Erivan rug *Armsite*

erre gul. A Turkmen gul consisting of an indented rectangle with a flower at the center and crosses at top and bottom. There are in-pointing arrowheads at the sides. In a variation, a diamond occupies the center.

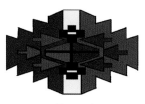

Erre gul

Ersari. A group of Turkmen tribes of northern Afghanistan and Turkmenistan. The Ersari emigrated from the eastern shore of the Caspian Sea in the seventeenth century to the valley of the Amu Darya river. Some scholars consider rugs specifically attributed to Bokhara as Ersari productions while others do not. The Kizil Ayak and Dali are considered subtribes of the Ersaris and the Chub Bash may be a subtribe. Ersari weavings include a larger design repertoire and variety of rug sizes than do the weavings of other Turkmen tribes. Some of these designs, such as botehs and minâ khâni, are of non-tribal origin. Turkmen rugs may have been attributed to the Ersari when there is no specific basis for attributing them to some other tribe. The main carpet of the Ersari, carrying the gulli gul, was a major rug export of Afghanistan in the late nineteenth century. See "Afghan," "Babaseqal," "Beshir," "Chakesh," "Chub Bash," "Dali," "Jengal Arjuk," and "Kizil Ayak."

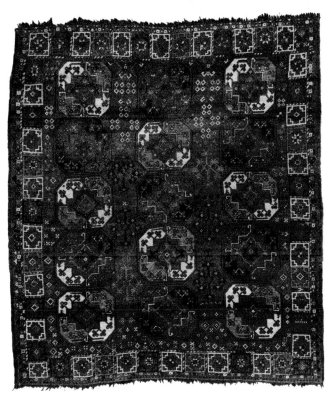

Ersari main carpet *Sothebys*

ertman gul, ertmen gul. A Turkmen gul used in the weavings of the Chaudor tribe and, possibly, those of the Yomud. The gul is a partially stepped diamond with projections terminating in a ram's horn. See "Chaudor."

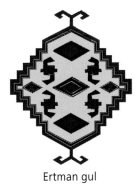

Ertman gul

Erzurum. A town of eastern Anatolia, southwest of Kars, that serves as a collecting point for eastern Anatolian village and nomadic rugs. Erzurum is, itself, a source of kilims. These are small prayer kilims with pointed or stepped mihrabs and multiple borders.

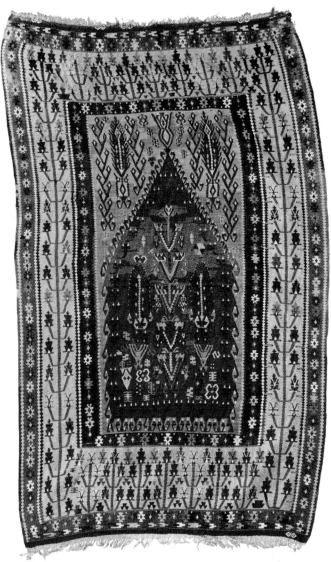

Erzurum prayer kilim *Sothebys*

escutcheon. A shield or similarly defined area displaying an armorial bearing. Escutcheons are sometimes included in the designs of specially commissioned rugs. See "armorial rugs" and "Girdlers' Carpet."

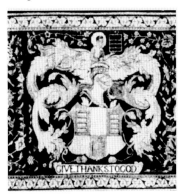

Escutcheon from the Girdlers' Carpet

Esfahan. See "Isfahan."

eshik tysh. A Kirghiz tent door hanging. See "ensi."

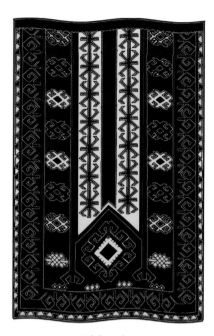

Eshik tysh

eslimi. See "islimi."

Esme. A town of western Anatolia near Uşak. Kilims are woven here, traditionally in shades of pink and gray. Recent kilims are in shades of brown.

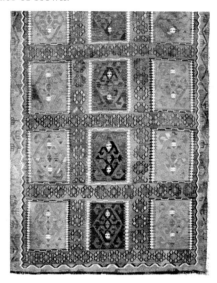

Esme kilim (detail) *Kazim Yildiz*

esparek (Persian), **larkspur, zalil.** A yellow dye obtained from the flowers of the yellow larkspur, *Delphinium zalil*. See "Delphinium zalil."

Estehbânât, Estebanat. A village south of Neyriz in Fars province, southern Iran. Rugs of Estehbânât are usually attributed to the Afshar.

"Esthetic" rugs. A design category of Chinese rugs that were introduced in the 1930s, consisting of Art Deco and Aubusson designs. See "Fette rugs."

etching, corrosion, erosion, oxidized. The loss of pile in colored areas where a dye or mordant was used that contains corrosive salts, usually areas dyed black or brown. Because etching suggests usage and age in a rug, the effect is sometimes imitated by clipping in contemporary rugs. See "inherent vice" and "consesrvation."

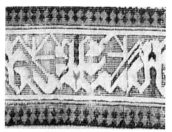

Etching *R. John Howe*

Ethiopia. A country of East Africa. Thick wool rugs in a discontinuous, two-strand, countered weft twining structure are woven in Ethiopia. Grass mats in a weft twining structure are woven by the Gurage people of Ethiopia.

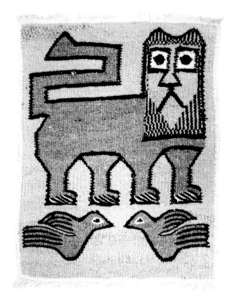

Ethiopian flatweave rug with the Lion of Judah *Wanderloot*

Ettinghausen, Richard (1905-1979). Curator of Eastern Art at the Freer Gallery, Washington, D.C., Professor of Islamic Art at New York University, and Consulting Chairman of the Department of Islamic Art of the Metropolitan Museum of Art, New York. He organized exhibitions of oriental rugs and wrote many scholarly articles on the subject.

euphorbia. A genus of plants flourishing in Anatolia and thought be a to source of yellow dyes in some Anatolian rugs.

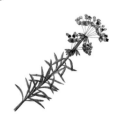

Euphorbia

Everu. A village southeast of Hamadan in western Iran producing rugs with the Herati pattern and copies of the Serabend design. These are coarsely woven, single-wefted rugs.

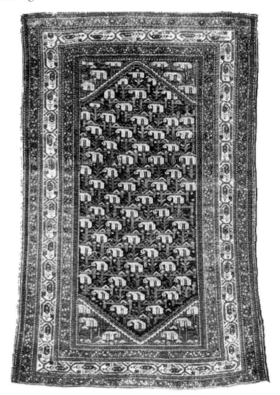

Everu rug *J. Barry O'Connell*

ewer, ibrik (Turk.). A water vessel with a handle and spout seen in side view as a motif in Near Eastern rugs. It is sometimes seen in prayer rugs and may allude to ritual cleansing. It is used as a small filler motif in tribal and nomadic rugs. See "filler motif."

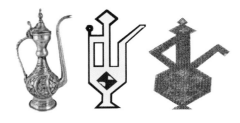

Ewers

extra warp patterning. Supplementary or non-structural warps for decorative patterning that may be continuous or discontinuous within the ground fabric.

extra weft knotted wrapping. A flatweave structure in which continuous or discontinuous supplementary weft is knotted (a true tie) on adjacent sets of warps. See "weft wrapping."

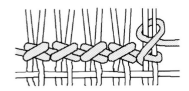

Extra weft knotted wrapping *After Tanavoli*

extra weft patterning. Supplementary or non-structural wefts for decorative patterning that may be continuous or discontinuous within the ground fabric.

extra weft pile wrapping. A fabric structure in which supplementary wefts wrap warps and where loops of weft, cut or uncut, form the pile. Such wefts can be continuous or discontinuous. "Symmetric knots" and "asymmetric knots" are actually systems of extra weft pile wrapping in which loops have been cut. See "knot."

Eye dazzler. A Navajo pattern of horizontally spiked or serrated concentric diamonds and spiked zigzags of contrasting colors.

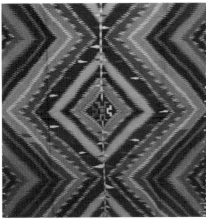

Eye dazzler (detail)

eyerlik (Turk.). A Turkmen saddlecloth or saddle rug. See "saddle cover."

Ezine. A town (formerly Avunya) south of Çanakkale in Anatolia serving as a collection point for rugs woven in the area. Typically, these rugs are red, blue, and yellow in complex geometric designs with arrows projecting from rectangular medallions, often surrounded by the leaf-and-goblet border. They are wool throughout and woven in small sizes. See "Turkey."

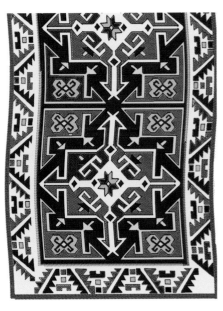

Ezine rug

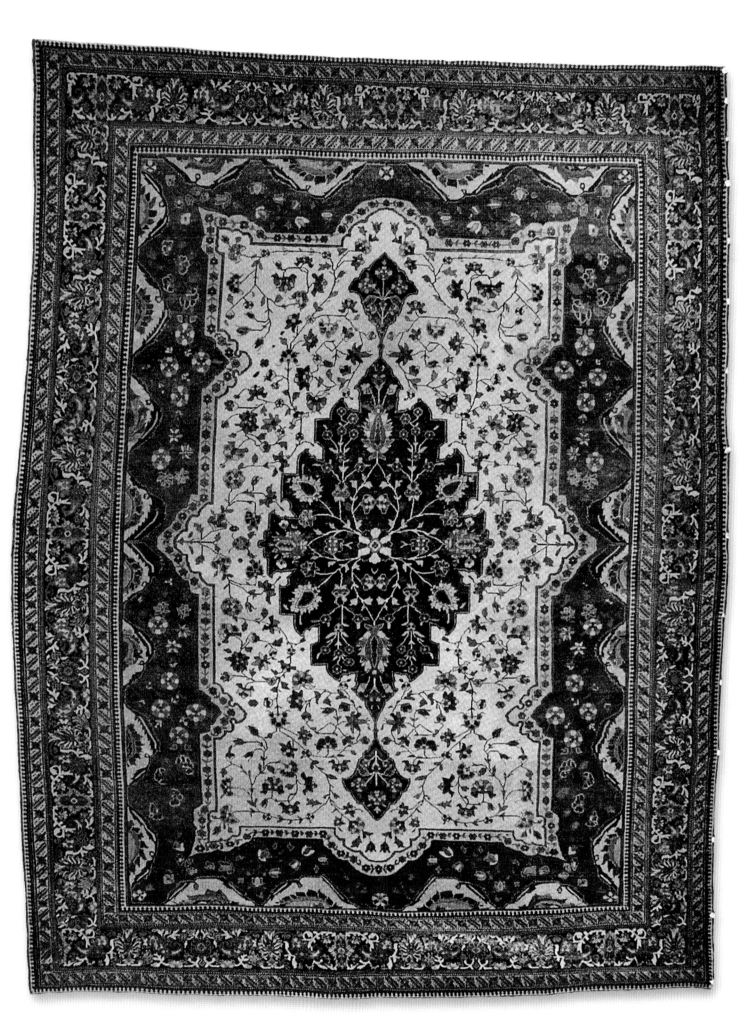

fabric. A construction, woven or otherwise, of spun or unspun fibers.

face. That side of a fabric which is exposed for viewing; the most decorative side of a fabric. A bag face is the pile side or decorated side of a bag that has been cut away from the flatwoven back. See "front."

Fachralo, Fekhraly. A town 25 miles southwest of Tiflis in the Caucasus. Fachralo rugs are classified as Kazaks. Many nineteenth-century rugs attributed to Fachralo have a medallion consisting of a horizontal rectangle superimposed over a lozenge so that a 10-sided figure is produced. The prayer format is common. Average density is about 64 symmetric knots per square inch. The average area for these rugs is 23 square feet. See "Kazak."

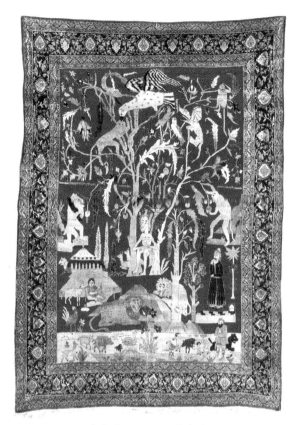

Tabriz fantasy rug *Sothebys*

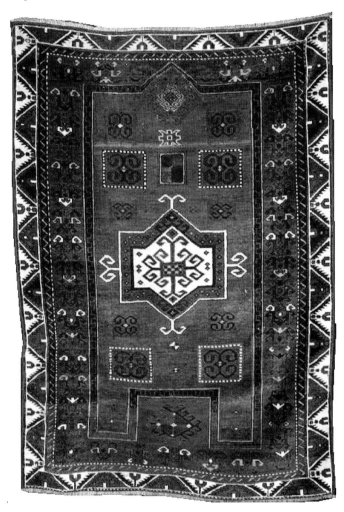

Fachralo rug *Simon Knight*

factory rugs. See "workshop rugs" and "decorative rugs."

fading. See "bleaching."

false selvage. See "selvage, false."

family prayer rug. See "saff."

fantasy rug. A rug with a design containing mythical or fantastic creatures. See "vak vak tree."

Farâhân, Feraghan, Ferahan. A plains area north of the city of Arâk in western Iran. Finely woven nineteenth-century rugs of this area have all-over patterns such as the Herati, Mina Khani, or Gol Hinnai. Most Farâhân rugs have asymmetric knots at densities from 60 to 160 per square inch. These rugs have a cotton foundation with pink or blue wefts. Vegetable dyes were used in their production. Green was more prevalent than in most Persian rugs. This green, described as "celadon" or "apple" was frequently corrosive. Some of these rugs may be referred to as "Farâhân Sarouks," but there is no unambiguous definition of this term.

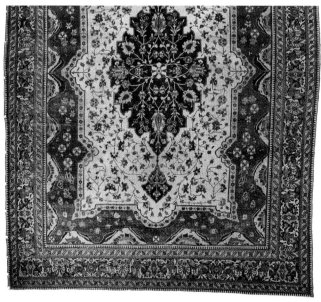

Farâhân rug (detail) *Grogan and Company*

farda (Turk.) A kilim with an empty red field used as a bed cover, often as a ritual bed cover in marriages. See "ruidjo."

Faridan. See "Feridân."

farmash. See "mafrash."

farangi gul, gul farang (Turk. and Persian, "European rose"). The western cabbage rose or related stylizations. See "cabbage rose" and "rose."

farrasie. A small flatwoven, brocaded rug or wall hanging of Pakistan, about 6 feet by 4 feet. The typical design consists of stripes containing geometrical patterns.

Fars. A province of southwest Iran on the Persian Gulf, including the southern range of the Zagros Mountains. The ancient ruins of Persepolis are located in Fars; the province's earlier name, Parsa, in its Greek form Persia, came to be applied to the whole country of Iran. The principal city, Shiraz, is an important rug trading center. Nomadic peoples inhabit the area. These include the Qashqa'i, Khamseh, Lurs, and some Afshars. Rugs have been woven in this province since the ninth century. Many rugs of Fars are of nomadic or tribal origin and woven on horizontal looms. Because of their glowing colors, fine weave, and varied designs, these nomadic pieces are prized by collectors. Nomadic weavings are wool throughout, while later village production is more coarsely woven on cotton warps. See "Afshar," "Khamseh Confederacy," "Lion of Fars," "Lurs," "Qashqa'i," and "Shiraz."

farsh (Arabic). Floor covering.

Fârsi. Persian designation of the Persian language.

Farsi Madan. A subtribe of the Qashga'i.

farsibaff. Asymmetric or Persian knot.

fast. See "colorfast."

Fatima. The daughter of Prophet Muhammad. See "Hand of Fatima" and "Islam."

Fatimid caliphate. An Islamic dynasty ruling North Africa and later Sicily, Egypt, and Syria between 909 and 1171 C.E., claiming descent from Fatima, the daughter of Muhammad.

Fayli Lurs. A subtribe of the Lurs living primarily on the eastern flanks of the Zagros mountains in Iran.

felt. A fabric of random matted animal fibers, usually wool, that adhere to each other after a process of kneading and compression. Scales on animal fibers allow fibers to move in only one direction. As a result, kneading and compression inextricably entangles the fibers. Warmth and moisture speeds this process. Some evidence suggests that felt making by nomadic peoples antedates woven fabrics. Nomadic herdsmen from Mongolia to the Balkans and south through Iran have, through recorded history, lived in tents made of felt.

Felt pieces were unearthed in Pazyryk dating from the third century B.C.E. See "keçe," "koshma," "namad," and "namda."

felt carpets. Felt carpets may consist of mosaic pieces stitched together, inlay structure, or appliqué, work. Inlay structure is used in Afghanistan, Iran, and Turkey to produce complex designs. There are early Chinese examples using this structure. Eighth-century felt rugs of China have been preserved in a treasury in Nara, Japan. Some Turkmen knotted carpet designs are thought to have originated from designs used in felt carpets. Felt rugs are sometimes ornamented with embroidery, fringes, or tassels. See "arbabash," "istang," "namda," "kiyiz," and "shyrdak."

feng huang. Chinese for "phoenix." "Feng" refers to the male phoenix and "huang" to the female. See "dragon and phoenix" and "simurg."

Ferahan. See "Farâhân."

Ferdows, Firadows, Firdaus, Firdous (Persian "Paradise"). A town of northeastern Iran that is a production and collection center for Arab rugs. These small rugs are woven on horizontal looms, are single-wefted, and use the asymmetric knot. Formerly these rugs were similar to Baluchi rugs, but quality has declined.

Feridân, Faridan. A district of Chahâr Mahâl in Iran. The district is a source of single-wefted, Bakhtiari panel design rugs.

fermesh. See "mafrash."

ferrous sulfate. An iron mordant. Iron mordants tend to darken colors and embrittle wool. See "mordant."

Fertek. A village of central Anatolia. Fertek is a source of all-wool prayer rugs and rugs with geometric medallions. In the early nineteenth century, rugs in the Mejidian style were woven in Fertek.

Fethiye. See "Makri."

Fette rugs. Rugs woven in Beijing and Tianjan in the 1920s and early 1930s and designed by Helen Fette for the American market. The rugs were woven by the Fette-Li Rug Company. Natural dyes in pastel shades were used in rugs with Chinese and Spanish motifs. These rugs were woven in circles, semicircles, and ovals, as well as rectangles. See "China."

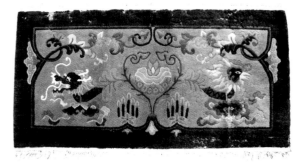

Fette rug *Peter Pap Oriental Rugs Inc*

Fez. A city of Morocco and a source of contemporary factory rugs, many in Persian designs.

fiber. Fiber is the fundamental constituent of fabrics. Natural fibers are classified by source as animal, plant, and mineral. Animal fibers are external (wool and hair), internal (tendons and sinews), and secreted filaments (silk). Plant fibers are seed and fruit hairs (cotton), leaf fibers (sisal), bast or stem fibers (flax and hemp), and bark and root fibers. Mineral fibers include metallic threads and asbestos. See "cotton," "flax," "hair," "metallic threads," "silk," "synthetic fibers," and "wool."

field. The portion of a rug design enclosed by a border, or the major portion of a rug without borders. The field may be unoccupied or contain medallions or an all-over pattern. See "design classification."

field repeat. A rug design in which the same motif or element is copied again and again and distributed over the field of the rug. Rugs with field repeats may also contain medallions. See "all-over pattern."

Figdor Garden Carpet. A small seventeenth-century Persian carpet attributed to Kerman. It is in the collection of the Vienna Museum für Angewandte Kunst. Its main border is missing. The carpet once belonged to Albert Figdor, an Austrian collector. The compartments of the garden are separated by streams containing ducks and fish. It is woven using the vase structure. Warps are cotton and there are two cotton wefts and one silk weft after each row of knots. The pile is wool and there are 196 asymmetric knots per square inch. Brocading of silver gilt wrapped silk is used in the rug. See "garden carpet" and "vase structure."

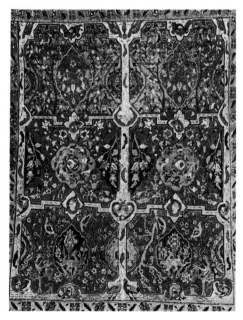

Figdor Garden Carpet (detail)

figural. A carpet in which representations of the human figure dominate the design. See "pictorial rug."

figure eight stitch. An overcasting stitch used for selvages containing two or more warps or warp bundles. The "8" is the path of the overcasting yarn as it passes around the warps.

Figure eight stitch

filé. A metallic strip or gilt paper wrapped around a yarn core. See "metallic thread."

filikli. A very shaggy rug from the area of Karapinar in Anatolia. Unspun Angora goat hair is knotted on four warps. Usually, the pile is natural white, but the rug may be dyed after weaving in a single color. See "tülü."

filler motifs. Small design elements such as florets, stars, geometric figures, and images of ewers, combs, and animals that are scattered around medallions or placed under the prayer niche in rug designs.

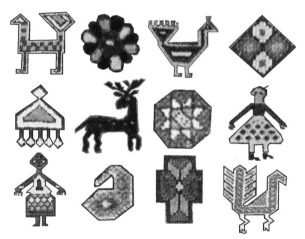

Filler motifs

fil-pai (Persian, "elephant's foot"). The principal octagonal gul associated with each of the Ersari subtribes. See "elephant's foot."

Finland. See "Scandinavian rugs."

Firdous. See "Ferdows."

Firozkohi. A Chahar Aimaq tribe of northern Afghanistan. They weave copies of marketable rugs and a variety of flatweaves decorated with weft float patterning.

Firuzâbâd. A town of southwest Iran and a source of millefleurs prayer rugs woven by the Kashkuli.

fisetin. A yellow flavone dye pigment obtained from fustic and sumac.

fish. Fish are represented in Chinese, Indian, Persian, and Turkish rugs. Fish have special significance in Chinese rugs.

When shown in pairs, fish symbolize good fortune or wedded bliss. They are also emblems of Buddha. The carp symbolizes profit or eminence.

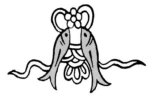 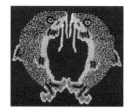

Fish

fish pattern. See "Herati pattern."

five-year plan rug, NEP rugs. Rugs woven in the Caucasus shortly after the Russian Revolution when rug-weaving co-operatives were first established. Such rugs may have synthetic dyes, lack abrash, and have rigidly rendered designs. See "kustar."

flag border. A border of segmented rectangles (kochak cross) used in Tekke and Salor jovals.

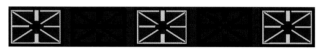

Flag border

flamskäv, flamskavnad (Swedish). "Flemish weave."A type of highly-prized Scandinavian tapestry woven on a vertical loom. These may include complex and curvilinear images. See "rya rugs."

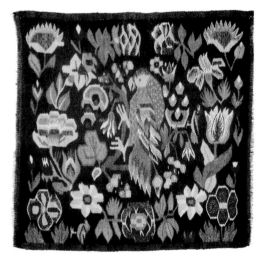

Flamskäv cushion cover *Sothebys*

flatweave. A textile woven without pile. See "cicim," "gadzhari," "jijim," "kilim," "sileh," "soumak," "suzani," "tapestry weave," and "verneh."

flavone or flavonol dyes. Yellow pigment derived from a wide variety of plants. See "luteolin" and "quercetin."

flax. *Linum usitatus-simum.* The fibers from the stalk of this plant are used to make yarn. See "linen.

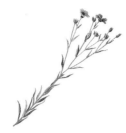

Flax

flea pattern. An all-over repeat pattern of very small botehs.

Fletcher Prayer Rug. A Persian prayer rug with Koranic inscriptions in major and minor borders, thought to be of the 17th century. Its size is 3 feet 6 inches by 5 feet 3 inches. It has a density of 552 asymmetric knots per square inch. Weft is silk. Warp is cotton. Pile is wool. There is some silver brocading. This rug is in the collection of the Metropolitan Museum of Art, New York.

flij. Narrow strips of fabric that are sewn together to make tents for nomadic tribes in Libya and Tunisia.

float weave. In a plain weave, carrying wefts over two or more adjacent warps or carrying warps over two or more adjacent wefts in a systematic manner producing, for example, twills or satins.

flocked. Any rug in which tufts are glued or cemented to a fabric backing.

flokati. A Greek rug of wool with a very shaggy pile with strands up to six inches long. These rugs carry no design or pattern and are usually of natural wool or dyed in bright colors.

floorcloth. Heavy wool or linen cloth or canvas used as a floor covering. The cloth may be painted or stenciled. Using floor cloths was an early American practice.

Floral carpet, Blossom carpet. A design classification of early Caucasian rugs. The oldest rugs of this design are eighteenth-century Caucasian carpets derived from the Dragon carpets. Early examples show a leaf lattice which contains palmettes and a variety of floral motifs.

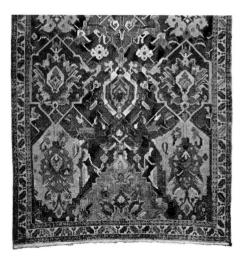

Floral carpet *Caucasian (detail)*

floral motifs. Floral motifs are a universal feature of oriental rug designs. Flowers are represented naturalistically, in many stylized forms, and in many levels of abstraction, all the way to the purely geometric. Within some cultures, specific floral motifs have symbolic meaning. This is particularly true of floral representation in Chinese rugs. Certain flowers are associated with particular countries and their rug designs, the tulip motif in Turkish rugs for example. See entries under specific flowers or floral designs.

floret, rosette. A stylized, generally symmetrical rendering of an overhead view of a flower blossom.

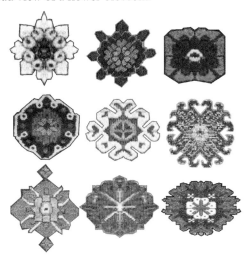

Florets
TOP ROW Persia, Shahsavan, Baluch. **MIDDLE ROW** Kurd, Lâdik, China.
BOTTOM ROW Karabagh, Kuba, Kuba.

floss, flosh, flos, (Turk.). Mercerized cotton polished to look like silk. Sometimes referred to as "Turkish silk."Rugs made of mercerized cotton.

flossa. See "rya rugs."

flying carpet, magic carpet. A legendary green, silk carpet that could carry King Solomon and his court to any location he desired. A similar carpet figures in the *Arabian Nights*. Researchers say that, to stay afloat in air, a sheet measuring about 10 cm. in length and .01 mm. thick would need to vibrate at about 10 hz. with an amplitude of about .25 mm.

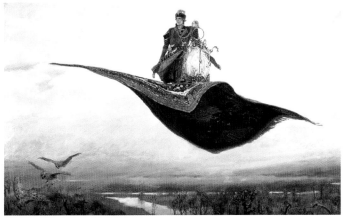

Flying carpet *Vasnetsov*

fo dog. See "fu dog."

forgery, rug. Rug designs are frequently copiedand this is typically acknowledged. A few rugsare deliberately created as forgeries meant to deceive the buyer as to age, origin and authenticity. These may be exposed by dye analysis and other scientific tests. See "Tuduc, Theodor."

format. A general reference to design or pattern. Format may also refer to the size or length-to-width proportions of a rug. See "shape ratio."

foshou. See "Buddha's hand."

Fostat. See "Fustat."

foundation. The combination of warps and wefts in the body of a rug.

foxglove. A plant of the genus *Digitalis*. Foxglove is a source of yellow dyes in Anatolian rugs.

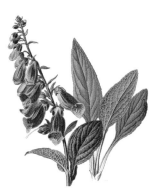

Foxglove

frach (Arabic farsh, "mat, bedding"). A bedding rug of Tunisia about 4 feet by 6 feet. The design often includes hooked diamonds and wide vertical strips at each side. The symmetric jufti knot is used followed by four or more wefts. Dominant colors are dark red, blue, and black.

fragments, rug. A severely damaged rug or a piece of a rug. Study of rug fragments from Pazyryk, Lou-lan, Fustat, and other archaeological sites has partially illuminated the ancient origins of pile rugs and their designs. Carbon dating of these fragments has pushed back the speculative time of origin of knotted pile rugs. Photographic techniques are used to reconstruct complete rug designs from fragments. Some fragments present designs of such beauty that they are aesthetically pleasing in themselves. Rug fragments are studied and collected for their rare or unusual designs, unusual structures, and their dyes. All of these properties provide information about their cultures of origin and commerce between cultures. See "archaeological sites."

France. See "Aubusson," "Gobelins," "moquette," and "Savonnerie."

frazada. A southwest American wool blanket.

Fremlin Carpet. An important Mughal carpet in the Victoria and Albert Museum carrying the arms of the Fremlin family of Kent, England. The carpet shows hunting scenes with a palmette border. Its size is 8 by 19 feet. It was probably commissioned in the early seventeenth century.

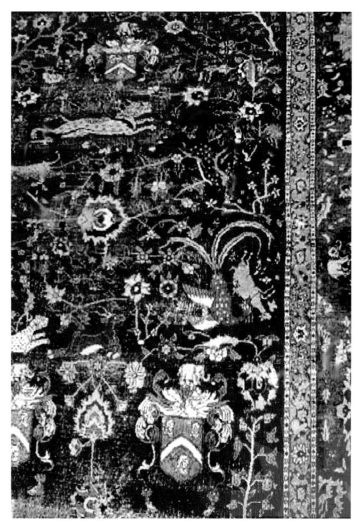

Fremlin carpet (detail) *Wikimedia Commons*

fret. Winding or interlaced designs, often characterized by right-angle turns. Fret designs are common in the borders of Chinese rugs. The wan symbol or swastika is connected by lines or "T" or rectilinear "S" (leiwen) shapes to form patterns. See "border" and "Greek key."

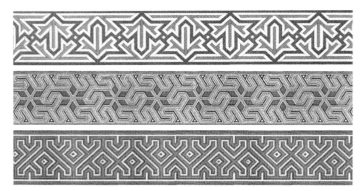

Frets (Near Eastern)

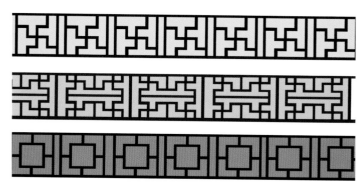

Frets (Chinese)

fret design, RKO rugs. Chinese rugs of East Turkestan, Ningxia and Gansu with designs consisting of bands of long parallel bars or dashes. These are in dark brown or dark blue on a red or yellow field. The rugs do not have side borders. The rugs were woven in the late 18th and early 19th centuries. Because the bands of dashes resemble sound waves in the RKO motion picture logo, they have been termed "RKO" rugs.

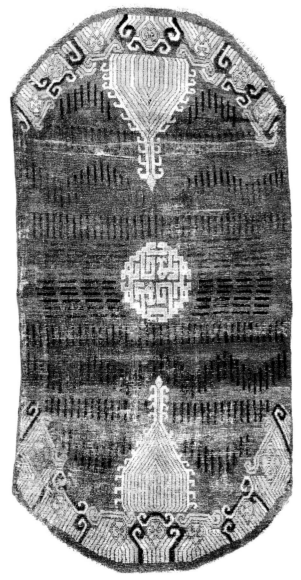

East Turkestan fret saddle cover RKO (detail) *Sothebys*

frieze. A carpet woven of nubbly or slubbed (excessively twisted) yarns.

fringe. Warps extending from the foundation at the ends of a rug. These warps are treated in various ways to prevent wefts and knots from unraveling. Artificial fringes may be attached to rugs with damaged ends as an unsatisfactory substitute. See "end finish" and "thrum."

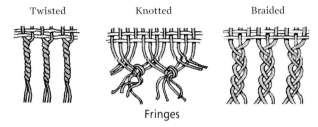

Twisted Knotted Braided

Fringes

front. That side of the rug normally placed upwards. In pile rugs, the side with the cut pile. See "design classification and description" and "face."

fu. A Chinese character symbolizing happiness that is occasionally used in a stylized form in Chinese rugs. See "shou" and "xi."

Fu

fu dog, fo dog, fu lion. A mythical animal with the mane of a lion, flowing tail, and mouth agape. Fu dogs are represented in Chinese architecture as guardians of sacred buildings. Images are used in China as temple guards. Fu dogs are represented on Chinese rugs. The female is shown with her paw on her young and the male is shown with his paw on a sphere.

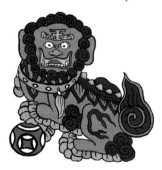

Fu dog *After Hackmack*

fugitive dye. The failure of a dye to retain its hue and shade. This failure may involve a change of hue as well as fading.

fulling. Thickening and shrinking woolen fabrics through heat, moisture, and pressure. The process causes felting in some of the fibers. See "felt."

fuschine. A magenta aniline dye invented by Hofmann and Nicholson in about 1858. This dye fades when exposed to light. See "dye, synthetic."

Fustat, Fostat. Fustat, near Cairo, was the seat of government in Egypt under the Umayyad and Abbasid Caliphates from the seventh to the ninth century. Excavations at this oldest Muslim center in Egypt have produced fabrics and fragments of imported rugs dating from the ninth century. Most fragments were of linen, but a few were fragments tied with the symmetric knot or fragments tied with the Spanish knot.

Fustat Carpet. A pile carpet, almost complete, allegedly found at Fustat. The carpet is approximately 6½ feet by 3 feet, with symmetric knots, and has an image in the field similar to tribal lion rugs. The carpet has been carbon-dated between the seventh and ninth centuries c.e. It is in the collection of the De Young Museum of San Francisco. See "Fustat."

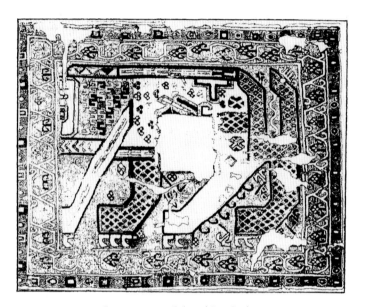

Fustat carpet *Oriental Rug Review*

fustic wood. *Cholorophora tinctoria* called old fustic or dyer's mulberry. A yellow dye used on wool is extracted from this wood.

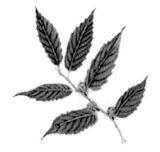

Fustic wood

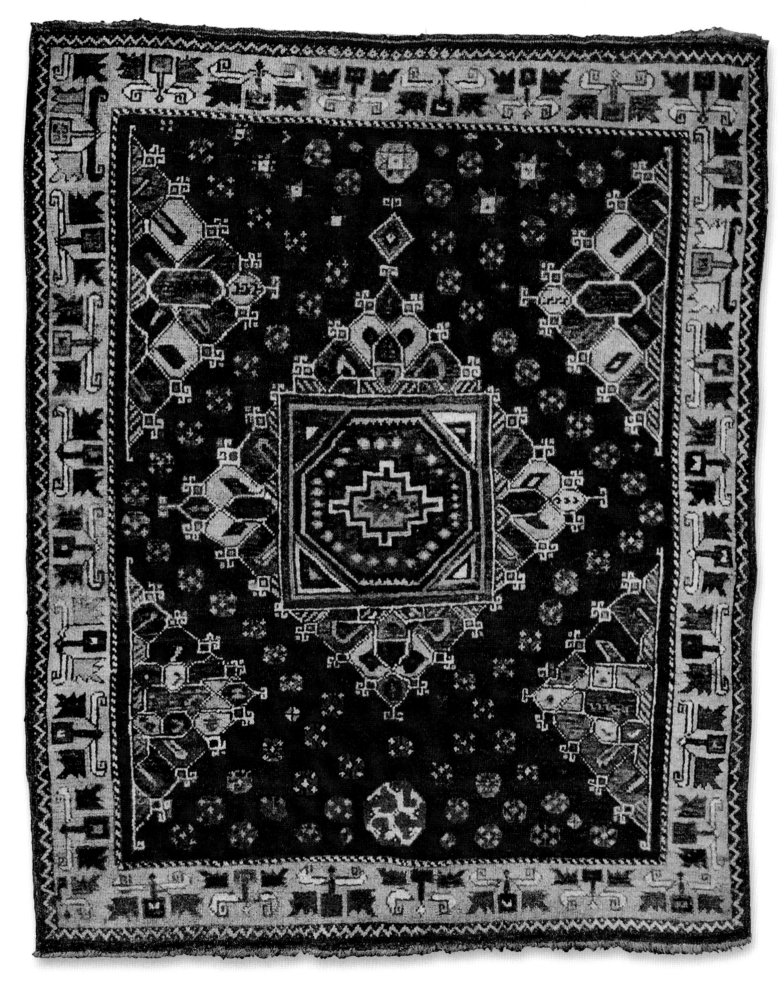

gabba. Appliqéd and embroidered rugs of Kashmir.

gabbeh, gaba, gabeh, khersak. Coarsely woven Persian rugs of tribal origin. Until recently, these were woven for domestic use and not for the market. Gabbehs were woven in southwest Iran and in Khurasan. Gabbehs of undyed wool are known in the rug trade as Shouli-Gabbehs, after the town of Shul Sanger near Shiraz. Most gabbehs are very brightly colored with synthetic dyes. Designs are simple geometric patterns or figures. Some designs are naive renderings of people, animals, and flowers. Asymmetric and symmetric knots are often used in the same rug. Usually there are four to six wefts between each row of knots. When taken from the loom, ends are folded over and hemmed, but this end finish may be altered or elaborated by dealers. Some gabbehs woven by the Lurs have pile on both sides. These are used as blankets and known as "gabbeh patuee." See "Fars."

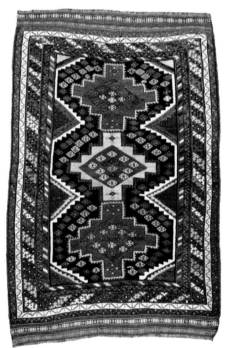

Qashga'i gabbeh *John Collins*

gadzhari. In Afghanistan, a flatweave of warp-faced bands or rugs made of such bands sewn together. This structure is used by Arabs, Ersaris, Pashtuns, and Kirghiz. The term is thought to be of Kirghiz derivation. See "alasa," "jijim," and "kanat."

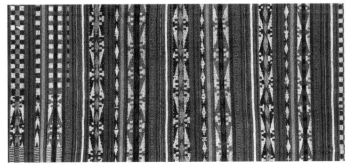

Kirghiz gadzhari (detail)

gage. See "gauge."

galeh (Persian). Bedding bag or mafrash. See "mafrash."

gali, qâli (Persian, "carpet"). See "halı."

gallery carpet. A long rug wider than 3½ feet.

gallic acid. An acid found in a wide variety of plants such as tea, tree bark, and oak galls that are used as dyes.

Gallup. A town of western New Mexico and a source of brightly colored contemporary Navajo long, narrow weavings or throw rugs woven on cotton warps.

Ganado. Navajo rugs of New Mexico from the Ganado area. Geometric figures in these rugs are woven with yarn dyed a dark red. A serrated or stepped diamond or crosses are a common motif. Ganado rugs first date from about 1915 and are associated with the Hubbell Trading Post. See "eye dazzler" and "Hubbell Trading Post."

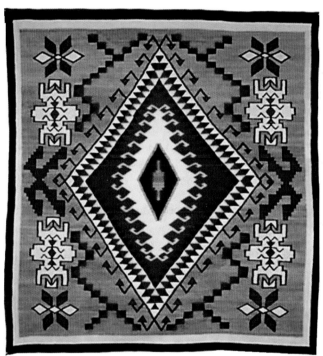

Ganado Navajo rug *Steve Getzwiller*

Gangchen (Tibetan, "snowland"). Contemporary rugs woven in Tibet by InnerAsia, a Tibetan rug production and marketing company. These rugs are woven using traditional Tibetan colors and design motifs.

Ganja. See "Genje."

Gansu, Kansu. A province of western China, including the city of Ningxia. The major weaving center is Ningxia, but rugs are woven in many smaller towns. Generally, rugs of Gansu are coarsely woven with about 36 asymmetric knots per square inch. Designs are usually rendered in blue on yellow, light red, or tan fields. Some Gansu rugs have wool wefts. Machine-spun cotton warps were first used in the province in about 1920. See "China" and "Ningxia."

garance (French). Madder.

garden carpet. Carpets with rectangular compartments containing floral motifs. The earliest of such carpets from the seventeenth century represented Safavid gardens. Their compartments are elaborations of the chahâr bâgh, the quartered garden. The compartments are delineated by rectangular water courses, often containing representations of fish and water fowl. There are rectangular pools or reservoirs at major intersections of the channels. Early garden carpet designs are highly variable, but a group of consistent design is attributed to Kurdistan of about 1800. See "Figdor Garden Carpet."

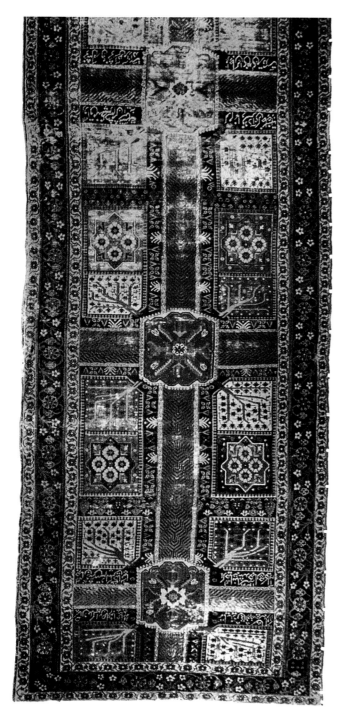

Garden carpet dated 1806 (detail) *Grogan and Company*

Garmsar. A town near Varâmin in north central Iran. Kilims of the area have an all-over pattern of variously colored hexagons. Weft wrapping is used to outline the hexagons. Warps are brown wool.

garmsir (Persian, "warm region"). Winter pasturage (on the plains) of nomadic tribes. See "qishlaq," "kishlak," and "transhumance."

Garrus design, Gerous design. "Garrus" was formerly a designation for Bijâr in northwest Persia as well as the name of a Kurdish subtribe of the area. A design of large Bijâr rugs of the nineteenth century consisting of a system of split leaf arabesques in red on a blue background. There are sixteenth-century rugs with a similar design. See "split leaf arabesque."

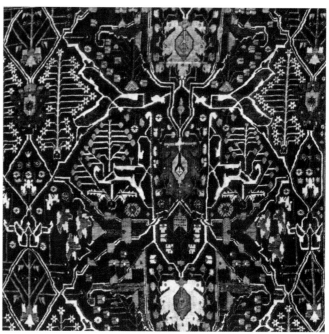

Garrus design (detail)

gauge, gage, pitch. The number of warps in a 27-inch width (ell) of woven carpet. Also, in commercial tufted rugs, gauge is the number of rows of pile yarn per inch. A ⅛ gauge is 8 rows per inch, ¹/₁₀ is 10 rows per inch, and so on. See "wire."

gauge rod. A rod used in pile weaving. Pile yarn is looped over the gauge rod and around warps. When the loops over the gauge rod are cut, a pile of consistent height is produced. See "Tibet," "tülü," and "Wilton."

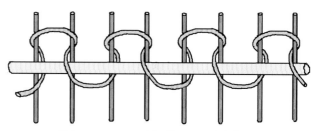

Using a gauge rod to tie symmetric knots

gaz. A woven Turkmen cradle. See "nanu."

Gaziantep, Aintab, Aintap. A town of southeastern Anatolia and a market center for locally woven cicims.

Gelveri. A town in south central Anatolia where rugs with star motifs and prayer rugs are woven.

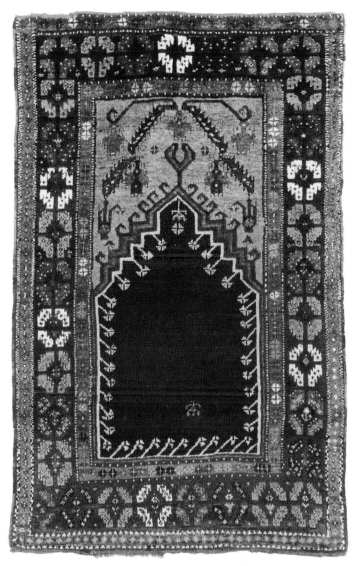

Gelveri prayer rug *Peter Willborg*

gem-set carpets. Carpets set with precious or semi-precious stones. Gem-set velvet carpets were woven in late 19th and early 20th century India. See "Gujarat" and "Spring Carpet of Chosroes."

gemyan (Turk.). The term used in Azerbaijan for soumaks carrying the S-shaped motif where these soumaks are made. Blue is usually the dominant color in these soumaks. These weavings are termed "verneh" in other areas of the Near East and "sileh" in the West. See "soumak."

Genje, Elisavetpol, Ganja. The city and khanate of Genje in the Caucasus became the city and province of Elisavetpol in Imperial Russia. Elisavetpol was renamed Kirovabad under Soviet rule, and has now reverted to Genje. Nineteenth-century rugs of this area are similar to Kazak rugs, though they may have a longer format. Designs consist of diagonal stripes, often containing botehs, all-over memling guls, and lattices. The density is about 57 symmetric knots per square inch. Average area is about 31 square feet. See "Caucasus."

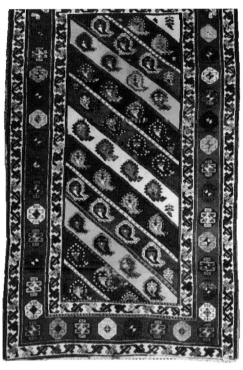

Genje rug *Grogan and Company*

geometric design. Designs that are rectilinear, stepped, or angular. Geometric designs are often dictated by coarsely knotted rugs that make it difficult to represent smoothly curving lines in a design and by the naive pictorial tastes of the weavers. The designs of village and tribal rugs are sometimes geometric interpretations of finely woven, curvilinear, urban designs. See "curvilinear designs."

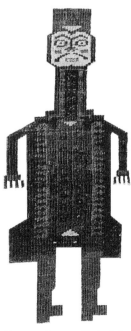

Geometric man (Baluchi)

Georgia. The Republic of Georgia (Georgian Sakartvelo, Russian Gruziya) is located in the western Caucasus. Tiflis (Tbilisi), the capital of Georgia was a major nineteenth-century market for Persian and Caucasian rugs. Nineteenth-century rugs woven in this area are classified as "Kazak." See "Caucasus," "Kazak," and "pardaghy."

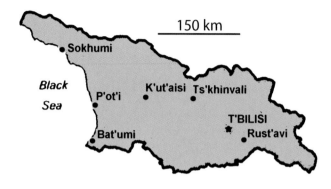

Georgia

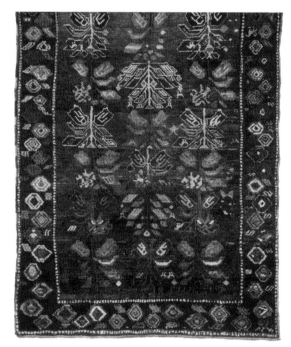

Georgian rug (detail) *Peter Willborg*

gereh (Persian, "knot"). This term refers to a linear measure in units of about 2½ inches. See "reg."

gereh zadan (Persian). To knot into fringes.

Germantown yarn. A commercial 3-ply wool yarn manufactured from 1864 to 1875 and then supplanted by a 4-ply yarn that is still available. These synthetically dyed yarns are used in rugs and blankets of the Navajos and Pueblos.

Germany. Production of hand-knotted rugs on a commercial basis began in Germany about 1850. Hand-knotting was displaced by power-loomed rug production in the early twentieth century. See "Bauhaus."

germesh, germetch. A Turkmen weaving hung across the yurt entrance beneath the engsi to keep ground dust out of the tent. They are of the same width as the engsi and of matching design. See "engsi."

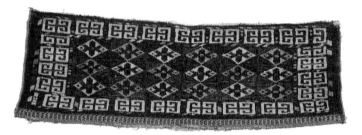

Ersari Germesh *R. John Howe*

Gerous. See "Garrus."

Gharaghân. A district of Hamadan. It is a source of rugs with large medallions and spandrels. Knots are symmetric on a cotton foundation with single wefts.

ghermez, germez (Persian *germez*). Red.

Ghilza'i, Gilza'i. A Pashtun tribe of southeast Afghanistan. They are thought to weave bands or strips of warp-faced brocade which they sew into fabrics. See "gadzhari."

Ghiordes. See "Gördes."

ghorband. In Afghanistan, a strap for loading pack animals and woven by Baluchi weavers.

Ghirlandaio medallion. Domenico Ghirlandaio was a 15th-century Italian artist whose works showed rugs with medallions similar to the following example. Such medallions were used in Bergama rugs. See "Bergama."

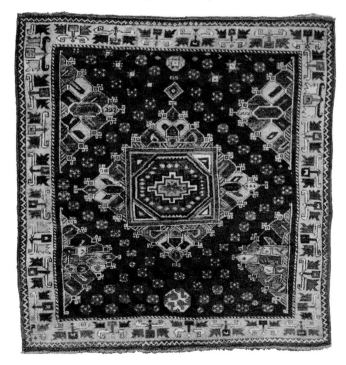

Ghirlandaio medallion rug (Bergama) *Sothebys*

Ghorian, Ghurian. A town of northwestern Afghanistan, west of Herat. Tekke Turkmen in the area weave prayer rugs and rugs with the Tekke gul.

Ghormaj. A small town of northwest Aghanistan. A source of small, coarsely-woven rugs in geometric designs with weft float brocaded kilim ends. The colors are suggestive of Baluchi rugs.

giaba. Small Caucasian pile rugs.

gillim. See "kilim."

gillimche. Persian for "small kilim."

Gilza'i. See "Ghilza'i.

Girdi. A Kurdish tribe of the Erbil plain. The tribe is a source of heavy rugs of lustrous wool. Designs are stars and memling guls. There is little current production.

Girdlers' Carpet. A Mughal rug, dated 1634, woven on commission in Lahore for a trade guild, the Girdlers' Company of London. It is a floral carpet, 24 feet by 8 feet. Five shields or coats-of-arms are arranged along the major axis. This masterpiece was woven in the reign of Shah Jahan and is in the collection of the Victoria and Albert Museum.

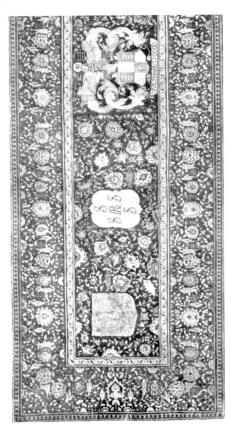

Girdlers' Carpet (detail)

girth. See "tent band."

gishlag. See "kışlak."

giyak. See "gyak."

Glaoua rugs. A local merchants' term for flatwoven rugs of the High Atlas in Morocco. These rugs have broad stripes and zigzag designs of weft twining, with some designs worked in pile knots. See "Ouaouzqite."

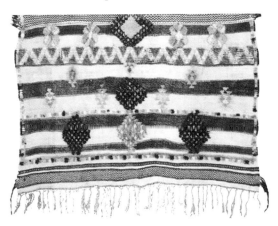

Glaoua rug (detail)   *H.J. Hakimian*

gloss. A sheen or high degree of light reflectance, present in silk, mercerized cotton, synthetic fibers, and some coarse wools. See "luster."

glossa. A type of Scandinavian rug. Specifically, a rya rug employing the symmetric knot. See "rya rugs."

Goa. Formerly a Portuguese colony on the west coast of India. Seventeenth century, so-called "Portuguese" rugs have been attributed to Goa. See "'Portuguese carpets.'"

goat. A member of the genus *Capra*. Hollow-horned ruminant mammals closely related to sheep. Goat hair is used in the warps and selvages of some tribal and nomadic rugs. See "Angora goat" and "Kashmir goat."

Gobelins. A family of dyers whose workshop was founded at Paris in the late fifteenth century. In the sixteenth century, tapestry weaving was begun at the workshop. In 1662, Colbert purchased the workshop in the name of Louis XIV. Fine tapestries and upholstery fabrics are woven at the works. Carpets were woven at the Gobelins beginning in 1825.

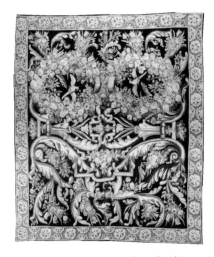

Gobelins tapestry   *Doris Leslie Blau*

Gogarjin. A village near Bijâr in northwest Iran. It is a source of double-wefted medallion rugs with spandrels, marketed as Bijârs.

Gohar Carpet. An important rug of Karabagh with a design related to both the Kasim Ushag and the Dragon Carpets. This rug is significant because it includes an inscription in Armenian by the weaver, Gohar, with a date variously interpreted as 1680, 1700, and 1732. The rug, however, may be of later production. The rug is 5 feet 11 in. by 11 feet 6 in. with 49 to 64 symmetric knots per square inch. See "Armenian rugs."

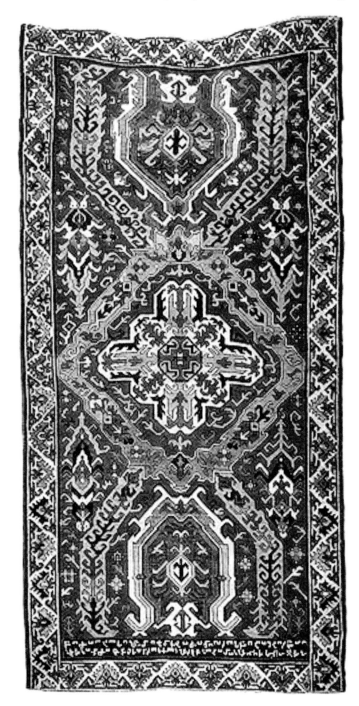

Gohar carpet

going-out-of-business-sale, GOOBS. A recent retail rug marketing practice in which a rug store owner announces a store closing with rug discounts, only to re-open with another name. This practice has been made illegal in some states.

Göklan Turkmen. A Turkmen tribe of Khurasan in Iran. The weavings of this tribe may have been incorrectly attributed to the Yomud. The major gul of the Göklan is thought to be an octagon with ram's horns similar to that of the Salor. A distinctive feature of their rugs is a symmetric knot tied over three warps used in design outlines. Another distinctive feature is the occasional use of red silk wefts. See "Eagle gul," "Imreli," and "Turkmen."

gol. See "gul."

gol hennae. See "guli hinnai."

gold thread. See "metallic threads."

gold washing. The process of bleaching red rugs to produce shades of yellow.

Golden Afghan. Originally, an Afghan rug with the Ersari gul that had been bleached from red to yellow. Now, rugs from Afghanistan are woven in shades of yellow to satisfy this demand of the western market. See "bleaching."

gollab. See "hook, weaver's."

Golpâyegân. Weavers of this town of west central Iran produce single-medallion rugs with red as the dominant color. They are woven with the asymmetric knot at about 65 knots per square inch.

Gombad-i Qâbus. A Turkmen market town of northeast Iran. It is a source of rugs with designs based on Turkmen guls. Foundations are wool. Knot densities are between 150 to 230 asymmetric knots per square inch.

gomden (Tibetan). Prayer mat.

Gonâbâd. A town of Khurasan in northeastern Iran, a minor source of coarsely woven rugs.

Goradis. A village in southern Karabagh in the Caucasus. Nineteenth century rugs attributed to this area often have a staggered, angular comet-shaped motif that may be derived from boteh. These rugs have a density of about 46 symmetric knots per square inch. Rug area is about 38 square feet.

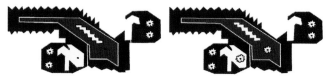

Goradis motif

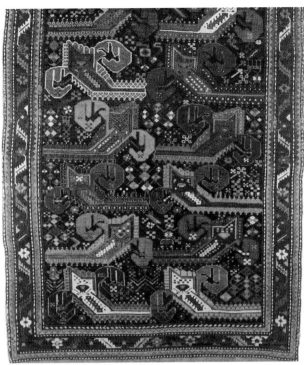

Goradis rug *Grogan and Ciompany*

Goran. See "Guran."

gorbaghe gul. See kurbage gul.

Gördes, Ghiordes, Yordiz. A town of western Anatolia to which many prayer rugs have been attributed. Rugs have been woven in the area of Gördes since the eighteenth century. The early prayer rugs have a curvilinear mihrab with panels at top and bottom of the mihrab and are woven with knot densities of about 100 to 200 symmetric knots per square inch. A floral border is typical. In the nineteenth century, copies of these rugs were woven in Kayseri, Hereke, Bandırma, and other locations. Some of these copies were treated to suggest great age. See "Kiz Gördes" and "Mejidian style."

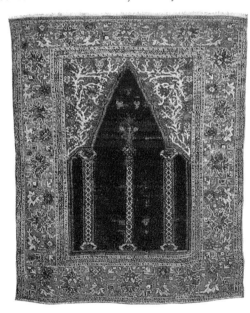

Gördes prayer rug *Huntimgton Museum of Art*

Gördes knot. See "symmetric knot."

Gorevan. A town in the vicinity of Heriz in Iran. The term "Gorevan" is used by the rug trade to denote quality rather than local attribution. A very coarsely woven rug with a Heriz pattern may be described as a "Gorevan." See "Heriz."

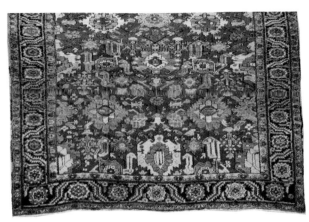

Gorevan rug (detail) *Peter Pap Oriental Rugs Inc*

goyo (Tibetan). Hanging door rug. See "ensi."

gray. A color formed by blending white and black. In oriental rugs, gray may be the result of a dye or the natural color of some sheeps' wool. Gray is produced by cochineal with an iron mordant.

Great Britain. See "England."

Greece. The weaving of kilims for domestic use is a folk craft in Greece. Designs were strongly influenced by the Turkish occupation. Weft substitution patterning is used in Greek flatweaves. There is a wide variety of flatweaves woven in the Greek islands, many of them decorated with embroidery. Knotted carpet production commenced with the repatriation of Greek weavers from Turkey at the end of the Greco-Turkish War in 1922. Knotted pile carpets were woven in Athens and Corinth up to the Second World War. See "berde," "bouharopodia," "churga," "Epirus," "flokati," "Kouskousse," and "Thessaly."

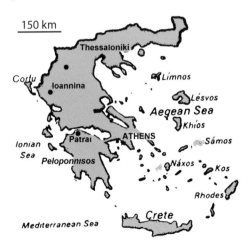

Greece

Greek cross. A cross with vertical and transverse members of equal length and intersecting at the center of each member. See "cross."

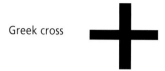

Greek cross

Greek key, Greek fret. A variety of reciprocal repeating border patterns, often found in architectural ornament, consisting of rectilinear wave forms, sometimes nested. See "fret" and "running dog."

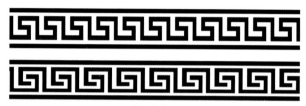

Greek key

green. A color of the visual spectrum. Where green is produced with vegetable dyes, the wool is usually dyed with indigo and over-dyed with yellow vegetable dyes such as esparek or pomegranate rind. Since yellow vegetable dyes fade faster than indigo, bright or forest green becomes sea green in older pieces. See "Prophet's green."

Gregorian date. A year, expressed in western numeric symbols, dating from the time of Christ, as adjusted by Pope Gregory in 1582. This is in distinction to Islamic dates which are based on a lunar year and commence with the Hijra of Muhammad in 622. See "Islamic dates."

greige goods. Undyed broadloom carpet.

grinning. A trade term describing the condition of a runner on stairs when the pile opens up to reveal the foundation where the runner crosses the projecting edge of a tread. See "cornrowing."

ground. The interlaced combination of warp and weft that is structurally essential to the fabric. In pile rugs, the "ground" may be referred to as the "foundation."

ground color. The dominant color of the field of a rug.

ground loom. See "carpet loom."

grun-tse (Tibetan). Knotted carpet.

guard stripe. Stripes or lesser borders on either side of the main border. See "bala-khachi" and "border."

Guergour carpet. A carpet of Algeria. These are primarily copies of Anatolian models with a single mihrab or opposing mihrabs. They are long carpets, four to six feet wide and up to 12 feet long. The field is red with designs in blue, green, yellow, and white. See "Algeria."

Guizhou, Kweichow, Kweihwa. A weaving center near Baotou of Inner Mongolia in China. Early rugs from this center are thought to be small, while larger carpets were woven there in the 1920s. Blue was the dominant color of these later carpets.

Gujarat, Gujerat. A state of western India and formerly a source of carpets. Baroda (now Vadodara) was a city in Gujarat. The Pearl Carpet of Baroda was commissioned by the Maharajah of Baroda circa 1865. It is about six ft. by nine ft. and covered with approximately 1.5 million seed pearls. The design includes emeralds, sapphires, diamonds, and gold on a silk and deer hide base. See "Ahmedabad," "Spring Carpet of Chosroes," and "India."

gul, gol (Persian, "flower, rose"). A motif of octagonal or angular shape used in Turkmen designs. Usually, the gul is repeated to form an all-over pattern in the field. Certain Turkmen tribes are associated with specific guls as emblems of the tribe. These are known as major guls and are used in the main carpets of the tribe. There are descriptions of guls under entries for specific Turkmen tribes.

The origin of the gul may be a flower representation as suggested by the Persian meaning of the word. Some believe the gul developed as a tribal symbol from animal designs with totemic significance. The Chinese cloud collar has been proposed as the ultimate source of the Turkmen gul. Roundels and filler motifs of very early Chinese silk fabrics have also been proposed as the ultimate source. See "cloud collar," "major gul," and "minor gul." See the following entries:

aina gul	gulli gul
ashik gul	Jengal Arjuk gul
ay gul	Karakalpak gul
"C" gul	kepse gulkurbage gul
chemche gul	Memling gul
chenâr gul	Sariq gul
dyrnak gul	Sekme gul
eagle gul	Tauk noska gul
erre gul	Tekke gul
ertman gul	Temirchin gul
farangi gul	turret gul
guli hinnai	Waziri gul

gülbudak (Turk., "rose branch"). A motif in central Anatolian kilims and Kurdish weavings. It has been interpreted as two opposing bird.

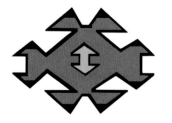 

Gülbudak

gul farang. See "farangi gul."

gul-i badam (Turk. "almond blossom"). A minor border common in Ersari pile weavings.

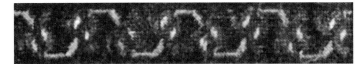

Gul-i badam

guli hinnai, gol henna, gul hennae. An all-over pattern of henna flowers, usually arranged in a repeated diamond format. See "henna."

Guli hinnai motif

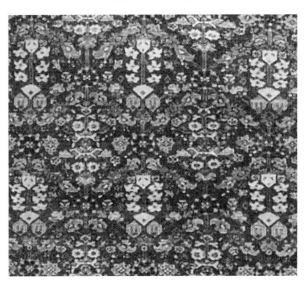

Guli hinnai from a Mahal carpet

gulli gul. A gul associated with the Ersari, Salor, and Saryq Turkmen tribes. Each quarter contains a clover leaf motif. There are many variations.

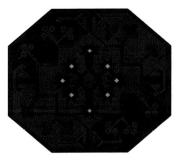 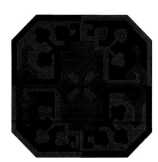

Gulli guls

Güney. A town of western Anatolia and a source of rugs with cotton pile on a cotton foundation. The symmetric knot is used.

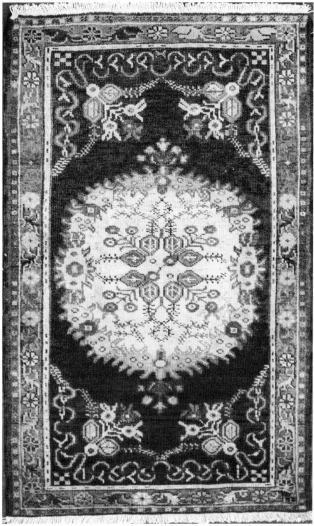

Güney rug

Guran, Goran. A Kurdish tribe of the Kermanshah district in Iran. The tribe is Shi'i Muslim. Some weavings are produced by the tribe.

gusfand (Persian). Sheep.

Gwalior. A city of north central India and a rug-weaving center since 1902. Contemporary rugs of this city have a knot density of about 210 knots per square inch.

gyabnye (Tibetan). A cushion cover with a pile face.

gyab-yol (Tibetan). A wall rug.

gyak, giyak (Turk.) Barberpole stripe.

Gyantse. A city of southern Tibet. A site of rug production since the nineteenth century.

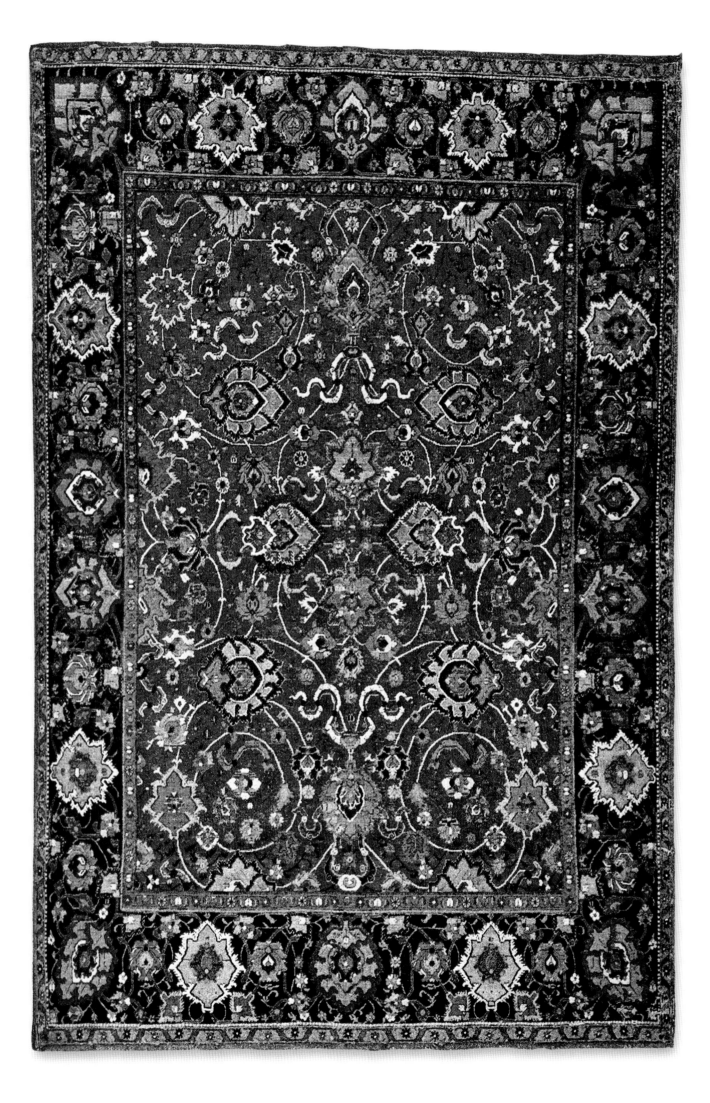

Hadith. So-called "Traditions of the Prophet"; reports of the recommendations and conduct of Muhammad and his companions, regarded as normative for the behavior of Muslims. Next to the Koran, the major source of Islamic law. See "Islam."

Haftbalâ (Persian, "seven plagues"). A tribe of Pashtun origin in Afghanistan, noted as rug weavers.

haft rang (Persian, "seven colors"). Dyed warps sometimes used in Senneh rugs. Seven colors were used to dye bands of warps. An Uzbeki ikat of seven colors and highly prized because of the complex dyeing process.

hair. Microscopically, hair is distinguished from wool in that hair contains a medulla or core consisting of a cellular structure of air pockets. In oriental rugs, some admixture of hair adds luster to the rug. Excessive hair diminishes the wearing quality of the rug. See "wool."

Hai. See "Iraq."

Haji Hanum. A prayer rug design in which a vase of flowers fills the area under the niche.

hajj. Pilgrimage to Mecca. See "Islam."

Hajji Baba Club. The first American society for the appreciation of oriental rugs founded in New York in 1932. The society takes its name from the Persian hero of an English novel by James Morier, published in 1824. Arthur Urbane Dilley was the first president of the society. Dilley was a rug dealer and author of **Oriental Rugs and Carpets**, published in 1931. Some members became prominent through collecting or rug scholarship. These include Maurice Dimand, Charles Grant Ellis, Jerome Straka, H. McCoy Jones, and Joseph McMullan. The society continues to foster understanding and appreciation of oriental rugs.

Hakkârî. A provincial capital of southeast Anatolia. Kurdish rugs and kilims are woven in the area by the Hartushi and Herki tribes.

Halep. See "Aleppo."

halı (Turk.), gali, qâli (Persian). A knotted pile carpet.

halıcı (Turk.). A rug dealer or rug maker.

Hamadan. A city and provincial capital in northwest Iran, ancient Ecbatana. Hamadan is the collection and shipping center of an important rug-weaving area. Hundreds of towns and villages in the region produce scatter size rugs and runners for export. Many of these towns and villages are populated by Kurds. Distinctive designs are associated with particular towns and villages in the region. The rugs of Hamadan are single-wefted and most of them have a cotton foundation. Early examples may have a wool foundation and a camel-colored field. The rugs have symmetric knots and are coarsely

woven with densities of about 40 to 100 knots per square inch. See "Bijâr," "Dargazin," "Kasvin," "Kurds," and "Zanjân."

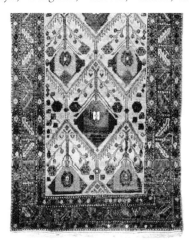

Hamadan rug (detail) *J.P. Willborg*

hamel. In Tunisia, a flatwoven blanket of about five feet by seven feet made of broad bands sewn together. In Algeria, a flatwoven tent partition about three feet wide by 12 to 15 feet long.

Hammersmith carpets. See "Morris, William."

hanbel. Moroccan for "kilim." Hanbels are floor coverings or blankets in a variety of flatweave structures. Designs are usually wide, heavily decorated stripes.

hand, handle. The overall impression of a rug or fabric when handled due to its density, flexibility, thickness, softness, and texture.

Hand of Fatima. An image of the palm and extended fingers in the upper spandrels of some prayer rugs, thought to suggest five principles of Islam (the "five pillars"): profession of faith, prayer, pilgrimage, fasting, and almsgiving. The hand images may also suggest the placement of hands during prayer. See "Fatima."

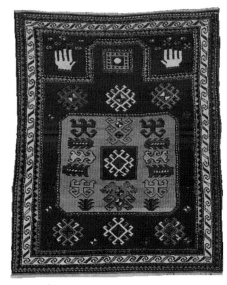

Hand of Fatima in a Kazak rug *R. John Howe*

hank. See "skein."

Hapsburg Prayer Rug. A sixteenth-century prayer rug of Cairo or, possibly, Bursa or Istanbul. It is four feet two inches by five feet eleven inches. Its knot density is about 360 asymmetric knots per square inch. The rug has a silk foundation and "S" spun wool pile, with some cotton pile detail. This rug is in the collection of the Vienna Museum für Angewandte Kunst.

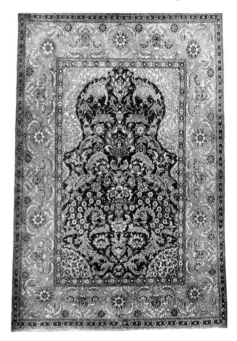

Hapsburg Prayer Rug

Harania tapestry. See "Harrânia tapestry."

hard spun, hard twist. See "angle of twist."

Haris. See "Heriz."

Harmon. A trade designation of quality for Romanian rugs with wool foundation and 130 knots per square inch.

Harrânia tapestry, Harania tapestry. Harrânia is a village near Cairo, Egypt. Harrânia tapestries are woven by children and young adults in a craft school in the village. The tapestries show naive images of people, animals, buildings, and scenes from the area. See "Wissa Wassef."

harshang (Turk., from Persian *kharchang,* "crab"), crab design, flaming palmette. A design of shield-shaped palmettes with foliate extensions (suggesting a crab) with interspersed florets or other floral elements. The harshang design may have originated in designs of Indo-Herat rugs. It is widely used in Persian and Caucasian rugs of the eighteenth and nineteenth centuries. See "palmette."

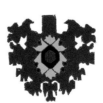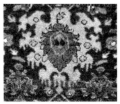

Harshang motif

Harsin. A town south of Kangâvar in Kermânshâh province and an archaeological site, in northwest Iran. The name is a trade term for a large production of Kurdish kilims of northwest Iran. These are single-piece kilims in a narrow format, often with eccentric wefts.

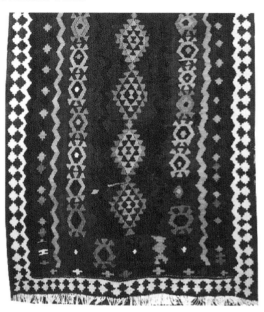

Harsin kilim (detail) *Peter Willborg*

Hartushi. A Kurdish tribe of the area of Hakkârî in northeast Anatolia. The tribe weaves pile rugs and kilims in clear blues and reds. These rugs have two or three wefts between each row of knots.

Hashtrud (Persian, "eight rivers"). A mountainous area of northwestern Iran southeast of Tabriz inhabited by Kurds and Shahsavan. Some rugs with a highly geometricized version of the Herati pattern are woven in this area.

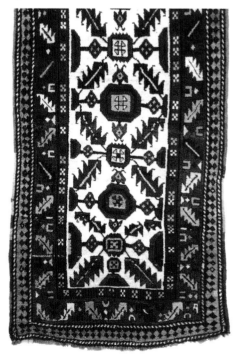

Hashtrud rug (detail) *Peter Willbog*

hatayi, khatayi (Turk., "Chinese, Cathayan"). An Ottoman decorative motif of a stylized lotus blossom with buds and feathery leaves. See "arabesque," "islimi" and "saz."

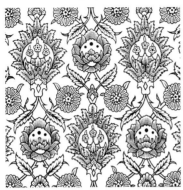

Hatayi

hatchli, hatchlu (Turk., haçlı "cruciform"). See "khatchli."

hausi design, hauzi design, havuzî design. A medallion used fequently in Kurdish rugs consisting of a rectangle with arrows projecting from each side. The design is thought to derive from a water tank or basin (*hauz*) or from an eight-lobed Anatolian medallion.

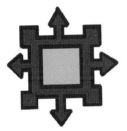

Hausi medallion

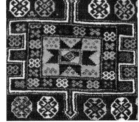

Bukhara-Carpets

hava. A comb for beating down wefts on the loom.

Havemeyer Carpet. A seventeenth-century floral cartouche compartment carpet attributed to Isfahan in Persia. This rug is woven with the vase technique. It is 16 feet 5 inches by 10 feet 8 inches. The asymmetric knot is used at a density of 272 per square inch. It is a bequest of Horace Havemeyer to the Metropolitan Museum of Art, New York.

havli (Turk.). Pile surface.

havuzî design. See "hausi design."

Hazara, Hazareh. A tribe of the Aimaq group in northwestern Afghanistan, noted for their flatwoven salt bags, saddle bags, and kilims. Also a related people of central Afghanistan, Shi'i Muslims who speak a variety of Persian. See "Aimaq."

hearth rug. Any small rug or mat used in front of a fireplace. In western countries, such rugs may be semi-circular. See "ojak-bashi."

heat set fibers. Yarns that have been heated to set the twist. This commercial treatment helps prevent the cut ends of pile from fraying or untwisting.

He-bei, Hopeh, Hopei. A province of northern China; capital, Tientsin. This province is a source of contemporary silk rugs. Either cotton or silk warps are used, but wefts are cotton. There is also major production of wool carpets in this province.

heddle. A harness used to raise alternating or selected warps on a loom.

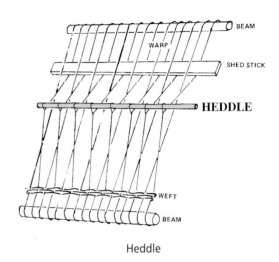

Heddle

Hegira, Hejira. See "Hijra."

Helvacı. Kilims of European Turkey and western Anatolia employing both slit tapestry and weft float brocade structures in the same weaving. Pastel colors are used with a variety of geometric design motifs.

Helvai Bijâr. Helvai is a Kurdish tribal name and a trade term denoting a Bijâr rug of higher quality.

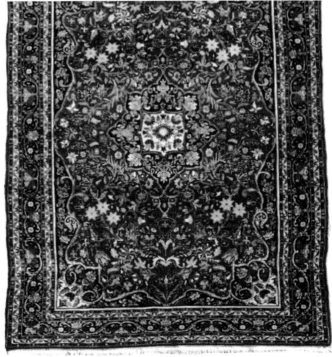

Helvai Bijâr rug (detail) *John Collins*

helwan. An Egyptian kilim of geometric designs woven in natural colors, attributed to the city of Helwan, south of Cairo.

hemp. A bast fiber of *Cannabis sativa*. Hemp is used for making rope or very coarse fabrics. In the Near East, the plant buds are smoked as hashish or bhang, while the leaves are smoked in the United States as marijuana or pot. Hemp has been used in the foundation of rugs of India and Afghanistan. It has been used for weftin older Chinese rugs and for warps in some Romanian kilims.

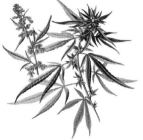

Hemp

henna. A shrub, *Lawsonia inermis*. The leaves of this shrub are a source of a reddish-brown or orange dye that has been used for rug wool. The dye is also used cosmetically to color the skin and hair. See "guli hinnai."

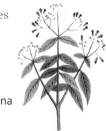

Henna

Herat. A city of northwestern Afghanistan, formerly a major city of Persia. Herat was among the oldest weaving centers of Persia. Some Safavid rugs of the sixteenth and seventeenth centuries have been attributed to Herat, though these attributions are disputed. Many of these carpets contain early forms of the "Herati pattern." Currently, Herat is a major collection and market center for Baluchi rugs woven in the area.

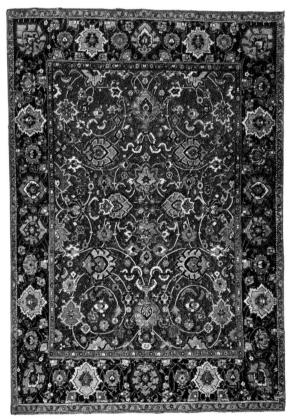

Herat carpet (16th/17th century) *Sothebys*

Herati pattern, fish pattern. A very common repeat field design consisting of a flower centered in a diamond with curving

lanceolate or sickle leaves located outside the diamond and parallel to each side. The sickle leaves sometimes have the appearance of fish. There are many versions of the Herati pattern, curvilinear and geometric, simple and complex. See "Nadir Shah" and "mâhi."

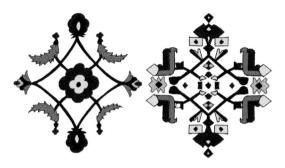

Herati patterns

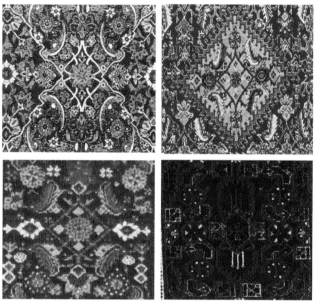

Herati patterns
TOP: Yazd, Qashqa'i. **BOTTOM:** Karabagh, Ersari

Herati border, samovar border. A common border consisting of palmettes or florets with divided tendrils at the base and lanceolate leaves hanging from the tendrils. The design may be curvilinear or geometricized. See "turtle border."

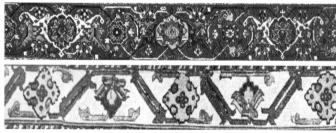

TOP: Herati border curvilinear
BOTTOM: Herati border geometricized

Hereke. A town in western Turkey about 45 miles from Istanbul. Commercial rug production began in Hereke in about 1843 with the establishment of court weaving workshops. Actual rug weaving did not begin until 1864. Early commercial production was of the highest quality, with asymmetric knots at densities reaching 800 per square inch. Copies were woven of classic Persian designs and of Gördes prayer rug designs. Production after World War II often combined a metal brocade field and high knot density in the same piece. Finely woven rugs of Bursa silk are produced in Hereke. The average grade is about 645 knots per square inch. The Hereke wool rug may be referred to as "Tokat" and typically has a knot density of about 230 symmetric knots per square inch on a cotton foundation. Rugs produced at the National Manufactory have the inscription "Hereke" woven into the border. The location and style of the inscription has varied. Currently the inscription, in Latin capitals, is in the top left border. Some very large rugs, woven in sections, were produced at the manufactory. See "Salting group."

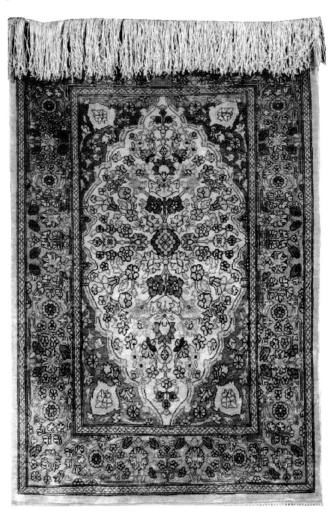

Hereke silk rug (detail) *Simon Knight*

Heriz, Herez, Heris, Haris. A town of Iranian Azerbaijan, about forty miles west of Tabriz. Rugs woven in Heriz and the nearby villages may be termed "Bakshaish," "Mehrabân," "Serapi," or "Gorevan," as well as "Heriz." These are trade designations of general quality rather than specific geographic attributions. Mehrabân and Serapi refer to the finer, more densely knotted rugs, while Gorevan refers to the lowest quality. Some nineteenth-century rugs of the Heriz area have all-over patterns of palmettes rather than the traditional large Heriz medallion. The traditional Heriz design is a geometric lobed medallion with pendants. Traditional Heriz designs are thought to be geometricized interpretations of Tabriz designs. The symmetric knot is used at densities of 30 to 80 per square inch. The foundation is cotton. See "Bakhshaish," "Bilverdi," "Gorevan," "Mehrabân," and "Serapi."

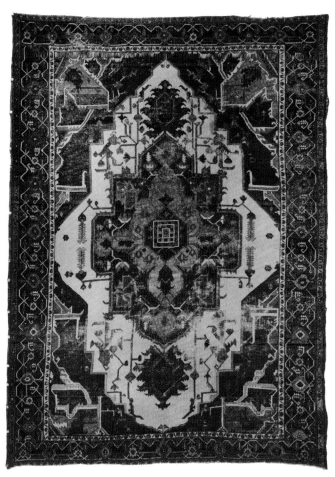

Heriz rug *Grogan and Company*

Herki. A tribe of the Kurds. The Herkis of southeastern Anatolia and northeastern Iraq weave rugs and flatweaves with the soumak structure. These rugs are in a long format. Production is relatively large. These tribes also weave a variety of animal trappings and functional items. See "Kurds."

Hetien. See "Khotan."

Hewraman. A Kurdish tribe of Kurdistan in Iran. Weavers produce rugs with designs derived from those of Senneh. See "Kurds."

hexagon. Any regular six-sided figure.

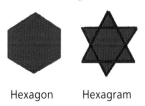

Hexagon   Hexagram

hexagram. A six-pointed star, the star of David.

hex-column. A vertical arrangement of stepped hexagons. This design is very common on nineteenth-century rugs of Shirvân in the Caucasus. Shirvân rugs of this design have an average density of 99 symmetric knots per square inch and an average area of 30 square feet. These rugs are more likely to be cotton-wefted than wool-wefted.

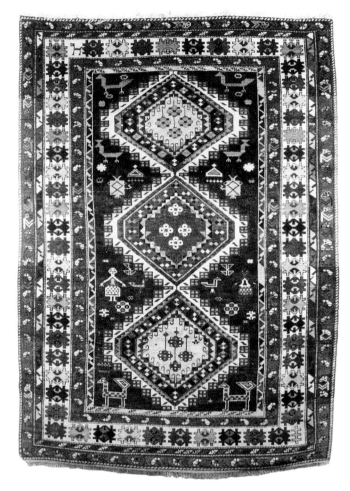

Shirvan hex-column rug *Grogan and Company*

heybe, heybeh (Turk.) Bag or saddle bag.

High Atlas. A mountain range of central Morocco. Berber tribes of the High Atlas weave small rugs. Dominant colors are red, gold and orange. A very narrow border surrounds a field of wide stripes containing geometrical motifs. Symmetric knots are tied on two warps. These rugs are of mixed pile and flatwoven structure. See "Morocco."

high-low loop. A trade term for a power-loomed carpet in which texture is achieved through loop pile of different height or cut pile and loop pile of different height. See "cut-and-loop" and "broche carpet."

Hijra, Hegira, Hejira. The emigration of Muhammad from Mecca to Medinah in September of 622 C.E. The Islamic system of dating begins with 622 C.E. as year 1. See " A.H." and "Islam."

Himachal Pradesh. A province of nothern India bordered by Kashmir, Uttar Pradesh, and Punjab. The province is a source of rugs woven by Tibetan refugees. These rugs have typical contemporary Tibetan designs and structure. The pile is wool on a cotton foundation.

Hispano-Moresque. Refers to the period of Muslim occupation of Spain from the eighth to the fifteenth centuries. Fabrics and rugs woven in Spain in this period reflect Islamic influence in their use of Arabic (esp. Kufic) script in decoration and in their geometric designs with Islamic motifs. See "mudejar" and "Spain."

historical rugs and textiles. See the following entries:
Ames Pictorial Rug
Anhalt Medallion Carpet
Animal Carpets of Leopold I
Ardabil Carpets
Chelsea Carpet
Coronation Carpet
Dudley Carpet
Figdor Garden Carpet
Fletcher Prayer Rug
Fustat Carpet
Fremlin Carpet
Girdlers' Carpet
Gohar Carpet
Hapsburg Prayer Rug
Havemeyer Carpet
Imperial Mughal Prayer Rug
Maggie and Jiggs Carpets
Marby Rug
Marcy Injoudjian Cope
Marquand Medallion Carpet
Medici Mamluk Carpet
Medici Ottoman Carpet
Paravicini Mughal Prayer Rug
Pazyryk Carpet
Poldi Pezzoli Hunting Carpet
Sackville Mughal Animal and Tree Carpet
Salting Group
Simonetti Rug
Strathmore Carpet
Swedish Royal Hunting Carpet
Topkapı Harem Medallion and Cartouche Carpet
Vienna Hunting Carpet
Vienna Portuguese Carpet
Widener Animal Carpet
Williams Admiral Carpet

Holbein carpets, dome and squinch carpets, wheel carpets. Turkish rugs with designs depicted in the paintings of Hans Holbein (1465-1524) and contemporaneous artists. Although originally attributed to Ushak, the origin of these rugs is being reconsidered. Large pattern Holbeins, showing large octagons inside squares with Kufesque borders (dome and squinch or wheel carpets), were probably woven in the

Çanakkale area. The field of small pattern Holbeins usually shows rows of diamonds or octagons with interlaced borders separated by vines and florets with a Kufesque main border. See "Alcaraz" and "Lotto carpets."

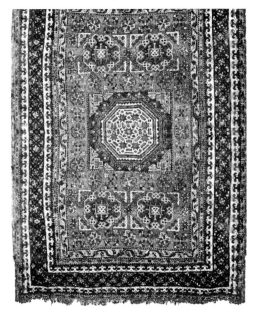

Holbein large pattern (wheel carpet)

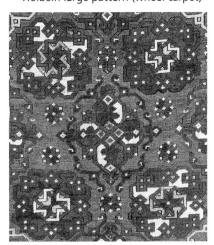

Holbein small pattern (detail)

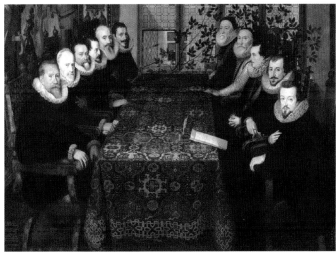

Detail of a Flemish painting of about 1604 showing a Holbein small pattern rug

Holland. In 1797, a royal factory for hand-knotted rugs was founded in Deventer. In 1887, a royal factory in Rotterdam began production of hand-knotted rugs. Handwoven rugs were produced in The Hague in 1900, and production of Wilton carpets began in Deventer in the same year. See "Dutch East India Company."

homespun. A textile with yarn spun by hand and woven by hand.

honeycomb. A compact arrangement of diamonds, hexagons, or octagons used as an all-over pattern. The cells may be occupied by floral motifs. This design is common in rugs of the northeast Caucasus. See "lattice" and "Williams Admiral Carpet."

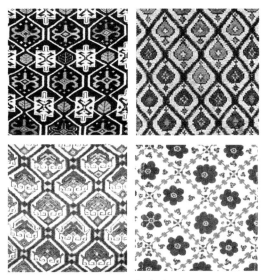

Honeycomb designs

hook, weaver's, gollab (Persian). A hooked tool used by rug weavers to pull yarn through the warps in tying knots. The shaft of the tool may be flattened and sharpened to form a cutting edge with which pile yarn is cut. See "kârdak."

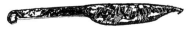

Hook, weaver's

hooked medallion. A medallion with projecting hooks. These hooks may project outwards or both outwards and inwards.

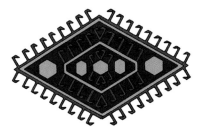

Hooked medallion

hooked rugs, draw-in rugs. Rugs produced by using a hook to draw yarn or strips of fabric through another fabric, usually canvas or burlap that has been mounted on a frame. The resulting surface is looped and may be clipped for a tufted or pile surface. Making hooked rugs is a domestic craft of English-speaking countries. The earliest hooked rugs are from about 1840. Hooked rugs are also made in China and India and are similar in structure to those of America and England. See "linsery-woolsey," "poked rugs," and "rag rugs."

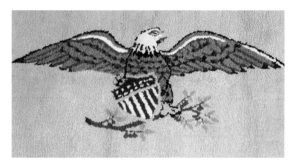

American hooked rug *Jason Nazmiyal*

Hopi. A Pueblo people of the American southwest who wove fabrics and blankets. They raised cotton as early as 1581 and reared sheep in the eighteenth century. See "Pueblo weaving."

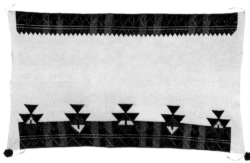

Hopi manta

horizontal loom. See "carpet loom."

horse. A common animal motif in oriental rugs. The horse is prominent in hunting carpets. In Chinese rugs, the horse may be a symbol of wealth and status.

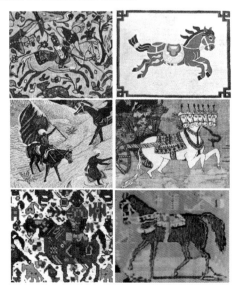

Horses
TOP: Persia, China. **MIDDLE:** Turkmenistan, India.
BOTTOM: Khamseh, Karabagh.

horse cover, horse blanket, chul (Turk.), **jol-i asb** (Persian), **shabrak** (Kurdish). A blanket placed under the saddle on a horse or that is used otherwise to cover a horse. Many horse covers have two pieces, called "pectorals" or "breast pieces," that cross over the horse's chest under the neck. See "ru-olâghi" and "zinpush."

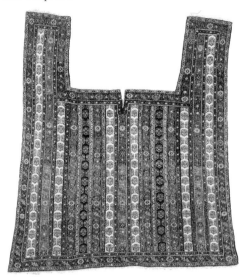

Horse cover (Kurd)

horsehair. Horsehair is sometimes used in the construction of tribal bags, particularly in Iran and Afghanistan. The sides of bags may be laced with coarsely spun or braided horsehair. Loops for the closure at the top of the bag may also be made of horse-hair.

Hotamiş. A town of south central Anatolia and a source of kilims.

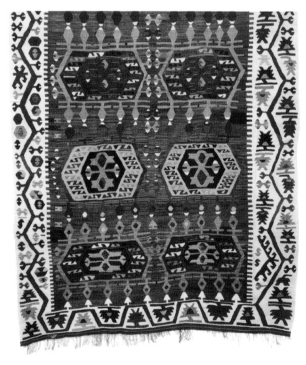

Hotamiş kilim (detail)

Hotien. See "Khotan."

houris. Beautiful virgins in Paradise who comfort faithful followers of Islam. See "Peri."

Hubbell Trading Post. A trading post founded by Don Lorenzo Hubbell in 1876 near the town of Ganado in Arizona. Hubbell traded with the Navajos for rugs of high quality, most of which were resold to the Fred Harvey Company. The area was a source of large rugs and many rugs were woven using a distinctive red termed "Ganado red." The trading post continues in operation. See "Ganado."

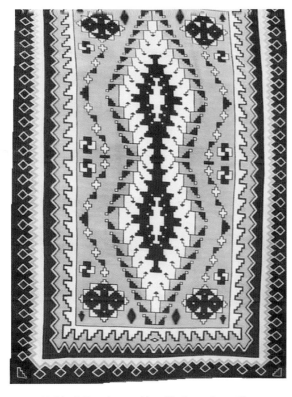

Hubbell Navajo rug (detail) *Steve Getzwiller*

hue, pure color. Color from the visual spectrum or combination of such colors. See "Munsell's color theory."

huli. A long flatweave blanket of Tunisia, including ornamented end panels.

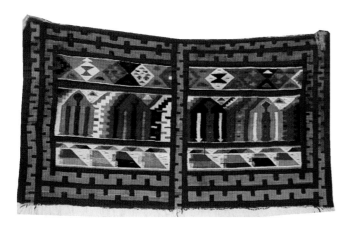

Huli end panel *R. John Howe*

Hunedoara. A region of Romania and a source of kilims.

Hungary. Kilims were woven in Hungary in the regions of Torontali and Kalocsa

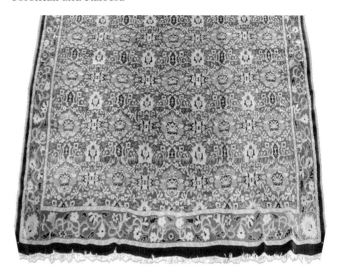

Hungarian carpet (detail) *Peter Pap Oriental Rugs Inc.*

hunting carpet. Persian carpets from the Safavid period and Mughal carpets showing hunting scenes, animals in combat or animals singly, usually within an intricate floral setting. Many of these are attributed to Kashan. A contemporary carpet with the same motif. See "animal carpet," "Imperial Silk Hunting Carpet," "Poldi Pezzoli Hunting Carpet," "Sanguszco group," "Swedish Royal Hunting Carpet," and "Vienna Hunting Carpet."

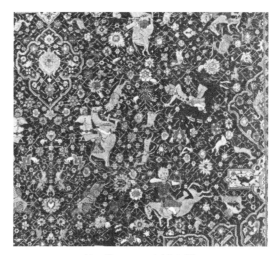

Hunting carpet (detail)

hurch (Persian khorj, cf. "khorjin"). Large double storage bag similar to a saddle bag but much deeper and wider.

husk matting. An early American mat made of braided corn husks.

Husseinabad. A village of the Hamadan area in northwest Iran. It is a source of rugs woven with the Herati pattern. See "Hamadan."

Hyderabad. A city of southern Pakistan and a source of contemporary rugs. Also, a city of south central India.

hydrophobic fiber. Synthetic fibers used in rugs that do not absorb water.

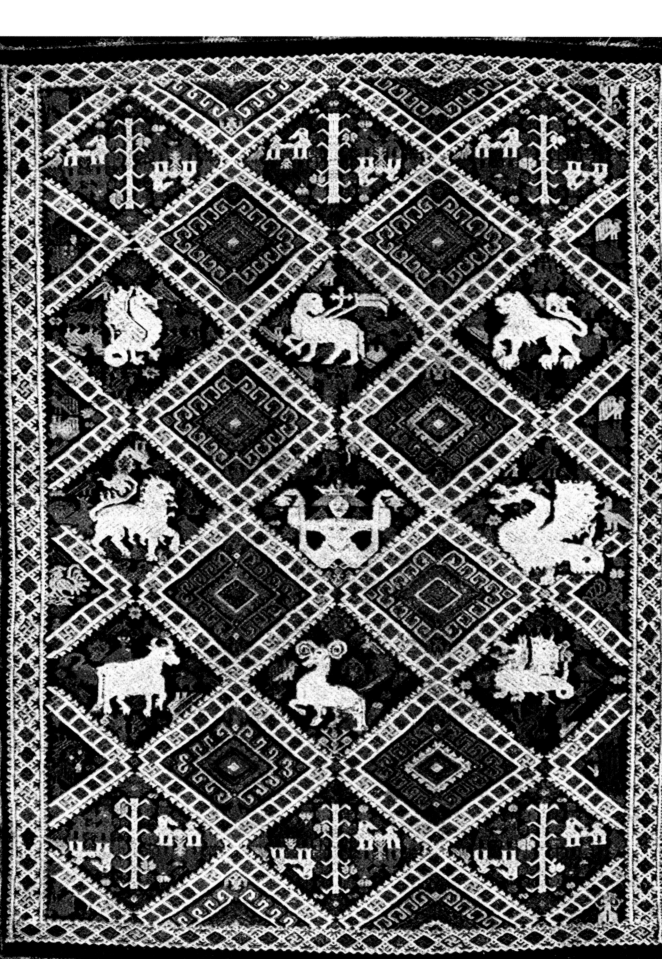

ian'. A narrow pile Caucasian runner about 3 feet wide and at least twice as long as it is wide.

ibrik. See "ewer."

I.C.O.C., International Conference on Oriental Carpets. An organization sponsoring periodic international conferences dealing with carpets and textile arts primarily of the Mideast and East. Seminars and research papers are presented along with special exhibitions.

ideogram, A written symbol directly representing an object or idea rather than a word or sound. Some ideograms are used in Chinese writing and are design elements in some Chinese rugs. See "fu," "shou," and "xi."

Igdir, Igdyr. A Turkmen tribe related to the Yomud.

iğsalik (Turk.) A Turkmen spindle bag.

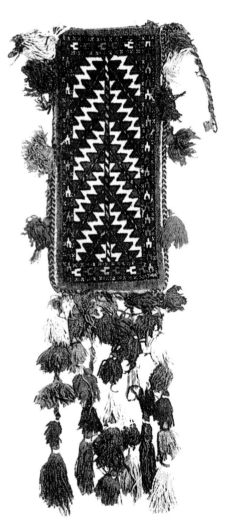

Iğsalik

ikat (Malay, "tie, bind"). A process in which fabric designs are created by tie-dyeing warps and/or wefts before they are used on the loom. A fabric produced by this process. During the nineteenth century, Uzbeks and Tajiks wove silk ikats for robe-like outer garments (chapan, chirpy, khalat). They used tie-dyed warps which tend to produce a vertical "smearing" of the design. Ikat patterns influenced the designs of some Ersari pile weaves. See "abr," "asab," "baghmal," "bandha," "haft rang," "maghmal," and "weft ikat blankets."

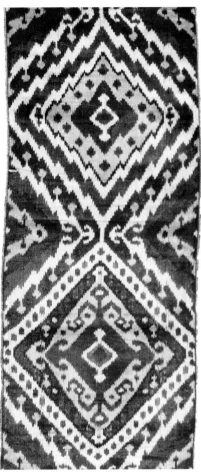

Uzbeki silk velvet ikat *Sothebys*

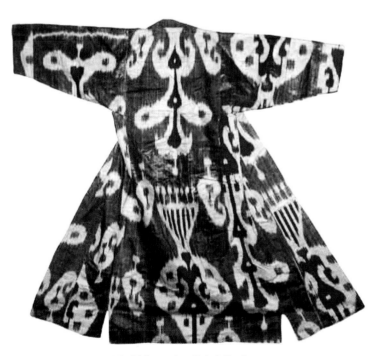

Uzbeki ikat robe *Uzbek Textile*

ilem tülü. See "tülü."

Imperial Mughal Prayer Rug, Vienna Millefleurs Prayer Rug.
A mille fleurs prayer rug attributed to eighteenth-century
Kashmir. A mihrab and cypresses frame a field of blossoms.
This rug has a silk foundation and wool pile. Its knot density
is 430 asymmetric knots per square inch. It is in the
collection of the Vienna Museum für Angewandte Kunst.
A very similar rug, formerly in the McMullan collection, is at
Harvard in Cambridge, Massachusetts.

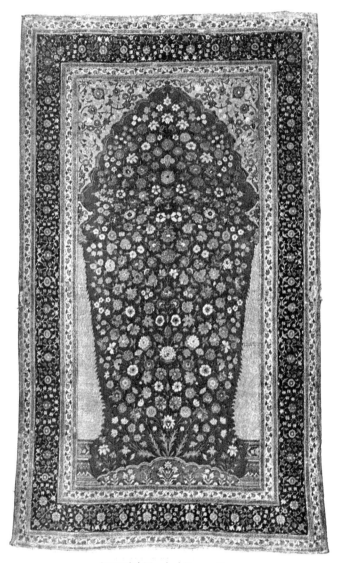

Imperial Mughal Prayer Rug

Imreli. A tribe of Turkestan. The name is derived from Eimur, a
sub-tribe of the Salor. Carpets and torbas were first attributed
to this tribe in 1980. Supporting evidence was never provided
and this attribution is considered questionable. See "eagle gul."

Inalu. A sub-tribe of the Shahsavan. See "Shahsavan." A village
in northwest Iran.

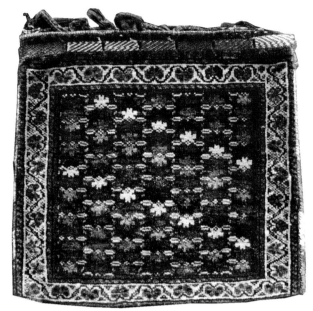

Inalu saddle bag *Michael Craycraft*

Incescu. A trade designation for central Anatolian rugs with a
long format from the area of Kayseri. These rugs have
multiple geometric medallions with yellow borders and red
fields. They have elems at either end.

India. The great period of Indian carpet weaving was from about
1550 through 1740. Rugs of this period are discussed under
the entry "Mughal carpets." The Persians defeated the
Mughals and sacked Delhi in 1739. Thereafter, Mughal power
rapidly declined and it was only the British East India
Company that fostered carpet production. Eighteenth-century
carpet production was quite small. The quality of rug weaving
deteriorated in the 1800s as factory production of copies
supplanted the oriental rug as a creative art in the hands of
craftsmen. In this period, prison labor was used to weave rugs
with Mughal designs. The rug production of India increased
significantly in the 1950s. In India, rugs are woven by men and
boys and not by women.

Contemporary Indian rugs consist of copies of Chinese,
Persian, Turkmen, and Aubusson or Savonnerie designs. They
are woven with asymmetric knots on a cotton foundation
with double wefts.

Nominal knot counts for contemporary rugs of India are
generally shown by two numbers separated by a slash. The
first number equals the number of weftwise or horizontal
knots in a nine-inch span divided by ten. The number
following the slash is the number of knots warpwise or
vertically in a nine-inch span divided by two. For example,
7/52 indicates 70 knots per nine inches weftwise and 104
knots per nine inches warpwise. To convert this indicator to
knots per square inch, multiply the first number by ten, the
second number by two and divide their product by 81. Thus,

$$(70 \times 104)/81 = 90 \text{ knots per square inch.}$$

Common knot counts are 4/30, 5/40, 7/52, 9/60 and 12/60. See "asan," "dhurrie," "dihari," "dulicha" "Mughal carpets," and "namda" See entries under the following geographical locations:

Agra	Jaunpur
Ahmedabad	Kashmir
Amritsar	Khamariah
Andhra Pradesh	Kutch
Benares	Lahore
Bengal	Mahabalipuram
Bhadohi	Masulipatam
Calcutta	Mirzapur
Deccan	Poona
Ellora	Rajasthan
Gujarat	Sharistan
Gwalior	Srinagar
Himachal Pradesh	Uttar Pradesh
Jaipur	Warangel
Jammu	

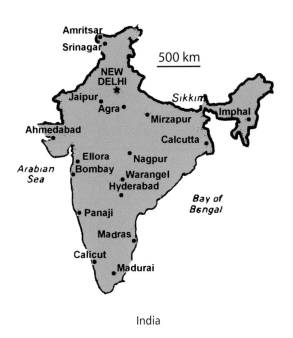

India

indigo. A blue vegetable dye derived from members of the pea family, *Indigofera tinctoria, Indigofera argentea*, or *Indigofera arrecta*. A yellow juice from the plant oxidizes to blue upon exposure to air. Indigo was chemically synthesized in 1880. When indigo is used in combination with some natural yellow dyes to produce green, the color may become blue-green with time as the yellow fades.

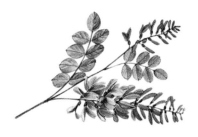

Indigo

indigotine. Indigo carmine, a water-soluble compound of indigo, formerly used as a textile dye.

Indo-. A prefix indicating that the rug was woven in India with a design characteristic of some other region, e.g., Indo-Persian or Indo-Chinese.

Indo-Herat, Indo-Persian. A large group of sixteenth and seventeenth-century rugs of disputed origin. These rugs were first attributed to India, but some scholars attribute them to Herat. They are predominantly red and green in color with designs generally including small floral elements, vines, animals, birds, and cloudbands. Warps are silk with three cotton or silk wefts between rows of knots. Knot densities are between 250 and 400 knots per square inch. See "'Portuguese' carpets."

Indo-Mir. Rugs woven primarily in Uttar Pradesh, India, with an all-over field pattern of small botehs. The designs are variations of those of Serabend.

Indo-Persian. See "Indo-Herat."

ingrain. All-wool, flatwoven, power-loomed carpets with reversible patterns. Two fabrics are interwoven so the design on the front is also on the back, but reversed in color. These carpets were woven from about the middle of the eighteenth century to the 1930s. Types are known as English, Kilmarnock, Kidderminster, Scotch, and Venetian.

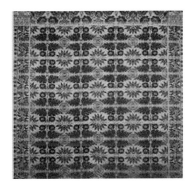

Ingrain carpet *Jason Nazmiyal*

inherent vice. In conservation, the propensity of a textile or any object to deteriorate because of the nature of the materials or structures used in its fabrication. The gradual embrittlement of fibers and loss of pile through the use of corrosive dyes or mordants is an example of inherent vice in oriental rugs. Some insurance policies cite damage due to inherent vice as an exclusion from coverage. See "etching."

Injilas. See "Enjelâs."

inscription. Script on an oriental rug. It may be a date, some religious or poetic sentiment, or a name of the donor, initial owner, or weaver of the rug. In court and factory rugs, inscriptions are usually enclosed by a cartouche in the field or border. In village and nomadic rugs, the inscription is usually not enclosed. Most inscription are Arabic or Persian, in Arabic script. Some are in Armenian or Slavic languages. See "Arabic calligraphy," "chronogram," "dating rugs," and "khan carpet."

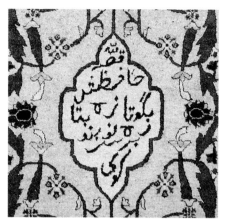

Inscription within cartouche

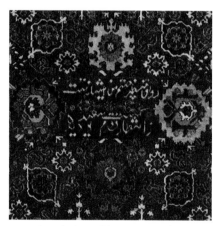

Inscription without cartouche

interior decoration. See "decorative styles."

inter-knotting. See "macramé."

interlocking wefts, interlocking tapestry. In a tapestry-woven fabric, wefts that reverse direction by passing around other wefts (usually of a different color) rather than by passing around warps. Double interlocking wefts are those that pass around two wefts in reversing direction. See "double interlocking wefts."

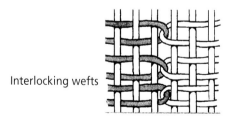

Interlocking wefts

ipekli (Turk., "silken"). Carpets with pile of mercerized cotton.

Iran. See "Persia."

Iraq. Rugs are woven in Kurdish communities of northern Iraq. Kilims are woven in the town of Hai in southern Iraq and these are termed "Hai." These are tapestry-woven in two vertical pieces and joined in the center. They have geometric designs. "Samawas" are embroidered blankets and rugs on a wool foundation. These are woven in villages of southern Iraq. Colors are bright and designs consist of densely-arranged geometric, floral, and animal motifs and images. Human figures are also shown. Since the 1930s, some pile rugs have been woven in Baghdad prisons. Designs have included maps of Iraq, the royal coat of arms, and ancient buildings. The quality of these rugs has declined in current production.

Ancient pile carpet fragments have been unearthed at the At-Tar Caves in Iraq. These fragments have been dated from the third century B.C.E. to the third century C.E. Different fragments were woven with the asymmetric knot, the symmetric knot, the Coptic knot, or the Senneh loop knot (an unusual knot producing pile on both sides of the fabric) and an unknotted cut loop. See "Erbil" and "Mosul."

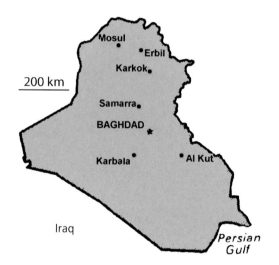

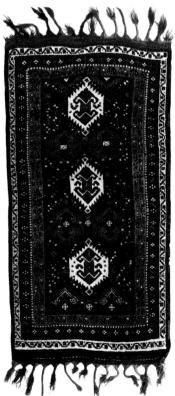

Iraqi Kurdish rug *CarpetView*

Ireland. From the middle to late eighteenth century carpets primarily of the Wilton type were woven in Ireland. See "Donegal."

iron mordant. See "ferrous sulphate" and "mordant."

Isfahan, Esfahan, Isphahan. A city of western central Iran and the capital of Persia under Shah Abbas and his Safavid successors. Magnificent court rugs were woven in Isfahan in the seventeenth and eighteenth centuries up to the Afghan invasion of 1722. After that, Iran's capital city was successively Mashhad, Shiraz, and finally Tehran. Isfahan regained some of its cultural and commercial prominence only in the 1920s.

Between the First and Second World Wars, carpets of fine workmanship and good design, but poor dyes, were woven in Isfahan. After World War II, very fine rugs with designs of the Safavid period were woven there. These rugs have knot densities up to 750 per square inch. Dyes were improved. Intricate floral medallion carpets or pictorial animal rugs were produced. The asymmetric knot is used and some later rugs are woven on silk warps or are entirely silk. Some notable twentieth-century weaver-designers of Isfahan include Emami, Sirafian, and Hekmet Nejad. See "kheft," and "Persia."

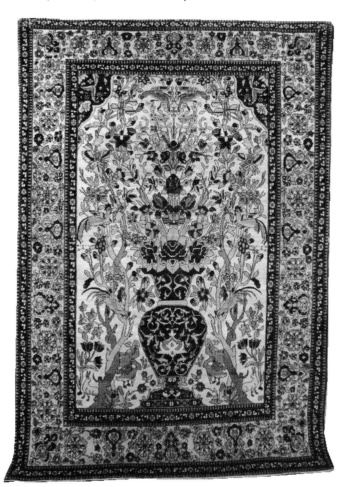

Isfahan rug *Grogan and Company*

Islam. Islam means "submission [to God]" in Arabic. Islam is a system of religious beliefs revealed to Muhammad (ca. 570-632 C.E.). There are five basic tenets or "pillars" of Islam.

1. Faith: the profession of faith is the shahâda: "There is no god but God (Allâh), and Muhammad is his Prophet." This phrase is frequently found calligraphed on mosques and other public buildings, textiles and other artifacts, sometimes in a highly stylized and barely legible form. One widespread style may be seen on the flag of Saudi Arabia.

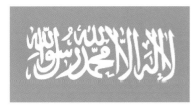

Profession of faith

2. Prayer: prayer is obligatory at five fixed times each day, regardless of where the worshipper might be, and is accompanied by gestures and movements performed in sequence known as rak'a. These movements include prostration, during which the worshipper places his hands and forehead on the ground: hence the convenience of a portable, individual prayer rug.

3. Charity: by alms-giving, the donor believes he purifies that portion of his wealth which he retains.

4. Fasting: abstinence from food, drink, and sex is required during daylight hours in the month of Ramadan. Because the Islamic calendar employs a lunar month, Ramadan rotates through the seasons of the year.

5. Pilgrimage: the believer with adequate means is obliged to make the pilgrimage to Mecca at least once in his lifetime. The pilgrimage (hajj) is made two months after Ramadan. Additional sites of pilgrimage for Shi'i Muslims are Najaf, Karbala (in Iraq), Qum, and Mashhabad (in Iran).

There are two great divisions of Islam, Sunnism and Shi'ism. Sunni Muslims accept the legitimacy of the rulers who succeeded Muhammad (the caliphs) by election. Shi'i Muslims or Shi'ites hold that the caliphate belongs only to the house and descendants of Muhammad, namely the twelve imams beginning with Muhammad's cousin and son-in-law, Ali. The Ismailis accept only the first seven of the imams. There are also differences in ritual and interpretation of scripture between the sects. See "Hadith," "Hijra," "Kaaba," "Koran," "prayer rugs," and "qibla."

Islamic dates. Dates are sometimes woven into rugs using Arabic calligraphy. These numbers translate as follows:

$$1 = I \qquad 2 = N \qquad 3 = \mu \qquad 4 = \varepsilon, \mu \quad 5 = O, O$$
$$6 = \gamma, q \quad 7 = V \qquad 8 = \Lambda \qquad 9 = q \qquad 0 = +, \bullet$$

Dates and other complex numerals are read from left to right, as in Western usage. The Islamic date is converted into a Gregorian date using this formula:

Islamic date + 622 - (Islamic date/33.7) = Gregorian date.
See "chronogram," "dates," "dating rugs," and "Gregorian date."

islimi, eslimi, rumi, selimi (Persian and Turk.) Design motifs based on leaf shapes and used in metalwork, ceramics, architectural ornament, textiles and carpets in the Near East. These arabesque forms are classified as simple islimi (*sade islimi*), winged islimi (*qanadly islimi*), forked islimi (*khacely islimi*), almond-shaped islimi (*butaly islimi*), plaited islimi (*khorme islimi*) and complex islimi (*islimi bendlik*). See "hatayi" and "saz."

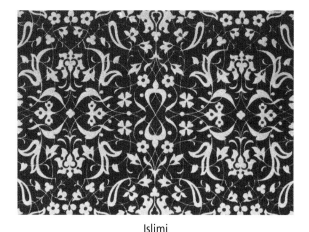

Islimi

Isparta. Isparta in southwestern Anatolia is a major commercial finishing center and market for Turkish rugs. Rugs are woven in Denizli and Afyon, some one hundred miles distant. Designs are copies of other Turkish rugs, Caucasian rugs, and Persian rugs. They are woven on a cotton foundation, many using the asymmetric knot. There is some warp offset. In the 1920s and 1930s, commercial rugs were woven in Isparta with Sarouk designs similar to those of rugs woven in Arâk and Mahallât. These rugs have slightly offset warps.

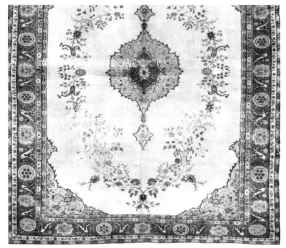

Isparta rug (detail) *Kaziim Yildiz*

isparek. See "esperek."

Isphahan. See "Isfahan."

Istanbul, Constantinople, Kumkapı, Koum Kapu. In Istanbul, Armenian weavers wove silk and metallic thread rugs. Designs were copies of great Persian rugs and other Turkish rugs. Some of the most famous Armenian weavers were Hagop Kapoukjian,

Zareh Penyamin, Garabed Apelian, and Tossourian. They wove rugs prior to the Second World War. Many of these rugs were signed. These rugs may be referred to as "Kumkapı."

More strictly, Kumkapı refers to rugs woven prior to the First World War by Turkish weavers employed by the Sultan. Kumkapı (Turk., "sandgate"), on the Marmara shore of the Istanbul peninsula, was the site of the workshops of the Sultan's master weavers. These include Kanatta, Nemzur, and Takouchi. See "Salting Group" and "Hereke."

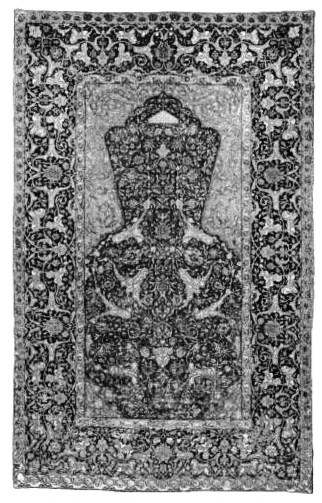

Kumkapı rug (silk and metal thread) *Sothebys*

istang. Appliquéd felt carpets of the Chechens in the Caucasus.

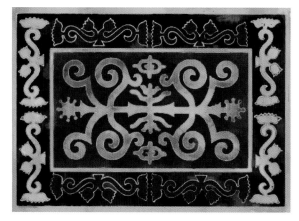

Istang *Wikipedia*

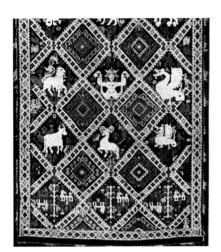

Italian rug of the early 19th century (detail) *Albert Sautier*

Italy. Rugs with the asymmetric knot were woven by Italian peasants in the eighteenth and nineteenth centuries. A variety of brocaded and embroidered textiles was produced for domestic uses. Most of these weavings were relatively narrow and were probably intended as furniture covers rather than as rugs. See "Abruzzi" and "Sardinia."

itea. In Cappadocia, Turkey, a simple kilim used as a clean surface in baking. These kilims are in shades of ivory and brown.

Ivrindi. A village in western Anatolia, west of Balıkesir. Rugs from this village use Caucasian designs and are woven in long, narrow formats.

Izmir, Smyrna. Izmir (formerly Smyrna) is a city on the west coast of Anatolia. Earlier rugs from Smyrna showed large floral motifs on rugs with a wool foundation. Later rugs were woven on a cotton foundation. No hand-knotted rugs are presently woven in Izmir, but the city is a collection and marketing center for rugs woven in the area.

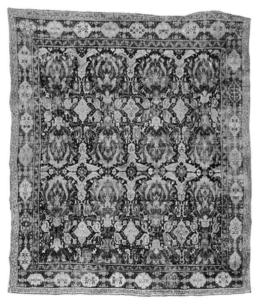

Smyrna rug *Sothebys*

Iznik ceramics. From the 16th century, tiles and pottery of superior quality have been produced in Iznik, Anatolia. The floral designs in these ceramics, especially tile work, are a likely source of some designs in Turkish carpets.

Iznik tile with Laleh Abbasi motif *Amir Mohtashemi*

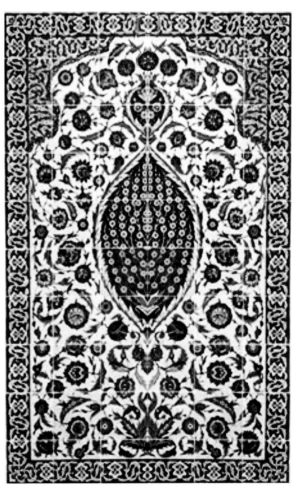

Iznik tile with mihrab *Yurdan*

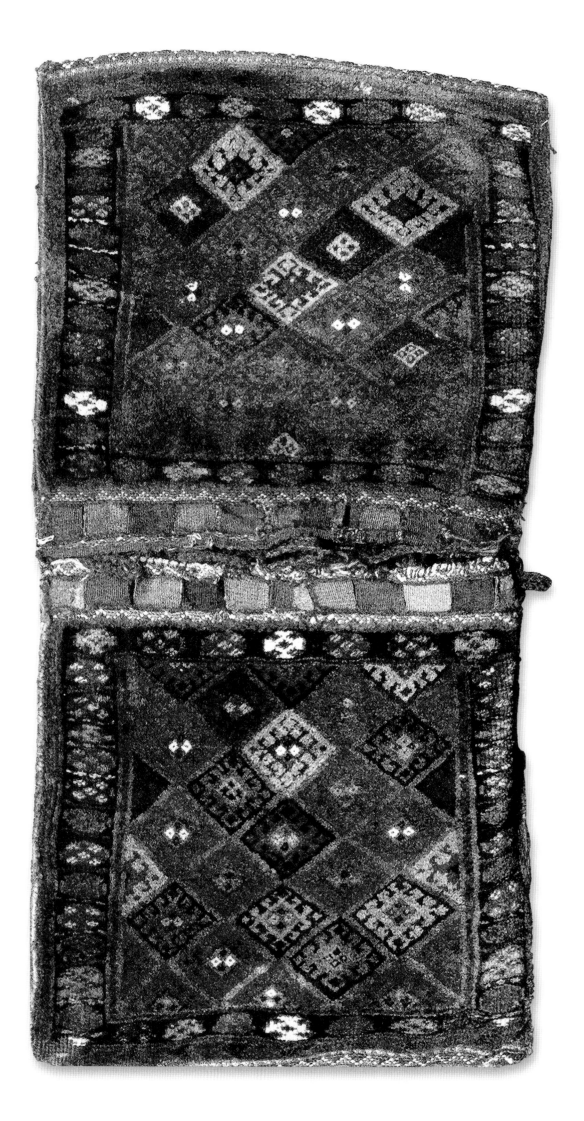

jabuye (Tibetan). Mats and pillows.

jacquard. A system of controlling color patterns on a loom consisting of punched cards or paper rolls and wires. The system was developed by J.M. Jacquard in 1804. The principle was later adapted for statistical tabulating.

Jaff. A tribe of the Kurds in Iran (north and west of Senneh) and eastern Iraq. Weavers of this tribe were the source of a great many bags woven in the 1920s and 1930s. Many of the pile bag faces survive and have designs of diagonal rows of hooked diamonds. Colors are green, blue, red, and brown.

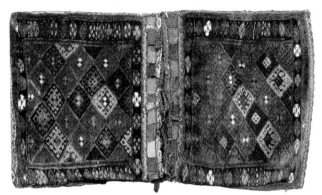

Jaff Kurd saddle bag *Sothebys*

jahâzi (Persian). A dowry rug.

Jaipur. A city of northern central India in the wool-producing province of Rajasthan. Rug weaving in prisons began in Jaipur in the middle of the nineteenth century. These rugs were copies of Mughal designs. Carpets are woven with single or double wefts, with single-wefted rugs of a finer weave. Contemporary carpets have asymmetric knots on a cotton foundation. The finer variety have a knot density of about 200 knots per square inch and are copies of other Near Eastern designs. The collection of the Jaipur Palace Museum includes many fine Mughal carpets.

jajim. See "jijim."

jaldar. A design of Pakistani rugs consisting of columns or lattices of diamonds.

jamkhani. See "dhurrie."

Jammu. A northern province of India, south of Kashmir. Rug production in the area is non-commercial except for that woven by Tibetan refugees who have settled in the area.

Jamshidi. A tribe of the Chahar Aimaq residing in Herat and northwestern Afghanistan. The tribe weaves copies of commercially popular designs. Jamshid is a legendary Persian ruler and patron of arts and crafts. See "Aimaq," "Kawdani," and "Takht-e Jamshid."

jânamâz, joi namaz (Persian). See "prayer rug."

Jan Begi. A Persian-speaking tribe located near Ghorian in northwestern Afghanistan. Members of the tribe weave rugs

with a distinctive motif of columns of blossoms, the minâ khâni pattern, that has been frequently copied.

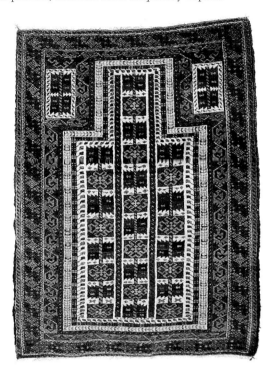

Jan Begi prayer rug

Jangalarik. See "Jengel Arjuk."

Jangal Areq. See "Jengel Arjuk."

Jan Mirzai. A Baluchi tribe of Zaveh in Khurasan, Iran. Some pile rugs have been attributed to them.

Jaunpur. A town of northeastern India (northwest of Benares) and formerly a minor carpet production center.

Jawalakhel. A town of Nepal where Tibetan refugees weave contemporary rugs on a cotton foundation.

Jehol. A region of Manchuria in China and a source of pile rugs in the 1930s. Designs were copies of those used in early Beijing and Tianjan rugs. Colors are blue, brown, white, and black. See "China."

Jengel Arjuk, Jangal Areq, Jangalarik. A village and tribe of the Ersari near Aq Chah in northern Afghanistan. Many of their rugs display a unique small, quartered gul. Also, a designation for prayer rugs with realistic floral designs sold in Kabul, Afghanistan. See "Ersari."

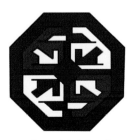

Jengel Arjuk gul

Jenkins, Arthur D. (1897-1988). An American publisher and collector of oriental rugs. He bequeathed a major collection of more than 250 rugs and nomadic weavings to The Textile Museum, Washington, D.C. He also collected books about oriental rugs and contributed more than 850 volumes to The Textile Museum Library. Jenkins served as President of the Board of Trustees of the Museum.

jerga (Spanish, perhaps from Arabic *khirqa*, "rag, duster"). An early American thick, coarse, twill-woven fabric of the southwest of hand-spun yarn, used as a floor covering. Simple plaid was a common design. A hooded tunic made of this.

jewelry asmalyk. A Yomud asmalyk in which there are stylized images of women's jewelry. There are very few of these asmalyks. See "asmalyk."

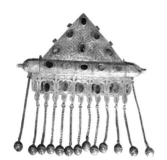

Turkmen jewelry

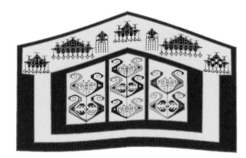

Jewelry asmalyk

ji. An antique, long-handled trident sometimes represented in Chinese rugs. See "bogu."

jijim, djidjim, dezhidzhim, jajim, cicim (Turk.). A flatweave of narrow, warp-faced strips sewn together or a warp-patterned weave. A flatweave with various brocade structures. The term is used ambiguously. In India, a printed cotton fabric used as a floor covering. See "alasa," "cicim," and "gadzhari."

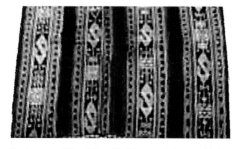

Shahsavan jijim (detail) *Manouchehr Haghighhat*

joi namaz. See "prayer rug."

Jokar. A town south of Hamadan in Iran. It is a source of medallion and spandrel rugs with the Herati pattern in the field.

jol, jol-i asb (Arabic, Persian). See "horse cover."

jollam. See "tent band."

jollar. A Turkmen tent bag that is much longer than it is wide, 2 feet by 6 feet, for example. One face may be pile and tassels may be attached. The bag is open on a long side. See "joval" and "torba."

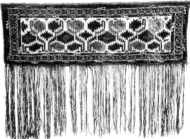

Jollar *Dr. Herbert J. Exner*

Jones, H. McCoy (1896-1987). A prominent American collector of tribal and village rugs. He was the founder and first President of The International Hajji Baba Society. He contributed rugs and textiles valued at more than three million dollars to the M.H. De Young Museum in San Francisco.

Josan. See "Jowzân."

Joshegan, Josheqân-e Qâli. A town in northern central Iran, thirty miles southwest of Kashan. Rugs have been woven in Joshegan since the eighteenth century. The design for which Joshegan is famed is an all-over lozenge pattern, each lozenge consisting of a geometricized floral motif. This design may include a small medallion and spandrels. The design has been widely copied. Rugs of the guli hinnai design are also woven in Joshegan and surrounding villages. The rugs are woven on a cotton foundation with a density of 100 to 200 asymmetric knots per square inch.

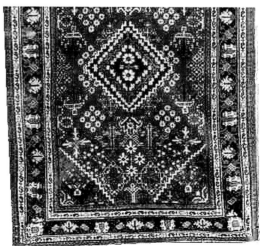

Joshegan rug *J. Barry O'Connell*

joval, chuval, çuval, juval, tschoval; toushak, doshak. A large Turkmen or Turkish storage bag, approximately 3 feet by 6 feet, one surface of which may be covered with pile, used to store clothing. The bag is open on a long side. Often, only the pile face has survived. See "ak chuval," "ala chuval," and "kizil chuval."

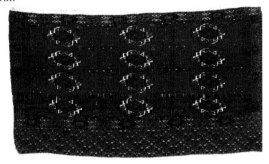

Joval face *Jerry Silverman*

jowz. (Persian) "walnut." A motif of an eight-pointed star within an octagon.

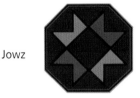

Jowz

Jowzân, Josan, Jozan. A village in northwestern Iran, southeast of Malâyer. Rugs from Jowzân and surrounding villages are similar to early twentieth-century Sarouks in design, but have symmetric knots. These are double-wefted rugs of about 200 symmetric knots to the square inch. The foundation is cotton and wefts may be blue. See "Malâyer."

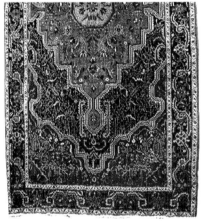

Jowzân rug (detail) *Peter Willborg*

Jozan. See "Jowzân."

jufti knot, double knot, doutakapi, Langari knot. A symmetric or asymmetric knot tied over three or more warps instead of the usual two warps. In Persian rugs, the jufti knot is used in solid colored areas of a rug, but not in design outlines. As a result, design outlines are more dense than solid colored areas. This can be felt by running one' fingers, warp-wise, across outlines in the rug. If an increased density is felt at the outline, the jufti knot is probably used in the rug. Erosion of outline or a change in yarn quality used in outlines confuses the results of this test. A very close inspection of the knots is definitive. See "Khurasan."

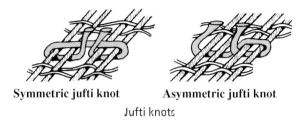

Symmetric jufti knot   **Asymmetric jufti knot**
Jufti knots

julgah. In Khurasan, "coarse wool."

julkhyrs. "Bearskin." An Uzbek carpet with very long pile, often made up of broad pile strips of different colors.

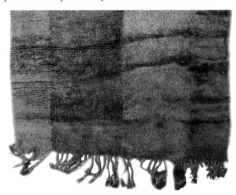

Julkhyrs (detail) *Peter Pap Oriental Rugs Inc*

jute. A bast fiber from the stem of the sisal plant *Corchorus capsularis* and *Corchorus olitorius*. Jute has been used in the foundation and sometimes in the pile (mixed with wool) of rugs from India. Jute was not used in pile rugs before the early nineteenth century. A few very old Chinese rugs have foundations of jute. It is used in some power loomed rugs as filler. Jute is more susceptible than other vegetal fibers to weakening through alkalis or bleaches. Jute is used in the manufacture of burlap.

jynne (Swedish). A flatwoven square cushion used during marraige ceremonies and festivals in church.

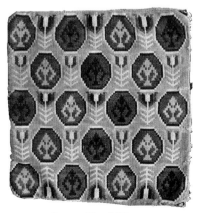

Jynne *Wendel Swan*

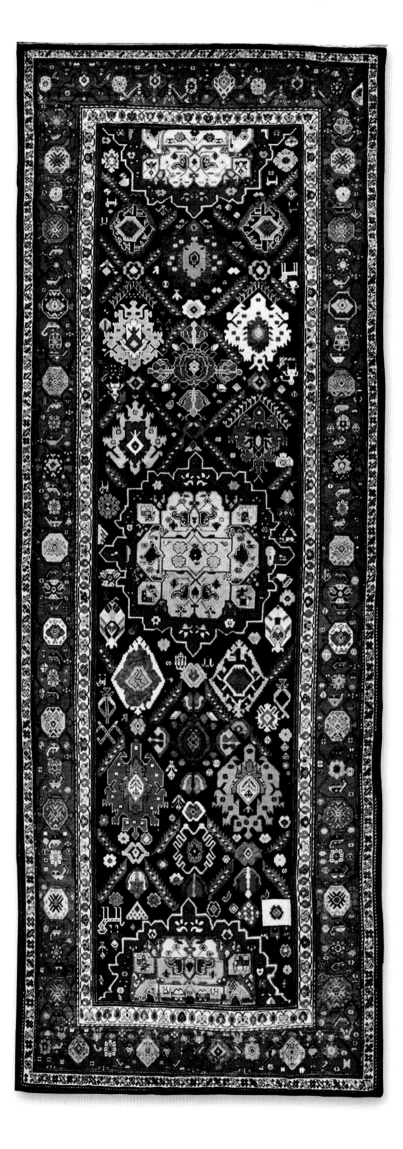

Kaaba, Ka'ba (Arabic, "cube"). A cubical stone building in Mecca, Saudi Arabia, a shrine since pre-Islamic times and the spiritual center of Islam. A venerated meteorite, the Black Stone, is embedded in the wall of the Kaaba. The top half of the Kaaba is covered with a black cloth (Kiswa) with a gold-embroidered calligraphic band running around it. The Kaaba is sometimes portrayed in prayer rugs. See "Islam."

kabal. A measure of a weaver's production in Tabriz, Iran, equal to 14,000 knots.

Kablstan. See "Cabistan."

Kabul, Kabol. The capital and largest city of Afghanistan. Before the Russian occupation of Afghanistan, the Kabul carpet bazaar was a primary source for new Afghanistan rug production and artificially aged Turkmen pieces. Many retail rug shops offered rugs to tourists. See "Afghanistan."

Kabud Râhang, Kabutarhang, Kabutarhan. A village north of Hamadan in northwestern Iran producing large rugs. These are single-wefted rugs on a cotton foundation. They are coarsely woven using the symmetric knot. The design is usually a red ground with a medallion and scattered floral sprays or a diaper pattern on a camel-colored ground.

kadife (Arabic *qatifa*, "plush, velvet"). Early Ottoman silk velvets. See "çatma."

Kağızman. A village near Kars in eastern Anatolia that was the source of rugs of modified Caucasian designs in lustrous colors on an all-wool foundation. These rugs are usually in a long format.

Kaimuri. A floral design used by weavers in the Kaimur Hills of India (south of Benares). The design is ultimately derived from Farâhân in Persia. The design consists of floral and leaf sprays in a columnar arrangement.

Kairouan, Qairawan. A city of north central Tunisia. Early nineteenth-century rugs of this region were prayer rugs with opposing niches. The area within the mihrabs is red. Some rugs had Kufesque borders. Later versions of the Kairouan rug were woven of naturally colored wool in shades of black, gray, brown, tan, and white.

kaikalak, tabak (Turk. plate). A motif in Anatolian rugs and other rugs consisting of four opposing ram's horns, usually with a diamond in the center. The horns tend to form a square with their tips curling inwards. See "birth symbol," "kochak," and "wurma."

Kaikalaks
1st and 2nd: Konya, Yalameh. 3rd and 4th: Moghan, Kazak

Kaitag embroideries. Embroideries of a small, multi-ethnic group of peoples known as Kaitag in an area northwest of Derbent in Daghestan. The emroideries are silk stitching on a hand-woven cotton fabric. Designs appear to be derived from Ottoman sources and from motifs found on local tombstones.

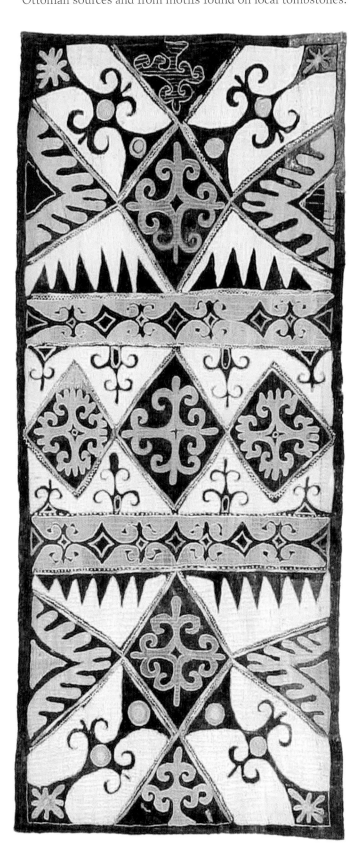

Kaitag embroidery *Jason Nazmiyal*

Kakaberu. A Kurdish tribe in the area of Senneh (Sanandaj), Iran. The tribe weaves rugs with large medallions. The rugs are double-wefted and coarsely knotted. Dark colors are used. The existence of this tribe is questioned. See "Kurds."

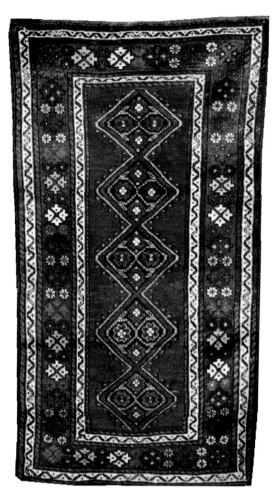

Kalârdasht rug (detail) *Simon Knight*

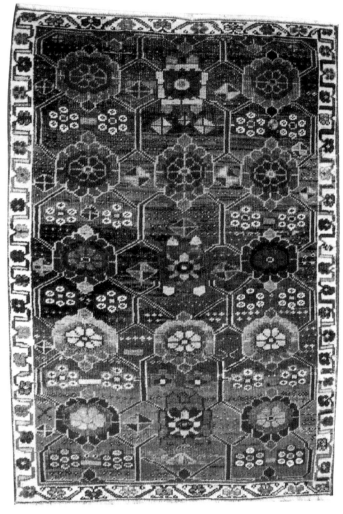

Kakaberu rug (detail) *Peter Willborg*

Kalâa, Kalâa des Beni-Rached. A village in Algeria south of Oran. Early rugs of this area were woven with long, vertical, octagonal compartments in the field and wide, striped kilim ends. The symmetric knot was used with seven to ten wefts between each row of knots.

kalamkâr, qalamkar (Persian *qalamkâr*, "engraving, print"). Cotton cloth of Iran and India patterned by mordant stamping and colored by painted or printed dyes. See "Masulipatam."

kalamkâr sofreh. An Iranian eating cloth made of printed cotton. See "sofreh."

Kalârdasht, Kelardasht. A valley of the Elburz mountains northwest of Tehran, Iran. Many rugs of this valley have large red medallions of the Memling gul with stepped outlining in white. Knot density is about 65 symmetric knots per square inch.

Kalât, Kalât-i Nâdiri. A village of northeastern Iran east of Quchân (now called Kabud Gonbad). It was the site of the stronghold and treasury of Nadir Shah Afshar, ruler of Iran from 1736 to 1747. Flatweaves, including sofrehs and bags, are woven in the area by people who claim descent from the Afshars and from Kurds resettled there by Nadir Shah Afshar. Their contemporary weavings are garishly colored with unstable dyes.

kalin (Turk.) General term for carpet in India (same word as qali, qâlin).

Kalhor. A tribe of the Lurs inhabiting the district of Kermanshah in Iran. They are Shi'i Muslims. This tribe is the source of some rugs.

kallegi, kalleghi, kalle'i, kelle, kelleghi, kelley (Persian, "headpiece"). A long narrow carpet in which the length is at least twice the width, 5 feet by 10 feet or 8 feet by 24 feet, for example. See "audience rug."

Kamo, Kamoo. A village of central Iran southeast of Nain, known for its sofrehs.

kampbaff. Rugs woven in Turkmen camps in Pakistan.

Kamsah, Kamseh. See "Khamseh."

kanat (Turk., "wing(s)"). Narrow bands woven in a variety of structures and then joined to form a rug. See "jijim."

k'ang cover. Chinese carpets of about five feet by eight feet or six feet by ten feet that are placed on top of the k'ang, a long brick stove used for household heating and on which people sit or sleep. See "blankets."

Kangal. A town of central Anatolia, southeast of Sivas, where yastiks are woven. These are on a wool foundation. Designs are simple geometric medallions, some with latch hooks.

Kansu. See "Gansu."

kantha. A traditional quilt of Bengal, India.

kap (Turk.). Any Turkmen bag.

kapan (Kurdish). Camel cover, often with tassels. See "ushter-i jol."

Kapristan. See "Gabistan."

kapunuk, kaplyk. A pile fabric decoration hung across the top and down the sides of Turkmen tent doors on the inside of the tent. These decorative pieces may have tassels in the center or ends. A curled leaf design is common in Ersari, Sariq, Tekke, and Arabatchi kapunuks.

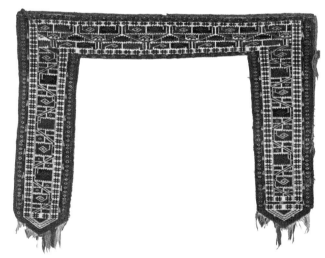

Tekke kapunuk *Sothebys*

kara. (Turk.) Black.

Karabagh. A mountainous region in the southern portion of the province of Genje (nineteenth-century Elisavetpol) in the Caucasus. The capital is the rug-producing center of Shusha. Nineteenth century rugs of this area have a great variety of designs. Some of the more common designs are the Chelaberd, Chondzoresk, Kasim Ushag, Lampa, and Herati. See entries for these terms. These are coarsely woven rugs with an average knot density of about 65 symmetric knots per square inch. The rugs of Karabagh tend to be the largest of the Caucasian rugs. Typically, they have an area of about 41 square feet and are in a long format. See "Caucasus" and "Shusha."

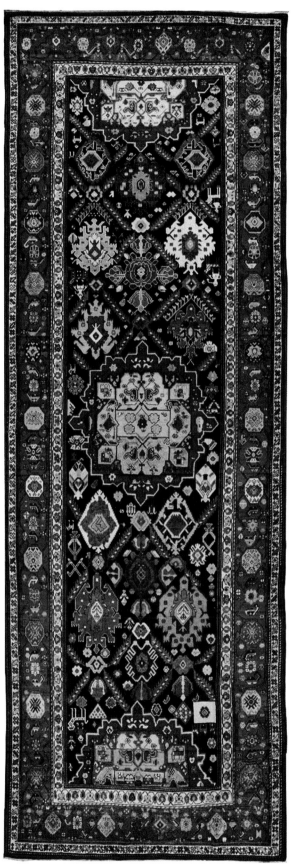

Karabagh rug (detail)

Karachi. A city of southern Pakistan. Karachi is a major source of factory rugs which are copies of Turkmen designs. See "Pakistan."

Karachoph, Karachov. A town south of Tiflis in the Caucasus. Nineteenth-century rugs attributed to this area are considered Kazaks and have a large central octagon medallion with two rectangles above the medallion and two rectangles below the medallion, a 2-1-2 pattern. The design resembles certain Anatolian rugs and probably has a Turkish origin. Caucasian rugs with this design typically have an area of 39 square feet and a knot density of 60 symmetric knots per square inch. See "Kazak."

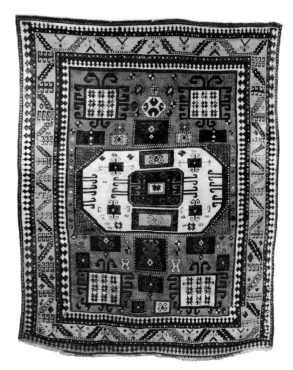

Karachoph Kazak *Grogan and Company*

Karachov. See "Karachoph."

Karadagh, Qaradagh. (Turk., "black mountains"). A mountainous region in northwestern Iran on the border of the Caucasus. Rugs with the Karadja design may be referred to as Karadagh when they are double-wefted rather than single-wefted. Kurdish rugs showing a Caucasian design influence are incorrectly termed Karadaghs.

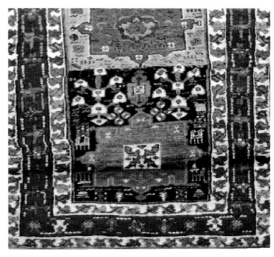

Karadagh rug (detail) *Peter Pap Oriental Rugs Inc*

Karadashli. A town of Turkmenistan and a source of Yomud weavings.

Karadja, Karaja, Qarâjeh. A town in Iranian Azerbaijan, near Heriz (between Tabriz and Ahar). Rugs attributed to Karadja have distinctive hooked hexagon medallions on rugs of a long format. They are single-wefted and use the symmetric knot at densities of about 65 to 130 per square inch on a cotton foundation.

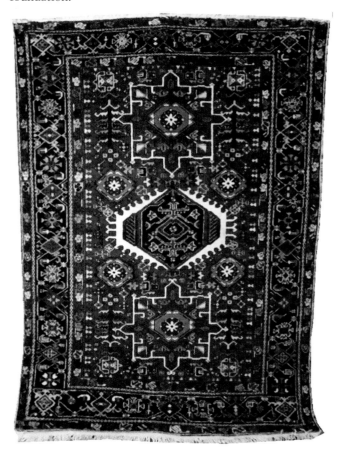

Karadja rug *Grogan and Company*

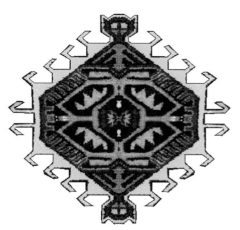

Karadja medallion

Karagashli. A village south of Derbend in the Caucasus. Nineteenth century rugs attributed to this village are classified as Kubas and have a motif consisting of dented quadrilaterals that may be considered geometricized palmettes. These are small rugs with an average knot density of 144 symmetric knots per square inch. See "Kuba."

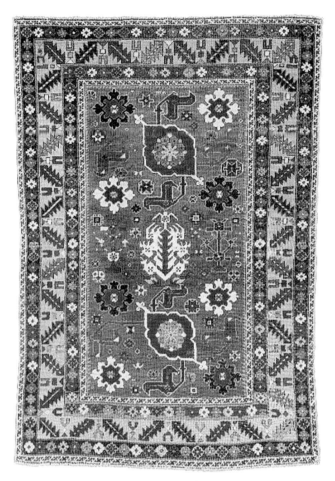

Karagashli rug *R. John Howe*

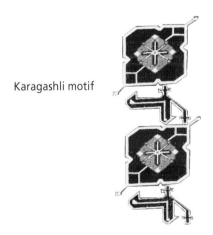

Karagashli motif

Karagöz, Karagös, Karagözlü. Rugs woven by a Kurdish tribe near Hamadan. These rugs have a cotton foundation and a knot density of about 130 symmetric knots per square inch. These rugs are single wefted. Early nineteenth-century rugs of this tribe have a lattice field with cells filled with floral motifs. Many of them have a camel-colored ground.

Karahisar. A designation for carpets woven in Afyon ("opium"), a village of west central Anatolia.

Karaja. See "Karadja."

Karakalpak, Karapapaks. (Turk., "black hat"). A Turko-Mongolian tribe primarily inhabiting the Oxus delta. They weave rugs and a variety of tribal functional pieces. Pile rugs attributed to the Karakalpak may have been woven by peoples who describe themselves as Uzbek Turkmen.

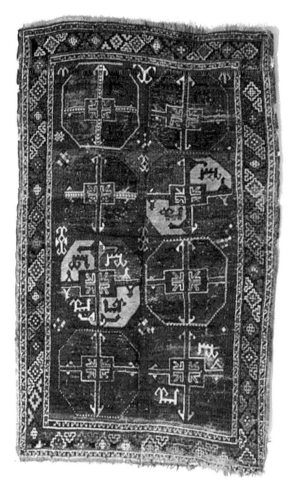

Karakalpak rug (detail) *Detlev Fischer*

Kara-Keçili (Turk., "with black goats"). A formerly nomadic tribe of western Anatolia who weave all-wool rugs in a square format. These rugs have all-over geometricized floral patterns.

Karakul. A primary breed of Asian sheep. Fleece color varies from black, gray, tan, and brown. Karakul caps, the typical cap of Afghan lambskin, are made from the skins of newborn or unborn Karakul lambs.

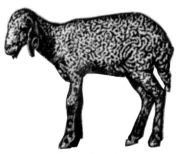

Karakul lamb

Karaman, Karamani, Karamanli. A Turkish term for the fat-tailed sheep. A town of south central Anatolia. It is the source of some pile rugs, but it is primarily known for the kilims woven in the area. These kilims or "Karamani" employ the slit weave structure. A distinctive design feature of these rugs is vertical borders consisting of black and red, finger-like, reciprocating rectangles. Skirts at top and bottom are common. Also, an obsolete term for any Turkish kilim.

Karaova. A designation for Milas rugs with fields consisting of a single, vertical, narrow panel or multiple, vertical, narrow panels.

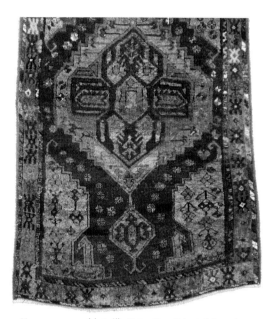

Karaman rug (detail) *Peter Pap Oriental Rugs Inc*

Karapınar (Turk., "black spring"). A village of south central Anatolia. Rugs from this village are all wool. Many are in runner format. The dominant colors are shades of red with some mustard yellow. The designs are geometric and often the medallions are eight-pointed stars inside octagons. Designs are similar to those of Caucasian rugs.

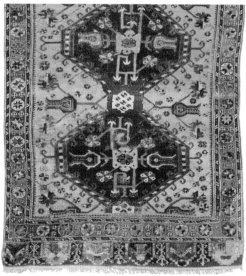

Karapınar rug (detail) *Sothebys*

kârdak (Persian). Carpet-trimming knife.

kargi (Turk.). A flat rod or slat that opens or closes a shed on a loom when the rod is rotated.

kâr-i sefide. In Afghanistan, designs containing white.

kâr-i surkh. In Afghanistan, designs rendered entirely in shades of red.

kara göz (Turk. "black eye"). A motif consisting of a cross within an octagon used in Anatolian rugs and Persian tribal rugs.

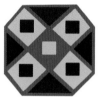

Kara göz

karolya (Turk.). Carpets used as bed covers. The size is about 5 feet by 6 feet.

Kars. A city of northeastern Anatolia near the border with the Caucasus. Rugs woven in the area of Kars have modified Caucasian designs. They are on an all-wool foundation. They are coarsely woven and similar to Kazaks in construction as well as design. For Kars rugs, reds tend to be burgundy rather that brick red as in Kazaks. Knot density is about 60 symmetric knots per square inch. Most kilims from the Kars area are long and narrow. Small prayer kilims with triangular mihrabs are also woven. Kilim warps are of brown wool and braided at the ends. Kurds in the area weave rugs, but their products are not generally distinguishable from other Kars rugs woven outside of workshops. Kars is a source of soumak bags that are woven without ground wefts.

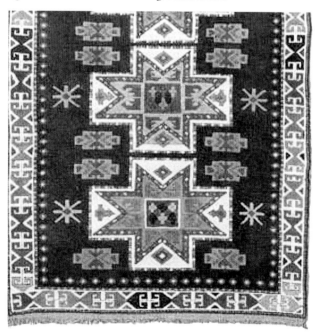

Kars rug (detail) *Turkish Cultural Foundation*

karshin. A Karakalpak, long, narrow bag for clothing.

Kashan. A city of north central Iran. Great court carpets were woven in Kashan during the Safavid period, but carpet weaving virtually ceased after the Afghan invasion in 1722. There was little weaving during the eighteenth and nineteenth centuries.

At the beginning of the twentieth century, carpet weaving was commenced using merino wool from Australia that had been spun in Manchester, England. These "Manchester" Kashans had velvety, glossy wool. They were woven until the early 1930s, the onset of world-wide economic depression. Thereafter, local wools were used.

Contemporary production is of double-wefted carpets on a cotton foundation with about 200 asymmetric knots per square inch. Silk is produced in the countryside surrounding Kashan and some silk rugs are woven in Kashan. Designs are primarily intricate floral medallion and spandrel types or designs similar to Sarouks. Many rugs are woven with a red field. Some notable twentieth-century weaver-designers of Kashan include Dabir Sanayeh, Shad Sar, Tafazzoli, and Madeh. These names may be used in referring to Kashan rugs. See "Dabir Kashan," "Manchester Kashan," "Mohtashem Kashan," and "souf."

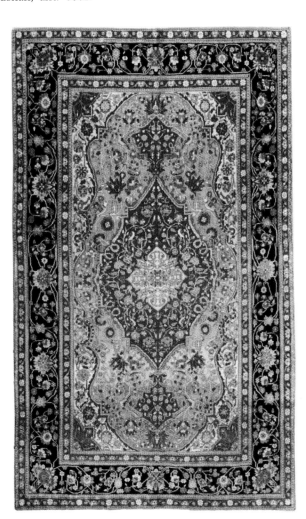

Kashan rug (detail) *Jason Nazmiyal*

Kashan medallion. The central medallion used in Kashan rugs. It is a diamond or pointed ovoid that may be slightly lobed or indented. It is filled with floral motifs and always has floral pendants at top and bottom.

Kashgai. See "Qashqa'i."

Kâshgar. A town of Eastern Turkestan, China, close to the border with Kirghizia. Silk carpets with gold and silver embroidery were woven in Kâshgar in the eighteenth century. Contemporary Kâshgar rugs use the symmetric knot on a cotton foundation and are double-wefted. See "Khotan" and "Yarkand."

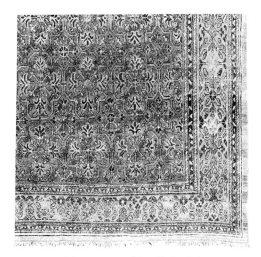

Kâshgar carpet (detail) *Sothebys*

Kashkuli, Kashguli, Qashguli. The Kashkuli Bozorg (Greater Kashkuli) and the Kashkuli Kuchek (Lesser Kashkuli) are tribes of the Qashqa'i Confederacy of southwest Iran. The more finely knotted rugs of the Qashqa'i are thought to be woven by the Kashkuli. Their rugs use the asymmetric knot. Wefts are usually dyed red. Warps are offset. Many of their rugs are woven in Firuzabad. Their designs include repeating boteh, Herati pattern, and an adaptation of the Indian Millefleurs prayer rug.

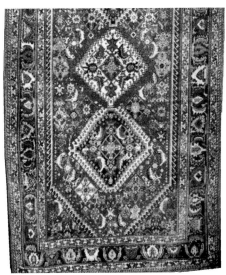

Kashkuli rug (detail) *Simon Knight*

Kâshmar, Turshiz. A town of Khurasan in northeastern Iran, southwest of Mashhad. A source of pictorial rugs based on Tabriz models. The central medallion and cartouches are filled with architectural views and images of ancient artifacts. The asymmetric knot is used on a cotton foundation. The town is also a collecting point for Baluchi rugs. See "Zirhaki."

Kashmir. The northernmost state of India, primarily Muslim in population. Kashmir was noted for the intricately patterned hand embroidered shawls produced there in the eighteenth and nineteenth centuries. These shawls used elaborate boteh motifs. In the early nineteenth century, these designs were copied on power looms in Paisley, Scotland and these machine-woven shawls displaced the Kashmir embroidered shawls in the market.

Kashmir pile rugs achieved prominence in the mid-nineteenth century. Contemporary Kashmir rugs are woven primarily on a cotton foundation, the better ones having a knot density of about 400 to 480 knots per square inch. Rugs are double-wefted with offset warps.

Most rugs are jufti knotted with outlines in regular knots. Some silk pile rugs are woven. Most designs are copies of early Persian carpets. Some are pictorial rugs with images of Hindu deities. See "gabba," "Khamariah," and "Srinagar."

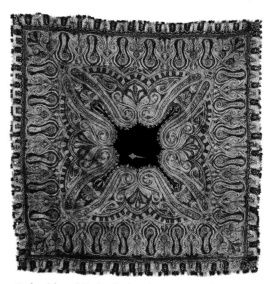

Embroidered Kashmir shawl *Grogan and Company*

Kashmir goat, Cashmere goat. A mountain goat, originally of the Himalayas in Kashmir. The underwool (pashmina) of this goat is fine and silky. Fibers are more rounded than sheep's wool and more likely to have roots and tapered ends. Kashmir goats are raised for their fiber in Australia, China, Iran, and Mongolia. See "Angora goat."

Kashmir kani. A Kashmir shawl of fine weave, hand-loomed from pashmina fiber (cashmere).

kashmiring. An embroidery stitch or soumak work used to replace or strengthen damaged areas of a rug when the rug is to be displayed rather than used as a floor covering.

kaşıklık. See "spoon bag."

Kasim Ushag. A design of nineteenth-century rugs of Karabagh in the Caucasus derived from Floral carpets and Dragon carpets, and ultimately from Anatolian medallion carpets. In this design, a large dented lozenge is enclosed by four hooked brackets. Rugs with this design are typically the smallest of the Karabaghs. Typical rug area is 33 square feet. The knot density is about 66 symmetric knots per square inch. See "Karabagh."

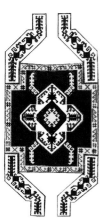

Kasim Ushag *medallion*

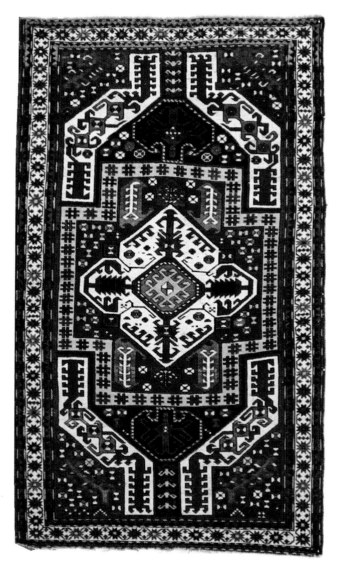

Kasim Ushag rug *Michael Craycraft*

Kasvin. See "Qazvin."

katchli. See "khatchli."

Kathmandu. The capital city of Nepal and a source of rugs woven by Tibetan refugees. See "Nepal."

katum, kathum (Tibetan). Pillar rug.

Kavak (Turk., "poplar"). A town of eastern central Anatolia, southwest of Sivas, where prayer rugs with stepped mihrabs are woven.

Kawdani, Koudani. A clan of the Jamshidi living in Jaffa Beg, near Kosh, north of Herat in Afghanistan. These people weave small prayer rugs with the tree-of-life design, very similar to those of the Baluch.

Kayseri, Keyserie. Formerly Caesarea, a rug production center in central Anatolia. In nineteenth-century rugs, white cotton was used with wool pile as a design accent. Rugs from the nearby town of Büyan are designated as Kayseri. Most rugs are copies of Turkish prayer designs such as the Gördes or copies of Persian designs. Many saff-design rugs are woven with pile of mercerized cotton. A cotton foundation is used with pile of wool, rayon, mercerized cotton, or, rarely, silk. Kayseri silk rugs have been woven with a knot density up to 450 knots per square inch. Contemporary wool rugs have knot densities between 80 to 120 symmetric knots per square inch. A few Kayseri rugs are woven with the asymmetric knot. Kayseri is also a source of kilims, many of them unusually wide. Their colors are pale blue, yellow, and green.

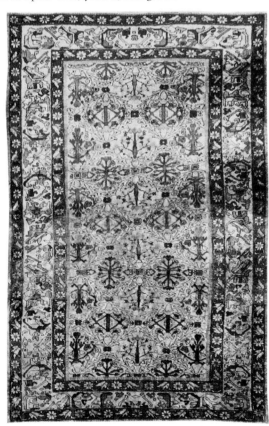

Kayseri rug *Jason Nazmiyal*

Kazak. An indefinite region of the south central Caucasus north of the Araxes River, south of the Kura River and including Tiflis and Erivan. Nineteenth-century rugs of this area have bold designs in bright colors. Kazak rugs are characteristically coarsely knotted with a density of about 40 to 60 symmetric knots per square inch. Average rug area is about 33 square feet. These rugs are wool throughout. There are from two to eight wefts between rows of knots, varying within the same rug. For most rugs, wefts are dyed red or pink. See "Borjalou," "Fachralo," "Karachov," "Lambalo," "Lori Pambak," "Memling gul," "Pinwheel Kazak," "Sevan Kazak," "Shield Kazak," "Shikli Kazak," "Star Kazak," and "Tree Kazak."

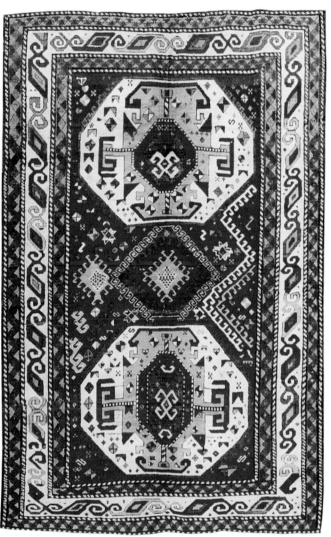

Kazak rug *Jason Nazmiyal*

Kazakh, Khazak (*Qazāq*). A Turkic people primarily inhabiting Kazakhstan (the Kazakh Republic of southern Russia), with scattered groups in Afghanistan and Central Asia. Older rugs attributed to the Kazakhs are in red and black with yellow highlights and are all wool. In these rugs, edge knots are symmetric, while ground knots are asymmetric. Geometric designs are used. The Kazakhs produce elaborate embroidery. They make screens of parallel reeds sewn together with which they surround the interiors of their yurts. The reeds are wrapped with threads to produce geometric designs similar to those of their rugs. Contemporary rugs are woven with either the symmetric or asymmetric knots. Contemporary factory rugs from the Kazakh Republic are woven on a cotton foundation. The Kazakhs make felt pieces with complex designs of inlaid and appliquéd felt. See "alasa," "baskur" and "reed screens."

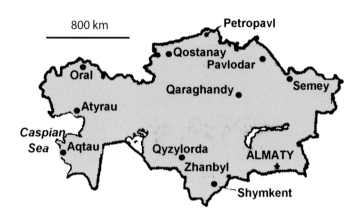

Kazakhstan

Kazan. A tribe of the Aq Chah in northeastern Afghanistan. They weave rugs with large gulli guls.

Kazvin. See "Qazvin."

keçe (Turk.) Felt.

Keçimuslu, Keçinuslu. A tribal group of western central Anatolia in the village of Keçimuhsine, west of Konya. Rugs woven by this group are all wool and triple-wefted. Designs are simple geometricized floral motifs on a red field, or prayer rugs.

kejebe (Turk.) A tent-like camel litter for the bride in a Turkmen wedding procession.

Kelardasht. See "Kalârdasht."

kelle. See "kallegi."

kellegi. See "kallegi."

kelley. See "kallegi."

Kemereh. Several villages south of Hamadan, including Lillihan and Reihân. Single-wefted rugs are woven in these villages.

kemha. Ottoman brocaded silks.

kemps. The coarsest fiber from sheep. Kemps contain a large medulla or hollow core, are brittle, and take dye poorly.

kenâreh, kenar (Persian, "edge-piece, border"). A runner 2½ to 3½ feet wide. See "audience rug."

Kepse gul, Kepche gul (Turk., "sheaf "). This is a complex gul, a horizontal lozenge of vertical bands with an octagonal

element in the middle. It is woven in diagonal rows on Yomut main carpets. It is thought to derive from the serrated leaf gul.

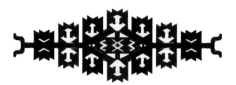

Kepse gul *After Moshkova*

Kerman, Kirman. A city and province of southeastern Iran. Rugs have been woven in Kerman since the Safavid period. In the early nineteenth century, Kerman was famed for its production of handwoven shawls. Major rug production began in about 1890. In the early 1900s most of Kerman's carpets were exported to America. The rugs of Kerman are woven on a cotton foundation with three wefts between each row of knots. Warps are offset. Knot densities tend to be high, between 150 and 400 asymmetric knots per square inch. Designs are intricate floral patterns. There are medallion designs, all-over designs, panel designs, prayer rugs, pictorial designs, and a diaper design. A very wide variety of colors is used in these rugs. Some notable twentieth-century weaver-designers of Kerman include Arjomand, Sherefat Khan, and Golam Hussein. See "laver."

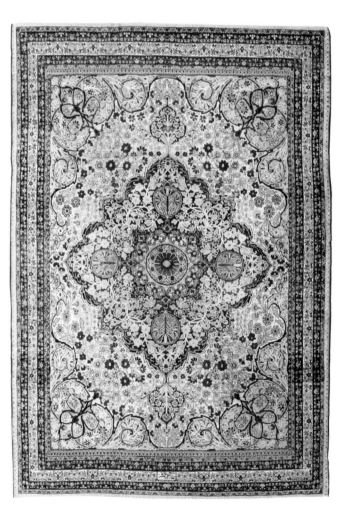

Kerman rug *Jason Nazmiyal*

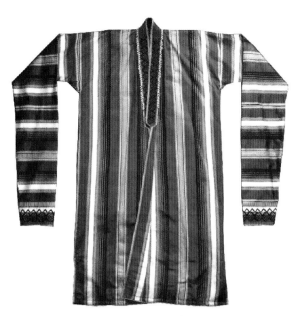

Khalat *Tara Perry*

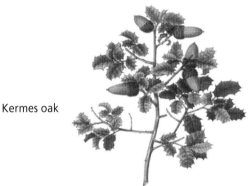

Kermes oak

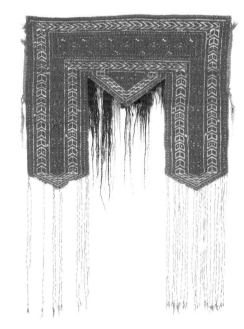

Khalyk *Alan Vartesian*

Kerman Armori. Kerman rugs bearing the coat of arms of the Shah of Iran.

Kerman Laver. See "Laver."

Kermanshah, Kirmanshah. A city and district of western Iran, on the road between Hamadan and Baghdad; currently called Bâkhtarân. The city is a market for wool and a source of Kurdish village rugs with the symmetric knot at densities up to 130 per square inch, often woven on a cotton foundation.

kermes (from Persian *qermez*, "red"), vartan garmir (Armenian). A red dye prepared from a scale insect, *Coccus ilicis* (also known as *Kermococcus vermilia*) which infests oak trees (*Quercus coccifera*). The insect encysts in galls which were harvested for the dye. Kermes was a major dye product of the southern Caucasus. This dye was very costly and was used only rarely in rugs.

kese. Turkmen tobacco pouch.

keshte. Central Asian embroideries. See "Suzanni."

kesi. See "k'o-ssu."

keyhole designs. See "turret design."

Keyserie. See "Kayseri."

khâbgâh (Persian). Bedding bag or mafrash. See "mafrash."

khaden (Tibetan). A rug used for sleeping or sitting.

khagangma (Tibetan). A sitting mat placed on top of another rug or a prayer mat.

Khailani. A Kurdish tribe of northeastern Iraq. The tribe is a source of large shaggy rugs with multiple columns of memling guls.

Khairabad. A village of north central Afghanistan (west of Kunduz) and a source of felt rugs produced and embroidered by Uzbeks.

khalat, chalat. An Uzbek man's robe, often striped ikat, and worn with overlong sleeves dangling loose. These are lined or quilted.

khali (Turkish from Persian qâli). The largest size of Caucasian pile rug or any Turkmen main carpet.

khali-balasi (Turk.). A size of Caucasian pile rug about 5 feet by 13 feet.

khalyk, chalik (Turk.). A Turkmen weaving, basically U-shaped or rectangular, and having one or more pendant triangles beneath the horizontal part of the weaving. It may be used as a camel trapping or curtain for a bride's litter. Most khalyks are of Tekke origin.

Khamariah. A town of Kashmir, India, and a source of rugs with designs based on Isfahan models.

Khamseh. A district of northwestern Iran, lying southwest of Zanjân. It is the source of small, low-quality rugs. The rugs are woven at densities of 30 to 65 knots per square inch. The foundation is cotton with single wefts.

Khamseh Confederacy (or League), **Kamseh Confederacy** (Arabic for "quintet" or "group of five"). A confederacy of five tribes inhabiting southwest Iran. They are the Ainalu, Baharlu, Baseri, Nafar, and Arab. Of these, the Arab is the largest group and by far the most productive rug weavers. The Confederacy, originally formed in the middle of the nineteenth century as a political counterpoise to the Qashqa'i, was disbanded in the 1960s.

Generally, yarns used by the Khamseh are more coarsely spun than those of the Qashqa'i. The Arab rugs are of medium to low quality with a shaggy pile and woven with the asymmetric knot. The Baseri rugs are woven with an asymmetric knot. The Baharlu weave some rugs with the asymmetric knot and others with the symmetric knot. There is no significant pile rug production from the Ainalu and Nafar. Khamseh designs are often all-over patterns of geometricized florets and animals scattered in a random manner over the field. The Nafar produce slit tapestry kilims of very fine weave. See "Fars."

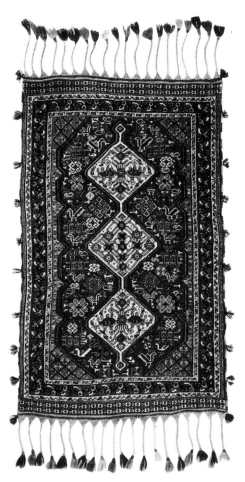

Khamseh rug

khan. A tribal leader or chieftan. The position is often hereditary.

khan carpet. A carpet with an inscription referring to a tribal khan or leader. The inscription may be a dedication or the name of the political leader for whom the rug was woven.

Kharaghan, Kharaqân, Gharaghan. A group of villages in Hamadan province of Iran, northwest of Sâveh. These villages produce single-wefted rugs with Kurdish designs.

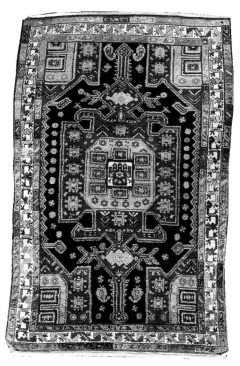

Kharaghan rug *Detlev Fischer*

kharak (Persian). Square ends of a mafrash. See "mafrash."

kharchang. See "harshang."

khatayi. See "hatayi."

khatchli, katchli, hatchlu, hatchli (Turk., "cruciform"). The cross formed by the four panels in the design of an ensi. See "ensi."

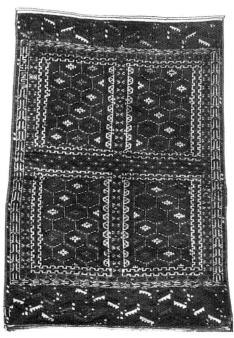

Yomud ensi with khatchli

Khazakh. See "Kazakh."

khersak. See "gabbeh."

kheshti. A Bakhtiari rug design of rectangular compartments each containig botanical motifs or a mhirab. A garden carpet design. See "Bakhtiari."

Khila. See "Chila."

khilin. See "ky'lin."

Khirghiz. See "Kirghiz."

Khiva. A city and district of Uzbekistan, south of the Aral Sea, formerly an independent khanate. Khiva was a nineteenth-century collection and shipping point for Turkmen rugs. Yomud Turkmen are settled around Khiva.

khod rang (Persian, "natural color"). Rugs woven in only natural colored wool (white, beige, gray, tan, brown) and called khod rang or panj rang (five colors). This term refers to a type of rug woven mainly in the Chahâr Mahâl region of Persia in the 1960s and 1970s.

Khorasan, Khorassan. See "Khurasan."

khorjin, kharjin, khordjin, khurdzhin (Persian). A saddlebag.

Khorramabad. A market center in Luristan, southwestern Iran. Rugs of the area are woven on cotton warps with designs of dark colors. Luri designs are used.

Khosru, Spring Carpet of. See "Spring Carpet of Chosroes."

Khosro (Khusrau, Kosru) **and Shirin.** Khosro was a king of Persia in about 590 C.E. Shirin was his queen. Their mythic love story has been told by many Persian poets. Kosru and Shirin and their adventures have been portrayed in rugs in naive and naturalistic styles.

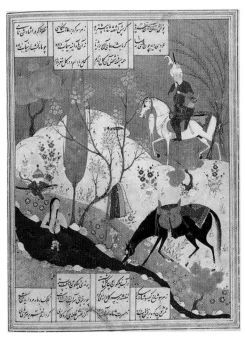

Khosru and Shirin from a Safavid manuscript

Khotan, Hetien, Hotien. A city of Eastern Turkestan in China. Written evidence suggests carpets were woven in Khotan as early as the seventh century. Production in 1870 was estimated at 5,000 carpets exported annually from Khotan and surrounding villages. Khotan is thought to be the source of most East Turkestan medallion rugs. Early rugs woven in Khotan are likely to have three wool wefts (two cable and one sinuous) between each row of knots. Some eighteenth or nineteenth-century Khotan rugs were woven with metallic threads. The ground or open areas of the field and border were executed in a metallic thread in a continuous weft wrapping structure, while motifs were rendered in pile, providing high relief for the design. Later Khotan rugs have a cotton foundation. Wool rugs have about 40 to 100 asymmetric knots per square inch. Silk rugs have densities up to 200 knots per square inch. See "ay gul," "Eastern Turkestan," "Kâshgar," and "Yarkand."

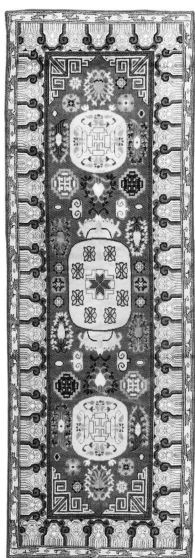

Khotan rug (detail) *Jason Nazmiyal*

Khoy. A town of Iranian Azerbaijan near Tabriz. Rugs from this town have designs based on Tabriz models.

khurdzhin. See "khorjin."

Khurasan, Khorasan, Khorassan. A province of northeast Iran. Historically, Khurasan included much of what is now southern Turkestan and northwestern Afghanistan. Herat was formerly a city of this province. Mashhad is now the leading rug-weaving center. The carpets of Birjand and the Qainat and Baluchi rugs of the area are marketed in Mashhad. Many rugs of Khurasan are woven using a distinctive bluish-red color and with the jufti knot. This knot is asymmetrical and open to the left. In the foundation, the pile yarn passes over three warps and under one warp before the left pile end rises to the surface. Northern Khurasan is a major wool-producing area of Iran. Many Kurdish rugs were woven in northern Khurasan. Formerly, Khurasan was a source of Baluchi weavings. See "Birjand," "Mashhad," "Qarai," "Qainat," and "Quchân."

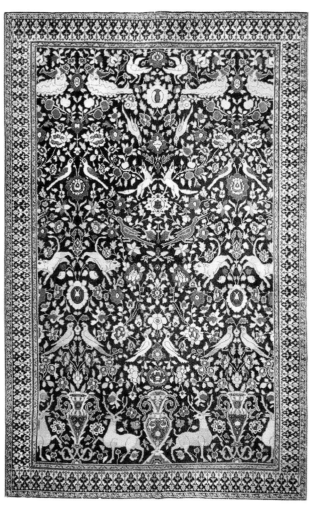

Khurasan rug *Jason Nazmiyal*

kiaba. A size of rugs of Shirvân in the Caucusus.

kibitka. See "yurt."

Kidderminster. A heavy, ingrain fabric with the design on both sides and used as a floor covering. This floor covering was first woven in the eighteenth century in Kidderminster, England. See "ingrain."

kif (Persian). A purse or bag.

kilim, gelim, kelim, khilim. A weft-faced plain weave in which the design is rendered by means of colored areas of discontinuous ground wefts. A tapestry woven fabric. See "eccentric weft," "interlocking weft," "neyestan," "slit weave," and "tapestry weave."

Kirghiz, Kirgiz, Kyrghyz. A Turkic ethnic group of Eastern Turkestan and Kirghizstan. They make felt pieces of complex design through felt inlay, appliqué, and embroidery. They weave ornamental warp-faced bands which they sew into gadzhari. They also make reed screens for yurt interiors of geometric designs by wrapping reeds with colored threads. Small rugs, pouches, and animal trappings are woven with knotted pile. See "bashtyk," "postaghi," and "shyrdak."

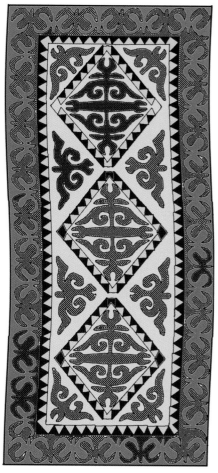

Kirghiz felt rug or shyrdak (detail)

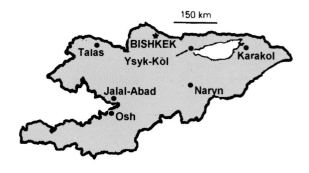

Kirghizstan

kırkbudak (Turk., "forty branches"). An Anatolian design motif consisting of a hooked diamond.

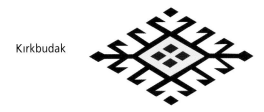

Kırkbudak

Kirman. See "Kerman."

Kirman-Laver. See "Laver."

Kirmanshah. See "Kermanshah."

Kirne. A village of northwestern Anatolia and a source of soumak weavings very similar to those of the Caucasus in structure and design.

Kirovabad. See "Elisavetpol."

Kırşehir. A town of north central Anatolia. Prayer rugs, prayer runners, and yastiks are woven in the town and area. These rugs are all-wool and the wool is usually glossy.

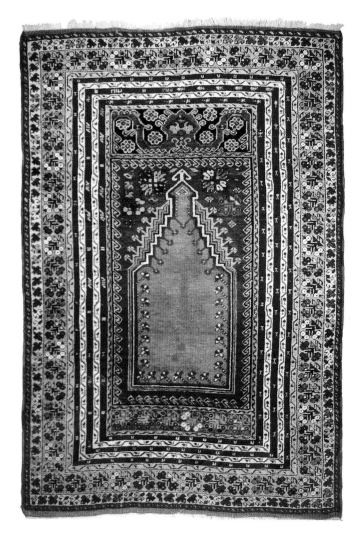

Kırşehir prayer rug *Wendel Swan*

kis, kız (Turk., "girl" or "bride"). Rugs named with this prefix are supposedly dowry pieces woven with special care by the bride in anticipation of the marriage. The term as used in the rug trade refers to design and not to origin.

kis-Gördes. Nineteenth and early twentieth-century Gördes double prayer rugs. See "Gördes."

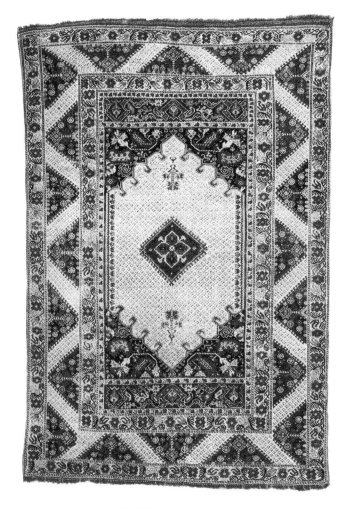

Kis-Gördes *Sothebys*

kışlak, kishlak (Turk.), **gishlag, qishlaq.** Winter pasturage (on the plains) of nomadic tribes. See "garmsir" and "transhumance." In Afghanistan, a mountain village.

kiyiz. Felt carpets of Daghestan in which designs are produced by colored felt pressed into the ground felt. See "arbabash."

kızil (Turk.) Red.

Kizil. A village and archaeological site in Eastern Turkestan where a fifth or sixth-century pile fragment was unearthed by Albert Von Coq in 1913. An unusual knot was tied on a single warp with both knot ends projecting from the same side of the warp.

Kızil Ayak, Kızil Ajak (Turk., "red foot"). A town in southern Anatolia. A Turkmen tribe thought to be a sub-group of the Ersari. Because of the similarity of structure and design, it may not be possible to distinguish some Kızıl Ayak from Chub Bash weavings. The major gul of the Kızıl Ayak is the tauk noska. Their minor gul is the chemche. Kızıl Ayak rugs are woven with the asymmetric knot open to the right. Warps are of light, undyed wool and wefts are brown. See "Ersari."

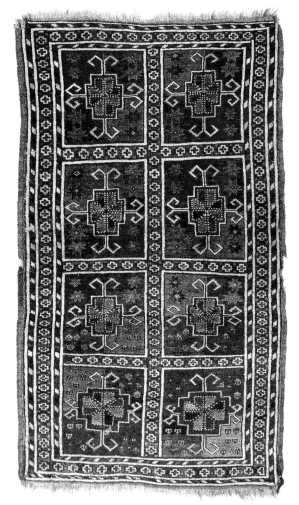

Kızıl Ayak rug

kızıl chuval. A red, flatwoven joval with pile strips.

knee caps. A garter-like animal trapping tied around the knees of horses and camels. Tassels and bells may be attached to knee caps. See "accessory objects" and "dizlyk."

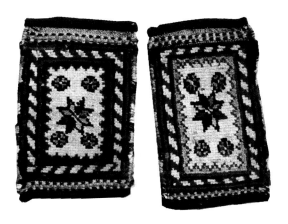

Kalârdasht camel knee caps *Manouchehr Highighat*

knitted carpet. An American hand-crafted rug made by sewing rag strips end-to-end. The strip is then knitted into a rug. There are contemporary machine-knitted rugs produced with a looped pile.

knockout. See "auction pool."

knot. A tie produced by interlocking one or more cords in such a way that one end of a cord passes through a loop in itself. Technically, the symmetric or Turkish and asymmetric or Persian knots in cut pile fabrics are not knots at all (because no tie is produced), but different systems of discontinuous supplementary weft wrapping. See "asymmetric knot," "Berber knot," "jufti knot," "macrame," "offset knots," "Senneh loop," "Spanish knot," "symmetric knot," "Tibetan knots," and "weft wrapping."

knot count. The number of knots per unit measure. Sometimes used synonymously for knot density. In counting knots, if there is little or no warp offset, then two nodes per knot are identified. If warp offset is so great that only a single node of each pair can be seen (one node per color instead of two nodes per color), then only one node per knot is counted in finding knot density. See "dihari."

knot density. In a knotted pile fabric, the knots per unit area. The product of the vertical or warp-wise knot count per linear unit measure multiplied by the horizontal or weft-wise knot count per linear unit measure. To convert knot density to different units, the following equivalents may be used: 100,000 knots per square meter = 1,000 knots per square decimeter = 65 knots per square inch.

There are rug fragments with extraordinarily high knot densities. One is an all-silk fragment of a Mughal carpet in the Metropolitan Museum of Art. It has a knot density of 2,516 knots per square inch. The highest knot density is that of an all-silk Hereke prayer rug with a density of about 4,360 symmetric knots per square inch. This rug was completed in about 1970. See "Bhadohi," "Egypt," "India," "gereh," "line," "Pakistan," and "reg."

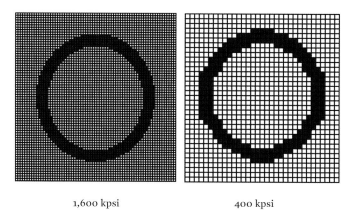

1,600 kpsi   400 kpsi

Appearance of a circle at different knot densities

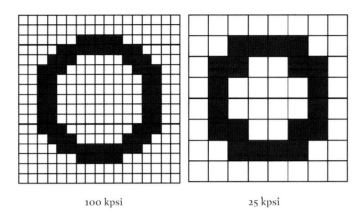

|100 kpsi|25 kpsi|

knot, marker. See "marker knot."

knot node. See "node."

knot ratio. In a knotted pile carpet, the vertical or warp-wise knot count per linear unit measure divided by the horizontal or weft-wise knot count per linear unit measure. This ratio is useful in comparing vertical knot compression or packing in different rugs. This ratio is characteristic for certain attributions. See "knot density."

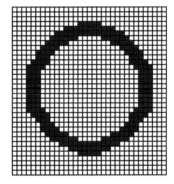 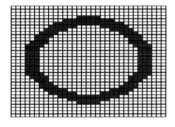

knot ratio of 1   knot ratio of 1.5

Appearance of a circle at different knot ratios

kochak, aina kotchak, kochanak (Turk.) Ram's horn, a design motif with many variations often used in Turkmen rugs. See "vurma" and "kaikalak."

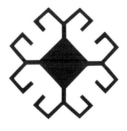 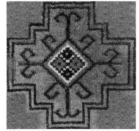

Kochak

Kochanak. See "kochak."

Kohistan, Koristan, Nuristan. An area of northwestern Pakistan around the city of Chitral and an adjacent area of Afghanistan, southwest of Wakhan. Natives of the area weave ornamental woolen shawls and small kilims.

koca baş (Turk. "big head"). A reversing leaf border common in rugs of Bergama and Çanakkale.

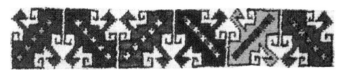

Koca baş border

kola-i chergh (from Persian kolâh-e charkh, "wheel-cap"). Flatwoven Turkmen bags, often with tassels, placed over the ends of bundles of tent poles when the tent is moved. See "ok-bash."

kolk. Persian for velvet pile.

Kolyai. A tribe of the Kurds in the area of Sonqur in northwestern Iran, about fifty miles west of Hamadan. Newer rugs have a cotton foundation and are single-wefted. Older rugs have a wool foundation. Colors tend to be bright. The Kolyais are a major source of Kurdish rugs. The Takht-e Jamshid design is common. See "Kurds" and "Takht-e Jamshid."

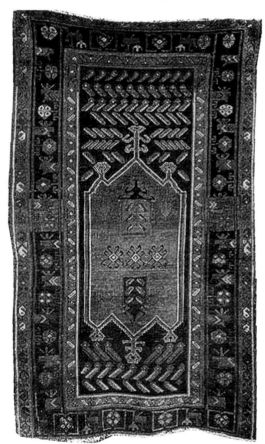

Kolyai rug *Detlev Fischer*

Kömürcü Kula. See "Demirci."

Konaghend, Konagkend, Ordutch-Konagend, A village 20 miles south of Kuba in the northeastern Caucasus. Nineteenth-century rugs attributed to this village often have an all-over honeycomb pattern surrounded by Kufesque borders. The typical knot density of this Kuba design type is

127 symmetric knots per square inch. The average area is 21 square feet. These rugs are usually twice as long as they are wide. See "Kufesque borders."

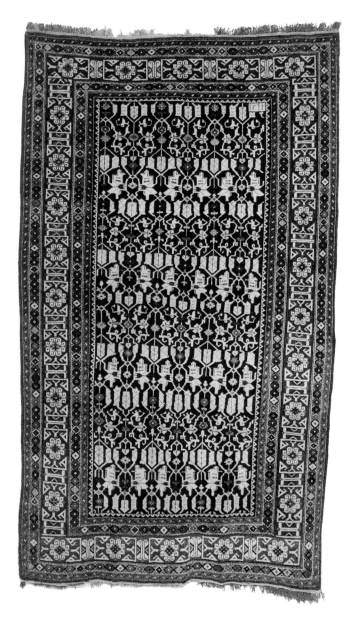

Konaghend rug *Grogan and Company*

Kongrat. See "Lakai and Kungrat embroideries."

kont. A Pakistani flatwoven rug with weft substitution patterning. Designs are horizontal rows of small geometric motifs.

Konya. A city of western central Anatolia (ancient Iconium). Rugs have been woven in Konya and the surrounding area from the time of the Seljuks (late eleventh century). Eighteenth and nineteenth-century rugs are of earth tones: brown, green, and mustard. Some have an apricot field. Contemporary production consists mainly of prayer rugs with a red ground, yastiks, and mat sizes. These may be woven in nearby towns such as Lâdik, Keçimusta, and Obruk.

Generally, Konya kilims are slit-tapestry woven and in two pieces. The soumak structure may be used to outline some designs. The most distinctive feature of Konya kilims is their white ground. Typically, the field is a column of brightly colored hexagons on a white ground.

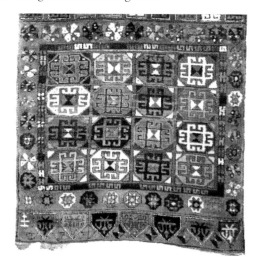

Konya yatak *Alberto Levi*

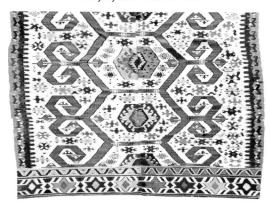

Konya kilim (detail) *Peter Pap Oriental Rugs Inc*

kooleh poshti (Persian). Knapsack.

kopan (Turk.) See "tülü."

Koran, Quran (Arabic qur'ân, "recitations"). The Koran is the Muslim scripture, consisting of the collected revelations of Muhammad in Arabic. It is divided into chapters called suras (surahs) and arranged sequentially from the longest to the shortest, with the exception of the Fâtiha ("opening sura"); this is a short invocation placed at the beginning and often distinctively illuminated. Quotations from the Koran are sometimes woven into rugs as inscriptions. There are pouches, special containers for copies of the Koran. See "Hadith" and "Islam."

Koran bag. A special container for the Koran.

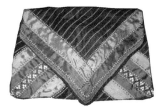

Turkmen Koran bag or pouch

Korani. A rug design of medallion and spandrels thought to derive from the designs in tooled leather bindings of the Koran. See "lachak toranj."

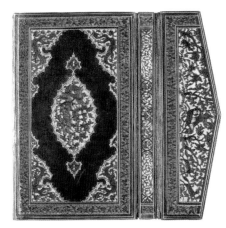

Koran cover

Kordi (Persian). Kurdish weavings.

Kords. See "Kurds."

Koristan. See "Kohistan."

kork (Turk.) Underhair of a goat or fine belly wool of a sheep.

koshma (Persian). Felt.

Kosru and Shirin. See "Khosru and Shirin."

k'o-ssu, kesi. Silk, tapestry-woven textiles of China. There are complete Chinese silk tapestry weaves from the sixth century and fragments from the fourth century. These textiles are extremely finely woven with sophisticated designs. They were woven in urban workshops for the reigning aristocracy. The fineness of weave permitted close copies of paintings, calligraphy, and other graphic works. Panels, curtains, and formal court garments were woven in this structure.

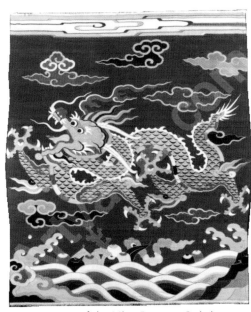

K'o-ssu of the Ming Dynasty *Sothebys*

Kotel. A town of eastern Bulgaria. Slit-weave kilims of the area are relatively coarse. Hooked diamonds are a common motif. See "Bulgaria."

Koudani. See "Kawdani."

Koum Kapu. See "Istanbul."

Kouskousse. An embroidered rug of Crete, usually made of undyed wool.

kovri. See "Doukhobor rugs."

koyun (Turk.) Sheep.

Kozak (Turk., "pine cone"). A town of western Anatolia. The small rugs woven in Kozak are all wool with striped kilim ends. Bright colors are used with designs suggestive of the central Caucasus.

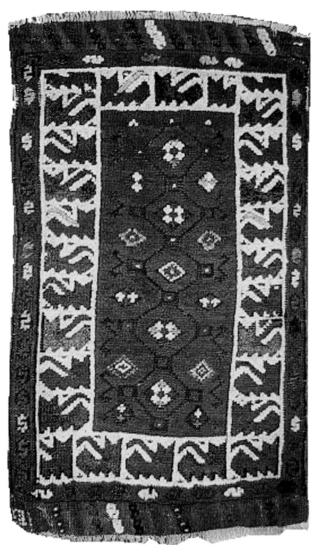

Kozak yastik *R. John Howe*

kpsd. Knots per square decimeter.

kpsi. Knots per square inch.

krabbasnar. A Swedish textile of extra weft patterning.

Krists. See "Chechens."

Kronstadt. See "Braşov."

Kuba. This city and district, south of Derbend in the northeastern Caucasus, was formerly a khanate owing periodic allegiance to Persia. Dragon carpets were once attributed to Kuba, but such attributions are now being reconsidered. Nineteenth century rugs of Kuba are small and comparatively finely knotted. They have an average knot density of 115 symmetric knots per square inch and a typical area of 27 square feet. Major design classifications are Alpan Kuba, Chichi, Karagashli, Konaghend, Perpedil, Seishour, Zejwa, and Turret or Keyhole. See entries under these names.

Kilims tentatively attributed to Kuba and the area are finely woven, slit-weave tapestry. A complete border surrounds the kilim. In a common design, the field is occupied by offset rows of medallions. The central portion of the medallion is a diamond with arrows projecting from both ends. See "Caucasus."

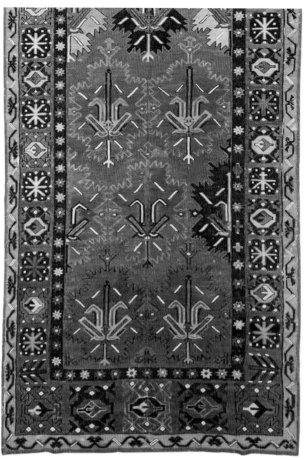

Kuba kilim (detail) *Jason Nazmiyal*

kufesque, kufic. Used to describe border designs that are thought to be derived from an Arabic script, characterized by elongated angular letters with serifs. Some of these borders, such as those of Holbein carpets, are thought to be highly stylized kufic renditions of "Allah" or a sequence of the characters lam and alif, evoking a mystical relationship with God. This derivation of the borders is disputed. See "Arabic calligraphy and script."

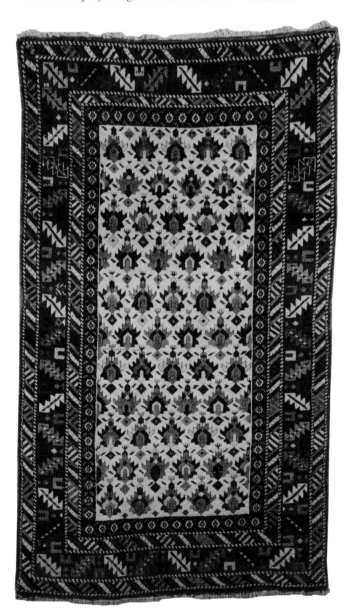

Kuba rug *Grogan and Company*

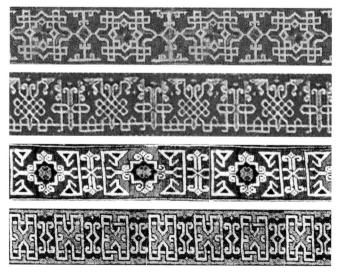

Kufesque borders
FROM TOP DOWN: Holbein, Holbein, Kuba, Lotto

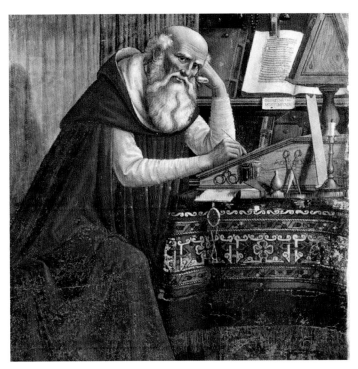

A Ghirlandaio painting of 1480 (detail) showing
a rug with Kufesque border

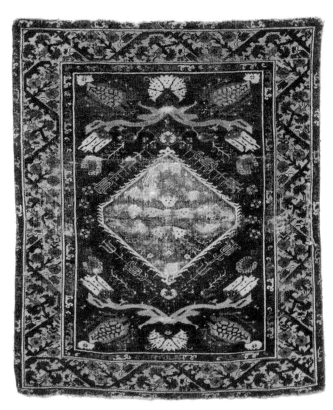

Kula rug *Grogan and Company*

Kuhi (Persian, "montagnard, from the mountains").
Tribespeople of the Kerman area west of Sirjan. Rugs of these
tribes are tied with the symmetric knot, double-wefted, and
with offset warps. Saddlebags are woven with pile on both
faces. See "Afshar."

kuilung. The central medallion of a Chinese carpet that
contains a dragon or flower. More specifically, kuilung refers
to an image of the dragon in an archaic form, sometimes
termed "foliate dragon."

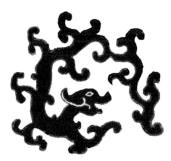

Kuilung (archaic dragon)

Kula, Kulah. A town of western Anatolia south of Demirci,
about eighty miles east of Izmir. There are eighteenth-century
rugs attributed to Kula. The designs are single-mihrab prayer
rugs similar to early rugs of Gördes, only the field is frequently
occupied by a vase of flowers. Early rugs have a knot density of
about 120 knots per square inch and later rugs have densities
of about 50 knots per square inch. After 1920, these rugs
declined in quality, using coarse weaves and garish colors.
Currently, rugs of higher quality are woven in Kula. Small
mazarlik-design rugs are also woven in Kula. See "Demirci."

Kum. See "Qom."

Kumkapı. See "Istanbul."

Kumyk. A Turkic-speaking people of northern Daghestan. The
tribe makes a flatweave termed dum. See "dum."

Kunduz. A provincial capital and rug market town of
northeastern Afghanistan. Rugs and bags woven in the
districts of Imam Saheb, Qala-i Zal, and Chardarah are sold in
the town or transported to the market in Kabul.

Kungrat. See "Lakai embroideries."

kurbage (Turk., "frog") gul, gorbaghe gul. Secondary field motif
in Turkmen rugs. See "chemche gul."

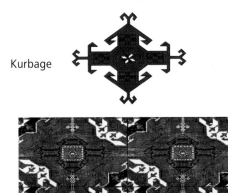

Kurbage

Kurbage in a Tekke rug

Kurdish village rugs. Rugs woven in the villages of Iranian Kurdistan. These are coarsely woven with the symmetric knot, usually on a wool foundation. Later rugs may have a cotton foundation. Often these rugs are abstract versions of classic patterns such as the Herati, Mina Khani, or harshang patterns. There is a wide variety of geometric designs, diamonds, Memling gul, and others used in these rugs. In the early twentieth century, many Kurdish runners were exported from the area. See "Kurds."

Kurds, Kords. The territory most densely populated by Kurds consists of adjacent areas of Iran, Iraq, Syria, Turkey, and Armenia. Communities and tribes of Kurds are scattered throughout the Near East. The Kurds speak an Indo-European language related to Persian. Major dialects are Kurmanji or Badiman in the north, and Sorani, of Sulaimani and Mahabad. Most Kurds are Sunni Muslims, though a significant minority is Shi'i. Generally, Kurds have settled into village and urban lifestyles, though a very few remain semi-nomadic.

Because of the great variety of designs and weaving structures used by Kurds and because they adopt or modify local weaving practices and designs, there are few overall characterizations of their weavings. Generally, geometric motifs or abstract designs are used. Wefts are two-ply, except in Turkey. Knot densities tend to be low to medium. Many Kurdish rugs of Turkey have been incorrectly described as "yörük."

Kurdish weavings of particular geographic areas are discussed under these entries: Bijâr, Cihanbeyi, Hakkari, Hamadan, Harsin, Iraq, Kermanshah, Khurasan, Kurdish village rugs, Mosul, Qazvin, Quchân, Rashwan, Sauj Bulaq, Senneh, Shavak, Siirt, Sonqur.

Kurdish weavings attributed to specific tribes are discussed under these entries: Dehbokri, Dizai, Girdi, Guran, Hartushi, Herki, Hewraman, Jaff, Kakaberu, Khailani, Kalhor, Kolyai, Mantik, Sanjâbi, Shikâk, Surchi.

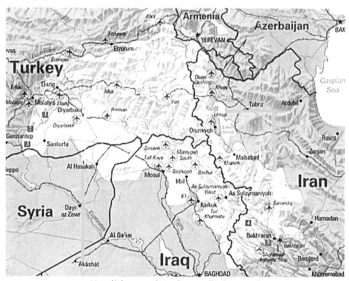

Kurdish populated area (light area)
Central Intelligence Agency

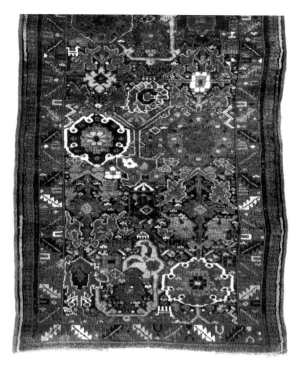

Kurdish rug *Moe Jamali*

Kurins. A language subgroup of the Lesghians of the northeastern Caucasus. See "Lesghi" and "Daghestan."

kustar. A movement of the late 19th and early 20th century in Imperial Russia to improve the quality of cottage industry production, including the weaving of rugs in the Caucasus. Kustar committees worked to remove bad dyes, increase the quality of rug-weaving, and promote more marketable designs. See "five-year plan rugs."

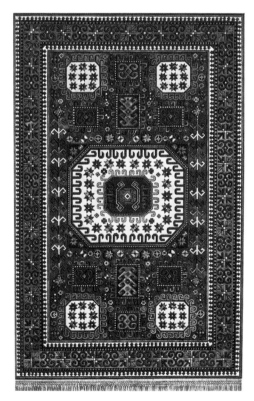

Kustar design for a Kazak rug

Kütahya. A town of western Anatolia near Ushak. A minor source of prayer rugs on cotton foundations and a trading center for rugs of the area.

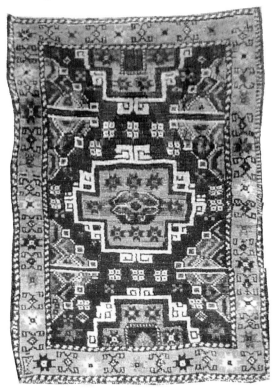

Kütahya yastik *R. John Howe*

Kutch. A district of Gurjurat in western India. A source of colorful beaded work, embroidery, and appliqué work on clothing, household decorations, and animal trappings.

Kweihwa, Kweichow. See "Guizhow."

ky'lin, khilin, kylin, chilin. A fabulous or mythological deer-like animal with flaming haunches sometimes portrayed in Chinese, Mongolian, and Tibetan rugs. In Persian carpets, ky'lins may also have characteristics of horses or lions.

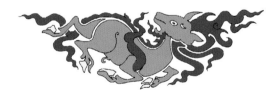

Ky'lin

kyongden (Tibetan). Fringed runner less than sixteen feet in length.

kyongring (Tibetan). Fringed runner greater than sixteen feet in length.

Kyrghyz. See "Kirghiz."

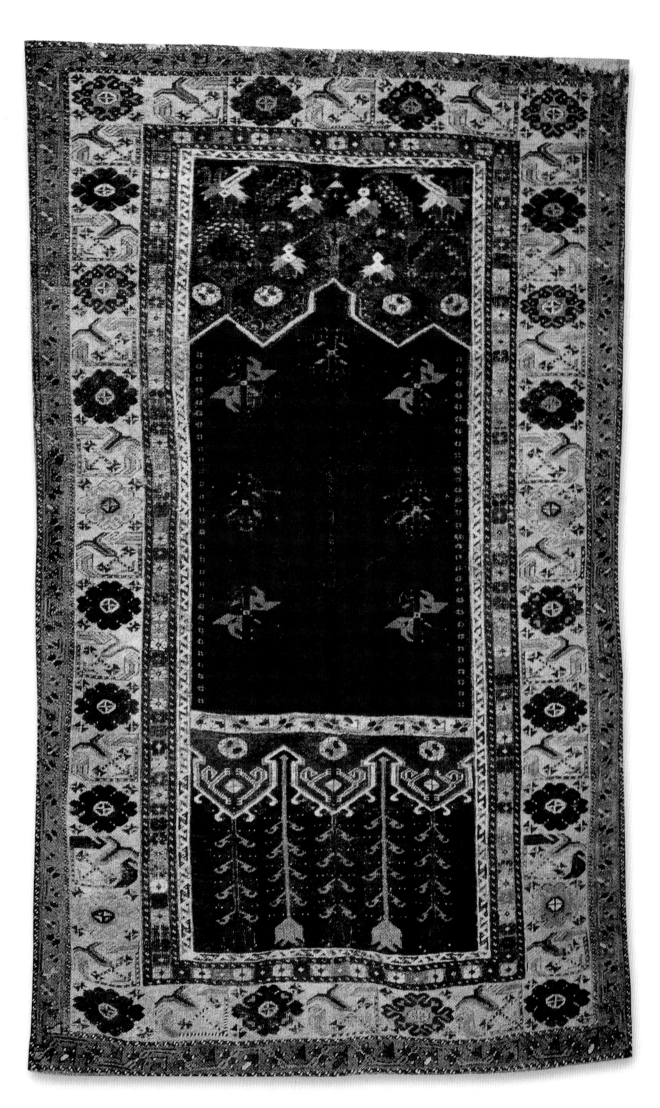

la Persian (thread). The number of singles in each foundation yarn in Nain rugs. These are 4 to 6 la, with four as the finest resulting in the finer weave.

lab-i Mazar (Persian, "edge of the tomb"). A border motif used by the Hazara of Afghanistan. It consists of a row of diamonds with points touching within two lines in white on a black background.

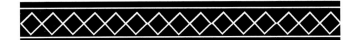

Lab-i Mazar border

Labijar. A town of northern Afghanistan near Sheberghân. Ersari Turkoman of Labijar weave rugs similar to those of Andkhoy. Older rugs of Labijar had distinctive minor borders of pink rosettes. See "Afghanistan."

lac. A red dye derived from a scale insect, *Coccus laccae*.

lachak toranj (Turko-Persian, "shawl, kerchief"). Any design with central medallions and corner elements of quartered medallions or spandrels. See "Korani."

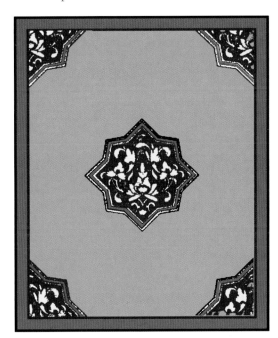

Lachak toranj

lackchi. In India, sinuous weft in rugs. See "sinuous weft" and "thari."

Ladakh. A part of Kashmir in India adjacent to Tibet. Formerly, native Ladakhis (related ethnically to the Tibetans) wove rugs with a looped pile. These are termed *stan*. Currently, Tibetan refugees in Ladakh weave rugs typical of contemporary Tibetan production.

Lâdik. There are a number of towns in Turkey called Lâdik. The town famed for rug weaving is in central Anatolia northwest of Konya. Formerly, rugs of this area were prayer rugs with

stepped mihrabs, triple-arch mihrabs, or two-column mihrabs. These designs have cross panels containing tulips. Dominant colors are shades of red and blue. Warp and weft of older rugs are wool with offset warps. These rugs have been attributed to Lâdik from the eighteenth century, with production declining since the First World War. There has been a recent boom in rug production and Lâdik is now a major rug-weaving center. Contemporary rugs are copies of Persian floral designs with densities between 140 and 160 symmetric knots per square inch. See "Turkey."

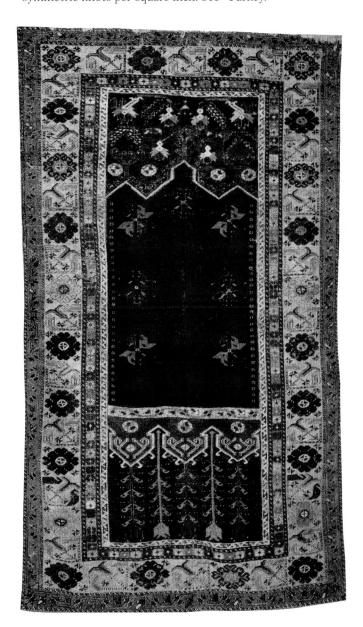

Lâdik prayer rug *Sothebys*

Laghari, Lokari. A village of northwestern Afghanistan, the source of weft-float brocaded kilims woven by Hazaras in the area. These kilims are woven in two halves in shades of red, white, and black. See "Afghanistan."

Lahore. A city of northeastern Pakistan in the province of Punjab, formerly India. Seventeenth-century rugs are attributed to Lahore, which was a major source of rugs for the

British East India Company. Prison rugs were woven in Lahore in the nineteenth century. Current production is primarily of rugs in Turkmen designs. See "Girdlers' Carpet" and "India."

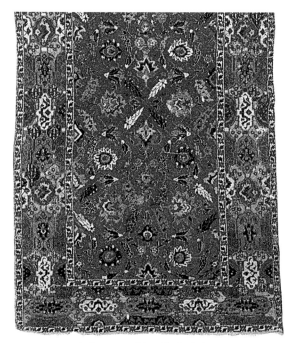

Lahore rug (detail) *Sothebys*

laicerul. A borderless kilim of Romania used as a wall covering. See "berdelik" and "scoarta."

Lakai and Kungrat (Kongrat) embroideries. The Lakai and Kungrat are subtribes of the Uzbeks of Uzbekistan and Tajikistan. They produce brightly-colored, heavily-embroidered, small household items. These include small panels (*ilgitsch*), pouches (*khalta*), wall hangings (*soyo gusha*), and suzanis. There are two decorative styles for these embroideries. The surface may be completely covered with fine silk cross-stitches producing rectilinear designs or the surface is ornamented with bold, distinct, chain-stitched, curvilinear floral motifs. See "soyo gusha," "suwari," and "Uzbeks."

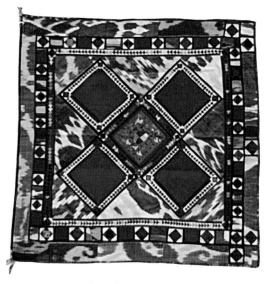

Kungrat ilgitsch *Grogan and Company*

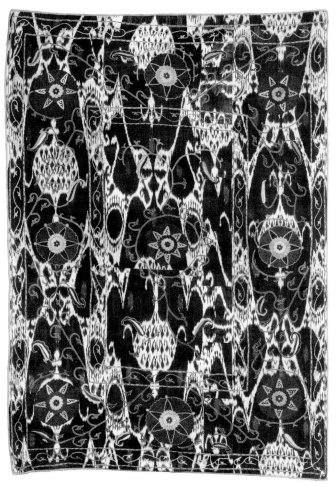

Lakai suzani *Sothebys*

Lake Van. See "Van."

lâle (Turk., from Persian). Tulip.

Laleh Abbasi ("Abbasi tulip"), **medahil** ("doorways"), **scepter head.** A reciprocating trefoil border motif. It is a tulip calyx (*lâle* in Turkish) that ranges from a curvilinear rendering to an extreme geometric abstraction consisting of a row of triangles with a diamond atop each triangle. See "reciprocating border" and "Iznik ceramics."

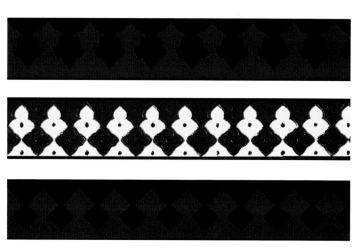

Laleh Abbasi borders

Lambalo. A nineteenth-century Kazak rug design similar to those of Talish rugs. These are rugs in a long format with multiple borders. The field may be empty or only sparsely occupied. See "Kazak."

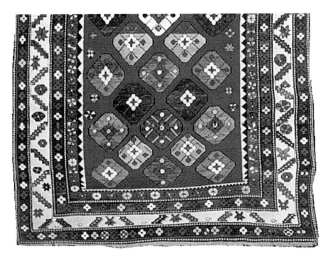

Lambalo Kazak rug (detail)

Lamberan. An area northwest of Karadja in Iranian Azerbaijan. It is a source of rugs with a hooked hexagon medallion similar to those of Karadja. The rugs are more coarsely woven than those of Karadja.

lamella. See "metallic threads."

lamp. The hanging oil lamp is a common motif in prayer rugs. It is placed close to, or hangs from, the apex of the mihrab. The motif may refer to hanging lamps in mosques or serve as the symbol of God who is described in the Koran as "the light of the heavens and the earth."

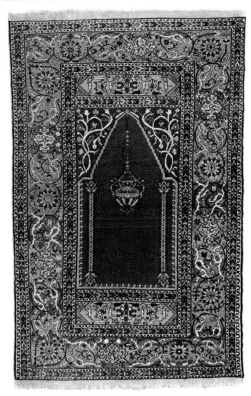

Prayer rug with lamp

Lampa, Lampas. A rug design of nineteenth-century Karabagh in the Caucasus. Rugs of this design have the longest format of Karabagh rugs; the shape ratio is about 3.70. The field contains medallions with eight lobes alternating with a flattened rectangular medallion in a columnar arrangement. These rugs have a knot density of about 60 symmetric knots per square inch. See "Karabagh."

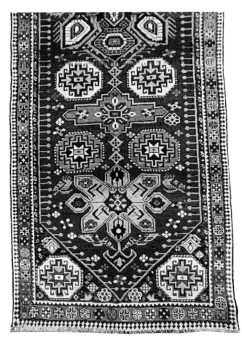

Lampa Karabagh rug (detail) *Michael Phillips*

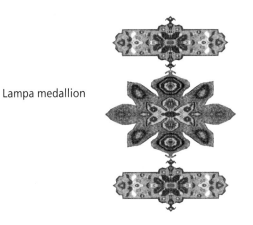

Lampa medallion

lampas. A fabric in which a pattern of supplementary weft floats is bound by a secondary binding warp which is supplementary.

lanceolate leaves, sickle leaves. A common floral motif in oriental rugs consisting of a narrow, curving, tapering leaf. Often, one or both edges are serrated. See "Herati pattern" and "sickle leaf design."

Lanceolate leaves

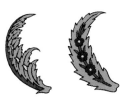

landscape carpet, cemetery carpet, mazarlık, ship carpet, türbe-lik. A group of Anatolian carpets with a distinctive design, first woven in the eighteenth century. In the nineteenth and early twentieth centuries, the major sources for rugs of this design were Kula, Gördes, and Kırşehir. The design consists of stylized houses or mosques and trees arranged horizontally. This horizontal arrangement is repeated in the field of the rug, usually a prayer rug. Since there is no evidence these rugs were used for funerary rites, the term "cemetery carpets" has no foundation. The designs were once thought to illustrate an Islamic cemetery (*mazarlık*). See "ayatalak."

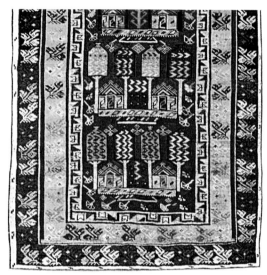

Gordes landscape carpet *Jason Nazmial*

Langari knot. See "jufti knot."

lanolin, wool fat. A fatty oil coating of sheep's wool. In commercial wool production, lanolin is a residue of the wool washing process. In wool rugs, lanolin adds luster and flexibility to wool fibers. Attempts to restore lanolin to old rugs are of doubtful value.

lappets. A common end design or elem design in Turkish rugs consisting of a row of five-sided figures or capped rectangles. The term "lappets" is derived from the folding ear flaps of a cap. The term is entirely Western.

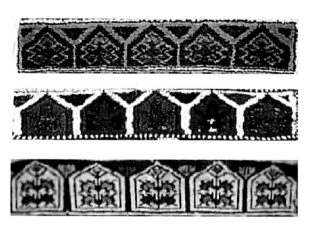

Lappets
TOP: *Karaman* **MIDDLE:** *Niğde* **BOTTOM:** *Aksary*

larkspur. See "esparek."

lassna. A type of Scandinavian rya rug in which warps are used for patterning.

latch hooks. A motif consisting of parallel projections with short, right-angle or acute-angle terminations pointed in the same direction. These are arranged on the sides of diamonds and other medallion figures or on the edges of broad stripes.

Latch hooks

lattice. An all-over pattern consisting of ogives, diamonds, hexagons, octagons, or rectangles. Usually the cells are filled by some floral motif. In classic Persian rugs, lattices are ogives formed by curving stems or vines. These rug designs may be composed of a lattice in one plane or of two or three planes of lattices superimposed. The three-plane lattice design is most common. Early versions of these designs are curvilinear, while later versions consist of diamonds or hexagons rather than ogives. See "diaper" and "honeycomb."

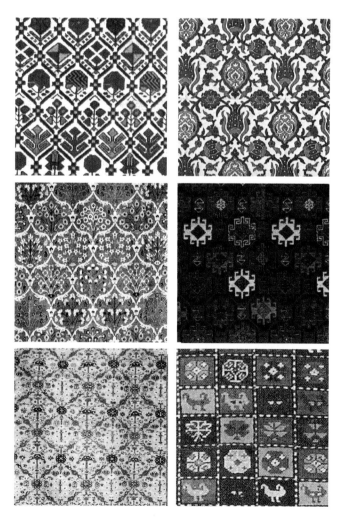

Lattices

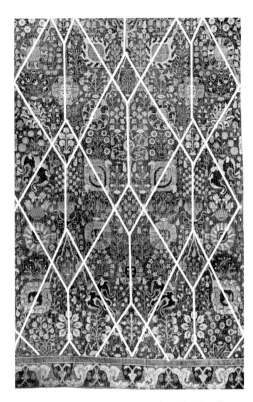

Latttices in a vase carpet (emphasized)

Laver, Lavar, Râvar, Raver. Râvar is a town north of Kerman in Iran. Finer quality rugs from the Kerman area are sometimes described as "Laver" (a corruption of Râvar), whether or not they were actually woven in Râvar. See "Kerman."

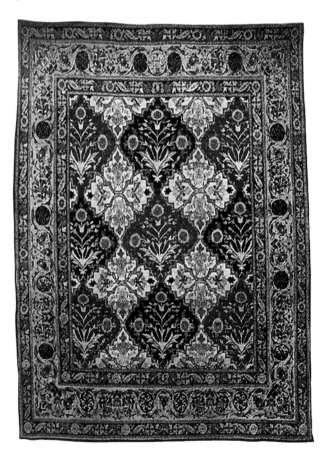

Laver Kerman *David Zahirpour*

lazy lines. Diagonal lines visible from the back of a knotted rug caused by successive rows of turnarounds of discontinuous wefts. This occurs when only a portion of the width of a rug is woven at one time.

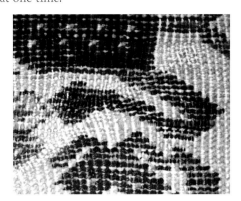

Lazy line (back of rug) *Rug Rag*

Lazgis. See "Lesghis."

leaf and calyx, leaf and goblet, wineglass. A border design used in Caucasian rugs, especially those of the Kazak region. Diagonal serrated leaves alternate with a geometricized calyx which suggests a goblet or wineglass.

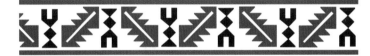

Leaf and calyx border

leiwen, lei wan. Means "thunder pattern." An ancient Chinese fret pattern.

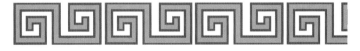

Leiwen

Lenkoran. A town and district on the Caspian Sea in the southeastern Caucasus. Lenkoran was once the capital of the khanate of Talish. The Lenkoran medallion may be a large geometricized calyx or derived from a dragon motif. The medallion may have two or four arms. This medallion has been used in the rugs of Kazak and Karabagh. Nineteenth-century rugs of Talish with this medallion have a knot density of about 69 symmetric knots per square inch, a shape ratio of about 2.21 and an area of about 34 square feet. See "Talish."

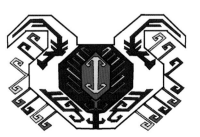

Lenkoran medallion

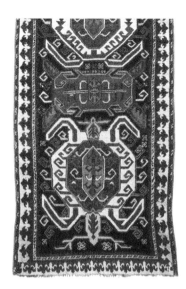

Lenkoran rug (detail) *Sothebys*

Lesghis, Lazgis, Lesgins. Any one of a group of Turkic mountain tribes inhabiting the northeast Caucasus. The Lesghis include the Avars, Darghis, Kumyk, and Kurins.

Lesghistan. See "Daghestan."

Lesghi star. A design of Shahsavan flatweaves, eastern Anatolian rugs, and Caucasian rugs. Although its use is widespread, this design is especially associated with nineteenth-century rugs of Daghestan. It is an eight-pointed stepped star with four radiating arrows. Daghestan rugs with this design have a knot density of about 99 symmetric knots per square inch, an area of about 33 square feet, and a shape ratio of about 2.01. See "Daghestan."

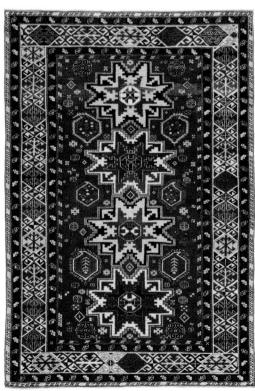

Lesghi star rug *Richard Rothstein & Co.*

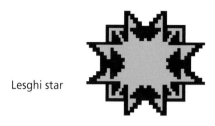

Lesghi star

level loop pile. A trade term for power-loomed carpet with a pile of loops in which all loops are of the same height. This is a hard-wearing structure used for carpets in commercial or high-traffic areas.

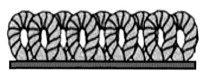

Level loop pile

Lhasa. A city of southern Tibet and the capital. Although rugs are woven in Lhasa, no specific structure or design characteristics are associated with these rugs. See "Tibet."

Libya, Tripolitania. The very few pile rugs woven in Libya appear to be modeled after those of Tunisia. A flatweave of strips sewn together, called "flij," is used to make a variety of functional items. Kilims are also woven. Designs are simple geometric figures.

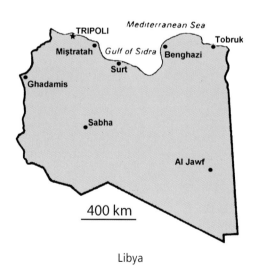

Libya

Lilân. See "Lillihan."

Lilehan. See "Lillihan."

Lillihan, Lilân, Lilehan. A town in Iran south of Arâk, about ten miles west of Khomein. Rugs of this town are similar in design to Sarouks and, like Sarouks, they were often painted. These are single-wefted rugs tied with the asymmetric knot at a density of about 65 per square inch. The foundation is cotton and wefts may be dyed red. Large numbers of these rugs were exported to the United States through the 1930s.

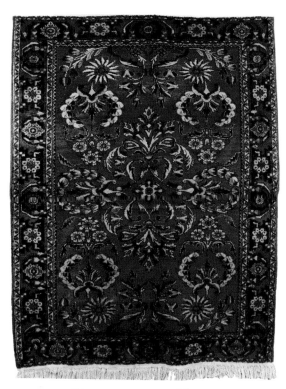

Lillihan rug *Grogan and Company*

lingzhi. A Chinese fungus growing at the base of trees and thought to bestow immortality when eaten. It is sometimes represented as a motif in Chinese rugs.

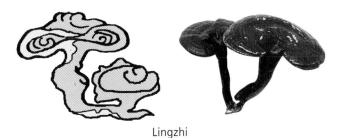

Lingzhi

line. A commercial measure of warp spacing and knot density in Chinese rugs. Line is the number of pairs of warps per linear foot. Since there is one knot for each pair of warps, the line number is the same as the number of knots per linear foot, weft-wise. Vertical knot count is assumed to be the same as the horizontal knot count. Thus, a 90-line rug has 7.5 knots per inch horizontally and vertically (90/12) and a knot density of about 56 knots per square inch (7.5 x 7.5). Common knot densities are 70, 80, 90, 120, 200, 250, and 300 line. See "China," "knot density" and "units of measure."

line count. The number of knots in one foot weftwise in a knotted pile rug. See "units of measure."

linen. A fabric made of yarn with fibers from the stem of the flax plant. Linen is not generally used in rugs, though it has been used in the warps of rugs of Donegal, rya rugs, and Polish rugs. See "flax."

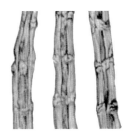

Microscopic view of linen fiber

linen tester. A small magnifying glass with a folding stand. The aperture in the base includes a one-inch scale to assist counting threads or knots.

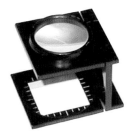

Linen tester

linoleum. A compound of linseed oil, cork, or sawdust and pigments rolled into sheets on a burlap backing. This floor covering was invented in 1863 and is still manufactured.

linsey-woolsey. A combination of homespun linen and wool used for rag rug backing prior to 1850 in the United States.

lion rugs of Fars. A group of pictorial nineteenth and twentieth-century rugs woven by tribes of Fars province, southwestern Iran. These rugs show primitive stylizations of lions. See "Fustat carpet."

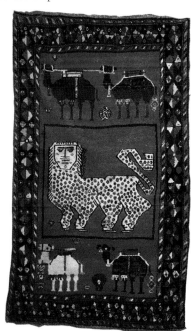

Lion Rugs of Fars *Parviz Tanavoli*

list carpets. American carpets in which strips of fabric (list) are used as weft. See "rag rugs."

listas. Early rya rugs were woven in narrow strips. The strips were then sewn together. Listas are the seams along which the narrow rugs were sewn. See "rya rugs."

logwood. A red to violet dye used in Chinese rugs and derived from the heartwood of *Haematoxylon campechianum*, a leguminous tree of Central America and the West Indies. See "brazilwood dye."

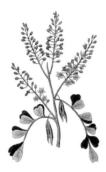

Logwood

lool, lule (Persian). Offset warps.

lool-baft, lule-baft (Persian). Completely offset warps.

loom. A frame used for weaving. Usually, the frame supports two beams to which warp ends are fastened. A system for raising alternate warps, a harness in effect, is termed the "heddle." A shed stick, a narrow board or lath, is used to open a passage through the warps, the shed, through which the shuttle, carrying weft, is passed. A reed, a form of comb the width of the loom, may be used to compress the wefts. See "backstrap loom," "carpet loom," "treadle loom," and "warp-weighted loom."

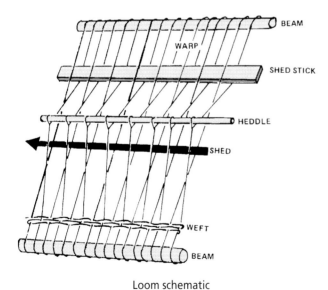

Loom schematic

loom drawing. A full-size color pattern of a rug design (usually one quarter of the rug) to be copied by the weaver on the loom. Graph paper is used with each cell representing one knot. Often, yarn samples for each color are attached to the loom drawing. See "design plate."

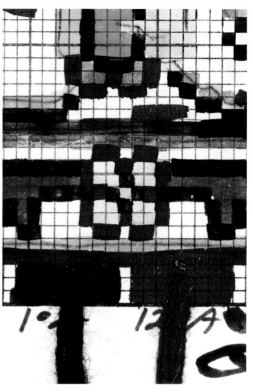

Loom drawing *Rug Rag*

loom time, time-on-loom. For commercial hand-knotted rugs, the time in the rug production cycle beginning with warping the loom, the weaving of an acceptable sample through the production of a saleable rug cut from the loom, but not washed, sheared, or finished. See "production cycle, rug."

loop pile. A pile of uncut loops. The symmetric and asymmetric knots are supplementary weft wrapping structures that may be continuous. When used in this manner, a loop may be formed between each pair of warps. If this loop is not cut, a loop pile is formed. For the asymmetric knot, this structure may be termed "Senneh loop pile." For the symmetric knot, this structure may be termed "Gördes loop pile." See "Senneh loop."

In power-loomed carpets, there are many variations of loop pile structure. These are described in the following entries: "high-low loop pile," "level loop pile," "scrolled loop pile," "tip sheared pile."

Senneh loop pile   Gördes loop pile

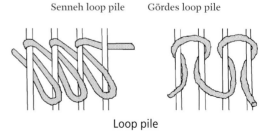

Loop pile

Lop Nor. An archaeological site in the Tarim Basin of Xinjiang in western China. In 1970 fabrics were discovered at this site dating from the first to third century C.E., the Eastern Han period. The find included fragments of woolen tapestries, patterned silks, and a fragment of a pile carpet. The fragment was woven using the Spanish knot. See "archaeological sites."

Lop Sanpra. An archaeological site in Xinjiang, China. A small, symmetric knotted, pile rug, a saddle blanket, was discovered at this site and carbon 14 dated from 1,715 to 2,290 years old. Associated artifacts at the site date the rug to the Han Dynasty. This rug is complete, measuring 2 feet 4 inches on each side. The field is a lattice and the main border is a leaf and vine motif. Colors are madder red, yellow, black, and blue. See "archaeological sites."

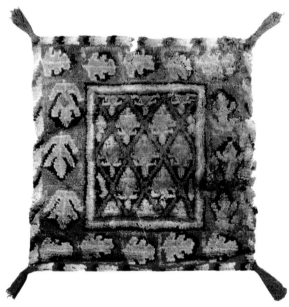

Lop Sanpra saddle blanket

Lorghabi, Lakharbi. Thought to be an Uzbek tribe of northwestern Afghanistan. Flatweaves in a wide variety of structures and some pile rugs have been given a Lorghabi attribution. Designs are the Memling gul or simple geometric patterns.

Lori Pambak. A town south of Tiflis (Tbilisi) in the Kazak region of the Caucasus. The Lori Pambak motif is a large octagonal medallion filled by two pairs of opposing calyxes, all joined at the base. This design evolved from an Anatolian medallion and is still used by Turkish and Kurdish weavers in the area of Kars. Nineteenth-century Kazak rugs with this design have a knot density of about 64 symmetric knots per square inch, an area of about 23 square feet and a shape ratio of 1.29. See "Kazak."

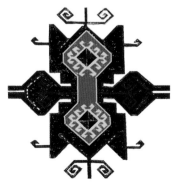

Lori Pambak motif

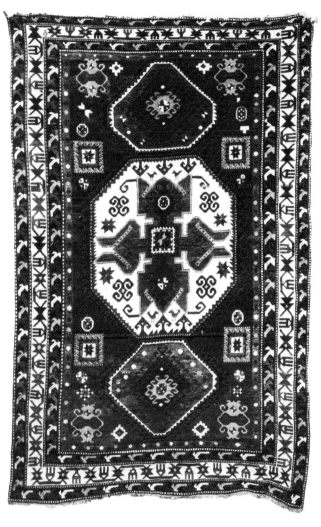

Lori Pambak rug *Sothebys*

Lors. See "Lurs."

Lotto. A group of rugs with a design appearing on rugs in the paintings of Lorenzo Lotto, a sixteenth-century Venetian painter, and other painters. These rugs, usually attributed to Ushak in Anatolia, were woven from the early sixteenth through the eighteenth century. Typically, the red field is occupied by an all-over yellow tracery or arabesque and there is a Kufesque border, although other borders are used.

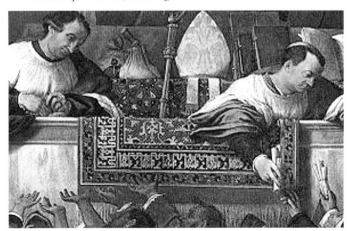

Detail of a painting by Lorenzo Lotto

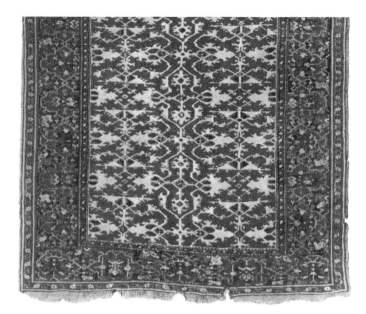

Lotto carpet (detail) *Dover*

lotus. The lotus flower is a Buddhist and Taoist symbol of perfection and purity. It is a design motif in Chinese rugs and may suggest summer. A stylized lotus flower has been proposed as the prototype for certain Turkmen guls. See "palmette."

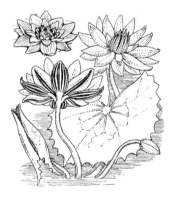

Lotus (nymphaeaceae)

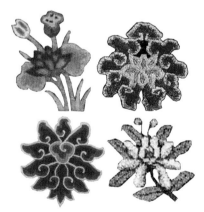

Lotus (various interpretations)

Lou lan. A group of archaeological sites in the Tarim Basin of Xinjiang, China. Sir Aurel Stein discovered a variety of textile fragments at these sites in 1913 through 1916, including patterned silks and fragments of pile carpets. These materials

have been dated to the Eastern Han period from the first to third centuries C.E. The carpet fragments have symmetric knots and features suggesting a Turkic origin. See "Lop Nor" and "Niya."

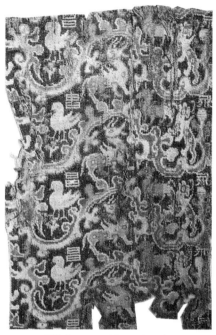

Silk fragment from Lou lan

lozenge. A diamond shape, an equilateral four-sided figure with two obtuse and two acute angles.

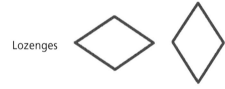

Lozenges

Lukachukai. A reservation trading post region of eastern Arizona. Navajos in the area weave small rugs with yei figures on a gray, tan, black, or red background. Dyes are synthetic.

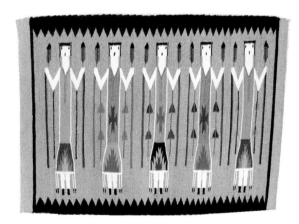

Lukachukai weaving with Yei figures *Steve Getzwiller*

lule. See "lool."

luminance. Brightness. That quality of a color differentiating light from dark.

lung. See "dragon and phoenix."

Lurs, Lors. An ancient people speaking an Iranian language, in the Zagros mountains of southwestern Persia. They are tribally organized and still to a great extent pastoral nomads. The Fayli Lurs of Luristan (principal town, Khorramabad) are usually divided into those living east of the Zagros (pish-e kuh) and those on the western slopes (pusht-e kuh). The Bakhtiari also belong to the Lurs. Southeast of Luristan, in Fars, are other Lurs tribes: the Mamasâni, the Boyer Ahmadi, and the Kuhgilu Lurs. There are also Lurs settled in the area of Varâmin. Their pile rug designs are often all-over hexagonal cells filled with a geometricized blossoms derived from the Minâ khâni pattern, or all-over diamond cells, each filled with a geometricized tree of life. Some rugs are woven with symmetric knots while other are woven with asymmetric knots.

The Lurs weave a variety of functional tribal pieces: saddle bags, salt bags, torbas, animal trappings, and carpets, using different flatweave structures. Some of their bags combine soumak, tapestry weave, and knotted pile within the same piece. See "Bakhtiari."

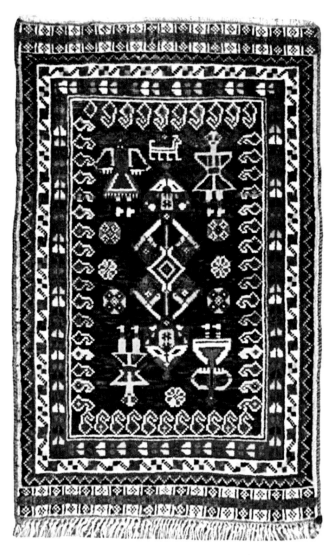

Lurs mat *John Collins*

luster, lusterizing. Luster is the extent of light reflectance or glossiness of rug pile. Lusterizing is a chemical treatment intended to enhance luster. When a lusterized rug is subsequently washed, it may appear exceptionally dull or "dead." This is a problem with some contemporary Chinese rugs. Sometimes rugs are made more lustrous by coating the pile fibers with glycerin. See "antique wash," "bleaching," "gloss," and "patina."

luteolin. A flavenol and the essential yellow dye component of Reseda luteola or weld. See "weld."

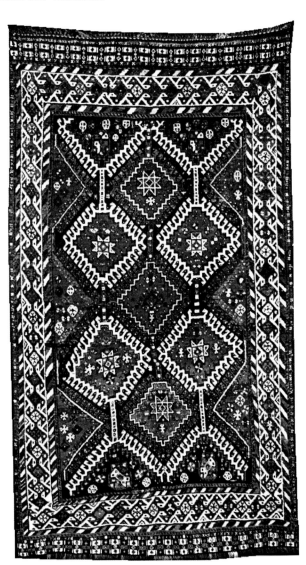

Lurs rug (detail) *Simon Knight*

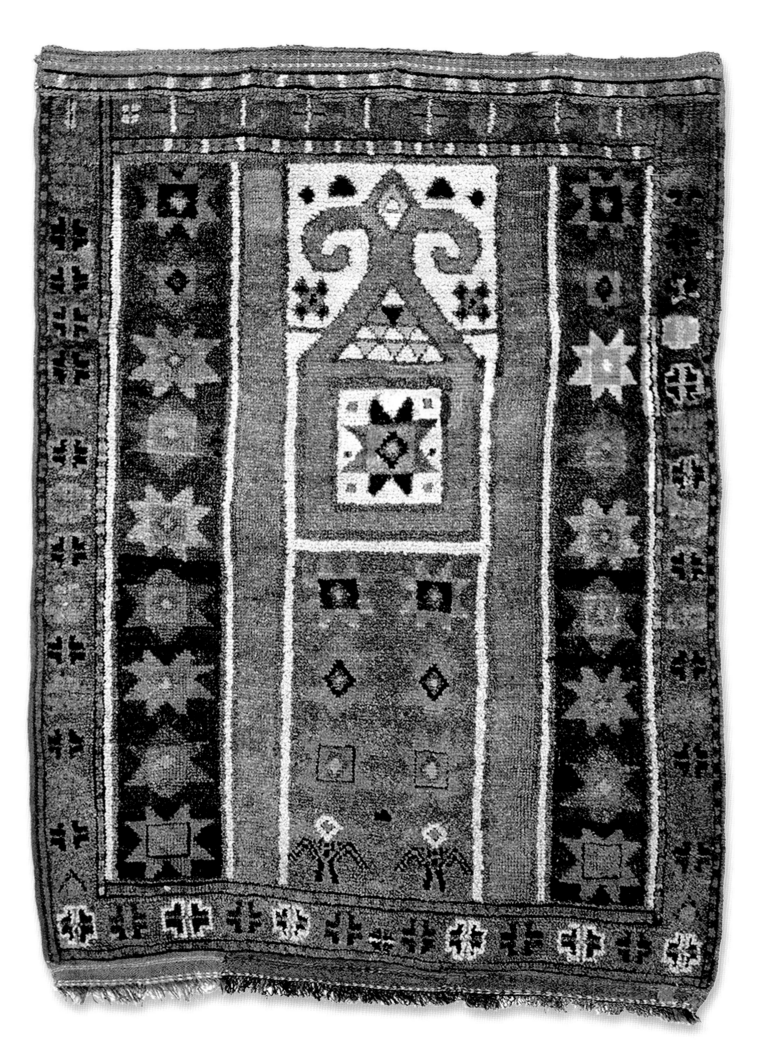

Maadid tribe. A tribe of Algeria. Rugs of this tribe were influenced by Turkish models. Later rugs are coarsely woven with seven to eight wefts between each row of knots.

macramé, (from Arabic *miqrama,* "embroidered coverlet or curtain," via Turkish, Italian, and French), **inter-knotting.** A term for knotted work. The fringe or warps extending from the end of a rug are often knotted in various ways to secure the fabric from unraveling.

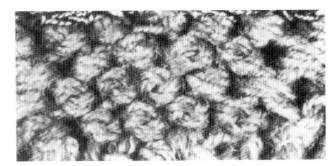

Macramé fringe

madder, garance. *Rubia tinctorum.* A widely distributed plant whose roots are used to produce a red to brown dye. Different mordants produce different colors with madder: aluminum for red, tin for orange, chromium for reddish brown, and iron for purple and black. Madder was largely displaced in the 1870s by the synthetic dye alizarin. See "alizarin."

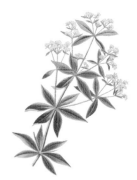

Madder

Maden. See "Çamardı"

mafrash (Arabic), **beshek, beşik** (Turk.), **farmesh, fermesh, galeh, khâbgâh** (Persian), **rakht-e khab pich** (Persian), **bedding bag.** A flat-woven bag in the form of a box, used to contain and transport bedding. Mafrash are not cradles nor used as such. Most mafrash are woven in tapestry or soumak structures. They are usually made in pairs, though not connected. The two sides and bottom are woven in one piece with the ends added. The bottom is normally a striped plain weave. They measure about three feet long and a foot high. Mafrash ends can be distinguished from saddlebag faces in that there are only top and bottom borders to a mafrash while borders completely surround saddlebag faces. Mafrash are woven by the Shahsavan of northern Iran, Afshars, and some Kurds. See "kharak" and "sar-andâz."

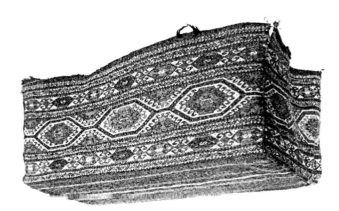

Mafrash *Jerry Franke*

Maggie and Jiggs Carpets. Three pictorial carpets woven in Kashan, Iran, in about 1925. These are all-silk rugs. The field contains cartoon characters of the American cartoonist, George McManus. In these rugs, a high level of weaving skill is lavished on a questionable design.

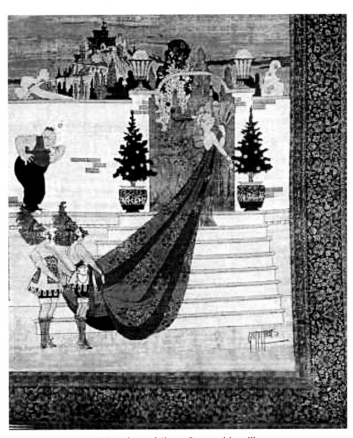

Maggie and Jiggs Carpet (detail)

maghmal (Persian, makhmal "velvet"). An ikat of silk velvet.

Maghreb. See "North Africa."

magic carpet. See "flying carpet."

Mahabad. See "Sauj Bulaq."

Mahabalipuram. A town south of Madras in India. Formerly a source of rug production in India since the mid-sixteenth century.

Mahal. A trade term for Sarouks of a second or lesser quality. See "Sarouk."

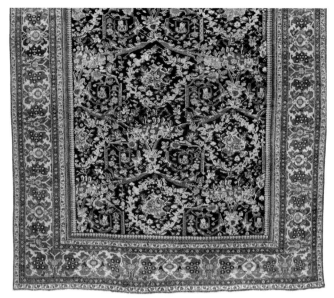

Mahal carpet (detail) *Sothebys*

mahfuri. See "qali-ha-yi-mahfuri."

Mahallât, Mahalat. A city of central Iran. Rugs woven in villages in the areas of Farâhân, Dulakhor, and Mushkabad of central Iran. Common designs are the Herati pattern and Sarouk patterns. Mahallât rugs are less densely knotted and have less depressed warps than other Sarouks woven in the same area. The knot density is about 30 to 65 asymmetric knots per square inch on a cotton foundation.

Mahvilât, Mahavallat. A town near Kâshmar in east Khurasan in Iran. It is a source of highly ornate medallion and spandrel rugs similar to those of Mashhad.

mâhi (Persian, "fish"). A term used in Hamadan, Iran, for the Herati pattern, referring to the shape of a stylized leaf. See "Herati pattern."

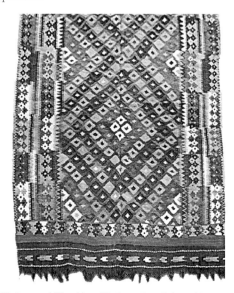

Maimana kilim (detail) *Peter Pap Oriental Rugs Inc.*

main border. See "border."

main carpet. The largest knotted pile weaving of a Turkmen tribe, with a design thought to contain the principal gul of that tribe. The principal gul is only used in its entirety; it is not halved or quartered. See "gul."

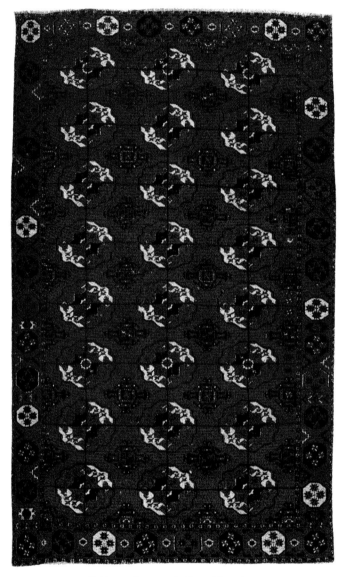

Tekke main carpet *Gerard Paquin*

major gul, primary gul. The gul associated with a specific Turkmen tribe and used in their main carpet. See "gul," "main carpet," and "minor gul."

makata. An embroidered or ornamented wall hanging imported from Turkey and popular with the Polish aristocracy from the 17th century.

makden (Tibetan). A rug used beneath the saddle.

mako (Persian). Weaver's shuttle.

Makri, Megri, Fethiye (now Fethiye). A seaport town of south-western Anatolia. Typically, rugs of this area have two or three vertical panels, each containing geometricized floral motifs or a tree of life. In the last quarter of the nineteenth century, medallion rugs with European roses in the Mejid style were woven in Makri. Wefts of Makri rugs are usually red and the selvage is often blue.

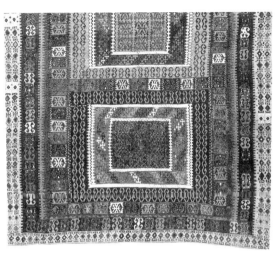

Malatya kilim (detail) *Sothebys*

Malâyer, Malyer. A town of northwestern Iran, south of Hamadan. Rugs of Malâyer and surrounding villages are single-wefted and more densely knotted than other rugs of the Hamadan area. Designs are geometric medallions, the Herati pattern, or designs similar to Sarouks. The symmetric knot at densities from about 25 to 130 knots per square inch is used on a cotton foundation, sometimes with blue wefts. See "Jowzân."

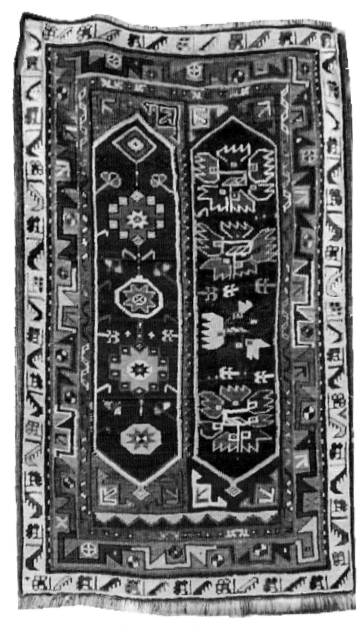

Makri rug *R. John Howe*

malacate. A spindle used by Indians and Spanish Americans of the American southwest. See "spindle."

Malatya. A town of central Anatolia. Malatya is a rug marketing center for village rugs and kilims woven in the region. Many of these are coarsely knotted rugs with geometric designs woven by Kurds.

Malatya kilims are exceptionally long, some reaching 15 feet. They are woven in two vertically matching halves. Mixed technique is used in these kilims, including slit tapestry weave, brocading, and soumak. Designs often consist of broad stripes containing geometric motifs or the sandıklı motif shown in the example. See "Yörük."

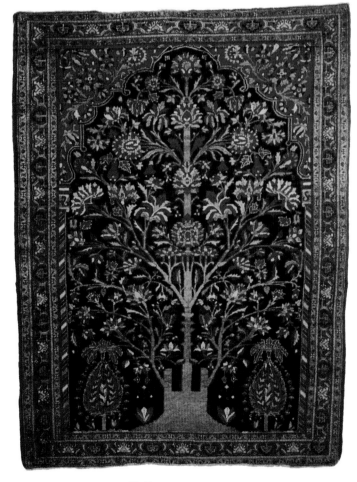

Malâyer prayer rug

mâlband (Persian). A strap used on pack animals.

Malyer. See "Malâyer."

Mamasâni, Mamassani. A tribe of the Lurs of southwestern Iran, settled to the northwest of Shiraz.

Mamluk carpets, Mameluk carpets. The Mamluks were soldiers and administrators of the Ayyubid sultanate of Egypt and Syria. They were originally imported as slaves from among the Turks of Central Asia and the Circassians of the Caucasus. They soon came to dominate the government, and in 1260 took control of the sultanate. They stemmed the advance of the Mongols in 1261, and ruled from Cairo until defeated by the Ottomans in 1517. Sitting athwart the Mediterranean and Red Sea-Indian Ocean trade routes, the Mamluk Empire prospered. Arts and crafts reflected that prosperity and cosmopolitanism, and also the continued contact of the Mamluks with the Persian Islamic culture of Iran and Turkestan.

The earliest of the Mamluk carpets have complex geometric designs. The early rugs tend to be in a long format with large geometric medallions. The dominant color of these carpets is a red, the dye source being lac. The colors include vibrant yellows, blues, and greens. The asymmetric knot is used in an all-wool rug with "S" spun yarns, rather than the more common "Z" spun yarns. There is one all-silk Mamluk in Vienna. The purely geometric Mamluk carpets continued to be woven in Cairo after the end of the Empire, along with Ottoman floral carpets. Later Mamluk carpets in the "compartment" or "chessboard" design have an all-over pattern of octagons linked by parallel radiating lines.

Many so-called "Mamluk" rugs are of problematic origin. One group of such rugs is attributed to the Maghreb, an area that now includes Morocco, Algeria, and Tunisia. Architectural ornament in Moroccan buildings contemporaneous with these rugs share design features with the rugs. See "Cairene carpets," "Chessboard rugs," "Compartment rugs," "Medici Mamluk," "Ottoman Empire," "Ottoman floral carpets," "para-Mamluk," and "Simonetti Rug."

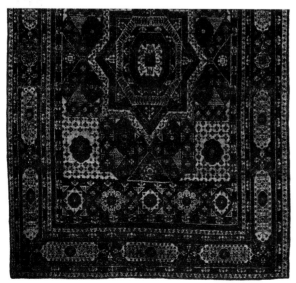

Mamluk carpet (detail)

Manastır. A trade designation for kilims from an area east of Izmir in western Anatolia. These are tribal pieces woven in contrasting colors with very evident abrash. The central portion of these kilims may be unornamented or sparsely ornamented. Some of these kilims are thought to be woven by Turks who repatriated from Bulgaria after World War I.

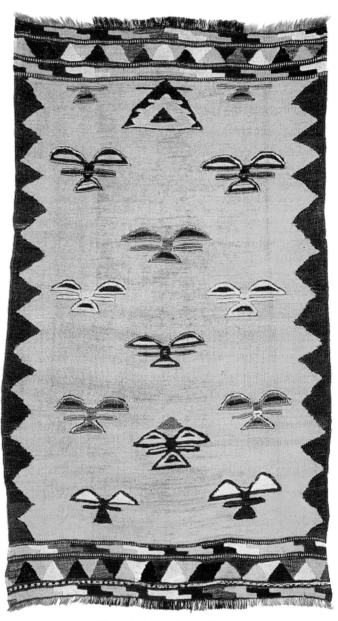

Manastır kilim *R. John Howe*

Manchester. A city in England known for its production of wool yarn. See "Merino."

Manchester Kashan. Rugs woven in Kashan in north central Iran from about 1890 to 1930. These rugs were woven of Australian Merino wool that had been processed in Manchester, England. See "Merino."

Mandarin yellow, Imperial yellow. An orange-tinted yellow in some Chinese carpets.

manguleh (Persian). Tassel.

manta. A man's shawl or blanket worn over the shoulders as a wrap. Navajo and Pueblo blankets were woven for this purpose. See "Saltillo," "serape," "shawl," and "poncho." See "Hopi."

Mantik. A Kurdish tribe of the Erbil plain in northern Iraq. The tribe is a source of kilims and bags in a weft-wrapping structure.

Manyas. A village of northwestern Anatolia. Rugs of Manyas have geometric designs and are often sold as Bergamas.

Maramures. A district of northern Romania. Many of the Maramures kilims have hemp warps. A warp sharing tapestry weave is used where wefts reverse direction on vertical lines. Often, side borders and end borders do not match. A common field design is packed, stepped diamonds containing subsidiary geometric motifs. See "Romania."

Marasali. A village south of Shemakha in Shirvân in the Caucasus. Nineteenth-century prayer rugs with large colorful botehs are attributed to this village. See "Shirvân."

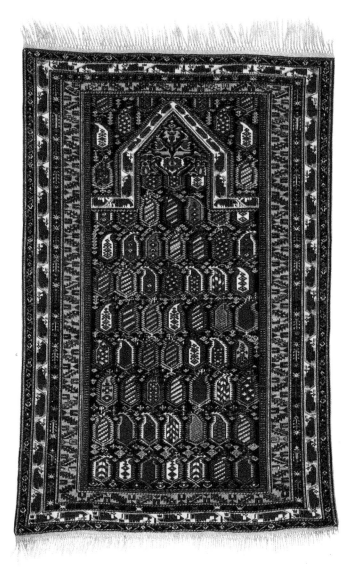

Marasali prayer rug

Marby Rug. A small rug of nomadic character found in the Church of Marby, Sweden, in 1925 and presently in the Statens Historiska Museum, Stockholm. The rug is dated to the mid-fifteenth century and was woven in eastern Anatolia or the south Caucasus. The design is two octagon medallions containing geometrically stylized birds thought to be derived from Chinese images of phoenixes. The rug is all wool with 52 symmetric knots per square inch on the front. The reverse side has widely spaced rows of asymmetric knots.

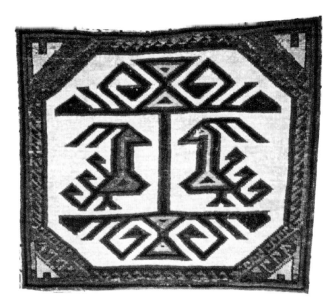

Marby rug medallion

Marcy Injoudjian Cope. An early seventeenth-century Persian pile weaving. This ecclesiastical mantle is thought to have been woven for Armenians in Persia during the reign of Shah Abbas. The cope shows the Crucifixion and the Annunciation along with Safavid floral motifs and borders. This weaving is in the collection of the Victoria and Albert Museum, London. Its width at the sleeves is 8 feet 5 inches and its length is 4 feet 11 inches. The weaving is silk with gold and silver brocade. The density is 650 asymmetric knots per square inch.

Markarian, Richard B. (1905-1989). An American rug dealer and collector. He was born in Turkey of Armenian extraction. During his life he assembled an important collection of Turkish, Caucasian, and Persian rugs, now belonging to the Markarian Foundation, Cincinnati.

marker knots. In Yomut weavings, knots of contrasting color may be tied at regular intervals down the centerline of the piece. A theory proposes that these knots mark the completion of either 10,000, 20,000, or 30,000 knots in the piece as a measure of work performed.

Marquand Medallion Carpet. A mid-nineteenth-century Anatolian hunting carpet. This carpet was formerly attributed to sixteenth-century Persia. It is presently classified in the Salting group. The rug has a red lobed medallion containing arabesques. The border contains cartouches with poetic inscriptions. The rug was the property of Henry G. Marquand and is now in the collection of the Philadelphia Museum of Art. Its size is 11 feet 9 inches by 5 feet 11 inches. The rug has a silk foundation with wool and cotton pile. It has a density of 520 asymmetric knots per square inch. See "Salting group."

Marrakesh, Marrakech. A city of central Morocco. Rug factories are located in Marrakesh and these produce copies of Turkish rugs. Tribal pieces are woven in the plains around Marrakesh. See "Morocco."

Martin, Fredrik Robert (1868-1933). A Swedish archaeologist and art historian and the author of *Oriental Rugs* before 1800. This early authoritative work was published in Vienna in 1906. He was the author of more than 40 publications, many dealing with Islamic arts. He participated in the preparation of the Munich Islamic Arts Exhibition of 1910.

Marvidiah rugs. Rugs woven by Jewish weavers in Jerusalem in the 1920s, often including images of Hebrew ritual objects and synagogues. See "Bezalel."

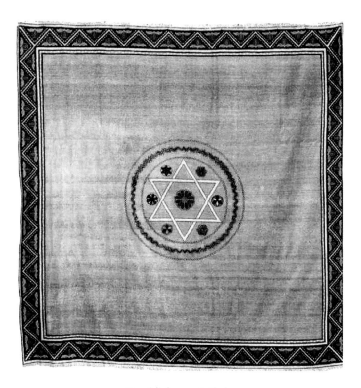

Marvidiah rug *Sothebys*

Mashhad, Mashad, Meshed. A city of northeastern Iran in the province of Khurasan. Carpet production began in Mashhad in the late nineteenth century. Mashhad is a source of rugs as well as a market for rugs of surrounding villages. Some rugs of Mashhad are woven with the symmetric knot, while most are woven with a Jufti version of the asymmetric knot on a cotton foundation. Most contemporary rugs are double-wefted. Many of these rugs have heavy cable wefts every 4 to 8 inches and these are visible on the back. Deep cochineal red predominates in Mashhad carpets. Usually, rugs are carpet sizes with medallion designs resembling those of Kerman.

Some notable twentieth-century weaver-designers of Mashhad include Amo Oghli, Saber, and Khadivi.

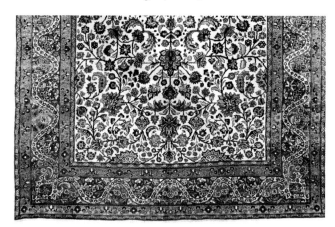

Mashhad rug *Richard Rothstein & Co.*

masho (Tibetan). A rug used on top of the saddle.

Maslaghan Mazlagan. A town in the Hamadan area of Iran. The design of rugs from this town is usually a hexagon medallion with spiked or stepped projections and spandrels. Geometricized blossoms occupy open areas. Typical knot density is 100 symmetric knots per square inch. Asymmetric knots may also be used. Very similar rugs are made in Noberan and Kerdar.

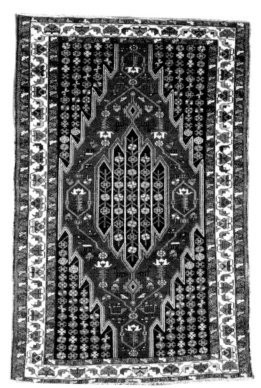

Maslaghan rug *Haliden*

masnad (Arabic). A large elevated pillow for royalty or the chief person present. This pillow was sometimes covered with a flatweave especially designed for this purpose. Also, a small rug for seating guests.

Masulipatam. A city on the eastern coast of India. The city is reputed to have been a rug-weaving center. There is no significant contemporary rug production. Masulipatam was a major source of printed cotton fabric known as kalamkar.

mat. A small fabric floor covering.

matandar. Indian for central medallion.

matn (Persian). Ground or field of a rug.

Maurchaq Mauri. Rugs woven in the village of Maurchaq and other villages on the northern border of Afghanistan. They are woven by Tekke and Sariq Turkmen. The Tekke gul is used on these rugs. Their knot density is about 175 knots per square inch.

mauri (Turk., "of Merv"). A trade designation for the best grade of contemporary Afghanistan carpets. These carpets have slightly offset warps with pile of singles yarn rather than double-plied yarn. See "mori."

mazarlık (Turk.). A Turkish carpet with images of trees and houses. It was incorrectly supposed that such carpets are used to enfold the dead when carried to a cemetery. The origin of the term was a reference to the supposed representation of a cemetery with cypress trees and gravestones. See "ayatalak" and "landscape carpet."

McMullan, Joseph V. (1896-1973). Joseph V. McMullan was a pipeline engineer and the second president of the Hajji Baba Club. He established an excellent collection of oriental rugs from the sixteenth to the nineteenth centuries. The collection included court rugs and many fine examples of village and nomadic rugs. Nineteenth century Turkmen and Turkish rugs were well represented in the collection. The greater part of the collection was left to the Metropolitan Museum of Art, New York, and the remainder to the Fogg Art Museum, Harvard, and to several other museums.

meander border. Any of a wide variety of continuous border designs that do not fill the band they occupy but alternate from side to side. Often, meander borders suggest a floral vine.

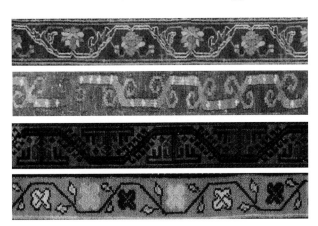

Meander borders
From top to bottom: *Khurasan, Kirşehir, Baluchi, Donegal*

measurement. See "units of measure."

Mecca Shiraz. A trade designation for higher quality rugs woven in Fars, Iran. See "Shiraz."

medahil. See "Laleh Abbasi."

medallion, shamsa (Arabic), **toranj** (Persian). A large enclosed portion of a design usually located in the center of the field. Common shapes are diamonds, octagons, ovoids, hexagons, and stars. Medallions may be lobed or stepped. Where there is a single central medallion, quarters of that medallion may be used as corners or spandrels in the rug. There may be several medallions or parts of medallions in rug designs.

Medallions are somewhat less common in tribal rugs than in urban rugs. Some of the medallion designs of Ottoman and Safavid court rugs are similar to contemporaneous designs of book bindings. One theory holds that the designs of the earliest medallion court rugs were derived from book bindings. See "korani," "matandar," "pendant," "pole medallion," and "quincunx."

medallion soumaks. Soumaks with a design of a column of large medallions, usually three or more. The medallion may be a diamond with inward pointing crosses, an eight-pointed figure of a diamond superimposed on a rectangle, a hooked diamond, or an octagon. See "dragon soumak" and "soumak."

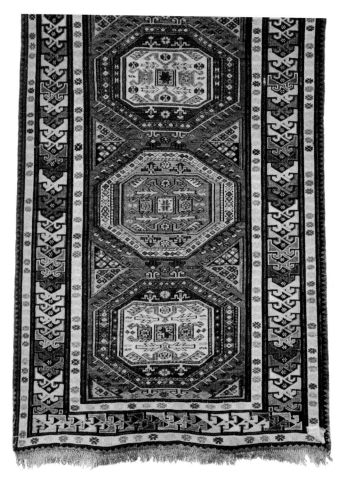

Caucasian medallion soumak (detail)
Grogan and Company

Medallion Ushak. Sixteenth and seventeenth-century rugs

woven in Ushak, Anatolia, with a circular central medallion with pendants. The medallion contains a quatrefoil. The field is red. These rugs are large and in a long format. Similar rugs were woven near Izmir during the same period, and these have darker colors and a lower knot density. See "Ushak."

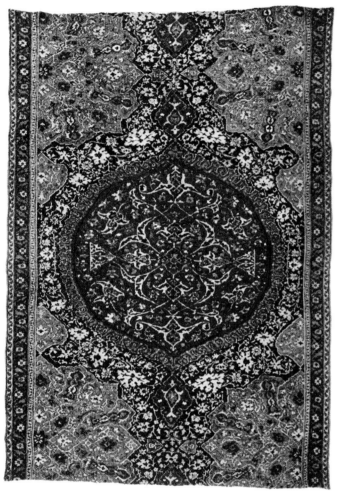

Medallion Ushak (detail)

Medici Mamluk Carpet. A recently discovered sixteenth-century Mamluk carpet from Cairo, Egypt. This carpet has three octagon medallions and is the largest Mamluk carpet, about 36 feet by 13 feet. It has the usual red ground of Mamluks and characteristic colors of yellow, green, and blue. The rug has a cartouche border. It is in the collection of the Palazzo Pitti in Florence, Italy.

Medici Ottoman Carpet. An early seventeenth-century Ottoman carpet attributed to Cairo. Purchase records indicate Cairo as the origin. It is a very large rug, about 32 feet by 9 feet, and in excellent condition. The design is basically two columns of green palmette quatrefoils on a red field. The foundation is all wool. The pile is wool except for areas of blue and white cotton. The rug is in the Palazzo Pitti in Florence, Italy.

Mediouna. A town near Casablanca in Morocco. Rugs woven in Mediouna are influenced by Persian designs and usually have three medallions. Borders are narrow, and intricate floral

motifs are worked into the overall design. The symmetrical knot is used with a density between 35 to 50 knots per square inch on a wool foundation. See "Morocco."

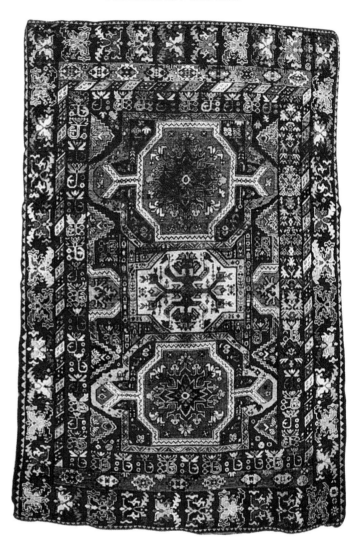

Mediouna carpet *Pickering/Yohe Collection*

meditation mat, prayer mat. A trade term for a small Tibetan pile mat about one and one-half feet square, used in Buddhist meditation. Some mats have an added heavy fringe. This term is sometimes used by auction houses to describe prayer rugs. See "Wangden."

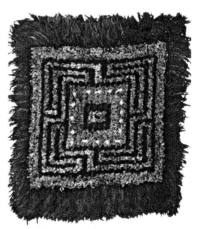

Wangden meditation mat

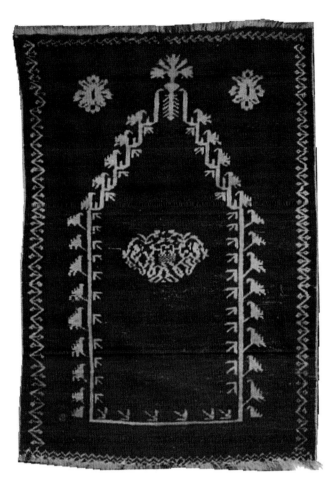

Medjidian style yastik *R. John Howe*

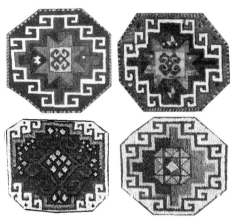

Memling guls
Top: *Kazak, Moghan* **Bottom:** *Kurd, Anatolian*

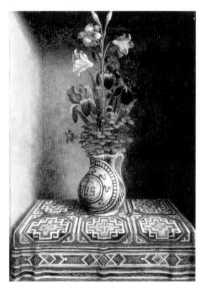

Still life by Memlinc with Memling gul rug
Wikimedia Commons

Medjidian style, Medjid. A design style employing naturalistic floral arrangements in imitation of European models and favored by Abdul-Mejid, Sultan of Turkey from 1839 through 1861. Some rugs of Gördes, Makri, and Milas were influenced by this style.

Megri. See "Makri."

mehraby (Turk. "with mihrab"). Azerbaijani term for "prayer rug."

Mehrabân, Mehriban, Mehrivan. A district north of Hamadan in Iran. Rugs from villages in this area are single-wefted with symmetric knots, often with a medallion on a camel-colored field. The foundation is cotton. Mehrabân is also the name of a village east of Tabriz. Mehribân also refers to a grade of Heriz rug between Heriz and Gorevan in quality.

Meimeh. See "Meymeh."

mekik (Turk.). Shuttle.

Melas. See "Milas."

Memling gul. A widely-used motif named after Hans Memlinc, a fifteenth-century Flemish artist whose paintings show rugs designed with the motif. The earliest Memling gul rugs were probably flatwoven.

mercerized. Cotton thread or yarn whose strength and gloss has been increased by treating it with alkali under pressure. See "art silk," "floss," and "ipekli."

Merino. A breed of sheep producing very fine wool. The Merino was first raised in Spain. Australian Merino wool is used in some rugs from Iran, Pakistan, China, and India. "Manchester" is Merino wool processed in Manchester, England. See "Manchester Kashan" and "sheep."

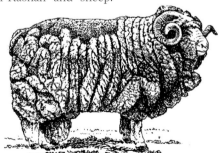

Merino ram

Merv, Marv, Mary. An oasis city of Russian Turkestan (Turkmenistan). In the eighteenth century, it was dominated by the Uzbeks, then by the Saryk and Salor Turkmen, and then by the Tekke after they defeated the Salor in about 1830. Russia occupied Merv in 1884. The area was a source of silk which was occasionally used in Tekke weavings. In the early twentieth century Merv was a major market center for Turkmen rugs, with thousands of rugs sold each week. See "Tekke" and "Salor."

Meshed. See "Mashhad."

Meshkâbâd. See "Mushkabad."

Meshkin. A town of northwestern Iran in Persian Azerbaijan north of Zanjân. Rugs of Meshkin have symmetric knots and are double-wefted on a cotton foundation. Knot density is about 65 per square inch. Caucasian designs are often used. They are similar to contemporary rugs of Ardabil. See "Ardabil."

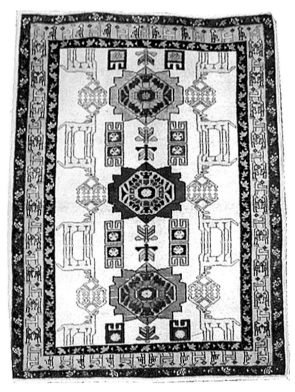

Meshkin mat *Manouchehr Haghighat*

metallic threads. Gold, silver, and other metals have been used in rugs in the form of wires and as flat ribbons wrapped around a fiber core. A metallic flat strip or a strip of gilt paper is termed "lamella." When lamella is wrapped smoothly around core yarn, the result is termed "filé." Aside from those described in literary references, the earliest rugs using metallic threads are the Polonaise carpets woven in sixteenth and seventeenth-century Persia and containing silver and gold threads. Some eighteenth-century rugs from Khotan and Kâshgar contain metallic threads. Metallic brocades were used in some rugs of Hereke woven in the first half of the twentieth century. Gold threads are used in some contemporary Kashmir carpets.

meter. See "conversion factors."

met hame, met hane. A design consisting of multiple borders, but an essentially unoccupied field. See "Talish."

metrah. Pile carpets woven for sale by male weavers of certain Algerian tribes. See "Algeria."

metric. See "conversion factors."

Meymaneh. See "Maimana."

Meymeh, Meimeh. A town in the area of Joshegan in northwest Iran. Rugs woven in this town have the traditional Joshegan design. The asymmetric knot is used at a density of about 65 per square inch on a cotton foundation. See "Joshegan."

miân farsh (Persian). The large, middle carpet in the traditional Persian carpet arrangement. See "audience rug."

Miâneh. A town of northwestern Iran southeast of Tabriz. The area is inhabited by Shahsavan. See "Shahsavan."

Middle Atlas. A range of mountains in central Morocco. Tribes of the Middle Atlas weave pile rugs in a long format with narrow borders. Designs include concentric diamond medallions or vertical or horizontal stripes occupied by diamonds and sawtooth designs. For these rugs, the symmetric knot is tied on four warps. See "Morocco."

Mihaliççik. A town of western Anatolia between Ankara and Eskişehir. A source of small prayer rugs with stepped or triangular mihrabs. Borders are wide and ewers, diamonds, and geometricized blossoms are used as filler motifs.

mihrab (Arabic). The prayer niche in a mosque wall indicating the *qibla* or direction of Mecca or a symbolic gateway, represented by an arch in a prayer rug.

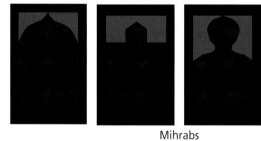

Mihrabs

Milanlu. A town and a source of Kurdish weavings in Khurasan, Iran.

Milas, Melas. A town of southwest Anatolia. Rug weaving may have begun in Milas as early as the seventeenth century. Designs of rugs from Milas and surrounding villages include prayer rugs with a diamond-shaped mihrab derived from Ottoman horseshoe-shaped mihrabs, rugs with vertical panels similar to those of Makri, and rugs with fields occupied by a vertical column of boxes or diamonds. Some Mejidian-style rugs were also woven in the area. Milas rugs are all-wool with red wefts. Most rugs are coarsely knotted with densities varying between 55 and 75 symmetric knots per square inch.

Currently there is no weaving in Milas itself, but only in the surrounding villages. See "Karaova."

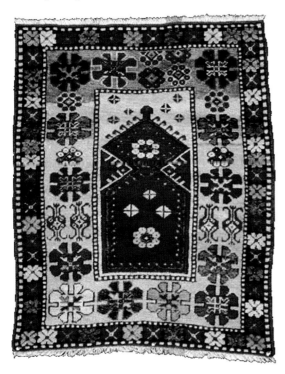

Milas prayer rug *James Allen*

Milcov. The highest commercial grade for Romanian carpets with a cotton foundation. Rugs so designated have a knot density of 194 per square inch.

mildew. See "dry rot."

millefleurs. A design composed of many flower blossoms. Often the millefleurs design occupies the field of a prayer rug with the field flanked by cypresses. Such rugs were woven in Mughal India and southwestern Iran. A similar design is used in some prayer rugs of Hereke in Turkey and by the Qaashga'i. See "Imperial Mughal Prayer Rug."

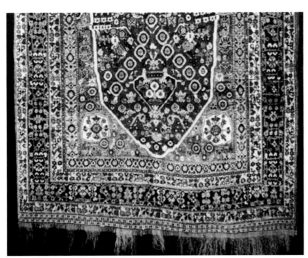

Qashqa'i millefleurs rug (detail) *Simon Knight*

mill end. A remnant or piece of power-loomed carpet of about 9 to 20 feet in length.

minä khäni (Persian). An overall pattern consisting of two or more flower blossoms connected by a diamond lattice. There are many versions of this pattern.

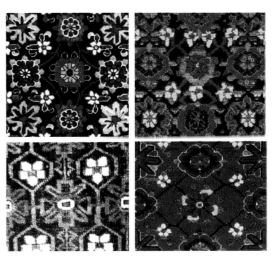

Minä khäni patterns
Top: *Persian, Lurs* Bottom: *Baluch, Ersari*

minbar, mimbar. Pulpit in a mosque; generally a structure consisting of an entrance door and a flight of steps.

Arabesques above a minbar door

mindar, minder (Turk. "cushion, padded mat"). A bolster or large pillow for seating.

Ming dynasty (1368-1644). Felt Sino-Mongolian carpets and bedding (in shades of red) have been dated to the 15th and 16th centuries. A very few Chinese pile rugs have been dated to the same period. See "kuilung" and "Ch'ing dynasty."

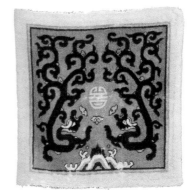

Chinese rug of the Ming dynasty *Wendel Swan*

Ming emblem. The phoenix and dragon motif. See "dragon."

minor border. The borders of a rug usually consist of one broad band or major border with narrower bands or stripes on both sides. These narrow bands or stripes are minor borders or guard borders.

minor gul, secondary gul. Motifs used generally in the weavings of Turkmen tribes. A minor gul is smaller than a major gul and may be used in combination with the major gul. See "gul" and "major gul."

mir-i boteh (Persian). A design of multiple rows of small botehs.

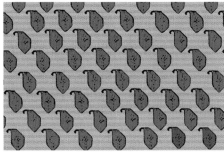

Mir-i boteh

mirror carpet. A carpet with an empty field. See "met hame."

mirror gul. See "aina gul."

mirror writing. Inscriptions in rugs that are mirror images of readable inscriptions. Mirror writing occurs when inscriptions are copied from the back of a rug by a weaver for whom the inscription has only design significance.

Mir Serabend, Saruq Mir, (from Mir-i Boteh). A grade of Serabend rug with asymmetric knots at a high density, fine wool, and a cotton foundation with blue wefts. Typically, the red field is covered by an all-over pattern of small blue botehs. See "Serabend."

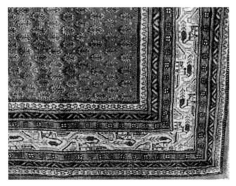

Mir Serabend (detail) *J. Barry O'Connell*

Mirzapur. A city and the major carpet production center of Uttar Pradesh in northeastern India. Finely woven rugs were produced in Mirzapur in the nineteenth century. Since about 1900, however, Mirzapur has been the source of a very large volume of coarsely woven rugs. Currently Persian, Chinese, and Aubusson designs are used, and often the rugs are sculptured. The asymmetric knot is used with a cotton foundation. See "Bhadohi" and "India."

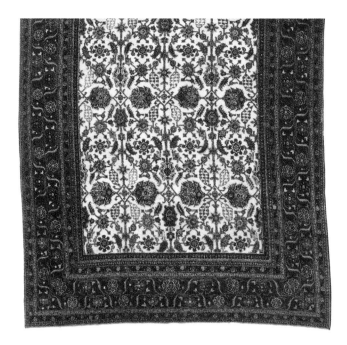

Mirzapur rug (detail) *Sothebys*

Mishkin. See "Meshkin."

mixed technique. Any fabric employing a variety of weaving techniques. For example, a Bakhtiari saddle bag may have the closure strip woven with the tapestry structure, the bag face woven with the soumak structure, including eccentric wefts, a panel at the bottom of the bag woven with symmetric pile knots, and weft twining delineating certain areas.

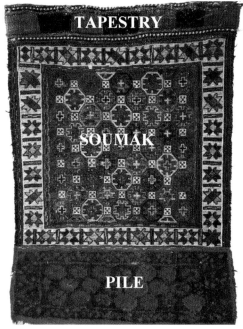

Mixed technique Bakhtiari saddle bag face

Moghal, Moghul. See "Mughal."

Moghän, Mughan. A plain southeast of the Caucasus range bordering Iran and Talish. Nineteenth-century rug designs from this region usually consist of Memling guls or hooked medallions. Typically, they have a knot density of 72 symmetric knots per square inch. They have a mean rug area of about 33 square feet and are about twice as long as they are wide. See "Caucasus."

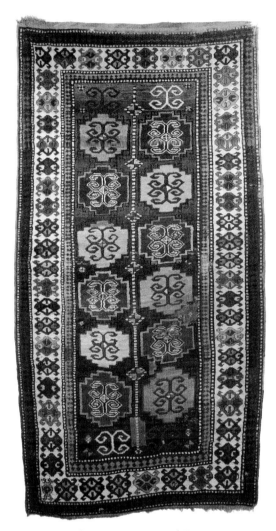

Moghän rug *Grogan and Company*

mohair, mouher (Turk. moher from Arabic mukhayyar, "by choice, deliberately" referring to the watered design of camlet which was produced "deliberately" and not by accident). Yarn or fabric made from the fleece of the Angora goat.

Mohajaran Sarouk. Large, fine Sarouk rugs woven between 1910 and 1930. A fine weave and lustrous wool were used in these rugs. They were not chemically washed and painted. A distinctive deep orange-red was used in the design. See "Sarouk."

Mohammad. See "Islam."

Mohtashem, Mochtachan, Motasham, Mohteshan Kashan (Persian *mohtashem*, "ceremonial," or a surname). A term used by the rug trade in referring to high-quality, late nineteenth-century and early twentieth-century rugs woven in Kashan, Iran. Mohtashem was supposed to be a weaver who was among the first to operate a factory weaving rugs of wool imported from Manchester, England. There are two silk prayer rugs inscribed Mohtashem and a wool rug with the Mohtashem

inscription dated 1905. It is probable that most of the rugs attributed to Mohtashem within the rug trade are from some other source. See "Manchester Kashan" and "Kashan."

moj. A southwest Persian tribal flatweave. These are woven in a balanced twill weave in several pieces and sewn together. Moj may have elaborate end tassels. Motifs are diamonds, squares, and vertical colored stripes. Moj are used as blankets or as coverings for bags and household goods in the tent.

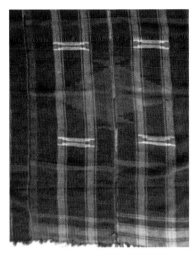

Lurs moj (detail) *Manouchehr Haghighat*

Moki. Early Spanish name for the Hopi Indians. A design for blankets woven by the Navajo consisting of alternating brown, indigo, blue, and white stripes.

mokata. A measure of a weaver's production in Mashhad, Iran, equal to 16,000 knots.

Moldova. A district of northeastern Romania and the former Moldavian Soviet Republic on the far side of the Prut river. Moldova is a source of kilims, usually with a green, brown, gray, or black field. Designs are floral motifs in red, pink, or mauve. Some designs are rendered more curvilinear through the use of eccentric wefts. Some pieces are dated or carry inscriptions using the Latin alphabet. There is extensive embroidery of household textiles and clothing. See "Bessarabia."

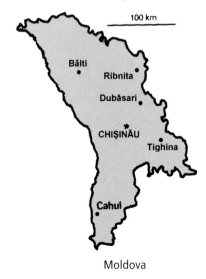

Moldova

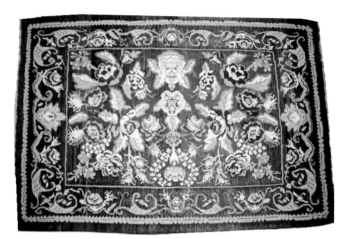

Moldova kilim *Peter Willborg*

Mongolia, Outer Mongolia, People's Republic of Mongolia.
Traditional rugs of Mongolia are quilted felt rugs (*shirdeg* or
toiruulga). There are similar felt tent flaps and mats (*olbog*).
The attribution of old pile rugs (*xives*) to Mongolia is highly
speculative. The earliest rugs so attributed are from the
nineteenth century. These rugs show Chinese design
influences. The field consists of small geometrical motifs in a
dense all-over pattern. Designs may include spandrels. Red
and pink are the dominant colors. Rugs are small. The
asymmetric knot is used and the foundation is cotton. Double
wefts are used and there is no warp offset. In 1925, a pile rug
factory was opened in Ulan Bator, the capital. There is
contemporary production of low-quality pile rugs in Chinese
designs with very bright colors on a cotton foundation.

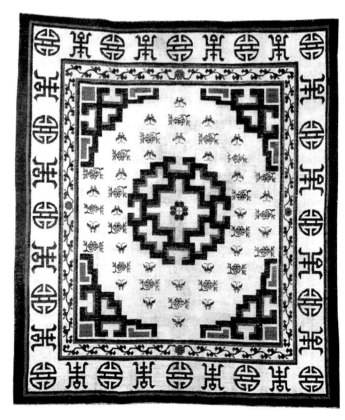

Mongolian rug *Alberto Levi*

Monistir, Manistir. A province of Macedonia and the supposed
source of some 19th and early 20th century pile prayer rugs.
This attribution is disputed.

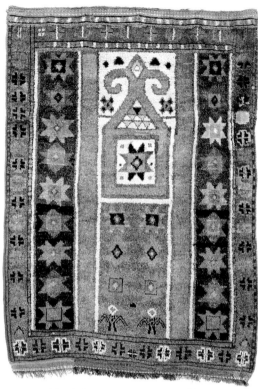

Monistir prayer rug *Peter Willborg*

monofilament. A long, continuous single fiber or filament. A
common feature of synthetic fibers, but only occurring
naturally in silk fiber.

Moorfields. The site of Thomas Moore's carpet factory in
London, England. This factory produced hand-knotted rugs
from about 1757 to 1806. Some of the carpets were designed
by Robert Adam. See "England."

moquette carpet. An eighteenth-century French velvet carpet
or an early American-made Axminster. In French, any
broadloom carpet. Also, a sixteenth-century Dutch woolen
velvet (mockado, moucade).

mordant. A compound used in dyeing that reacts with the dye
and fiber to fix the dye permanently to the fiber. Acid dyes
require basic mordants and basic dyes require acid mordants.
Most natural dyes are weak acids. Different mordants produce
different hues and shades from the same dye. Common
mordants are aluminum sulphate, potassium alum, copper
sulphate, ferrous sulphate, potassium dichromate, stannous
chloride, dried yoghurt, and urine. See "alum mordant,"
"chrome mordant," "copper mordant," "iron mordant," and "tin
mordant."

Moreidari. A group of possibly Timuri origin that live among
the Baluchis in Afghanistan and learned rug-weaving from
them. See "Baluchi."

moresque. In power-loomed cut pile carpets, where yarns of different colors are combined for a pepper-and-salt effect.

mori, mouri. Derives from "Merv." A trade term describing the weave of certain Pakistani and Indian rugs, specifically the absence of warp offset in these rugs. The term may also describe a common Turkmen design of the Tekke gul. This design is used in rugs of India, Pakistan, and Afghanistan. See "mauri."

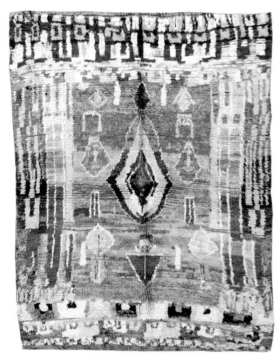

Moroccan rug *Jason Nazmiyal*

Morocco (from Arabic *maghreb*, west), Berber rugs. Morocco is a Muslim country of northeast Africa on the Atlantic and Mediterranean coasts. The urban population is a mixture of Arabs and Berbers, with Berbers comprising a majority in the countryside. Berbers ascribe magical properties to the motifs of their weavings.

Some Hispano-Moresque rugs may have been woven in Morocco. The Berber knot, tied on multiple warps is similar to the Spanish knot tied on a single warp, a feature suggesting a Moroccan origin of the Spanish knot. Moroccan rugs have not been reliably dated earlier than the nineteenth century, although rug weaving has been practiced in Morocco for many centuries.

Most Moroccan rugs have symmetric knots and a few have asymmetric knots or Berber knots. Early rugs are on an all-wool foundation while later rugs have a cotton foundation. The earliest rugs are based on Anatolian designs, usually with an arch or niche at both ends. They are more coarsely knotted and more brightly colored than the Anatolian rugs. Many current designs are derived from Persian models.

Rugs using weft skip plain weave, weft twining, soumak structure, and tapestry structure are woven in Morocco. Some of these flatweaves may be ornamented with metal sequins. Since 1919, Moroccan rugs have been labeled "M.A.R.O.C." or "Maroc." See "asachu," "Berber knots," "Beni M'Guild," "Beni M'tir," "boucherouite," "Chiadma," "gtifa," "High Atlas,"

"Marrakesh," "Mediouna," "Middle Atlas," "Ouaouzquite," "Oulad Bou Sbaa," "Rabat," "tharashna," "Zaiane," and "Zemmour."

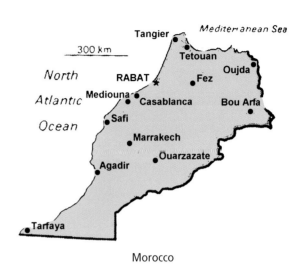

Morocco

Morris, William (1834-1896). An English designer, artist, writer and social activist. Hammersmith, a company he founded, produced machine woven carpets beginning in 1875, but his concern for quality craftsmanship prompted him to weave hand-knotted carpets, beginning in 1878. The symmetric knot was used with a cotton foundation. Only about 100 carpets were woven according to the designs of Morris and his assistant, Henry Deale. The carpets used floral motifs with vines and arabesques, remotely derived from Persian models. Blues and madder reds were dominant colors. His trade mark, woven into the carpets, consists of a hammer, the letter "M" or parallel wave forms, or combinations of these elements. These trademarks were woven into Morris hand-knotted rugs between 1878 and 1881. William Morris was the founder of the Arts and Crafts Movement. See "Arts and Crafts."

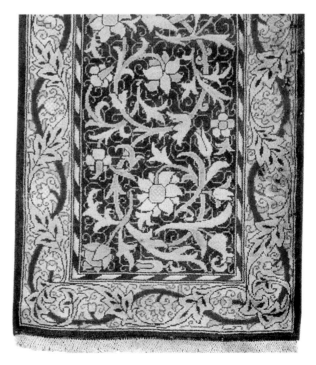

William Morris rug (detail) *Sothebys*

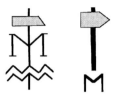

William Morris (Hammersmith) trademarks

mosaic carpet. See "compartment rug."

Moshkova, Valentina G. (1902-1952). An Uzbeki scholar of Turkmen and Central Asian rugs. She cataloged the guls, motifs and designs of tribal weaving and described the functions of these weavings. She was an ethnographer. Her major work, *Carpets of the People of Central Asia*, is the foundation of the study of these weavings.

mosque (Arabic *masjid*, "place of prostration"). A Muslim place of worship. A dome and minaret are common architectural features of mosques. See "landscape carpet," "mihrab," "minbar," "Qibla," "squinch," and "wakf."

Mosul, Mossul. A city of nothern Iraq, primarily Kurd in population. Mosul is an obsolete trade designation for Persian Kurdish rugs. Also, Mosul may refer to a rug size of about 6½ feet by 3¼ feet.

moth. See *"Bombyx mori,"* "carpet moth," "casemaking moth," and "silk."

mother-and-daughter boteh. A design found in Qashqa'i, Khamseh and some other rugs consisting of small botehs inside large botehs.

Mother Goddess of Anatolia. See "Çatal Hüyük."

motif. A significant or distinctive design element or figure in a rug or weaving. A repertoir of motifs is characteristic for specific tribal, village, and urban rugs. These motifs vary over time, tending from the complex to the simple and the curvilinear to the geometric. Motifs are subject to borrowing and re-interpretation, which leads to some confusion in rug attribution. See "design" and "attribution." See "boteh," "elibelinde," "endless knots," "filler motifs," "florets," "gul," "Herati pattern," "kaikalak," "memling gul," "mina khani," "Motif Variation Examples," "muska," "palmettes," "tree of life," "vurma."

Moud. See "Mud."

mountain carpet. A prayer rug with a reentry design at the bottom of the field. This may be a "turret" or "keyhole," a rectangle, triangle, or arch. See "Bellini rugs" and "turret design."

mouri. See "mori."

Mourzouck. In India, a dhurrie made of coir, sometimes mixed with jute or sisal.

Mucur, Mudjar. A town of central Anatolia near Kırşehir. Mucur is a source of saffs and prayer rugs with stepped and pointed mihrabs. Mihrabs may be nested and there is often a cross-panel above the mihrab. The main border may consist of rectangles occupied by geometricized blossoms. Earlier rugs have muted shades of red, green, and brown.

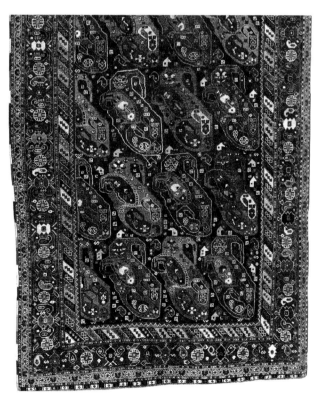

Khamseh Mother-and-daughter botehs (detail) *Sothebys*

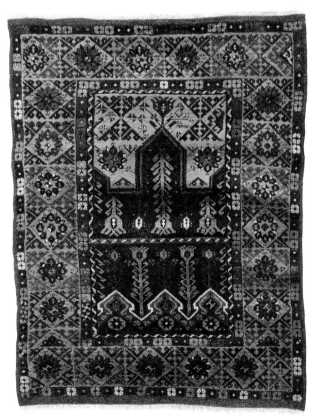

Mucur prayer rug *Sothebys*

Mud, Moud, Mud-e Dahanâb. A village of the Qainat near Birjand in northeastern Iran. Carpets of the village are typically dark blue with an arabesque medallion design or the Herati pattern. The asymmetric jufti knot is used at densities from 130 to 290 knots per square inch on a cotton foundation. See "Birjand."

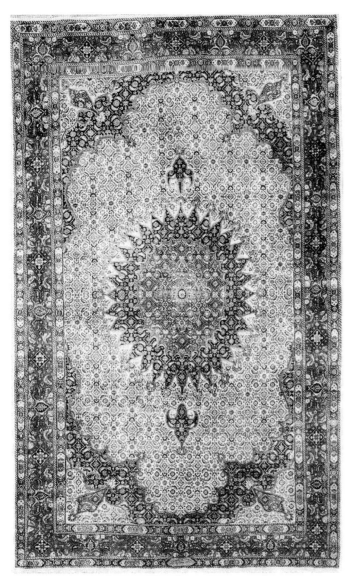

Mud carpet (detail) *J. Barry O'Connell*

mudejar. Muslims living under Christian rule, therefore, art created by such Muslims, usually for Chrisian patrons. A design style consisting of a synthesis of Christian and Muslim motifs in Hispano-Moresque architecture, furnishings, and rugs. See "Alcaraz."

Mudjar. See "Mucur."

Mughal carpets. Carpet weaving first achieved prominence in India during the Mughal dynasty, founded by Babur (1483-1530). Babur was of Turko-Mongol descent (a scion of the Timurid dynasty of Herat), and the terms "Mughal" or "Mogul" are derived from "Mongol." Persian carpet weavers settled in India in the early sixteenth century. Some of the earlier rugs attributed to India may have been woven in Herat. The grandson of Babur, Akbar (1556-1605) set up extensive carpet-weaving workshops to produce carpets for his palaces. Carpets were woven in Lahore, Agra, and Fatehpur Sikri. The earliest surviving whole Mughal carpets were woven in the seventeenth century.

In the reign of Akbar's son Jahangir (1605-1627) trade in carpets with England was undertaken through the British East India Company. During Jahangir's reign, carpet design departed from the early Persian models and became increasingly naturalistic. The greatest Mughal carpets were woven during the reigns of Jahangir and Shah Jahan (1628-1658). In the time of Shah Jahan, the Girdler's Carpet was woven on commission in Lahore and a silk rug was woven with the extraordinary knot density of 2,550 knots per square inch. A fragment of this rug is in the collection of the Metropolitan Museum of Art. Carpet designs of this period were influenced by contemporary European engravings and paintings of flowers.

Mughal rugs include those with naturalistically rendered flowers on a crimson field, pictorial carpets, and carpets with stylized floral elements similar to Persian Safavid carpets. See "Ames Pictorial Rug," "Fremlin Carpet," "Girdler's Carpet," "Imperial Mughal Prayer Rug," "India," "Millefleurs carpets," "Paravicini Prayer Rug," "'Portuguese' carpets," and "Widener Animal Carpet."

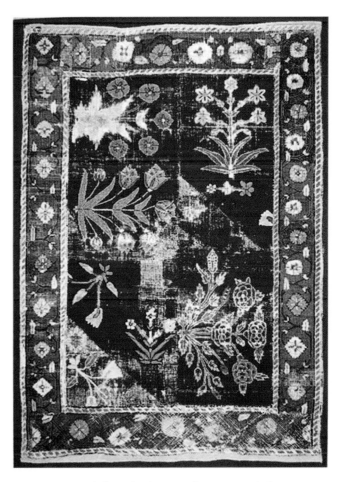

Mughal rug (17th century) *Jason Nazmiyal*

Mughal grotesques. See "vak-vak tree."

Mughan. See "Moghân."

Muhammad. See "Islam."

Munsell's color theory. Munsell's color theory is based on psychological perceptions rather than on physical measurements. Hue, chroma, and value are used to describe each color in this theory. All colors can be located in a conceptual sphere. The vertical axis indicates value with light or white at the top and darkness or black at the bottom. Degree of rotation around the axis indicates hue or color from the visual spectrum. Chroma or saturation, the admixture of white, black, or gray, is indicated along a horizontal radius from the axis to the surface of the sphere, with the most saturated or vivid colors at the surface. There is a special notation for this color theory. See "chroma," "hue," and "value."

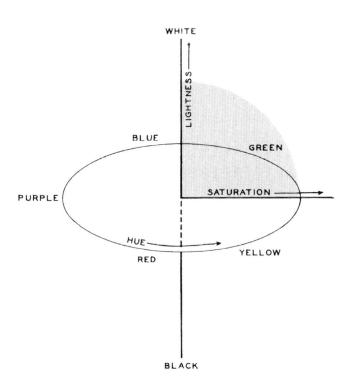

Munsell's color sphere

Murdschekar, Murcha Khort, Murcheh Khurt. A village between Isfahan and Joshegan in central Iran. Murdschekar rugs are in the Joshegan or Herati patterns. The symmetric knot is used at densities of about 130 to 135 knots per square inch on a cotton foundation.

Mureş. A region of central Romania. A trade designation for a grade of Romanian rugs employing Persian designs. These rugs have a cotton foundation with a knot density of 129 knots per square inch. This region is also a source of kilims. See "Transylvania."

murex dye. A dye extracted from a Mediteranean mollusc used to produce Tyrian or royal purple.

murgi (adjective from Persian *morgh*, "chicken"). Geometricized images of chickens occur in south western Persian rugs, particularly those of the Khamseh Confederacy. Rugs in which this motif is dominant may be termed "murgi rugs."

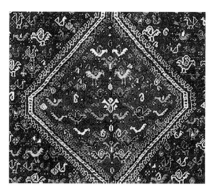

Murgi (Khamseh rug medallion) *Peter Willborg*

mushaki kilims (Persian *mushak*, "rocket"). A kilim woven in Muteh, a village northwest of Isfahan in Iran. The kilims have ornamented, horizontal, parallel stripes. The stripes have pointed ends, suggesting a rocket.

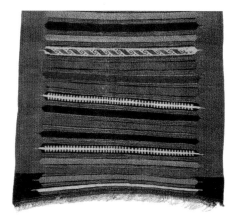

Mushaki kilim *Parviz Tanavoli*

Mushkabad, Meshkâbâd. An area east of Arâk in northeastern Iran. Mushkabad is a trade designation for the lowest grade of modern Sarouks. The term does not refer to a place of origin. See "Sarouk."

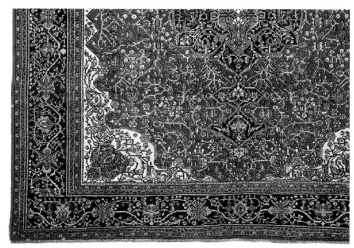

Mushkabad rug (detail)

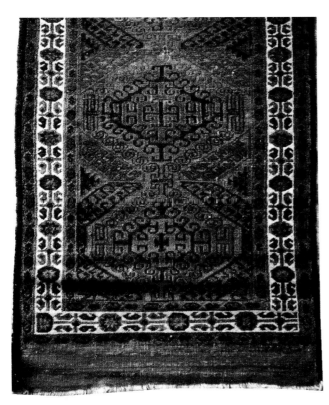

Mushwani rug

Mushwani. A Pashtun tribe of northern Afghanistan. The Mushwanis weave large rugs in a dark color palette. The colors are usually dark blue, dark brown, black, and dark red with highlights of white. The basic field design consists of diamond latch hook medallions. Often, these rugs are finely woven with knot densities greater than 100 asymmetric knots (open to the left) per square inch. The symmetric knot is used in some rugs.

muska (Turk., "amulet," from Arabic **nuskha**, "prescription, talisman"). A triangular design figure, supposed to have magical properties, derived from the shape of a pouch or amulet used to carry Koranic inscriptions, religious or shamanistic relics. Often drawn as a pyramid built up of triangles and used as a filler motif.

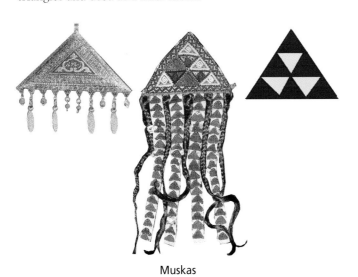

Muskas

Mut. A town south of Karaman in southern Anatolia. Mut is a source of kilims with concentric hooked or sawtoothed diamonds. These kilims are woven in a single piece and may be without edge borders. Colors are bright and contrasting. The ground color is usually red.

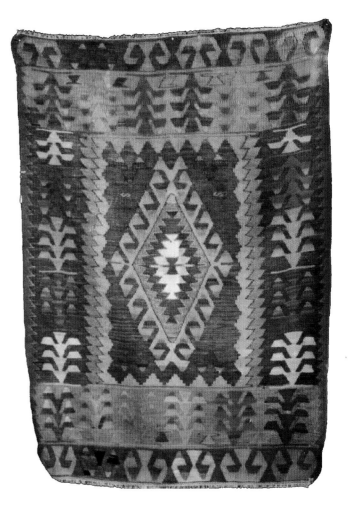

Mut kilim *Simon Knight*

Myers Coupled-Column Prayer Rug. An early eighteenth-century central Anatolian prayer rug with three arches. The arches are supported by pairs of columns. A floral panel spans the area above the arches. The field is red. Blue cartouche-like elements fill the main border. The top of the rug, according to design, was woven first. The rug is 3 feet 8 inches by 5 feet 6 inches. It is all wool with a density of about 90 symmetric knots per square inch. It is in the collection of the Textile Museum, Washington, D.C.

Myers, George Hewitt (1875-1957). George Hewitt Myers was a rug collector and the founder of The Textile Museum, Washington, D.C. Myers established the Museum in 1925 and managed its operations and collection. By the time of his death the collection included more than 500 rugs, many of them fine antiques, and thousands of textiles. See "Textile Museum, The."

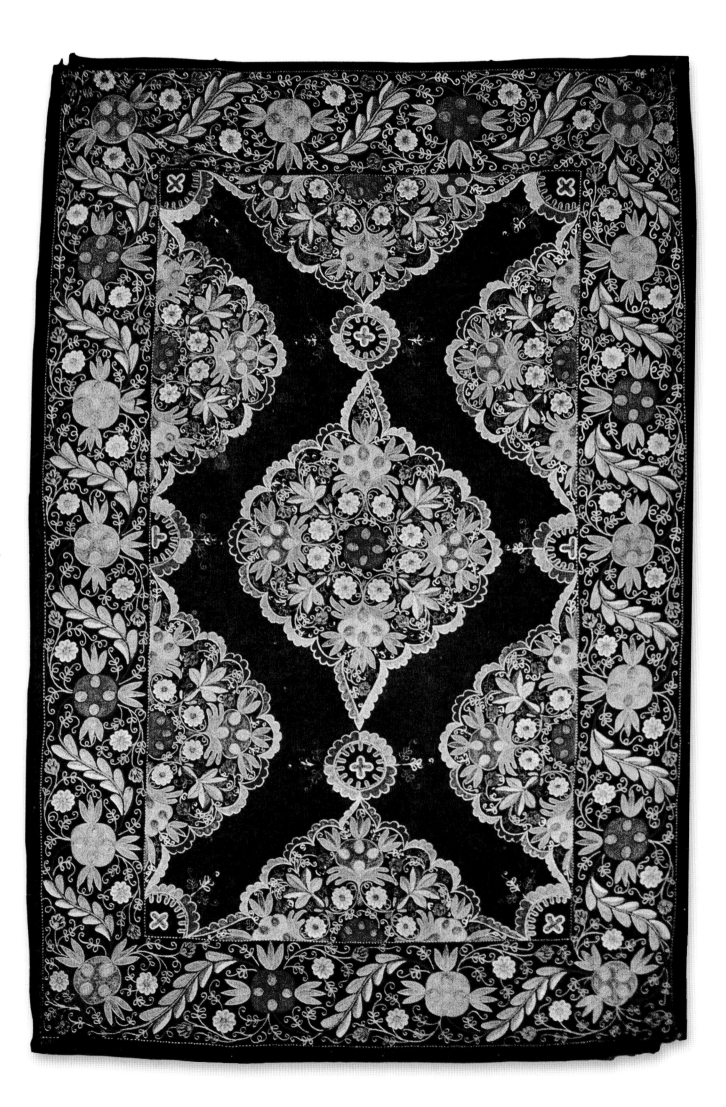

Nain Rug Origins & Description Guide

Persian rugs > Persian rug guides > Rug origins > Nain rugs

View all our fine <u>Nain rugs</u>.

Nain is a town 150km to the east of <u>Isfahan</u> in central Iran; it is relatively new to the carpet world compared to ancient weaving centres such as <u>Kashan</u>, Isfahan and <u>Yazd</u>. Although it started out producing Isfahan carpets, in the mid 1930s Nain began developing its own style. Very fine and precise designs were created due to the high quality of the workshops in the area. Fathollah Habibian (1903-1995) ran one of the most famous Na'in workshops and is widely regarded as 'the father of Nain rugs'. Producing fine carpets with his brother Mohammed since his school days Fathollah Habibian is responsible for the design and weaving of some of the world's finest Nains.

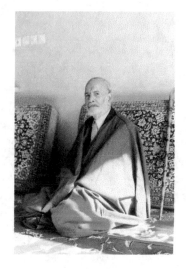

Fathollah Habibian (1903-1995)

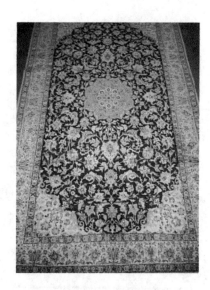

Nain rugs usually have a cotton foundation with a very soft wool or wool & silk pile. The majority of Nain rugs have at least some silk detail. Quality is measured not only in knots per square inch (KPSI) which averages about 300 but also in LAA. LAA is a Farsi term referring to the number of threads that make up each fringe. A Nain with a LAA of 9 is considered a good quality rug (yet is the lowest quality of true Nains) while a LAA of 4 the best. LAA is related to KPSI as it allows tighter knotting.

Learn About | Persian Habibian Nain Rugs

The Habibian rug is one of the most prestigious carpet types to emerge during the 20th century, and they are still offered today. The master weaver Fatollah Habibi (1903-1995) is generally regarded as the

father of Nain rugs and one of the city's best weavers. Persian Nain Habibian rugs feature outstanding designs and construction to match.

The first Persian Habibian rug was sold sometime before 1920. While studying in Nain, the master weaver Fatollah Habibi, who specialized in weaving aba overcoats for men, sold his first carpet in the city of Isfahan for a reputed sum of 100 tomans or $21, a price that would have been a tremendous amount of money for the time. Together with his brother Mohammed, the Habibi brothers opened their first carpet weaving workshop in 1920. Although Nain has never been as large as neighboring Isfahan and other weaver centers, the Habibian Nain name gained an international following that put the rural county on the international carpet weaving map.

Since the Habibian workshop was founded, Persian Nain Habibian carpets have been manufactured with a cotton foundation and exceptionally soft Kurk wool pile. The quality rating of a Persian Habibian rug is generally determined by the type of cotton yarn used for the warp. Thinner warp threads are used to produce the finest Persian Nain Habibian carpets that are woven with 650 knots per square inch or more. Nola rugs that use three strands of three-ply yarn are classified as 9-Lah rugs. These rugs average between 175 and 250 knots per square inch. Shisla or 6-Lah rugs use three strands of two-play yarn and average between 300 and 400 knots per square inch. However, the finest and rarest Persian Nain Habibian rugs are Charla quality, which are made with two stands of two-ply yarn that have been joined together to produce a 4-Lah rug.

The tradition of the Habibian rug continues today at the Habibian Naeen Carpet Company where Habibian Nain carpets are still produced with the guidance of Fatollah's grandson Mahmud Reza Habibi Naini. Habibian Nain rugs feature elegant floral medallions, exemplary geometry and the perfect combination of construction and design. The quality and aesthetic perfection of Habibian rugs have made Nain one of the world's top carpet-producing cities for the past 50 years.

Nadir Shah. Shah of Persia from 1736 to 1747. He expelled the Afghan invaders from Iran, defeated the Ottoman Turks, and invaded India. His capital was Mashhad. According to tradition, during his reign, he brought weavers from Herat to Farâhân. These weavers are thought to have fostered the spread of the Herati pattern.

Nafar. A tribe of the Khamseh Confederacy. See "Khamseh Confederacy."

Nahâvand, Nehâvend, Nihâvand. A town of the Hamadan region in northwestern Iran. The town is a source of large rugs with geometricized versions of Sarouk designs. For some rugs, the border design penetrates the field. The dominant color is blue. These rugs are single wefted with the symmetric knot on a cotton foundation.

Nain. A town of central Iran. From the 1930s, very densely knotted rugs were woven in Nain. Knot densities are between 200 and 800 asymmetric knots per square inch. Designs are similar to Isfahans or are based on Safavid models. Foundations are cotton or silk. Motifs are highlighted with outlines of ivory silk in wool pile rugs. Some all-silk rugs are woven in Nain. Some notable twentieth-century weaver-designers of Nain include Habibian and Mofidi.

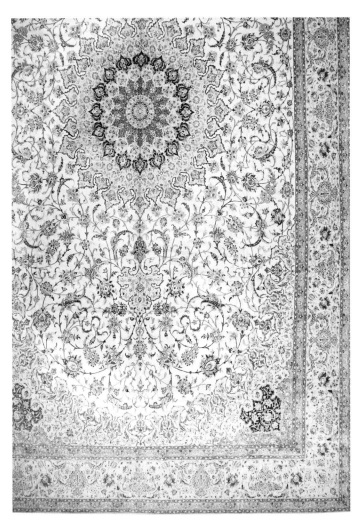

Nain rug (detail) *Jason Nazmial*

Najafabad. A city of central Iran and the source of medallion rugs with asymmetric knots of 120 to 475 per square inch.

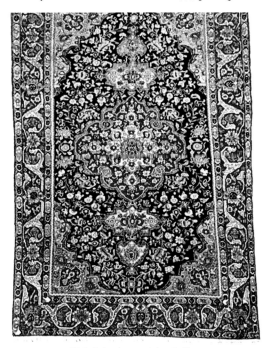

Najafabad rug *John Collins*

nakh (Persian, "thread"). Cotton.

Nakhchivan. An autonomous republic within the republic of Azerbaijan. Cotton and silk are agricultural products. Rugs of Nakhchivan have structure and colors similar to rugs of Karabagh.

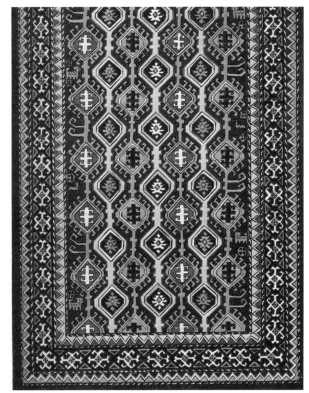

Nakhchivan rug design (detail)

nakhlai. A looped pile rug of northwest Pakistan.

Naldag border. A common border in Saryk rugs.

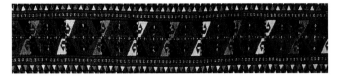

Naldag border

namad. A Turkmen felt rug, usually with bold designs.

namakdan. See "salt bag."

namâz (Persian). Muslim ritual prayer.

namazlik (Turk.). Prayer rug.

namda, numdah, numud. A felt carpet of India. Designs are appliquéd to the rug or created with colored wool during felting. See "felt."

nanu (Persian), *gaz* (Turk.) A woven cradle. See "salıcak."

nap. Technically, nap is distinguished from pile in that nap is produced as a finishing process by raising fibers from the woven surface, while pile is the cut ends or loops of supplementary yarns or elements.

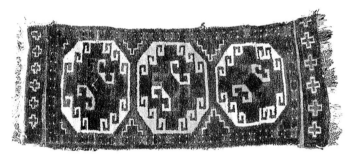

Napramach face *J. Barry O'Connell*

napramach. An Uzbek bag for household utensils. Also used as a sitting pillow in the same manner as a balisht.

naqsh (Persian). A design, cartoon, or pattern for a carpet. See "cartoon," "design plate," and "talim."

narcissus. In China, the narcissus symbolizes winter. It may be represented in Chinese rugs.

Narcissus *After Hackmack*

Nasrâbâd. A trade term for rugs originating southeast of Isfahan. These rugs are thought to be of Luri origin. Warps are of goat hair or cotton.

nassâj (Persian). Weaver. See "bâfandeh," "ostâd," and "shâgird."

natural dyes. See "dye, natural."

Navajo rugs, Navaho rugs, Navajo blankets. Pueblo Indians wove cotton fabrics in the American southwest. Fragments of their weavings date from 700 C.E. After a rebellion against the Spaniards in 1680, some Pueblo Indians migrated northward and settled with the Navajo, who learned their weaving techniques. The Pueblo and Navajo wove wool blankets.

The earliest Navajo blankets date from the late eighteenth century. In 1805, a group of Navajo were massacred in a cave in New Mexico by the Spaniards in retaliation for raids on Spanish settlements. The earliest examples of Navajo blankets were found in this cave.

Most Navajo blankets are tapestry-woven wool. Indigenous designs are stripes or simple geometric designs. Plain stripes were most common until the internment of about 7,000 Navajos by the U.S. Government at Bosque Redondo from 1864 to 1868. Bosque Redondo, Spanish for "circle of trees," is a barren site shared by Fort Sumner on the Pecos River in New Mexico.

The internment marked a change in the stylistic tradition of the Navajo blanket. The third phase Chief's blanket developed after the Bosque Redondo experience. The simple stripes of the bayeta serape were increasingly replaced with stripes containing geometric motifs. After Bosque Redondo, the Navajo received commercial yarns and dyes as partial annuity payments. At the same time, the Navajo began weaving for trade.

By 1890, a heavier fabric with borders was woven and the Navajo rug had evolved from the blanket in response to market demand. Pictorial rugs were woven for trade with images of houses, bows and arrows, railroad trains, and tribal symbols and gods. Most contemporary weavings originate on Navajo reservations in northern Arizona.

See "bayeta," "bayeta serape," "blanket dress," "Chief blanket," "child's serape," "Churro," "Eye Dazzler," "Germantown yarn," "manta," "Moki," "Navajo twill weaves," "Navajo wedge weave," "Pueblo weaving," "poncho," "pound blanket," "sandpainting rug," "Saxony," "serape," "spirit trail," "Storm pattern," "yeibichai," and "yei rugs."

See entries under these locations: Chinle, Coal Mine Mesa, Crystal, Gallup, Ganado, Hubbell Trading Post, Lukachukai, New Lands, Pine Springs, Shiprock, Teec Nos Pos, Two Gray Hills, Western Reservation.

Navajo twill weaves. Navajo blankets, rugs, and saddle blankets in which a twill structure is used. Herringbone, diamond, and zigzag designs are common. Undyed wool is used in these weavings. See "twill."

Navajo wedge weave, pulled warp. A tapestry weave structure used by Navajos in some of their blankets between about 1870 and 1900. The weaver forces warps into a diagonal direction and then packs wefts so the warps remain diagonal. With this structure, different colored wefts produce a zigzag effect. The edges of the blankest are slightly scalloped because of the distortion of the warps.

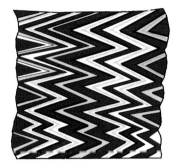

Navajo wedge weave (detail)

navâr (Persian). A band or strap.

navmal (Kurdish). A warp-faced, striped flatweave with designs of weft wrapping, of the Kurds of northern Khurasan.

needlepoint rugs. Needlepoint is generally executed with the tent stitch (continental stitch) or cross stitch, using crewel yarn on canvas. "Petit point" is needlepoint with more than eight stitches per inch and "gros point" is needlepoint with eight or less stitches per inch. Contemporary needlepoint carpets are commercially produced in China, India, and Portugal for export to the European and American markets. For Chinese needlepoint, the fineness of stitching ranges up to 400 stitches per square inch. See "Arraiolos," "chain stitch," "cross stitch," and "embroidered rugs.

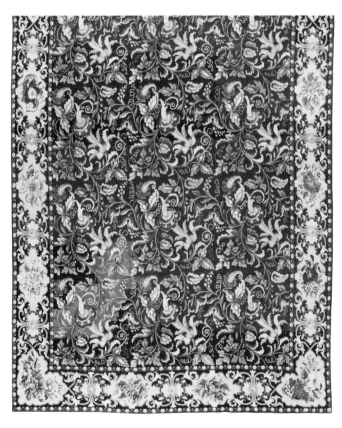

English needlepoint rug *Jason Nazmiyal*

Nehâvend. See "Nahâvend."

Nepal. A country located on the northern border of India and the southern border of Tibet. The major urban and weaving centers are the capital Kathmandu, Pokhara, and Patan. Tibetan carpets are woven in Nepal by refugees from Tibet who immigrated in 1959 and 1960. Rugs are woven in the traditional Tibetan manner with many traditional designs, though bright synthetic colors are used. The pile is Himalayan wool on a cotton foundation. The typical size is 3 feet by 6 feet. Commercial importers may describe these rugs as "Tibetan" even though they are woven in Nepal. See "Jawalekhel" and "Tibet."

NEP rug. New Economic Plan rug. See "five-year plan rug."

New Lands. A recently settled area for Navajos in Arizona. Since 1980, weavers of the area have produced rugs with designs outlined in eccentric wefts.

New Zealand wool. Wool from New Zealand widely used in commercial rug production and thought to be superior to most other commercial rug wools.

neyden, nyeden (Tibetan). A small rug used for sleeping.

neyestan (Kurdish). Kilims with an all-over diamond motif woven by Kurds of North Khurasan.

Neyshâbur. See "Nishâpur."

Neyriz, Niris, Niriz. A town and lake of southwest Iran. The town of Neyriz is a minor source of rugs in the tree-of-life medallion design woven in the style of the Qashqa'i. The town is a minor collection point for Afshar and other tribal rugs. Knot density is about 65 to 100 asymmetric per square inch on a cotton foundation.

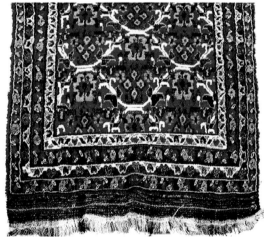

Neyriz rug (detail) *Haliden*

niche, niche rugs. The mihrab or arch in a prayer rug or saff. A rug with a niche. See "mihrab" and "prayer rug."

Nichols carpets. In 1924, Walter Nichols founded Nichols Super Yarn and Carpets in Tientsin, China. His firm wove heavy, strong carpets with a cotton foundation and wool selvages. Warps are fully offset (Chinese closed back) with the asymmetric knot. Many of these rugs were in the Art Deco style and this style has been closely associated with his name.

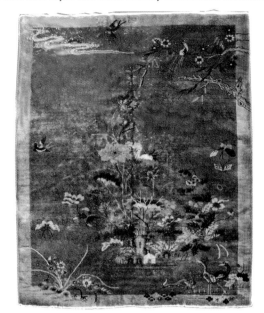

Nichols Chinese rug *Peter Pap Oriental Rugs Inc*

Niğde. A town of south central Anatolia. A rug-weaving center and collection point for prayer rugs and kilims. Kilims from the Niğde area tend to have wide borders. The borders usually contain a zigzag stripe that may be hooked or connected to florets. Medallions are often hexagons, sometimes hooked. See "Turkey."

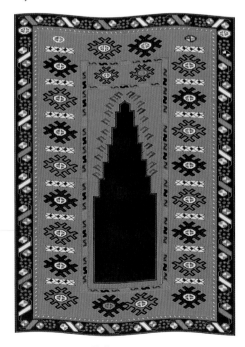

Niğde prayer rug

Nihâvand. See "Nahâvand."

nim-lool (Persian). Semi-offset warps.

Nim suzanni. A half-sized suzanni.

Ningxia, Ninghsia. A city of Gansu province in western China.

There are literary references to Ningxia rugs from 1692. A group of rugs has been attributed to eighteenth-century Ningxia. These rugs have a grey-brown margin and are in a variety of designs, with the designs typically rendered in blue on a yellow field. This attribution has been disputed. Three-ply, machine-spun warps were used after 1920. Late nineteenth-century and early twentieth-century rugs of Ningxia were coarsely woven, with about 40 asymmetric knots per square inch on a cotton foundation. Machine-spun warps of this period were six to eight ply. The field is usually yellow with the design in blue. See "China" and "Gansu."

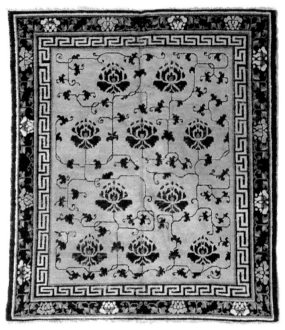

Ningxia rug *Alberto Levi*

Niris. See "Neyriz."

nishan. A measure of a weaver's production in Kerman, Iran, equal to 160 knots.

Nishâpur, Neyshâbur. A town east of Mashhad in northeastern Iran and a major archaeological site of pre-Islamic culture in Iran. It is a wool market and a rug collection center.

Niya. An archaeological site along the Silk Route in Xinjiang, China, on the southern edge of the Taklamakan Desert. In 1959, a wool pile carpet fragment was unearthed at the site. The fragment has been dated to about 100 B.C.E. See "China."

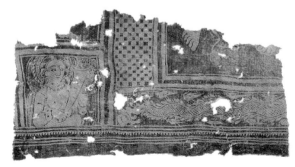

Batik textile *Niya*

Noberân, Nowbarân. A town of the Hamadan region in northwest Iran. It is a source of rugs with a large diamond medallion and spandrels. The diamond outline is vertically spiked. See "Maslaghan."

node. One loop of a pile knot around a warp when viewed from the back of a rug.

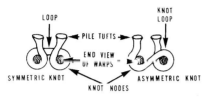

Nodes

nomadic rugs. Rugs woven by sheep-herding peoples who live in tents or temporary dwellings and move with their herds between summer and winter pasturage. Summer pasturage is usually a highland or mountainous area and winter pasturage is a low-land or valley area. This kind of pastoral economy ("transhumance") is found particularly among the Lurs and Qashqa'i in Iran, and the Turkmen and Kirghiz in Afghanistan and Turkestan. Small rugs are woven by nomadic peoples because of the difficulty of moving large looms. Larger rugs are woven only in long formats because of the short beams used in nomadic looms. Often, a ground loom is used.

Nomadic rugs are generally all wool. Warps are sometimes naturally brown or black wool because these wools cannot be dyed for pile. With some exceptions, weaving and knot density are coarse rather than fine. Nomadic peoples weave a variety of special function pieces in addition to rugs. These may include saddlebags, tent bags, special containers for personal items, ornamental weavings for the tent, and animal trappings.

Designs tend to be repeats of geometric elements that are traditional tribal motifs. However, some nomadic rugs have been influenced by court or urban designs. Because nomadic rugs are not woven from a cartoon, corners are not planned exactly and usually there is some mismatch or asymmetry of the border design at the corners of the borders (unresolved corners). See "transhumance" and "tribal rugs."

non-directional design. A rug design that is aesthetically pleasing when viewed from any vantage point. Most geometric designs and all-over designs are non-directional. Designs with both lateral and vertical symmetry are non-directional. See "directional design."

North Africa. Also collectively called "the Maghreb" (Arabic, *al-maghrib*, "the west"). See "Algeria," "Egypt," "Libya," "Morocco," and "Tunisia."

Norway. See "Scandinavian weaving."

Nowbarân. See "Noberân."

Nukha, Nucha, Shaki, Sheki. A town in northern Genje province on the southern slopes of the Caucasus range. The district, formerly a khanate, is known as Sheki. The principal town, called Nukha during the Soviet period, was also known as Sheki in earlier centuries and again from the 1970s. Nineteenth-century rugs of this area are classified as Genje. The town was also a source of silk embroideries. See "Genje."

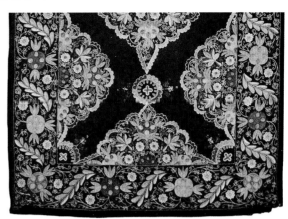

Nukha (Sheki) embroidery

numud. See "namda."

numdah. See "namda."

Nurata. A town of central Uzbekistan and the source of rugs and suzannis. Some of the rugs have early forms of a Turkmen gul with animal and bird images.

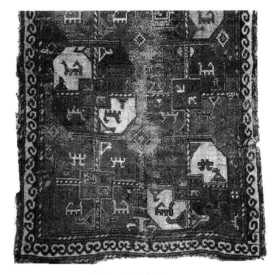

Nurata Uzbek rug

Nuristan. See "Kohistan."

nyeden. See "neyden."

nylon. Nylon is a commercial name for polyamide. A plastic derived from petroleum. This synthetic fiber is used in more than 80% of American made rugs. Nylon is less expensive and easier to dye and clean than wool. It is more stain resistant than wool and has better wear resistance. Some nylons are excessively glossy and some have poor soil-hiding properties. Nylon is crimped before spinning and may be heat set after spinning.

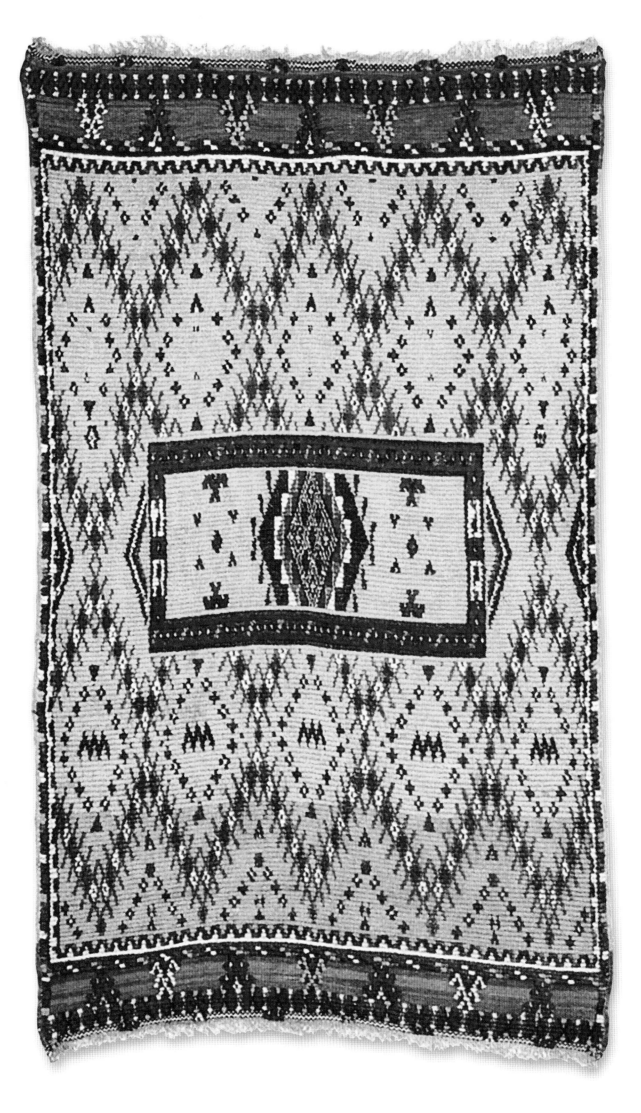

oak bark, oak galls, acorn shells. Oak bark, oak galls, and acorn shells are used as a source of brown and black dyes. See "etching" and "dye, natural."

oblique interlacing. A system of braiding producing a flat, over-and-under interworking of elements. Such braiding is sometimes used with warps at rug ends. See "braiding" and "plaiting."

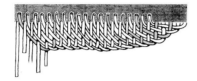

Oblique interlacing

Obruk. A town of south central Anatolia. Obruk is a source of coarsely woven pile rugs of nomadic character and of fine kilims. From the late nineteenth century, prayer kilims have been woven in Obruk. Mihrabs are pointed and hooked. A tree-of-life motif is usually located in each spandrel. See "Turkey."

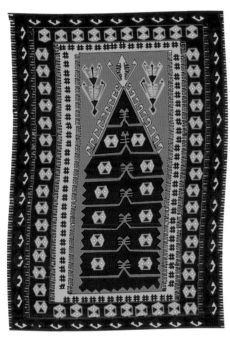

Obruk kilim

OCM. Oriental Carpet Manufacturers, Ltd., a major British rug trading company formed in 1907 by European rug traders in Izmir (then Smyrna), Anatolia. The company operated rug factories and commissioned rug production in Turkey, Persia, Turkestan, India, China, and the Caucasus.

octagon. Any regular eight-sided geometric figure.

octagram. An eight-pointed star. This may take the form of superimposed squares or a cross with triangular cut-outs at the end of each arm.

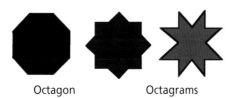

Octagon   Octagrams

odjakhlik. See "ojakbashi."

odshak bashi. See "ojakbashi."

offset warp. See "warp offset."

offset knots. In hand-knotted pile weaves, knots are usually tied on pairs of warps so that knots are in columns on the same pair of warps. Knots may be occasionally tied on warps so that adjacent columns of knots are connected. These knots are offset by one warp or staggered. Offset knots are sometimes used in Turkmen and Kurdish pile weaves to achieve particular curving design effects. They are also found in some early Chinese rugs and Moroccan rugs. See "packing knots" and "qtifa."

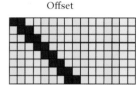

No offset   Offset

Smoothing effect of offset knots

Oghuz Turkmen, Oğuz. A Turkic people of the eleventh century, tracing their ancestry back to the legendary Oghuz Khan. One branch of the Oghuz Turkmen founded the Ottoman Empire upon the dissolution of the Seljuk Empire. The present-day Turks of Turkey and Azerbaijan and the Turkmen trace their ancestry to the Oghuz. The term is sometimes used as an ethnic and linguistic designation for the southwest Turks in general, as distinct from the Uzbeks, Kazakhs, Kirghiz, etc., of the northeast. Turkish *oghuz* means "brave, robust, simple, honest, peasant." See "Ottoman Empire," "Seljuk," and "Turkey."

ogive. A pointed arch or two such arches joined to enclose a space.

Ogiv

Ogurjali. Thought to be an early Turkmen subtribe of the Yomut, settled on the eastern coast of the Caspian Sea.

Oğuz. See "Oghuz Turkmen."

ojakbashi, odshak bashi, odjakhlik, ojak giragi (Turk. "hearth-head"). A Turkmen rug intended to surround the hearth. It has a U-shaped form. A square cut-out accommodates the fireplace. Examples are of Yomud origin. Small square mats may also be described as hearth rugs.

ok-bash (Turk., "arrow head"). Tent pole cover. This is a pouch that fits over the ends of tent poles to hold them together when Turkmen tents are taken down and moved. See "kola-i chergh."

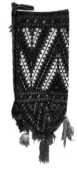

Ok-bash

olduz, yildiz. (Turk.) Star.

olefin. Olefin is a plastic and petroleum derivative. This synthetic fiber is colorfast and abrasion resistant. It is also stain resistant. Olefin fibers have poor crush resistance. Olefin fibers are used primarily in loop pile rugs.

Olt. A river and district of southern Romania. A trade designation of quality for a Romanian rug woven on a cotton foundation with 160 knots per square inch.

Oltenia. A region of southwest Romania and a source of fine kilims. Motifs are floral vegetation and birds. These motifs are randomly located in the field. The field is often black and designs are executed in red, white, green, and blue. Eccentric wefts are used to produce the designs. See "Romania."

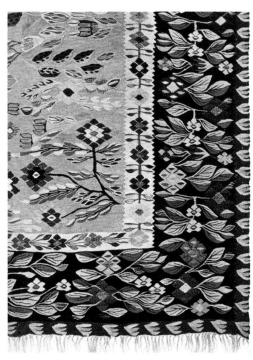

Oltenian kilim (detail)

O.N.A.T. Office National de l'Artisanat Tunisien. A government organization of Tunisia controlling most contemporary rug production.

onion skin. Onion skins have been used as a source of yellow dyes. See "natural dyes."

önlük (Turk. "for the front"). Apron.

onurga. See "Temirchin gul."

open back. When wefts are visible from the back of contemporary Chinese rugs, the structure may be referred to as "open back." In this case, the loop of the asymmetric knot encircles the warp nearest the front of the rug. See "closed back."

opposed arch prayer rug. Any prayer rug with opposing arches or mihrabs at each end. The arches are complete, and this feature is thought to distinguish these rugs from other small rugs with separated spandrels so the field touches the border at the ends of the field. There is a group of such small rugs

from the seventeenth century attributed to Ushak or Romania. See "Tintoretto rug" and "Transylvania."

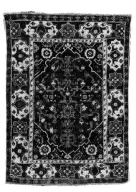

Opposed arch prayer rug

orange. A portion of the visual spectrum between yellow and red. In oriental rugs, natural orange may derive from henna or madder.

Orange II. An acid azo dye synthesized in 1876.

Ordutch-Konagend. See "Konagend."

O.R.I.A. Oriental Rug Importers Association. This trade association was formed in 1931 to promote the interests of oriental rug importers. It has about 80 members and is headquartered at the Oriental Rug Industry Center of America in Secaucus, New Jersey. See "Oriental Rug Trade Statistics."

oriental-design rug. A machine-made rug with oriental rug designs. See "oriental rug."

oriental rug. An indefinite term. Originally, this term applied only to hand-knotted pile rugs woven in the Near East and Asia. In current usage, the term includes all hand-knotted pile weaves used as rugs, regardless of origin, as well as many of the flat-woven rugs of the Near East and Asia. "Persian rug" is sometimes used incorrectly as a synonym.

Oriental Rug Importers Association. See "O.R.I.A."

Oriental Rug Retailers of America. See "O.R.R.A."

orlon. A synthetic fiber of polyacrylonitirle. Orlon fibers resemble silk.

orphan rugs. From 1884 through the end of the First World War, thousands of Armenians died in ethnic struggles between Christians and Muslims in Turkey. Orphanages were founded for the homeless Armenian children where they were employed in weaving rugs. There are examples bearing inscriptions from Aintab (present-day Gaziantep) in south central Anatolia and from Agin in eastern central Anatolia.

O.R.R.A. Oriental Rug Retailers of America. This association was founded in 1970 to support the interests of retail oriental rug dealers. Members subscribe to a code of ethics and must be involved in the retail rug business. Headquarters of the association are in Portland, Oregon.

Ortaköy. A town of central Anatolia. A source of small rugs in bright colors. See "Turkey."

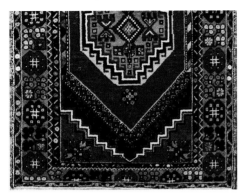

Ortaköy rug *Kazim Yildiz*

osmulduk. See "asmalyk."

ostâd, usta, ustad, ustadh (Persian). Master craftsman. May be applied to a rug weaver. See "nassâj" and "shâgird."

Ottoman Empire. A Turkish empire from about 1281 to 1924. Founded by Osman, this empire began in western Anatolia and southeastern Europe (Thrace). With the conquest of Constantinople (thenceforward called Istanbul) in 1453, it became a major world power. The Ottoman Empire reached its greatest extent under Suleiman the Magnificent (1520-1566), when it included territories from the frontiers of Austria to the frontiers of Persia. Architecture, painting, metalwork, tilework, ceramics, and weaving flourished during the reign of Suleiman. During this period, the earliest of the great Ottoman court rugs were woven at Istanbul and Bursa. See "Ottoman floral carpets," "Suleiman the Magnificent," and "Turkey."

Ottoman floral carpets. Rugs woven in Cairo, dating from the sixteenth century through the seventeenth century. These rugs used curvilinear designs of naturalistic vegetation and were woven with the asymmetric knot. Yarn in these rugs is "S" spun, a structural feature peculiar to North African rugs. Designs of the court rugs are thought to derive from Ottoman illumination and tilework. See "Mamluk carpets" and "Rhodian carpets."

Oulad Bou Sbâa. A tribe settled southwest of Marrakesh in Morocco. Their rugs are woven with a red or orange field using geometric motifs with some geometricized human figures. These rugs may be referred to as "Chichaoua" after a town in the area. Knot densities are very coarse, averaging about 15 or 20 symmetric knots to the square inch. See "Morocco."

Ouaouzquite. A tribe inhabiting the High Atlas and Siroua mountains of Morocco. The tribe produces weaving of mixed structures, flatweaves with pile bands or pile borders, as well as pile rugs. Many of their rugs have an all-over diaper or diamond pattern. Others show simple geometric motifs with geometricized objects or animals. Knot densities are very coarse, averaging about 15 to 20 symmetric knots per square inch. See "Glaoua rugs" and "Morocco."

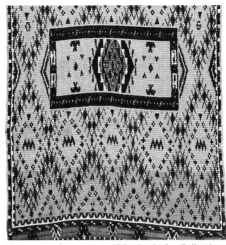

Ouaouzquite carpet *Pickering/Yohe Collection*

outlining. A line marking the limits of a shape or figure. Contrasting colors are often used to outline designs or motifs in oriental rugs. More rarely, different stitches or fibers are used for this purpose, silk on wool, for example. See "double outlining."

ovadan. A curled leaf field and border design used in kapunuks and torbas by Chaudor, Tekke, Saryk, and Salor Turkmen. See "curled leaf border."

overcasting. A treatment of rug edges consisting of a yarn that wraps edge warps or interweaves with edge warps and that is not continuous with foundation weft. See "edge finish."

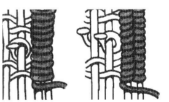

Whip stitch   Figure eight stitch   Ornamental

overdyeing. The use of two different natural dyes on the same fiber to achieve some other color. The most common example is blue overdyed with yellow to produce green.

overlay brocading. Brocade in which supplementary wefts float on the fabric's front surface to produce the design. See "sileh."

overlay-underlay brocading. Brocade in which supplementary wefts float on both sides of the fabric. Wefts float on the front to produce the design and on the back where they are not needed. See "cicim."

Owlâd, Pashkuhi. Owlâd is a clan of the Lurs around the village of Naghân (Naghun) in southwest Iran, south of Shahr-e Kord. Pashkuhi is a trade term for their rugs. Owlâd rugs have geometric designs, usually all-over patterns in dark colors. Wefts are red cotton. Owlâd also refers to a group of six Turkmen tribes: the Khoja, Shikh, Sayyid, Ata, and Mujevur.

oxidized. See "etching."

Özbeks. See "Uzbeks."

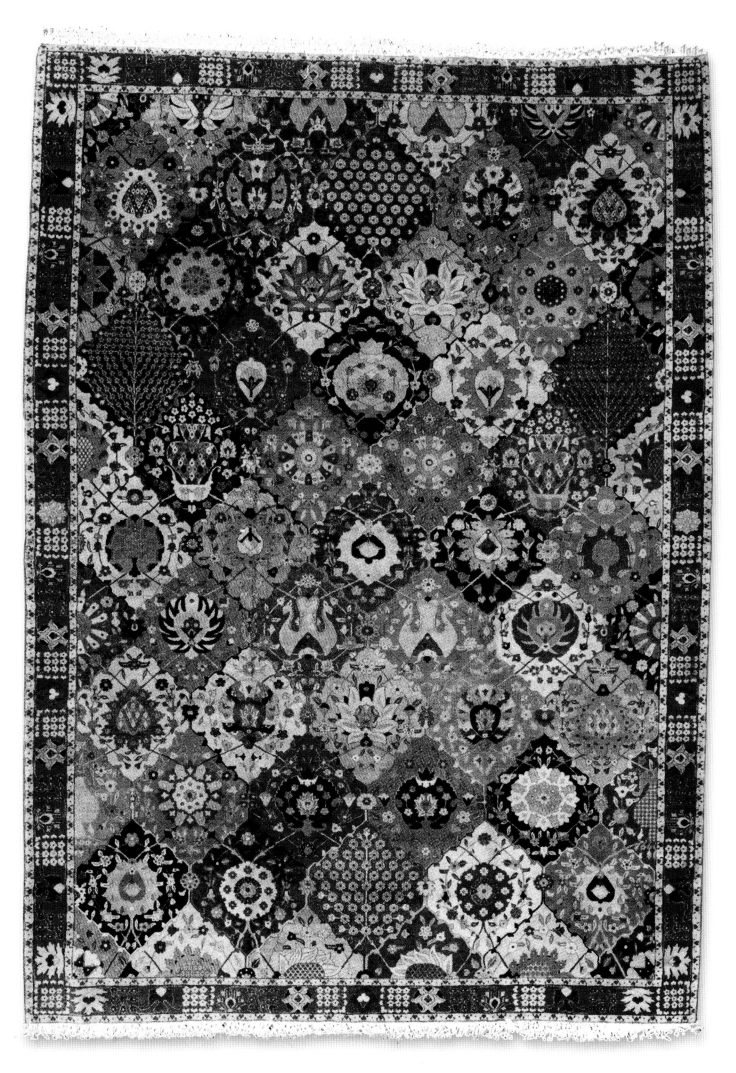

packing bag. See "mafrash."

packing knot. Pile knots inserted with no weft between an adjacent row of knots. Such knots may be offset by one warp or fall directly within a column of knots. Packing knots have been used in Chinese rugs to create certain design effects. See "offset knots."

padding. See "underlay."

painting, enhancement. Applying dye, stain, or color to the front of the rug after the rug is woven. Exposed foundation where the pile is worn may be painted to conceal wear.

Paisley. A design of botehs derived from Kashmir shawls. These shawls were copied in early nineteenth-century factory production in Paislely, Scotland. See "boteh," "Kashmir," and "shawl."

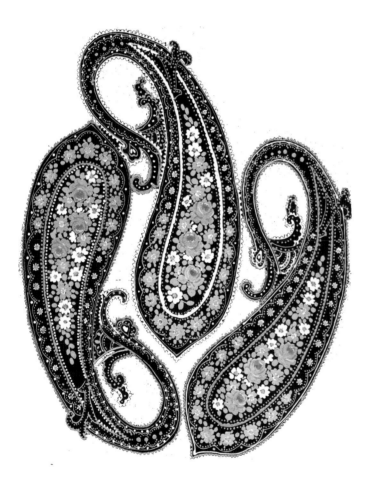

Paisley

Pakistan. A country bordered by India, Afghanitan, and Iran. Pakistan was formerly a part of India and became independent with the partition of India in 1947. It comprises the states of Sind, Punjab, Baluchistan, Northwest Frontier Province, and part of Kashmir. About 77% of the population is Sunni and 20% is Shi'ia. Virtually all contemporary pile rugs woven in Pakistan are intended for export. Until recently, rug designs were copies of or variations of Turkmen models ("Bohkara" designs). Now, some copies of Persian rugs are woven. Rug-

weaving centers are Lahore, Karachi, Hyderabad, and Peshawar. Rug weaving in Pakistan is organized as both factory and cottage production.

Rugs of Pakistan are woven on a cotton foundation with the asymmetric knot. The cheapest grades may have jute wefts. Wools are local or blended with New Zealand or Australian wool for the finer grades of rugs. Where designs copy Persian models, offset warps are used, while warps are not offset for the "Bokhara" designs. Knot densities for Pakistani rugs are expressed as: (knots per horizontal inch)/(knots per vertical inch). Thus, 11/22 equals 11 x 22 or 242 knots per square inch. The term "doubles" in referring to knots of Pakistani rugs means that the vertical knot count is twice the horizontal knot count. Pakistani rugs have knot densities ranging from 40 to 350 knots per square inch.

Wool flatweaves are produced in Pakistan for domestic use. These are termed "farrasie" and "palesk." See these entries: "Bahawalpur," "Bannu," "Hyderabad," "Karachi," "Lahore," and "Peshawar."

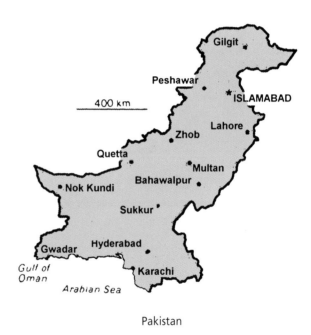

Pakistan

Palace carpet. A trade term for a carpet larger than 14 by 24 feet.

palampore. A bed curtain or fabric wall hanging of India.

palâs, pallas, pelas (Persian, "old rag"). A striped flatweave or coarse rug. In Afghanistan, a flatweave of goat hair used for tents and large sacks. Also, a kilim of the Caucasus. This term has a range of meanings varying with usage in different languages.

palesk. A flat-woven rug of Pakistan made from rope-like yarn of wool or goat hair and usually dyed brown These rugs are woven in Chitral in northwest Pakistan. Geometric designs are sometimes used. See "Pakistan."

palmette. A very common conventionalized motif based on the lotus flower and spread leaves. The flower is shown in side view. There are a great many interpretations of this motif. See "lotus" and "Shah Abbasi motif."

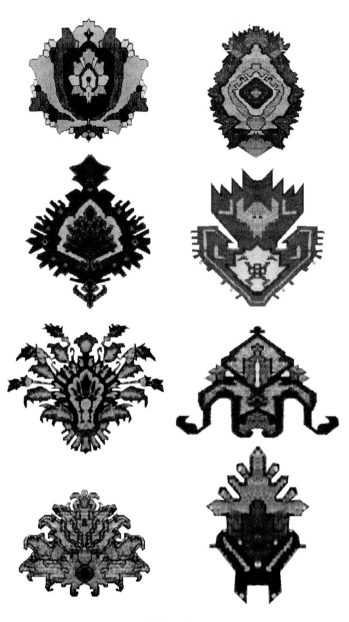

Palmettes

palmette border. Any border in which the dominant motif is palmettes.

Panderma. See Bandırma.

panel. A rectangular area, the width of the rug, that is below and/or above the primary field. The inclusion of one or two panels is a design feature of some prayer rugs. See "alınık," "elem," "huli," "takhta," and "yaprak."

panja. In India, a heavy metal comb used to beat down wefts and knots.

panj mihraba. Means "five mihrabs." A trade term for an Afghanistan prayer rug in which a panel above the main mihrab contains a row of smaller mihrabs. See "Chichaktu."

panj rang (Persian). Five colors. See "haft rang" and "khod rang."

Paotou. See "Baotou."

Paradise park carpet. Large carpets with fields filled with trees, birds, and animals, suggestive of Paradise.

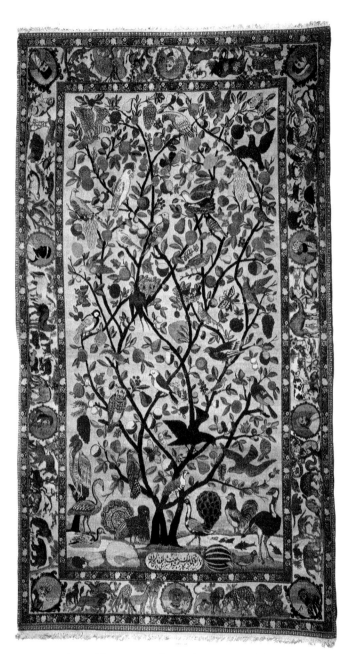

Laver Kirman paradise park carpet *Sothebys*

para-Mamluk. A group of fifteenth and sixteenth-century rugs. Their field design is usually a 2-1-2 medallion arrangement, each medallion containing a complex, central star. The ground is red and most other design features of the field are green, blue, brown, yellow, and purple. In construction, these rugs have an asymmetric knot open to the left with "Z" spun yarn (Mamluks have "S" spun yarn). These rugs have been attributed to Cairene workshops, Damascus, and Anatolia. See "Cairene carpets," "Chessboard rugs," "Compartment rugs," "Egypt," and "Mamluk."

Paravicini Mughal Prayer Rug. The field of this seventeenth-century Mughal prayer rug is dominated by a large, naturalistically drawn plant with blossoms similar to those of a marigold. The spandrels are white and contain blossoms. A floral vine occupies the main border. It is 3 feet 3 inches by 5 feet. The foundation is silk and the pile is fine wool. The density is 1,956 asymmetric knots per square inch. This rug is in the Pincket Collection, Grimberg.

pardaghy. In Georgia in the Caucasus, a kilim used as a cover.

pardeh. See "ensi."

parmakli (Turk.). A motif of Turkish kilims consisting of rhoms, ovals or other figures with horizontal, parallel extensions suggesting fingers (*parmak*). These kilims are woven in some towns of western Anatolia.

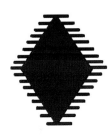 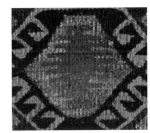

Parmakli

Pârs. A designation for ancient Persia. A variant of "Fârs," the southwestern province of Iran, the capital of which is Shiraz.

pashm (Persian). Wool or the woolly underhair of goats.

pashmina. Pashmina is a fine, downy, under wool from Himalayan goats or fabrics made from this wool. Some Mughal rugs were woven from pashmina in Kashmir and northern India.

Pashkuhi. See "Owlâd."

Pashtun, Pathan. An ethnic group making up about half of the population of Afghanistan. Their language is Pashto (Pushtu), of the Iranian family. There is a significant Pashtun minority in Pakistan. Rug-weaving Pashtun tribes include Durrâni, Ghilza'i, Haftbala, Mushwani and Shirkhâni.

patchwork carpet. A carpet composed of scraps from other carpets.

patina. The softening of colors and increased sheen that sometimes occurs with usage in oriental rugs. See "gloss."

patka. In India, a sash or court girdle.

pattern. Used synonymously with "design," but "pattern" suggests repeating elements. See "design" and "motif."

patuee. See "gabbeh."

Pâzuhki, Pâziki. A Kurdush tribe in Khurasan and Varamin in Iran and the source of all-wool rugs with the symmetric knot.

Pazyryk Carpet. A knotted pile carpet found at Pazyryk in the Altay mountains of Siberia in 1949. The carpet was unearthed in a Scythian burial site. The rug has been carbon-dated to about 300 B.C.E. Its survival was due to the permanently frozen condition of the soil in which it was found. Its size is about 6 feet by 6 feet with a knot density of approximately 225 symmetric knots per square inch. Dye analysis showed that the blue dye contained indigotin. The red dye contains carminic acid derived from Indian lac. The source of the brown dye could not be determined. The design has some similarity to ornamental motifs of Babylonian architecture. This rug demonstrates that pile knotting is a very ancient craft.

There is considerable speculation about the origin of the Pazyryk carpet. It has been attributed to early Turkmens, "proto"-Armenians, Persians, and Assyrians. Some scholars think that the rug came into the hands of the Scythians through trade or conquest.

Older fragments of knotted pile carpets have been found at other Scythian burial sites. One such fragment has asymmetric knots with a density of about 400 knots to the square inch and is thought to be one or two hundred years older than the Pazyryk carpet. See "Altai culture."

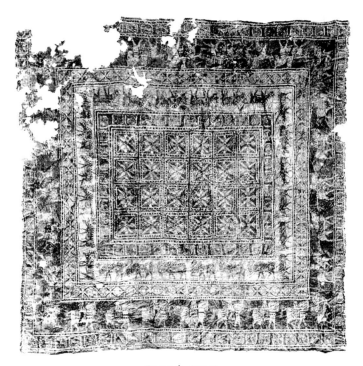

Pazyryk carpet

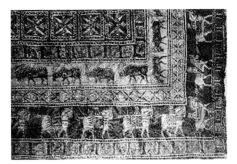

Pazyryk carpet (detail)

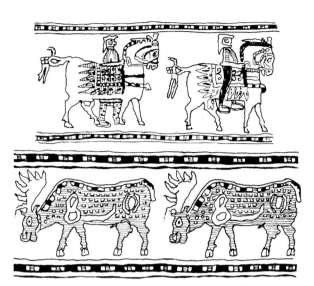

Line rendering of Pazyryk border motifs

peach. This fruit and its blossoms are sometimes used as a motif in Chinese rugs. The peach symbolizes longevity and the blossoms symbolize spring.

Peach and peach blossom (Chinese)

peacock. The peacock is associated with paradise and may also symbolize royalty. It is shown in Chinese rugs. In classical Mughal and Persian rugs, the peacock is represented naturalistically. In tribal rugs it may be highly stylized, as in the Akstafa peacock motif occurring in Iranian, Caucasian, and Turkish rugs. See "Akstafa peacock."

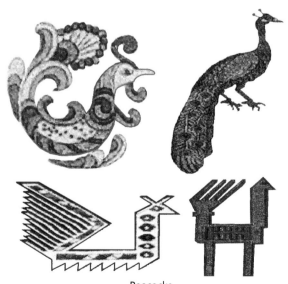

Peacocks
TOP: *China, India* **BOTTOM:** *Shirvan (Akstafa), Shahsavan*

Peacock rug. A rug of 17th-century India with peacocks in the field.

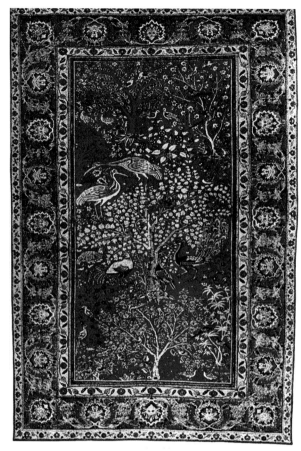

Peacock rug

pearl. One of the "eight precious things" associated with Confucianism. The pearl symbolizes perfection and is used as a motif in Chinese rugs. In some rugs, two dragons are shown fighting over a flaming pearl. See "chintamani."

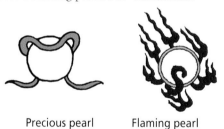

Precious pearl   Flaming pearl

pearl border. A guard stripe used in Chinese rugs consisting of lightly colored disks (pearls) on a dark blue or black stripe.

Pearl Carpet of Baroda. See "Gurjarat."

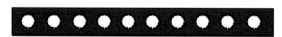

Pearl border

pech (Turk., from Persian, "twist, bend"). Swastika.

pectinated line. A line with short parallel, straight projections, as the teeth of a comb. Such lines are sometimes found in rug designs. See "ciliated line."

peech baf (Persian pich bâf, "twisting weave, zigzag weave"). Soumak weave. See "soumak."

Peking. See "Beijing."

pelas. See "palâs."

pelt rug. A rug that shows an animal pelt or a rug made in imitation of an animal pelt.

pendant. A small stylized flower or floral cluster at the top and bottom of a central medallion. The medallion is usually ovoid or diamond shaped. Medallions with pendants are thought to derive from Safavid court designs used on book covers.

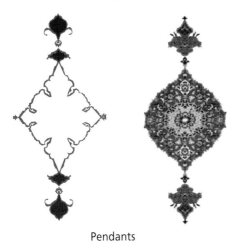

Pendants

pendeh. An older trade term used to describe Turkmen weavings of indefinite origin.

Pendeh khatchli, Pende khatchli. Pende or Pendjeh (properly Penjdeh, from Persian *panj deh*, "five villages") is an oasis surrounded by several villages in Turkmenistan near the border with Iran and Afghanistan. The Pende khatchli is an ensi with a distinctive panel containing turret-like figures and is probably of Saryq origin.

penjerlik. See "jollar."

penny rugs. See "dollar rugs."

pentagram. A five-pointed star.

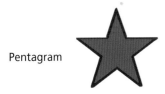

Pentagram

peony. This flower is a common motif in Chinese rugs. It may symbolize riches, honor, beauty, love, or spring. It is often used in the borders of Ningxia rugs. The peony is naturalistically represented in Mughal carpets.

perde. Kilim strips or patches sewn together. Also, a curtain.

Pergamum. See "Bergama."

peri. Persian for "fairy." Winged peris are sometimes portrayed in Safavid carpets.

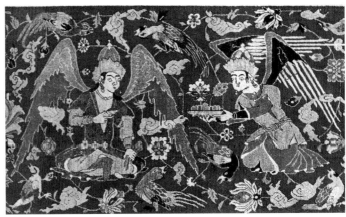

Peris

Perpedil, Perepedil, Pirabadil. A town southeast of Kuba in Daghestan, the Caucasus. Rugs of this area are classified as Kuba. Nineteenth-century rugs attributed to this town have a design of stylized ram's horns or flower calyxes, often with a Kufesque border. The Kuba Perpedil is the most densely knotted design type of the nineteenth-century Caucasian rugs. They average 167 symmetric knots per square inch. Typical rug area is about 22 square feet. Their shape ratio is 1.34. Warps are wool but wefts may be cotton or wool. See "Caucasus," "Kuba," and "vurma."

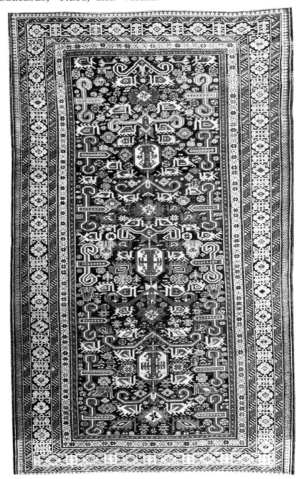

Perpedil rug *Jason Nazmiyal*

Perpedil motif

Persepolis rug. Rugs of Iran depicting bas reliefs or ruins of ancient Persepolis near Shiraz in Iran. Some of these rugs are woven by the Qashqa'i. Designs are copied from nineteenth-century French lithographs or engravings. Some rugs include inscriptions in French taken from the captions for the lithographs or engravings. See "Zirhaki."

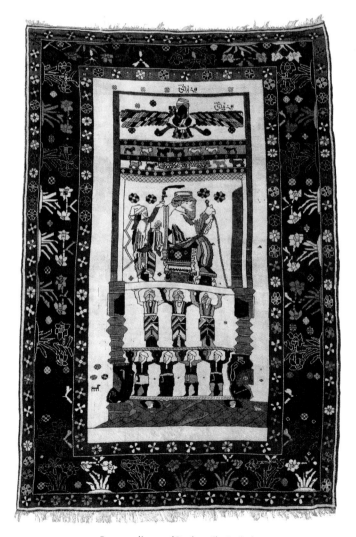

Persepolis rug (Qashga'i) *Sothebys*

Persia, Iran. Irân is the Persian term used by Iranians for their country. From the time of the ancient Greek wars with the Persians, western countries have referred to Iran as "Persia" or a variant of this in their own languages. In 1935, Reza Shah requested western diplomats to refer to "Iran," and this is now in general use as the geopolitical term. "Persia" continues to be used, however, especially in historical and cultural contexts.

Rugs may be classified according to socioeconomic modes of production as court or atelier rugs, factory or commercial rugs, cottage industry or village rugs, and nomadic or tribal rugs. All of these modes of production have been used in Persia.

The earliest carpet fragments in Persia date from about 600 B.C.E. See "Shahr-i Qumis." The Fustat Carpet, found in Egypt and dated to the ninth to tenth century, has been attributed to Persia. See "Fustat Carpet." Fragments of cut-loop pile from the ninth to tenth century, one in the Victoria and Albert Musueum, London, have been attributed to Persia. A zilu of Persian origin carries a date translated as 1405 and earlier ones in Leningrad are dated to the thirteenth century. See "zilu."

Although the earliest rugs of Persia were probably nomadic, the oldest extant complete rugs are those of the court. Court rugs are characterized by carefully planned and sophisticated design and great craftsmanship in construction. Court rugs were woven in Persia under the Safavid Dynasty from 1501 through 1722. In human effort, these were probably the costliest rugs ever woven. Designs of great curvilinear intricacy were used in the vase carpets. Silk and silver and gold metallic threads were used in the Polonaise carpets. Medallion carpets (thought to derive from book cover designs) were developed during this period. See entries for "Ardabil carpet," "Nadir Shah," "Polonaise carpets," "Qajar Dynasty," "Safavid," "Shah Abbas," "Shah Tahmâsp," and "vase carpets."

Nomadic rugs, more than other types, are made for use rather than for sale. Often, they are woven on ground looms and are all wool. Designs may derive from ancient tribal traditions or from urban or court motifs that have been reinterpreted. Primary sources of Persian nomadic rugs are the Afshars, Bakhtiaris, Baluch, Khamseh Confederation, Lurs, Shahsavan, and Qashqa'i. See entries under these names.

Village rugs are usually woven for the market and are influenced by market preferences for size, color, and design. Village rugs are sometimes woven by settled nomads and tribal motifs may persist in their rug designs. They are usually woven on vertical looms and may have a wool or cotton foundation. Many rug-weaving villages in Persia are cross-referenced at the end of this entry.

Factory rugs are woven for commerce and based on cartoons or patterns so that rugs woven from the same cartoon have almost identical designs, even though they are hand-knotted. These rugs may achieve the highest standards of design and construction or they may be of the lowest marketable quality. There was a boom in Persian factory carpet production beginning in the late nineteenth century. Rugs woven by PETAG or Zeigler and Co. in Tabriz are examples of factory production. The two world wars temporarily depressed rug production.

In 1935, the Iran Carpet Company was formed under state sponsorship. Its goal is to raise rug quality and serve as a guarantor of loans to village rug-weaving cooperatives. It provides washed and dyed wool to weavers and buys and markets carpets. It controlled about 3 percent of Iranian rug production in the 1970s.

There is a long history of flatweaves in Persia. Highly complex kilims of hunting scenes and intricate floral designs were woven of silk and metal threads in the sixteenth and seventeenth centuries. These were interlocking and warp-sharing weaves and not slit tapestry weaves. See "Polonaise."

For tribal weavings, kilim designs usually have little relationship to the designs of pile rugs of the same tribe. Kilims of Persian Azerbaijan have multiple hexagonal medallions and ends of braided warps. Kilims of north central Persia have designs of closely packed diamonds. The Laleh Abbasi border is frequently used. These kilims are woven on a cotton foundation. Kilims of western Persia are woven in and around Sanandaj by Kurds. These are the most intricate and finely woven contemporary Persian kilims. See "Senneh." Flatweaves are described under specific Persian tribal and geographic entries.

In 1979, Muhammad Reza Shah Pahlevi was forced from the throne of Iran. A fundamentalist Islamic régime assumed power. This régime has been as hostile as its predecessors to regional and tribal autonomy. The Iran-Iraq war, the United States embargo on Iranian imports, and government austerities and repression have reduced rug production. The descriptions of rug production and marketing centers in this Lexicon generally refer to Iran before the Islamic revolution.

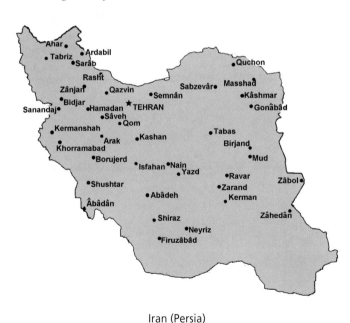

Iran (Persia)

Geographical entries for Persia or Iran are under the following place names:

Abâdeh	Azerbaijan
Ahar	Baba Haidar
Alamdâr	Barjid
Arâk	Bakhshaish
Ardabil	Baluchistan
Ardakân	Behbehân
Asadâbâd	Bibikabad

Bidgeneh	Nasrâbâd
Bijâr	Neyriz
Bilverdi	Nishâpur
Birjand	Noberân
Boldaji	Qain
Borujerd	Qainat
Bowanat	Qazvin
Chahal Shotur	Qoltuq
Chahâr Mahâl	Qom
Chahâr-râ	Quchân
Chenâr	Râvar
Joshegan	Reihân
Jowzân	Rasht
Kabud Râhang	Rosveh
Kalârdasht	Rudbâr
Kalât	Sabzevâr
Kamoo	Sarâb
Karadagh	Sarouk
Karadja	Sauj Bulâq
Karagâz	Sâveh
Kashan	Seistan
Kâshmar	Semnân
Kemereh	Senneh
Kerman	Serabend
Kermanshah	Shahr-e Bâbak
Khamseh	Shahr-e Kord
Kharaghan	Shahr-i Qumis
Khorramabad	Shâlamzâr
Khoy	Shiraz
Khurasan	Shushtar
Lillihan	Sirjân
Lamberan	Sonqur
Mahalât	Sultanabad
Mahvilât	Tabas
Malâyer	Tabriz
Mashhad	Tehran
Maslaghan	Taimeh
Mehrabân	Tâleghân
Meshkin	Tuysarkân
Meym	Ushvân
Miâneh	Varâmin
Milanlu	Vordoveh
Mud	Wiss
Murdschekar	Yalameh
Mushkabad	Yazd
Mussabad	Zâbol
Nahâvand	Zâgheh
Nain	Zanân
Najafabad	Zarand

Persian. The official language of Iran (Persia) and the native tongue of a majority of the population. One of the Indo-European family of languages. Modern or New Persian (pârsi, fârsi) is descended from Old Persian, in which the cuneiform inscriptions of Cyrus and Darius were written. After the

verse, may be found calligraphed on metalwork, textiles, and other artifacts from the sixteenth century onward; earlier inscriptions are more likely to be in Arabic. "Persian" as an adjective also designates cultural aspects of Iranian history and contemporary life, e.g., Persian literature, art, carpets (but Iranian banks, frontiers, policy).

Persian knot. See "asymmetric knot."

Persian rug. A rug from Persia (Iran). Incorrectly used as a synonym for "oriental rug."

Persian yarn. A commercial designation for soft-spun, three-ply yarn made up of medium twist two-ply wool yarns.

Peshawar. A city and rug-weaving center of northern Pakistan. The quality of rugs woven in the area is considered lower than that of rugs woven in Karachi and Lahore. See "Pakistan."

PETAG. An acronym for Persische Teppich-Gesellschaft (Persian Carpet Company). A company in Tabriz that produced fine reproductions of antique rugs from about 1911.

phulkari (Hindi, "flowers embroidery"). A ceremonial wedding cloth of Rajasthan, India, of cotton embroidered with silk.

pibiones. See "Sardinia."

pick. A single weft passing through warps.

picker. An individual who regularly purchases rugs at auctions, house sales, and flea markets and resells these rugs to dealers.

pictorial rug. A rug whose field is occupied by naturalistic or realistic representations of people, places, or things other than conventionalized design motifs. Because these rugs are not generally popular, Iranian dealers refer to them as *naqsh-e ghalat*, meaning "wrong design." There are village examples with naive execution and formal carpets with fine drawing that were woven from cartoons in Kirman and Tabriz. Persian examples depict large animals such as horses, camels, and lions, tales from Persian literature and folklore, and kings and historical personages. Beginning in the nineteenth century, many pictorial rugs were woven in China. See "aksi," "Maggie and Jiggs Carpet," and "Zirhaki."

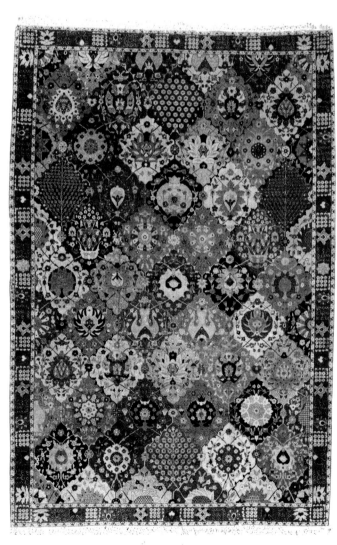

PETAG Tabriz carpet *Sothhebys*

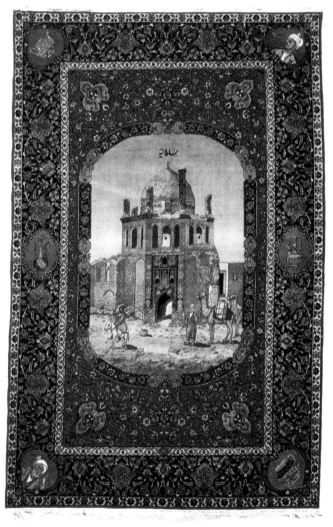

Tabriz pictorial rug *Sothebys*

phoenix. See "dragon and phoenix" and "simurg."

pile. The loops or cut ends of supplementary yarns anchored in a fabric. More specifically, the sheared fibers rising from the foundation of a hand-knotted rug. See "nap" and "tufted."

pile height. The length of pile measured from the foundation to the pile end.

pill, pilling. To form into small fuzz balls. Some rugs are subject to pilling.

pillar rug. A long, narrow Chinese pile rug designed to be wrapped around a pillar or column. The design is not complete unless the edges of the rug abut. Accordingly, there are no side borders on these rugs. The dragon is a common dominant design in pillar rugs. These rugs were used in Buddhist temples in northern China, Mongolia, and Tibet. See "katum."

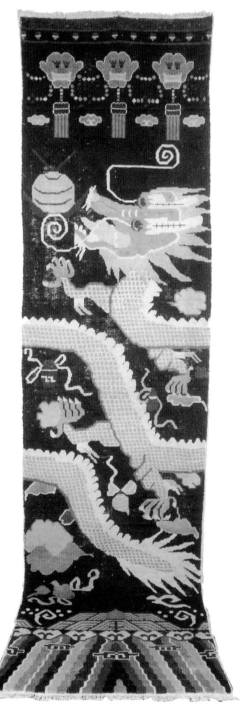

Pillar rug *Grogan and Company*

pillow, pillow cover. See "agedyna," "gyabhye," "jynne," "mindar," "pushti," "ussada," and "yastik."

Pinesprings, Wide Ruin, Burnt Water. A cluster of Navajo weaving centers in southwest Arizona and a source of rugs with natural dyes. Rugs of the 1930s from this area are without borders. They have broad stripes containing diamonds or zigzags. The dominant colors are shades of brown and tan.

Pinner, Robert H. (1925–2004). Robert Pinner was a co-founder of Hali magazine, founder of the International Conference on Oriental Carpets, and a scholar of oriental rugs, Turkmen weavings in particular. He authored many articles and catalogs and the book *Turkoman Studies I.*

Pinwheel Kazak. A repeated pinwheel or swastika design fills the field of this nineteenth-century rug attributed to the Kazak region of the Caucasus. These rugs are all wool, red wefted, and woven with a density of about 53 symmetric knots per square inch. The mean knot ratio of this design is .94 and their average area is about 46 square feet. See "Caucasus" and "Kazak."

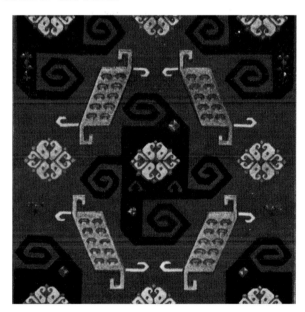

Pinwheel Kazak motif

piqué. The appearance of yarns of contrasting colors plied together.

Pirabadil. See "Perpedil."

Pirot kilims. A village of Serbia, formerly known as Şarköy, noted for its nineteenth and early twentieth-century kilims in characteristic colors of magenta-red, blue, blue-green with some white, and yellow. Currently, these kilims may be described as Şarköy or Thracian kilims through confusion with the Turkish town of Şarköy, named after the former Serbian town, where refugees from the frontier live and, according to some, weave kilims.

pitch. See "gauge."

plain soumak. See "soumak."

plain weave. The simplest interlacing of warp and weft in which there is only one weft in each of two sheds composed of alternating warps. See "warp-faced" and weft-faced."

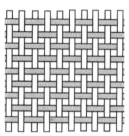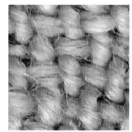

Plain weave

plain weft wrapping. See "soumak" and "weft wrapping."

plaiting. This term may be used synonymously with braiding, but is more correctly used in referring to structures created by oblique interlacing of two or more sets of elements in two or more directions, as distinguished from braiding, which is oblique interlacing of one set of elements in one direction. See "braiding."

plug. A piece from another rug sewn or woven into a hole in a rug as a repair.

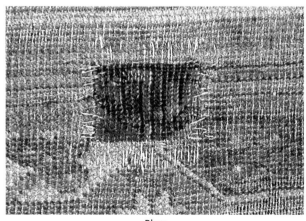

Plug

plum blossom. The plum blossom, a five-petaled flower, is a motif in Chinese rugs. It may symbolize winter and overcoming obstacles.

Plum blossom

plush. A power-loomed fabric in which cut pile consists of singles (unplied yarn) and the pile is longer than that of velvet.

ply. Two or more singles yarns spun or twisted together make a ply or plied yarn. Also termed "doubled yarn." See "spin" and "winder plied."

poked rug. A rag rug made off of a frame by pushing short pieces of fabric through a backing fabric. See "hooked rug" and "rag rug."

Poland. In the seventeenth and eighteenth centuries, pile rugs were woven in Lwow, Poland (now L'vov, Ukraine). Some of these rugs had linen warps and most were woven in naturalistic floral designs. Kilims are the traditional floor covering of Poland. Designs are geometricized floral motifs, ornamented stripes, or adaptations of western floral designs.

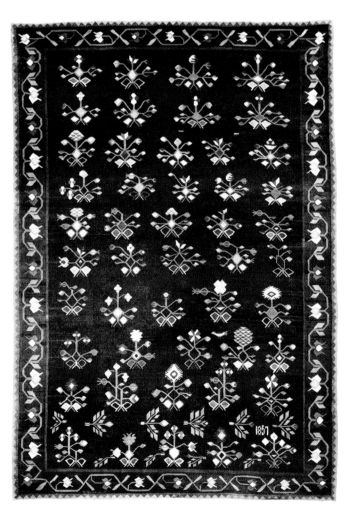

Polish kilim (detail)

polasi. See "Doukhobor rugs."

Poldi Pezzoli Hunting Carpet. A Persian medallion hunting carpet with border inscriptions in the Poldi Pezzoli Museum in Milan, Italy. Its size is about 18 feet by 12 feet. Woven into this rug is an Islamic date the equivalent of 1542/43. This dating is questioned.

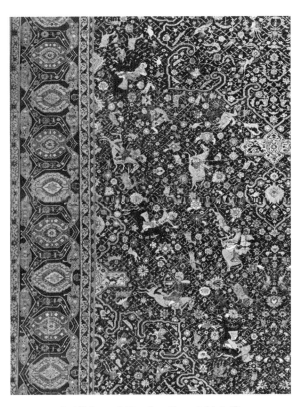

Poldi Pezzoli Hunting Carpet (detail)

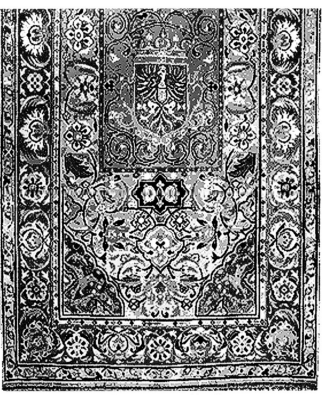

"Polonaise" carpet (detail)

pole medallion. A design in which central medallions are arranged vertically and connected by a pole, stripe, rod, or trunk. This arrangement may suggest a tree-of-life.

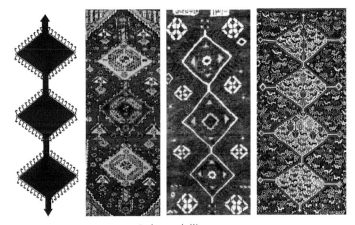

Pole medallions
FROM LEFT TO RIGHT: design type, Gorevan, Kazak, Khamseh

"Polonaise." A group of seventeenth-century Persian carpets woven in silk and brocaded gold and silver. There are over 200 examples extant. They are so named because examples of this group were first exhibited by Count Czartoryski of Poland, and some of those displayed his family arms. Examples bear the coat of arms of other Polish families. Evidence suggests these rugs were woven in Kashan or Isfahan.

Kilims of hunting scenes and intricate floral designs of silk and metallic threads were woven in the same period. These were not slit weave tapestry, but interlocking weft and warp-sharing weaves. These weavings may be referred to as "Polonaise" kilims.

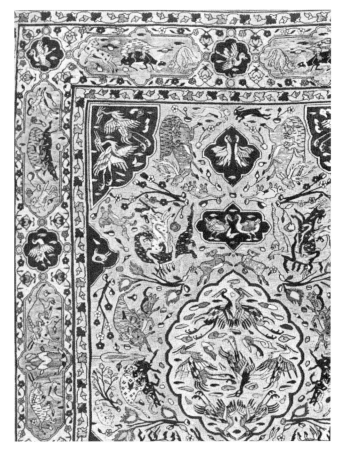

"Polonaise" kilim (detail)

polyester. A polymer of polyhydric alcohol and a polybasic acid. A synthetic fiber derived from petroleum. Polyester resists abrasion, but is not resilient. It dyes well and is stain resistant. It is produced as a staple (cut) fiber and not as a monofilament. Polyester has a tendency to "fuzz" or "pill" when exposed to traffic and it is difficult to clean.

polypropylene. A synthetic fiber used in tufted Chinese rugs and in some Wilton weaves from Belgium. See "synthetic fiber."

pomegranate design. The pomegranate is thought to symbolize fertility in the East and Near East. The pomegranate tree is a common motif in rugs of Eastern Turkestan, where it is used as an all-over design. In eastern Chinese rugs, the pomegranate may be shown partially opened with seeds exposed. This motif is termed *liuka baiza*. Pomegranates have been represented in Mughal rugs. Alpujarra rugs of Spain depicted the pomegranate as a symbol of Granada (granada is Spanish for "pomegranate").

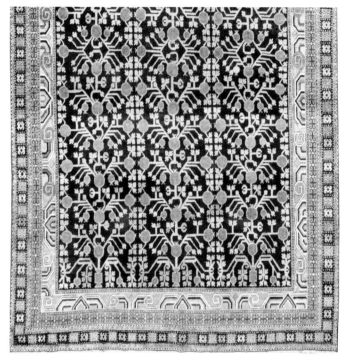

Eastern Turkestan rug with
pomegranate design (detail) *Jason Nazmiyal*

pomegranate dye. The rind of the pomegranate, *Puncia granatum*, is used to produce a yellow dye.

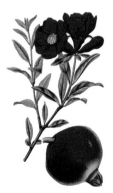 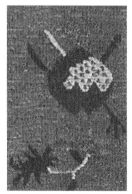

Pomegranate   Pomegranate (Tibet)

Ponceau 2R dye. A bright red acid azo dye synthesized about 1880. It is found in some Turkmen rugs.

poncho. A Mexican or southwestern rectangular garment consisting of two parts that are stitched together down the center with a slit left open for the head. The sides are open when the garment is worn on the shoulders. See "shawl" and "serape."

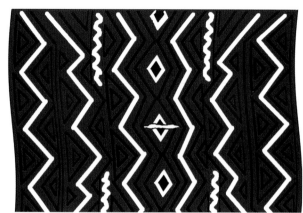

Poncho (Navajo) *Doris Leslie Blau*

pool, auction. See "auction pool."

pooling, watermark. Irregular darkened areas in cut pile power-loomed carpets where pile has reversed direction due to high traffic.

Poona, Pune. A district in western India, near Bombay. In the late nineteenth and early twentieth century, high quality carpets were woven in a prison in Poona.

Pope, Arthur Upham (1881-1969). An American scholar of Iranian history and culture. He was the author of numerous publications. His most significant work was the six-volume *Survey of Persian Art*, published in 1938. This work included a history of carpet-making in Persia.

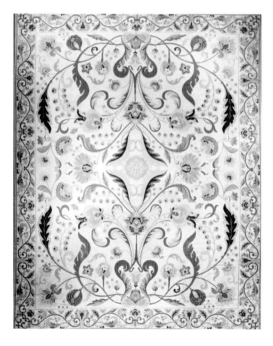

Portuguese needlework carpet *Doris Leslie Blau*

Portugal. Portugal has a long tradition of needlework rugs. Designs are stylized floral and animal motifs, usually with a central floral medallion. A yellow ground is common. See "Arraiolos."

"Portuguese" carpets. A small group of sixteenth and seventeenth-century carpets, of disputed origin, characterized by a large medallion and spandrels showing vessels occupied by men (possibly in western dress), a drowning man, and fish. These rugs are Persian knotted, usually on a cotton foundation. Knot densities range from 200 to 380 knots per square inch. They were termed "Portuguese" carpets because they supposedly depicted the drowning of Bahadur Shah while visiting the Portuguese fleet at Goa in 1537. However, the scene may refer to other historical events. They have been attributed to Mughal India and to northern Persia. See "Vienna Portuguese Carpet."

poshti. See "pushti."

postaghi. A long-pile Kirghiz sleeping rug.

Postavarul. A contemporary commercial grade of Romanian rug woven on a wool foundation with a knot density of 155 knots per square inch.

post knotting. Areas of a rug in which knots have been replaced or new designs have been introduced after the rug was initially knotted. This occurs when date inscriptions are changed to make the rug appear older. See "dates."

potassium dichromate. See "chrome mordant."

pound blankets. Navajo blankets made between about 1890 and 1920 of very poor quality that were sold to traders who bought them by weight at so much per pound.

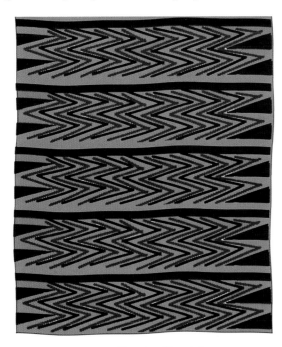

Pound blanket (Navajo)

power loom. Any automated loom not powered by hand or foot movements. The fly shuttle, invented in 1745, was an essential component of the standard power loom. In 1785 the Cartwright power loom was invented and gradually began to supplant the hand loom in western countries. See "Bigelow, Erasmus B."

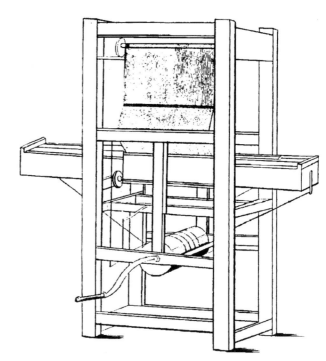

Cartwright's power loom

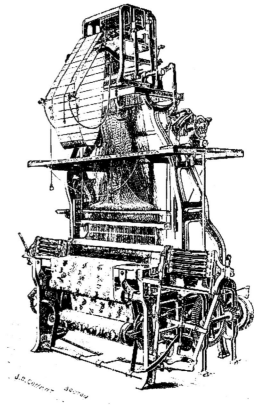

Power carpet loom with jacquard controls
Wikimedia Commons

prayer mat. See "meditation carpet."

prayer rug, mehraby, namazlik, seccade (Turk.), **sajjâda, sedjade, sejjadeh** (Arabic), **jânamz, dzheinamaz, jaynamaz, joi namaz** (Persian), **niche rug.** A rug with a representation of a mihrab (prayer niche) or "gateway to paradise." Columns may be shown supporting the arch and a lamp may be shown hanging from the apex of the arch. Some prayer rugs show other religious or talismanic objects. These may include ewers (for religious ablutions), muskas, the "hand of Fatima," mosques, and the Ka'ba. A double prayer rug (a design taken from bookbinding) is one with a niche at either end as a mirror image. Although most prayer rugs were woven in Anatolia, the motif occurs throughout Muslim countries, including Turkestan and India. The prayer rug is not necessarily used for prayer, as any clean area is sufficient for this purpose. See "alınık," "Fletcher Prayer Rug," "gomden," "hand of Fatima," "Hapsburg Prayer Rug," "Imperial Mughal Prayer Rug," "Islam," "landscape carpets," "Marasali," "Meyers Coupled-Column Prayer Rug," "mihrab," "namazlik," "opposed arch prayer rug," "Paravicini Mughal Prayer Rug," "saff," and "vertical multi-niche prayer rugs."

primary colors. Red, blue, and yellow. Other colors of the visual spectrum are combinations of these colors.

primary gul. See "major gul."

production cycle, rug. For commercial hand-knotted rugs, the steps from design on graph paper through weaving, the finishing steps of shearing and washing to preparation for shipment of the saleable rug in the source country. This cycle typically requires from 12 to 18 months. The production cycle for a sample rug typically requires from 6 to 8 months. The production cycle for a dhurrie typically requires 4 to 6 months. See "loom time."

program line, program goods. A trade term for factory, hand-knotted rugs of the same design, but in different sizes, shapes, and colorways available on a continuing basis. See "continuity line."

Prophet's green. Shades of green derived from combinations of indigo blue and yellow obtained from different vegetable sources. This was thought to have been the color of Muhammad's banner, now in Istanbul.

provenance. The source, origin, or history of ownership. When applied to rugs, provenance may refer to the place of origin, the weavers of the rug and the time of origin, as well as the history of ownership. See "attribution."

provocation. Deliberately making a false or misleading attribution to encourage debate or research. See "attribution."

pu (Persian). A row of knots in a carpet.

pud (Persian). Weft.

Pueblo weaving. Pueblo Indians had been weaving cotton fabrics from about 700 C.E. when the Spanish settled in New Mexico in 1598. By the 1630s, the Pueblo were weaving blankets with wool from Spanish sheep. Some of the Pueblo, who were enslaved by the Spanish, rebelled, deserted, and joined the Navajo. The Pueblo taught the Navajo weaving and sheep rearing. By 1706, the Navajo were weaving wool blankets. Generally, Pueblo wool fabrics are more loosely woven than those of the Navajo. The Pueblo used a weft-faced plain weave while the Navajo used both a plain weave and a twill weave. Hopis and Zunis are Pueblo Indians. See "Navajo rugs."

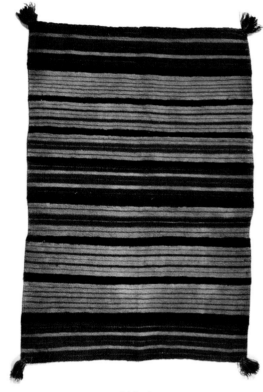

Zuni blanket

pul donneh (Persian pul-dân, "money-holder"). In Afghanistan, a narrow bag of about 2½ feet by 10 inches, used to store money.

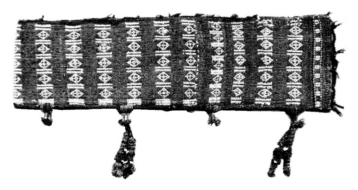

Baluchi pul donneh *Allen Arthur*

pulled-warp structure. See "Navajo wedge weave."

pulo. A tie dying technique used in Tibet that produces a pattern of small dots, crosses, or small concentric circles in a wool fabric called *nambu*. Gansu rugs of China of the 12th to 14th century with this field repeat are described as pulo design rugs, as are a few similarly designed 20th-century Tibetan and Chinese rugs.

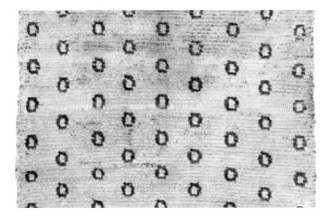

Tibetan pulo design sleeping rug (detail) *Alberto Levi*

Punjab (Persian *panj âb*, "five rivers"). The plain of the upper Indus and its tributaries. Formerly a province of India, now primarily within the borders of Pakistan. See "Lahore" and "Amritsar."

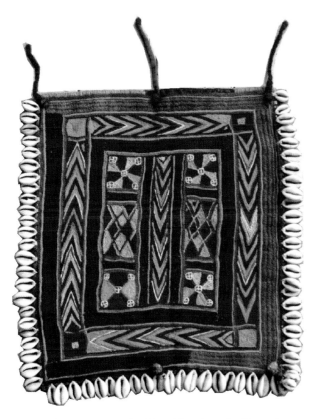

Punjabi women's embroidered head scarf *Allen Arthur*

purdah. See "ensi."

purpurin. A constituent of the dye derived from madder. It is an anthraquinone that is pinkish-red by itself. It provides more intense colors in combination with different metals. See "alizarin" and "madder."

pushti, poshti. Adjective from Persian *posht* "back." A mat of about 3 feet by 2 feet or a pillow.

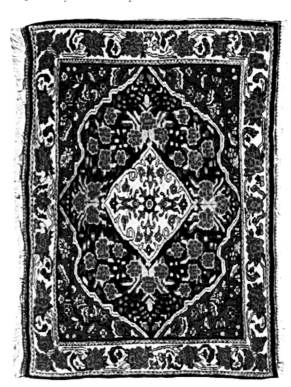

Bijar pushti *John Collins*

puttees (Persian *pâ-tâveh*). Cloth leggings or bands wrapped around the lower legs, as worn by Middle Eastern men. One end of each band may be ornamented. Tassels connected to the bands are used as ties.

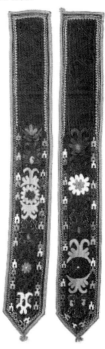

Afghanistan puttees *R. John Howe*

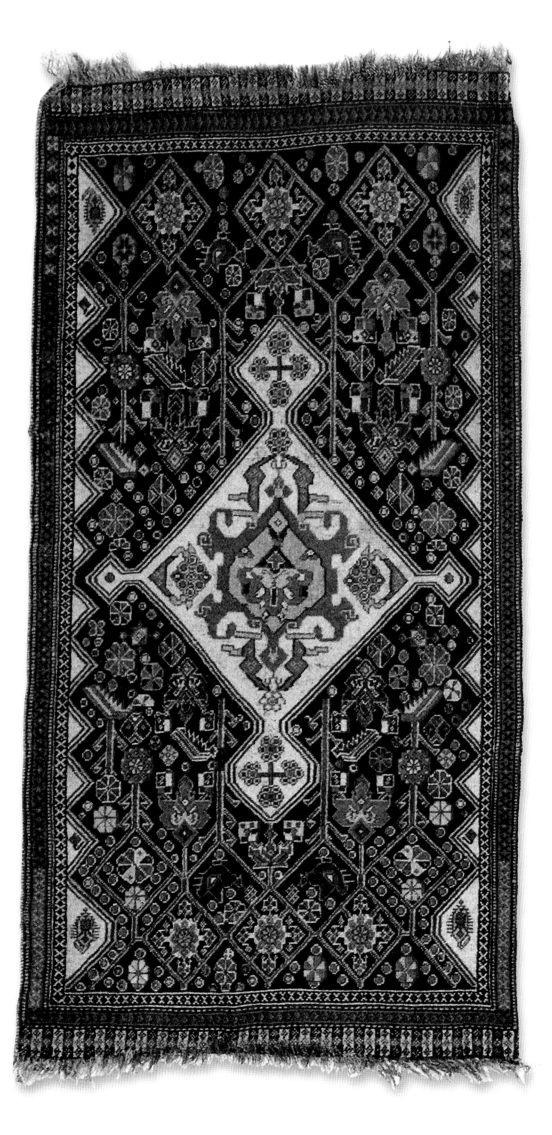

Qain, Qâyen. A city of northeastern Iran. Formerly a source of felt carpets and pile rugs with boteh designs. Between World Wars I and II, many carpets were woven in Qain. These were analine dyed and used the Jufti knot.

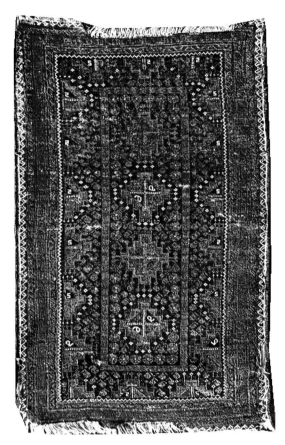

Qain rug *Michael Craycraft*

Qainat, Qâyenât. A mountainous area of southern Khurasan, Iran. Former and contemporary rug-weaving centers in the Qainat include Gonâbâd, Qain, Durukhsh, Birjand, and Mud. Birjand and Mud are sources of current rug production in the area. See entries under these names.

Qairawan. See "Kairouan."

Qaisar. A town of northwestern Afghanistan, west of Maimana. Uzbeks in the town weave rugs with variations of designs used in ensis. These are double-wefted rugs tied with the asymmetric knot.

Qajar dynasty. The Qajars were a branch of the Turkmen who came to prominence under the Safavids and rose to power in northern Iran after the collapse of the Zand dynasty of Shiraz (1751-1796). They conquered the south, recovered Khurasan from the Afsharids, but lost Iran's possessions north of the Aras river by 1828, after two wars with Russia. Qajar Iran, with its capital at Tehran, was thus more or less the same in territory as present-day Iran. The dynasty lasted from 1796 until 1925. In the last few decades the ruler's absolute power was repeatedly challenged, notably by the Constitutional Revolution (1906-11) and the coup d'état of Reza Khan (1921;

Reza Shah Pahlavi from 1925). Culturally speaking, the Qajar period in Persia effectively means the nineteenth century.

There was considerable artistic development in the reign of Fath Ali Shah (1797-1834), and many fine textiles were produced, particularly by the traditional royal workshops. Under Naser od-din Shah (1848-96) increased contact with Europe brought a boom in international demand for Persian rugs; from the 1870s there was a great increase in the number of looms in Iran, and in carpet exports. Many factory rugs woven in this period were in Herati, offset boteh, minâ khâni, and shah abbasi designs. Floral medallion designs, imitations of classic Persian designs, and pictorial rugs were also woven. Government attempts in this period to prevent the use of synthetic dyes were largely futile. See "Senneh" and "Ziegler."

Qala-i Nau. A town of northwestern Afghanistan, northeast of Herat, inhabited by Sunni Hazaras. Formerly, a source of fine kilims, weavers now produce pile rugs with variations of ensi designs.

Qala-i Zâl. A town of north central Afghanistan, northwest of Kunduz. The town is inhabited by Ersaris. Designs of their rugs are all-over stars or diamonds and Turkmen guls. These rugs have offset warps. Quality standards for these rugs are very high.

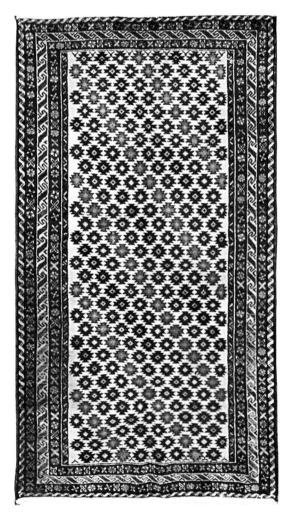

Qala-i Zâl (detail) *Issam Al-Lahham*

qâli (Persian). A pile rug.

qâli-ha-yi-mahfuri (Persian). Sculptured rugs.

qalamkâr sofreh. See "kalamkâr sofreh."

qâlin. A Turkmen carpet with a size greater than 9 feet by 6 feet.

qâlincha. A Turkmen rug with a size less than 9 feet by 6 feet.

qalyândân. A deep, rectangular bag specifically intended to hold a *qâlyân* or *nargilah* (water pipe). The size is about 20 inches by 14 inches. Such bags were woven by the Afshars.

qanât (Turk., "wing"). A Mughal tent wall panel. These decorative panels were created in a variety of techniques. Many surviving examples contain an arch or mihrab. Also, a system of irrigation.

Qaradâgh. See "Karadagh."

Qaragözlü. See Karagöz.

Qarâjeh. See "Karadja."

Qarqin, Qarqeen. A town of north central Afghanistan, west of Mazâr-e Sharif. Also, a Turkmen tribe. Contemporary rugs of Qarqin are the cheapest and lowest in quality of Afghanistan rugs. Some of these rugs may have hemp wefts. Various undistinguished Bokhara designs are used.

Qashqa'i, Kashgai. The Qashqa'i are a confederacy of tribes of Fars province, southwest Iran. The confederacy was formed in the eighteenth century. The major tribes are of Turkmen origin, having settled in the region perhaps as early as the eleventh century. These tribes did not assume the name "Qashqa'i" before the sixteenth century. The tribes include the Amaleh, Darashuri, Fârsi Madân, Kashkuli Bozorg (Greater Kashkuli), Kashkuli Kuchek (Lesser Kashkuli), and Shish Boluki.

Many Qashqa'i have settled in villages and towns. Their rugs are more directly influenced by market demands. These rugs are more coarsely woven than older nomadic tribal pieces and often have cotton warps. Typically, nomadic tribal rugs are all wool. Wefts are double and dyed with madder. The asymmetric knot, open to the left, is used. The knot density range is about 70 to 170 per square inch. Ends are finished with a plain weave with brocade. A barber pole stripe is typically used to finish the selvage. The Qashqa'i medallion consists of a hexagon or diamond with four projecting hooks inside of a hooked diamond. In earlier versions, the hexagon and projections are curvilinear while later versions are rectilinear. The source of this medallion has been differently ascribed to the pendant of medallions of Safavid rugs, the mina khani design, and the hooked octagon in Holbein carpets. This medallion is used on many Qashqa'i rugs and bag faces. Other Qashqa'i rugs show a field completely filled with randomly placed small elements. These are geometricized blossoms, leaves, animals, birds, and human figures.

Qashqa'i kilims are woven in one piece, with cotton sometimes used as highlights in an otherwise wool fabric. Laleh Abbasi and sawtooth borders are common, usually entirely framing the field. Panels are common at the ends of these kilims and sometimes include brocading. The Amaleh and Darashuri are subtribes noted for their kilims. See "Fars," "Kashkuli," "Shiraz" and "Shish Boluki."

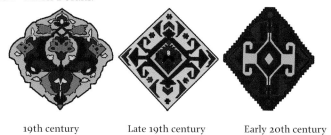

19th century   Late 19th century   Early 20th century

Qashqa'i medallions

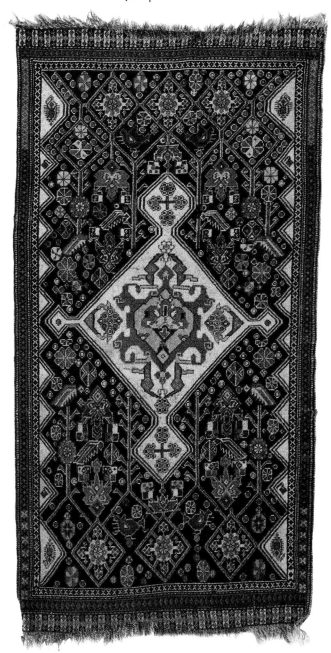

Qashga'i rug *Donald N. Wilber*

Qashqa'i frieze, vani. A border used primarily at the ends of southwestern Iranian tribal flatweaves and pile rugs. The border is used commonly by the Qashqa'i. The border suggests a line of dominoes and consists of alternating squares of light and dark colors, often blue and white. Within each square are dots or small rectangles, often five or nine in number. These square motifs are called "vani."

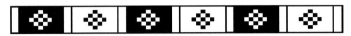

Qashqa'i frieze

Qashguli. See "Kashkuli."

qâshoqdân (Persian). See "spoon bag."

Qâyen. See "Qain."

Qâyenât. See "Qainat."

Qazaq. See "Kazakh."

Qazvin, Alvand, Kasvin, Kazvin. A city in northern Iran. It was formerly the capital of the Safavid empire in the mid-sixteenth century. It was probably the design source for rugs such as the Sanguszko carpet in the Metropolitan Museum of Art. The city was a source, between the First and Second World Wars, of medallion rugs very similar to Sarouks. The foundation is cotton and the knot density is between 130 to 200 knots per square inch. Kasvin is an American trade designation for rugs woven in the city of Hamadan. Alvand and Ecbetana are European trade designations for the same rug. Structurally, they are distinguished from the rugs of the Hamadan area in that they are double-wefted rather than single wefted. A wide variety of flatweaves are woven in the Qazvin and Sâveh areas. These may be termed "Zarand" weavings by dealers. See "Hamadan," "Sâveh," and "Zarand."

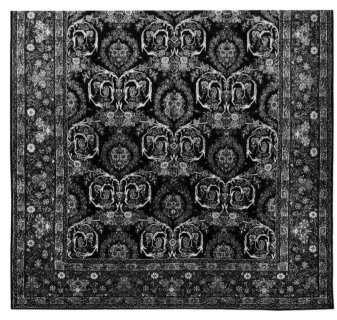

Qazvin rug *Jason Nazmiyal*

Qibla, Quibla. The direction of Mecca. The wall of a mosque that includes the mihrab.

qishlaq. See "kışhlak."

Qoltuq. A town of northwest Iran, lying southwest of Zanjân. It is inhabited by Kurds and is a source of rugs with medallions with pendants and spandrels. The foundation is cotton, double-wefted, and the typical knot density is about 130 knots per square inch.

Qom, Kum, Qum. A city of northwest central Iran. Carpet production in Qom did not begin until about 1930. Rugs of Qom are similar to those of Kashan, except that all-over designs are used more frequently than medallion designs. Boteh, tree-of-life, and panel designs are found. Qom is noted for its finely-woven, all-silk rugs, often in a compartment design. Wool carpets are on a cotton foundation. Typical knot density is about 325 asymmetric knots per square inch. Notable twentieth-century weaver-designers of Qom include Rashti Zâdeh, Arsalâni, and Ahmad Archang. See "Persia."

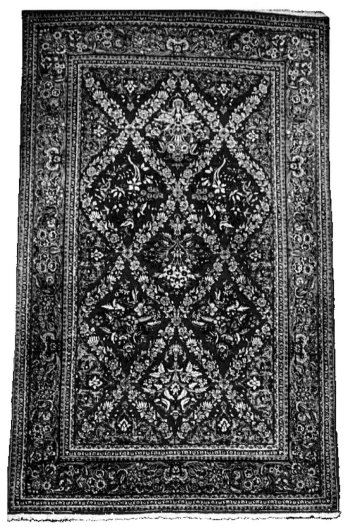

Qom carpet *Simon Knight*

qtifa, qtif (Arabic *qatifa*, "velvet, plush, pile"). In Morocco, a pile rug. The dominant color is red. Simple geometric motifs are asymmetrically arranged in the field. The Turkish knot is used, sometimes in columns offset by one warp. Many shoots of red wefts alternate with the rows of knots. Warps are of goat hair. In Tunisia and Algeria, a heavy-pile sleeping rug woven by a reggam. The symmetric knot is used in rows separated by four to six shoots of wefts. These are long-pile weaves used as mattresses or blankets. The dominant color is red. Designs consist of large packed diamonds or eight-pointed star medallions. See "Algeria," "Morocco," "reggam," and "Tunisia."

quality. As a term of the rug trade, quality refers to knot density, without regard to other rug properties such as design, color, type of wool, and so on. Thus higher quality, for the rug trade, means higher knot density for the particular type of rug. Used in this sense, quality is descriptive rather than judgmental. See "knot density."

quarter. One quarter of a yard or 9 inches. A unit of measure for carpet widths in America. Twenty-seven inch carpeting would be known as ¾. Also, one quarter of a non-directional rug, usually 4 by 6 feet, woven as a sample by manufacturers. See "weaver's square."

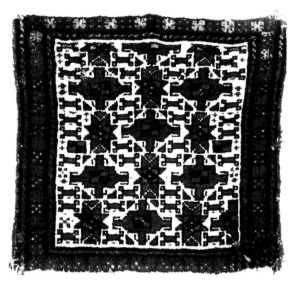

Quchân Kurdish bag face

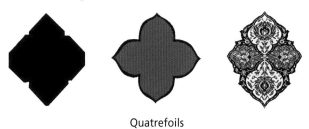

Quatrefoils

quatrefoil. A design or motif of four symmetrically arranged quadrants. A medallion of symmetrical quadrants or four lobes. See "trefoil."

Quchân, Quchon. A city and wool market of northern Khurasan, formerly known as Khabushân, northwest of Mashhad in Iran. The city and surrounding area are inhabited by Kurds, descended from those deported from Kurdistan in the seventeenth century. Kurdish weaving of north Khurasan has been described as Quchân Kurd. Rugs from this area are all wool, woven with a symmetric knot, and have traditional Kurdish designs. Local wool is used, and is finer than the wool used in Kurdish rugs from western Iran. A wide variety of flatweave structures are woven by Kurds of this area. These include tapestry weaves, soumak weaves, embroidery, and brocade. Functional weavings include kilims, vernehs, jijims, sofrehs, bags of all types, and animal trappings. Darreh Gaz and Kalât-i Nâdiri are towns not far from Quchân. Both Kurdish and Afshar weavings are sold in Kalât-i Nadiri. Darreh Gaz is inhabited by Za'farânlu Kurds and is a minor market for Kurdish weavings. See "Kalât," "Khurasan," and "Kurds."

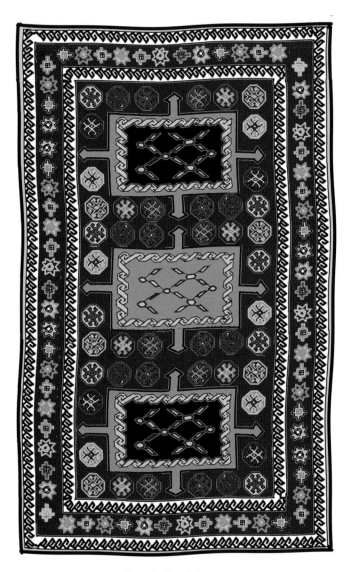

Quchân Kurdish rug

quercetin. A water soluble yellow dye obtained from the bark of trees and from other vegetable sources. See "yellow."

Quibla. See "Qibla."

quincunx, two-one-two, 2-1-2. Any field design or border pattern consisting of five elements arranged in a 2-1-2 pattern as the five spots on a pair of dice. This is a common arrangement of medallions in rugs, one medallion in the center and a medallion (often smaller) in each of the four corners. Examples are Karachoph Kazaks and certain Bergama, Holbein, and Beshir rugs

Qum. See "Qom."

Quseir al-Qadim. An archaeological site in Egypt near the Red Sea. Excavations between 1978 and 1982 produced pile carpet fragments. These were tied with the asymmetric knot at a density of 52 per square inch. The fragments were dated to the 13th century.

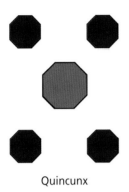

Quincunx

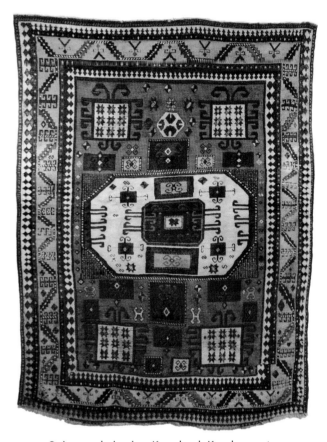

Quincunx design in a Karachoph Kazak carpet

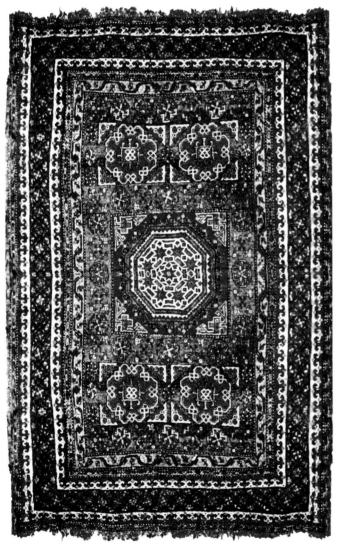

Quincunx design in a Holbein carpet

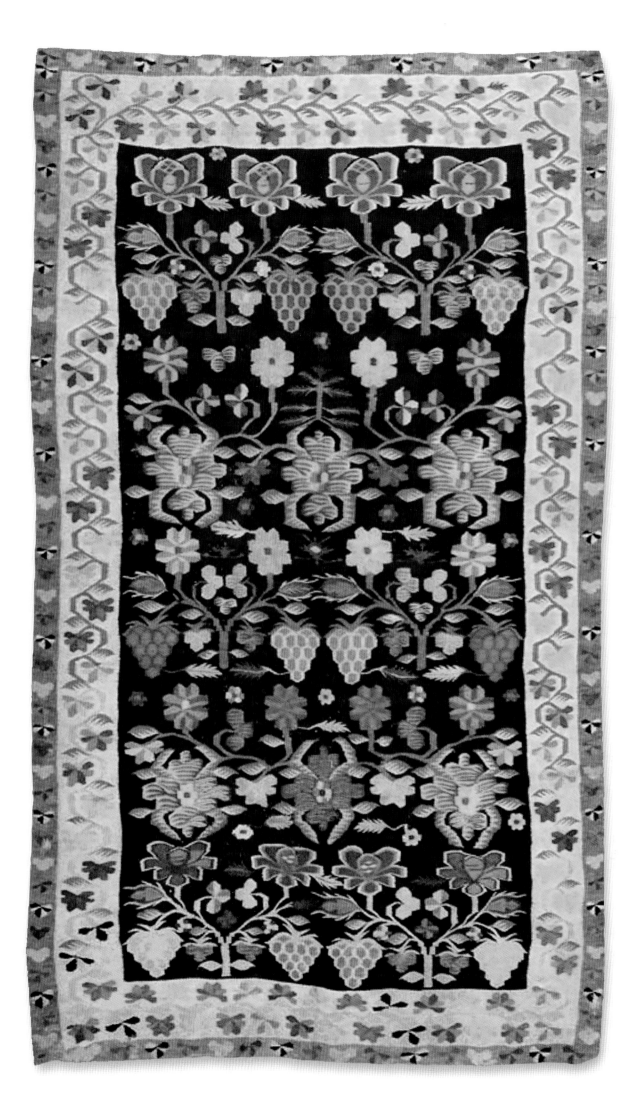

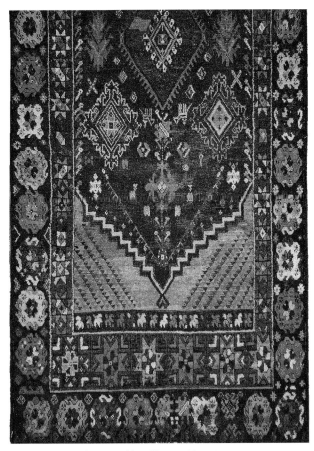

Rabat rug (detail) *Brooklyn Museum*

Rabat. A city of Morocco on the Atlantic coast. Rabat rugs, woven since the eighteenth century, are long and narrow to fit the main rooms of Moroccan urban homes. Usually, a small field is surrounded by many borders such that about two thirds of the rug consists of borders. Designs are reinterpretations of Turkish models. These rugs have symmetric knots on an all-wool foundation in older rugs and a cotton foundation in contemporary rugs. Knot densities range from 40 to 60 symmetric knots per square inch. Contemporary factory rugs are woven in Rabat. See "Morocco."

rack, rug. A metal structure used for hanging and displaying rugs in retail stores. The most common structures are swinging arm racks and sliding panel racks. These racks are manufactured to carry rug sizes of 6 by 9 feet, 8 by 10 feet, and 9 by 12 feet.

rag rugs. In Egypt, rag rugs are woven of rag strips about one inch wide sewn together end-to-end. These strips are used as weft in weaving rugs of simple stripes or checks. Similar rugs were woven in the United States in the eighteenth and nineteenth centuries. See "boucherouite," "drugget," "hooked rug," "list carpets," and "poked rug."

rainbow border. A border used in Chinese rugs, consisting of parallel, wavy stripes of different colors radiating from the edge of the field to the edge of the rug. Sometimes the border is used only at the bottom of the rug in conjunction with the sacred mountain motif. See "sacred mountain motif."

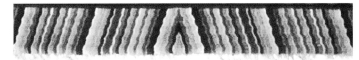

Rainbow border

raj. See "reg."

Rajasthan. Rajasthan is a region of northwest India adjacent to Pakistan. Jaipur, Bikaner, and Ajmer are rug-weaving centers of the region. Knot densities of contemporary rugs are about 144 to 225 knots per square inch. Bikaner and Ajmer were the source of very finely woven rugs at the turn of the century. See "Jaipur."

rakhat, rakkat (Persian *rakht*, "bedding"). A long, narrow bag, about 2 feet by 4 feet, and open on the long side, woven by the Afshars. This weaving is used as a bedding bag.

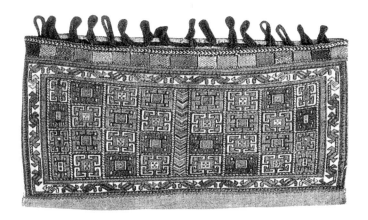

Rakhat *P.R.J. Ford*

rakht-e khab pich. See "mafrash."

rakkat. See "rakhat."

Rambouillet-Merino sheep. A variety of sheep introduced to the American Southwest in about 1859. This variety crossbred with and replaced Churro, the earlier variety of sheep brought to the New World by the Spaniards. The wool of the Rambouillet-Merino was of shorter staple, more kinky, and greasier than that of the Churro. These qualities made the wool difficult to spin and dye manually and thus discouraged domestic production of hand-spun blankets and rugs. See "sheep."

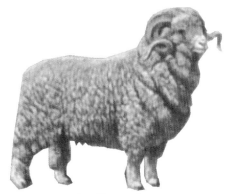

Rambouillet-Merino ram

random sheared. In power-loomed loop pile carpets, shearing some areas to produce cut pile while leaving other areas of loops intact. Sheared areas are darker in appearance.

rang (Persian). Color, dye.

rang-raz (Persian). Dyer.

rang shodeh (Persian, "colored, painted"). A painted rug.

rank badges, (Chinese, "*buzi*") Embroidered fabric panels, usually silk, of about 30 by 30 centimeters. These were worn over the chest by members of the Chinese Imperial aristocracy and showed different animals denoting rank of the wearer.

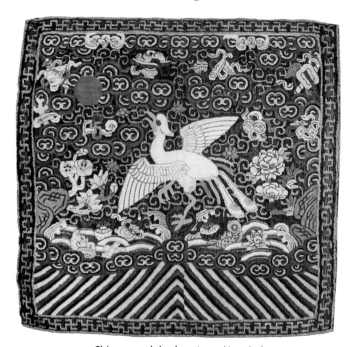

Chinese rank badge *Jason Nazmiyal*

Rasht, Resht. A city of Iran near the southwest coast of the Caspian Sea. It was a source of wall hangings, animal trappings and rugs made of appliquéd or inlaid fabrics and embroidered silk. Some of these textiles have been dated to the eighteenth century. The Persian term for this work is *gol-duzi-ye Rasht*, "flower embroidery of Rasht."

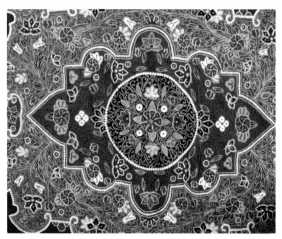

Rasht embroidered panel (detail) *Haliden*

Rashwan. A Kurdish tribe in Iran that weaves rugs, bags, and kilims. Also, a trade term applied to kilims from south central Anatolia in an area between Kayseri and Malatya. Most of these kilims have large, concentric diamond medallions. The diamonds have geometricized pendants. Warps are wool. Some cotton, silk, or gilt yarns may be used as supplementary wefts.

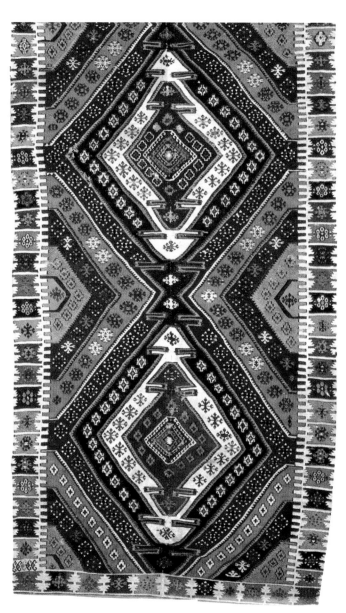

Rashwan kilim (detail) *Sothebys*

rataya. In Morocco, a saddle cover.

Râvar. See "Laver."

Raver. See "Laver."

reciprocal brocading. A brocade in which two complete rows of patterning wefts are woven between ground wefts.

reciprocating border. A two-part interlocking and repeating design, each part exactly complementary and congruent, fills the border. Two or more colors are used. See "crenellated border," "fret," "Laleh Abbasi," and "sawtooth border."

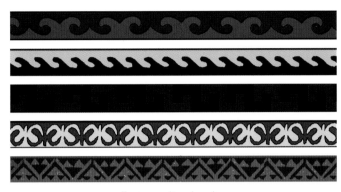

Reciprocating borders

red. That portion of the visual spectrum with the longest frequency. Natural sources of red dye in oriental rugs include Brazilwood, cochineal, kermes, lac, logwood, and madder. See entries under these names.

red carpet. Traditionally, a long red carpet unrolled at an entrance way to welcome an especially honored guest. Now used metaphorically to describe a special welcoming or reception ceremony.

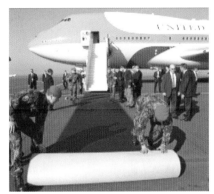

Rolling out the red carpet

reduced. A rug that has been cut down in size to remove damaged areas or to fit a particular space.

reed. A part of a loom used to compress wefts. The reed is a frame extending across the width of the loom containing finely-spaced dividers of reed or metal. Warps pass between the dividers. On Near Eastern carpet looms, the same function is served by using a heavy comb.

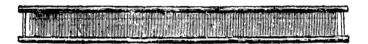

Reed from a loom

reed screens, chikhs. Reed screens are made for tent interiors by Kazakhs, Kirghiz, Durmien Uzbeks, and several Kurdish tribes. Patterns are formed by wrapping colored yarns around each reed. The reeds are then twined together. There are door screens, partition screens, and screens that surround the tent between the trellis and the felt exterior. The longest screens are about fifteen feet long and five feet high. One theory holds that the screen designs were copied in kilims which served similar purposes. This theory suggests that these kilims were intended to be viewed horizontally rather than vertically. A related technique is used in round wicker military shields (kalkan) of sixteenth and seventeenth-century Turkey.

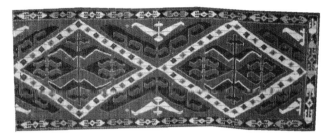

Reed screen (Kirghiz)

re-entrant design. See "Bellini rugs," "turret design," and "mountain carpet."

reg, raj (Persian *rag*, "row, course"). Knots per gereh (about 2.75 inches). Twenty reg would be approximately 53 knots per square inch.

reggam. A reggam is a male weaver of pile rugs on commission for wealthy tribal families in Tunisia and Algeria. Rugs woven by a reggam are highly prized. Designs are traditional. The practice of the reggam has virtually ended and women produce contemporary weavings in these countries.

Reihân. A village southeast of Arâk in Iran. The village is a source of single-wefted rugs with red fields and all-over designs derived from the Herati pattern.

repair. Rug repair includes those steps taken to strengthen a damaged rug so it can be returned to use. See "conservation" and "restoration."

Reseda luteola. See "weld."

reserve price. A minimum price for an item to be auctioned set by the auctioneer or owner. At auction, a sale is rejected if it falls below this price. Reserve prices may or may not be announced prior to the auction.

Resht. See "Rasht."

resilience. The capacity of carpet pile to resume its original position after exposure to traffic.

resist dyeing. Dyeing fabric or yarn by coating non-dye areas with a mechanical resist such as wax or a chemical resist such as acid. When the fabric or yarn is placed in the dye bath, no dye is absorbed in the resist areas. Resist substances are subsequently removed.

restoration. An attempt to return an object to its original, first, or earlier condition. A true restoration of a weaving requires the same type of fiber, yarn, dyes, and structures used in the original.

ret, retting. Soaking flax or hemp to separate the fiber from woody tissues by partial rotting.

reverse soumak. See "soumak."

reversible rugs. See "double knotted."

Reyhanlı. A village of southeast Anatolia near the Syrian border. Kilims of this village date from the middle of the nineteenth century. Early examples are very finely woven with excellent drawing. These kilims are long, narrow, and woven in two pieces. Warps are of white wool. Supplementary wefts may be cotton in white areas. Sometimes, silk, metallic thread, feathers, and even human hair have been woven into these kilims.

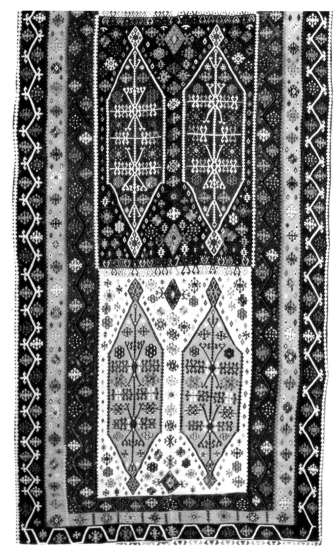

Reyhanlı kilim (detail) *Sothebys*

Reza Shah Pahlevi (Pahlavi). Reza Shah (1877-1944) ruled Iran from 1925 to 1941. During his reign, the carpet industry in Iran grew rapidly through finely-woven export carpets. Formal Iranian workshop carpets reached very high standards of quality through his encouragement of the industry.

Rhodian lily. A geometricized lily or tulip showing the angled calyx bracketed by two leaves. This motif is alternated with large rosettes in the borders of Ladik prayer rugs. Iznik ceramics, on which the motif appears, were once erroneously attributed to Rhodes.

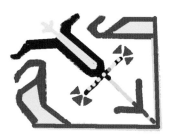 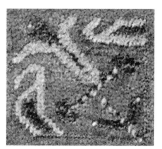

Rhodian lily

rhomb, rhombus. An equilateral parallelogram with oblique angles. A diamond.

rhomb motif. Any design in which the diamond shape is dominant. More specifically, a central, serrated diamond motif in Saltillo sarapes. See "baklava design."

rhubarb. Rhubarb leaves are a source of yellow to copper-red dyes in rugs of China and India.

Rhubarb

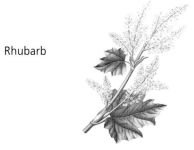

ring, auction. See "auction pool."

Rio Grande blankets. Wool blankets woven in the nineteenth century in the area of the Rio Grande and its tributaries in Colorado and New Mexico. These blankets were woven on Spanish haciendas and ranches. Originally, designs were stripes. Later motifs derived from Saltillo serapes. Colors were that of undyed white and brown wool. Early examples used natural dyes for red, yellow, and blue. Early examples are woven of Churro wool and later examples are woven of a mixture of Merino and Churro wool. See "colcha embroidery," "jerga," "servant blankets," and "Vallero blankets."

risheh (Persian). Fringe.

Roccelline dye. A red azo dye derived from naphthol. This synthetic dye, invented in the late nineteenth century, has been used in oriental rugs.

rofu (Persian, "darn, repair"). A repair made so as not to be evident.

rölaken. Eighteenth and nineteenth-century Swedish wall-hangings, bedcovers, and cushions in a tapestry weave of double interlocking wefts. Designs are brightly colored geometric figures and geometricized images of people and animals. See "agedyna."

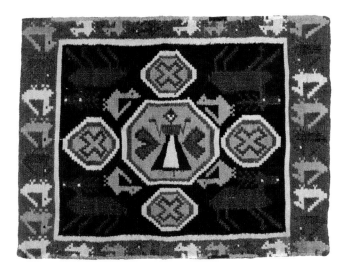

Rölaken cushion cover *Sothebys*

roll crush. Weft-wise bands of flattened pile. Usually, roll crush disappears when the carpet is unrolled and the pile is exposed to normal traffic. Steaming removes roll crush in wool and nylon pile.

Romania. Modern pile rug production in Romania was begun by Armenian refugees after the First World War. In the 1920s and 1930s, workshops in Romania wove fine copies of Caucasian and Turkish pile rugs. These copies were so convincing that some were purchased as authentic by major museums. Significant pile rug weaving for export began about 1950 and increased significantly with the lowering of United States tariffs in 1975. Rugs are woven by cooperatives in a variety of grades, in Persian, Turkish, and Caucasian designs. Steel frame looms are used. These looms permit very regular shapes and a highly consistent weave. Knot density varies between 25 and 200 knots per square inch, depending on grade. Generally, the asymmetric knot is used for Persian designs and the symmetric knot is used for Turkish and Caucasian designs. Rugs are woven on either a wool or cotton foundation. Grades are Braila, Bran, Braşov, Bucureşti, Dorna, Harmon, Milcov, Mureœ, Olt, and Postavarul. See entries under these names. See "Tuduc."

The oldest dated Romanian kilim was woven in 1789, but the tradition is much older. Romanian kilims have been influenced by the period of Turkish rule beginning in the sixteenth century. Kilims (*scoarta* in Romanian) were used in peasant homes as table cloths, bed covers, and wall hangings. Only wealthier families used them as floor coverings. Many Romanian kilims employ eccentric wefts and this permits a more naturalistic rendering of the floral and animal motifs used in these weavings. Some older examples show naive renderings of human figures. Typically, the field is in a contrasting color to the wide borders. Older kilims are all wool while contemporary products are wool wefted on cotton

warps. Currently, there is a large volume of Romanian kilims imported into the United States. Designs are modifications of traditional motifs with non-traditional pastel colors. See "Banat," "Dobruja," "Hunedoara," "laicerul," "Maramures," "Moldavia," "Oltenia," "Transylvania," and "Walachia."

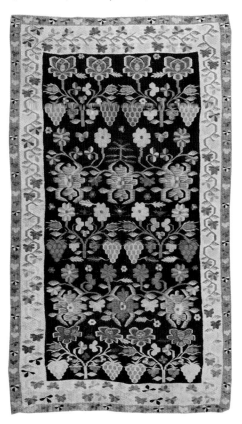

Romanian kilim (detail) *Jason Nazmiyal*

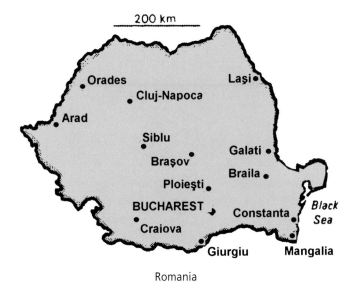

Romania

room-size rug. Large rugs intended to cover most of the floor of a room in a Western dwelling. Typical sizes are from 8 by 10 feet, 9 by 10 feet, 10 by 14 feet, up to 14 by 24 feet. These sizes are not traditional Islamic carpet sizes, but sizes and proportions developed for the Western market in Iran in the late nineteenth century. See "palace carpets" and "rug sizes and shapes."

rose motif. The rose is a common motif in oriental rugs. It is prominent in Turkish rugs in the Mejid style, Senneh kilims of Persia, and Karabagh rugs of the Caucasus. Clusters and sprays of roses are common in Aubusson and Savonnerie rugs. See "cabbage rose" and "farangi gul."

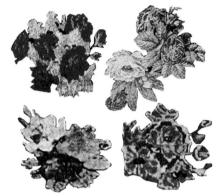

Roses
TOP: *Karabagh, Bessarabia* **BOTTOM:** *Qashqa'i, Sarouk,*

rosette. A stylized, generally symmetrical rendering of an overhead view of a flower blossom. See "floret."

rosette border. Any border featuring an overhead view of repeated, large stylized blossoms. The blossoms may be geometricized.

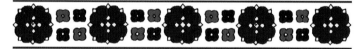

Rosette border (Talish)

Rosveh. A town of southeast Iran in the Feridan district. Rugs woven here have highly stylized floral patterns, almost a posterized effect. Rugs of this area are woven by the Bakhtiari.

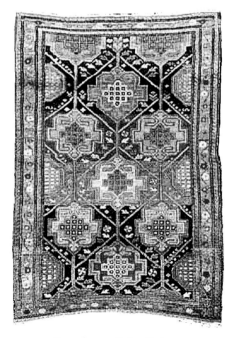

Rosveh rug *Detlev Fischer*

roundel. Any circular motif. Sometimes used to refer to rosettes.

roving. A filler in rag carpets. Also, a slightly twisted roll of fibers prepared for spinning.

rows per inch, RPI. The number of tufted or pile rows per inch. An indicator of rug quality.

royal. An indefinite trade term suggesting high quality in rugs.

Royal Bokhara. In the rug trade, a supposedly superior grade of Turkmen rug or rug with Turkmen designs. The meaning is indefinite. The term may refer to Tekke main carpets.

RPI. See "rows per inch."

Rudbâr. A town of Iran northwest of Qazvin and a source of rugs in different sizes with white, gray, or pink wefts. The Herati pattern with central medallion is a common design. The symmetric knot is used on a cotton foundation with single wefts.

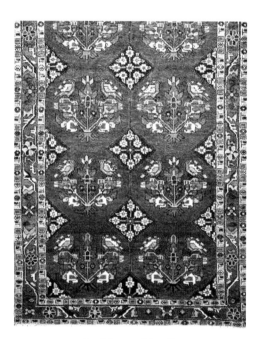

Rudbâr rug (detail)

rufarsh (Persian). Carpet covers used by wealthy persons in Iran in the early twentieth century.

rug (from Old Norse, *rögg*, shaggy). Any fabric floor covering. Some distinguish between a carpet and a rug, the latter being less than 8 by 10 feet in size.

rug classification. The most widely used system of rug classification is by country or region of origin. Other systems are based on design type, mode of production, historical development, and structure.

For classification according to country or regional origin, rugs may be grouped as Persian, Turkish, Caucasian, Chinese, Indian, and so on. A study employing this classification is *Oriental Rugs: A New Comprehensive Guide* by Murray L. Eiland.

For classification according to design type, rugs may be grouped as geometric designs, floral designs, pictorial designs, compartment designs, and so on. A study employing this system of classification is *The Oriental Carpet* by P.R.J. Ford. In categorizing old and classic rugs by design type, groups may be named after European artists whose works first portrayed a rug of that design type. Examples are Bellini, Crivelli, Holbein, Lotto, Memling, and Tintoretto.

For classification according to mode of production, rugs may be grouped as court rugs, factory rugs, village rugs, and nomadic rugs. A study employing this system of classification is *Oriental Carpets from the Tents, Cottages, and Workshops of Asia* by Jon Thompson.

For classification according to historical development, the history of rugs is considered with emphasis on the development and evolution of design styles. A study that relies, in part, on this system of classification is *Oriental Carpets* by Kurt Erdmann.

For classification according to structure, rugs are divided into pile and flatwoven categories. Because structural variation is much greater in flatweaves than in pile rugs, classification by structure is often employed in the study of flatweaves. Flatwoven rugs may be grouped as kilims, soumaks, vernehs, and so on. An example is *From the Bosporus to Samarkand: Flatwoven Rugs* by Anthony M. Landreau and W.R. Pickering.

rug designs. See "design classification and description."

rug names. There is no system for naming rugs, nor is there any consistency among rug scholars and researchers in naming rug types or classifications. As examples, pile rugs and flatweaves have been named after:

Contemporary Places
Tabriz
Ushak

Archaic Places
Senneh
Persepolis

Imaginary Places
Cabistan
Karastan

Tribes
Qashqa'i
Navajo

Ethnic Groups
Tajik
Kazakh

Empires
Mughal
Ottoman

Animal Designs
Eagle Kazak
Murgi Rugs

Plant Designs
Garden Carpets
Millefleurs

rug production cycle. See "production cycle, rug."

rug rack. See "rack, rug."

rug sizes and shapes. See entries under these names:
area rug
baby
carpet
çeyrek
circular carpet
corridor carpet
dozar
gallery rug
ian'
kallegi
kenâreh
khali
kiaba
mat

ruidjo, ruijo (Tajik-Persian *ruijô*, "bed cover"). A Central Asian embroidered wedding bedspread or sheet. Embroidered ornamentation forms a wide U-shaped band along three edges of the fabric with the center left unornamented.

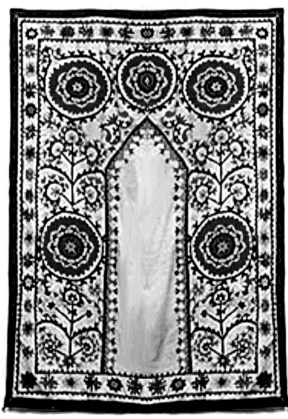

Ruidjo (detail) *Donna Larsen*

ru-korsi, sofreh-ye ru-korsi (Persian). Flatwoven stove covers, approximately one yard square. Most ru-korsi were woven in Khurasan and Varâmin in Iran or western Afghanistan. See "sofreh."

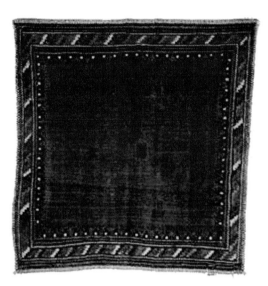

Afshar ru-korsi *J. Barry O'Connell*

rukhazal. See "Avar."

rum, rumden (Tibetan). Pile rugs.

rumâl (Persian). In India, a decorated cloth used to cover food or gifts. In Kashmir, a square shawl.

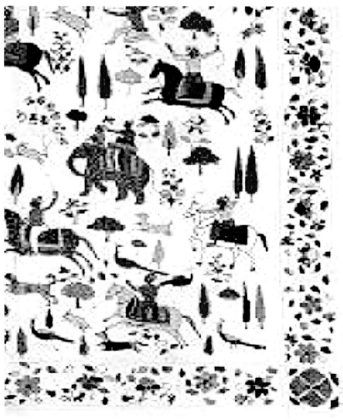

Rumâl of India (detail)

rumi. See "islimi."

runner. Any long narrow rug, generally less than 3½ feet in width. See "corridor carpet," "ian," and "kallegi."

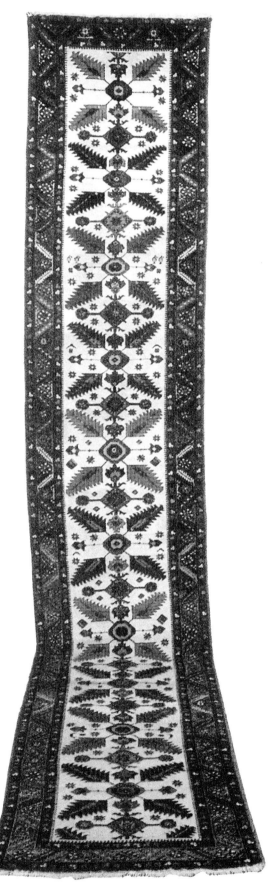

Southwest Persian runner *Grogan and Company*

running. See "bleeding."

Running dog, Seishour border. A border of repeated wave shapes, similar to a Vitruvian scroll. In some interpretations, it is a reciprocating border. Geometricized versions may be termed "Greek key" or "Greek ware." This border is frequently used in Seishour rugs in shades of blue.

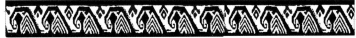

Seischour border

Greek key

Vitruvian scroll

Running dog borders

ru-olâghi (Persian). A donkey cover. Such a cover is distinguished from a horse cover in that it has only one pectoral piece, rather than two.

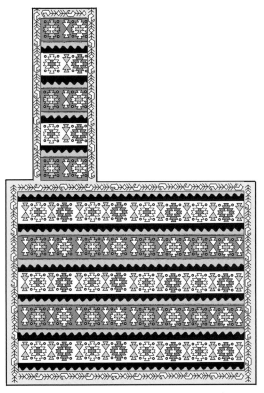

Ru-olâghi *Kurdish*

Russia, Commonwealth of Independent Nations, Union of Soviet Socialist Republics (U.S.S.R.). In 1991 the Union of Soviet Socialist Republics dissolved and was replaced in part by the Commonwealth of Independent Nations. At the present time, it is not clear which of the former republics of the U.S.S.R. will remain within this Commonwealth and which will seek complete independence. Descriptions of some weavings are under separate entries for the republics and other descriptions of weavings are under entries for ethnic groups. See these geographic entries: Armenia, Azerbaijan, Bessarabia, Caucasus, Georgia, Moldavia, Turkmenistan, Ukraine, Western Turkestan. See these entries for ethnic groups: Avar, Chechens, Cherkess, Karakalpak, Kazakh, Kirghiz, Tajik, Turkmen, Uzbeks.

ruyi clouds. In Chinese, ruyi means "as you wish." A Chinese cloud motif that is symmetrically lobed as compared to the drifting cloud motif which has a trailing, tail-shaped segment. Ruyi clouds are used in earlier Chinese rugs than are drifting clouds. See "chi."

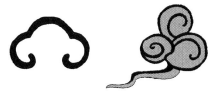

Ruyi cloud   Drifting cloud

ru-zini (Persian). See "saddle cover."

rya rugs, flossa weave. A coarsely knotted rug of Scandinavia. The oldest examples are of undyed wool and very shaggy. Later examples include yellow and red dyed yarns. There may be from 5 to 20 wefts between each row of knots. They were originally used as bed covers and sometimes had pile on both sides. Wool pile is used on linen or cotton warps. Some eighteenth-century rya rugs were tied with the symmetric knot. Geometric patterns and geometricized flowers, animals, and human figures are typical designs. See "glossa," "lassna," "listas," "Scandinavian weaving," and "trensaflossa."

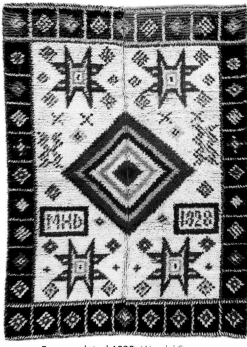

Rya rug dated 1828 *Wendel Swan*

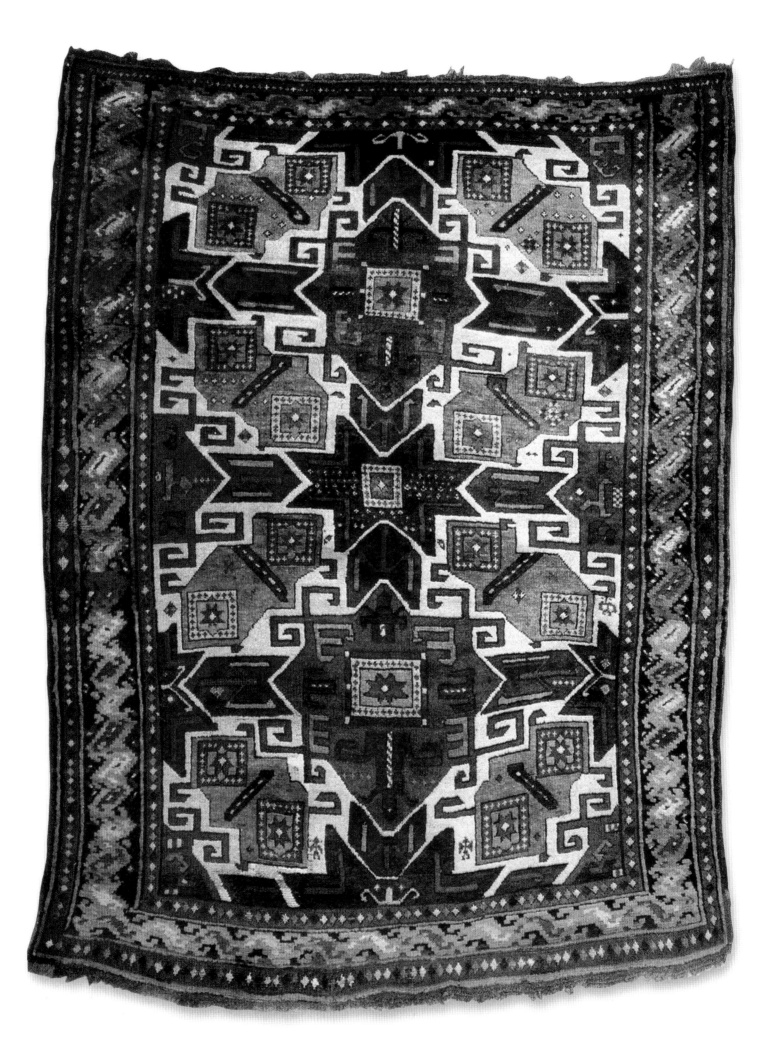

sabbâgh (Arabic-Persian). Dyer.

sabden, saden (Tibetan). Large floor rug.

sabz (Persian). Green.

Sabzevâr. A town of northeastern Iran. Carpets woven in the town are similar to those of Mashhad. Medallion with pendants is a common design, usually with a red ground. Asymmetric knots are tied on a cotton foundation.

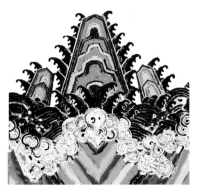

Sacred mountain motif

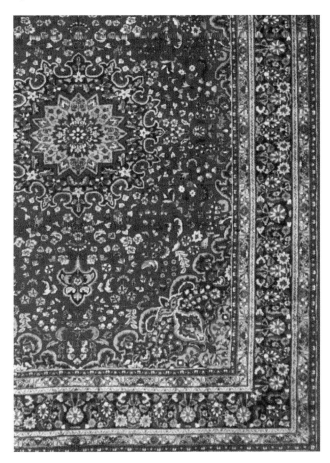

Sabzevâr carpet (detail) *ecarpetgallery*

saçak (Turk.) Macramé, or braided finish for rug ends.

Sackville Mughal Animal and Tree Carpet. An early seventeenth-century Mughal carpet in the collection of the Metropolitan Museum of Art, New York. This rug has a field of naturalistically drawn shrubs, trees, animals, and birds. The main border is filled with cartouche-like elements that are seen in tile work from early seventeenth-century Agra. It is 9 feet 6 inches by 27 feet 4 inches. It has a cotton foundation and wool pile. The density is 110 asymmetric knots per square inch

sacred mountain motif, shoushan fuhai. A motif common in Chinese rugs consisting of several tiers of mountains above clouds, and these in turn, above a rainbow border. Waves may be shown cresting the mountains. This motif extends all the way across the bottom of the rug or across both top and bottom. More rarely, the motif is used on all four sides. See "rainbow border."

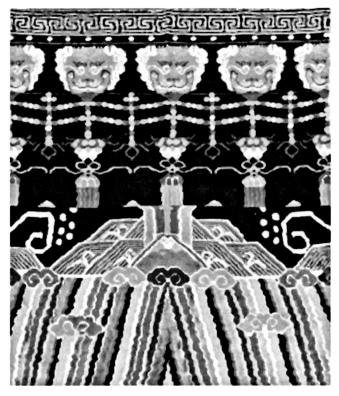

Pillar rug with sacred mountain motif *Grogan and Company*

sadden. To add ingredients to the dye bath which mute or darken the color.

saddle bags, heybe, heybeh (Turk.), **khorjin** (Arabic-Persian). Two bags or pouches connected so they can be thrown over the back of a horse, donkey, or camel or carried over the shoulder of a person. Sometimes there is a slit in the fabric connecting the two bags (bridge). This slit may be fitted over the pommel or horn of the saddle to hold the saddlebags in place. The outside faces may be pile or any of a variety of flatweave structures, while the inside faces are usually weft-faced plain weave. Bags are usually woven of a single continuous strip; the warps are continuous. The two ends are folded upwards to make the bags. As a result, when pile faces are used, the direction of pile is reversed in relation to the design on one of the bag faces. A variety of closure systems are used, but the most common is a series of loops that pass through each other or loops that pass through slits in the fabric to seal the bag. Typically, a pair of bags is about two feet by seven feet. See "bag."

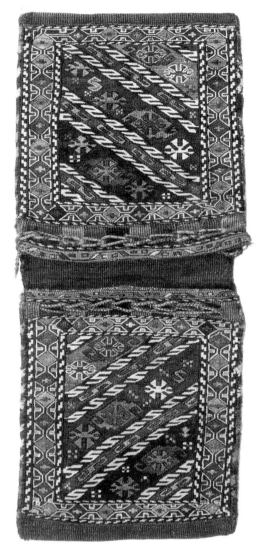

South Persian saddle bag *Grogan and Company*

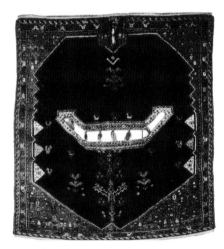

Senneh saddle cover *Grogan and Company*

saddle cover, cherlyk (Turk.), **eyerlik** (Turk.), **saddle blanket, ru-zini** (Persian). A blanket, sometimes pile, placed over the saddle. Often, there are holes or slits for the pommel and cantle. Some are made in two pieces. Outline shapes vary according to different tribal, urban or ethnic origins.

saden. See "sabden."

sadranji (from Persian *shatranji*, "checkerboard"). An all-cotton rug, similar to a dhurrie, woven by prisoners in Afghanistan. See "dhurrie."

saerzini bycyknapramach (Turk.). Bicycle seat cover. These have been woven in pile.

Safavid, Sefavid. The Safavid dynasty ruled Persia from 1502 to 1722, when Persia was conquered by Afghans. During this period, Persian carpet design reached its zenith. The earliest dated carpet from the Safavid Period carries a date translated as 1522-1523. Kashan is thought to be the source of fine silk hunting carpets and Isfahan was probably the source of Polonaise carpets. Large medallion carpets are attributed to Tabriz and vase carpets have been attributed to Kerman. Some floral carpets are thought to have originated in Herat. The Safavids set up carpet factories and many Safavid carpets were exported to India, Turkey, and Europe. See "hunting carpets," "Persia," "Polonaise carpets," " 'Portuguese carpets', " "Sanguszko carpets," "Abbas I, Shah," "Tahmâsp, Shah," and "vase carpets."

saff, saph (Arabic, "row, rank"), family prayer rug. Literally, row or rank. A prayer rug containing multiple niches in a row, sometimes referred to as a family prayer rug. Examples were woven throughout the Mideast. There are kilims employing this design. The design may be derived from arcades or series of arches used in mosques rather than from the mihrab itself. See "prayer rug" and "vertical multi-niche prayer rug."

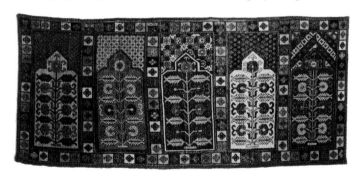

East Turkestan saff *Grogan and Company*

safflower. The flowers of the safflower, *Carthamus tinctoria*, produce a yellow dye. This dye may have been used in some early rugs of China, India, and Tibet.

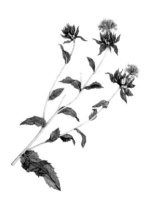

Safflower

saffron. The stigmas of the plant, *Crocus sativus*, which are used to produce a yellow dye. Saffron may have been used to dye some early rugs of China, India, and the Balkans. See "crocin" and "crocus."

"S" group. A group of Turkmen weavings characterized by asymmetric knots open to the left, highly offset warps, long pile, highlights of bluish-red or pink silk, and an overall color of rust red to brick red. Up to thirty percent of the pile surface may be silk in these weavings. Such Turkmen weavings were attributed to the Salor tribe. The exclusive attribution of weavings with this cluster of technical features to the Salor is questioned. See "Salor."

Sahend. A trade designation of recently manufactured Tabriz carpets suggesting higher quality.

sainak. A Turkmen motif consisting of two outward-facing ram's horns. This motif is used in the borders of ensis.

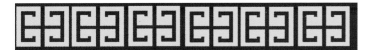

Sainak

sajjâda, sejjadeh (Arabic). Prayer rug.

Sâliâni, Sal'yany. A town located south of Baku on the Kura River and east of the Moghân steppe. Rugs of this area are classified as Baku rugs. See "Baku" and "Caucasus."

Salar Khani. A subtribe of the Baluchi. Their rugs often present variations of major Turkmen guls treated as medallions. See "Baluchi."

Salât (Arabic). Muslim ritual prayer.

salıncak, salachak, salatchyk (Turk.). Cradle or hammock. The term has also been used for prayer rugs in which the corners above the mihrab are not completed so the rug is not rectangular. The top of the rug has three sides, is triangular, or is arched. See "nanu."

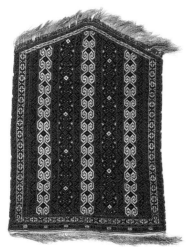

Yomud salıncak *Sothebys*

Salor, Salur. Thought to be the oldest of the Turkmen tribes; there are historical references to the Salor from the eleventh century. In the early nineteenth century, the Salor inhabited the area around Merv in Turkestan until their defeat by the Tekke and Persians in the 1830s. Some Salor now live in Afghanistan. The attribution of their weavings is problematic. Originally the Salor gul, consisting of an octagon with turret-like projections, was believed to identify their work. There is evidence that other tribes used this gul in their own weavings after the defeat and dispersion of the Salor in the 1830s. Some believe that only the "S" group weavings are Salor in origin while weavings with the Salor gul that do not have "S" group features were woven after the defeat of the Salor and should be attributed to the Tekke or Saryk. See "'S' group" and "Turkmen."

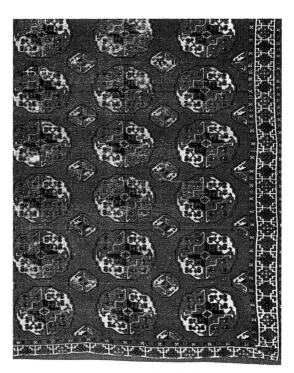

Salor main carpet (detail) *Sothebys*

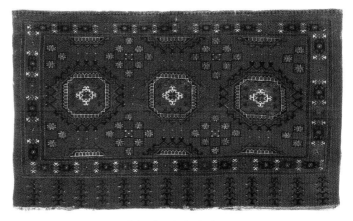

Salor joval *Sothebys*

Salor gul. See "turret gul."

salt bag, namakdan (Persian *namak-dân*, "salt-holder"). A bag of distinctive shape with a neck or spout. It is used to store salt or grain. Most salt bags are of different flat weave structures, but some have pile faces. Typically, salt bags are about 20 inches high and 16 inches wide. These bags are most commonly attributed to the Afshars, the Bakhtiyari, the Baluch, the Lurs, and the Shahsavan.

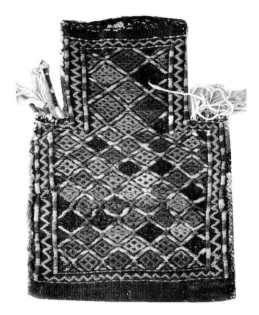

Shahsavan salt bag *Manouchehr Haghighhat*

Saltillo. A town of northern Mexico and the site of a fair in which very finely woven serapes were traded. These serapes were woven by Tlaxcalan Indians settled in Parras, San Esteban and other towns. Production of these serapes began in the early seventeenth century. Wool wefts were used with cotton warps. The structure is usually a plainweave with discontinuous wefts forming small slits with single dovetailing. Designs consisted of horizontal stripes with zigzags, stepped diamonds, and vertical stripes with diamond medallions. See "Tlaxcalans."

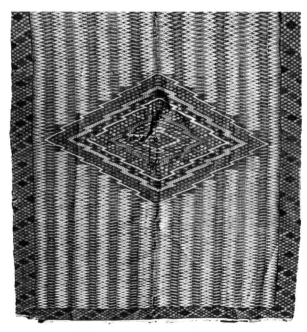

Saltillo serape *Grogan and Company*

Salting group. Rugs with arabesques, animals, cloud bands, and borders with cartouches containing inscriptions. This group of rugs was first attributed to sixteenth-century Persia. This attribution has been questioned in favor of a Turkish origin. Recent dye analyses have tended to confirm a Persian origin. These rugs are woven with the asymmetric knot. Warps are wool or silk. There are highlights of gold and silver threads. This group of rugs is named after a rug given by George Salting to the Victoria and Albert Museum, London. See "Marquand Medallion Carpet."

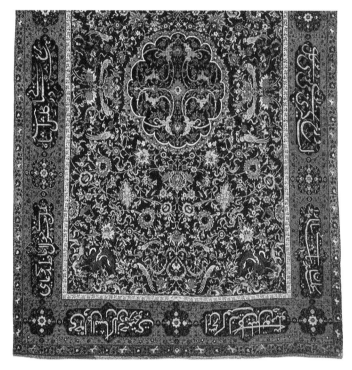

The Salting carpet

Saltiq. A sub-tribe of the Ersari inhabiting an area of northern Afghanistan. Their early rugs have a rosy field color. The design consists of a version of the gulli gul repeated with a continuous tree-like motif within the field on either side of the rug. Later rugs have simplified guls without the tree motif.

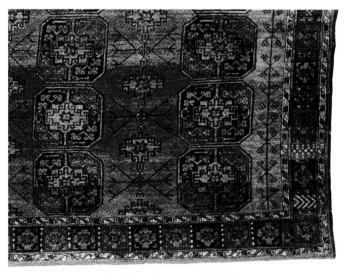

Saltiq main carpet (detail)

Salur. See "Salor."

Sal'yany. See "Sâliâni."

Saman. A Bakhtiari panel design rug woven in the area of Chahâr Mahâl in Iran. The panels are diamond shaped. See "Bakhtiari."

Samangân, Aibak, Aybak. A province and town of north central Afghanistan and formerly the source of flatweaves made by Uzbeks and Arabs in the area. See "Afghanistan."

Samarkand, Samarqand. An ancient khanate and city of western Turkestan. Located on the eastern trade route between Tashkent and Herat, Samarkand was a market for rugs, but not a major weaving center. Some Uzbek weavings may have originated in or around Samarkand. Rugs woven in Kâshgar, Khotan, and Yarkand have been erroneously attributed to Samarkand. See "Eastern Turkestan."

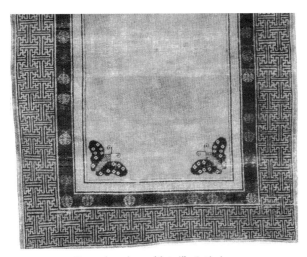

Samarkand rug (detail) *Sothebys*

Samawas. See "Iraq."

samovar border. See "turtle border."

sampler, vagiereh, wagireh (Persian *vâgireh*). A small rug woven with parts of different designs to show the variety of designs available to a prospective rug buyer or as a weaver's guide.

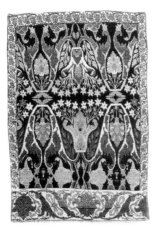

Sampler or Vagiereh (Bijar) *Dr. Herbert J. Exner*

samples, set of samples. A set of rugs, usually 6 by 9 feet, representing a broader range of programmed rugs. A sample rug is shown to a customer in a retail store. The customer may then select a rug, on the basis of the sample, from a range of as many as 20 to 50 different rug sizes and colorways. See "special order."

Sanandaj. See "Senneh."

sandık (Turk., via Persian from Arabic *sundûq*). Chest, coffer, or box.

sandıklı motif. A box-shaped or rectangular motif. Each rectangle or compartment has a wide border. The center of the compartment may be filled by the elibelinde motif.

sandıklık (Turk.). Storage chest cover of pile or flatwoven fabric.

sandpainting rug. A Navajo rug with designs from Navajo ceremonial sandpainting. In sandpainting, images and designs with religious significance are created with colored sand. Sandpaintings are destroyed shortly after they are created. See "yei rugs."

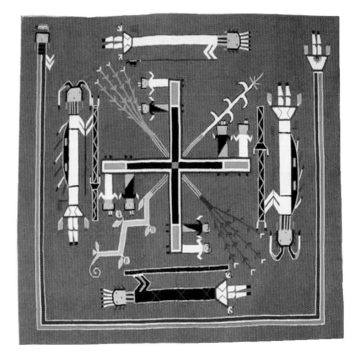

Navajo sandpainting rug *Steve Getzwiller*

Sanguszko group. A group of about fifteen sixteenth and seventeenth-century Safavid carpets of disputed attribution within Persia. They are named after the Polish expatriate, Prince Roman Sanguszko, who possessed an outstanding example. This carpet was for many years in the Metropolitan Museum of Art, New York. These are medallion rugs that show animals and birds, some in combat, within a floral setting. These rugs are woven with the vase structure. See "Persia" and "Safavid."

Sanjâbi, Senjâbi. A Kurdish tribe of the Kermanshah district in

Iran. The tribe was formerly a source of rugs, many with the Herati pattern, and a variety of functional weavings. The foundation is usually cotton with the symmetric knot.

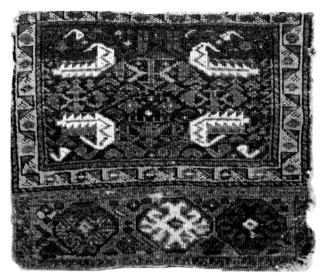

Sanjâbi bag face *Mete Mutlu*

Sanjan. See "Zanjân."

saph. See "saff."

sar (Tibetan). A three-cornered pile weaving placed underneath the crupper of a horse. Also, the name of a village in Tibet.

Sarâb, Serab. A town of northwest Iran between Tabriz and Ardabil. The trade term , "Serapi," derives from this name. Weavers in the area produce runners with repeating diamond or hexagon medallions on a camel-colored field. The field around the medallions may be filled with a lattice or short, angled, parallel hatch lines. The symmetric knot is used at a density of about 50 per square inch. The rug may have an all-wool or wool and cotton foundation. See "Serapi."

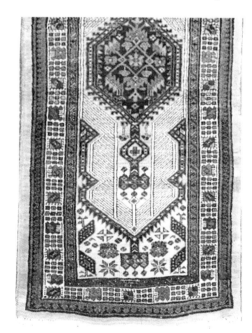

Sarâb rug (detail) *Grogan and Company*

Saraband. See "Serabend."

sar-andâz (Persian). Square ends of a mafrash. See "mafrash."

sarape. See "serape."

Sarband. See "Serabend."

Sardinia. A large island off the west coast of Italy. Peasant weavings of Sardinia include tapestry-woven "*tapinu de mortu*" or burial rugs, used as coffin covers. Bed covers are woven in the "*pibiones*" technique which produces a looped pile, sometimes voided to emphasize designs. The most common peasant weavings of Sardinia are long, narrow, densely-emboidered bench covers. Motifs are flowers, birds, and soldiers on horseback. See "Italy."

sardsir (Persian, "cool region"). Summer pasturage (in the mountains) of nomadic tribes. See "transhumance," "yayla," and "yaylak."

Sar-e Pol, Sari-Pul. A province and town of northern Afghanistan south of Sheberghân and a market for flatweaves woven in the area by Hazaras, Uzbeks, and Pashtuns.

sari. (Turk.) Yellow.

sari gira. A border design used by the Ersari. It is a series of reversing stepped gables.

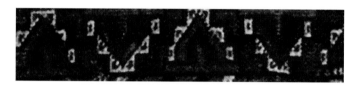

Sari gira border

Sarikeçili. A Turkmen tribe of central and southern Anatolia, some of whom are still nomadic. They produce flatwoven bags and fabrics with geometric motifs.

Sariq, Saryk, Sarukh. The Sariq are a Turkmen tribe of southern Turkestan. Many have settled around Penjdeh and others have settled in northern Afghanistan. Early Sariq rugs have symmetric knots, while very late rugs may have asymmetric knots. Their rugs are double-wefted with offset warps. Late pieces, after 1880, have a purple-brown, brown, or purple field. Earlier pieces have a crimson red field with cotton and silk highlights. The earliest pieces are all wool with an orange-tan field. The most common Sariq gul is a stepped octagon with a central hexagon. The Sariq Temirchin gul is an octagon with a distinctive row of fish-like elements in each quarter and a rectangular central medallion. In Afghanistan, the Sariqs weave the Sariq Mauri using the turret gul. Other contemporary production consists of patterned felts. See "temerchin gul" and "Turkmen."

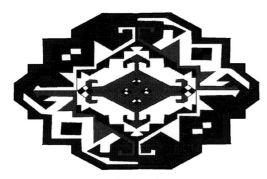

Sariq gul

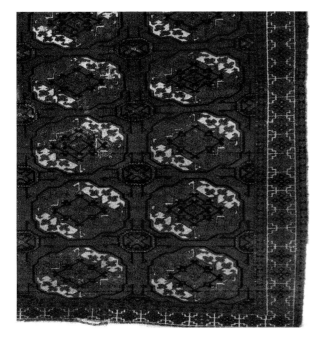

Sariq main carpet (detail) *Sothebys*

Şarkışla. A town of central Anatolia, between Sivas and Kayseri, and a minor source of pile rugs since the eighteenth century. These rugs may have a lattice pattern of serrated diamonds or other geometric motifs.

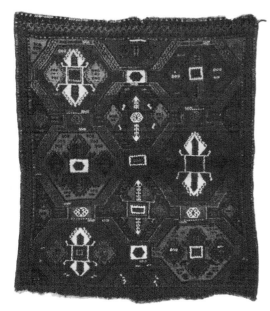

Şarkışla rug *Grogan and Company*

Şarköy. A town that was formerly a part of Bulgaria and is now Pirot, in Serbia. The town and its area have been the source of finely-woven kilims, sometimes referred to as Thracian through confusion with the Turkish town of Şarköy. These kilims employ eccentric wefts in representations of floral and animal motifs. See "Bulgaria," "Kotel," and "Pirot."

Sarouk, Sarouq, Saruq. A village north of Arâk, Iran. Rugs with certain designs woven in Arâk, surrounding villages, and the plains of Farâhân are designated as Sarouks within the rug trade. Nineteenth-century rugs of this area often employed an all-over design of the Herati or Gul Hennai patterns. These were woven with about 100 asymmetric knots per square inch on a cotton foundation. Some smaller Sarouks and Farâhâns of very fine quality were woven in the same period.

In the late nineteenth century, factory rugs were woven in imitation of Tabriz models, using floral medallions. These rugs had higher knot densities on a cotton foundation with offset warps. Knots are asymmetric and wefts are blue. The medallion design was dominant until after the First World War, when Sarouk rugs were woven with detached floral sprays. This design was extraordinarily popular. However, the colors of these rugs were not attractive in the American market. During the 1920s and 1930s, certain dyes of most imported Sarouks were stripped and painted in darker shades. Currently, Sarouk designs of detached floral sprays are used in rugs woven in India, Romania, and China. "Mahal" may be used to describe a second grade of Sarouk and "Mushkabad" may be used to describe the lowest grade of Sarouk. See "Farâhân," "Josan," "Mahal," and "Mohajaran Sarouk."

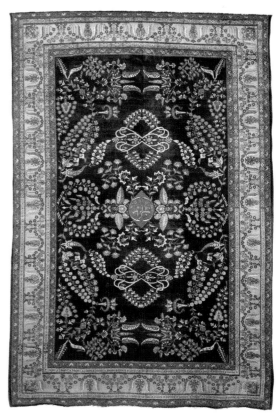

Sarouk rug *Sothebys*

Sarts. An indefinite term applied by the nomadic Turks of Central Asia first to the settled Iranian (Tajik) inhabitants of the oasis towns (e.g. Bokhara and Samarkand), later to the settled Turks (chiefly Uzbeks). See "Uzbeks."

Saruq. See "Sarouk."

Sarukh. See "Sariq."

Saruq Mir. See "mir Serabend."

Saryk. See "Sariq."

sash. See "cummerbund."

satrangi. See "dhurrie."

saturation. Color intensity, and particularly the absence of admixture of white, black or gray. See "Munsell's color theory."

Sauj Bulâq, Mahâbâd. A town in the mountains of northwest Iran, south of Lake Urmiyeh, and a source of Kurdish rugs woven with red wefts and dark colors. The symmetric knot is used on a cotton foundation.

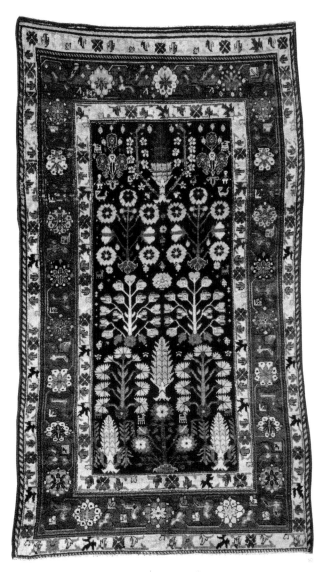

Sauj Bulâq rug *Sothebys*

Sâveh. A small town of northwest Iran near Hamadan. Rugs of this town are woven on a cotton foundation with a knot density of about 65 symmetric knots per square inch. Shahsavan in the area produce a variety of flatweaves.

Savonnerie (French, "soapworks"). The Savonnerie rug workshops were established in Paris by Pierre Dupont in 1628 with the support and protection of Henry IV. Initially, orphans were apprenticed as weavers. Rugs were woven on large vertical looms. A symmetric knot was used on linen warps. Output of the workshops was for royal palaces, state gifts, and special commissions. Designs were created under the supervision of court artists. Designs consisted of naturalistic floral arrangements, military motifs, heraldic references, and some architectural motifs. Some rugs were sculpted to accentuate designs. The period of greatest productivity was from about 1650 to 1789, when the French Revolution interrupted production. In 1825, the Savonnerie workshops were relocated to the Gobelins. The Savonnerie workshops have continued production to the present. See "Aubusson" and "Gobelins."

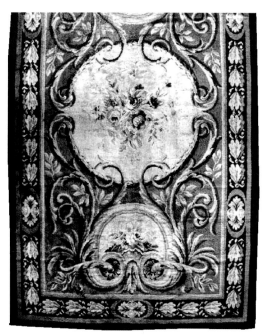

Savonnerie rug (detail) *Doris Leslie Blau*

sawtooth. Suggesting the serrated edge of a saw. A series of triangles forming a simple reciprocating border in oriental rugs. See "reciprocating border."

Sawtooth border

Saxony. A contemporary carpet made of high-density, heat-set fibers. A high-pile Wilton. Also, a power-loomed carpet in which twisted singles are placed so closely that the sheared surface gives the impression of velvet. Also, a type of fine, three-ply yarn imported from Germany and England in the mid-nineteenth century and used in some Navajo blankets.

saz (Turk., "reed, bullrush" or "enchanted forest"). An Ottoman floral design style consisting of long, feathery leaves, rosettes, and palmettes. See "arabesque," "hatayi," and "islimi."

Saz

S-border. Any border consisting of sequential or overlapping "S" or "Z" shapes. See "ajdaha," "dragon and phoenix" and "'S' motif."

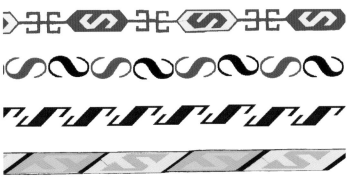

S-borders

scaling in rug design. Scaling in rug design occurs when the same design is used in weaving rugs of different sizes and shapes. Commercially, rugs are produced in standard sizes, for example 9 feet by 12 feet and 6 feet by 9 feet. The length to width proportions are different for these rugs. For a 9 by 12, the shape ratio is 1.33, and for a 6 by 9, the shape ratio is 1.5. Because of this change in shape ratio, some adjustment of the design must be made in size reduction. Additional scaling problems are introduced by the need for symmetrical border designs at corners and by the fact that the same design from a large rug cannot be drawn as finely when reduced in size for a small rug using the same knot density. See "program line" and "shape ratio."

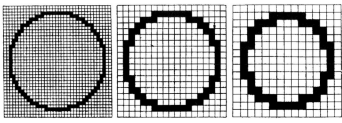

Scaling a circle from fine to coarse knot density

Scandinavian weaving. Rya (pile) rugs and bedcovers are woven in Norway, Sweden, Finland, and Iceland. The earliest literary references are in fifteenth-century Finnish inventory records. The earliest rugs were woven in natural wool colors, with later rugs including yarn dyed yellow and red. Floral designs, deer, horses, birds, naive images of humans, tulips, and hearts are common motifs. Rya rugs used as bedcovers had pile on both sides, with one side carrying designs. A variety of flatweaves were woven, including cushion covers, bed covers, sleigh blankets and bench covers. Different tapestry weave structures were used. See "agedyna," "billdrev," "drätt," "flamskäv," "glossa," "jynne," "lassna," "listas," "röllakan," "rya," and "täcke."

scatter rug. Any small rug that can be easily placed as a decorative accent. Also a rug from 2 by 4 feet up to 4 by 6 feet.

scepter head. See "Laleh Abbasi."

scissor bags. Bags about 4 inches wide and 16 to 20 inches long used to hold sheep-shearing scissors. These are woven by the Shahsavan and some other tribes. The bags may be of knotted pile, soumak, or mixed technique. Most are flatwoven. The Shahsavan term for these bags is *qirkhlig*.

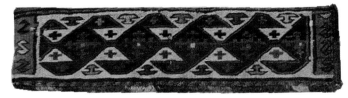

Shahsavan scissor bag *R. John Howe*

Schürmann, Ulrich (1908-1995). A German barrister and scholar of oriental rugs. He is primarily noted for his study of Caucasian rugs and Central Asian rugs. His *Caucasian Rugs*, published in 1964, focused collectors' and researchers' attention on nineteenth and early twentieth century rugs of this region.

scoarta. Romanian for "bark" and for "kilim." See "Romania."

scorching. In the commercial production of hand-knotted rugs, random wool fibers project from the back of the rug when it is taken from the loom. This fuzzy wool may be burned with torches to give the back a smooth, clean, finished appearance.

scorpion motif, toplu çengel (Turk., "ball with hooks"). A diamond with projecting hooks or a rectangle with appendages.

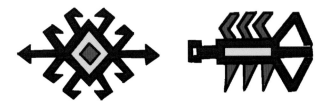

Scorpion motifs

Scotland. Records indicate carpet weaving as early as 1590 in Scotland. Many towns and cities were sites of rug production by the mid-eighteenth century. Scottish weavers produced so much ingrain carpet that it became known as "scotch carpet." Chenille carpets were first manufactured on equipment invented in Scotland in about 1830. Scotland is a major source of power-loomed rugs.

scrolled loop pile. High and low loop pile forming relief patterns, usually leaf or floral designs in the rug.

sculpting, embossing, qali-ha-yi-mahfuri. In carpets, the creation of relief by trimming pile height, especially to accentuate design or color change. Sculpting is a common feature of twentieth-century Chinese rugs and of Indian copies of Chinese rugs.

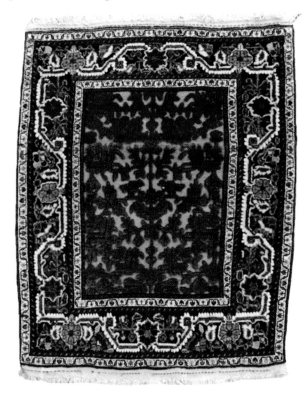

Rug with sculpting (Josan)

seccade (Turk. from Arabic, "prayer rug"). In the rug trade, a rug measuring approximately 4½ feet by 6½ feet.

secondary gul. See "minor gul."

sedjade (Arabic). See "prayer rug."

Sefavid. See "Safavid."

sefid (Persian). White.

segusha. See "soyo gusha."

Seishour, Seischour. A village in the northern part of the Kuba region, possibly Zeikhur. The Seishour cross and the Seishour rose, a design employing the European or cabbage rose, occur most frequently in nineteenth-century rugs attributed to this village.

    The "running dog" border in blue is often found in these rugs. The Seishour cross has been referred to as the "St. Andrew's cross." Typically, the knot density for this design type is 102 symmetric knots per square inch. The rug area is about 30 square feet. Most rugs are all wool, but about 25 percent are cotton wefted.

    The Seishour rose design, with a field of cabbage roses,

typically has a knot density of about 84 symmetric knots per square inch. The rug area is about 31 square feet. These rugs are all wool. See "Caucasus" and "Kuba."

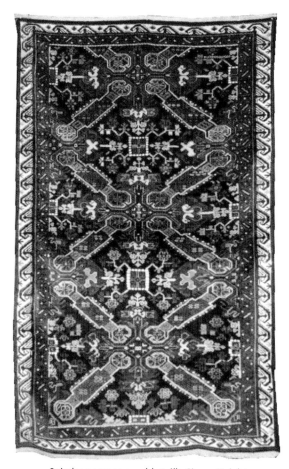

Seischour cross rug (detail) *Simon Knight*

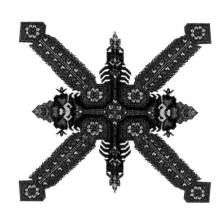

Seishour cross medallion

Seistan, Sistân. An area of eastern Iran and western Afghanistan (chief town, Zâbol). The area is inhabited by Baluchis who weave small rugs in a variety of geometric designs. Designs include all-over patterns, prayer rugs and pictorial rugs, of highly stylized human and animal figures. See "Baluchi."

Seishour border. See "running dog border."

sejjadeh. See "prayer rug."

Seklers, Székelys. An ethnic group of Hungarian origin inhabiting a part of Transylvania in Romania. They weave kilims with wool wefts on hemp warps. Designs are rhomboids, stepped diamonds and zigzags. The kilims are woven in halves on horizontal looms and then sewn together. See "Romania."

Sekme gul. A rectangle containing two concentic, stepped diamonds. It is a gul used in Tekke weavings

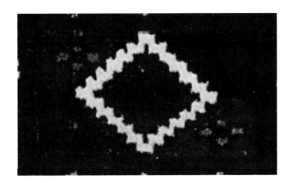

Sekme gul

Selçuk. A town near Konya in Anatolia and the source of small, all-wool carpets, predominantly red. Three elongated hexagons occupy the field. The hexagons contain crosses.

Selendi. A town and district of western Anatolia. Seventeenth-century Selendi rugs have been found in Transylvania churches. Many of these have a white ground. Some are so-called "scorpian" design rugs, more likely palmettes than scorpions.

selimi. See "islimi."

Seljuk. The Seljuks were a dynasty of Oghuz Turkmen origin who founded an empire including Persia, Anatolia, Mesopotamia, and Syria in the eleventh century. Their state in Anatolia survived until the end of the thirteenth century. Some carpets and carpet fragments discovered in mosques in Turkey early in the twentieth century are thought to be of Seljuk or post-Seljuk production, of the thirteenth or fourteenth-century. They consist of stylized geometric floral patterns, some with border designs related to the Kufesque border. The overall character of these rugs suggests later Turkmen designs.

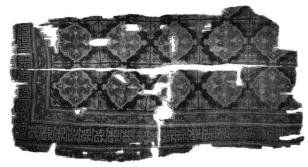

Seljuk rug fragment from the 13th century *Wikimedia Commons*

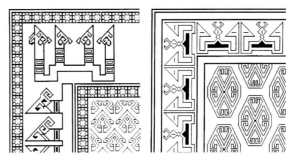

Seljuk rug designs

selvage, selvedge. The warp-wise or side edges of a rug where wefts reverse direction. The selvage may be a complex structure of multiple warps and additional wefts that are not part of the rug foundation. Usually, a selvage consists of two pairs of edge warps and may consist of up to five pairs. See "band-e kenâreh" and "overcasting."

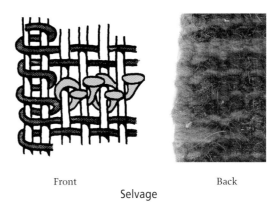

Front   Back

Selvage

selvage, false. Cords sewn or woven parallel to a rug edge to replace or reinforce original edge warps. Some new rugs, mainly from Pakistan, are woven without additional edge warps and false selvages are sewn on off loom.

semi-antique. A rug between fifty and one-hundred years old. See "antique."

Semnân. A town of northern Iran. Rugs of this town copy Safavid designs with some all-over patterns. The foundation is cotton with a knot density of about 160 asymmetric knots per square inch.

Senjâbi. See "Sanjâbi."

Senneh, Sanandaj. Senneh (now Sanandaj) is a city of northwest Iran in Kurdistan. The Kurds of Senneh wove a very fine carpet with knot densities up to 400 symmetric knots per square inch. The foundation is cotton except for a few antique rugs with a silk foundation. These rugs are single-wefted with offset warps. Warps are sometimes dyed in brightly colored bands (haft rang). Designs are the Herati pattern, all-over botehs, and medallions. Very fine horse and saddle blankets were woven. Current production is of much lower quality.

Senneh kilims are woven in other areas of Persian Kurdistan, as well as Senneh. The typical size is about four feet by five feet. Wool is used except when cotton or silk is occasionally used for highlights. Warps are sometimes dyed in brightly colored bands. These are single-piece kilims and extremely finely woven with the slit-weave tapestry structure and employing eccentric wefts. Warps are usually cotton in the finer examples. Designs are intricate floral patterns, often in light green and light red. The Herati pattern is common. It is often used to fill medallions. Senneh kilims have borders on all sides. Patterns include all-over botehs and stripes occupied by blossoms and vines. The designs of Senneh kilims are thought to have been influenced by patronage of the Qajar dynasty during the early nineteenth century. See "Kurds" and "Qajar dynasty."

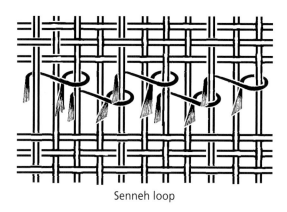

Senneh loop

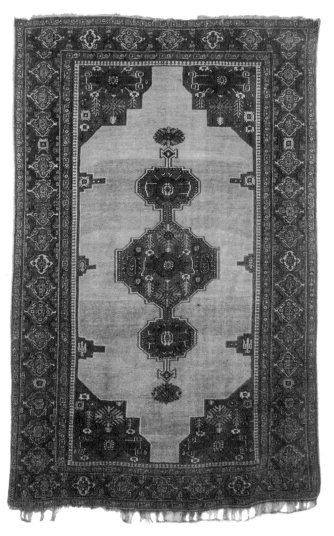

Senneh rug *Grogan and Company*

Senneh knot. See "asymmetric knot."

Senneh loop, Coptic knot. A pile structure used in rug fragments found at Fustat and At-Tar. Supplementary cut weft passes under one warp, over the next warp, and over and around the third warp. Each segment begins on the warp where another segment ends so that two weft ends rise above every third warp, forming the pile. The structure is similar to an asymmetric knot except that it encompasses three warps and not two warps. See "At-Tar" and "Fustat."

sennit. Braiding or oblique interlacing of a narrow structure such as a cord or band.

Serab. See "Sarâb."

Serabend, Saraband, Sarband. A district located southwest of Arâk in western central Iran. Rugs from villages in this area typically have an all-over small boteh pattern, often on a light red or dark blue field. Most of these rugs have symmetric knots and are double-wefted with a cotton foundation. See "mir Serabend" and "shekeri border."

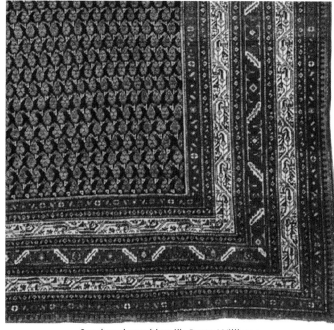

Serabend rug (detail) Peter Willborg

serape, sarape. Large Mexican blankets woven in two pieces and stitched together in the center. Single-piece blankets woven by Navajos. See "bayeta serape," "poncho," and "Saltillo."

Serapi, Serabi ("from Serab"), Serab. A rug woven in the Heriz area of northern Iran. "Serapi" is a trade term used only in America. Some define Serapi as a Heriz rug between 100 and 200 years old. The Serapi may also be defined by its design. This consists of a medallion with pendants and spandrels in the corners of the rug. The medallion is generally hexagonal with a stepped border made up of staggered squares. The field color is often a light madder red or light blue with a contrasting color for the medallion. The design may be derived from early Konya models. These rugs use the symmetric knot and are single-wefted. See "Heriz."

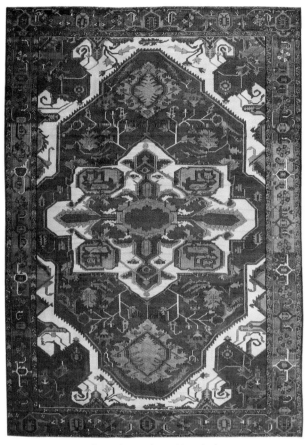

Serapi rug *Jason Nazmiyal*

Serbia. Serbia, formerly a part of Yugoslavia, was the source of slit weave kilims in the nineteenth century. Vegetable dyed wool wefts were woven on hemp or cotton warps. By the beginning of the twentieth century, commercial factory production of kilims had overtaken folk weaving and traditions and design quality declined. See "Pirot kilims" and "Şarköy."

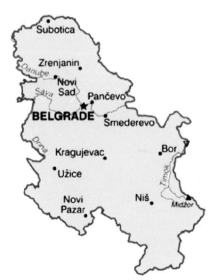

Serbia

serging. Binding of heavy yarn, often done by a specialized machine, on any edge of a carpet to prevent unraveling.

servant blankets, slave blankets. From the seventeenth century through the late nineteenth century, the Spaniards of the American Southwest acquired servants through warfare with the Navajos. These Indian servants (*sirvientes*) were sometimes employed by Spanish households in weaving blankets. Such blankets are extremely rare. Technical characteristics include two-ply warps, lazy lines, and synthetic dyes. See "Rio Grande blankets."

set of samples. See "samples."

set match. A vertically and horizontally symmetric rug pattern which permits easy alignment of butted edges of power-loomed carpet with minimum wastage of carpeting. See "drop match."

Sevan Kazak, Sewan Kazak, Shield Kazak. A group of nineteenth-century rugs attributed to the Lake Sevan district of the Kazak region with field medallion designs in a variety of cruciform shapes. This design is used in rugs attributed to Kuba and Shirvân, as well as those attributed to Kazak. For rugs of this design attributed to Kazak, the mean knot density is 58 symmetric knots per square inch and the area is about 34 square feet. These are all-wool rugs and about 70 percent have red wefts.

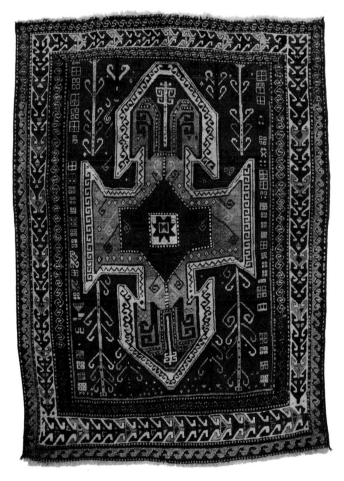

Sevan Kazak rug *Grogan and Company*

sezar (Persian). Three zars. A rug approximately 7½ feet by 5 feet.

shabadan (from Persian *chamadân* or Russian *chemodan*, "portmanteau"). A Kazakh kit bag. See "chavadan."

shabrak (Kurdish). Horse cover with breast pieces.

shadda. A flatwoven cover of the Caucasus, usually brocaded.

shade. A hue with an admixture of black. See "hue," "tint," and "tone."

shaffi. A Baluchi textile covering for stacked bags and provisions.

shag. Long pile on the back of some rugs to provide insulation or softness.

shâgird (Persian). Apprentice. May be used to describe an apprentice weaver. See "nassaj" and "ostâd."

shag rug. Any rug with long, shaggy tufts. More formally, a rug with pile at least ¾ inch in length.

Shah Abbas I. See "Abbas I, Shah."

shah abbasi motif. A symmetrical palmette with two sprays at the top. This motif is used in borders and in combination with other floral elements as an all-over repeat in the field.

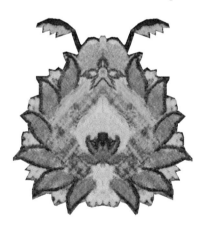

Shah Abbasi motif

shahr (Persian). Town.

Shahr-e Bâbak. A town of central Iran, between Rafsanjân and Neyriz. It is settled by Afshars. Rugs of the area have single or multiple geometric medallions, roughly diamond shaped. The dominant color is brownish red. These rugs have a cotton foundation with a knot density of about 130 per square inch.

Shahr-e Kord, Shahr Kurd. A town of Chahâr Mahâl in southwestern Iran. It is the source of Bakhtiari panel design rugs that are double-wefted and have cotton foundations. In the mid-1970s, Shahr-e Kord had 2,297 weaving shops and fifty spinning and dyeing shops. See "Bakhtiari."

Shahr-i Qumis. A Sassanian archaeological site in northern Iran, west of Dâmghân. Two important carpet fragments were found at the site between 1967 and 1970. One is a piece of flatwoven brown and white wool. It is double-woven, so the simple design appears in reverse on the back. The second piece is a looped pile fragment. It is of white wool. The pile weft does not encircle any warps. These fragments are dated to 600 C.E. See "archaeological sites."

Shahsavan, Shahsevan, Shahseven (Turko-Persian "those who love the King"). A confederation of Turkish-speaking tribes, settled mainly in northwest Iran in or around Moghân, Hashtrud, Miâneh, Khamseh, Bijâr, Qazvin, Sâveh, and Varâmin. See entries under these names. Shahsavan means "those who love the Shah," a title which according to legend was conferred by Shah Abbas on warriors drawn from the tribes to protect Persia's northern border. Weavings of the Shahsavan consist mainly of flatwoven rugs and flatwoven functional pieces such as saddle bags, mafrash, and animal trappings. Most of their work is tapestry woven or soumak (weft wrapping). Shasavan pile carpets are rare.

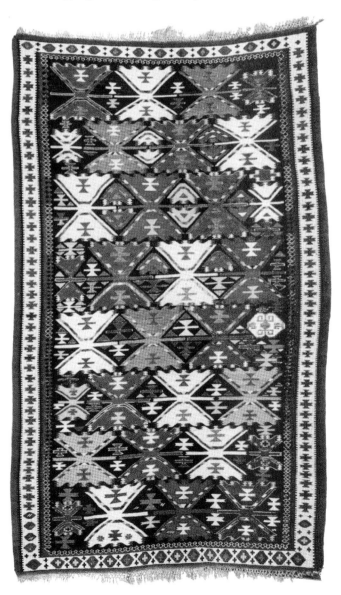

Shahsavan kilim *Roger Hilpp*

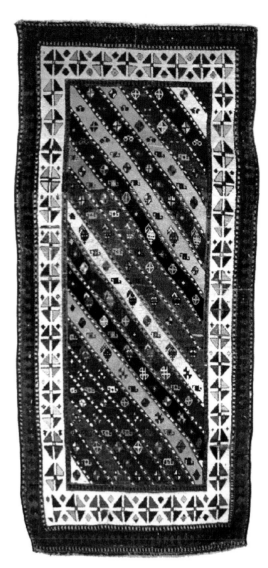

Shahsavan pile rug (detail)

Shah Tahmâsp. See "Tahmâsp, Shah."

Shaker rugs. An American nineteenth-century rug made up of bits of rag threaded onto yarn and then sewn to a canvas backing. Abstract designs were used.

Shaki. See "Nukha."

shâl (Persian). Shawl.

Shâlamzâr. A village of Chahâr Mahâl in central Iran. It is a source of rugs with the Bakhtiari panel design and vase designs. These rugs are double-wefted. See "Bakhtiari."

shâl termeh. Woolen shawls woven in Kerman and Mashhad in Persia during the Safavid period. See "shawl."

shamsa. See "medallion."

Shamshadnee. A town in the Kazak region of the Caucasus and a source of Kazak rugs in the nineteenth century. See "Kazak."

Shanghai. A city of China near the mouth of the Yangtse River. The first Chinese plant for machine spinning yarns was set up in Shanghai in 1890. Shanghai is a major weaving center for contemporary rugs. Wool rugs from Shanghai have a knot density of about 33 to 56 asymmetric knots per square inch. A wide variety of designs are used, including reinterpretations of Aubusson designs. Shanghai is also a source of silk pictorial rugs. See "China."

Shantung, Shandong. A province of northeast China on the Yellow Sea. Contemporary rug production of Shantung consists of copies of Persian designs, finely knotted (100 to 200 asymmetric knots per square inch) and with a short pile. See "China."

shape ratio. The length of a rug (warpwise) divided by its width (weftwise). A rug 10 feet by 8 feet would have a shape ratio of 1.25. The shape ratio is a convenient way of comparing rug formats even though rug areas are different. The shape ratio may be characteristic of a particular attribution.

shaped carpets. Any carpet of unusual shape and intended for some highly specific purpose. A group of Mughal carpets with a red ground and a design of realistic flowering plants. These carpets at the Jaipur Treasury and the Calico Museum, Ahmedabad, were probably woven in the time of Shah Jahan. They have been proposed as fountain or arch surrounds and as floor coverings for an unusually-shaped tent. See "table carpet."

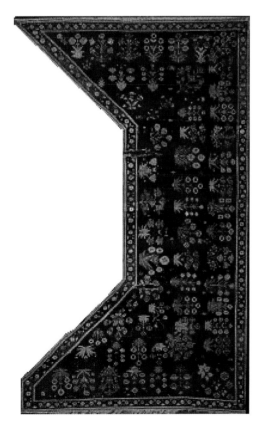

Mughal shaped carpet *R. John Howe*

shaqqeh (Persian, "cleft"). The term is used to describe repeat designs that are cut in half. For example, a series of diamonds becomes a series of triangles.

Sharistan. A district of northern India and a minor source of rugs and shawls. In the early 20th century, Sharistan was a center for contract workshop rug production.

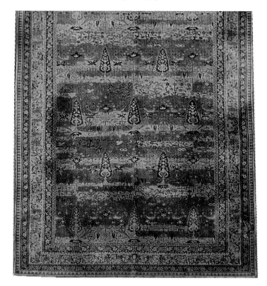

Sharistan rug (detail) *Grogan and Company*

Shakhrisabz. A town in Uzbekistan and a market and production center for floral and vine suzanis. See "suzani."

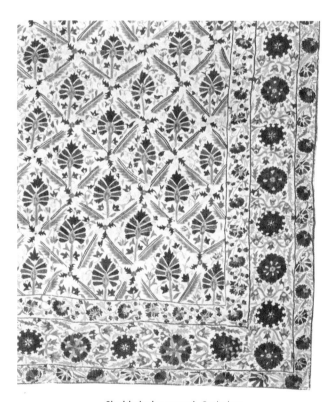

Shakhrisabz susani *Sothebys*

Sharkh. A town of northern Afghanistan. The town is a source of rugs with the Tekke gul and variations. These rugs are double-wefted with offset warps. See "Afghanistan."

shavadan. See "chavadan."

Shavak. A semi-nomadic Kurdish tribe in an area north of Malatya in eastern Anatolia. The tribe weaves runners with lustrous pile, strong colors, and Caucasian designs. Weavers also produce kilims, bags, and cicims.

shawl. A simple garment wrapped around the head and shoulders, usually a square or rectangle. See the following entries:
    Chief's blanket
    doruka
    kashmir
    manta
    Paisley
    poncho
    rumâl
    Saltillo
    shâl termeh
    tápalo
    tahdun
    tilma

Sheberghân, Shibarghân. A town and provincial capital in northern Afghanistan. Formerly, it was a major rug market for production in the area up to the 1960s. Both quality and quantity of production in the area have declined.

shed. The opening formed through the warps when alternate warps are raised to permit the shuttle and wefts to pass through the warps. There is one shed for each set of warps, depending on whether even or odd numbered warps are raised.

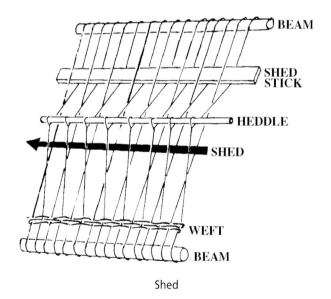

Shed

shedde carpet. A flatwoven carpet of Azerbaijan.

sheep. There are two varieties of sheep that are the primary sources of wool in the Near East and Asia. These are the fat-tailed sheep (*Ovis platura*) and the fat-rumped sheep (*Ovis steatopyga*). The fat-tailed or dumba sheep is most common in the Near East and North Africa. The fat-rumped sheep is common in Central Asia. Both the fat-tailed and fat-rumped sheep are found in China. See "Ak Karaman," "Churro," "karakul," "Merino," "Rambouillet-Merino," and "wool."

Shekarlu. A Luri-led subtribe of the Qashqa'i confederacy, no longer existing as a tribe. Pile rugs attributed to this tribe have a white ground border.

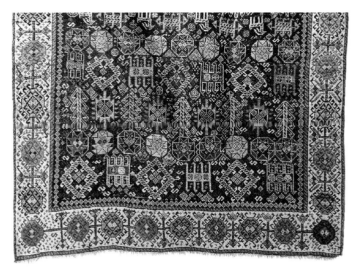

Qashqa'i Shekarlu rug (detail) *Detlev Fischer*

shekeri border. A highly stylized meandering vine border used in Serabend rugs. There are many variations of this border.

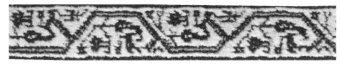

Shekeri border

Sheki. See "Nukha."

Shemakha. The former capital of Shirvân in the Caucasus. The soumak, a flatweave employing a weft wrapping structure, takes its name from this town. See "Caucasus" and "Shirvân."

Shemle motif. A hexagon with horns or hooks used in Salor and Saryk weavings.

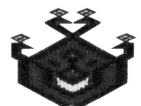

Shemle motif

Sherkat Farsh. An Iranian governmental agency to foster quality carpet production through the use of natural dyes, higher knot densities, and better grades of wool.

Shesh Boluki. See "Shish Boluki."

Shibarghân. See "Sheberghân."

Shield Kazak. A south Caucasian rug with an allover pattern of diagonally arranged, shield-shaped motifs with hooked extensions. The same design is found in some rugs of Shirvân.

Shield carpet, Caucasian. A group of Caucasian carpets, primarily of the 19th century, with field repeats of shield-shaped palmettes. These are often woven with silk or silk and cotton foundations.

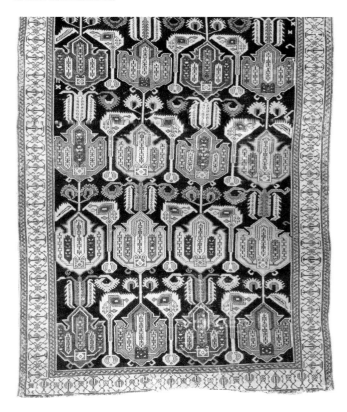

Caucasian shield carpet (detail) *Sothebys*

Shi'i, Shi'a, Shi'ite. See "Islam."

Shigatse. A town of southern Tibet. The town is second to Gyantse as a former source of higher quality Tibetan rugs. Typically, rugs were woven at a knot density of about 50 per square inch. See "Tibet."

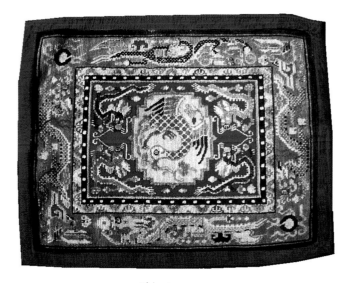

Shigatse rug

Shikâk. A Kurdish tribe of northern Azerbaijan and a source of high quality rugs in the early twentieth century.

Shikargah. A silk fabric of India embroidered with silk or gold threads portraying a hunting scene. Also, a carpet showing a hunting scene.

Shikli Kazak. A group of nineteenth-century rugs from the Kazak region in the Caucasus with designs consisting of a large central lozenge medallion surrounded by six large palmettes. See "Caucasus" and "Kazak."

ship carpet. See "landscape carpet."

Shiprock. A contemporary Navajo weaving area of northwest New Mexico. This is a source of yei rugs, those with images derived from sand paintings of spirits. The dominant color is some shade of brown. See "yei rugs."

Shiraz. The capital city of the province of Fars in southwest Iran. Shiraz is a major market for rugs woven in the province. The term "Shiraz" is used to describe rugs made anywhere in Fars. See "Fars," "Khamseh," and "Qashqa'i."

shirazi, schiraci (German). Selvage.

shyrdak. A Kirghiz felt rug in which differently colored layers of felt are pressed together to create the design.

shireki. Two-sided. A flatwoven cover of the Kerman area about 5 ft. by 8 ft. and usually patterned with a lattice design.

Shirkhâni. A Pashtun tribe occupying an area west of Herat in Afghanistan. Tribal weavers produce rugs with a tree-of-life motif similar to those of the Baluchis.

shirred rugs. American rugs made of accordion-pleated strips of fabric stitched to a backing.

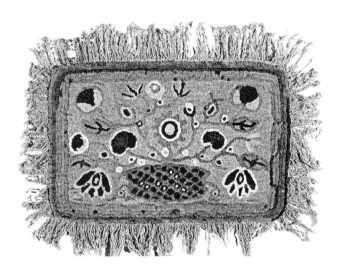

Shirred rug *Ronnie Newman*

Shirvân. Shirvân was formerly a khanate in the central eastern Caucasus, with its capital at Shemakha. Rugs of nineteenth-century Shirvân typically have about 113 symmetric knots per square inch. Their area averages about 28 square feet. They are wool warped and may have either cotton or wool wefts. Many of these rugs are woven in the prayer design with a lattice or

rows of stylized flowers or blossoms occupying the field. Design types are Afshan, Akstafa, Bijov, Chajli, and Marasali. See entries under these names.

Kilims attributed to Shirvân are slit tapestry structure and are woven in a single piece. Usually, there are no borders. Wide bands filled with hexagons alternate with narrow bands of varying designs in a typical kilim. Shirvân is also the name of towns of Khurasan and of Kermanshah in Iran. See "Caucasus."

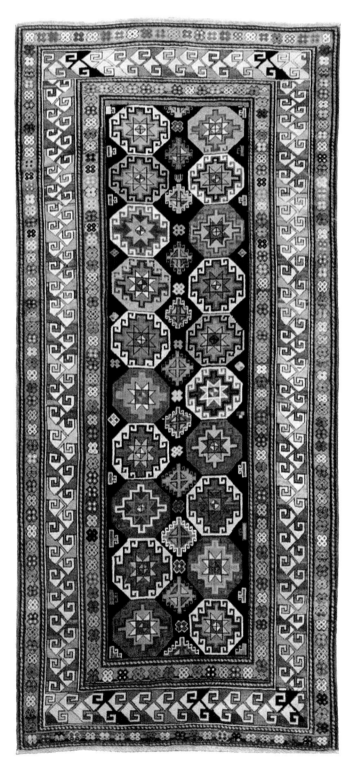

Shirvân rug (detail) *Jason Nazmiyal*

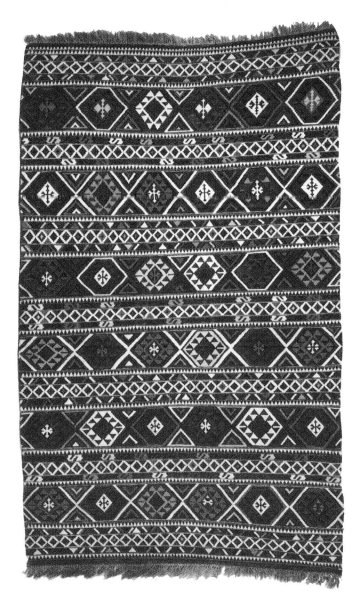

Shirvân kilim *Sothebys*

Shish Boluki, Shesh Boluki, Shish Boluki, meaning "of the six districts," is a tribe of the Qashqa'i Confederacy in southwest Iran. Members of the tribe weave all-wool rugs with asymmetric knots, red wefts, and offset warps. The four-armed "Qashqa'i medallion" is often used in the center of a field of blossoms. The blossoms are connected by lateral branches across the field. Spandrels occupy the corners. See "Qashqa'i."

shoot, shot, pick. A weft or the passage of a weft through a warp shed.

short warped. Any weaving designed and woven so that warps are shorter than wefts.

shotima. Checker board design of Tibetan rugs.

shotor (Persian). Camel.

shotori (Persian). Camel-colored or naturally brown sheep's wool.

shou. A number of Chinese characters symbolizing long life. The most common is circular in form, but there are many elongated variants. The character is sometimes used as a central medallion or a repeated border element in Chinese rugs. See "fu" and "xi."

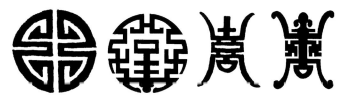

Shou (four forms)

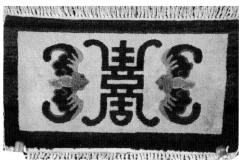

Chinese mat with shou

shoulders. When a rug mat or underlay is too small for the rug, a step forms where the rug extends over the edge of the mat onto the floor. This step is termed "shoulders." Shoulders expose the rugs to excessive wear along the raised edge.

shoushan fuhai. Chinese for "longevity hill" and "happiness sea." This is the sacred mountain motif. See "sacred mountain."

Shrub rugs. A group of seventeenth-century Persian rugs attributed to Kerman. The field of these rugs is occupied by flowering and leafy shrubs in offset rows or columns. Similar designs occur in some Mughal rugs. See "Dudley Carpet."

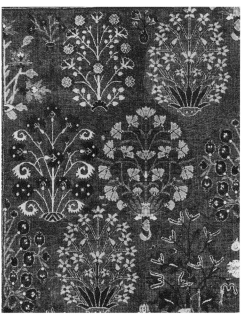

Shrub rug (detail)

Shulaver Kazak. A group of nineteenth-century long rugs from the Kazak region with designs consisting of columns of hexagons or columns of diamonds. See "Kazak."

Shusha. The capital of Karabagh in the Caucasus. Shusha was noted for the high quality and large production of the rugs woven there in the nineteenth century. Large rugs were woven on commission in Shusha. Designs included boteh, minâ khâni, and Herati patterns. Cochineal was used in many of the rugs. See "Caucasus."

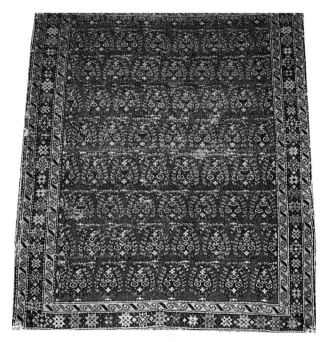

Shusha rug (detail) *Azerbaijan Rugs*

Shushtar. A town of Khuzestan, at the foot of the Zagros range, in southwest Iran. Bakhtiaris in the area weave distinctive kilims with broad, unoccupied, camel-colored borders. The Laleh Abbasi motif is used for the inner borders. The field usually consists of widely-spaced diamond medallions arranged on a central pole or connecting lines. Warps are brown wool. The kilims are woven using a double interlocking weft tapestry structure.

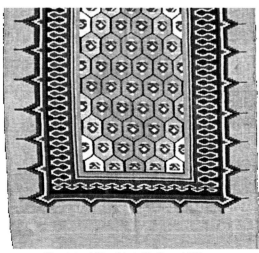

Shushtar kilim (detail) *Peter Willborg*

shushtari (Persian). A cloth wrapping for clothes taken to or from a public bath.

shuttle. A device of wood or metal used to carry wefts through the warps in weaving. The shuttle may contain a spool or winding of weft yarn.

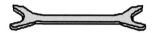

Stick shuttle to hold yarn windings

shyrdak. A Kirghiz felt rug. See "Kirghiz."

Siebenbürgen rugs. See "Transylvanian rugs."

sickle leaf design. A design of large curving lancelolate leaves and palmettes used in some sixteenth and seventeenth-century vase-technique Persian rugs. See "lanceolate leaves."

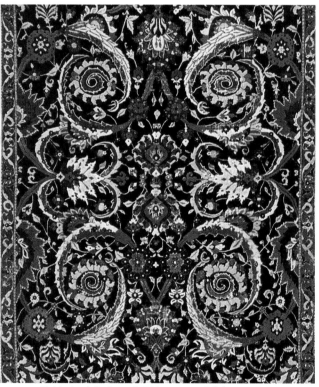

Sickle leaf design of 17th-century Isfahan carpet

signature flag. A small cartouche, usually in the rug border, containing the name of the commercial rug weaver or designer.

Siirt. A provincial capital of southeast Anatolia and a source of blankets woven by Kurds. These blankets (**battaniyas**) are woven of undyed mohair in black, white, gray, and tan and are striped. The seeming pile surface is not true pile but mohair nap "teased up" from heavy wefts. See "Turkey."

Sikkim. A small country located on the southern border of Tibet between Nepal and Bhutan. Rug production in Sikkim began with the immigration of Tibetan refugees in the early 1960s. Tibetan rugs are woven in Sikkim by these refugees.

sileh, sili, zili. This term has a different meaning in western countries than it does in Near Eastern countries and Russia. Caucasian flatweaves with the S-shaped dragon motif with a supplementary weft float are termed "sileh" in the West. The structure consists of an overlay brocade with binding warps on plain weave. Typically, extra wefts float over three or five warps before passing under a single warp. Normally, two ground wefts are skipped as the extra weft is moved vertically to fill in an area. A ribbed appearance is usual where the plain weave is completely covered by extra weft. This structure may be confused with reverse soumak.

In Russia and the Caucasus, Caucasian flatweaves with a bird motif woven in a combination of soumak and tapestry structures are termed "sileh," as are square covers of the Caucasus woven with supplementary weft floats. See "gemyan" and "verneh."

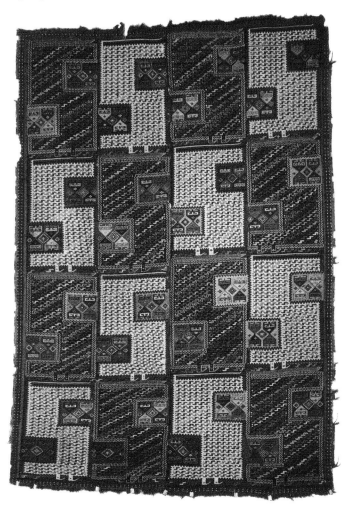

Sileh (Western terminology) *Grogan and Company*

silk. Very fine fibers drawn from the cocoon of the moth *Bombyx mori*. The triangular cross-section of these fibers accounts for the prismatic luster of silk yarn and silk fabric. Filament from the cocoon is about 1/1,200 inch in thickness and from 800 to 1,200 yards in length. Wild or tussar silk, from a variety of moth species, is collected and processed in remote areas of the Near East and Asia. Tussar silk is usually gray, but it can be brown or orange depending on the particular moth species.

Tussar silk does not accept dye well.

One method of distinguishing silk from mercerized cotton is to burn a very small quantity. Silk does not easily sustain a flame and forms a small ball of ash. The smoke smells of burnt feathers. Cotton burns easily and brightly and forms a very fine ash. The smoke smells of burnt paper. See "art silk," "*Antheraea pernyi*," "floss," "kemba," "mercerized cotton," "Silk Road," and "silk weighting."

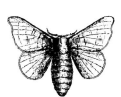 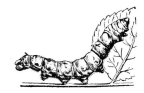

Silk moth and larva

silk accents, silk touch. Small amounts of silk used in the pile of a wool rug to enhance the design.

Silk Route, Silk Road. An ancient overland network of trade routes between China, the Mideast, and Mediterranean countries, originating about 200 C.E. Along this route, eastern spices, Chinese silk, fabrics, and porcelain were traded for western goods. The cloud band and dragon motifs entered the Near Eastern design repertoire from China through trade of the Silk Route. Buddhism entered China along this route. Through various alternates, the route extended from Xi'an in China to Kâshgar in Turkestan. The inner Asian empires formed by Turk and Mongol nomads were based on their power as guardians of the Silk Route and the profits from tolls and services. Archaeological sites along the route have produced fragments of ancient textiles. See "Map of the Silk Route."

silk touch. See "silk accents."

silk weighting. A process through which silk absorbs metallic salts from baths. This is done to increase its weight and thus, its value. Usually, compounds of tin are used. The process weakens and embrittles the silk. Silk weighting was not used in China until about the beginning of the twentieth century. See "weighting."

silver thread. See "metallic thread."

singles, singles yarn. A yarn consisting of unplied fibers all spun in the same direction.

Simonetti Rug. A sixteenth-century Mamluk rug in the collection of the Metropolitan Museum of Art, New York. It is in a long format with the field occupied by a column of five medallions. The center medallion consists of an eight-pointed star. A lobed roundel and an octagon medallion are above and below the center medallion. The border consists of ornamental cartouches. The dominant color is red. The rug is all wool with about 100 asymmetric knots per square inch. Its size is 29 feet 7 inches by 7 feet 10 inches. See "Mamluk."

simurg, symurge, senmurv (Turk., from Persian *simorgh*). A mythical and benevolent bird similar to the phoenix. In Persian mythology, the simurg (bird) and simar (serpent) are analogous to the phoenix and dragon. See "dragon" and "dragon and phoenix."

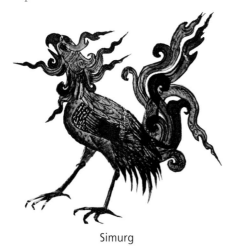

Simurg

Sındırgı. A town of northwestern Anatolia, southeast of Balıkesir. Rugs made in and around this town are similar to those of Yağcıbedir.

sinekli (Turk., "fly-spotted"). An all-over repeat pattern of very small blossoms or circles.

singles yarn. An unplied yarn consisting of fibers all spun in the same direction.

Sinkiang. See "Eastern Turkestan" and "Xinjiang."

sinuous weft. When warps are offset, wefts are alternately straight or bending in their passage through the warps. The bending weft is termed a "sinuous" weft and the straight weft is termed a "cable" weft. See "cable weft" and "lackchi."

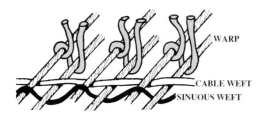

Sinuous weft

Sirjân, Sirjand. A town and valley of southeast Iran lying between Kerman and Neyriz. The town is also called Sa'idâbâd. Afshars are settled near Sirjân and the town is a market for their rugs. These rugs are double-wefted, with the weft of blue cotton and the warp of cotton or wool and squarish in format. A common design consists of a highly geometricized central floral medallion with a geometricized floral cluster in each corner. Another design is a lattice of diamonds, each containing stylized blossoms. Sirjân is a source of very fine soumak rugs and bags woven by Afshars. See "Afshar."

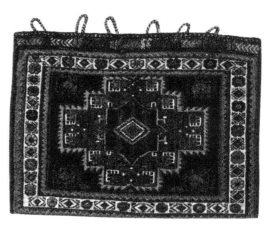

Soumak tubreh (Sirjân area) *P.R.J. Ford*

Sistân. See "Seistan."

Sivas, Sevas. A city in north central Anatolia. Rugs are woven in the city and surrounding villages. A prison in the city is the source for some rugs woven in Persian designs by prisoners. Older rugs of Sivas are all wool. Cotton is increasingly used in the foundation. Rugs have symmetric knots except for those woven at a government-operated weaving school. There, rugs with Persian designs are woven with the asymmetric knot. Prayer rugs from this area have stepped mihrabs. A typical Sivas rug design consists of three rectangular panels, each of a different color and each containing a stepped medallion. Broad vertical striped areas are also common. A meandering vine carnation border with leaves and rosettes is common in rugs of the Sivas district.

Eighteenth and nineteenth-century kilims, woven between Sivas and Malatya, have designs of compartments or rectangular medallions (sandıklı motif). Saffs were also woven in the region. All these kilims have borders and were woven in a single piece. Contemporary prayer kilims are woven in the Sivas area. These prayer kilims have an apricot or salmon-colored border. Warps are white. See "Turkey" and "Zara."

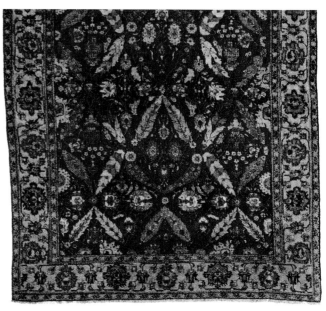

Sivas rug (detail)

sizes, rug. See "rug sizes and shapes."

sizing. Starch or glue added to yarns or fabrics to increase their smoothness, stiffness, or bulk. Sizing is sometimes used in oriental rugs. The loss of sizing in a new rug may be noticed when it is washed for the first time and it becomes loose and floppy. See "weighting."

skein, hank. A loose coil of yarn, not in a ball or on a spindle.

skip plain weave, weft or warp substitution. A plain weave in which elements (warp or weft) float or skip over two or more other elements. In a weft-faced fabric, wefts regularly interlace to form patterning on the front of the fabric and skip areas on the back of the fabric. These are ground wefts and not supplementary wefts.

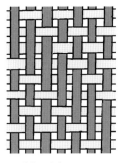

Skip plain weave

skirt. See "elem."

sky door. See "cloud collar."

slave blankets. See "servant blankets."

sleeping rugs. See "blankets."

slit weave. A tapestry weave in which wefts of different colors reverse direction on adjacent warps. Where several rows of wefts reverse direction on the same adjacent warps, a slit in the fabric results. See "kilim" and "tapestry weave."

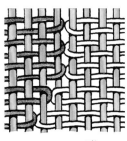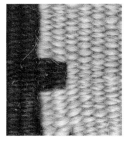

Slit weave tapestry

smatt. In Morocco, a saddlebag. These have a large square opening in the bridge. See "saddlebag."

"S" motif. "S" or "Z" shapes are common motifs in tribal and nomadic rugs. They may be used singly or as a chain (sometimes overlapping) or series in borders and ends of rugs. The motif is thought to represent the dragon. See "ajdaha," "S-border," and "dragon and phoenix."

Smyrna. See "Izmir."

"Smyrna" rug. A reversible Axminster rug manufactured in the United States in the late nineteenth and early twentieth century.

sofreh, soffreh (Persian from Arabic *sufrah*, "provisions, tablecloth"), **sofra** (Turkish). Any small blanket or cover. More specifically, a small, flatwoven, rectangular cloth to be laid on the ground, on which food is prepared or served. The size is about 1½ feet by 4 feet. Many examples are of Kurdish or Baluchi origin. See "dastarkhan," "qalimkar sofreh," "ru-korsi," and "tea sofreh."

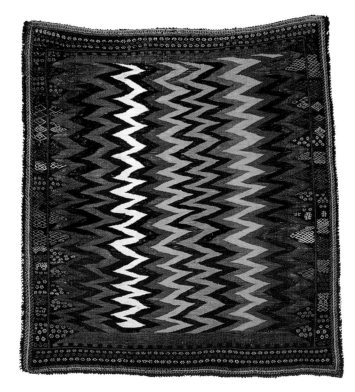

Sofreh (Afshar) *Manoucher Haghighhat*

soft spun. See "angle of twist."

soldat border. A border of nested forks used in Turkmen weavings.

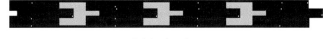

Soldat border

Sonqur. A town of southern Kurdistan in Iran and a source of Kurdish rugs. See "Kolyai."

sophora griffithii. A tree growing in the Near East, the flowers of which are used to prepare a yellow dye. This dye is used in rugs of Baluchistan.

sophora japonica. A tree growing in the Orient, the flowers of which are used to prepare a yellow dye. This dye is used in Chinese rugs.

souf technique. A rug with a flatweave ground and designs executed in pile. See "sculptured."

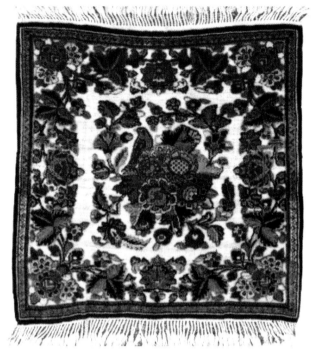

Souf technique Kashan mat *John Collins*

soumak, soumac, sumak. A plain weft wrapping structure. A flatweave in which the weft encircles groups of warps. The encirclement is usually horizontal, though it may be diagonal with loops staggered across warps. There may be vertical movement of weft in the direction of the warps, forming a column of loops, in some weavings. Usually, wefts are supplementary, discontinuous, and move horizontally, looping four warps forward and two warps backward, for example. A movement of two warps forward and one warp backward produces a finer weave.

In plain soumak, all rows of wefts loop in the same direction. In countered soumak (countered weft wrapping), the direction of looping is reversed for alternate rows, producing a herringbone effect. In reverse soumak (vertical weft wrapping), what is normally the back of the weaving becomes the face. In this case, the face is composed primarily of columns of loops and loose thread ends for differently colored weft areas appear on the side where forward looping occurs. The soumac weave may be used without ground weft. Horizontal, diagonal, and vertical weft wrapping may occur in the same piece.

Soumak structures are common in weavings of the Near East and Central Asia. Functional pieces, bags, and animal trappings are soumak woven, as are rugs, blankets, and mats. The Shahsavan and Kurds excel in the use of this structure. Soumak bags without ground wefts were woven in the area of Kars and Van in Anatolia. There are many nineteenth-century Caucasian soumak rugs. The soumak structure was used in some nineteenth-century Swedish weavings. The term "soumak" is thought to derive from the town of Shemakha in the southeastern Caucasus. See "dragon soumak," "gemyan," "medallion soumaks," "sileh," "verneh," and "weft wrapping."

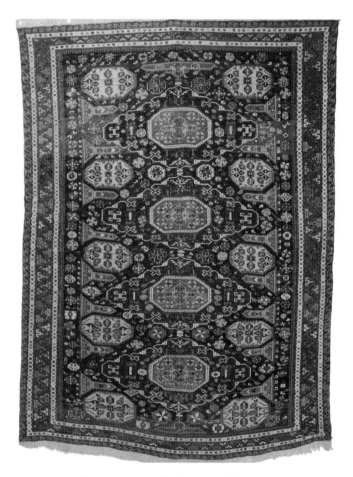

Caucasian soumak *Grogan and Company*

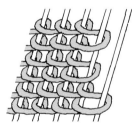
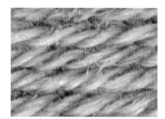

Plain soumak

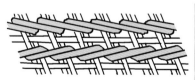
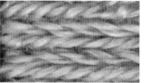

Countered soumak

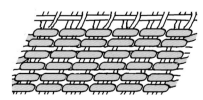

Reverse soumak

Christian, and folk motifs and copies of Turkish motifs

Many rugs bearing coats of arms have survived and these have been used to date rugs from the early part of the fifteenth century. Often these armorial rugs have Kufesque borders. Rugs influenced by Turkish styles have large octagon medallions or Holbein or Lotto designs. In the sixteenth and seventeenth centuries, Turkish styles became dominant. In the eighteenth and nineteenth centuries, copies of Aubusson and Savonnerie carpets were woven using the Turkish knot. See "Admiral carpets," "Alcaraz," "Alpujarra," "Cuenca," "Hispano-Moresque," "Mudejar," "Spanish knot," "Star carpets," "Williams Admiral Carpet," and "wreath carpets."

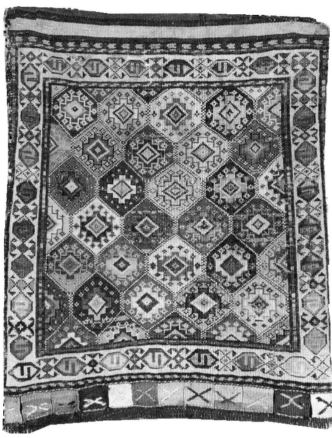

Reverse soumak Caucasian bag *Grogan and Company*

Soyo gusha, segusha. Lakai wall hanging or bedding decoration, often of fine silk needlework and sometimes V-shaped. See "Lakai."

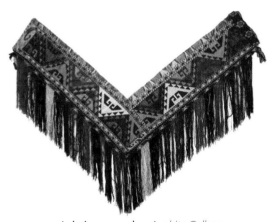

Lakai soyo gusha *Anahita Gallery*

Spain. Most of the Iberian peninsula was under Muslim rule from the eighth until the thirteenth century. The Muslims were finally expelled in 1492. Records show that Spain was an important rug production area from the twelfth century. Existing Spanish cut-pile rugs from the fifteenth through the seventeenth centuries were woven with knots tied to single warps. Knots are in staggered rows, usually with a single three-stranded weft. Mudejars (Moors, i.e. Muslims of Arab or Berber origin who remained in Spain after the Christian reconquest) wove rugs in two styles: a synthesis of Islamic,

spandrel. Designs spanning the corners of a rug inside the borders. In central medallion rugs, the spandrel is often a quarter of the medallion. The areas in either corner of a rug above a mihrab. See "corner."

Spandrels

Spanish knot. A pile knot tied on a single warp and staggered or offset on adjacent warps. This knot is thought to have originated in North Africa. Coptic weavers in the eighth and ninth centuries used a similar knot. See "Senneh loop."

Sparta. See "Isparta."

special order. The ordering of a rug by the retailer from a wholesaler to serve a customer who purchased a rug on the basis of a sample. See "samples."

spectrophotometry. In spectrophotometry, a solution is produced from sample dyed material. A curve from the spectrum of this solution is then compared to reference spectra curves of different dyes to identify the dye in the sample. This method is used with increasing success to identify dyes used in oriental rugs as more reference spectra are developed from dyes. See "chromatography."

spin. The relative direction of twist of yarns, "Z" spun or "S" spun. When conceptually superimposed over the yarn, the diagonal line in the "Z" or "S" parallels the direction of spin. An "I" or "U" is sometimes used to indicate unspun yarn. Most yarns have singles that are "Z" spun. These singles are usually "S" plied to make up the yarn. In conventional notation, "Z2S" means two Z-spun singles are plied with an S spin. In oriental rugs, "S" spun singles are found almost exclusively in weavings from North Africa and in weavings from the western Arabian peninsula. See "ply" and "winder plied."

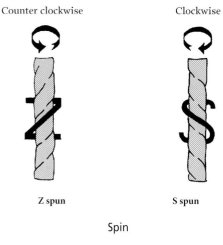

Spin

spindle. A wooden rod, usually tapering about 8 to 12 inches in length. A disk acts as a flywheel. Yarn is wound on the spindle as it is spun and drawn from the distaff. The distaff is another rod on which unspun fiber is mounted. See "malacate" and "spinning wheel."

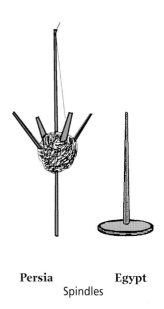

Spindles

Spindle bag. See "iğsalik."

spinning, machine. Machine spinning of yarns began in England in the eighteenth century. The machine was called a spinning jenny. During the nineteenth century, machine-spun yarns displaced hand-spun yarns in all major weaving centers. The approximate date at which machine-spun yarns were introduced to a rug-weaving area can be used in dating rugs

from the area, depending on the yarn used. Hand spun yarns have greater variation in thickness and angle of twist than machine-spun yarns. See "dating rugs" and "hand-spun."

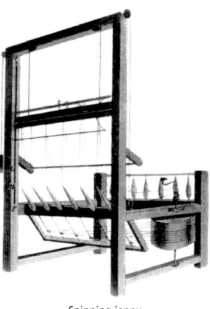

Spinning jenny

spinning wheel. The foot-operated spinning wheel, familiar in Europe and America, is not used in the Near East. Rather, small hand-operated spinning wheels are used to spin yarn in small towns and villages. Nomadic peoples rely on the spindle in spinning yarn. See "çıcrık" and "spindle."

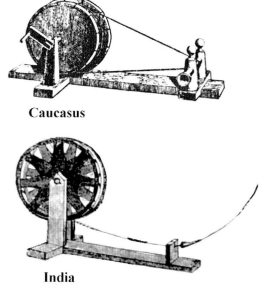

Spinning wheels

spirit trail. A very thin line connecting the field of a Navajo rug to the edge of the rug. Some weavers believe the line permits the "creative spirit" of the weaver to escape from the rug.

split leaf arabesque. A common motif used in both borders and fields of rugs. It is the basis of the Garrus design in Bijâr rugs. See "arabesque."

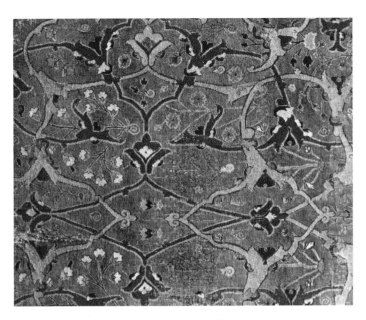

Split leaf arabesque (Garrus)

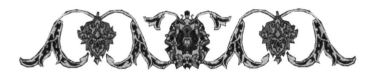

Split leaf arabesque border (Isfahan)

spoon bag, qâshoqdân (Persian), kaşıklık (Turk.). A bag used to hold spoons, knives, and small articles. The bags are often woven with netting and tassels on a band to be hung around the neck of a camel.

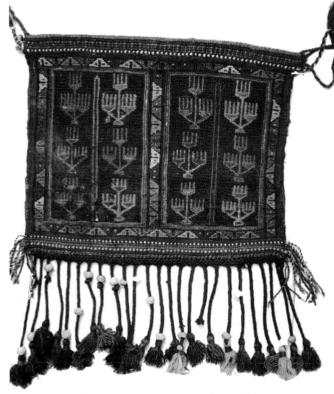

Afshar spoon bag *Manouchehr Haghighat*

Spring Carpet of Chosroes (Khosru), Baharestan. An immense carpet mentioned in historical sources as belonging to the Sassanian King Chosroes II. This carpet in his palace at Ctesiphon, possibly a flatweave, was said to be brocaded with gold and silver thread and adorned with pearls and other gems. It may have been an ancient example of the garden carpet design.

sprouts. In power-loomed rugs. yarn ends extending above the pile that were not properly cut in shearing. To correct the defect, sprouts should be cut and not pulled.

squinch. One of four arches thrown across corners of a square or octagonal room to create a zone of transition on which a dome may then be constructed. "Squinch" may also refer to corner brackets in Turkish rugs.

Srinagar. The capital of Kashmir and a weaving center from the fifteenth century. Srinagar was the source of handwoven shawls based on boteh patterns in the early nineteenth century. These were later reproduced by machine in Paisley, Scotland. Rug production in Srinagar became significant in the late nineteenth century. The city is the source of the finest contemporary Kashmir rugs. These are all-silk rugs and part-wool and part-silk rugs. See "Kashmir" and "shawl."

S-spun. Yarn spun in a clockwise direction. The diagonal in the "S" suggests the direction of spin. See "spin."

stains. The same property of wool that makes it receptive to natural dyes makes it susceptible to staining. There are many effective stain removal recipes addressed to specific staining substances. However, there is always a risk that such recipes will also affect dyes in a rug. No stain removal compound or procedure should be used before testing it on the dyes on a very small portion of the back of the rug.

stair rod. A rod of brass or wood fastened to the back of each step to hold a stair runner in place.

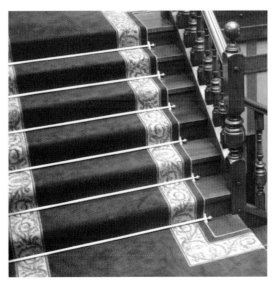

Stair rods in use *Stairrods Ltd.*

staple. The average length of fibers in a yarn.

star. A conventional figure of three or more points radiating symmetrically from a common center. See "Crivelli rugs," "hexagram," "Lesghi Star," "octagram," "olduz," "pentagram," "Star carpets," "Star Kazak," "Star of David," "Star of Solomon," "Star Ushak," and "Vallero blankets."

Star carpets. A group of fifteenth-century Spanish rugs attributed to Alcaraz. These rugs have single or multiple columns of large, complex, 24-pointed stars, each star within an octagon. These stars are similar to those in Crivelli rugs.

Star Kazak. A group of nineteenth-century Kazak rugs with a design of large, eight-pointed stars. The mean knot density for rugs of this design type is 68 symmetric knots per square inch and the area is about 34 square feet. These are all-wool rugs with red wefts. Star Kazaks may be classified as types A through D. See "Caucasus."

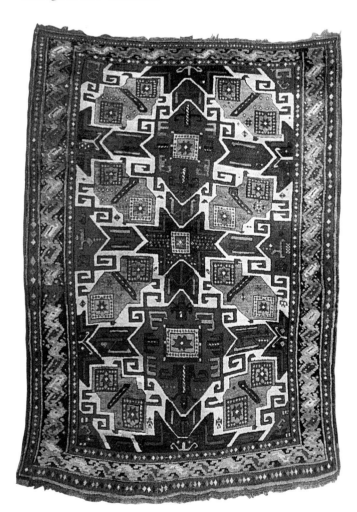

Star Kazak *Sothebys*

Star of David. A six-pointed star. A hexagram.

Star Ushak. A pattern of large, eight-lobed, blue stars filled with yellow arabesques alternating with indented diamonds on a red field. Rugs with this design were woven in sixteenth and seventeenth-century Ushak workshops in Anatolia. These were usually large rugs of about 14 by 7 feet. They are all-wool rugs with the symmetric knot at a density of about 90 knots per square inch. Star Ushaks are represented in early Italian paintings. The earliest such picture was painted by Paris Bordone in 1534. See "Ushak."

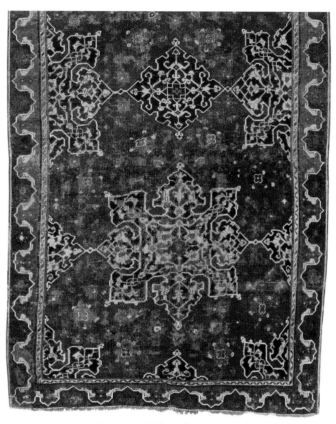

Star Ushak (detail) *Sothebys*

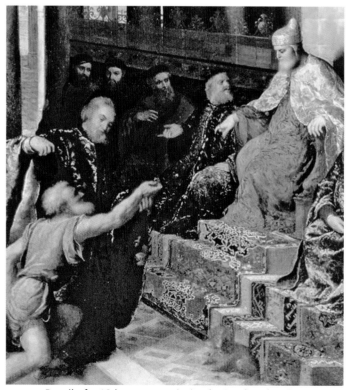

Detail of a 16th-century painting by Bordon showing a stair carpet with a Star Ushak design

Star of Solomon. A six-pointed star. A hexagram.

stepped. An outline of staggered or offset right angles. A stepped outline may be used for medallions, geometric figures, a mihrab, or images in a rug. In some cases, a stepped outline is dictated by the coarseness of knotting in a rug.

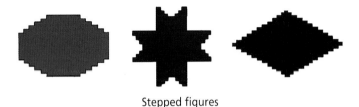

Stepped figures

stitch. A complete movement of an element through a fabric or the element that remains after such a movement. Within the rug trade, stitch refers to knot count as in stitches per inch.

Storm pattern. A Navajo rug design originating in the Tuba City area. In earlier versions, it consists of a central rectangle and four corner rectangles (quincunx), each with horizontal parallel projections. Zigzag lines or lightening bolts connect the corner rectangles (houses of the wind) to the central rectangle (center of the world). In later versions, various motifs may be substituted for the rectangles. See "Navajo rugs."

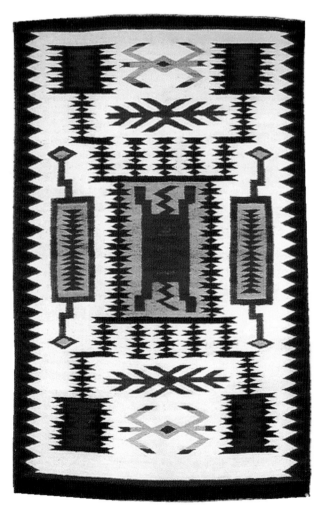

Storm pattern *Steve Getzwiller*

strap. See "band."

Strapwork carpets. A group of seventeenth-century Persian carpets with arabesque designs of solid color bands. The bands contain a floral vine. The bands form an all-over pattern of vertical columns of overlapping spirals. Also, later rug designs with strap-like lattices. See "Jaipur Strapwork Carpet."

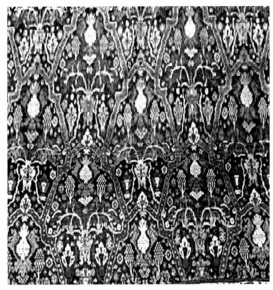

Bijar strapwork carpet (detail) *John Collins*

Strathmore Carpet. A copy of an Indo-Persian carpet woven in England in the early seventeenth century. It includes the monogram of John Lyon. The foundation is hemp and the symmetric knot is used with a density of 60 knots per square inch.

striped. In fabrics, parallel lines or bands of color, pattern, or texture.

stripping. Bleaching a rug so that it may be dyed another color.

structural analysis. See "technical analysis."

structure. The composition and specific arrangement of elements constituting a fabric. Strictly, this is distinct from "technique" which is the process through which a structure is created. Different techniques can produce the same structure. See "technique."

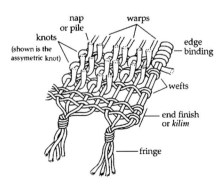

Knotted pile rug structure *Jacobsen Rugs*

Suiyuan. A province of Inner Mongolia in China where there is rug production. Its capital is Guizhow. See "Baotou," "China," and "Guizhow."

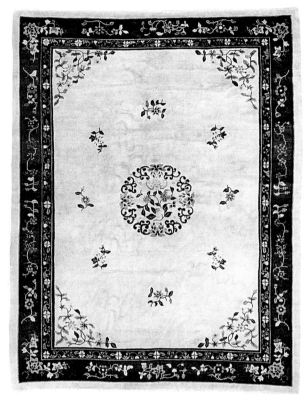

Suiyuan rug *Peter Willborg*

Süleyman I "the Magnificent." Sultan of the Ottoman Empire from 1520 to 1566. He expanded the empire to its greatest geographic extent. Architecture, painting, calligraphy, book production, ceramics, and weaving achieved great artistic development in his reign. Carpets were woven in imperial workshops. These carpets were woven with the asymmetric knot. Many finely woven prayer rugs have been attributed to the reign of Süleyman I.

Sultanabad. See "Arâk."

Sultan's head prayer rug. A prayer rug in which there are curvilinear indentations in the upper part of the mihrab arch, creating the impression of head and shoulders. The arch peaks with reversing curves.

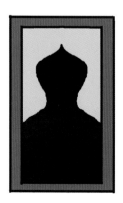 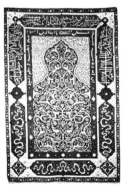

Sultan's head prayer rug

sumac. The wood of the sumac tree, *Rhus* family, may have been used as a yellow dye in rugs of China

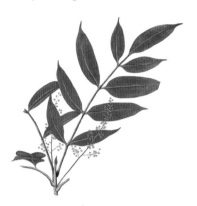

Sumac

sumach. See "soumak."

sumak. See "soumak."

Sunburst Kazak. See "Chelaberd."

Sunni. See "Islam."

"super" Chinese rugs. A trade term for contemporary Chinese rugs with 90-line knot density, ⅝-inch pile height and a closed back. See "China."

supplementary warp or weft, extra warp or weft. A weft that is not structurally essential to a fabric, but is added to create a textured or ornamental effect. See "eccentric weft."

supplementary weft float patterning. Ornamentation of a ground fabric with supplementary wefts, continuous from selvage to selvage, that skip over two or more adjacent warp.

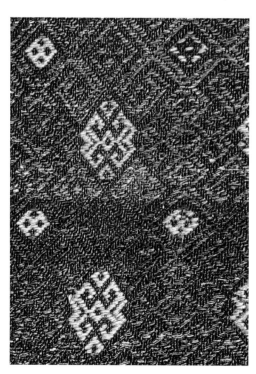

Karabagh supplementary weft float patterning *R. John Howe*

Surakhany, Surhanni. A town east of Baku on the Apsheron peninsula in the Caucasus. Nineteenth-century rugs of this area are classified as Baku rugs. See "Baku."

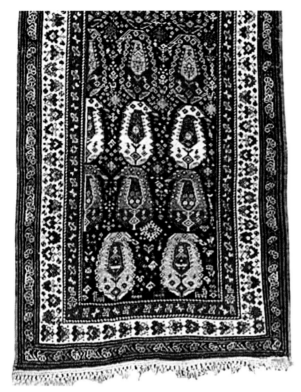

Surakhany rug (detail) *J. Barry O'Connell*

Surchi. A Kurdish tribe of northeastern Iraq. The tribe was a minor source of rugs, bags, and kilims.

Surhanni. See "Surakhany."

surme'i (Persian, from *sormeh*, "antimony"). Bluish-black, dark blue.

suwari. A small, shield-shaped, silk-bordered, decorative hanging of the Uzbeks.

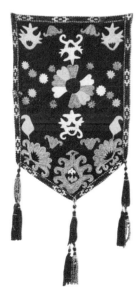

Suwari *Thomas Cole and John Wertime*

suzan (Persian). Needle.

suzanduz (Persian, "needlework"). Coarse needlework patterning. The term is incorrectly applied to the soumac weave.

suzani, suzanni (Persian). Dowry pieces of embroidered needlework used as wall hangings, curtains, and bed covers. Most were woven in an area within present-day Uzbekistan. Bukhara, Samarkand, Tashkent, and the town of Shahrisyabz (Shahr-i sabz) were primary sources. The most finely embroidered suzanis were from Sharhrisyabz. Most consist of silk embroidery on cotton panels which are sewn together. The most common design consists of large and small red roundels with interconnecting vines and arabesques in green and blue. Wide borders contain similar designs. Finer suzanis are attributed to the nineteenth century, before they became articles of trade in the twentieth century.

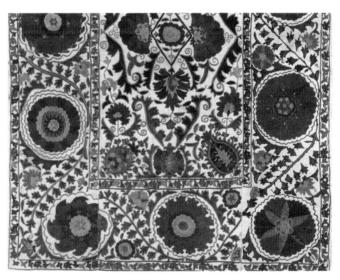

Uzbeki suzani (detail)

swastika, pech (Turk., from Persian), **pinwheel, triskellion, wan** (Chinese). An ancient and primitive design shared by many cultures of three or more radiating arms, all crooked or spiraled in the same direction. In some cultures, this symbol represents the sun. See "Pinwheel Kazak," "triskellion," and "wan."

Chinese   Caucasian   Native American

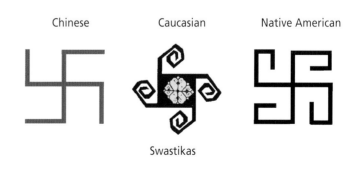

Swastikas

swastika border. A border of linked swastikas often found in Chinese rugs.

Swastika border

Sweden. See "Scandinavian weavings."

Swedish Royal Hunting Carpet. A sixteenth-century silk Persian carpet in the Royal Palace in Stockholm, Sweden. It is in the Royal Collection. There is an eight-pointed central star medallion with pendants surrounded by cloud bands and mounted hunters pursuing different animals. The medallion and spandrels contain dragons and phoenixes. The main border is occupied by scrollwork, blossoms, and small birds and animals. This carpet is all silk except for some areas of brocaded metal thread. Its size is 18 feet by 9 feet.

symbolism in rugs. Some designs or motifs have a long tradition of usage in oriental rugs. In some cases, symbolic meaning is attributed to these designs or motifs. There is considerable ambiguity in interpreting such symbols due to historical change or loss of symbolic meaning. This change or loss of meaning can occur because of:
- inter-cultural borrowing of motifs
- passage of time and changing circumstances of those societies using the designs or motifs
- design evolution of the symbol, often through progressive abstraction

Through tradition, weavers continue to use symbols long after symbolic meanings are lost. Symbolic meaning may be incorrectly supposed where a design has been used for purely aesthetic reasons. Some believe there is a continuous design tradition relating certain bronzes of eighth to sixth-century B.C.E. Luristan to motifs (the animal head column) in contemporary southwest Iranian weavings. See "animal head motif."

The iconography of prayer rugs is comparatively unambiguous. The mihrab represents the mihrab in the mosque wall facing Mecca. Handprints in the spandrels suggest the placement of hands in prayer and the five fingers, the five pillars of Islam. Hanging lamps, ewers, and kufesque borders all allude to ritual objects or the mosque. In some prayer rugs, the Ka'ba is represented. There is extensive religious symbolism in Chinese rugs. See "Buddhist symbols," "Confucian symbols," and "Taoist symbols."

Talismanic symbols suggest direct magical power. The muska represented in Turkish rugs is an example. Tribal weavers of Moroccan rugs ascribe protective powers to the motifs in their rugs.

Totemic symbols derive from animals associated with tribal identity: the Ak Kuyunlu (white sheep) and Kara Kuyunlu (black sheep) Turkmen are examples. The two-headed animal image on the Tauk Noska gul is another example.

Tamgas are livestock brands. These have been recognized in nomadic rugs and may signal a tribal identity.

Related to totemic symbols are heraldic symbols or blazons. These, too, are found in rugs, not only those commissioned by Europeans, but also in the rugs of Near Eastern royalty. See "Admiral carpets" and "Kerman armori."

Of all rugs, those of the Chinese have a repertoire of symbols with the most explicit meanings. Different flowers, animals, fruits, and objects have clear symbolic references. See "China."

There are universal symbols, such as the tree-of-life, that are used again and again in many forms. Universal symbols have many different meanings. Attempts to specify the meaning in a particular context are often arbitrary. See "animal motifs," "birth symbol," and "floral motifs."

symmetric knot. The Turkish (Turkbaff), Ghiordes, or Gördes knot. This knot is tied on two warps as shown.

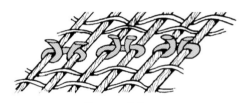

Symmetric knot

symurge. See "simurg."

synagogue rug. A pile rug commissioned for use in a synagogue. It may be used as a Torah curtain. Such rugs may show Hebraic ritual objects. Hebrew inscriptions may be included in the design. See "Bezalel."

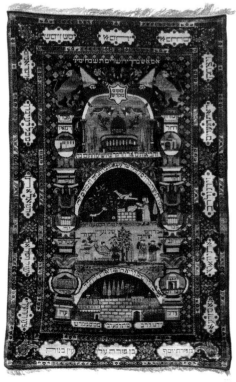

Kashan synagogue rug   *Sothebys*

synthetic dye. See "dye, synthetic."

synthetic fibers. See "acrylic," "nylon," "olefin," "orlon," and "polyester."

Syria. Aleppo, a city of northwest Syria, was a collecting point for rugs woven by certain Kurdish tribes and kilims woven by Kurdish or Bedouin tribes. See "Aleppo."

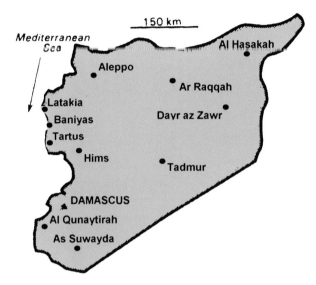

Syria

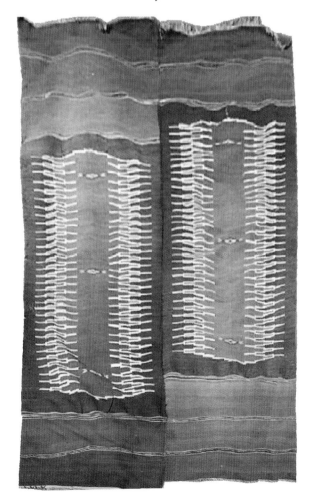

Syrian kilim *Peter Pap Oriental Rugs Inc*

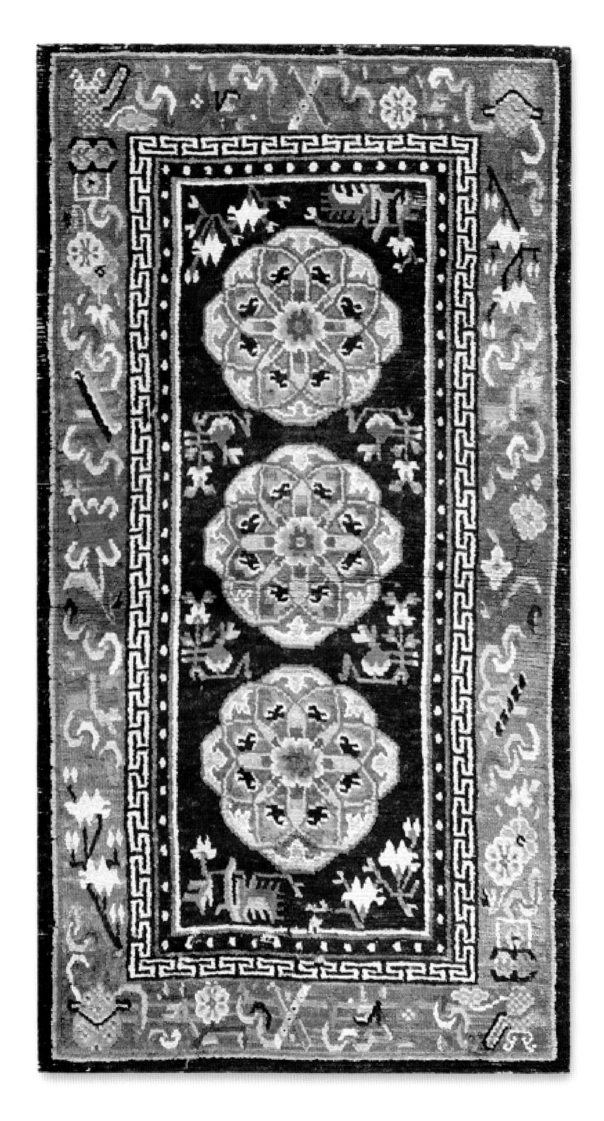

tabachi, dead wool. This term refers to wool removed from a sheepskin in a tannery by a chemical process rather than by shearing. Such wool does not accept dyes well.

tabak (Turk. "plate"). A term used by weavers of Ezine for the kaikalak motif. See "kaikalak."

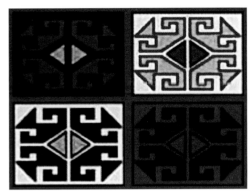

Tabak *kaikalak*

Tabas. A town of southwestern Khurasan in Iran (not the village in southeastern Khurasan) and a source of rugs with medallion designs similar to those of Nain, though not as finely woven. The knot is asymmetrical on a cotton foundation with wool pile and silk accents.

Tabassaran. A people of the Lesghi language group inhabiting Daghestan in the Caucasus. They are known as weavers of fine rugs. As recently as 1984, Tabassaran women brought their rugs for sale in a monthly market in Derbend. Also, an area within Daghestan. See "Caucasus" and "Daghestan."

Taba Tabriz. A contemporary, thick Tabriz rug of rust and ivory with hunting or Safavid medallion designs.

table carpet. Circular and cruciform pile rugs woven for the European market in sixteenth and seventeenth-century Cairo. Earlier rugs have Mamluk designs and later rugs have Ottoman designs. See "rug sizes and shapes."

tablet weaving, card weaving. The use of punctured cards through which warp passes to produce warp twining. Turning the cards creates sheds for weft. This method of weaving is often used for bands, belts, and straps. Warp twining occurs when warps are crossed or twisted after the passage of a weft. Tablet-woven bands may be edge sewn to create larger fabrics. See "jijim."

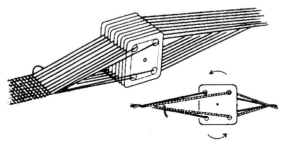

Tablet-woven band

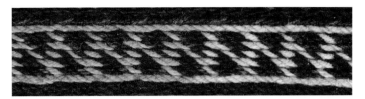

Tablet-woven band

Tabriz. A city of northwestern Iran and the capital of Iranian Azerbaijan. Carpets may have been woven in Tabriz from the fifteenth century. Tabriz was the market center for rugs forming Persia's great export trade beginning in the mid-nineteenth century. Rugs woven about this time in Tabriz were in traditional court designs and used harsh wool. Modern rugs woven in and around Tabriz are factory products. They are usually double-wefted with a cotton foundation and a symmetric knot. Knot densities range from about 40 to 400 knots per square inch. Some silk rugs were woven in Tabriz. Many designs are used, including medallions, hunting designs, prayer designs, and pictorial rugs. Notable early twentieth-century weaver-designers of Tabriz include Sadakiani and Faradji. See "Tabriz Haji Jalil," "PETAG," and "Taba Tabriz."

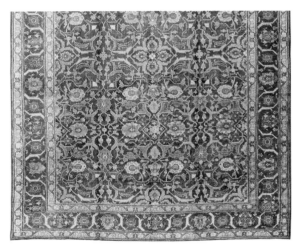

Tabriz carpet *Jason Nazmiyal*

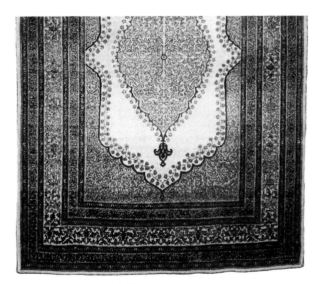

Tabriz Haji Jalil rug *Grogan and Company*

Tabriz Haji Jalil. A putative designer of Tabriz rugs from the late 19th century. High-quality Tabriz rugs may be so attributed even though there is no conclusive evidence Haji Jalil actually existed.

tacheh (Persian). An Iranian tribal bag. Sizes vary but are typically 3 feet by 3 feet. Tachehs may be woven in pairs. Often, there is pile on about a quarter of the surface. This pile surface can be viewed when the bags are filled and stacked.

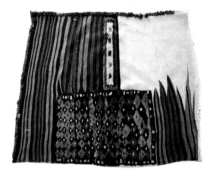

Lurs tacheh face *Manouchehr Haghighat*

täcke (Swedish). A flatwoven bedcover or blanket.

Tadjiks, Tadzhiks. See "Tajiks."

Tafrash, Tafresh, Tafrish. A town of nothwestern Iran. The town is a source of rugs with medallions, pendants and arabesques. The field is usually red. The asymmetric knot is used on a cotton foundation with single wefts.

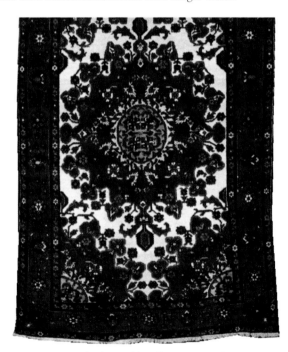

Tafrash rug (detail) *Simon Knight*

tafta (From Persian *tâfta*, "twisted, spun;" English "taffeta" derives from this.). Early Ottoman single-color silk satins.

Taghan Daulatabad. An Afghan rug of the Ersari type distinguished by a large gul containing fork-like elements in each quarter of the gul. See "Ersari."

Taghan Daulatabad rug *Gul*

taght baft (Persian *takht-bâft*, "board weave"). A rug structure with flat (not offset) warps.

Tahmâsp, Shah. Shah Tahmâsp (1524-1576) was the son of Shah Isma'il, founder of the Safavid dynasty in Persia. The greatest of the Persian carpets, including the Ardabil, were woven in his reign. In this period, there was important carpet production in Kashan, Tabriz, Kerman, Isfahan, Herat, and Mashhad. See "Persia."

tahdun. In Morocco, a Berber woman's mantle. These are usually striped, often with a white ground.

Taimani, Tiamani. A sub-group of the Chahar Aimaq inhabiting the southern slopes of the Hindu Kush in Afghanistan. Significant rug production by the Taimani began after World War II. Most designs are geometric all-over repeats. Some Turkmen guls are used. The dominant color is purple, with brown and blue. These are all-wool rugs woven with the asymmetric knot with average densities of about 40 knots per square inch.

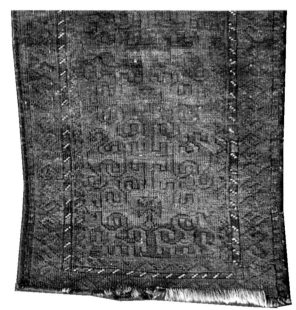

Tiamani pushti face (detail) *Michael Craycraft*

Taimeh. A village south of Josan in the Hamadan area. Rugs of this village are double wefted with the symmetric knot on a cotton foundation. The Herati pattern is used with a medallion and spandrels.

Tajiks, Tadjiks, Tadzhiks. A Persian-speaking ethnic group inhabiting Tajikistan and an adjacent area of Afghanistan (Badakhshân), and the cities of Bokhara and Samarkand. Attribution of weavings to this group is problematic. See "ikat."

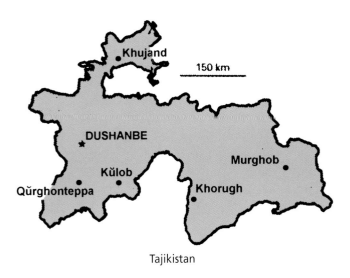

Tajikistan

takheb (Tibetan). Animal trapping. Specifically, a forehead cover.

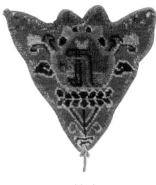

Takheb

Takht-e Jamshid. Kurdish "throne of Jamshid" design. A medallion design with the outline of three, narrow, vertically-aligned and touching hexagons. The Persian term takht-e Jamshid refers to the ruins of Persepolis. See "Jamshidi" and "Kolyai."

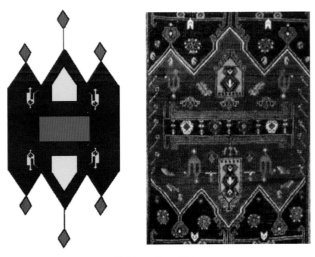

Takht-e Jamshid

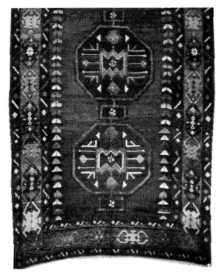

Tâleghân rug (detail) *Manoucher Highighat*

Tâleghân. A district east of Qazvin in northern Iran and a source of small medallion rugs, some including gul-like motifs. A symmetric knot is used at a density of about 65 knots per square inch with cotton warps and cotton or wool wefts. These rugs are single wefted.

talim (Persian, from Arabic *ta'lim*, "instruction"). A written description of the numbers of pile knots and their colors to create a specific design. Used in the production of workshop rugs. This system has been used in the production of rugs of Kashmir and Pakistan. See "cartoon," "buli," and "naqsh."

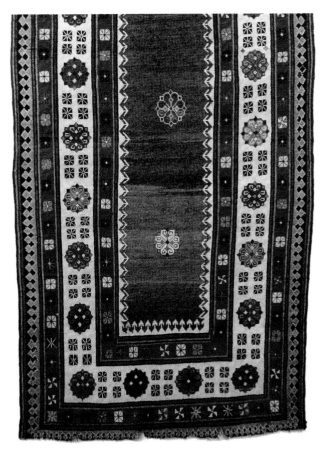

Talish rug (detail) *Grogan and Company*

Talish, Talysh. An area of the southeastern Caucasus bordering Iran. Nineteenth-century rugs of this area tend to have a long format. Many have empty or almost empty fields. Lenkoran is the major city and the Lenkoran medallion is used in many of the rugs. Many Talish rugs have a primary border design of a large blossom alternating with four florets. Knot density for Talish rugs is about 83 symmetric knots per square inch. The knot ratio is about 1.1. The average rug area is 30 square feet and the shape ratio is about 2.24.

Kilims attributed to Talish have bright colors, designs of all-over stepped diamonds or hexagons, and Laleh Abbasi borders. These kilims are woven in a single piece and ends have a macramé finish. See "Caucasus" and "Lenkoran."

Tamerlane, mark of. See "chintamani."

tamga, damga (Turk.), **wasm** (Arabic). Nomadic livestock brand, which may also be a tribal emblem woven into rugs.

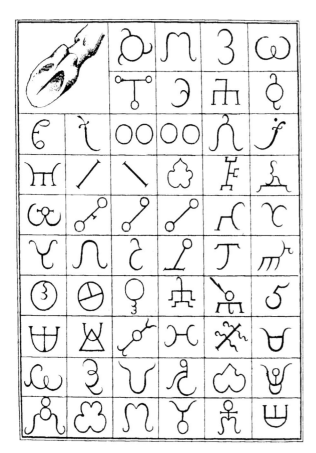

Horse brands of the Circassians *Tamga*

tanchra (Arabic *tanshira*, "bed-spread"). A thick rug, formerly woven in Algeria, used as a mattress. The rug has a loop pile of rope-like yarn.

tang (Persian, "tight; cinch"). A strap or band used on pack animals.

tanka. Tibetan Buddhist images painted, woven, embroidered, or appliquéd for use as banners or wall hangings.

Taoist symbols, Daoist symbols. The Taoist religion was founded by the sixth-century B.C. Chinese philosopher Laotse. In this religion, there are eight immortal spirits in human form. These spirits are represented by eight symbols sometimes used in Chinese rug designs. These symbols are the fan, the sword, the staff and gourd, the castanets, the basket of flowers, the flute, the tube and rods, and the lotus pod or flower. See "Buddhist symbols" and "Confucian symbols."

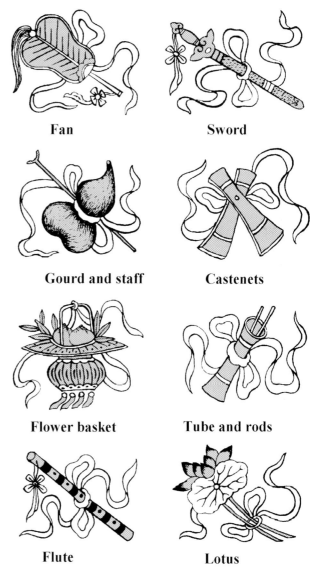

Taoist symbols

tápalo. A woman's shawl woven in the nineteenth century in the American Southwest. See "shawl."

tapestry weave. Any one of a variety of weft-faced weaves in which the pattern or design is created by colored ground wefts that are not usually continuous from selvage to selvage. See "eccentric weft," "dovetailed," "interlocking weft," "slit weave," "kilim," and "warp sharing."

tapestry yarn. A trade designation for four-ply, hard-spun wool yarn.

tapiglyph. A pseudo-scientific term for an image in carpets.

tapinu de mortu. See "Sardinia."

târ (Persian). Warp.

tarhalt, tahrart, tharart. In Morocco, large, coarsely-woven transport sacks.

tarfaft. A Moroccan flatwoven rug used in tents.

Taşpınar (Turk., "stone spring"). A village in south central Anatolia and the source of carpets, most of which have elongated medallions and a dark blue field.

tassels. Bundles of yarn in the form of brushes. Tassels are common in tribal weavings. They are used on animal trappings, bags and the edges of rugs.

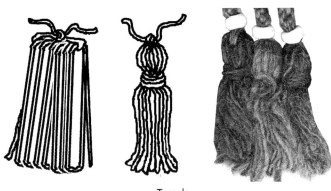

Tassels

tauk noska gul (Turk., "chicken design gul"). A Turkmen gul used by the Kizilayak, Ersari, Arabachi, Yomut, and Chodor tribes. This gul contains two small animals in each quadrant. In early versions, the animal has two heads. Its origin has been assigned to eleventh-century Luristan.

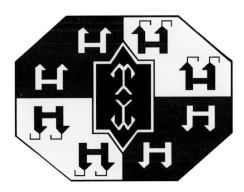

Tauk noska gul *After Moshkova*

T-band. A border in Chinese rugs, consisting of a continuous band of T-shapes alternating toward and away from the field. Sometimes the band is rendered with a three-dimensional effect.

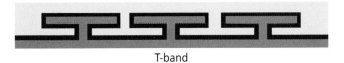

T-band

Tcherkess. See "Cherkess."

Tchetchens. See "Chechens."

Tchitchaktu. See "Chichaktu."

tea. Tea leaves have been used as a brown or tan dye, especially to darken other colors in rug repairs.

tea sofreh, dining sofreh. A long, narrow weaving, about 10 in. by 8 ft., used as a cloth for eating off. It may be mistaken for a section of a tent band.

technique. The process through which a fabric structure is created as distinct from the structure itself. Different techniques may produce the same structure. See "structure."

technical analysis. The identification and systematic description of structural properties and dyes in a rug. Technical analysis includes identification and description of:

Function	Dimensions
Warp, weft, pile	Fiber type Direction of spin Angle of spin Ply (number of elements) Angle of ply Color
Warp Weft	Offset (degrees of rotation of alternate warps) Linear warp count for flatweaves Number of wefts between rows of knots Sinuous and cable wefts Linear weft count for flatweaves
Knot	Type Vertical and horizontal knot count Pile length
Flatweave structure	Tapestry Soumak Other
End structure Edge structure	Unusual features Dyes and colors Condition

Microscopic examination of yarns and fibers and chemical and spectrophotometric and other chromatographic analyses of dyes are being used with increasing frequency. The results of technical analyses are useful in attribution, dating, and restoring rugs. Technical analysis is also useful in ethnographic and historical research. See "attribution" and "Oriental Rug Technical Analysis and Description Form."

Teec Nos Pos. Means "circle of cottonwood." A Navajo weaving area of southeast Utah and northeast Arizona. Designs often consist of diamond medallions and wide borders containing geometric motifs. See "Navajo rugs."

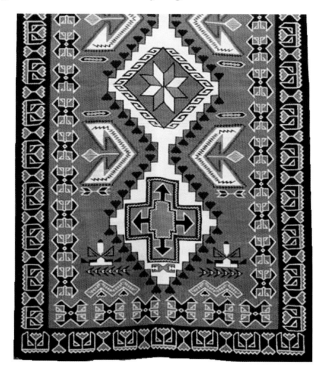

Teec Nos Pos Navajo rug *Steve Getzwiller*

Tehran. A large city in north central Iran and the capital of modern Iran. Tehran is a major market for Persian rugs. Some floral design rugs and modern pictorial rugs are woven in the city. These rugs have asymmetric knots at densities from 130 to 325 per square inch on a cotton foundation. Notable early twentieth-century weaver-designers of Tehran include Hadj Muhammad Djafar and Farschi. See "Persia."

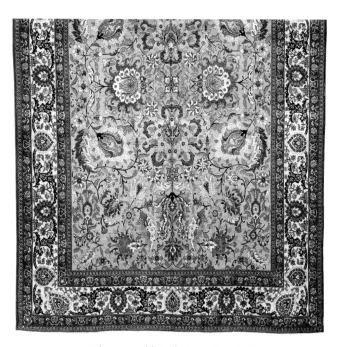

Tehran rug (detail) *Jason Nazmiyal*

Tekáb-Bijár. Copies of Bijár rugs woven by Afshars in the Bijár area.

Tekke. A Turkmen tribe currently inhabiting Merv and the surrounding area in Turkestan, an area along either side of the border between Turkestan and northeastern Iran and areas around Herat in Afghanistan. Tekke rugs are woven with the asymmetric knot and are usually double-wefted, though a few are single-wefted. Rugs have about 150 knots per square inch and dark blue overcasting of the selvage. Tekke torbas may be very finely knotted. The traditional Tekke gul is an indented octagon. See "Turkmen" and "main carpet."

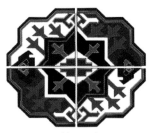

Tekke gul

temerchin gul, onurga. An octagonal gul in early Sariq main carpets and in some old Ersari carpets. The most distinctive feature of the gul is a motif consisting of four overlapping angelfish shapes in each quarter of the gul.

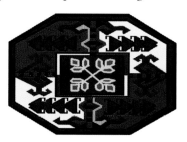

Temerchin gul

tent band, baskur, bou, girth, jolam, yolami, yup. A Turkmen tent band. Decorative tent bands, typically about 45 feet in length and 6 to 18 inches wide, are arranged around the interior circumference where the yurt roof meets the sides. A wide variety of weaving structures are used for the bands, including knotted pile, warp float brocade, and embroidered felt. Tassels may be added to the band. In some tent bands where pile is used for decoration, the knot nodes may not be visible from the back of the band because they are concealed by additional wefts.

tentering, blocking. When rugs are taken from the loom and are not rectangular or do not lie flat, they may be wetted and dried on a stretching frame to correct the shape. The problem usually returns when the rug is washed.

teppetology (cf. Latin *tapete*, "carpet"). A pseudo-learned term for the study of rugs.

teppetomorph. A series of images purporting to show the evolution of a design or motif.

teppetophilia. Collecting and studying oriental rugs. A pathological extension of the hunter-gatherer instinct. A diminished capacity for normal social relationships is symptomatic.

tereh Assur. See "weeping willow design."

textile. Any woven (loomed) fabric.

Textile Museum, The. In the United States, The Textile Museum in Washington, D.C. is the leading institution for the collection and study of oriental rugs. Founded in 1925 by George Hewett Myers, the collection began with his contribution of 275 early rugs. His family home became the museum's first building. A conservation laboratory, library, and museum store were added as the collection grew to 18,000 items. The Museum is the center for conferences, classes and research for oriental rugs and other textiles.

texture. The tactile quality of the surface of a fabric, without regard to color or design. Its roughness, smoothness, hardness, softness, resilience, and so on. Texture is the combined result of the fabric structure and the types of yarn and fibers used. See "hand."

tezgâh (Turk., from Persian dastgâh). Loom.

tharart. See "tarhalt."

tharashna. Morrocan large, pile carpets that serve as tent floor covering or bedding.

thari. In India, cable (straight) weft in rugs. See "cable weft" and "lackchi."

Thessaly. A region of eastern Greece. Tapestry woven kilims, bed covers and pillow covers are woven in the region. Designs are stripes containing geometric motifs, serrated concentric diamond medallions and naive rendering of human figures. Colors are bright and contrasting. See "Greece."

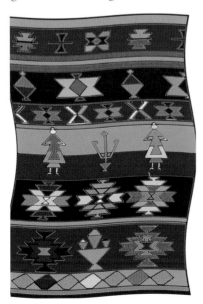

Thessaly kilim

Thibet. See "Tibet."

thigyarbya (Tibetan). A pile throne chair back rest used by chief lamas.

Thrace. See "Bulgaria" and "Şarköy."

thread count. The number of warps or wefts per linear measure or their product per unit area measure.

throne back. See "chair cover."

thread counter. A magnifying scope with several scales used to count threads (or knots) in a textile. See "linen tester."

Thread counter

throw rug. A small rug used as a cover for furniture or as a blanket.

thrum. The fringe of warp yarns on a carpet when it is cut from the loom or the remaining warp yarns left on the loom when the rug is removed.

Tiamani. See "Taimani."

Tianjin, Tianjan, Tientsin. An industrial city and port in northern China and the major production center for Chinese rugs, beginning about 1910. By 1929, there were about 300 workshops and factories weaving rugs on contract for American and European firms. Most production was for the American market. Prior to 1924, much of the wool used in Tianjin rugs was hand-spun. Rugs were woven with traditional motifs adapted to western tastes. A blue field with white, yellow, or gold designs was most popular. The field was often empty or occupied by asymmetrically placed floral sprays. Sometimes small rounded medallions were used or a centrally placed large rounded medallion. Borders were absent or consisted of elaborate Chinese motifs. Copies of Aubusson and Savonnerie rugs were woven, together with some pictorial rugs of inferior quality. See "Beijing," "China," and "Fette rugs."

Tibet, Thibet. Tibet, in Inner Asia, is bordered on the south by Nepal, Bhutan, and Burma, on the west by India, and on the north and east by China. The earliest archaeological finds of pile fragments in Tibet have been carbon-dated to 1700 B.C. There are rugs tentatively dated to the seventeenth century with reliable dating of rugs beginning in the 1880s. There are records of factory or commercial rug production from the late eighteenth century.

Tibetan rug design has been primarily influenced by that of China and, to a lesser extent, by East Turkestan. Some traditional indigenous folk motifs are used. Certain colors in Tibetan rugs have been associated with their function. Orange and gold are used in rugs for religious ceremonies. Maroon is often used in monastery floor coverings. Tiger skins were prized by ancient Tibetan nobles and officials. Thus older pile carpets, woven to represent tiger skins, are thought to be badges of authority. There are many examples of early Tibetan rugs in a checkerboard design.

Older Tibetan rugs, with a few exceptions, are all wool. Many of the older rugs have a red fabric edging and backing. Rugs are woven with a distinctive weft wrapping technique. Continuous supplementary weft is looped around two warps and then once around a gauge rod. After a series of loops are formed on the gauge rod in the colored yarn desired, the loops are cut and the gauge rod removed. Rows of cut weft are alternated with multiple rows of ground weft. The result is a pile structure that suggests overlapping shingles or lap strakes on a wooden boat hull. Some Tibetan rugs are woven with the symmetric knot. Knot densities vary from 20 to 140 per square inch. Older rugs are more coarsely knotted. Contemporary rugs are often sculptured after they are removed from the loom.

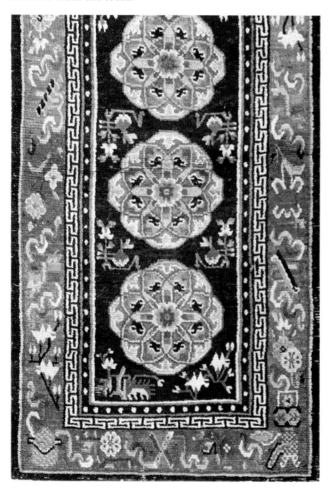

Tibetan rug *Jason Nazmiyal*

In 1959, with the assertion of Chinese control over Tibet, many Tibetans fled to Nepal, Bhutan, and India. There, in refugee camps, they began significant commercial production of rugs in the Tibetan weaving technique. Designs in these rugs are highly variable, with a few traditional design still used. Modern dyes are used and these are not selected in the harmonious combinations of vegetable dyes. These rugs have a knot density of about 50 per square inch and are well constructed. Recently, rugs have been commissioned in Tibet

and woven using traditional methods and designs and vegetable dyes in a manner analogous to the DOBAG project in Turkey. See "butterfly saddle rugs," "den," "dorje," "drumze," "dzo ke-thil," "Gangchen," "goyo," "gyabnye," "gyab-yol," "Gyantse," "jabuye," "katum," "khaden," "khagangma," "kyongden," "kyongring," "makden," "neyden," "rum," "sabden," "sar," "Shigatse," "takheb," "tanka," "thigyarbya," "Tsang," "tsogden," "tsuktruk," and "yak hair rugs."

Tiffany, Louis Comfort (1848-1933). The son of a highly successful New York jeweler. He became an outstanding designer of domestic accessories and interior decorations. He is especially noted for his work in glass. He collected oriental rugs and marketed them in the United States. His catalogs of rugs published in 1906 and 1908 contain primarily eighteenth and nineteenth-century Turkish prayer rugs.

tiftik (Turk., from Persian taftik, "mohair"). Angora wool.

tiger rugs. A large group of Tibetan rugs woven in imitation of tiger skins. See "Tibet."

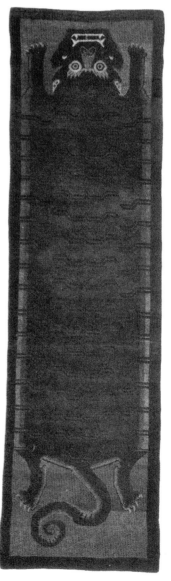

Tibetan tiger runner *Ivory Friedus*

tile carpets. White ground Turkish carpets thought to derive from a repetitive field of square designs used in Turkish tiles. Examples are Bird Ushak and Chintamani Ushak carpets. Also, compartment rugs with compartments shaped like tiles. See "compartment rugs."

tiles. See "carpet tiles."

tilma, conga. A short serape.

time-on-loom. See "loom time."

Timuri. Possibly a sub-group of the Chahar Aimaq. "Timuri" means attributed to or descended from Tamerlane. The Timuri inhabited eastern Iran and are thought to have inhabited Afghanistan. Superior weavings were produced by the Timuri of Khurasan. Their pile weavings are often classified as Baluch. Their rugs often employ a panel design with each panel containing abstract floral motifs. The asymmetric knot is used. See "Aimaq" and "Dokhtar-e Gazi."

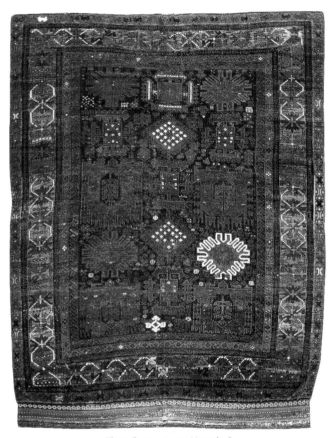

Timuri rug *Jason Nazmiyal*

tin mordant. Tin in the form of stannous chloride is used as a mordant. For yarns that have been dyed and mordanted already, additional tin mordant brightens the colors. Excessive tin mordant embrittles wool.

tint. A hue with an admixture of white. See "hue," "shade," and "tone."

Tintoretto rug. A vague term applied to Anatolian rugs with a small central medallion, arches at both ends, and a red field.

So named for the sixteenth-century Venetian artist who portrayed such a rug in a painting. The painting is in the Brera Gallery in Milan. See "opposed-arch prayer rug."

tip fading. Bleaching in pile ends due to the use of dyes that are particularly sensitive to sunlight.

tip sheared loop pile. Power loomed rugs in which there is both cut and loop pile creating designs of different textures.

tiraz (Arabic, from Persian, "embroidery"). The earliest commercial fabrics produced by Near Eastern workshops under the Caliphs. Tiraz also refers to early Islamic textiles with Arabic script woven or embroidered in the fabric.

Tlaxcalans. Indians of central Mexico who migrated to the American Southwest under Spanish protection. They settled in the Saltillo area and were the original weavers of the Saltillo sarapes. See "Saltillo."

tobreh, toobreh (Persian). See "tubreh."

Tokat. See "Hereke."

tomb cover. Ornately decorated cloths are sometimes used to cover tomb caskets when caskets are displayed. Usually, these are not pile weavings.

tone. A color not found on the spectrum such as gray and brown. See "hue," "shade," and "tint."

tone-on-tone, ton-sur-ton (French). In broadloom carpets, two or more shades of the same color used together.

tools, weaving. See the following entries:

beater	loom
bobbin	mako
çıkırk	malacate
comb	mekik
distaff	panja
gauge rod	shuttle
hava	spindle
hook, weaver's	spinning wheel
kârdak	suzan

top. The edge of a rug opposing the edge towards which the pile lies. The edge of the rug at the top of the loom and woven last.

Topkapı Harem Medallion and Cartouche Carpet. An early sixteenth-century Persian carpet. This is one of a pair woven contemporaneously. A central lobed medallion lies on a field of complex tile-like compartments. The carpet is 24 feet 6 inches by 9 feet 8 inches. The foundation is cotton with three wefts. The pile is wool and the asymmetric knot is used at a density of about 125 per square inch. This carpet is in the collection of the Museum für Angewandte Kunst, Vienna.

toplu çengel (Turk.). See "scorpion motif."

toranj (Persian). Medallion of a rug.

torba (Turk.). A long, rectangular, shallow bag, open on a long side, hung from Turkmen tent struts. A torba is smaller than a joval. Pile knotting is normally used on only one face of a torba.

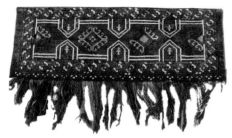

Ersari Torba

torbak. In Khurasan, Iran, a small belt bag or shoulder bag. A diminutive form of "torba."

toushak. See "joval."

transhumance. The movement of peoples and their livestock seasonally from lowlands to mountainous areas. This pastoral nomadism was formerly the source of many rugs and special-purpose weavings using traditional ethnic or tribal designs, vegetable dyes, and woven structures. See "garmsir," "kişlak," "nomadic rugs," "sardsir," and "yaylak."

Transylvania, Siebenbürgen rugs. Turkish rugs of the sixteenth through eighteenth centuries found in Protestant churches in Romania and Hungary. Similar rugs were found in Anatolia. These rugs were imported from western Turkey and were gifts to churches to celebrate weddings, funerals, and other special occasions. Of about 300 published examples, about one-third are opposed arch prayer rugs, one-third are Lotto designs, with the remainder Bird Ushak, prayer rugs, and other.

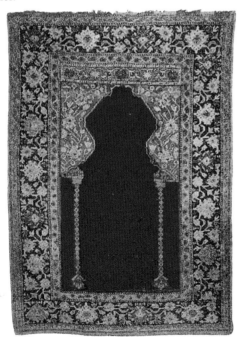

Transylvanian rug *Huntington Museum of Art*

Transylvanian flatweaves. See "Braşov" and "Seklars."

treadle loom. A loom in which foot-operated treadles raise or lower warp harnesses so the weaver's hands are free to move the shuttle. These looms are not generally used for weaving knotted pile carpets.

tree of life. A pervasive motif in oriental rugs, occurring in many variations, naturalistic, geometricized, and abstract. Generally, any primary design motif with a long vertical axis and horizontal or upward pointing limbs. See "Baluchi," "cypress," "vak-vak tree," and "weeping willow design."

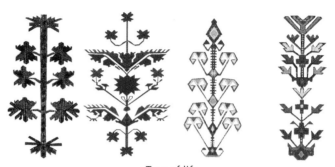

Tree of life
LEFT TO RIGHT *Baluchi, Yağcıbedir, Kağızman and Genje*

Tree Kazak. A Kazak design type of small trees in the field of the rug. See "Kazak."

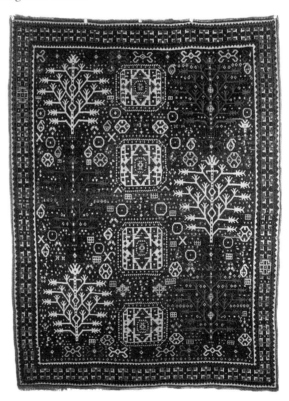

Tree Kazak rug (detail) *Grogan and Company*

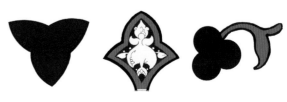

Trefoils

trefoil. A design motif of three elements. A stylized representation of a three-lobed leaf. This motif may be used as a reciprocating border. See "Laleh Abbasi" and "quatrefoil."

trensaflossa. A voided pile weave of Sweden. Designs are executed in pile while the background is flatwoven. See "souf."

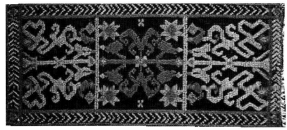

Trensaflossa

tribal rugs. Generally, a tribe is a political structure whose members consider themselves as a separate social grouping. They may share a common ancestral lineage. They rule themselves, defend each other from outsiders, share a common lifestyle and identity. Their weavings often suggest this identity through specific design or structural features. Rugs are woven by tribal members from a wide variety of Near Eastern ethnic groups. Generally, tribal rugs are characterized by traditional motifs employed by nomadic members as well as by those settled in villages. See "nomadic rugs."

triclinium. See "audience rug."

trigram. A Chinese and Korean symbol of eight different arrangements of three parallel lines or line segments. These trigrams represent heaven, earth, wind, fire, water, mountain, thunder, and clouds. The trigrams are often shown surrounding yin yang. Trigrams have been used in Chinese rug designs. See "yin yang."

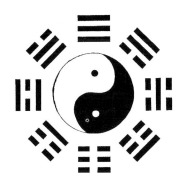

Trigram surrounding yin yang

Tripolitania. See "Libya."

triskelion. A motif of three arms radiating from a center and bent in the same direction. See "swastika."

tristvav (Swedish). Double cross stitch needlework.

Tsang province. A province of southern Tibet including the urban centers of Lhasa, Gyantse, and Shigatse. This province was the source of the greatest volume of Tibetan rugs and of rugs of the highest quality. Most carpets were woven in the towns with wool provided by nomads.

tschoval. See "joval."

tsherga. See "cerga."

tsongden (Tibetan). A long temple runner.

tsuktruk (Tibetan). A large, shaggy pile sleeping blanket made of narrow pieces sewn together.

tubreh, tobreh, toobreh (Persian *tubareh*). A small shoulder bag or a nose bag for feeding animals.

Tuduc, Theodor (1888-1983). A Romanian rug restorer and weaver of rug reproductions. Tuduc was born in Cluj, Transylvania and died in Bucharest. Much of his weaving was done in his workshop in Brasov between 1919 and 1945. His exact rug reproductions and creations were aged artificially and sold through intermediaries as authentic. Many of his reproductions were acquired and displayed by prominent museums. Tuduc's reproductions include white-ground Chintamani carpets, Transylvanian (Siebenbürgen) carpets, a Lotto carpet, Spanish armorial carpets, and a rug bearing the arms of Queen Elizabeth I of England. The name "Tuduc" has become synonymous with historical rug forgeries.

tüfek baş (Turk.) Gun cover.

tuft. Supplementary cut or looped weft that is not wrapped completely around warp. See "pile."

tufted rugs. Rugs of wool or synthetic yarns inserted by hand or machine in a cotton backing and then clipped. The back of the rug is coated with latex to lock the yarn in place and additional fabric backing is provided. Such rugs are commercially produced in China and the Phillipines.

tuğra (Turk.). A stylized monogram of a Sultan affixed to a firman or decree.

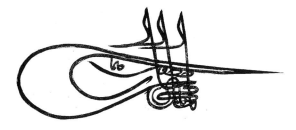

Tuğra of Bayezid II

Tuisserkhân. See "Tuysarkhân."

tulip motif. See "Laleh Abbasi."

tülü, kopan. *Tülü* is Turkish for "long haired." A sleeping rug of Central Anatolia. These are rugs with a very long cut pile or looped pile, usually woven around Konya. They are coarsely woven of lustrous wool with simple geometric designs. *Çeki* ("pulled") tülü are those carpets in which supplementary wefts do not encircle warps, but are only interlaced and pulled from the front of the carpet to create long, looped pile. Short loop pile rugs are made using a gauge rod. *Ilme* ("looped") tülü are knotted, long pile carpets. There are court examples of such rugs. See "filikli."

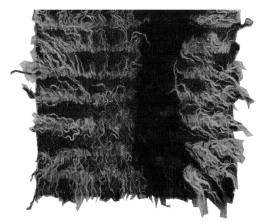

Tülü (detail) *Turkish Loom*

tun (Persian). Warp.

Tunisia. Tunisia is bounded on the west and south by Algeria and on the east and south by Libya and on the east and north by the Mediterranean. In Tunisia, pile carpets are woven on horizontal looms using the Turkish knot. Carpets from Kairouan, a town in central Tunisia, and the surrounding area are woven by women. These all-wool carpets have a short pile. Designs are based on Anatolian models and motifs and usually include a large central medallion with pointed ends. These ends may be stepped. Flower motifs are geometricized. One type of Kirouan carpet is termed the *alloucha*. This carpet is in colors of white, beige, brown, and gray, originally of undyed wool. Some carpets are woven in Bizerte which imitate Kairouan styles.

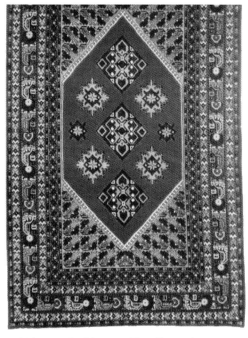

Kairouan Tunisian rug (detail) *R. John Howe*

The *qtifa* is a long-pile rug woven by men in central and northwestern tribes. This rug was not intended for trade, but for local use. It is all wool with each row of knots separated by four to eight wefts. The field is usually occupied by large, eight-pointed stars and hooked diamonds. The dominant color is red. The *qtifa* is a large rug, measuring about five by ten feet. See "Kairouan" and "qtifa."

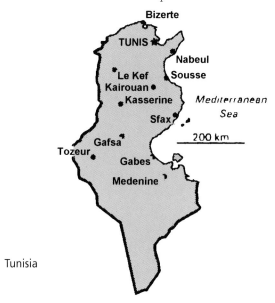

Tunisia

Tunisian flatweaves. Tunisian flatweaves are woven on horizontal and vertical looms by tribal women. The *hamel* is a blanket about five feet by seven feet composed of bands sewn together. These bands may be ornamented with diamonds, triangles and chevrons. The *ûsâda* is a cushion or bag about 1½ by 3 feet made of bands in a manner similar to the *hamel*. The *klim* is woven in blanket and mat sizes. Originally it was striped only. Later versions may be ornamented by diamonds and triangles. The *bost* is a saddle blanket about three feet square. Older versions have a red panel in the center. The *mouchtiya*, *bakhnûg*, *tajîrâ*, and *ketfîya* are shawls. See "huli."

türbelik. *Türbe* is Turkish for tomb or mausoleum. See "landscape carpet."

Turkbaff. See "symmetric knot."

Turkestan. See "Eastern Turkestan" and "Western Turkestan."

Turkey. Modern Turkey includes Istanbul (formerly Constantinople) and the adjacent European area on the west side of the Sea of Marmara, and the large Asiatic territory of Anatolia on the east side of the Sea of Marmara. The earliest Turkish rugs and fragments are from the Seljuk period in the thirteenth century. Designs in some of these rugs suggest Turkmen origins or influences.

The Ottoman empire gradually absorbed the mini-states that emerged in Anatolia after the decline of the Seljuks. The earliest Anatolian rugs, through the eighteenth century, tend to have Z-spun, red wefts. Most surviving Ottoman rugs woven prior to 1800 were products of workshops in Bergama, Gördes, Lâdik, Ushak, and other locations in Anatolia. There

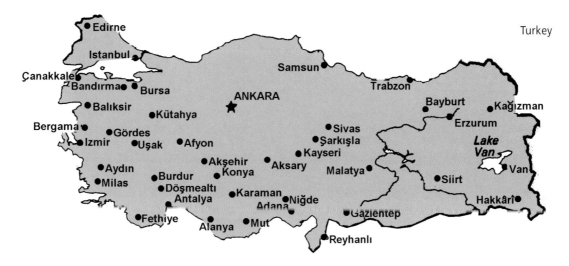

Turkey

are some early village and nomadic rugs, but their dating and attribution are problematic.

Most nineteenth and twentieth-century Turkish rugs are coarsely woven with a knot density below 50 knots per square inch. With few exceptions, the symmetric knot is used. Most rugs are woven on a wool foundation with a cotton foundation increasingly used from the turn of the century. Wefts are usually unplied, with two shoots between each row of knots. Some silk rugs have been woven in Turkey. Designs tend to be prayer rugs and medallions rather than all-over patterns.

There was a marked decline in rug production from the founding of the modern Turkish republic in 1923 until the 1950s. On December 1, 1928, Turkey officially adopted the Latin alphabet. Newspapers and other publications were required to be printed in western script rather than Arabic script. This change in written usage was soon reflected in Turkish rug inscriptions. The vast majority of Turkish flatweaves are Anatolian. Structures used for these flatweaves include kilim, cicim, zili, and soumak. See "Anatolia," "DOBAG," "Holbein carpets," "Lotto," "Mamluk carpets," "Mejidian style," "Oghuz," "Ottoman floral carpets," "Ottoman Empire," "Rhodian carpets," "Seljuk," "Süleyman I 'the Magnificent'," "Transylvania rugs," and "Yörük."

There are entries under the following Turkish geographical references:

Ada-Milas	Bursa	Fethiye
Adana	Çal	Gaziantep
Afyon	Çamardı	Gördes
Aksaray	Çan	Güney
Akşehir	Çanakkale	Hakkârî
Alanya	Cappadocia	Helvacı
Antalya	Cihanbeyli	Hereke
Aydın	Dazkiri	Hotami
Ayvacık	Dereköy	Isparta
Balıkesir	Diyarbakır	Istanbul
Bandırma	Döşemealtı	Ivrindi
Basmakçı	Edirne	Izmir
Bayburt	Erzurum	Kağızman
Bergama	Esme	Kangal
Bünyan	Ezine	Karak
Burdur	Fertek	Karaman

Karapınar	Manyas	Sivas
Kars	Mihaliççik	Taşpinar
Kavak	Milas	Ürgüp
Kayseri	Mucur	Ushak (Uşak)
Kirne	Mut	Van
Kırşehir	Niğde	Yağcıbedir
Konya	Obruk	Yahyalı
Kozak	Ortaköy	Yeşilhisar
Kula	Rashwan	Yüncü
Kütahya	Reyhanlı	Yuntdağ
Ladik	Şarkışla	Zara
Makri	Selçuk	Zeyve
Malatya	Siirt	
Manastır	Sindirgı	

Turkey work. Needlework used to create looped or cut pile on a preexisting foundation, accessory pile. This technique was popular in the seventeenth and eighteenth centuries in England and used to imitate knotted carpets. In the eighteenth century, Turkey work was used synonymously for "oriental rugs."

Turkish knot. See "symmetric knot."

Turkmenistan, Turkmenia. Formerly the Turkmen Soviet Socialist Republic; capital Ashkhabad. Bordered by the Caspian Sea on the west, Iran on the south, Afghanistan on the southeast, and Kazakhstan and Uzbekistan on the north and northeast. Turkmenistan is considered a part of Western Turkestan. See "Ashkhabad," "Chardjou," "Karadashli," and "Western Turkestan."

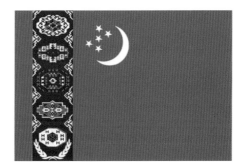

Turkmenistan national flag with tribal guls

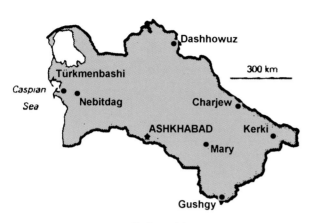

Turkmenistan

Turkmen, Türkmen, Turkoman. Turkic-speaking Muslims inhabiting Turkmenistan, northern Afghanistan, and northern Iran. Important Turkmen tribes include Chaudor, Ersari, Salor, Saryk, Tekke, and Yomut. See entries under these names. Formerly nomadic and warlike, they have increasingly adopted a semi-sedentary or settled way of life since the turn of the century. The Turkmen trace their origin to the Oghuz.

Turkmen women weave rugs for domestic use and the market. Rug weaving for the western market became a significant part of Turkmen economy in the late nineteenth and early twentieth centuries. Most Turkmen weavings are in shades of red or reddish brown with spare highlights of white, blue, green, and yellow. The usual design element is a repeated octagon or gul associated with specific tribes. Wool is used throughout in most weavings, but there are occasional silk pile pieces and pieces in which silk is used in small areas as a highlight. Functional weavings for domestic use include bokches, jovals, torbas, ensis, khorjins, tent bands, asmalyks, and other animal trappings. See entries under these names.

Turkmen flatweaves. Turkmen flatweaves include large carpets of brocading. These carpets have elems in plain weave or with brocade. They have been attributed to the Goklan, Tekke, and Yomut. The Yomut weave a slit weave tapestry with brocade. These fabrics have parallel rows of chevrons, all in the same direction. Slit weave tapestry kilims in all-over patterns are attributed to the Kizil Ayak and Dali Ersari. Tent bands are common Turkmen flatweaves. Most are warp-faced with warp float or supplementary weft patterning. There are soumaks attributed to the Tekke, Yomut, and Ersari Turkmen. See "girth" and "yup."

Turkoman. See "Turkmen."

turmeric, curcuma. The root of Curcuma tinctoria, used to prepare a yellow dye in India.

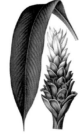

Turmeric

turnarounds. In reweaving foundation, new warp reverses direction when it passes from one column of knot nodes to the next column of knot nodes. New weft reverses direction when it passes under a knot. These reversals of direction are termed, "turnarounds."

turret design, keyhole design. A medallion consisting of a rectangle opening into an octagon at one or both ends. The medallion occurs in late Kazak and Shirvan rugs of the Caucasus and in some early Anatolian rugs from Divrigi. The shape may be derived from a mihrab or, possibly, from some architectural plan or structure. See "Bellini rugs."

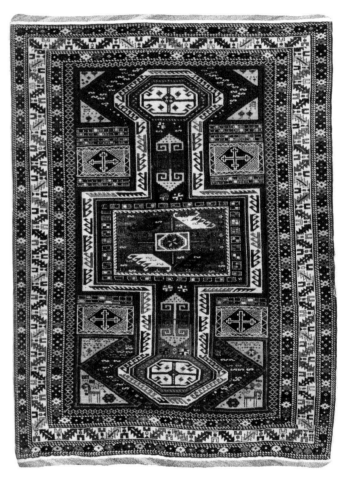

Turret medallion rug (Shirvan) *Sothebys*

turret gul. An octagon gul with projections around the perimeter which is used in weavings by the Salor, Sariq, Ersari, and Kizil Ayak Turkmens. It was associated with the Salor in early rug literature and was sometimes called the "Rose of Salor."

Turret gul *After Moshkova*

Turshiz. See "Kâshmar."

turtle border, samovar border. A palmette border used in Sarouks and other rugs. In some versions, detail within the larger palmettes is minimal and the shape suggests the shell of a turtle. This border is often used with the Herati pattern in the field in Persian rugs. See "Herati border."

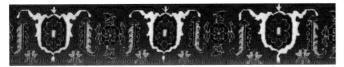

Turtle border

tus ki'z (Kazakh), **tush ki'iz** (Kirghyz). Fabric decorative tent hanging.

tussar silk. See "silk."

Tuysarkân, Tuisarkân, Tuisserkhân. A town of western Iran near Hamadan. It is a source of carpets with geometricized medallions with pendants. Medallion and spandrels have serrated edges. The field is dark blue with geometricized floral motifs. Rugs are single wefted with a few double wefted. The symmetric knot is used on a cotton foundation.

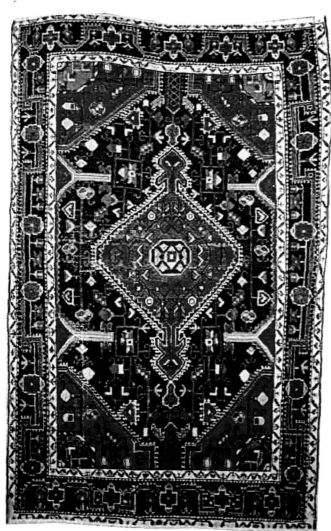

Tuysarkân rug (detail) *Woolley and Wallis*

twill weave. A basic diagonal weave in which warps consistently skip two, three, four, or five wefts or wefts consistently skip two, three, four, or five warps. See "Navajo twill weaves

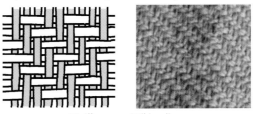

Twill weave *Wikipedia*

twining. See "weft twining" and "tablet weaving."

twist. In broadloom carpets, the turns per inch for pile yarns, typically about four to six turns. Also, in technical analysis, the direction of the ply of multiple-ply yarns, as distinct from the spin of each individual ply. See "angle of twist."

Two Gray Hills. A Navajo weaving area in northwestern New Mexico. A source of finely woven rugs with borders and medallion designs with spandrels. Colors are white, black, brown, tan, and gray. Some of these tapestry weaves are particularly fine. See "Navajo rug."

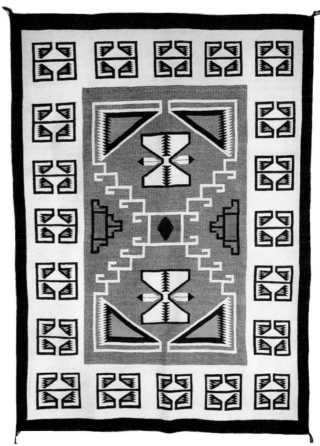

Two Gray Hills Navajo rug *Steve Getzwiller*

two-one-two, 2-1-2. See "quincunx."

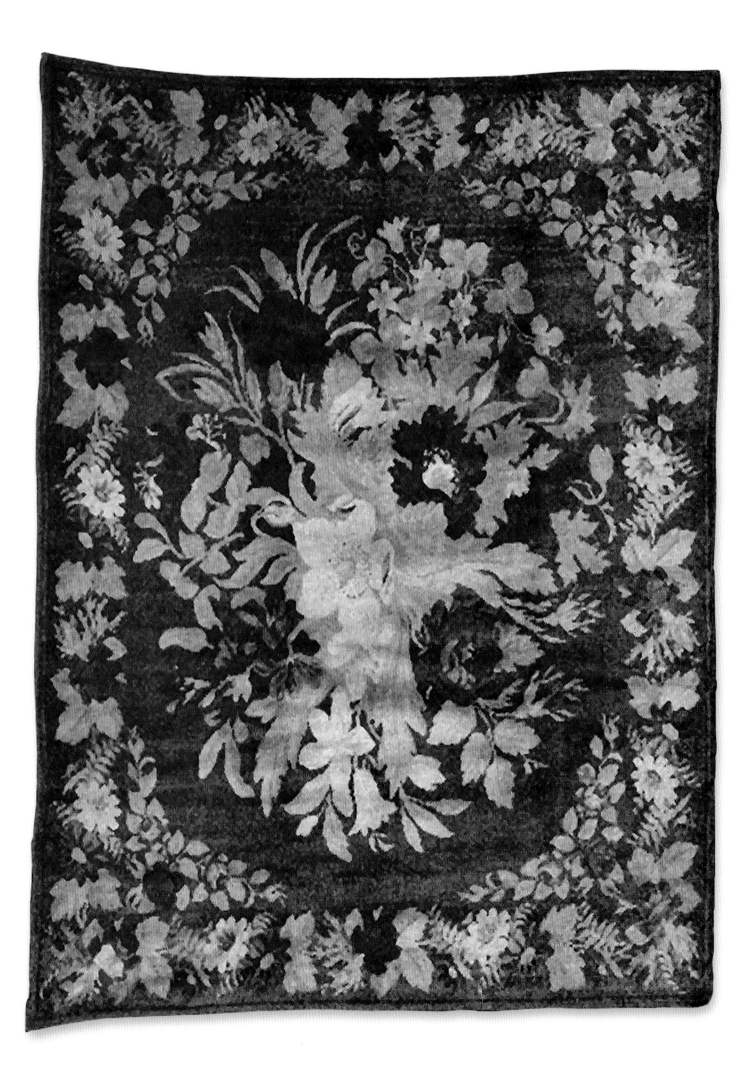

Uighurs. An ancient eastern Turkic people inhabiting portions of Xinjiang or Eastern Turkestan. They produce some pile and felt carpets for their own use.

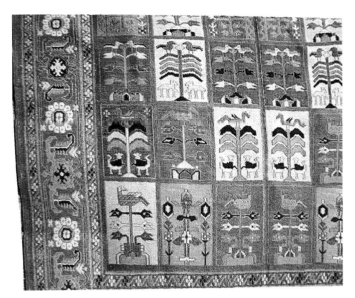

Uighurs rug (detail) *Mehmud Abliz*

Ukraine (Slavic, "borderland"). Ukraine, formerly the Ukrainian Soviet Socialist Republic, lies south and west of Russia, bordering the Black Sea. Pile rugs have been woven in manor houses and factories in the Ukraine since the seventeenth century. Floral motifs, possibly derived from Savonnerie models, are typical of early pile rug production. Pile rugs were woven in weaving cooperatives or artels after the Russian revolution. Tapestry woven kilims in geometric and floral designs were produced, some with Cyrillic inscriptions. The Ukraine is best known for elaborate embroidery work. As a folk craft, embroidery was used extensively on garments, bedclothes, curtains, and furniture coverings. Much of this embroidery comes from the Poltava and Kiev regions.

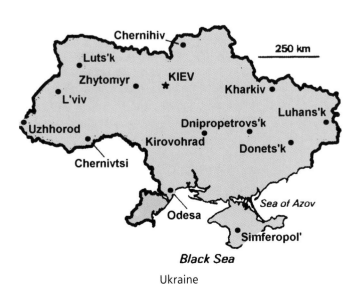

Ukraine

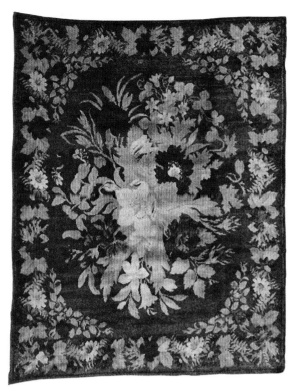

Ukranian rug *Sothebys*

ultraviolet light, UV. A portion of the electromagnetic spectrum with a frequency shorter than visible light and longer than X rays. The colors in fabrics are bleached over time by exposure to light, especially ultraviolet light. Ultraviolet light is an important component of sunlight, light from metal-halide (halogen) lamps, and fluorescent lamps. Protection of fabrics exposed to ultraviolet light from these sources is provided by UV-blocking screens over windows, by UV-blocking plastic over the fabric, by UV-blocking shields over artificial light sources, by using especially manufactured low-UV lamps, by low light intensity, and by limiting the time the fabric is exposed to light. Often a combination of these methods is used in museums. See "conservation."

umbrella. One of the eight emblems of Buddha. The umbrella is represented in Chinese rugs and symbolizes the authority of the state and the protection of the state.

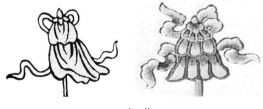

umbrella

underlay, padding. Material placed under a carpet or rug to protect it from friction with the floor and to provide resiliency and insulation. Common underlays are made of jute or hair (felted), urethane (bonded scrap or un-bonded), and rubber waffle. Special underlays are manufactured to prevent area rugs from slipping over wall-to-wall carpeting. In some cases, quality of underlay is measured in weight per unit area.

Union of Soviet Socialist Republics. See "Russia."

units of measure. See "conversion factors." See the following entries:

beat up	line count
bis	mokata
bhutan	nishan
cotton count	quarter
denier	reg
dihari	rows per inch
ell	sezar
gauge	shape ratio
gereh	stitch
kabal	thread count
knot ratio	warp sett
kpsd	wire
kpsi	yarn size
line	zar

universal motifs. Some motifs are used throughout the Middle East in rug-weaving cultures. These motifs include the Herati pattern, Minâ khâni pattern, memling gul, and boteh. See entries under these names

unlocked tapestry. Slit tapestry structure. See "kilim."

unresolved corners, unreconciled corners. Where borders with repeating motifs meet at the corner of a rug, the intersection of the designs can be so arranged that all four corners of the rug are symmetrical and similar. Where this does not occur, the corner is described as "unresolved." Vertical or horizontal borders may override each other or motifs may be incomplete or irregularly executed at the corner. Unresolved corners are characteristic of tribal and nomadic rugs. They may occur in some village rugs and more rarely in commercial rugs.

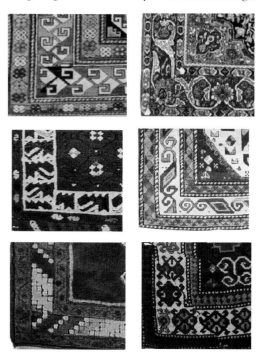

Unresolved corners

Urgench. A city of Uzbekistan and a weaving and market source of Uzbeki rugs.

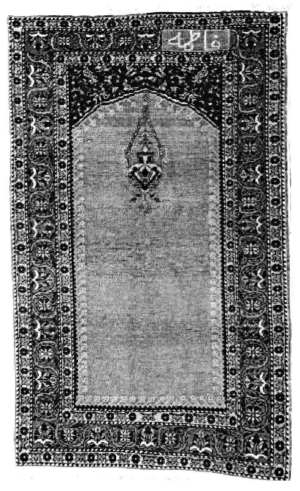

Ürgüp prayer rug *CarpetView*

Urumqi, Urumchi. A city in Xinjiang and a source of contemporary silk rugs with fields brocaded in gold-wrapped thread. Also, the location of a museum with early Chinese textiles.

Ürgüp. A town of Cappodocia in central Anatolia and a source of small rugs, predominantly brownish-gold and reddish-orange. Some rugs from Ürgüp were woven with Mejidian designs. The town is a major contemporary marketing center for Turkish rugs. Foundations are all wool or cotton.

Ushak, Oushak, Uşak. A town of west central Anatolia. Rugs have been woven in Ushak since the fifteenth century. Ushak rugs were widely used on the floors of mosques. The earliest Turkish prayer rugs are attributed to Ushak in the sixteenth century. Seventeenth-century Ushak prayer rugs have opposing niches at the ends of the rug. Many great carpets are attributed to Ushak and the surrounding area. These include the Medallion Ushak, Star Ushak, the Bird Ushak, Crab Ushak, the Chintamani Ushak, and Holbein and Lotto carpets. See entries under these names. From the beginning of the nineteenth century, the quality and quantity of Ushak rug production declined. See "Transylvania" and "Turkey."

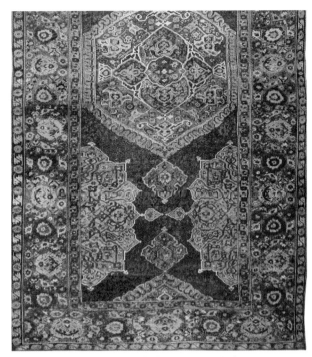

Medallion Ushak *Jason Nazmiyal*

ushter-i jol (Baluchi). Camel cover.

Ushvân. A village of Hamadan province in Iran, northwest of Nehâvand, and a source of rugs with a large diamond medallion with pendants and spandrels. The edges of the medallion and spandrels are serrated. The dominant color is red.

Üsküdar, Scutari. Eastern (Asiatic) Istanbul. Nineteenth century court rugs were woven in Üsküdar and it was also a source of early Turkish velvets. See "Istanbul."

ussada. In Morocco, a cushion.

ustad. See "ostâd."

Uttar Pradesh. A province of northwestern India and the area of greatest contemporary rug production. Most of these rugs have knot densities from about 120 to 245 knots per square inch. Rug weaving centers are Agra, Bhadohi, and Mirzapur. See entries under these names. See "Indo-Mir."

UV. See "ultraviolet light."

Uzbeks, Üzbeks, Özbeks. A people of Turkestan and northern Afghanistan, mainly inhabiting Uzbekistan. Settled Uzbeks of the oasis cities, formerly referred to as "Sarts," are an amalgamation of different Turkic groups and Turkicized Tajiks. Their weavings include a very wide variety of techniques. Their all-wool rugs have a long pile and are in colors of red, orange, and black in geometric designs (triangles, diamonds, and rectangles), often with the ram's horn motif. Some Uzbek pile rugs are woven in strips of about two and one-half feet by eight to ten feet. These rugs are woven with the symmetric knot tied so it skips a warp rather than being tied on two adjacent warps. Wefts in these rugs are behind rows of knots, as well as above

and below each row of knots. As a result, knot nodes are not easily visible from the back of the rug.

There are many Uzbek flatweaves. The Uzbeks weave silk ikats. Their needlework includes suzanis and other highly skilled embroidery. Functional flatweaves of the Uzbeks include kilims, animal trappings, saddle bags, the kergi or kit bag, animal trappings, duppi or skull-cap, shaikalt or small bag for tea, wall hangings, bedclothes, and garments. See "Bukhara," "julkhyrs," "Lakai and Kungrat embroideries," "Nurata," "Shakhrisabz," "suwari", "suzani," and "Urgench."

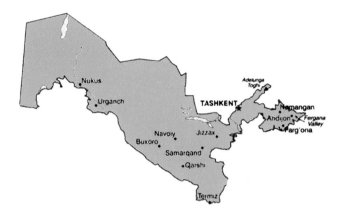

Uzbekistan

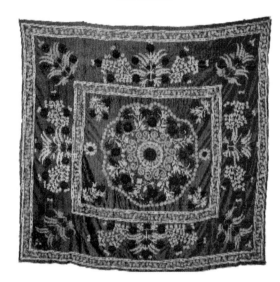

Tashkent suzani *Uzbek Textile*

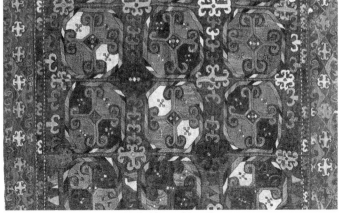

Uzbeki rug (detail)

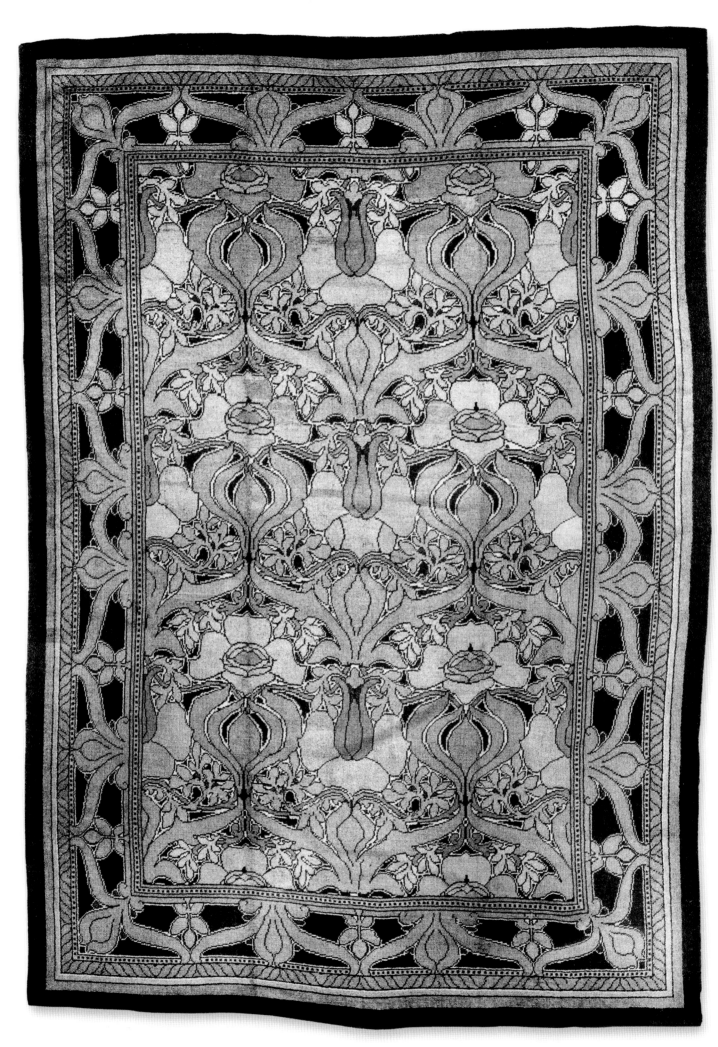

vâgireh (Persian, "copy, sampler"), **vagiereh, wagireh.** A sample rug. See "sampler."

vajra. See "dorje."

vakıf. See "wakf."

vak-vak tree, vaq-vaq tree, Mughal grotesques. A mythical tree in which the limbs terminated in heads of different animals. These heads talked. According to legend, such a tree informed Alexander the Great of his early death. The tree is depicted in Mughal and early Persian miniatures. The tree is a motif in some Mughal rug fragments. There are fifteen of these red-ground fragments showing writhing animals and monsters, some with other animals issuing from their mouths. There are other fragments on a blue ground. They are dated to the late 16th or early 17th century.

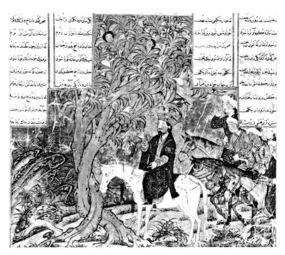

Alexander talking to the Vak-vak tree

Vallero blankets. Nineteenth century Rio Grande blankets in a variety of designs, but all including one or more Vallero stars. This is an eight-pointed star composed of eight diamonds. Most of these blankets were woven as two pieces and sewn in the middle. See "Crivelli star" and "Rio Grande blankets."

Vallero star

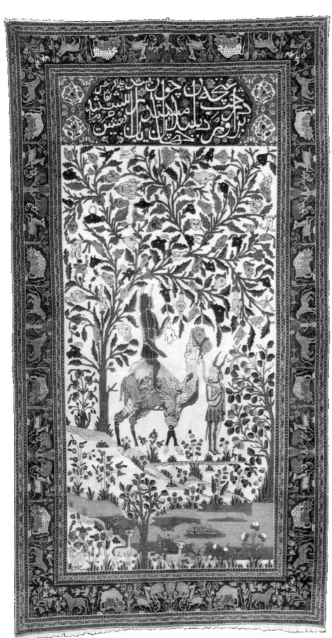

Vak-vak tree in a 20th-century Kashan rug
R. John Howe

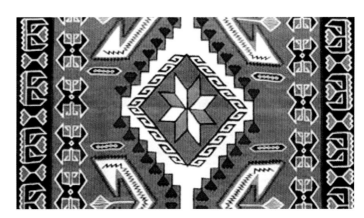

Navajo blanket with Vallero star (detail) *Steve Getzwiller*

value, color. The lightness or darkness of a color apart from the admixture of white or black. See "Munsell's color theory."

Van. A town near Lake Van in the Kurdish-settled region of eastern Anatolia. The area is the source of many kilims. Early kilims from the area were woven as a single piece while later examples are joined in the middle. A common design consists of all-over hooked hexagons. These kilims have borders. Many contemporary kilims have a white background with a very wide variety of designs.

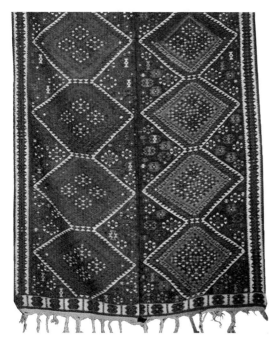

Van kilim *Simon Knight*

vani. See "Qashqa'i frieze."

Varâmin, Veramin. Varâmin is a town about 30 miles southeast of Tehran in Iran. Kurds and Turks living in this plains area weave pile rugs and flatweaves. Some rugs are woven with an asymmetric knot on a cotton foundation at densities from 130 to 225 per square inch. The minâ khâni design is common. Torbas, saddlebags, and salt bags from the area often have a motif resembling the Sariq gul. Memling guls are also common. The "S" motif is sometimes used in the main border of pile rugs. Slit-weave kilims from the area often include a narrow brocade band of connected S's or rosettes at top and bottom. In many kilims, motifs are outlined with a weft-wrapping structure. See "Garmsar."

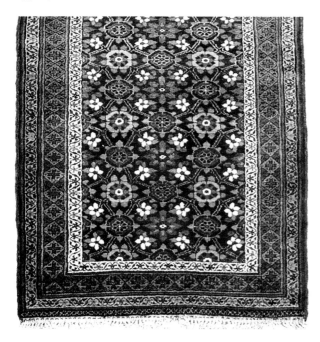

Varâmin rug (detail) *Peter Pap Oriental Rugs Inc*

vartan garmir (Armenian). Kermes.

vase. One of the eight emblems of Buddha. The vase is depicted on Chinese rugs and symbolizes a vessel of virtue.

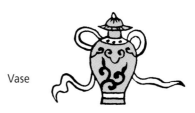

Vase

Vase carpet. Carpets with a field filled by flowers and tendrils or a lattice with a vase included as part of the design. More specifically, sixteenth and seventeenth-century Persian carpets with floral designs springing from vases. These rugs may have superimposed systems of arabesques. Orientation of the design is such that it can be viewed properly from only one direction. The origin of these rugs within Persia is problematic. They have been attributed to Kerman.

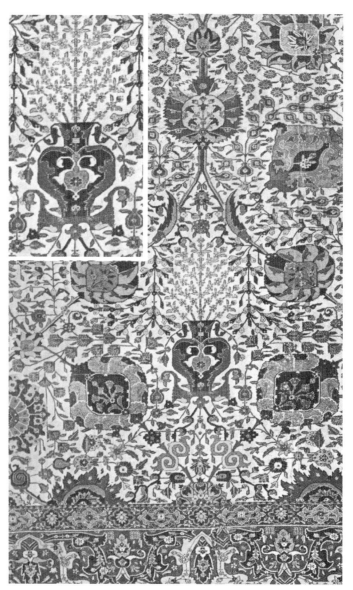

Vase carpet (detail)

Vase carpet structure. A structure used in certain sixteenth and seventeenth-century Persian vase carpets and other carpets. Warps are cotton and wefts are wool, cotton, or silk. Three wefts are used after each row of knots, two of wool and one of cotton or silk. Warps are completely offset. Wool pile and an asymmetric knot open to the left are used in this structure.

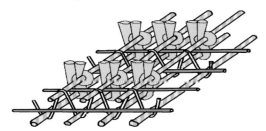

Vase structure *After Thompson*

vat dye. A dye soluble only in a reduced form and that is applied in that form and is fixed to the fiber only when exposed to oxygen. See "indigo."

velence, velençe (from Spanish "Valencia"). A wool cloth or blanket in a plain weave that has been heavily napped by combing. The combing pulls out the wefts. Colors are white, blue, and yellow.

velour. Any fabric with a cut pile or nap surface.

velvet. A fabric with an extra-warp woven pile structure. Velvet may suggest silk pile. There were Mughal and Ottoman velvets that were designed and used as carpets. See "çatma," "kadife," and "maghmal."

velveteen. A fabric with an extra-weft woven pile structure.

Venetian. A warp-faced carpet woven by machine in strips. Usually striped or checked. These carpets were woven in widths of 36 inches.

Veramin. See "Varâmin.

verneh, verné. This term has one meaning in western countries and another in Near Eastern countries and Russia. In western countries, verneh refers to Caucasian flatweaves of a variety of structures that are not soumak, tapestry, or silehs (western definition). In Near Eastern countries and Russia, a verneh is a Caucasian flatweave with the S-shaped dragon motif and soumak structure with a supplementary weft float. See "gemyan" and "sileh."

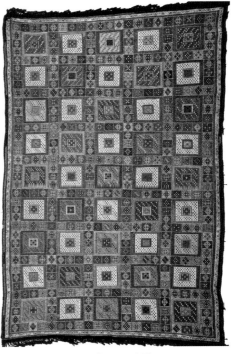

Verneh *Russel Fling*

vertical loom. See "carpet loom."

vertical multi-niche prayer rugs. A prayer rug or kilim with a vertical arrangement of three to five niches on the same vertical axis. Such prayer rugs or kilims are woven in central and south central Anatolia. See "prayer rug" and "saff."

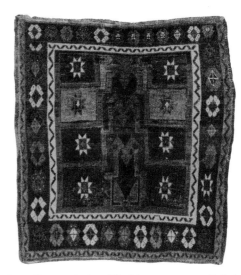

Anatolian vertical multi-niche prayer rug *Sothebys*

vertical wefts. An ambiguous term that may refer to supplementary yarns parallel to structural warps in some tapestry weaves. See "eccentric wefts."

vicuña. A South American Camelid producing a very fine and expensive hair. Cloth woven of the same.

Vienna Hunting Carpet. An early sixteenth-century Persian, all-silk carpet showing hunters on foot and on horseback attacking a variety of animals. Peris occupy the border. This rug may have been woven in Kashan. The rug measures about 23 feet by 11 feet. The knot density is about 785 per square inch. There is some silver brocading. This carpet is presently in the Museum für Angewandte Kunst, Vienna. There is a smaller, but very similar carpet in the Museum of Fine Arts, Boston.

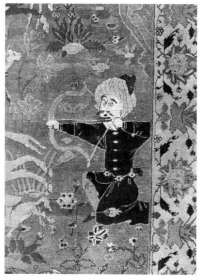

Vienna Hunting Carpet (detail)

Vienna Millefleurs Rug. See "Imperial Mughal Prayer Rug."

Vienna Portuguese Carpet. A late sixteenth-century carpet of India or Persia. Its size is about 20 feet by 10 feet. The asymmetric jufti knot is used in its construction on a cotton foundation. There are about 304 knots per square inch. This is a medallion rug with corner pieces that show what appear to be Portuguese caravels at sea occupied by Europeans. This carpet is presently in the Vienna Museum für Angwandte Kunst. See "'Portuguese' carpets."

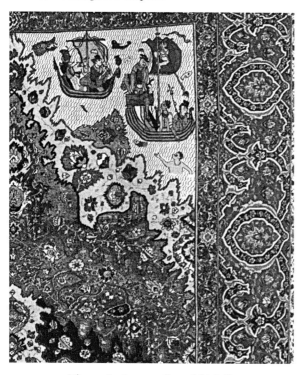

Vienna Portuguese Carpet (detail)

vilayet (Turk., from Arabic). A major administrative division of the Ottoman Empire and present-day Turkey, headed by a *vâli* (governor) and an elective council. A vilayet is subdivided into *kazas*, each headed by a *kaymakam*.

village rugs. Village rugs, as distinct from nomadic rugs, are usually woven on vertical looms. As distinct from workshop rugs, no cartoon or talim is used as a design guide. Border designs at corners may not be reconciled; there may be design mismatch at the corners. Village rugs may be woven by semi-nomadic peoples. Their rugs are likely to include traditional tribal motifs. However, these motifs may be changed, repeated, or enlarged to accommodate the larger rugs woven on village looms. Design idiosyncrasies in these rugs may include small motifs randomly placed within more formal medallion or all-over repeat patterns. See "cottage rug industry," "nomadic rugs," "tribal rugs," and "workshop rugs."

virgin wool. Wool that has never been used for another man-made product.

vishapagorg. Armenian for "dragon carpet." The term often refers to the Chondzoresk Kazak rug. Other Caucasian rugs have been so called. See "Chondzoresk."

Vist, Viss, Wiss. A town near Hamadan in Iran and a source of rugs with single wefts and a cotton foundation. Geometric designs are used on a red ground, often medallions of hooked diamonds alternating with hooked hexagons.

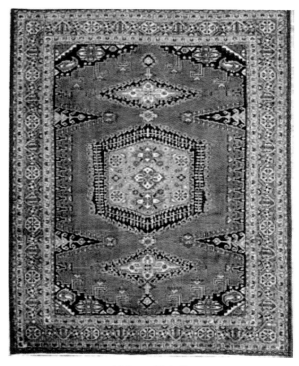

Vist rug (detail)

Vitruvian scroll. See "running dog."

voided pile. A weaving in which the design is produced or emphasized by contrasting flatwoven and pile areas. See "souf technique" and "trensaflossa."

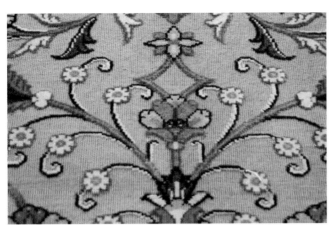

Qom rug with voided pile *Faresalesman*

Von Bode, Wilhelm (1845-1929). Though trained as a barrister, Von Bode became an art historian and museum curator. He studied and wrote about paintings and sculpture. His major work on carpets is ***Antique Rugs from the Near East***.

Vordoveh, Vardâvard. A village some twenty-five miles southwest of Hamadan. The characteristic design of this village is a medallion octagon or diamond with large, elaborate pendants on a camel-colored ground.

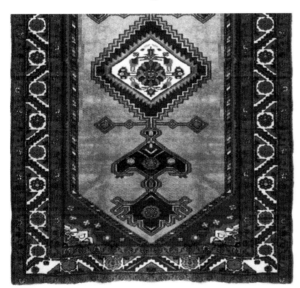

Vordoveh rug (detail) *Edward Koch*

Voysey, Charles F.A., (1857-1941). Voysey was an English architect and designer of the Arts and Crafts movement. He designed houses, wallpaper, and carpets. In 1897, he was commissioned to design hand-knotted carpets made in Donegal. His designs incorporated field repeats of stylized subjects from nature. His original carpets are sought after and highly valued. See "Arts and Crafts."

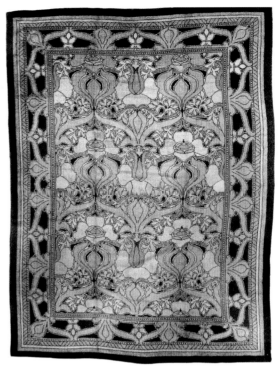

Donegal carpet designed by Voysey *Sothebys*

vurma, wurma (Turk.). Ram's horns or a design displaying ram's horns. See "kochak" and "Perpedil."

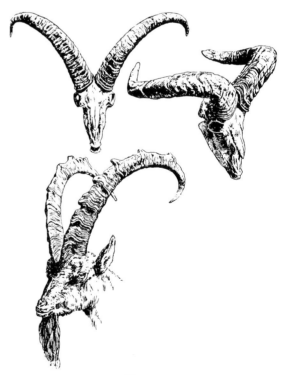

Vurma

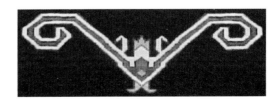

Perpedil motif

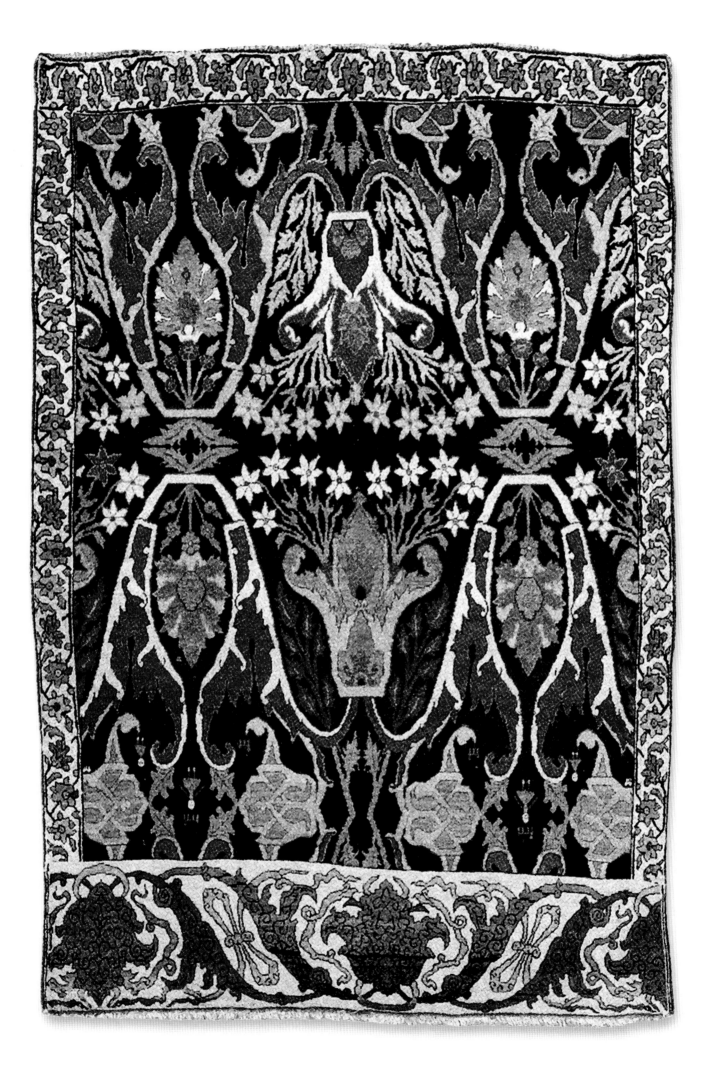

wagireh. See "vâgireh," "sampler."

wakf, vakıf (Turk., from Arabic *waqf*). A pious endowment, an inalienable gift of money, land, rugs, or other property (especially religious manuscripts and Korans) to a mosque or other charitable establishment, according to Islamic practice. Because of the practice of wakf, rugs as old as the fourteenth century have been found in Turkish mosques.

Walachia. A region of southern Romania producing some kilims. Older kilims may be striped with embroidered motifs and others may have designs of tapestry-woven naive images of humans and animals. See "Romania."

wall-to-wall carpeting. Any broadloom carpet fixed to the floor and entirely covering the surface.

walnut. Walnut husks are sometimes used for black or brown dyes.

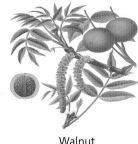

Walnut

wan (Chinese). Swastika. The Chinese symbol for "ten thousand." See "Chinese fret" and "swastika."

Wangden. A Tibetan village in the Nyang river valley and the source of meditation mats. See "meditation mat."

Warangal. A city of the province of Andhra Pradesh in southern India. Some old silk rugs were woven in Warangal. There is some production of lower-quality contemporary rugs in this city.

warp. Warps are the initial structural components of loom-woven fabrics. Parallel warp yarns run the length of the loom. Wefts are woven through the warps and pile knots are tied to the warps.

warp beam. The beam on which warp is wound or attached opposite the breast beam. On a vertical loom, the higher beam. On a horizontal loom, the beam farthest from the weaver's first weft. See "beam."

warp-faced. In a balanced plain weave, warps and wefts are equally visible. In a warp-faced fabric, warps are more closely spaced than wefts and wefts are concealed. Tribal straps and bands are often warp-faced. Turkmen and Uzbek ikat is usually warp-faced. See "tablet weaving."

warping the loom. The process of fixing the warps to the loom to achieve the desired warp count and warp tension. Special skill is required in this process. See "warp tension."

warp knots. Knots used to connect lengths of warp. In pile rugs, warp knots may be visible from the front of the rug. Warp knots may be colored to conceal them and only become visible the first time a new rug is washed.

warp offset, depressed warp, warp depression. A set of warps can be held in the same plane by tight, supporting wefts (cable wefts) while alternate warps are permitted to lie in another plane due to loose and bending wefts (sinuous wefts). Alternate warps are seen to be depressed from the back of the rug. Warps may be offset to the extent that one warp may lie on top of another. In this case, only one warp node per knot is visible from the back of the rug. Where there is a 45 degree warp offset, both knot nodes are visible from the back, but one node is much smaller than the other. See "cable weft" and "nim-lool."

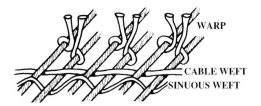

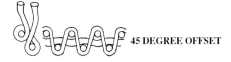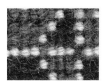

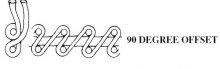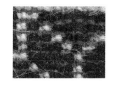

Warp offset

warp patterning. The use of warps in a variety of structures (extra-warp, warp float) to create designs or patterns.

warp sett. Number of warps per inch or centimeter. A measurement used in the technical analysis of flatweaves.

warp sharing, dovetailed. In a tapestry weave, wefts of differently-colored adjacent areas which reverse direction on the same warp. This structure does not have the slits produced in a tapestry weave where wefts of adjacent area reverse direction on different warps.

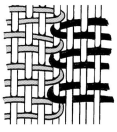

Warp offset

warp tension. In rug weaving, the stretching or tensile stress of warps on the loom to facilitate the weaving process. Even or equal tension across all warps is essential to produce a rectangular rug without wrinkles.

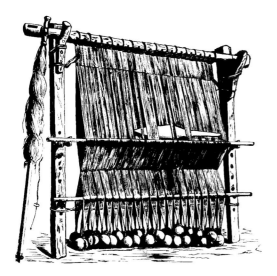

Warp-weighted loom *Scandanavian*

warp-weighted loom. The vertical warp-weighted loom is one in which warps are attached to weights that provide tension for the warps. Wefts are pushed upwards to the top of the loom. Weaving proceeds from the top of the loom downwards. Tapestry-woven fabrics were woven on such looms in ancient Greece, Egypt, and Anatolia. Warp weights have been discovered at archaeological sites in Anatolia. Such looms have been used until recently in Scandinavia.

Horizontal warp-weighted looms have been used up to the present in the Near East and North Africa. On these looms, weaving proceeds in the usual way, from the bottom up. One end of the warps is attached to the breast beam and the other end passes over one or more additional beams and is attached to weights. It is theorized that eccentric wefts are a common feature of fabrics woven on warp-weighted looms.

war rugs, war aksi. See "Afghanistan war rugs."

washing to bleach. Rugs may be washed in chemical solutions to soften (bleach) colors and to increase the luster of fibers. See "antique wash" and "bleaching."

washing to clean. Rugs should be washed in detergents with a pH of less than 7.5, such as sodium laurel sulfate (trade name "Orvis"). Before washing, the rug should be tested for running or bleeding dyes. Wash water should be at room temperature. Weak areas of the rug should be supported by patches. After washing, ample rinsing is required to remove all traces of the wash solution. Changes in rugs due to washing include altered shape, exposure of warp knots, bleeding or running, and loss of sizing in the foundation. See "wicking."

wasm. See "tamga."

watermark. See "pooling."

wazir (Arabic). Government official or minister.

Waziri. A design used in Aghanistan rugs, influenced by Western tastes, that includes a non-traditional octagonal gul and may include a square motif on four sides of the gul. This design is woven by Ersaris.

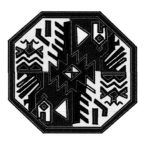

Waziri (non-traditional) gul

wazra (Arabic, "loincloth, skirt"). A blanket with a brown center and stripes woven in Tunisia.

weaver's hook. See "hook, weaver's."

weaver's knot. A knot (also known as the sheet bend or mesh knot) often used in hand-made nets.

weaver's square. The smallest unit of a rug design from which the whole rug design can be reconstructed. In many formal rug designs, one quarter of the rug includes the design for the whole rug when it is used to create mirror images across the central major and minor axes of the rug. For field designs where there is an all-over repeat pattern only, the weaver's square may be much smaller. See "quarter."

webbing end. In most oriental pile rugs, a flatwoven strip at both ends of the rug. This strip may be plain or ornamented.

webbing moth. See "carpet moth."

wedding blanket. Simple striped blankets of the nineteenth-century American southwest that were gifts of the groom's family at weddings.

wedge weave. See "Navajo wedge weave."

weeping willow design, Bid Majnún (Persian), **tereh asshur.** A common design of geometricized willow trees, cypresses, and flowering trees on rugs of Bijâr, Zanjân, and Ushak.

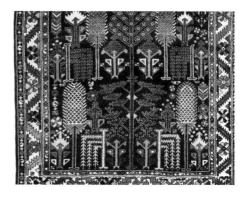

Bakhtiari rug (detail) with weeping willow design
Richard Rothstein & Co.

weft. Wefts are yarns woven through warps. Wefts are horizontal or crosswise yarns when the fabric is viewed on the loom. In pile rugs, there may be one or more wefts between each row of knots. Wefts help to lock knots in place. Wefts and warps make up the foundation. Wefts may be either structural or supplementary. See "eccentric wefts," "foundation," "supplementary weft," and "weft wrapping."

weft chaining. A weft wrapping structure similar to crochet work in which weft loops are pulled through each other as they pass around warps.

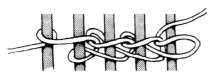
Weft chaining

weft-faced. In a balanced plain weave, warps and wefts are equally visible. In a weft-faced fabric, wefts are more closely spaced than warps and warps are concealed. Because of the warp spacing dictated by pile knotting, kilim ends are usually weft-faced.

weft float. A structure in which weft skips over warps to create a pattern or design. A continuous weft float produces a countered design in warps on the reverse side of the fabric.

weft ikat blankets. Rio Grande blankets of the early nineteenth-century southwest. Wefts were tie-dyed in indigo to produce simple designs. See "ikat."

weft substitution patterning. The use of wefts, continuous or discontinuous, of different colors to substitute structural wefts to create a design or pattern. The substitute wefts may float on the back of the weaving. See "Baluchi."

weft twining. A structure in which two wefts pass across warps, twisting together after each warp or at regular intervals. Twining may be countered or uncountered. Direction of twist around the warps is described as "S" or "Z." There are many different systems of twining and these are used widely in ethnic weavings of North Africa and the Near East. See "Ethiopia," "Glauoua rugs," and "tablet weaving."

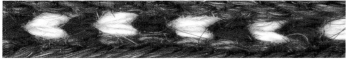
Weft twining

weft wrapping. Any of a wide variety of structures in which wefts are wrapped around warps, encircling them, rather than interlacing warps. Many forms of weft wrapping are used in oriental rugs and ethnic weavings. This classification of weft wrapping is useful.

1. Simple weft wrapping. The weft wrapping is ground weft. In plain weft wrapping, each row of weft moves in the same direction through progressive looping as in the soumak structure.

    In simple variable weft wrapping, there is variation in the looping in subsequent rows. This variation may be due to a change in loop direction. The direction of subsequent rows may be reversed (countered) as in soumak structures, producing a herringbone effect.

2. In knotted weft (not to be confused with extra weft pile wrapping used in pile rugs), the weft wrapping is ground weft. A true knot is formed around warps. The resulting structure often has a net-like appearance.

3. Compound structures. Weft wrapping is supplementary and used with an interlacing ground weft.

    In plain extra weft wrapping, a looping weft is used that may or may not be variable as in the soumak structure.

    In extra weft pile wrapping, the so-called symmetric knot, asymmetric knot, Spanish knot, and other rug knots are used. Symmetric and asymmetric knots may be wrapped continuously, to produce a loop pile, or they may be discontinuous, to produce cut pile. See "eccentric wefts," "knots," and "soumak."

weighting. Yarns and fabrics may be impregnated with mineral salts, gum, starch, or other substances to increase their bulk and weight. See "silk weighting" and "sizing."

weld, dyer's weed, dyer's rocket. The plant *Reseda luteola*, the stalks, leaves, and flowers yield a yellow dye.

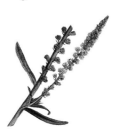
Weld

Western Reservation. A Navajo weaving area including Tuba City in Arizona. Rugs of the area have black, brown, or white fields with black or gray borders. The Tuba City Storm Pattern consists of central and corner rectangles containing serrated or spiked columns. Zigzag lines join the corner rectangles with the central rectangle.

Western Turkestan, Russian Turkestan. Western Turkestan comprises the former Republics of Kazakhstan, Kirghizia, Tajikistan, Turkmenistan, Uzbekistan, and the border area of northern Afghanistan. Rug-weaving peoples in this territory include Turkmen tribes, Khazakhs, Uzbeks, and a wide variety of other ethnic groups. See entries under "Beshir," "Bokhara," "Kazak," "Khiva," "Kirghiz," "Tajiks," "Turkmenistan," "Turkmen," and "Uzbeks."

wheel. One of the eight emblems of Buddhism. It is pictured in Chinese rugs and symbolizes the cyclical essence of life.

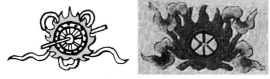

Wheel (Chinese)

wheel carpets. See "Holbein carpets."

whey. A product of sour milk used with madder to produce a salmon-red dye. See "madder."

whip stitch. A simple stitch used in overcasting and to lock the final weft in rug ends.

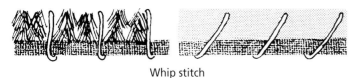

Whip stitch

white. Achromatic or without hue. In rugs, white is usually the natural color of wool or cotton. Either fiber may be bleached. In some pile weavings, bleached wool has become brittle, resulting in etching. Cotton or white silk may be used for highlights in some pile weaves.

wicking. When a rug is washed and soiled water evaporates from a white fringe, the fringe may be discolored tan or yellow. This problem may be solved by washing the fringe again to remove the soil. See "washing to clean."

widdle marks. Carpet stains due to soiling by pets.

Widener Animal Carpet. A seventeenth-century Mughal carpet in the collection of the National Gallery, Washington, D.C. This carpet shows no repeat pattern in the field. Animals include the elephant, tiger, cheetah, crocodile, rhinoceros, and mythological beasts. Human faces are shown within cartouches in the main border. The rug is 6 feet 3 inches by 13 feet 3 inches. The foundation is cotton and the pile is wool. The density is 288 asymmetric knots per square inch.

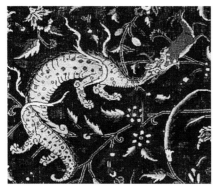

Dragon from the Widener Animal Carpet

Wide Ruin. See "Pinesprings."

Williams Admiral Carpet. A fifteenth-century Spanish carpet in the collection of the Philadelphia Museum of Art. This carpet has a lattice field of octagons and diamonds. The octagon cells are filled with floral motifs and birds. Three medallions on the field are heraldic blazons of Don Enriquez, Admiral of Castile. An inner border of lattices is surrounded by a kufesque border that also includes naive images of animals and human figures. There are end panels outside the borders containing other naive images. The carpet is 19 feet 1 inch by 8 feet 9 inches. The foundation and pile are wool. The Spanish knot is used at a density of 100 per square inch. See "Admiral carpets" and "Spain."

willow. See "weeping willow."

Wilton. A broadloom carpet made on a Jacquard system loom. A loop pile is formed over a flat rod or wire and cut during the weaving process. The process was developed in Wilton, England in about 1740. Originally, Wilton carpets were woven only in narrow widths, which were then stitched together. There were also hand-knotted Wilton carpets beginning in 1825 when Wilton acquired the Axminster looms and other equipment. Wilton hand-knotted carpets (termed Axminster) were still in production in 1924. See "Axminster" and "Brussels."

winder plied. Z-spun yarns that have been loosely S-plied by winding the yarn into a ball from a reel. Winder plied yarn is used for rug pile. In spin and ply notation, winder plied may be indicated by "w" as in Z2Sw. See "spin" and "ply."

wine glass border. See "leaf and calyx."

wire. For some power-loomed carpets, the number of rows of pile per warp inch. Also, that part of a power loom on which pile loops are formed. See "gauge" and "rows per inch."

Wiss. See "Vist."

Wissa Wassef, Ramses. Wissa Wassef founded an art school near Cairo, Egypt in 1952. The art school became a source of tapestries woven by children. These tapestries show naive representations of village scenes, animals, and family life. See "Egypt," "Harrânia."

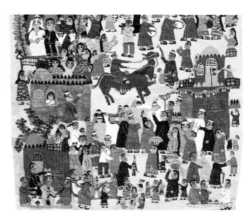

The Children Museum of Indianapolis *Wissa Wassef tapestry*

woof. Weft.

wool. The finest fiber from the coat of sheep. True wool fiber lacks a medulla or hollow central core. The fiber is solid. The most important qualities in wool are fineness, fiber length, and natural color. These qualities are primarily determined by the breed of sheep. The fineness of wool fibers ranges from a thickness of 1/3000 inch to 1/275 inch. The Merino and its crossbreeds regularly produce the finest wool, but fine wool is also taken from the first shearing of lambs from many breeds. Breeds producing coarse wools are generally found in the Middle East. Fairly coarse wools have better wear resistance than fine wools. Carpet wools have a diameter of about 35 to 40 microns.

Natural sheep wool may be colored brown, fawn, yellow, black, and gray, as well as white. The natural colors of wool have been exploited in rug designs. Wool fibers are covered with microscopic scales. These scales assist adherence in felting and spinning. Fibers without these scales from pelt-bearing animals are considered hair. Some hair in carpet wool adds gloss, but is undesirable in quantity because it dyes poorly. Some wool fibers or staple are as long as 20 inches. Longer staple is grown on the shoulder, while shorter staple is grown on the rump of the sheep. See " hair," "kemps," "pashmina," "sheep," "shotori," "tabachi," "woolen," and "worsted."

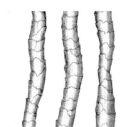

Microscopic view of wool fiber

woolen. A wool yarn of mixed staple that has been carded. Fibers are neither as long nor as parallel as worsted yarn. See "worsted."

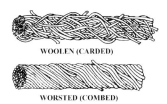

WOOLEN (CARDED)

WORSTED (COMBED)

wool fat. See "lanolin."

workshop rugs. Hand-knotted oriental rugs woven for market according to cartoons, talims, or samples. Usually many rugs copying the design are produced in a factory setting. Large, permanent looms in factories permit production of large rugs to market demand. Warp tensioning systems on these looms result in improved quality and more predictable quality than is possible with primitive looms.

Workshop rug designs tend to be formal and curvilinear. Because designs are carefully planned and followed, border corners are smoothly reconciled. Workshop rugs have been faulted because of their lack of design spontaneity. Some designs, however, have achieved great artistic merit. Many of these rugs are woven of the finest materials according to the highest technical structural standards. The modern workshop or factory system of rug production began in Persia in the late nineteenth century. Most contemporary oriental rugs are woven through this system. See "cottage industry," "Chinese rugs," "decorative rugs," "OCM," "PETAG," and "Ziegler and Co."

worsted. A wool yarn of long staple with fibers that have been combed prior to spinning. Combing produces more parallel fibers than carding. See "woolen."

wreath carpets. Sixteenth-century rugs of Alcaraz, Spain. Most of these rugs have green wreaths on a red field. The wreaths are in single or multiple columns. Each wreath is filled with arabesques. These rugs use the Spanish knot. See "Spain."

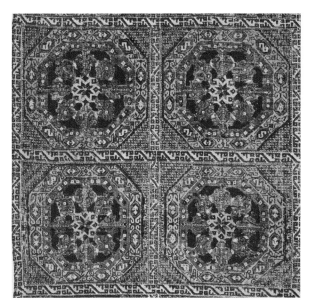

Wreath carpet (detail)

wufu. See "bats."

X

Xi. A Chinese character and symbol for happiness. This character is sometimes used in Chinese rug designs. A pair of such characters suggests wedded happiness. See "fu" and "shou."

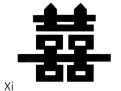

Xi

Xinjiang, Sinkiang. See "Eastern Turkestan."

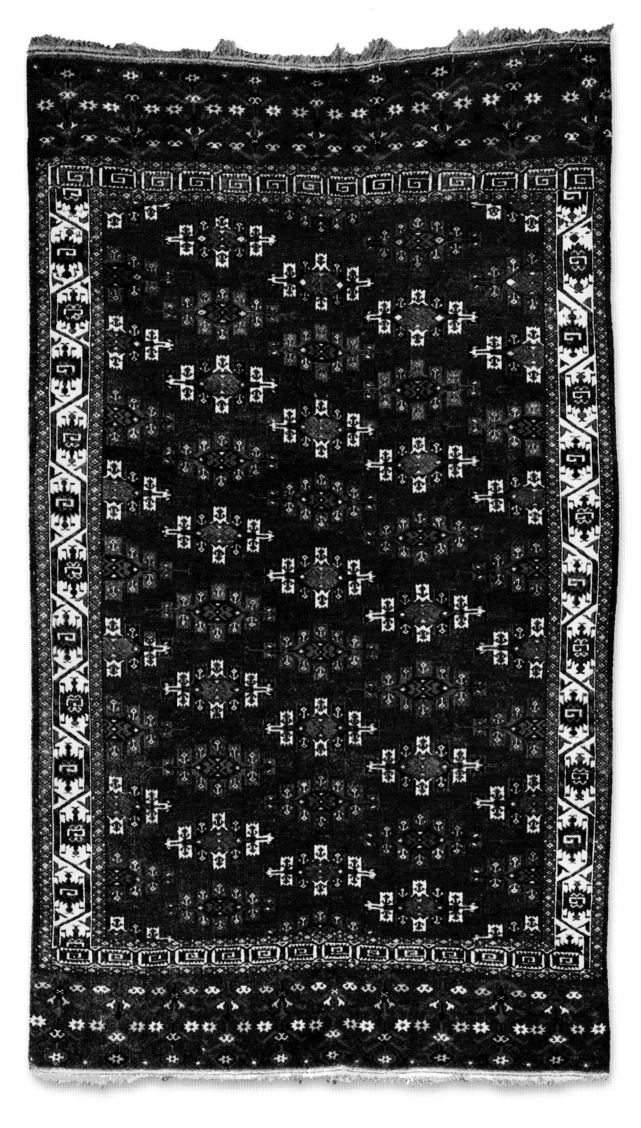

Yağcbedir. Village rugs made in the area of Balikesir and Bergama in northwestern Anatolia. Dominant colors are dark blue and red. Common designs are a hexagon medallion with stepped ends filled with geometricized flowers and a prayer rug with stepped mihrab filled with eight-pointed stars. Contemporary designs include copies of the Eagle Kazak. Narrow runners with geometricized blossoms on a dark blue field are also woven. Warp ends are plaited and tasseled. Knot densities are between 40 to 50 symmetric knots per square inch. Some older examples may have a line of variously dyed Angora wool knotted on the back of the rug. Currently, production in the area is increasing.

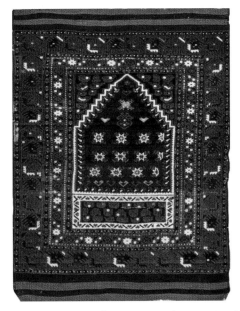

Yağcbedir prayer rug (Bergama area) *Jason Nazmiyal*

yağlık (Turk.) Napkin. Some of these have been elaborately embroidered.

Yahlameh. See "Yalameh."

Yahyalı. A town near Niğde in central Anatolia. Rugs made in the neighborhood of this town are generally in red, blue, and yellow. The typical rug includes a hexagon or diamond medallion with pendants (sometimes in the form of hanging lamps) on a red field.

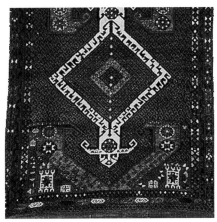

Yahyalı rug *James Allen*

yak hair rugs. Pile rugs and blankets of yak under-hair are woven in Tibet, Mongolia, and Bhutan. Such rugs are usually very shaggy, small and black. Yak hair is black, brown-gray, or white. Goat hair and sheep's wool may be mixed with yak hair in these weavings.

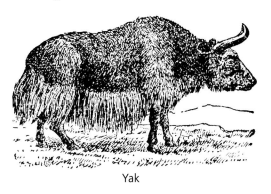

Yak

yak-gereh (Persian, "single knot"). Asymmetric knot.

Yalameh, Yahlameh. Village rugs woven in an area southeast of Chahâr Mahâl, Iran. These rugs include motifs of the Qashqa'i, Lurs and Khamseh. Three stacked latchhook diamond medallions are typical. Colors are brighter than most southwest Persian rugs. Yalamehs are relatively finely woven and many are of large size.

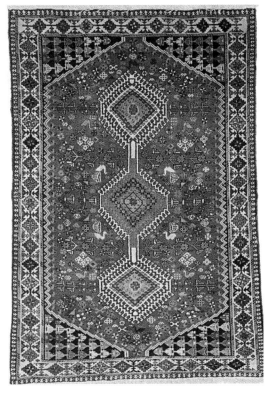

Yalameh rug (detail)

yamany. A Kurdish slit-weave tapestry woven cover of the Caucasus. See "bar."

yaprak (Turk., "leaf"). Panel or section of a rug.

Yaqub Kahani. A subtribe of the Baluchi and weavers of floor rugs and a few prayer rugs.

yarachitme (Turk., "half-weave"). Asymmetric knot.

Yarkand, Yarkant. A city of Eastern Turkestan (presently called Shache) on the Yarkand River about one-third of the way between Kâshgar and Khotan (Hotan). Yarkand has been a lesser source of rugs than Khotan and Kâshgar. Old Eastern Turkestan rugs with a pomegranate and vase design were assigned to Yarkand, but this attribution has been questioned. These rugs usually have asymmetric knots and two blue wefts in a cotton foundation. Older Yarkand rugs have highly offset warps. See "Kâshgar" and "Khotan."

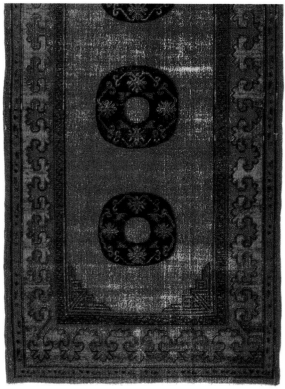

Yarkand rug *Sothebys*

yarn. A single or multiple ply of combed or carded filaments that have been spun or twisted to form a continuous strand. Yarns of different types are used in the warp, weft, and pile of oriental rugs. See "angle of twist," "crewel yarn," "fiber," "hand-spun," "machine spinning," "Persian yarn," "spin," "warp," and "weft."

yarn-sewn rugs. See "embroidery rugs."

yarn size. Yarn size is the equivalent of yarn count, yarn fineness, or yarn density. It is a number that is a multiple of a standard length in one pound of yarn. The standard length depends on the type of fiber. In all cases, the larger the size number, the smaller the yarn size. A size 2 yarn contains twice the standard length in one pound of yarn, a size 3 yarn contains three times the standard length in one pound of yarn, and so on. For example, size 1 worsted yarn contains 560 yards to a pound, size 2 contains 1,120 yards to a pound, size 3 contains 1,680 yards to a pound, and so on. See "cotton count" and "denier."

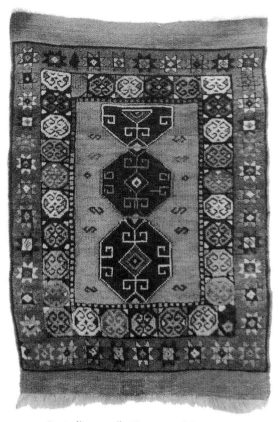

Anatolian yastik *Grogan and Company*

yastık (Turk.). A small Anatolian cushion face or pillow about three feet long by about one and one-half feet wide. The pile faces, without backs, are often used as mats.

yatak. (Turk., "bed"). Anatolian shaggy-pile rug made as a sleeping mat.

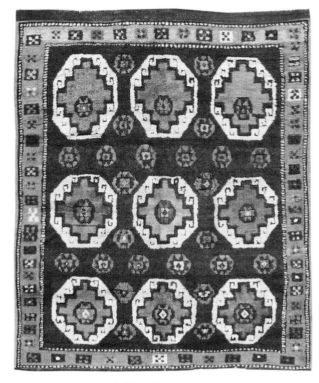

Yatak (detail) *Jason Nazmiyal*

yaylak, yayla, yaylah, yeylaq, yilag (Turk.) Summer pasturage (in the mountains) of nomadic tribes. See "sardsir" and "transhumance."

Yazd, Yezd. A city of central Iran. Older rugs of Yazd used the Herati design. Recent production consists of medallion designs similar to those of Kerman. Dominant colors are red, blue, and white. Warps are cotton and wefts are cotton or wool. Knot densities are about 100 to 200 asymmetric knots per square inch.

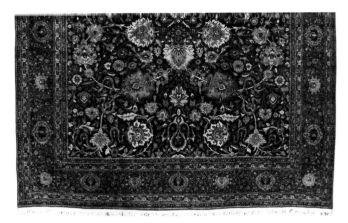

Yazd rug (detail) Sothebys

yazma (Turk.) Hand-printed or hand-painted cloth; bed cover.

yei rugs. Navajo rugs portraying the spirit intermediaries between god and man that are shown in Navajo sand painting. In some rugs, three sides of the field are outlined by the elongated body of the "rainbow goddess." See "sandpainting rugs."

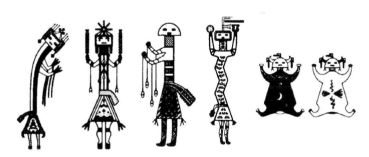

Yei figures

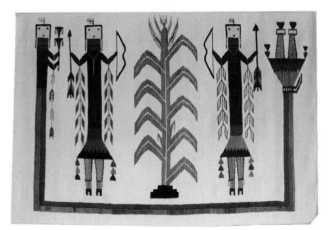

Yei Ship Rock rug *Steve Getzwiller*

yeibichai. Navajo rugs portraying dancers impersonating yeis or spirits.

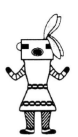 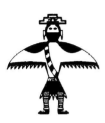 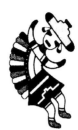

Yei dancers

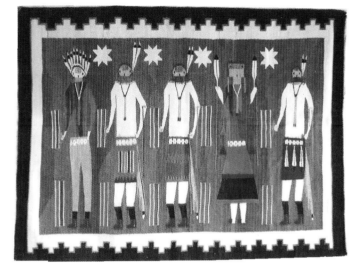

Yeibichai rug *Steve Getzwiller*

yelaq. See "yaylak."

yellow. A color of the visual spectrum. There are a wide variety of plant sources for natural yellow dyes in oriental rugs. Generally, yellow vegetal dyes have greater susceptibility to fading than other colors. See entries under these names: artemesia, buckthorn, chamomile, daphne, delphinium zalil, esparek, euphorbia, flavone, fox glove, fustic, onion skin, pomegranate, saffron, safflower, sophora japonica, sumac, turmeric. See "dye, natural" and "quercetin."

Yerevan. See "Erivan."

Yerkes, Charles Tyson (1837-1905). American financier, public transportation owner, and collector of oriental rugs in Chicago. His important collection of rugs was sold by the American Arts Association in 1910. The catalog for the auction was written by John K. Mumford.

yeşil (Turk.) Green.

Yeşilhisar (Turk., "green castle"). A town of south central Anatolia, between Kayseri and Niğde, and a source of long-pile, lower-quality rugs often with a pink field.

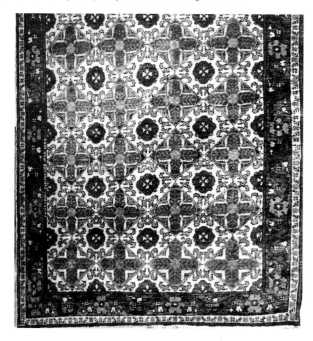

Yeşilhisar rug (detail) *Kazim Yildiz*

Yezd. See "Yazd."

yilag. See "yaylak."

yin yang. An oriental symbol of universal polarities: light and dark, male and female, good and evil, material and spiritual. The presence of a dot of dark color within the light area and a dot of light color within the dark area symbolizes the admixture of opposites in the real world. This symbol has been used in rugs of China and Eastern Turkestan. Yang is associated with the male or sun and yin with the female or moon. See "trigrams."

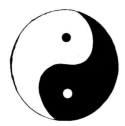

Yin yang

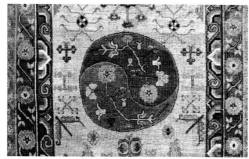

Chinese rug with yin yang,

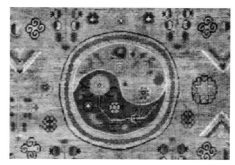

Khotan rug with yin yang

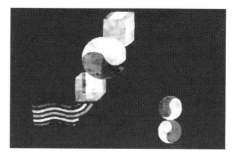

Chinese art deco rug with yin yang *Doris Leslie Blau*

yolami. See "tent band."

yolluk (Turk., "path-piece"). A carpet runner.

Yomud, Yomut. A Turkmen tribe occupying lands in Iran extending from the southeastern corner of the Caspian Sea and in Russian Turkestan along the eastern shore of the Caspian Sea. Subtribes include the Atabei, Djafarbei, Ogurjali, and Igdyr. Their primary guls are the Dyrnak, Tauk Noska, and Kepse. In the earliest rugs, guls are arranged in vertical columns. In later rugs they are in offset rows. A wide variety of borrowed motifs are used in bags and special-purpose weavings.These weavings include jovals, torbas, asmalyks, engsis, bokches, and tent bands.

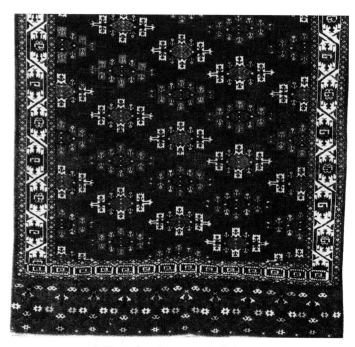

Yomud main carpet *Sothebys*

A wider range of colors is used in the weavings of the Yomud than in the weavings of other Turkmen tribes. The dominant color is a brownish red. The main borders usually have a white background. Both the asymmetric and symmetric knots are used in Yomud weavings. The symmetric knot is the more common. Typically, there are 100 to 150 knots per square inch in Yomud rugs. See "eagle gul," "Igdir," "marker knots," "Ogurjali," and "Turkmen."

yorgan yüzü. Turkish embroidered quilt cover.

Yörük, Yürük. (Turk.) Pastoral nomads of Anatolia who identify themselves as Yörük and who share an identity with certain tribes. These people are thought to have Turkmen origins. Their weaving techniques include pile weaves, brocade, tapestry weave, soumak, and tablet weaving. Their weavings are all wool. Motifs are mainly geometric floral and animal abstracts. Yörük rugs are woven in a very wide variety of designs and colors. Their weavings are strongly influenced by those of surrounding peoples. Kurdish rugs have been mistakenly attributed to the Yörük.

Yugoslavia. See "Bosnia," "Şarköy," and "Serbia."

yük perdesi, (Turk. "cargo cover"). An embroidered or otherwise decorated dust sheet draped over bags in a tent.

yün (Turk.) Wool.

yün-chien. See "cloud collar."

Yüncü. A nomadic tribe of northwest Anatolia near Balıkesır; the source of kilims of simple, bold and archaic designs. Dominant colors are red and blue.

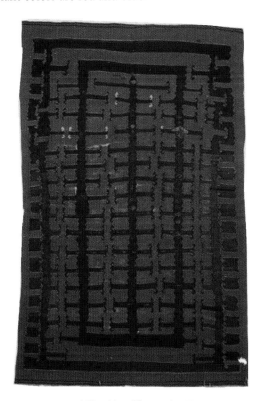

Yüncü kilim (detail) *R. John Howe*

Yuntdağ. A mountainous area south of Bergama in western Anatolia. The area is inhabited by peoples of Turkmen descent. They weave brightly colored rugs of geometric designs, many suggestive of Caucasian designs. The DOBAG project (contemporary vegetable-dyed rugs) originated in theYuntdağ. See "DOBAG."

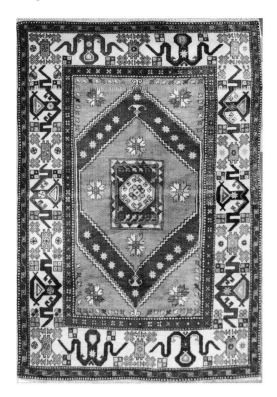

Yuntdağ rug (detail) *KazimYildiz*

yup. See "tent band."

yurt. (Turk., "home (land)"), **öy** (Turkmen, "house"), **kibitka** (Russian), **ger** (Mongol). Technically, yurt is the ground on which a Turkmen tent is erected, but the term is often used to refer to the tent itself. A tent-like structure common to the Turkmen, Mongols, Kazakhs, Kirghiz, and other Inner Asian nomads. It consists of a wooden latticework frame surrounded by reed mats and covered with heavy felt. Various ropes and bands are used to hold the structure together and a variety of weavings are used as functional or decorative structures in connection with the yurt. See "alachiq," "engsi," "germesh," "kapunuk," "reed screens," and "tent band."

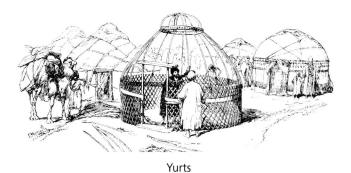

Yurts

Yürük. See "Yörük."

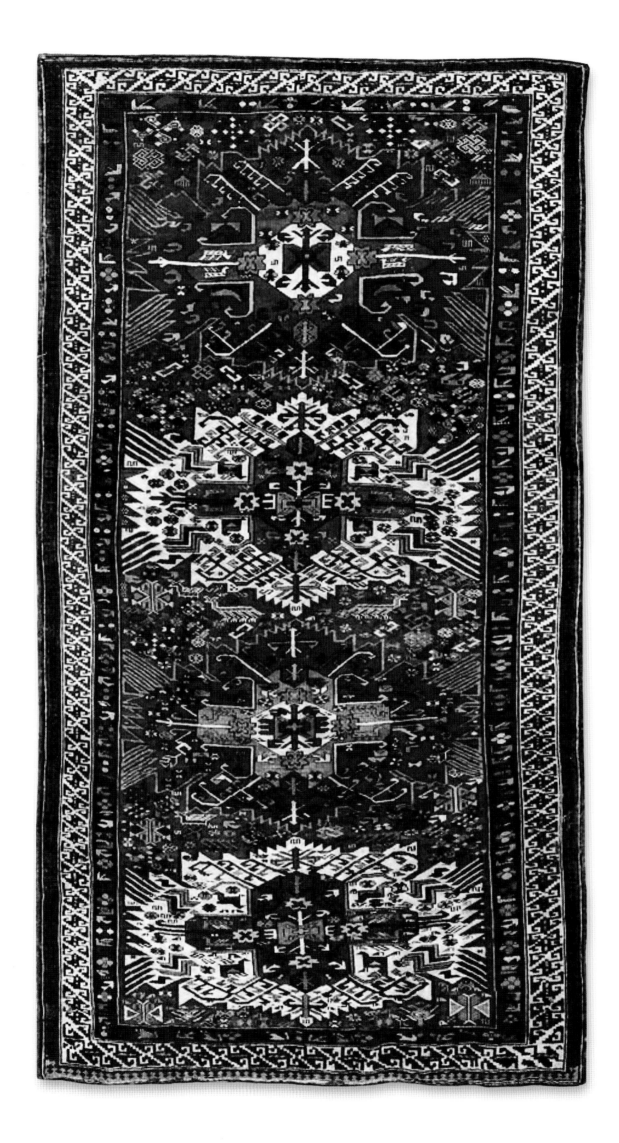

Zabol, Zabul. An Iranian town, the provincial capital of Seistan, close to the border of Afghanistan. Rugs of this area are woven by the Baluch. The field design of these rugs usually consists of some small repeated motif. Similar rugs are woven in Chakhansur. See "Chakhansur."

Za'farânlu Kurds. See "Quchan."

Zâgheh. A village of northwestern Iran, west of Hamadan, and a source of medallion rugs with serrated spandrels on a field with the Herati pattern or botehs. These rugs are single-wefted with the symmetric knot on a cotton foundation. There are other places named Zâgheh in Iran near Bijâr, Khorramâbâd, and Qom.

Zahir Shahi. A rug design used in Afghanistan consisting of alternate columns of diamonds and linked hexagons, often on a white field. The design was introduced by King Zahir Shah in the 1940s.

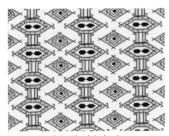

Zahir Shahi design

Zaiane. A tribe of the Middle Atlas Mountains of Morocco. Some of their pile weavings are very shaggy and are used for bedding or cloaks (*hendira*). The long pile obscures the design and the back is displayed because it better reveals the design. Colors are red, black, and white. Symmetric knots and Berber knots may be found in the same rug. Zaiane weavers also produce flatwoven rugs with designs of diamonds, horizontal stripes, or stripes containing diamonds. These sometimes have very narrow bands of pile. See "Morocco."

Zakatala, Zakataly. A group of villages of northern Azerbaijan in the Caucasus. All-wool, symetrically knotted rugs of this area have designs of vertical stripes with chevrons or variations of Kazak designs. Many Zakatala rugs are woven with yarn that is S-spun and Z-plied. See "Caucasus."

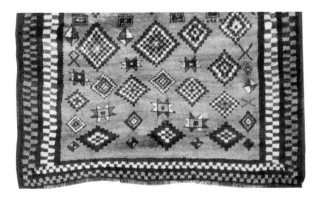

Zakatala rug (detail) *Sothebys*

zalil. See "esparek."

Zanjân, Sanjan, Zenjan. A town of northwestern Iran, the capital of the Khamseh district, about halfway between Tabriz and Tehran. Zanjân is a source of Kurdish village rugs. It is also a source of rugs woven in imitation of Bijars. The symmetric knot is used on a cotton foundation. Both single-wefted and double-wefted rugs are woven around Zanjân. See "Khamseh."

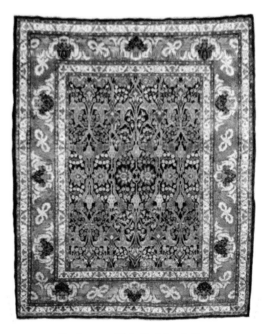

Zanjan rug (detail) *John Collins*

Zapotec rugs. The Zapotec are an indigenous people, primarily of the state of Oaxaca, Mexico. They weave mats on backstrap looms and tapestry woven rugs and blankets on large looms. Designs are stripes and diamonds.

zar (Persian, from Arabic *dhar*, "forearm, cubit"). Obsolete Persian linear measure of about 41 to 44 inches. Also (Persian *zar*), gold. In Turkish, zar means "curtain, thin cloth, head-to-foot veil." See "reg."

Zara. A village of eastern Anatolia near Sivas and the source of rugs usually with a design of ornamented vertical stripes. Older rugs of Zara are very finely knotted on an all-wool foundation. Within each stripe is a complex meander or vertically arranged botehs.

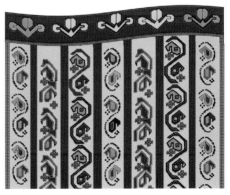

Zara rug (detail)

Zarand. A district of northwest Iran. Zarand is thought to be the source of kilims woven in the warp sharing tapestry technique on cotton warps. This weaving technique permits the use of prominent vertical lines in the design. Designs suggest Caucasian motifs. It is also the source of medallion and spandrel rugs with a single wefted cotton foundation and the symmetric knot. See "Qazvin" and "Sâveh."

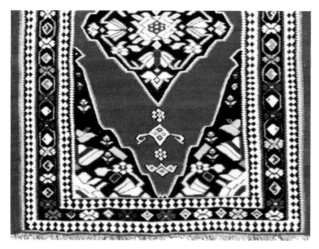

Zarand kilim (detail) *Peter Willborg*

zarbia. See "zerbiya."

zarcharak (Persian *zar'-chârak*, "one-and-one-quarter zar"). A rug size of about 4½ feet by 2½ feet.

zard (Persian). Yellow.

zaronim (Persian). A rug of about five feet by three feet. Literally, one and one-half zar (in length).

Zeikhur. See "Seishour."

Zejwa, Zeyva. A village south of Kuba in the Caucasus. Nineteenth century rugs attributed to this village have multiple medallions, similar to the Chelaberd, which consist of a cruciform shield with radiating hooks. Average knot density is 90 symmetric knots per square inch. Rugs with this design are the largest of Kuba rugs, averaging 40 square feet. The foundation is usually all wool.

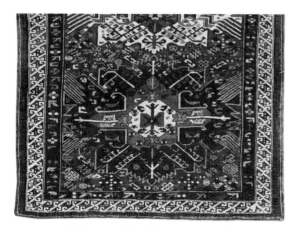

Zejwa rug (detail) *Jason Nazmiyal*

Zei-i Sultan. See "Zill-i Sultan."

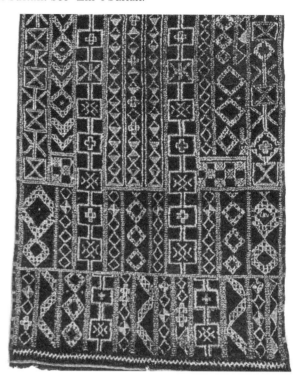

Zemmour rug (detail) *Pickering /Yohe Collection*

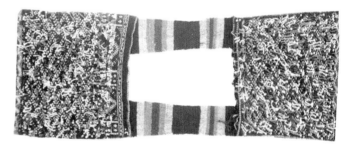

Zemmour saddle bag *Lloyd Rowcroft*

Zemmour. A Berber tribal group of Morocco. Their weavings include pile rugs and flatwoven mats, blankets, pillows and saddlebags. Red is the dominant color. Designs are horizontal stripes or rows of simple repeated geometric motifs. There may be a vertical design strip at the edges of their weavings, but complete borders are not used.

Zenaga. A tribe of Morocco. Their rugs display geometricized plants, animals, and domestic objects.

Zenjan. See "Zanjân."

zerbiya, zerbia, zarbia. A borderless carpet of eastern Morocco, roughly striped or including small, scattered motifs. Red is the dominant color. It measures about 6 feet by 12 feet. See "Morocco."

Zeyve. A town of western Anatolia and a source of small rugs with geometric designs. Red is the dominant color. The foundation may be cotton or wool and cotton. Many of these rugs are sold as Çal rugs. See "Çal."

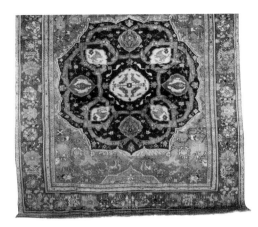

Ziegler Mahal rug *Grogan and Company*

Ziegler and Co. In 1883, the British firm of Ziegler and Co. of Manchester set up an office in Tabriz for the importation of Persian rugs. Ziegler began placing orders with rug weavers in and around Sultanabad and was purchasing the product of 3,000 carpet looms by the beginning of World War I. These rugs were of medium quality and known as Mushkabads or Mahals to the rug trade. The economic depression after World War I ended this major production and trade in Persian rugs.

zigzag. A sharply angular reversing design such as a sawtooth, often used in borders.

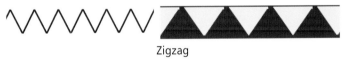

Zigzag

zili. See "sileh."

Zill-i Sultan, Zei-i Sultan. A common design of all-over repeats of vases with floral sprays. ***Zell os-Soltân*** (Arabic, "shadow of the emperor") was the title of Mas'ud Mirzâ, a Qajar prince who governed Iran's southern provinces during the late nineteenth and early twentieth centuries.

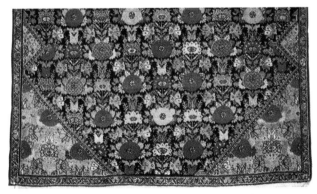

Zill-i Sultan rug Northwest Persia *Sothebys*

zilu (Persian). An Iranian weft-faced flatwoven rug. The structure includes two sets of warps and pairs of wefts. Contemporary zilus are all cotton. Most zilus have blue and white designs. Some designs are intricate and may include Koranic inscriptions. There is a Persian zilu with a date translated as 1556.

zinpush (Persian, "saddle cover"). In Azerbaijan, embroidered silk or velvet ceremonial horse covers.

zin-i asp (Persian, "horse saddle"). In Afghanistan, a saddle cover with an opening for the pommel.

Zipper selvage

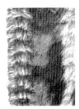

zipper selvage. A distinctive edge finish of a group of Kurdish rugs of eastern Anatolia in which the selvage wrapping is looped warp-wise between paired edge warps, creating the appearance of a closed zipper.

Zirhaki (Persian *zir-khâki*, "subterranean, underground"). A design used in Tabriz and Kashmar, Iran. It consists of flowers with urns and vases. The Iranian version may include architectural motifs and medallion views of ancient buildings. See "Persepolis rug."

zoomorphic. Having the form of stylized animals. Often used to describe motifs in oriental rugs. See "animal head," "Akstafa peacock," and "murgi."

Zoroastrianism. A religion of ancient Persia with adherents in India (the Parsees) and the Caucasus. Zoroaster (Zarathustra) was a prophet who taught the worship of Ahura Mazda as the source of good. The principal symbol and center of Zoroastrian ritual was the sacred fire. Zoroastrian motifs, often suggestive of fire or flame, have been recognized in oriental rugs. See "boteh."

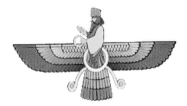

Zoroastrian symbol or Faravahar

Z-spun. Yarn spun in a counter-clock wise direction. The diagonal line in the "Z" suggests the direction of spin. Singles in almost all oriental rugs are Z-spun. See "S-spun."

Zig-spun

Zuni. See "Pueblo weaving."

Zurhuri. A tribe of Arab origin settled near Farah in Afghanistan and the source of contemporary rugs with geometricized floral motifs.

Museums with Notable Oriental Rug Collections

United States
Armenian Library And
Museum of America
65 Main Street
Watertown, MA 0247
(617) 926-2562

Museum of Fine Arts
465 Huntington Avenue
Boston, MA 02115
(617) 267-9300

The Art Institute of Chicago
111 South Michigan Avenue
Chicago, IL 60603
(312) 443-3600

The Brooklyn Museum of Art
200 Eastern Pkwy
Brooklyn, NY 11238-6099
(718) 638-5000

The Cleveland Museum of Art
11150 East Boulevard
Cleveland, OH 44106
(216) 421-7340

The Detroit Institute of
Arts Museum
5200 Woodward Avenue
Detroit, MI 48202
(313) 833-7900

De Young Museum
50 Hagiwara Tea Garden Drive
San Francisco, CA 94118
(415) 750-3600

The Getty
1200 Getty Center Drive
Los Angeles, California 90049
(310) 440-7330

The Hispanic Society of
America
613 West 155th Street
New York, NY 10032-7597
(212) 926-2234

Indianapolis Museum of Art,
4000 Michigan Road,
Indianapolis, IN 46208-3326
(317) 923-1331

The Los Angeles
County Museum of Art
5905 Wilshire Blvd
Los Angeles, CA 90036
(323) 857-6000

The Metropolitan
Museum of Art
1000 5th Avenue
New York, NY 10028
(212) 535-7710
The Textile Museum
2320 S Street Northwest
Washington, DC 20008-4088
(202) 667-0441

Canada
The Royal Ontario Museum
100 Queens Park
Toronto, ON M5S 2C6
(416) 586-8000

Textile Museum of Canada
55 Centre Avenue
Toronto, ON M5G 2H5
(416) 599-5321

United Kingdom
The Burrell Collection
2060 Pollokshaws Rd
Glasgow G43 1AT
0141 287 2550

The National Museum of
Scotland
Chambers Street
Edinburgh EH1 1JF
0300 123 6789

Victoria & Albert Museum
Cromwell Road
London SW7 2RL
0871 971 5939

The Whitworth Art Gallery
Oxford Road
Manchester,
Lancashire M15 6ER
0161 275 7450

Austria
Vienna Museum für
Angwandte Kunst
5 Stubenring, Vienna,
Austria
43-1-711-360

Oriental Rug Internet Sites

Informational sites

R. John Howe: Textiles and
Text
rjohnhowe.wordpress.com

The Textile Museum
textilemuseum.org

The Richard E. Wright Reports
richardewright.com

Turkotek
turkotek.com

Tea and Carpets
tea-and-carpets.blogspot.com

New England Rug Society
ne-rugsociety.org

Marla Mallett
marlamallett.com

SpongoBongo
spongobongo.com

Jozan
jozan.com

**Oriental rug organization
sites**

American Conference on
Oriental Rugs (ACOR)
acor-rugs.org

International Conference on
Oriental Carpets (ICOC)
icoc-orientalrugs.org

Oriental Rug Importers
Association
oria.org

Oriental Rug Industry Center
of America
oricarugs.com

Oriental Rug Retailers
Association of America
orrainc.com

RUGMARK Foundation
goodweave.org

Bibliography

Baluch
Azadi, Siawosch, *Belutsch Tradition,* Klinkhardt & Biermann, Munich, 1986

Black, David and various authors, *Rugs of the Wandering Baluchi*, David Black Oriental Carpets, London, 1976

Boucher, Jeff W., *Baluchi Woven Treasures*, Jeff W. Boucher, Alexandria, Virginia, 1989

Konieczny, M.G., *Textiles of Baluchistan*, Trustees of the British Museum, London, 1979

Caucasus
Burns, James D., *The Caucasus Traditions in Weaving*, Court Street Press, Seattle, 1987

Der Manuelian, Lucy, *Armenian Rugs,* University of Michigan, 1983

Der Manuelian, Lucy and Murray L. Eiland, *Weavers, Merchants and Kings,* Kimball Art Museum, Fort Worth, 1984

Ellis, Charles Grant, *Early Caucasian Rugs,* The Textile Museum, Washington D.C., 1975

Razina, Tatyana, and Natalia Cherkasova and Alexander Kantsedikas, *Folk Art in the Soviet Union,* Abrams/ Aurora, New York, 1990

Schürmann, Ulrich, *Caucasian Rugs*, Washington International Associates, 1974

Stone, Peter F., *Rugs of the Caucasus: Structure and Design,* Greenleaf Co., Chicago, 1984

Tschebull, Raoul, *Kazak,* The Near Eastern Research Center, New York, 1971

Wright, Richard, *Rugs and Flatweaves of the Transcaucasus,* Pittsburgh Rug Society, Pittsburgh, Pa., 1980

Wright, Richard, and John T. Wertime, *Caucasian Carpets and Covers,* Hali Publications Limited, London, 1995

Yetkin, Serare, *Early Caucasian Carpets in Turkey,* Oguz Press Limited, London, 1978

China
Allane, Lee, *Chinese Rugs A Buyer's Guide,* Thames and Hudson, London, 1993

Eiland, Murray L., *Chinese and Exotic Rugs,* New York Graphic Society, New York, 1979

Hackmack, Adolf, *Chinese Carpets and Rugs,* Publishers La Libraire Française, Tientsin, 1924

Hyman, Virginia Dulany and William C. C. Hu, *Carpets of China and Its Border Regions,* Ars Ceramica Ltd., Ann Arbor, Michigan, 1982

Larsson, Jr., Lennart, *Carpets from China, Xinjiang & Tibet,* Shambhala Publications, Boston, 1989

Leitch, Gordon B., *Chinese Rugs,* Tudor Publishing Co., New York, 1928

Lorenz, H.A., *A View of Chinese Rugs,* Routledge & Kegan Paul, London, 1972

Rostov, Charles I. and Jia Guanyan, *Chinese Carpets,* Harry N. Abrams, Inc., New York, 1983

Europe
Faraday, Cornelia, *European and American Carpets and Rugs,* The Dean Hicks Company, Grand Rapids, Michigan, 1929

Geliazkova, Nevena, *Bulgarian Textiles,* F. Lewis, Leigh-on-Sea, 1958

Haslam, Malcolm, *Arts and Crafts Carpets,* Rizzoli, New York, 1991

Lanier, Mildred B., *The English and Oriental Carpets at Williamsburg,* The Colonial Williamsburg Foundation, Williamsburg, 1975

Makris, Kisos A., *The Handwoven Fabrics of Thessaly,* National Organization of Hellenic Handicrafts, Athens, 1961

Nylén, Ann-Maja, *Swedish Handcraft,* Nostrand Reinhold Company, New York, 1977

Oliviera, Baptista de, *História e Técnica dos Tapetes de Arriolos,* Lisboa, 1979

Oprescu, George, *Peasant Art in Roumania,* The Studio, Ltd., London, 1929

Parry, Linda, *William Morris Textiles,* The Viking Press, New York, 1983

Rheims, Maurice, *The Flowering of Art Nouveau,* Harry Abrams, New York

Ribaric, Jelka Radaus, *Yugoslavia/Croatian Folk Embroidery Designs and Techniques,* Van Nostrand Reinhold Company, New York, 1975

Sautier, Albert, *Italian Peasant Rugs,* Gli Editori Piantanida - Valcarenghi, Milan, 1923

Sherrill, Sarah B., Carpets and Rugs of Europe and America, Abbeville Press, New York, 1996

Trilling, James, *Aegean Crossroads,* The Textile Museum, Washington, D.C., 1983

Weeks, Jeanne G. And Donald Treganowan, *Rugs and Carpets of Europe and the Western World,* Chilton Book Company, Philadelphia, 1969

Willborg, Peter, *Flatweaves from Fjord and Forest,* David Black Oriental Carpets, London, 1984

India

Chattopadbaya, Kamaladevi, *Carpets and Floor Coverings of India,* Taraporevala, Bombay, 1976

Cohen, Steven, *The Unappreciated Dhurrie,* David Black Oriental Rugs, London, 1982

Desai, Chelna, *Ikat Textiles of India,* Chronicle Books, San Francisco, 1987

Dhamija, Jasleen and Jyotindra Jain, *Handwoven Fabrics of India,* Mapin Publishing, Pvt., Ahmedabad, India, 1989

Gans-Ruedin, E., *Indian Carpets,* Rizzoli, New York, 1984

Haque, Enamul, *Woven Air, The Muslin and Kantha Tradition of Bangladesh,* Whitechapel Art Gallery, London, 1988

Strong, Roy and various authors, *The Indian Heritage,* Victoria and Albert Museum, London, 1982

Kurd

Biqqs, Robert D., *Discoveries from Kurdish Looms,* Northwestern University, Chicago, 1983

Eagleton, William, *An Introduction to Kurdish Rugs,* Interlink Books, New York, 1988

Stanzer, Wilfried, *Kordi,* Adil Besim, Vienna, 1988

North Africa

Ammoun, Denise, *Crafts of Egypt,* The American University in Cairo Press, Cairo, 1991

Brown, Luane and Sidna Rachid, *Egyptian Carpets,* The American University in Cairo, 1985

Fiske, Patricia L., W. Russell Pickering and Ralph S. Yohe, *From the Far West: Carpets and Textiles of Morocco,* The Textile Museum, Washington D.C., 1980

Reinisch, Helmut., and Wilfried Stanzer, *Berber,* Helmut Reinisch, Graz, 1991

Reswick, Irmtrud, *Traditional Textiles of Tunisia,* University of Washington Press, 1985

Sieber, Roy, *African Textiles and Decorative Arts,* The Museum of Modern Art, New York, 1972

Stone, Caroline, *The Embroideries of North Africa,* Longman, Harlow, Essex, 1985

North America

Bowen, Dorothy Boyd and various authors, *Spanish Textile Tradition of New Mexico and Colorado,* Museum of International Folk Art, Santa Fe, 1979

Burnham, Dorothy K., Unlike the Lillies: *Doukhobor Textile Traditions in Canada,* Royal Ontario Museum, Toronto, 1986

Dedera, Don, *Navajo Rugs,* Northland Publishing, Flagstaff, AZ, 1990

Dockstader, Frederick J., *Weaving Arts of the North American Indian,* Harper Collins Publishers, Inc., New York, 1993

James, George Wharton, *Indian Blankets and Their Makers,* Dover Publications, Inc. New York, 1920

Kahlenberg and Berlant, *The Navajo Blanket,* Praeger Publishers, Los Angeles, 1976

Kaufman, Alice, and Christopher Selser, *The Navajo Weaving Tradition,* E. P. Dutton, Inc., New York, 1985

Von Rosenstiel, Helene, *American Rugs and Carpets,* William Morrow and Company, New York, 1978

Persia

Adamec, Ludwig H., *Historical Gazetteer of Iran,* 4 volumes, Graz, 1976-89

Aschenbrenner, Eric, *Oriental Rugs,* Volume 2, Persia, Battenberg Verlag, Munich, 1981

Atlas-e râh'hâ-ye Irân (Road atlas of Iran), Tehran, 1360/1981

Beattie, May H., *Carpets of Central Persia,* Sheffield City Art Galleries, Sheffield, 1978

Bier, Carol, *Woven from the Soul, Spun from the Heart,* The Textile Museum, Washington, D.C., 1987

Defense Mapping Agency, Gazetteer of Iran, 2 volumes, 2nd Edition, Washington, D.C., November 1984

de Franchis, Amadeo and John T. Wertime, *Lori and Bakhtiyari Flatweaves,* Tehran Rug Society, Tehran, 1976

Dhamija, Jasleen, *Iran's Crafts,*

Farabi University, Tehran, 1979

Edwards, Cecil A., *The Persian Carpet,* Duckworth, London, 1975

Farhang-e joghrâfiyâ-ye Irân (Geographical dictionary of Iran), Iranian Army General Staff, 10 volumes, Tehran, 1328-32/1949-53

Hillmann, Michael Craig, *Persian Carpets,* University of Texas Press, Austin, 1984

Ittig, Annette and various authors, *The Carpets and Textiles of Iran,* The Journal of The Society for Iranian Studies, Vol. 25, Nos. 1-2, 1992

Lefevre, Jean, *The Persian Carpet,* Lefevre & Partners, London, 1977

Opie, James, *Tribal Rugs of Southern Persia,* James Opie Oriental Rugs, Inc., Portland, 1981

Tanavoli, Parviz, *Bread and Salt - Iranian Tribal Spreads and Salt Bags,* Ketab Sara Company, Tehran, 1991

Tanavoli, Parviz, *Lion Rugs of Fars,* The Textile Museum, Washington, D.C., 1983

Tanavoli, Parviz, *Shahsavan,* Rizzoli, New York, 1985

Various Authors, "Carpets," Encyclopaedia Iranica, Vol. IV (1990), 834-96, Vol. V (1991), 1-9; also at *iranicaonline.org*

Willborg, Peter, *Hamadan,* J P Willborg AB, Stockholm, 1993

Wulff, Hans E., *The Traditional Crafts of Persia,* The M.I.T. Press, Cambridge, MA, 1966

Tibet

Denwood, Philip, *The Tibetan Carpet,* Aris and Phillips Ltd., Warminster, England, 1974

Myers, Diana K., *Temple, Household, Horseback: Rugs of the Tibetan Plateau,* The Textile Museum, Washington, D.C., 1984

Rutherford, Tom and various authors, *Woven Jewels,* Pacific Asia Museum, 1992

Turkestan/Central Asia

Blackwell, Basil, *Ikats - Woven Silks from Central Asia,* Basil Blackwell Ltd., Oxford, 1989

Dovodov, N., *Carpets and Carpet Products of Turkmenistan,* Turkmen Carpet Company, U.S.S.R., 1983

Hoshko, Y., *State Museum of Ethnography and Crafts under the Ukrainian Soviet Socialist Republic Academy of Sciences,* Mistetsno Publishers, Kiev, 1976

Lefevre, Jean and Jon Thompson, *Central Asian Carpets,* Lefevre & Partners, London, 1976

Maksisov, V. and Y. Sarakin, *The Kirghiz Pattern,* Russia, 1986

Morosova, A. S., and various authors, *Folk Art of Uzbekistan,* Gafur Gulyam Literature and Art Publishing House, Russia, 1979

Tzareva, Elena, *Rugs & Carpets from Central Asia,* Aurora Art Publishers, Leningrad, 1984

Turkey

Acar, Belkis Balpinar, *Kilim-Cicim Zili-Sumak Turkish Flatweaves,* Eren, Istanbul, 1983

Aslanalpa, Oktay, *One Thousand Years of Turkish Carpets,* Eren, Istanbul, 1988

Atil, Esin, *The Age of Sultan Süleyman the Magnificent,* Harry N. Abrams, New York, 1987

Balpinar, Belkis and Udo Hirsch, *Carpets in the Vakiflar Museum Istanbul,* Verlag Uta Hulsey, West Germany, 1988

Balpinar, Belkis and Udo Hirsch, *Flatweaves of the Vakiflar Museum,* Istanbul, Verlag Uta Hulsey, West Germany, 1982

Brüggemann, W. and H. Bohmer, *Rugs of the Peasants and Nomads of Anatolia,* Verlag Kunst & Antiquitäten, Munich, 1983

Frauenknecht, Bertram, *Early Turkish Tapestries,* Frauenknecht, Nürnberg, 1984

Gazetteer of Turkey, 2 volumes, 2nd Edition, Washington, D.C., September 1984

Iten-Maritz, J., *Turkish Carpets,* Kodansha International, New York, 1977

Landreau, Anthony N. and Ralph S. Yohe, *Flowers of the Yayla,* The Textile Museum, Washington, D.C., 1983

Levey, Michael, *The World of Ottoman Art,* Charles Scribner's Sons, New York, 1975

Petsopoulos, Yanni, *Tulips, Arabesques and Turbans,* Abbeville Press, New York, 1982

Zipper, Kurt and Claudia Fritzsche, *Turkish,* Antique Collectors' Club Ltd., Munich, 1989

Turkmen

Harvey, Janet, *Traditional Textiles of Central Asia,* Thames and Hudson Ltd., London, 1996

Loges, Werner, *Turkoman Tribal Rugs,* Humanities Press, Atlantic Highlands, N.J., 1980

Mackie, Louise and Jon Thompson, *Turkmen,* The Textile Museum, Washington D.C., 1980

Moshkova, V.G., *Rugs of Central Asian Peoples in the Late 19th and 20th Centuries,* Tashkent: Fan, 1970

O'Bannon, George W., *The Turkoman Carpet,* Duckworth, London, 1974

O'Bannon, George W., *Kazakh and Uzbek Rugs from Afghanistan,* George W. O'Bannon, Pittsburgh, 1979

O'Bannon, George W., William A. Wood, William Irons, Paul Mushak, *Vanishing Jewels: Central Asian Tribal Weavings,* Rochester Museum and Science Center, Rochester, 1990

Parsons, R. D., *The Carpets of Afghanistan,* Oriental Textile Press, Antique Collector's Club, Woodbridge, Suffolk, 1985

Pinner, Robert, *The Rickmers Collection - Turkoman Rugs,* Staatliche Museen zu Berlin, Berlin, 1993

Pinner, Robert and Michael Franses, *Turkoman Studies I,* Oguz Press Limited, London, 1980

Survey Texts and Exhibition Catalogs

Bacharach, Jere L. and Irene A. Bierman, *The Warp and Weft of Islam,* The Henry Art Gallery, Seattle, 1978

Bennett, Ian, *Rugs & Carpets of the World,* A & W Publishers, New York, 1977

Black, David, *The Macmillan Atlas of Rugs and Carpets,* Macmillan Publishing Company, New York, 1985

Denny, Walter B., *Oriental Rugs,* Smithsonian Institution, Washington, D.C., 1979

Denny, Walter B., *Sotheby's Guide to Oriental Rugs,* Simon & Schuster, New York, 1994

Denny, Walter B. and Daniel Walker, *The Markarian Album,* The Markarian Foundation, Cincinatti, 1988

Dilley, Arthur Urbane, *Oriental Rugs and Carpets,* J.B. Lipincott Company, New York, 1959

Dimand, Maurice S., *The Ballard Collection of Oriental Rugs,* Ballard, 1935

Dimand, Maurice S., *Oriental Rugs in the Metropolitan Museum of Art,* New York, 1973

Eiland, Murray L., *Oriental Rugs: A New Comprehensive Guide,* Little, Brown & Co., Boston, 1981

Eiland, Murray L., *Oriental Rugs from Pacific Collections,* Murray L. Eiland and the San Francisco Bay Area Rug Society, 1990

Ellis, Charles Grant, *Oriental Carpets in the Philadelphia Museum of Art,* Philadelphia Museum of Art, 1988

Erdmann, Kurt, *Oriental Carpets,* The Crosby Press, Fishguard, Wales, 1976

Erdmann, Kurt, *Seven Hundred Years of Oriental Carpets,*

Faber and Faber Ltd., London, 1970

Ford, P.R.J., *The Oriental Carpet,* Harry Abrams, New York, 1981

Franses, Michael and various authors, *Orient Stars,* E. Heinrich Kircheim, Stuttgart, 1993

Herbert, Janice Summers, *Affordable Oriental Rugs,* Macmillan Publishing Co., 1980

Herbert, Janice Summers, *Oriental Rugs,* Macmillan Publishing Co., 1982

Hopkins, Mark, *Through the Collector's Eye,* Museum of Art, Rhode Island School of Design, Providence, 1991

Hubel, Reinhard G., *The Book of Carpets,* Washington International Associates, 1979

Jacoby, Heinrich, *How to Know Oriental Carpets and Rugs,* Allen & Unwin, London, 1987

King, Donald and David Sylvester, *The Eastern Carpet in the Western World,* Arts Council of Great Britain, London, 1983

Opie, James, *Tribal Rugs,* The Tolstoy Press, Portland, 1992

Revere, Glenn, *All About Carpets,* Tab Books Inc., Blue Ridge Summit, Pennsylvania, 1988

Riboud, Krishna, *In Quest of Themes and Skills - Asian Textiles,* Marg Publications, Bombay, 1989

Stone, Peter F. and various authors, *Mideast Meets Midwest,* The Chicago Rug Society, Chicago, 1994

Stone, Peter F., *Tribal & Village Rugs: The Definitive Guide to Design, Pattern & Motif,* Thames & Hudson, London, 2007

Summers, Janice, *Oriental Rugs The Illustrated World Buyers' Guide,* Crown Publishers, Inc., New York, 1994

Thompson, Jon, *Carpet Magic,* Barbican Art Gallery, 1983

Volkmann, Martin, *Alte Orientteppiche,* Callwey, Munich, 1985

Von Bode, Wilhelm and Ernst

Kühnel, *Antique Rugs from the Near East,* Cornell University Press, Ithaca, New York, 1984

Von Rosenstiel, Helene and Gail Caskey Winkler, *Floor Coverings for Historic Buildings,* The Preservation Press, Washington, D.C., 1988

Ware, Joyce C., *The Official Price Guide: Oriental Rugs,* House of Collectibles, New York, 1992

Special Function Weavings

Azadi, Siawosch and Peter A. Andrews, *Mafrash,* Dietrich Reimer Verlag, Berlin, 1985

DeLuca, Leonardo and various authors, *Cavalieri D'Oriente - Horse and Saddle Covers,* Leonardo DeLuca, Rome, 1992

Ettinghausen, Richard, *Prayer Rugs,* The Textile Museum, Washington D.C., 1974

Hegenbart, *Rare Oriental Woven Bags,* Adil Besim, Vienna, 1982

Mackie, Louise, *Prayer Rugs,* The Textile Museum, Washington, D.C., 1974

Reinisch, Helmut, *Gabbeh,* Hali Publications, London, 1986

Reinisch, Helmut, *Saddle Bags - Sattel Taschen,* Verlag Für Sammler, Graz, 1985

Flatweaves and Textile Structure

Baizerman, Susan and Karen Searle, *Finishes in the Ethnic Tradition,* Dos Tejedoras, St. Paul, MN, 1978

Beaumont, Roberts, *Carpets and Rugs,* Scott, Greenwood & Son, Ludgate Hill, 1924

Birrell, Vera, *The Textile Arts,* Harper & Brothers, New York, 1959

Burnham, Dorothy K., *Warp and Weft: Textile Terminology,* Royal Ontario Museum, Toronto, 1980

Collingwood, Peter, *The Maker's Hand,* Lark Books, Ashville, NC, 1987

Collingwood, Peter, *The Techniques of Rug Weaving,* Watson-Guptill Publications,

New York, 1978

Cootner, Cathryn, *Flatwoven Textiles,* The Textile Museum, Washington, D.C., 1981

Emery, Irene, *The Primary Structure of Fabrics,* The Textile Museum, Washington D.C., 1980

Evers, Inge, *Felt Making,* Lark Books, Ashville, N.C., 1987

Landreau, Anthony N. and W.R. Pickering, *From the Bosporus to Samarkand: Flatwoven Rugs,* The Textile Museum, Washington, D.C., 1969

Mallett, Marla, *Woven Structures,* Christopher Publications, Atlanta, 1998

Monreal, Luis, *The Conservation of Tapestries and Embroideries,* The Getty Conservation Institute, The J. Paul Getty Trust, 1989

Petsopoulos, Yanni, *Kilims,* Rizzoli, New York, 1982

Sabahi, Taher, *Sumakh,* Leonardo De Luca, Rome, 1992

Seiler-Baldinger, Annemarie, *Textiles,* Smithsonian Institution Press, Washington, D.C., 1994

Stone, Peter F., *Oriental Rug Repair,* Greenleaf Co., Chicago, 1981

Tennant, Emma, *Rag Rugs of England and America,* Walker Books, London, 1992

Zielinski, Stanislaw A., *Encyclopedia of Hand-Weaving,* Funk and Wagnall, New York, 1959

Other References

Atlas avtomobil'nykh dorog SSSR (Road atlas of the USSR), Moscow, 1981

El-Said, Issam and Ayse Parman, *Geometric Concepts in Islamic Art,* World of Islam Festival Publishing Company Ltd., London, 1976

Judd and Kelly, *Color-Universal Language and Dictionary of Names,* National Bureau of Standards, 1976

Korwin, Laurence, *Textiles as Art,* Laurence Korwin, Chicago, 1990

Lamm, Carl Johan, *Carpet Fragments,* National Museum, Uddevalla, Sweden, 1985

Lucie-Smith, Edward, *Dictionary of Art Terms,* Thames and Hudson, London, 1984

Neff, Ivan C. and Carol V. Maggs, *Dictionary of Oriental Rugs,* Van Nostrand Reinhold, New York, 1977

O'Bannon, George, *Oriental Rugs: A Bibliography,* The Scarecrow Press, Inc., Metuchen, N.J., and London, 1994

Storey, Joyce, *Manual of Dyes and Fabrics,* Thames and Hudson, London, 1978

The Times Atlas of the World, Seventh Comprehensive Edition, Times Books Limited, Edinburgh, 1989

Wilber, Donald M., *A Descriptive Catalogue of Dated Rugs and of Inscribed Rugs,* The Near Eastern Art Research Center, 1989

Periodicals and Journals

Afghanistan Journal, Center for Afghanistan Studies, University of Nebraska, Omaha

The Decorative Rug, Oriental Rug Auction Review, Inc., Meredith, New Hampshire

Ghereh, Turin, Italy

Hali, Hali Publications Limited, London

The Journal of the Society for Iranian Studies, New York

Oriental Carpet and Textile Studies, Islamic Department of Sotheby's and OCTS Ltd., London

Oriental Rug Review, Oriental Rug Auction Review, Inc., Meredith, New Hampshire

Rug News, Museum Books, Inc., New York

The Textile Museum Journal, Washington, D.C.

Graphics Sources

The following individuals, companies and organizations generously gave permission for the use of graphic materials.

Mehmud Abliz
Issam Al-Lahham
James Allen
Anahita Gallery
Allan Arthur
authenturk
Azerbaijan Rugs
Doris Leslie Blau
Carpet Collection Petter Haug
Carpetview
John Collins
Michael Craycraft
Dilmaghani & Co.
ecarpetgalley
Dr. Herbert J. Exner
Faresalesman
Detlev Fischer
Russel Fling
P.R.J. Ford
Foundation for Kurdish Library & Museum
Jerry Franke
Ivory Friedus
Steve Getzwiller Navajo Rug
Grogan and Company
Richaed Golder, Jr.
Manouchehr Haghighat
Roger Hilpp
R. John Howe
Huntington Museum of Art
Michael Isberian
Jacobsen Rugs
Moe Jamali
Jozan
Simon Knight
Edward Koch
Donna Larsen
Alberto Levi
Hagop Manoyan
Mete Mutlu
Jason Nazmiyal
Ronnie Newman
J. Barry O'Connell
Peter Pap Oriental Rugs Inc.
Gerard Paquin
Tara Perry
Michael Phillips
Pickering/Yohe Collection
Mr. and Mrs. Steven Price
Richard Rothstein & Co
Lloyd Rowcroft.
Rug Rag
Grover Schiltz
Jerry Silverman
Sothebys
Stairrods Ltd.
John Stockwell
Wendel Swan
Parviz Tanavoli
Treadway Gallery
Turkish Cultural Foundation

Turkish Loom
Uzbek Textile
Alan Vartesian
Julie Grant Weiss of Wanderloot
Wikipedia
Wikimedia Commons
Donald N. Wilber
Peter Willborg
Woolley and Wallis
Kazin Yildiz
Yurdan

Publications

Akar, Azade, *Authentic Turkish Designs,* Dover Publications, Inc., New York, 1992

The Art Institue of Chicago Exhibition of Oriental Rugs, The Art Institue of Chicago, Chicago, 1922

Bode, Wilhelm, Vorderasiatische Knüpfteppiche aus Älterer Zeit, Verlag Von Hermann Seeman Nachfolger, Leipzig, 1902

D'Addetta, Joseph, *Treasury of Chinese Design Motifs,* Dover Publications, Inc., New York, 1981

D'Awimes, Prisse, *Arabic Art in Color,* Dover Publications, Inc., New York, 1978

Dowlatashi, Ali, *Persian Designs and Motifs,* Dover Publications, Inc., New York, 1979

Elwanger, W.D., *The Oriental Rug,* Dodd, Mead & Company, New York, 1921

Gillow, Norah, *William Morris Designs and Patterns,* Crescent Books, New York, 1988

Guérinet, Armand, *Les Modules et les Tapisseries de la Manufacture Nationale des Gobelins,* Librairie D'Art Décoratif, Paris

Hatton, Richard G., *Handbook of Plant and Floral Ornament,* Dover Publications, Inc., New York, 1960

Hawley, W.M., *Chinese Folk Designs,* Dover Publications, Inc., New York, 1949

Hackmack, Adolf, *Der Chinesische Teppiche,* L. Friederichsen & Co., Hamburg, 1921

Heck, J.G., *The Complete Encyclopedia of Illustration,* Park Lane, New York, 1979

Hicks, Amy Mali, *The Craft of Hand Made-Rugs,* Mc Bride-Nast & Co., New York, 1914

Holt, Rosa Belle, *Rugs Oriental and Occidental,* A. C. McClurg & Co., Chicago, 1901

Horn, Diane Victoria, *African Nomad Designs,* Stemmer House Publishers, Inc., Owings Mills, Maryland, 1992

Jones, Owen, *The Grammar of Ornament,* Dover Publications, Inc., New York, 1987

Leconte, Emile and Ernest Clerget, *Sourcebook of Elegant Historic Ornament,* Dover Publications, Inc., New York, 1995

Mirow, Gregory, *A Treasury of Design,* Dover Publications, Inc., New York, 1969

Nahigian Brothers, *Oriental Rugs in the Home,* Nahigian Brothers, Chicago, 1913

Orban-Szontag, Madeleine, *Southwestern Indian Designs,* Dover Publications, Inc., New York, 1992

Planet Art, Beverly Hills, CA, 1996

Roth, H. Ling, *Ancient Egyptian and Greek Looms,* Bankfield Museum, Halifax, 1913

Sarre, Friedrich, and Hermann Trenkwald, *Oriental Carpet Designs in Full Color,* Dover Publications, Inc., New York, 1979

Sietsma, Robert, *Oriental Designs,* Hart Publishing Company, Inc., New York, 1978

Stone, Peter F., *Oriental Rug Repair,* Greenleaf Co., Chicago, 1981

Stone, Peter F., *Rugs of the Caucasus: Structure and Design,* Greenleaf Co., Chicago, 1984

The Tiffany Studios Collection of Notable Oriental Rugs, The Tiffany Studios, New York, 1907

Walton, Perry, *The Story of Textiles,* John S. Lawrence, Boston, 1912

Wilson, Eva, *Islamic Designs,* Dover Publications, Inc., New York, 1988

Woodhouse, Thomas, *The Handcraft Art of Weaving,* H. Frowde, London, 1921

The World Factbook 1995, Central Intelligence Agency, Washington, D.C., 1995

Map of the Middle East   Approximate locations of rug-weaving ethnic groups and tribes are shown in red.

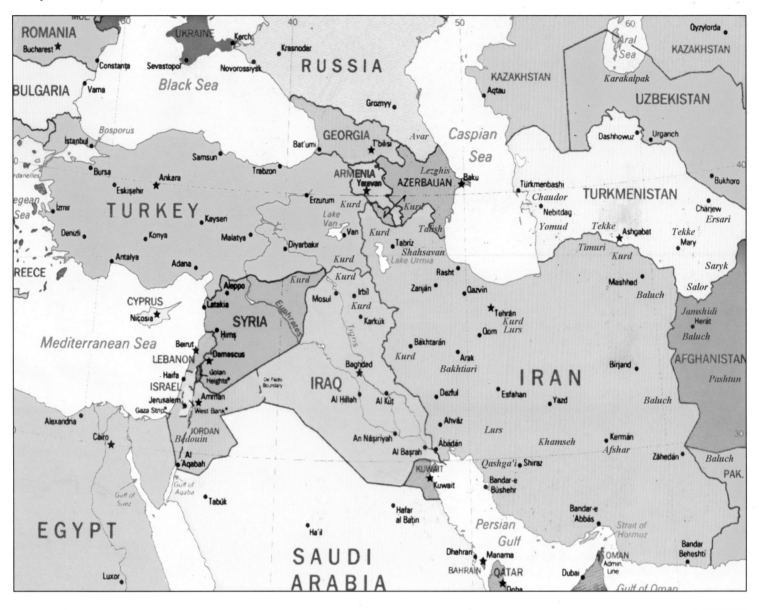

Map of the Silk Route

← Silk, Tea, Porcelain, Spices

Gold, Silver, Glassware, Carpets, Jewels, Wine →

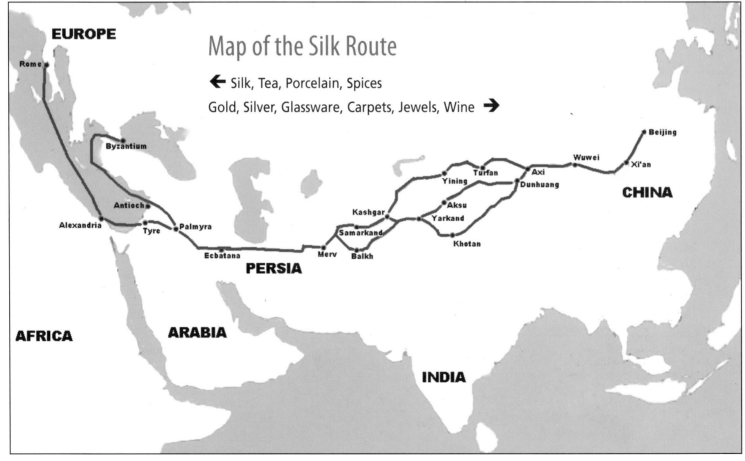